The American City: An Urban Geography

McGRAW-HILL SERIES IN GEOGRAPHY
JOHN C. WEAVER, *Consulting Editor*

VERNOR C. FINCH was Consulting Editor of this series from its inception in 1934 to 1951.

The
American
City An urban geography

Raymond E. Murphy

Professor of Economic Geography
Clark University

MCGRAW-HILL BOOK COMPANY

New York
St. Louis
San Francisco
Toronto
London
Sydney

THE AMERICAN CITY: AN URBAN GEOGRAPHY

Library of Congress Catalog Card Number 65-24894

44070
34567890 HD 732106987

Cover photograph
The city of tomorrow:
General Motors Futurama
(New York World's Fair)

Preface

MANY books dealing with various facets of cities and with the great problems that face cities have been published in recent years. The author of the present book does not attempt to discuss all these aspects or to deal with all the great urban problems. Instead, the book is based on a concept of urban geography that he has been following for several decades and has found both interesting and productive.

The American City: An Urban Geography presents the field of urban geography in a form which the author considers well suited to geography students at both graduate and higher undergraduate levels. It may be of interest, too, to urban planners, and to academicians in various fields in which the city plays an important role. The layman who wishes to look more penetratingly at his city may also find the book of interest.

The different aspects of urban geography are so interrelated that presentation of the subject in a strictly logical order is hardly possible. The arrangement followed in this book is one that the author has found workable, but it is certainly not the only or necessarily the best sequence. In some chapters, cities are considered without regard for interior variations—for example, in the chapters on the urban economic base, on classifications of cities, and on locations of cities; other chapters deal primarily with the interior patterns of cities. But for a number of topics it has been found convenient to treat intercity patterns and intracity patterns in a single chapter.

The book is designed to be used without supplementary reading. Nevertheless, a reading list is included at the end of each chapter representing books and articles that the student specializing in urban geography will probably wish to consult or to have in his library, and that the instructor may desire to have on reserve for his class. An attempt has been made to restrict each list to books and journals that are available, but a few out-of-print books are listed that are considered valuable enough to be worth ordering in microfilm or xerox form. The lists are far from complete, of course, since the literature of urban geography is large and still growing. Within the span of a single school year or even one semester, the instructor will find that new references will appear which should be added. The superior student is likely to bring in from his own reading new references and ideas that are relevant though not covered in the book. Indeed, in graduate courses, the volume may well be used largely as basic assigned material, thus liberating as much class time as possible for discussion of possible research topics and current urban problems.

Fortunately, for most classes using the book, a local city is available as a laboratory. Many ideas are best tried out through field mapping and testing. Moreover, census volumes and other data sources give opportunities for as many outside exercises as course time permits. There is hardly a topic discussed in the book that will not benefit from assigned exercises in the field or in the library.

One of the most interesting aspects of urban geography is that it includes so many topics that can be investigated in the field and from available data. The tremendous opportunities for research are emphasized throughout this book, as well as the many ways in which urban geography research can be applied to community problems. Not infrequently, a working arrangement can be effected with the local planning board or with other civic organizations which will benefit both the students and the community.

There is no attempt to introduce the more sophisticated quantitative statistical techniques, except to some degree through the reference lists at the ends of the chapters. This does not mean that such methods are considered of little value. On the contrary, the employment of advanced statistical techniques has added much to the urban geographer's research range and promises to open up still wider vistas for the future. But the details of such techniques are beyond the scope of this volume, which concentrates on concepts, data sources, and general research methods.

And there are various other omissions. For example, some of the people who read the manuscript of this book felt that it should begin with a general discussion of the phenomenon of urbanism. But the subject is discussed so voluminously in newspapers, magazines, and books that such a preliminary statement hardly seemed necessary. In fact much of this book deals with urbanism. Moreover, such an introductory discussion, valuable though it might be to the teacher or student, would be out of keeping with the general purpose of the book, which is to present urban geography more as a field of inquiry than as an established body of knowledge.

A book such as this is founded on the research and writing of many people. Some of these people are given credit in citations, but the author has drawn upon many works not specifically cited. To all these contributors to the field of urban geography, the author expresses his debt. More particularly, he is indebted to the many students who have taken part in his classes in urban geography. These former students are far too numerous to be given credit individually, though their contributions have been substantial. The author wishes particularly, however, to thank Carolyn J. Ryan of the University of Connecticut who, as a graduate student, read each of the various chapters in semifinal draft; Roland J. Fuchs of the University of Hawaii who used the material in a year's course in urban geography; and Lane J. Johnson of Wayne State University who read the entire manuscript critically. Lastly, the author wishes to thank his long-suffering wife, Marion Murphy, for her aid and her forbearance.

Raymond E. Murphy

Contents

The American City: An Urban Geography

1

The urban inquiry

MOST people prefer to live in or near cities, or at least in areas that are sufficiently city-like to be described as urban, and the preference is growing. This is a universal characteristic and one that is very evident in the United States. Unfortunately, there is no universally accepted distinction between urban and rural. Even in the United States the distinction is a questionable one, but most people follow the lead of the Bureau of the Census which defines certain types of areas as urban. The people living in these areas are considered to constitute the urban fraction of our population. A primary fact of American urban geography is the striking rise in this proportion over the years (Figure 1.1). In 1900 it amounted to 40 per cent; in 1960, according to the latest Census Bureau definition of urban, the proportion was 70 per cent. It is still increasing.

Interest in that acme of urbanism, the city, has grown accordingly. Urban and suburban problems often dominate the domestic news; and there has been an increasing demand in recent years for a department of urban affairs comparable to the Department of Agriculture, a demand finally met by a bill signed by President Johnson in September, 1965. In response to the growing interest in urban matters *The American City: An Urban Geography* has been written. It is a geographic inquiry into the American urban scene.

Scope of Urban Geography

Urban geography deals with the spatial aspects of urban development. Primarily, the focus is upon cities, but this focus is broadened to include all areas that are sufficiently city-like in housing density and land-use characteristics to be referred to as urban, and even to include non-urban areas as they relate to cities. The concern is with

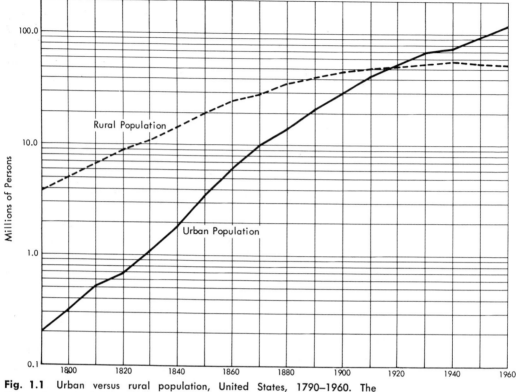

Fig. 1.1 Urban versus rural population, United States, 1790–1960. The Census Bureau's definition of urban was altered substantially between the 1940 and 1950 censuses, and the somewhat more liberal urban definition is reflected in the trends of the two curves after 1940. (Data from the U.S. Bureau of the Census.)

determining in the field or through plotting of data in the office the areal patterns associated with urban centers and in explaining these arrangements.

Throughout this book, urban centers will be dealt with at two levels. The urban geographer is concerned with cities as entities—their locations, characters, growth, relations to the countryside and to each other. But he is at least equally interested in patterns of the city's interior—land-use patterns, social and cultural patterns, patterns of circulation, patterns of the natural environment—all as they exist in interrelation and interaction in the urban area. In all this, he is concerned primarily with the search for generalizations—generalizations about cities and the interiors of cities—and

only secondarily with the cities as individuals.

But the interest is not confined to the contemporary scene. The urban geographer reaches into the past to find explanations of present areal arrangements and to investigate patterns of the past. He is interested, too, in using his methods to predict the futures of urban areas. Moreover, although urban geography is not urban planning, the urban geographer's findings can be of great value in urban planning.

Urban Geography and Neighboring Fields

The city and other urban areas are studied by workers from a number of disciplines. Some of the fields represented are not very close to urban geography. The engineer, for example, is interested in street paving, sewage disposal, and a host of other matters that are of only secondary concern to the geographer.

But other fields have more definite points of contact and even of overlap with urban geography. Sociologists with urban interests carry out studies, some of which are hard to distinguish from the work of urban geographers; note should be taken, too, of the research of rural sociologists who have dealt with areas bordering the city. Some economists focus on the city and on urban problems, either as economists per se or as land economists, and may contribute studies of value to urban geography. Research on urban problems is being done, too, by political scientists, and some of it is useful in the urban geography effort. The city planner carries on activities that often amount to urban geography research, but his primary concern must be with the city by which he is employed. He must plan for this area and work to have his plans put into action. The urban geographer, with his emphasis upon interrelated areal patterns, contributes a somewhat different point of view from any of the others, but there is no hard and fast line setting off his field.

The Literature of American Urban Geography

The overlapping of urban geography with various neighboring fields is reflected in the literature cited throughout this book. Just as several studies by urban geographers have been widely quoted and used by sociologists, planners, and others, so, too, scholars in adjacent fields have contributed many studies of value in urban geography. And, although the primary concern of the book is with the American city, some studies of foreign urban areas are discussed where they contribute findings or methods considered especially applicable to the Amer-

ican scene. The literature of urban geography, as pointed out in the Preface, is a rapidly growing one, indicating something of the vigor of this new field.

Preview of the Book

The book may be briefly outlined as follows: The introduction (Chapter 1) is followed by a chapter which deals with basic concepts and definitions. Here the distinction is made between urban and rural, and the *geographic city* or *real city* is contrasted with the corporate or legal city. Also introduced is terminology developed by the United States Bureau of the Census and the Bureau of the Budget. The geographer can collect a certain amount of data on his own, but, in order for him to generalize successfully, the data for various cities must be available and must be in comparable form. It is important, therefore, that the corporate city be distinguished from those other city areas for which the Census Bureau gives and has given data: the standard metropolitan statistical area and its ancestors, and the urbanized area. Chapter 3 introduces concepts and definitions of areas in the outer portion of the urban agglomeration—suburbs, satellites, and the rural-urban fringe.

Cities commonly serve areas around them. This relationship is considered in Chapters 4 through 7. The first of these deals with various types of service areas, particularly newspaper areas and retail and wholesale market areas, and with the general regions that cities may be considered to dominate. The idea of service areas is carried further in Chapter 5, a discussion of cities as central places and of a general theory of location of urban centers that is based on the center's services to the country around it. Such considerations lead, naturally, into attempts that have been made to rank cities in various orders in a hierarchy on this basis. These are discussed in Chapter 6. Still another way to look at the relations of cities to the areas around them is to analyze the cities according to the activities that bring money into the urban area and those that serve only the urban area itself. The values and implications of such urban economic base studies are discussed at some length in Chapter 7.

Cities as functional units form the basis for several systems of city classification which are presented in Chapter 8. The distribution and characteristics of various functional classes of cities are considered in Chapter 9.

Chapter 10 deals rather directly with people in the city—how cities are characterized by number and density of population, how population maps are made, and how the changing population pattern can be studied. Other types of social and cultural patterns, too, are discussed. This chapter in a sense spans the gap between studies which deal with cities as units and those in which variations within the interior of the city occupy the center of the stage.

Chapter 11 introduces the reader to urban land-use maps, in preparation for the series of chapters that follows. The construction and properties of such maps are considered, as well as their possible value in arriving at generalizations regarding land-use patterns of the city's interior. Such closely related topics as valuation data, zoning, and urban renewal are briefly discussed.

Chapters 12 through 19 deal with urban land uses and activities. Chapter 12 presents a theoretical consideration of the arrangement of land uses in the city. Then, in Chapter 13, transportation in relation to the city is considered, particularly the various types of transportation and the intracity patterns they generate. Commercial activities of cities and of the city interior are discussed in Chapter 14; and, in Chapter 15, the central business district is treated at some length. Chapter 16 deals with manufacturing at the intercity and intracity levels, and Chapter 17, with problems of manufacturing expansion. In Chapter 18, urban residential patterns are discussed, both from the standpoint of variations from city to city and from that of the interior of the city, and the neighborhood concept is evaluated. In the concluding chapter of the series (19) other urban activities and land uses are discussed. Here, urban patterns based on education, religion, recreation, and city government are considered, as well as the significance of vacant land to the future of the city.

Finally, in Chapter 20, growth of the political units of urban agglomerations is discussed. The chapter concludes with a consideration of one of the greatest problems faced in connection with United States cities: just how to get the many political units making up the average great urban agglomeration to work together as an efficient whole.

Morphology, Function, and Evolution

In connection with urban geography research, the terms *morphology, function,* and *evolution* often are used.

In morphological studies the form elements of the urban area are of chief concern: the arrangement of streets and railroads, the forms of buildings, in fact the whole urban landscape. Though the emphasis may be upon the current scene, morphological studies often deal with the development of forms and patterns of the present city or other urban area through time, in short, with evolution. This line of attack has been particularly popular in Europe, where a long history has left abundant traces of the past in the landscape. In settlement morphology, for example, the researcher reaches back into history for explanations of present form characteristics. In spite of the briefer time span involved in American history, this approach should be of interest in the United States as well.

Function presents two sides: the role of

the city as the focus of its region, and the inner diversity of function within the city. Urban planning deals to a large degree with this inner differentiation of functions, but there are many opportunities along this line, also, for scientific geographic research. Geographers both in America and abroad have done valuable work on what might be called the quantitative analysis of function. Examples of such studies will appear throughout this book.

In practice, morphology, function, and evolution are virtually inseparable. A morphological study in which function plays no part is hard to imagine; so, too, is a functional study where form elements do not enter in at all. And in most morphological and functional studies, evolution is brought in to some degree.

Orientation of the Book

All three approaches are represented in this book, though morphology and function are stressed more than evolution. They are fundamentally more geographic, though evolution is by no means unimportant. A knowledge of the evolution of the urban landscape can give depth to studies of the present scene, which is, after all, just one cross section through time. But no one book can accomplish everything, and the primary concern of this one is to present methods of analyzing and interpreting the American city of today. This in itself is a sufficient task. Moreover, the techniques and ideas applied to the present urban scene can be adapted to studies of urban areas as they existed in earlier stages of development.

The book deals with the American city as a type rather than with American cities individually. Of course, in a sense, every city is unique, but they have much in common, and what one can learn about the American city as a type should help anyone interested in understanding any individual American city. In short, a primary goal of

the urban geographer is to arrive at sound generalizations about the city, and a constant concern of this book is with methods of study that will yield such generalizations.

The unique aspects of the city are of least concern in this book. For example, there is no chapter on site characteristics—landforms, soils, bedrock conditions, climate. Site attributes are often very important in understanding a particular city, but they differ so much from city to city that the study of such topics does not contribute materially to knowledge of the American city as a type.

Consider, for example, relief features. Geographers at one time wrote about river junction cities and mountain gap cities. Yet the precise relief details of the site of one river junction city or mountain gap city are often so unlike those of another of similar type that such knowledge is of little value in building up a generalized picture of the American city. To date, worthwhile generalizations regarding urban adjustments to site do not appear to have been developed. Some day they may be. But in the meanwhile about all that can be said is that the individual city often shows pronounced adjustments to its own particular site conditions.

For similar reasons, the historical factor in urban geography does not form the subject of a chapter. No two cities have had exactly the same history. It is undoubtedly true that certain common features of cities synchronize with countrywide developments in economic history. But little is available in the literature thus far pointing out such features and the precise historical periods or events with which they can be correlated.

Studies that attempt complete coverage of a single city may be of high quality and contribute much that is of value. But unless they involve new concepts or new techniques that can be used in the study of other cities they will be referred to only briefly if at all in this book, since it is primarily a book of concepts and research methods.

Finally, the book is based on the American city rather than on cities in general. Cities are likely to be so different in different culture areas that an attempt to generalize without limiting the locale could lead only to superficiality. Moreover, much can be gained through working with data for comparable areas, and an attempt to deal with the world city or even with all those in areas of Western culture would mean working with varying statistics based on areas variously defined, with the added problem, of course, of varying languages.

The Urban Inquiry

An idea that is stressed frequently in this book is that urban geography is not so much an established body of facts and generalizations as it is a field of inquiry. Many questions are asked that are not answered, and the reader should find numerous ideas to try out on his home city or in broader programs of research.

Just how can urban geography be used to advance knowledge, to serve mankind, and, more immediately, to solve local, practical problems? All of these levels of inquiry are important. But more than anything else it is hoped that this book will lead the reader to look more inquiringly at the city, to ask questions, and to ponder ways these questions might be answered through research.

Selected References

Andrews, Richard B.: *Urban Growth and Development: A Problem Approach*, Simmons-Boardman Publishing Corporation, New York, 1962.

Beaujeu-Garnier, Jacqueline, and Georges Chabot: *Traité de Géographie Urbaine*, Librairie Armand Colin, Paris, 1964.

Bollens, John C., and Henry J. Schmandt: *The Metropolis: Its People, Politics, and Economic Life*, Harper & Row, New York, 1965.

Chapin, F. Stuart, Jr.: *Urban Land Use Planning*, 2d ed., University of Illinois Press, Urbana, Ill., 1965.

Conzen, N. R. G.: "Scandinavian Approach to Urban Geography," *Norsk Geografisk Tidskrift*, vol. 12, pp. 86–91, 1949.

Dickinson, Robert E.: *City and Region: A Geographical Interpretation*, Routledge & Kegan Paul, Ltd., London, 1965.

————: "Scope and Status of Urban Geography: An Assessment," *Land Economics*, vol. 24, pp. 221–238, 1948.

————: *The West European City*, Routledge & Kegan Paul, Ltd., London, 1951.

Duncan, Otis Dudley, W. Richard Scott, Stanley Lieberson, Beverly Duncan, and Hal H. Winsborough: *Metropolis and Region*, The Johns Hopkins Press, Baltimore, 1960.

Fisher, Ernest M., and Robert M. Fisher: *Urban Real Estate*, Holt, Rinehart and Winston, Inc., New York, 1954.

Freeman, T. W.: *Geography and Planning*, Hutchinson University Library, London, 1958.

Gibbs, Jack P. (ed.): *Urban Research Methods*, D. Van Nostrand Company, Inc., Princeton, N.J., 1961.

Gist, Noel P., and Sylvia Fava: *Urban Society*, 5th ed., Thomas Y. Crowell Company, New York, 1964.

McKenzie, R. D.: *The Metropolitan Community*, McGraw-Hill Book Company, Inc., New York, 1933. (Out of print but can be ordered in xeroxed form from a library that has a copy.)

Mayer, Harold M.: "Geography and Urbanism," *Scientific Monthly*, vol. 73, pp. 40–42, 1951.

———— et al.: "Urban Geography," in Preston E. James and Clarence F. Jones (eds.), *American Geography: Inventory and Prospect*, Syracuse University Press, Syracuse, N.Y., 1954, pp. 142–166.

———— and Clyde F. Kohn (eds.): *Readings in Urban Geography*, The University of Chicago Press, Chicago, 1959.

Norborg, Knut (ed.): Proceedings of the IGU Symposium in Urban Geography, Lund, 1960, *Lund Studies in Geography*, Ser. B, Human Geography, no. 24, Royal University of Lund, Sweden, 1962.

Ratcliff, Richard U.: *Urban Land Economics,* McGraw-Hill Book Company, Inc., New York, 1949.

Smailes, Arthur E.: *The Geography of Towns,* Hutchinson University Library, London, 1953.

U.S. Bureau of the Census. *Census of Population: 1960,* vol. I, *Number of Inhabitants,* 1961.

Whittlesey, Derwent: "A Geographer's Approach to Urban Study," *Scientific Monthly,* vol. 73, pp. 42–44, 1951.

CHAPTER

2

Basic concepts
and definitions

URBAN geography, like other fields of knowledge, is based in large part on concepts and on attempts to approximate these concepts through definitions. Many concepts and definitions will be dealt with in this book. Though nearly all are important, some are so basic that they must be introduced early. Indeed, certain concepts might be said to form the very foundations upon which study of the American city is built. The *urban* concept is basic to such study, and of course *the city*, itself, is a primary concept.

What is a city? What do we mean by urban? Undoubtedly a city is an urban area, but certainly not all urban areas are cities. Most people think of cities as densely settled separate entities of considerable size,[1] often with important economic and social functions. Urban areas range downward in size from unquestioned cities to smaller and smaller urban places. Somewhere on the downward scale, we find places that have such small populations and are so rural that they can in no sense be considered urban. This gradual transition is what some have called the urban-rural continuum. The concern of urban geography is primarily with cities and secondarily with lesser urban areas and places.

Urban versus Rural

The terms urban and rural usually are conceived of as opposites. Urban suggests busy streets lined with houses, stores, factories, and the like; rural connotes the open countryside, with farmhouses and their surrounding fields or even expanses of woods and wasteland. But these are the clear-cut extremes. Actually, urban areas often grade almost imperceptibly into rural areas; there

[1] Throughout this book the size of a city will be used to refer to its population total unless otherwise specified.

8

is no natural or universally agreed upon boundary between them.

The census definition of urban population Since the Bureau of the Census is charged with counting and classifying the United States population, its bases for separating urban from rural are of particular interest. It is a distinction the Census Bureau has to apply periodically in order to be able to report the numbers of urban, as contrasted with rural, residents in various parts of the country. The relative proportions of urban and rural population are considered to have many ramifications in the economy of the country and in the daily lives of its people. According to the Census Bureau's 1960 definition, the urban population comprises all persons living in the following:

(*a*) places of 2,500 inhabitants or more incorporated as cities, boroughs, villages, and towns (except towns in New England, New York, and Wisconsin).

(*b*) the densely settled urban fringe, whether incorporated or unincorporated, of urbanized areas [for details on the outlining of the urban fringe of urbanized areas see pp. 25 to 30.]

(*c*) towns in New England and townships in New Jersey and Pennsylvania which contain no incorporated municipalities as subdivisions and have either 25,000 inhabitants or more, or a population of 2,500 to 25,000 and a density of 1,500 persons or more per square mile.

(*d*) counties in states other than the New England states, New Jersey, and Pennsylvania that have no incorporated municipalities within their borders and have a density of 1,500 persons per square mile. [Actually, this rule is applicable to only one specific case: Arlington County, Virginia.]

(*e*) unincorporated places of 2,500 inhabitants or more.

According to the Bureau of the Census the 1960 urban population consisted of the following: (1) the 106,308,257 inhabitants of the 4,699 incorporated places of 2,500 inhabitants or more; (2) the 5,106,083 inhabitants of the 620 unincorporated places of 2,500 inhabitants or more; (3) the 3,313,- 559 residents of the 125 urban towns and townships and 1 urban county; and (4) the 10,540,851 persons living in urban-fringe areas outside urban places.

The Census Bureau's definition refers to the numbers and densities of people, rather than to their occupations, and concern with land use is only incidental. But the definition does involve the location of places and areas which are urban or urbanized to some degree, and thus it is basic to urban geography. The urban geographer may not like certain aspects of the definition, but he must work with it if he is to make use of the enormous amount of urban data assembled by the Census Bureau.

Is the rural-urban contrast obsolete? The whole rural-urban contrast is often criticized as arbitrary and outmoded. The idea, it is felt, dates back to the days when there really were sharp differences between city and country. But today, it is argued, with good highways and automobiles, with telephones, radios, and television, farm people enjoy essentially all the amenities of the city dweller, so that farm life is often not materially different from city life. Moreover, in many sections of the country there is a growing rural non-farm class. Some of these people live in fringes around cities that are too small to have urbanized areas. Others are in clusters too small to fall within the urban classification, and still others in single houses scattered over the countryside. They may be productive workers or retired older people. At any rate they do not depend upon farms for a living. They have sometimes been referred to as "exurbanites."

No definition of urban will suit everyone, and the Census Bureau's usage must be regarded as a practical compromise. Very possibly some of the objections to the present definition will be met by the Census Bureau in the future. The Bureau's 1940 definition of urban was altered substantially for the 1950 census, and the latter definition in turn was revised in various details for the 1960 census (see Figure 1.1).

Effects of variations in local governmental structure One thing must always be kept in mind in evaluating the Census Bureau's definitions. Governmental structure, involving divisions and boundaries, varies greatly from state to state and sometimes even within states. This fact vastly complicates the Bureau's efforts to use essentially similar methods in all parts of the country so that results for one area will be comparable to those for any other area.[2]

Our definition not a universal one Finally, it should be noted that the Census Bureau's definition of urban population is far from being a universal one. Other nations have other ideas about the distinction between urban and rural. It is obvious, therefore, that world data on urbanism, and country comparisons based on the degree of urbanization, should not be taken too literally. Differing cultures and differing economies complicate the picture. It is hard enough to arrive at an acceptable distinction between urban and rural for the United States.

The City: Concepts and Realities

It is difficult, also, to say just how the terms urban and city are related. Obviously they are related, though nowhere in Census Bureau publications does one find an attempt to equate urban areas with cities. At least it can be said that all urban areas as outlined in the census definition are either cities or are city-like in most of their attributes. Thus, places of only 2,500 population, whether or not they are incorporated, are likely to be small replicas of cities, with commercial establishments, urban services

such as water supply and sewerage, and livelihoods that are not directly dependent upon the land. Even the fringes of urbanized areas are city-like in that housing normally approximates the densities of city housing, and non-residential land is likely to be devoted to commerce, industry, transportation, recreation, or other functions related to the central city. And the towns, townships, and counties described in items c and d of the Census Bureau's urban definition (page 9) are presumed to be city-like in their housing densities.[3]

Urban versus city Though urban geography should deal with all urban areas, both large and small, the primary concern of American urban geographers has been with cities. This brings us to the problem of defining the term city. Even though it is agreed that urban areas are city-like in housing density and in function, yet few people would consider an isolated built-up area of 2,500 inhabitants a city. This is because, whether we realize it or not, most of us have in mind a rough minimum size for a city.

Popular Concept

The popular concept of a city is based chiefly upon obvious size. If one is driving across the country and approaches a large, built-up area he may think, "I am coming to a city." If the assemblage is somewhat smaller, however, he may conclude that it is a town or village. In each case he will be applying a sort of size rule. But the size rule may vary. To someone who comes from an area of great cities, a place of 25,000, 30,000, or even 50,000 population may seem little more than a large village. On the other hand, to someone who has been living in an

---

[2] For example, see Appendix A for a discussion of the unique governmental structure that prevails in New England. See, also, discussion of minor civil divisions in footnote 11 of this chapter.

[3] Small New England cities, and New England towns that the Census Bureau now classes as urban under a special rule, furnish some notable exceptions to these generalizations. Portions of some of these unit areas are decidedly rural (see Fig. 2.6).

area where urban centers are few and small, such a place may seem like a real city.

Perhaps, more astutely, the visitor will think also of functions, which though not unrelated to size are an even better measure of a city. He may see business blocks and factories and row upon row of closely spaced houses, and he may infer from what he can see of the size and activities of the agglomeration that this will be a good place to buy a suit of clothes, or to see a play, or to consult a specialist about eye troubles he has been having.

The Legal City

But "city" is more than a subjective, personal concept having to do with function, size, or areal extent. It has a legal meaning, too. If an urban cluster has a population of 20,000 to 25,000, it is probably a legal city, incorporated as a city according to the laws of the state in which it is situated.[4]

Whether a person thinks in terms of size or of both size and functions, he is applying a sort of preconceived and personal yardstick, and in a general way this works. Large urban clusters with a substantial development of business establishments usually are cities in both the popular and legal senses, but there are some interesting variations.

Not all large urban places have city charters Not all places avail themselves of the privilege of incorporating as cities even though they may be large enough to do so. Oak Park, Illinois, a village bordering the corporate city of Chicago on the west, long

had the reputation of being the largest of these urban centers that did not choose to incorporate. It had a population of 61,093 in 1960.[5] Brookline, Massachusetts, a town in the Boston Standard Metropolitan Statistical Area, is a New England example. Surrounded by other municipalities having city charters and with a population of 54,044 in 1960, Brookline has preferred to keep its town form of government. Still another example is Norristown, Pennsylvania, long known as the largest borough in the Commonwealth. The people of Norristown simply have not wanted a city charter even though the borough's population is close to 40,000. Such large towns or villages are unusual, though not rare. As a rule, if an agglomeration consists of a single corporate unit and has a population of 25,000 or more, it is a city in the legal as well as the popular sense.

There are other fairly substantial urban clusters that special influences have prevented from becoming legal cities. Occasionally, a single-company town will remain unincorporated even after it reaches a considerable size. Weirton, West Virginia, the home of a steel company, was long in this category, but Weirton was incorporated in 1947. Kannapolis, North Carolina, with a population of 34,647 in 1960, home of the Cannon Mills (household textiles), is a present-day example. Some urban areas established to carry out government projects have been slow to become incorporated. Oak Ridge, Tennessee, with a population of 30,229 in 1950, was long the best-known example of this type, but it was incorporated in 1959.

Advantages of studying large urban centers Although it is well to understand the variations in the way the word city is used, it is a matter that will not concern us greatly in this book. We shall be dealing

[4] Actually, the required size varies from state to state, and in some states several classes of cities are differentiated. In Kansas, for example, 100 people living close together and meeting certain specified requirements may incorporate as a third-class city. In Pennsylvania, on the other hand, a third-class city must have a population of 10,000 or more. In both states, a considerably larger population total is required for second- or first-class status.

[5] Since the 1960 census, Oak Park has been outdistanced as an unincorporated village by a neighbor, Skokie, Ill.

chiefly with urban agglomerations that are unquestionably cities. This is largely a matter of practicality. Standardized statistical data are extremely helpful, almost a necessity, in the study of the city. Urban centers of 20,000 or 30,000 population exhibit many of the features and problems of cities, but the Census Bureau gives only limited information for places of this size. Much more detail is given for cities of 50,000 or more, and still more for cities of even larger size classes.[6]

The corporate city as the basic element

The central and dominant unit of any substantial urban agglomeration is the incorporated or corporate city, which we have called here the legal city.[7] The corporate city has boundary lines fixed by law and is governed as a unit, having either a mayor and board of aldermen or a city manager and a city council. This is the city the world knows by a specific name—Boston, Peoria, or Middletown—and it is the city for which the Bureau of the Census has for many decades given a population total. Since the corporate city acts as a unit in many respects, it must be recognized as a real entity. It is a region in the geographic sense in that administrative activities involving various city services and controls prevail throughout the area and normally stop at the boundary.

Changes at border of corporate city

Frequently there is little visible change to mark the edge of the corporate city, since, more often than not, built-up areas occur on both sides of the city line. In fact, the casual motorist is not likely to know when he has crossed the line. If he is on an important street and watches carefully, he may see, as he enters the city, a sign giving the city's name. But it is a common experience to enter or leave a city without knowing that one has crossed the boundary.

There are various other changes coincident with the edge of the city. At the city limits, the nature of the paving may change, and city buses may have turnaround locations. The city fire department and the city police do not continue their activities across the line unless special arrangements have been made for them to do so. The city may, and often does, refuse to sell water to householders just across the city line. But the extreme boundary of a city service often has no expression in the landscape.

Sometimes more substantial changes reflect the difference in government on the two sides of the city line. A subdivision may stop at the line, or, owing to different zoning laws, the sizes of building lots and the nature of land use may change abruptly. Sometimes there are factories, located just outside the city rather than in it, taking advantage of the city's marketing facilities while avoiding high city taxes. It is interesting to see for any specific city just what city-line changes can be found in the field or detected on air photographs.

Legal status of the corporate city

The legal status of the corporate city is not always a simple one. Sometimes the city and county coincide, as they do in Philadelphia, San Francisco, and Denver. Sometimes, as in St. Louis and Baltimore and the cities of Virginia,[8] the city is completely independent of any county. But these are exceptions to the general rule, and in this book we are not looking for exceptions, though we cannot fail to recognize that they exist. The typical American city is a specially incorporated segment of a county, as

[6] Urban geographic research is not restricted to large cities. In smaller cities, through mapping and sampling, it is possible to gather much of one's own data, and comparative studies of small cities may yield interesting generalizations.

[7] Frequently there are several corporate cities of substantial size in one urban agglomeration (see p. 14). One is likely to be overwhelmingly dominant, however.

[8] In Virginia, by state law most cities are independent of the counties which surround them (see discussion on pp. 428–429).

South Bend is a segment of St. Joseph County, Indiana; Los Angeles, a part of Los Angeles County, California; and Moscow, an incorporated city in Latah County, Idaho.

The Geographic City

Although the corporate city is the traditional heart of the urban agglomeration, it generally forms only a part of a much larger contiguously built-up urban area. For many cities this is a fact so obvious as to be widely recognized. The population of Boston, for example, 697,197 in 1960, is an entirely inadequate expression of the Boston agglomeration of some 2.5 million. In like manner, no one would seriously contend that Pittsburgh's 1960 population total of 604,332 really described the population cluster at the junction of the Monongahela and Allegheny Rivers. In each case the population figure given is that of the corporate or legal city; the population of the entire urban agglomeration of which the corporate city is the heart is two or three times that of the corporate city.

The contiguously built-up area in and around the corporate city has been variously called the *real city*, the *brick and mortar city*, the *physical city*, and the *geographic city*. The last of these is a term which has been in use by geographers for several decades. It refers to the built-up area extending in all directions until significantly interrupted by farms, forest, or other nonurban land, or by water bodies.

The concept of the geographic city can be better appreciated if one imagines looking down at a city from a plane flying at 10,000 feet elevation. At this height, one can readily pick out the solidly built-up area that marks the main body of the city. In places, particularly where major highways lead away from the city, urban development juts outward between peninsulas of rural land. But generally the edge is one of transition: residences and other urban

buildings—sometimes singly, sometimes in clusters—are found farther and farther apart with distance outward. The edge of the geographic city is not a sharp one; indeed, the whole idea does not lend itself in practice to exact definition. Nevertheless, it has value as a concept.

Boundaries of the geographic city versus those of the corporate city The boundaries of the geographic city bear no consistent relationship to those of the corporate city. The corporate city may be larger than the geographic city. Probably everyone will recall driving into a city where, after passing a city-limits sign, he passed through woods and open fields for a short distance. Much more often, though, the geographic city is larger than the incorporated city, and a person entering the city will travel some distance in built-up urban sections before reaching the city line. In fact, the area of continuous urban development of the average large American city extends far beyond the boundaries of the legal city.

The terms *overbounded city, underbounded city,* and *truebounded city* have been applied to these several situations.[9] In the overbounded city the legal city is larger than the geographic city. In the underbounded city the geographic city is the larger of the two. The truebounded city, with the geographic and legal cities coinciding, is probably never actually attained.

Changing relative positions of corporate city and geographic city boundaries The corporate city and the geographic city may have coincided fairly well at one time. More often the city line originally extended beyond the edge of the geographic city: the city was overbounded. But, over the years, with the prodigious expansion of urban populations, the city limits have usually

[9] See International Urban Research, Institute of International Studies, *The World's Metropolitan Areas*, Berkeley, Calif., 1959, pp. 6–9.

been left far behind. This does not mean that the corporate city did not attempt to keep up; often pieces have been annexed here and there as the real city expanded. But usually this process has been accomplished with increasing difficulty. Small neighboring communities may have objected to being annexed by the major city, and often it has been impossible, or at least impracticable, to force them to submit to annexation.[10] Hence, the incorporated city has become, through the years, less and less expressive of the real urban agglomeration. Again and again, we shall be dealing with problems engendered by the central city's failure to keep up with the growth of the geographic city.

Less commonly the opposite situation prevails. The city through annexation may extend its boundaries beyond the geographic city boundaries. This is particularly true in certain states, such as Oklahoma and Texas, where annexation is a simple procedure. Oklahoma City has annexed so much surrounding territory that it extends into five counties and, at the time of writing, had by far the largest area of any city in the country.

Variety of civil units making up the geographic city The geographic city normally has one dominant corporate city. But occasionally it may have a second such city large enough to rival the major center, and sometimes even a third. In any event, in addition to the core city or cities the geographic city may include a variety of political odds and ends. Small incorporated cities may be present, as well as still smaller urban units variously known as towns or boroughs or villages. On the other hand, some of the outlying portions of the built-up area may remain simply parts of a township or county.[11]

---

[10] This is particularly true in New England where boundaries have been essentially frozen for many years (see Appendix A).

[11] The terminology of minor civil divisions is sur-

Relationships between political units and the geographic city are explored further in the final chapter of the book.

Urban Area Ideas Used by the Census Bureau

But the geographic city, useful though it is as a concept, is impractical, since it cannot be defined exactly and hence no data are available for it. Having, no doubt, some such concept as the geographic city in mind, but wishing to build an area out of statistical units, officials of the U.S. Bureau of the Census, early in the present century, introduced the metropolitan area idea. It began with the metropolitan district, but this eventually was replaced by two areas defined by the Bureau of the Budget: the standard metropolitan area and, later, the standard metropolitan statistical area. Somewhat different is a Census Bureau creation, the urbanized area, introduced for the first time for the 1950 census. It is intended as a basis for a more exact separation of urban population from rural population near our larger cities than was formerly possible.

The Metropolitan Area Idea

The term *metropolitan area* is widely and often very loosely used. To many, the

---

prisingly varied. Magisterial districts, election districts, election precincts, boroughs, villages, Indian reservations, and other such divisions replace or supplement townships in some states. In Mississippi, townships are replaced by "beats"; and, in Louisiana, there are parishes instead of counties, with the parishes in turn divided into police jury wards. In most of New England, towns and cities take the places of townships (see Appendix A). In the state of Washington, where the existing minor civil divisions were considered unsuitable for statistical purposes because of frequently changing boundaries, the Census Bureau established for the 1950 census a system of "census county divisions" (see Introduction, *Census of Population: 1960,* vol. I, *Number of Inhabitants,* 1961). Census county divisions have since been developed for a number of other states.

word *metropolis* suggests only the very largest cities, and terms like *metropolitanism* and *metropolitanization* are thought of chiefly in connection with such places as New York, Chicago, and Los Angeles. More commonly, however, metropolis is used to refer to any place that is large enough and important enough to serve as a sort of regional capital. But there is by no means full accord on this point.[12]

The term metropolitan area is used in a much less pretentious way—applied to almost any city and the area it is presumed to dominate. Ideally, the metropolitan area consists of a recognized, substantial population nucleus and the adjacent areas of countryside and scattered urban development that have a community of interests with the nucleus.

Several types of areas have been defined by government bureaus in attempts to approximate this metropolitan area concept. Three of them—the metropolitan district, the standard metropolitan area, and the standard metropolitan statistical area—are logically discussed in succession; and we shall find that there is also a popular use of the term metropolitan area which, for any particular city, does not necessarily coincide with any of the definitions arrived at in Washington.

Metropolitan District

Even before the era of the automobile and the correlated rapid suburban development, it was realized that data for the city alone often told only part of the story. A larger area was needed for statistical purposes. Just how much to include was a debatable point, but certainly much more than the central, incorporated city was necessary if the new area were to express the city at all realistically. To meet this obvious

need the Census Bureau developed the metropolitan district definition, first used in the 1910 *Census of Population.*

The metropolitan district as a first step
The term metropolitan district was not used after the 1940 census, but it is discussed here for two reasons. First, it represents the original attempt of the Census Bureau to delimit some sort of urban area that would be more realistic than the incorporated city alone; and, second, anyone using data from the census of 1940 or earlier needs to know the major differences between the metropolitan district and its successor, the standard metropolitan area.[13]

The metropolitan districts of 1940
The metropolitan district was redefined in various ways from one census period to another, but for our purposes it will suffice to discuss metropolitan districts as they were in 1940. In that year they were defined for every incorporated city having a population of 50,000 or more, though in some cases two or more such cities were included in one district. In general, the metropolitan district included, in addition to the central city or cities, all adjacent and contiguous minor civil divisions or incorporated places having a population density of 150 or more persons per square mile (Figure 2.1).

Limitations of the metropolitan district
Two major faults in the metropolitan district concept culminated, eventually, in the definition of a new type of area. In the first place, many kinds of data available locally are collected by counties rather than by the minor civil divisions which were the building blocks of the metropolitan dis-

---

[12] See discussion in Otis Dudley Duncan, W. Richard Scott, Stanley Lieberson, Beverly Duncan, and Hal H. Winsborough, *Metropolis and Region,* The Johns Hopkins Press, Baltimore, 1960.

[13] The British "conurbation," though similar in extent to the American urbanized area (see pp. 24–32), is essentially an aggregation of minor administrative divisions and therefore is more like our former metropolitan district than any other type of area we have outlined (see T. W. Freeman, *The Conurbations of Great Britain,* Manchester University Press, England, 1959).

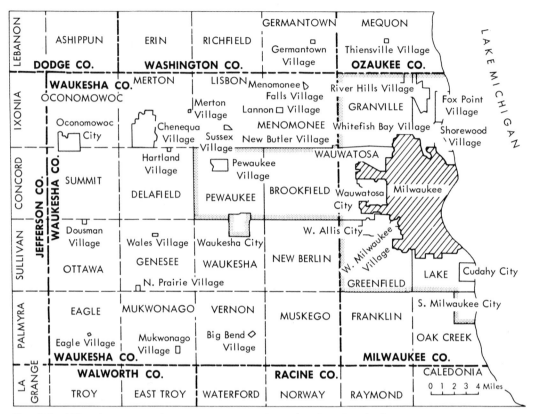

Fig. 2.1 Milwaukee Metropolitan District, 1940; the Milwaukee Standard Metropolitan Area, 1950; and the Milwaukee Standard Metropolitan Statistical Area, 1963.

The Milwaukee Metropolitan District is outlined by a shaded strip on the map. Minor civil divisions were the building blocks of the metropolitan district. In addition to the central city, Milwaukee, the district included all adjacent and contiguous minor civil divisions or incorporated places having a population density of 150 or more persons per square mile. The names of such divisions shown on the map are those in use in 1940.

In contrast, counties formed the building blocks of standard metropolitan areas, used for the 1950 census, and of the standard metropolitan statistical area, in use in 1960. The Milwaukee Standard Metropolitan Area consisted of Milwaukee County and Waukesha County. The Milwaukee Standard Metropolitan Statistical Area at first consisted only of these two counties. Milwaukee County was automatically included since it contained the only central city. The decisions to include Waukesha County and, later, in 1963, Ozaukee County, were based on tests of metropolitan character of each of these counties as well as the criterion of social and economic integration with the central city. Only the southernmost third of Ozaukee County appears on the map.

trict.[14] As a result, the possibilities of correlating local data with metropolitan district

[14] This is not true for New England where the town is more important as a statistical unit than the county (see Appendix A).

data were limited. In the second place, it was felt that, in delimiting the metropolitan district, too much emphasis had been placed upon population density and not enough upon social and economic integration with the central city and upon other measures of metropolitan character. Consequently, the standard metropolitan area was defined in 1949.

The Standard Metropolitan Area

A fundamental characteristic of the standard metropolitan area was that, except in New England, it consisted of a county or a group of contiguous counties which contained at least one city of 50,000 inhabitants or more. As originally defined:

> . . . In addition to the county, or counties, containing such a city [a central city], or cities [central cities], contiguous counties are included in a standard metropolitan area if according to certain criteria they are essentially metropolitan in character and socially and economically integrated with the central city [15] [Figure 2.1].

The area could cross state lines.

The central cities of standard metropolitan areas As the Census Bureau pointed out, not all cities of 50,000 or more in a standard metropolitan area were necessarily central cities. The largest city of the standard metropolitan area was considered the principal central city. Any other city of 25,000 or more could qualify as a central city if its population was one-third or more as great as that of the principal central city. There was the limitation, however, that no more than three cities were considered central cities in a standard metropolitan area, and the largest cities were automatically the ones chosen. The name of every central city in the area was included in the name of the standard metro-

politan area, except in the case of the New York–Northeastern New Jersey Standard Metropolitan Area, in which Newark and Jersey City, though central cities, were not included in the name.[16]

The standard metropolitan area as a standardized statistical unit The metropolitan district was not the only statistical area that was rendered obsolete by the standard metropolitan area. There were several others, used for different purposes and by various agencies. For example, there were the industrial areas of the Census of Manufactures and the labor-market areas of the Bureau of Employment Security. The idea was that the new type of area should replace all of these. Through the use of a standard area the various types of data for which the other areas had been used would become comparable. Moreover, as was pointed out earlier, the use of county units meant that more local data collected only at the county level would be available for comparison with the federally assembled data.

The standard metropolitan area in New England In New England, the city and town are administratively more important than the county (see Appendix A), and data are compiled locally for such minor civil divisions. Therefore, cities and towns were used as the building blocks of standard metropolitan areas, rather than counties, as was done for the remainder of the country. In addition to the central city, or cities, all adjacent cities and towns were included that met certain requirements. It was felt that the tests for metropolitan character used for counties in standard metro-

---

[15] U.S. Bureau of the Census, *Census of Population: 1950*, vol. I, *Number of Inhabitants, 1952*, p. xxxiii. The criteria on which metropolitan character and social and economic integration were based are not given here since they vary only in minor respects from those for the more recent standard metropolitan statistical area which are enumerated on pp. 18–21.

[16] The New York–Northeastern New Jersey Standard Metropolitan Area was an exception to the general rule in a second respect. Newark and Jersey City were classed as central cities though they fell short of meeting the criterion that a second or third central city should have at least one-third as great a population as the largest central city.

politan areas outside New England (for instance, the number and proportion of non-agricultural workers) were inapplicable. Instead, a population density criterion was used: 150 persons or more per square mile, or 100 persons or more where strong integration with the central city was evident. As a result the standard metropolitan area in New England was essentially the same as the former metropolitan district.

The Standard Metropolitan Statistical Area

For the 1960 census the standard metropolitan area was replaced officially by the standard metropolitan statistical area; this term, it was felt, more accurately described the purpose for which the area was established (Figures 2.1 and 2.2).[17] The definitions of the two areas differ only in minor details.

The standard metropolitan statistical area outside of New England: General requirements The standard metropolitan statistical area outside of New England is similar to the former standard metropolitan area in most respects. However, though most standard metropolitan statistical areas include at least one city of 50,000 inhabitants or more, this is not an absolute requirement as it was for the standard metropolitan area. Instead, two cities with contiguous boundaries and with a combined population of at least 50,000 (often referred to as *twin cities*) may serve the purpose if they constitute, for general economic and social purposes, a single community, and if the smaller of the two has a population of at least 15,000. Champaign–Urbana, Illinois, and Muskegon–Muskegon Heights, Michigan, are examples of twin cities that form standard metropolitan statistical areas under this rule.

There is also the provision that where two or more adjacent counties each has a city of 50,000 inhabitants or more (or twin cities such as those just described) and if the cities lie within 20 miles of each other (city limits to city limits), they will be included in a single standard metropolitan statistical area unless there is definite evidence that the two urban areas are not economically and socially integrated. The Albany–Schenectady–Troy, New York, Standard Metropolitan Statistical Area is an example of cities linked in this way.

Criteria of metropolitan character Every standard metropolitan statistical area outside New England consists of at least one county. Criteria of metropolitan character are used in determining whether other counties should be added to this central county.[18] The criteria of metropolitan character relate primarily to the attributes of the county as a place of work or as a home for a concentration of non-agricultural workers. Specifically, these criteria are:

1. At least 75 per cent of the labor force of the county must be in the non-agricultural labor force.

2. In addition to criterion 1, the county must meet at least one of the following conditions:

   (*a*) It must have 50 per cent or more of its population living in contiguous minor civil divisions with a density of at least 150 persons per square mile, in an unbroken chain of minor civil divisions with such density radiating from the central city in the area.

   (*b*) The number of non-agricultural workers employed in the county must equal at least 10 per cent of the number of non-agricultural workers employed in the county containing the largest city in the area, or be the place of employment of 10,000 non-agricultural workers.

   (*c*) The non-agricultural labor force living in the county must equal at least

---

[17] U.S. Bureau of the Budget, *Standard Metropolitan Statistical Areas*, 1964.

[18] See "Criteria of Metropolitan Character" and "Criteria of Integration," *ibid.*, pp. 1–3; footnotes in that bulletin give further details.

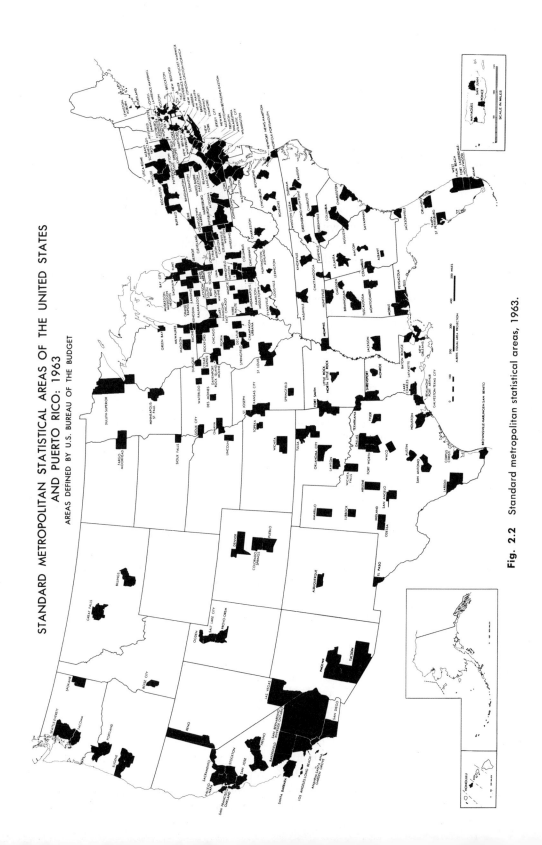

STANDARD METROPOLITAN STATISTICAL AREAS OF THE UNITED STATES
AND PUERTO RICO: 1963
AREAS DEFINED BY U.S. BUREAU OF THE BUDGET

Fig. 2.2 Standard metropolitan statistical areas, 1963.

10 per cent of the number of the non-agricultural labor force living in the county containing the largest city in the area, or be the place of residence of a non-agricultural labor force of 10,000.

Criteria of integration　Criteria of integration, too, are used in deciding whether or not a county should be included. They relate primarily to the extent of economic and social communication between the outlying counties and the central county. A county is regarded as integrated with the county or counties containing the central cities of the area if either of the 'following criteria is met:

1. If 15 per cent of the workers living in the county work in the county or counties containing the central cities of the area, or
2. If 25 per cent of those working in the county live in the county or counties containing the central cities of the area.

Only where data for criteria 1 and 2 are not conclusive are other related types of information used as necessary. These include newspaper circulation reports prepared by the Audit Bureau of Circulations, analysis of charge accounts in retail stores of central cities to determine the extent of their use by residents of the contiguous county, delivery service practices of retail stores in central cities, official traffic counts, the extent of public transportation facilities in operation between central cities and communities in the contiguous county, and the extent to which local planning groups and other civic organizations operate jointly.

Titles of standard metropolitan statistical areas　The titles of standard metropolitan statistical areas are based on much the same principles as those of standard metropolitan areas. Normally, only one name is used, that of the largest city in the area, and in any event the name of the largest city always appears first in the standard metropolitan statistical area title. Up to two names may be added to the title, however, "on the basis and in the order" of the

following criteria: (1) if the city or cities have at least 250,000 population each; (2) if the additional city or cities have a population of one-third or more of that of the largest city and a minimum population of 25,000. There is one exception to these rules: where two cities qualify through having a combined population of 50,000 (referred to earlier as twin cities) both names are used. All cities named in the titles are central cities. Besides the city names, all standard metropolitan statistical area titles include the name of the state or states. The standard metropolitan statistical area, like its predecessor the standard metropolitan area, may cross state lines. New York City is represented by a separate standard metropolitan statistical area instead of being linked with northeastern New Jersey as it was in the standard metropolitan area.

The standard metropolitan statistical area in New England　In New England the standard metropolitan statistical area, like the standard metropolitan area that preceded it, is made up of cities and towns rather than counties. Thus the Worcester, Massachusetts, Standard Metropolitan Statistical Area included, in 1963, the city of Worcester and twenty-one towns. The Boston Standard Metropolitan Statistical Area included seventeen cities (only one a central city) and 61 towns (see Appendix A). As elsewhere in the country, the requirement of at least one central city of 50,000 or greater population may be met by twin cities totaling at least 50,000 inhabitants as described on page 18. The Lewiston–Auburn, Maine, Standard Metropolitan Statistical Area is an example of this. The population-density requirement for determining which contiguous cities and towns should be added to a New England standard metropolitan statistical area is simpler than it was in the case of the standard metropolitan area: it is merely one hundred persons per square mile. In general the same criteria of integration are applied to

New England towns and cities as are applied to counties elsewhere in the country.[19]

Permanence of Standard Metropolitan Statistical Areas

Through 1963, 219 standard metropolitan statistical areas had been officially outlined in the United States and Puerto Rico. Most of the standard metropolitan statistical areas are the same in extent as the former standard metropolitan areas, but a substantial number of the areas have undergone changes. Moreover, one of the facts that should be kept in mind about standard metropolitan statistical areas is that, like the standard metropolitan areas, they are constantly subject to review. Changing conditions or a more thorough application of the criteria may result in the addition or deletion of counties (or cities or towns in New England) from certain areas or may make new standard metropolitan statistical areas advisable.

Evaluation of the Standard Metropolitan Statistical Area

The standard metropolitan statistical area has some serious disadvantages from the point of view of the geographer,[20] yet it is regarded by many as a very useful device.

Disadvantages The disadvantages of standard metropolitan statistical areas are readily apparent. Except in New England the areas are made up of county units. As a result an area may exclude sections that are essentially part of the city and include others where the connection is remote. For

instance, some minor civil divisions that are obviously parts of the geographic city may be excluded from the standard metropolitan statistical area because they are just across the line in a county that, as a whole, fails to meet the requirements. More often, however, the inclusion of whole counties brings in substantial outlying sections which are entirely agricultural or even sparsely settled forest regions or desert.

Two examples may make this point clearer. One is the Duluth, Minnesota–Superior, Wisconsin, Standard Metropolitan Statistical Area—7,591 square miles with a 1960 population of 276,596 (Figure 2.2). St. Louis County, Minnesota, in which Duluth is situated, extends northward to the international boundary. Though in addition to Duluth there is an isolated urban complex on the Iron Ranges, the county includes thousands of square miles of forests. Even more striking is the San Bernardino–Riverside–Ontario, California, Standard Metropolitan Statistical Area, which is more than three times as extensive as the Duluth–Superior Standard Metropolitan Statistical Area. Its several small cities and other intensively used areas are dwarfed by vast expanses of desert wasteland.

Still another limitation of standard metropolitan statistical areas must be pointed out. Counties vary so greatly in area that comparisons of standard metropolitan statistical areas on the basis of extent are of little significance, except possibly in New England, where minor civil divisions rather than counties are the building blocks of the areas.

Advantages In view of its obvious faults, why is the standard metropolitan statistical area so popular among workers in many fields? Certainly, it is a simple and easily used statistical unit, and yet in most cases is reasonably expressive of the modern city or city cluster. Population of the more rural sections of the standard metropolitan statistical area counties (and of New Eng-

[19] A town (or city) in New England is regarded as integrated with the central city or cities if 15 per cent of the workers living in the town work in the central city or cities or if 25 per cent of those working in the town live in the central city or cities.

[20] What is said here applied equally well to the standard metropolitan area.

land cities and towns) is likely to be small, so comparisons based upon purely economic and demographic statistics, unrelated to area, are reasonably valid. A comparison of standard metropolitan statistical areas on the basis of total population, for example, is not much affected by the great variations in area, but comparison on the basis of persons per square mile of land area or on any basis that involves relating economic data to area is unsatisfactory.

Most of all, research workers rely on the data for the standard metropolitan statistical areas because many United States census data are available only for these areas or are available in much greater detail for these areas than for any smaller areal units. At the same time, outside of New England, many more data are collected locally by counties than by smaller divisions and hence are available by standard metropolitan statistical areas. It follows, therefore, that fruitful comparisons are possible involving these local data and the Federal data for standard metropolitan statistical areas.

Evaluation of the New England standard metropolitan statistical areas In any comparative studies such as those mentioned, the special method used in outlining the standard metropolitan statistical areas in New England must be kept in mind. Since they are based on minor civil divisions instead of counties, the standard metropolitan statistical areas come closer to representing the geographic city in New England than they do elsewhere in the country. Totals for a New England standard metropolitan statistical area, therefore, are likely to represent a more nearly accurate expression of the city and the area it serves than do totals for standard metropolitan statistical areas elsewhere. And, for comparative studies of data not involving land areas, the differences between the New England and other standard metropolitan statistical areas probably are not serious.

Standard metropolitan statistical areas and city prosperity The metropolitan district, the standard metropolitan area, and the more recently defined standard metropolitan statistical area are statistical areas only, having no administrative significance whatever. Thus it would seem that whether the Census Bureau delimited such an area or not, or whether an extra county were added to the existing standard metropolitan statistical area (or an extra town or city in New England) or an old one dropped, the change would have little direct effect on the community.

But the standard metropolitan statistical area is not that unimportant. For one thing, it is a matter of pride for people when their city has a standard metropolitan statistical area for the first time, and even citizens of larger cities like to have their standard metropolitan statistical areas as large as possible. Moreover, the fact that a city has a standard metropolitan statistical area or that its standard metropolitan statistical area is enlarged is given some consideration in advertising campaigns and the like and even in locating factories. One chamber of commerce claimed that certain national chain stores locate only in standard metropolitan statistical areas, and that television stations outside these census areas have greater difficulty in obtaining advertising revenue. It was even claimed that a certain urban center had been bypassed in planning the course of an interstate highway because it lacked standard metropolitan statistical area status. To some extent, therefore, the Census Bureau's decisions regarding these statistical areas may actually affect a city's prosperity.

Standard Consolidated Areas

The standard metropolitan statistical area idea has been carried one step further. Standard consolidated areas have been established in recognition of the special importance of the country's two major population clusters, centered in the New York City and Chicago areas (Table 2.1). The standard consolidated areas are much the same in extent as the former New York–Northeastern New Jersey Standard Metropolitan Area and the Chicago Standard Metropolitan Area. The chief advantage of the new system, first used in 1960 Federal publications, is that now data will be avail-

The Metropolitan Area: Local Usage

We have been discussing definitions set up by government bureaus to approximate the metropolitan area concept. As used in the average city, however, the term metropolitan area may not follow established Census Bureau usage, or at least the current usage. It is likely to be applied to the territory the city dominates or the territory the

Table 2.1   Standard consolidated areas and their constituent parts, 1963

Standard consolidated areas	Constituent parts
New York–Northeastern New Jersey Standard Consolidated Area	New York, N.Y., Standard Metropolitan Statistical Area Newark, N.J., Standard Metropolitan Statistical Area Jersey City, N.J., Standard Metropolitan Statistical Area Paterson–Clifton–Passaic, N.J., Standard Metropolitan Statistical Area Middlesex County, N.J. Somerset County, N.J.
Chicago, Ill.–Northwestern Indiana Standard Consolidated Area	Chicago, Ill., Standard Metropolitan Statistical Area Gary–Hammond–East Chicago, Ind., Standard Metropolitan Statistical Area

SOURCE: U.S. Bureau of the Budget, *Standard Metropolitan Statistical Areas*, 1964, p. 43.

able for each of the two consolidated areas as a whole and also separately for four standard metropolitan statistical areas in the case of the New York–Northeastern New Jersey Standard Consolidated Area and for two standard metropolitan statistical areas in the case of the Chicago, Illinois–Northwestern Indiana Standard Consolidated Area. Thus each of the two consolidated areas can be looked at as a whole and also there is some basis for differentiating its interior. This can be accomplished to some degree through the use of data by counties, but greater detail is available by standard metropolitan statistical areas.

city's administrators and businessmen feel the city should dominate—a sort of *Lebensraum*, as it were—whether or not this is in accord with the Bureau of the Budget definition. In this respect, it is essentially synonymous with the term "greater city"—e.g., Greater Reading. For reasons of convenience in obtaining statistics, however, the metropolitan area, even in popular usage, is generally conceived of as made up of administrative units, sometimes counties, but often parts of counties such as townships, boroughs, and the like.

Frequently, the locally used metropolitan area concept is determined by inertia.

Members of the city's chamber of commerce and other local people may have been well pleased with the metropolitan district and hence got into the habit of considering it their metropolitan area. Since the metropolitan district consisted of minor civil divisions it had a relatively fine texture and may have appealed to them as realistic. The standard metropolitan area when it appeared in the 1950 census may not have been so appealing, nor the present standard metropolitan statistical area. The built-up area just across a county line may be excluded under these definitions since the adjacent county as a whole does not quite meet the requirements for inclusion in the city's standard metropolitan statistical area, whereas under the metropolitan district concept it would have been included. For reasons such as these, some cities may still use the metropolitan district version of their metropolitan area, or possibly some modification of the metropolitan district, or they may have a locally accepted metropolitan area even though they are too small ever to have had a metropolitan district or a standard metropolitan area outlined by any Federal agency.

The example of Metropolitan Dayton Some examples may help to make the point clear. The following is quoted from a booklet issued a few years ago: [21] "For planning purposes, Metropolitan Dayton includes Montgomery County (of which Dayton is the county seat) and the urbanized portions of adjoining Greene County." The Dayton Standard Metropolitan Area included Montgomery and Greene Counties; the Dayton Standard Metropolitan Statistical Area, as defined in 1958, included also Miami County, Ohio. Obviously, therefore, Metropolitan Dayton, as described in the quotation, included only part of the standard metropolitan area or of the standard metropolitan statistical area. As far as

[21] *Metropolis,* Ford Foundation, New York, 1959, p. 28.

the "urbanized portions" of Greene County were concerned, the definition probably referred to some of the built-up areas of Greene County contiguous to Montgomery County. It is likely that only certain minor civil divisions of Greene County were included. Planners usually prefer to work with civil divisions rather than with unorganized built-up areas since some sorts of data—at least population totals—are available by minor civil divisions. In short, the Metropolitan Dayton referred to in the brochure appears to be based on local usage rather than on current Census Bureau usage.

Moscow, Idaho, Metropolitan Area A somewhat different usage of the term metropolitan area is found in Moscow, Idaho, population 11,183 in 1960, the small city in which the University of Idaho is situated. There, people speak of their metropolitan area in spite of the fact that no standard metropolitan statistical area has been delimited for Moscow or is likely to be for such a small city in the foreseeable future. No doubt their trade area is what they have chiefly in mind.

The standard metropolitan statistical area gaining acceptance There is a tendency, however, in a city large enough to have a standard metropolitan statistical area, for the Census Bureau usage to become accepted. The overwhelming argument for acceptance is that, for the standard metropolitan statistical area, just as for its predecessor, there is such a wealth of statistical data available.

The Urbanized Area

The standard metropolitan statistical area, valuable though it may be, has certain deficiencies when it comes to separating urban from rural population. Often it includes too much area that is essentially rural. On the other hand, where a central city of a standard metropolitan statistical area is located at the edge of a county, there may be a built-up area just across the county line that is outside the statistical area and yet is unquestionably urban. Some type of division was needed that would approximate more closely the actual urban areas. It should, to a large degree, disregard political boundaries, thus approaching the geographic city concept. Most of all, it should give a better basis for separating urban from rural population in the vicinities of our larger cities than the standard metropolitan statistical area definition. To serve this purpose the Census Bureau set up a new category, the urbanized area, for the 1950 Census.

The Urbanized Area of 1950

Central cities As defined for the 1950 census, each urbanized area included at least one city of 50,000 inhabitants or more. This was automatically a *central city*. In addition, the second and third most populous cities of the urbanized area were classified as central cities, provided that each had a population at least one-third that of the largest city and a minimum of 25,000 inhabitants. All central city names appeared in urbanized area titles except in the case of the New York–Northeastern New Jersey Urbanized Area, in which Newark and Jersey City, though the second and third central cities of the urbanized area, were not included in the name.[22] Like the standard metropolitan area, an urbanized area could cross state lines. The Huntington–Ashland Urbanized Area, for example, involved three state lines, extending from West Virginia into Kentucky and Ohio.

Urban fringe But it was the area between and beyond the central cities that presented the real problems of definition. The *urban fringe*, as it was called, was that

[22] These two cities were peculiar in another respect: neither had a population equal to one-third the population total of the principal city, New York. Nevertheless, they were considered central cities.

part of an urbanized area which lay outside the central city or cities. It consisted of a contiguous area made up of certain levels of incorporated places, unincorporated territory that met a specified dwelling-unit density, and territory devoted to non-residential urban uses, functionally related to the central city. Also included were non-contiguous areas lying within a mile or two of the main contiguous urban area and meeting the required residential density.[23]

Applying the definition The outlining of the urbanized areas is an interesting example of the way in which geographic techniques may be applied by a government bureau. The job, which had to be completed prior to the beginning of enumeration for the 1950 census, was carried out by the Geography Division of the Bureau of the Census. It required intensive office study of maps, air photographs, and other sources, followed by careful field checks to

[23] According to the Census Bureau the following types of areas were included in the urban fringe for 1950 if they were contiguous to the central city or cities or if they were contiguous to any area already included:

1. Incorporated places with 2,500 inhabitants or more in 1940 or at a subsequent special census conducted prior to 1950.

2. Incorporated places with fewer than 2,500 inhabitants containing an area with a concentration of 100 dwelling units or more with a density in this concentration of 500 units or more per square mile. This density represents approximately 2,000 persons per square mile and normally is the minimum found associated with a closely spaced street pattern.

3. Unincorporated territory with at least 500 dwelling units per square mile.

4. Territory devoted to commercial, industrial, transportational, recreational, and other purposes functionally related to the central city.

Also included were outlying non-contiguous areas with the required dwelling unit density located within 1½ miles of the main contiguous urbanized part, measured along the shortest connecting highway, and other outlying areas within ½ mile of such non-contiguous areas which met the minimum residential density rule.

make sure that the criteria were followed and that the boundaries would be identifiable by census enumerators.

Detailed boundaries   The final product was a map for each city of 50,000 or more inhabitants showing the urbanized area in detail (Figure 2.3). An interesting property of all 1950 urbanized area maps was that successive sections of the boundary were numbered to correspond to streets, political boundaries, railroads, and the like, and the features to which the numbers applied were listed in a supplementary key.[24]

The Urbanized Area for 1960

Delineation based on 1960 census   It was decided to delineate the urbanized areas for 1960 in terms of the 1960 census results rather than prior to the census as had been done for 1950 (Figure 2.4). For this purpose a peripheral zone around each 1950 urbanized area and around each city that was presumably approaching a population of 50,000 was recognized.[25] Within unincorporated parts of this zone, small enumeration districts were established, each usually including no more than 1 square mile of land and no more than seventy-five housing units (for a discussion of enumera-

[24] Note, for example, the following description of a portion of the Peoria, Ill., Urbanized Area boundary for 1950: "Main urbanized part: (1) Corporate limits of Peoria, (2) Sheridan Rd., (3) West Glen Ave., (4) Edgebrook Dr., (5) Endres Ave., (6) Clara Ave., (7) Knoxville Ave. (State Hwy. 88), (8) Property line of North Moor Municipal Golf Course, (9) Sheridan Rd., (10) North Moor Rd., (11) Prospect Rd., (12) corporate limits of Peoria Heights, (13) C.R.I. & P.R.R., (14) extension of Cardinal Ct., (15) Peoria–Woodford County line, (16) Peoria-Tazewell County line, (17) corporate limits of East Peoria, (18) U.S. Hwy. 24, (19) East Peoria Stockyards Rd., (20) T.P. & W.R.R., . . ."
[25] There are a few urbanized areas where there are twin central cities that have a combined population of at least 50,000. These twin central cities are the same as those recognized for standard metropolitan statistical areas (see p. 18).

tion districts in general, see Appendix B).

Those enumeration districts meeting specified criteria of population density were included as well as adjacent incorporated places. Since the urbanized area outside of incorporated places was defined in terms of enumeration districts, the boundaries of the urbanized area for the most part followed such features as roads, streets, railroads, streams, and other clearly defined lines which could be easily identified by census enumerators in the field. Often these do not conform to the boundaries of political units (Figure 2.5).

Types of areas included in urban fringe, 1960   According to the Census Bureau, an urbanized area, in addition to the central city or cities, also contains the following types of contiguous areas, which together constitute its urban fringe:

1. Incorporated places with 2,500 inhabitants or more
2. Incorporated places with less than 2,500 inhabitants, provided each has a closely settled area of 100 dwelling units or more
3. Towns in the New England States, townships in New Jersey and Pennsylvania, and counties elsewhere which are classified as urban (See page 9.)
4. Enumeration districts in unincorporated territory with a population density of 1,000 inhabitants or more per square mile. (The areas of large non-residential tracts devoted to such urban land uses as railroad yards, factories, and cemeteries are excluded in computing the population density of an enumeration district.)
5. Other enumeration districts in unincorporated territory with lower population density provided that they serve one of the following purposes:
    (*a*) To eliminate enclaves
    (*b*) To close indentations in the urbanized area of one mile or less across the open end
    (*c*) To link outlying enumeration districts of qualifying density that were no more than 1½ miles from the main body of the urbanized area.

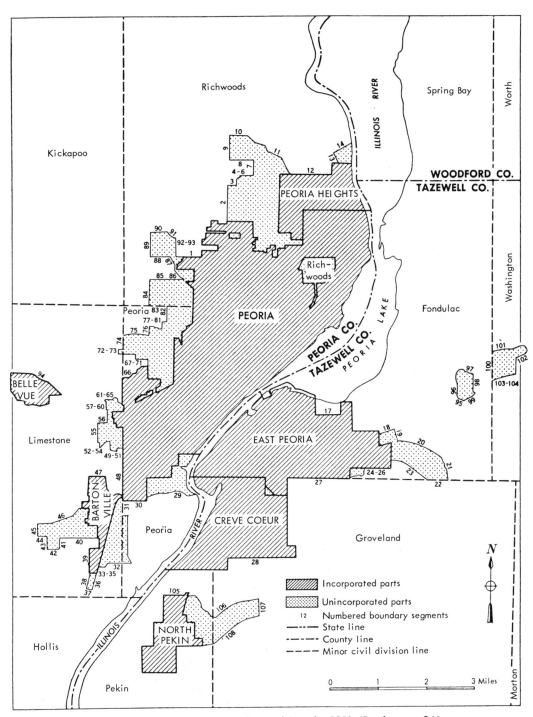

Fig. 2.3 The Peoria, Illinois, Urbanized Area for 1950. (See footnote 24.)

URBANIZED AREAS OF THE UNITED STATES AND PUERTO RICO: 1960

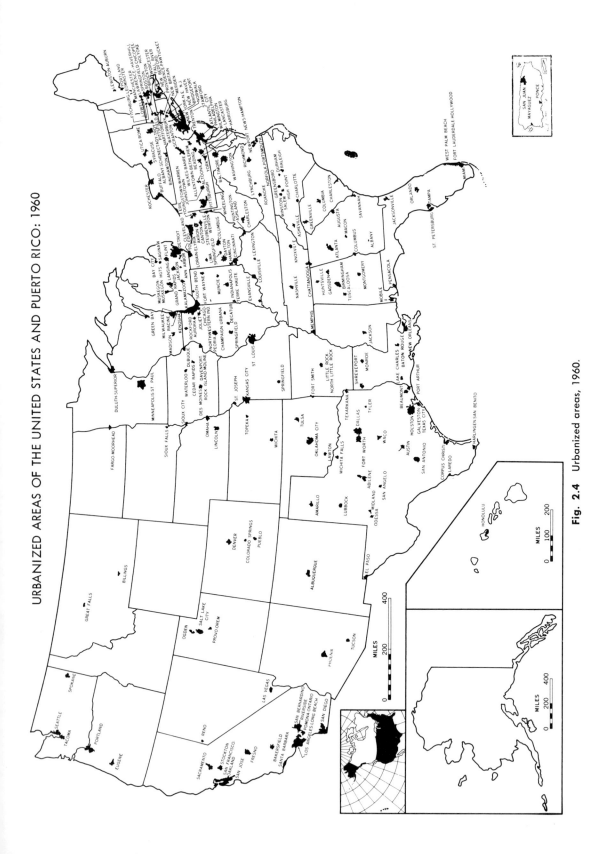

Fig. 2.4 Urbanized areas, 1960.

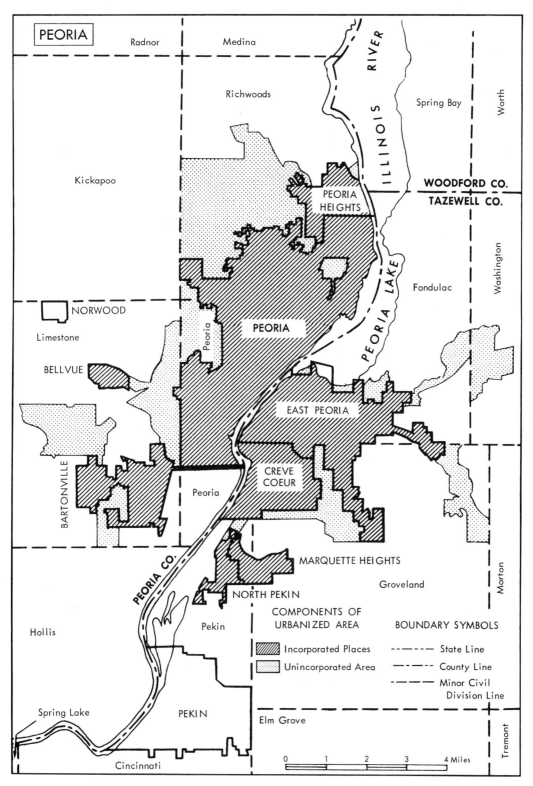

Fig. 2.5 The Peoria, Illinois, Urbanized Area for 1960. Compare with the Peoria Urbanized Area, 1950, Figure 2.3. Note that there are no outlying noncontiguous areas. Very few such areas appear on any of the 1960 maps.

1960 versus 1950 urbanized areas
The boundaries of the urbanized areas for 1960 do not conform to those for 1950, partly because of actual changes in land use and density of settlement and partly because of relatively minor changes in the rules used to determine the boundaries. According to the Census Bureau, the changes in the rules include the following:

1. The use of enumeration districts to construct the urbanized areas in 1960 resulted in a less precise definition than in 1950 when the limits were selected in the field (compare the 1950 and 1960 maps of the Peoria Urbanized Area, Figures 2.3 and 2.5). On the other hand, the 1960 procedures produced an urbanized area based on the census results rather than an area defined about a year before the census, as in 1950.

2. Unincorporated territory was included in the 1960 urbanized area if it contained at least 1,000 persons per square mile, which is a somewhat less exacting criterion than the 500 dwelling units per square mile of the unincorporated areas included in 1950.

3. The 1960 areas include those entire towns in New England, townships in New Jersey and Pennsylvania, and counties that are classified as urban in accordance with the criteria listed in the section on urban-rural residence (see pages 9 to 10). The 1950 criteria permitted the exclusion of portions of these particular minor civil divisions.

In spite of these changes, however, the urbanized areas of 1950 and 1960 are based on essentially the same definition, and according to the Census Bureau the figures for a given urbanized area for the two years may be used to measure the population growth of that area.

Names of urbanized areas Any city in an urbanized area which is a central city of a standard metropolitan statistical area (see pages 17 and 20) is also a central city of the urbanized area. With but two exceptions, the names of the central cities appear in the titles of the areas. The central cities of the New York–Northeastern New Jersey Urbanized Area are the central cities of the New York, Newark, Jersey City, and Paterson–Clifton–Passaic Standard Metropolitan Statistical Areas. Likewise, the central cities of the Chicago–Northwestern Indiana Urbanized Area are the central cities of the Chicago and Gary–Hammond–East Chicago Standard Metropolitan Statistical Areas.

Evaluation of the Urbanized Area

Urbanized area versus other city areas
Let us take a more critical look at the urbanized area. The Census Bureau refers to the urbanized area as the physical city in contrast to the legal city (the incorporated city) and the metropolitan community (the standard metropolitan statistical area). Urbanized areas are likely to be the thickly settled portions of the standard metropolitan statistical areas. Though in a few instances small segments of urbanized areas extend outside standard metropolitan statistical areas, in 1960, according to the Bureau of the Census, only 1 per cent of the population of urbanized areas lived in these small extensions. On the other hand, 15.8 per cent of the total population of all standard metropolitan statistical areas lived outside urbanized areas.

Limitations of the urbanized area In several respects, the urbanized area has limitations. First, any political unit, such as a city, town, village, or borough, that is recognized by the Census Bureau as incorporated is included as a whole in the urbanized area. This sometimes results in the inclusion of considerable areas that are not really urban. The problem is particularly serious in New England, where some of the smaller cities and a few towns that the Census Bureau now classifies as urban have extensive areas of rural land included in them (Figure 2.6). But it is significant, too, in a few cities in sections of the country where annexation is easy, especially in Texas and Oklahoma. Oklahoma City's great areal expansion was mentioned earlier

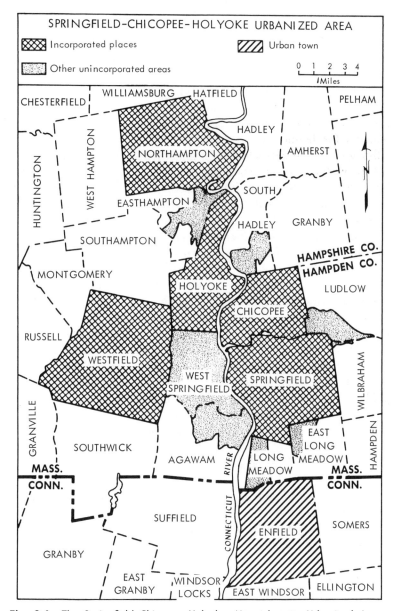

Fig. 2.6 The Springfield–Chicopee–Holyoke, Massachusetts, Urbanized Area illustrates some of the worst faults of the urbanized area idea as applied in New England (see Appendix A). Three central cities—Springfield, Chicopee, and Holyoke—form the core of this urbanized area. Westfield is included because it is incorporated as a city even though it has only 26,000 people in an area of 47 square miles; and Northampton, with 30,000, presents a similar anomaly. Each includes many square miles that are essentially rural. Enfield, though not incorporated as a city, is included in accordance with the Census Bureau rule that a New England town is regarded as urban if it has a total population of 25,000 or more. Enfield had a population of 31,000 in 1960 so it is included in its entirety. It, too, includes considerable land that is not really urban. The net effect of this inclusion of whole New England towns where they are incorporated as cities or where they meet certain Census Bureau rules is that unduly large urbanized areas may result.

(page 14). Much of the area annexed by Oklahoma City is rural.

A second criticism has to do with the nature of the boundaries of urbanized areas. For convenience in identification, the Bureau used streets and roads and similar features for boundaries in 1950. In 1960, although the boundaries had been smoothed out, they still followed much the same features. When such a boundary is used, the houses on one side of the street or road lie inside the limits of the urbanized area whereas those on the other side are excluded. Such boundaries have been called unrealistic, since a street or road characteristically unites rather than separates the houses that line it. Yet it is hard to see how the use of these or similar distinctive features can be avoided.

Finally, the urbanized area could not be expected to have the general comparative statistical value of the standard metropolitan statistical area. The latter is made up of counties throughout most of the United States, and many local as well as Federal data are available for it that are lacking for the urbanized area.

The urbanized area as an expression of the geographic city The major objective of the Census Bureau in setting up urbanized areas was to provide a better separation of urban and rural population around the larger cities. This has undoubtedly been accomplished, although there is still a considerable uncounted fraction of urban population in the fringe areas around cities of less than 50,000 population.

All in all, however, the urbanized area is a useful statistical unit. It expresses fairly well the shape of the whole urban agglomeration,[26] and the population total of the urbanized area probably better represents the reality of the city than any other figure available. There is another virtue of the

[26] For a marked exception to this statement see Fig. 2.6.

urbanized area. Even though the exact basis for outlining the urbanized area has changed since 1950, comparison of the urbanized area maps of any city for 1950 and 1960 gives a reasonably accurate impression of the way the city is expanding.

Urban Statistics

Much of this chapter has been devoted to setting the stage for what is to come. We have dealt with the fundamental distinction between urban and rural and with the differences between the corporate or legal city, on the one hand, and the geographic city and metropolitan area concepts on the other. Most of the chapter has been devoted to a description of the several statistical areas that have been defined to represent the modern urban agglomeration more realistically than the legal city, which is itself a statistical as well as an administrative area.

The Census Bureau and urban statistics The emphasis on statistical areas underlines the fact that statistical data are basic to the study of cities. The U.S. Bureau of the Census is the chief source of comparable city data, and such data carry the greatest promise of making possible broad, valid generalizations regarding the city. We might, therefore, examine briefly the data that are available for the various areas representing the city.

The decennial Census of Population is the most widely used source of census data. The character and value of the statistics vary with population total and with the type of urban statistical area. Information on some general characteristics such as sex, race, age, and housing is available in the Census of Population and the Census of Housing for places of as few as 1,000 inhabitants. There is considerably more information, however, for places of between 2,500 and 10,000 population, and so on up the scale. A much larger number of items is available for places of over 100,000 and even more for cities of 250,000 population or more.

The two census statistical areas—the standard metropolitan statistical area and the urbanized area—also differ in the extent and kinds of published data available. More information is published for standard metropolitan statistical areas than for urbanized areas or corporate cities. For example, the standard metropolitan statistical area is the only urban area for which data are given in the "Detailed Characteristics" section of the Census of Population.

The Census of Manufactures and the Census of Business are taken at approximately five-year intervals. Though general data are given for places of 10,000 or more in the Census of Manufactures, detailed breakdowns are published only for standard metropolitan statistical areas. Census of Business data are available in some detail for standard metropolitan statistical areas and for the larger corporate units. For these censuses no information is given by urbanized areas.

There is much variety in the several census publications which cannot be gone into here. In addition to data for the types of units approximating the city as a whole, statistics are published by census tracts and by city blocks.[27] But data for the city as a whole and for units of the city are so varied and can be used in so many different ways that no attempt is made to go into the possibilities here. They are discussed in greater detail in appropriate sections throughout the book.

A last point might be made regarding the value of Census Bureau urban statistics. Not only do these data make possible comparisons of cities on the basis of gross totals, but they permit also an examination of the

[27] See Appendix B for details regarding census tracts and city blocks and the data available for each.

changing structure of our urban areas. One simple approach to this, for example, is represented by calculations of the proportions of the population of urbanized areas that live in the central city or cities, as contrasted with the proportions living within the areas but outside the central cities. How are these proportions changing over the years? Similar studies are possible on a broader basis with respect to standard metropolitan statistical areas, and we shall find that interesting work has been done in this way regarding the suburbanization of people and of manufacturing.

Other sources of data Of course, the Census Bureau is not the only source of urban data. Much research in urban geography can be based on field mapping and on collection of data by individuals. Some urban statistics are available, too, from state and municipal sources, and the U.S. Bureau of Public Roads in cooperation with state highway departments has conducted a number of origin and destination surveys. For several cities, too, research organizations have carried out broadly conceived studies which have involved a great deal of data gathering, particularly data relative to transportation. Notable examples of such work are the *Chicago Area Transportation Study* and the *Pittsburgh Area Transportation Study.*

Megalopolis

Though some of the concepts and definitions discussed in this chapter may seem complex, reality is even more so. Cities and standard metropolitan statistical areas and urbanized areas rarely exist in isolation. In some sections of the country they occur in a continuous array, interlocking and almost without a break. The standard consolidated areas discussed earlier in the chapter are examples of this situation, but there is a large area in Eastern United States that furnishes an even better illustration. It has been recognized for some time that there is a belt of almost continuous urbanization stretching from Boston to Washington, D.C., of which the New York–Northeastern New Jersey Consolidated Area is only a part. Open spaces in this 600-mile belt are limited and exist chiefly as appendages to urban areas. Functionally, the region consists entirely of cities and areas oriented toward cities.

Jean Gottmann began to study this area after the 1950 census figures became available. He noted that a continuous belt of standard metropolitan areas stretched from Virginia to New England. If, for New England, the standard metropolitan areas were considered to consist of counties, as they do elsewhere, then the urbanized belt would continue as far as southern New Hampshire. He noted, too, that many of the counties adjacent to this belt of standard metropolitan areas had unusually high densities of population as well as many attributes of urbanization. He also noted that, even when some of the neighboring counties were relatively thinly peopled, they were often tied economically to the big cities so

near at hand. Gottmann applied the term "Megalopolis" to this extensive area, and has described it in a book.[28]

Selected References

Freeman, T. W.: *The Conurbations of Great Britain,* Manchester University Press, Manchester, England, 1959.

Gottmann, Jean: *Megalopolis: The Urbanized Northeastern Seaboard of the United States,* The Twentieth Century Fund, New York, 1961.

Hoyt, Homer: *World Urbanization: Expanding Population in a Shrinking World,* Urban Land Institute, Technical Bulletin 43, Washington, D.C., 1962.

International Urban Research, Institute of International Studies, *The World's Metropolitan Areas,* Berkeley, Calif., 1959.

Klove, Robert C.: "Metropolitan Areas: A Review of Three Recent Publications," *Economic Geography,* vol. 37, pp. 267–275, 1961.

U.S. Bureau of the Budget, *Standard Metropolitan Statistical Areas,* 1964.

U.S. Bureau of the Census, *Census of Population: 1960,* vol. I, *Number of Inhabitants,* 1961.

[28] Jean Gottmann, *Megalopolis: The Urbanized Northeastern Seaboard of the United States,* The Twentieth Century Fund, New York, 1961.

CHAPTER **3**

Suburban agglomerations and the rural-urban fringe

IN the preceding chapter it was pointed out that the central city is usually only part of an urban complex, and that attempts have been made by Federal agencies to approximate that complex through defining metropolitan areas and the urbanized area. One characteristic of the urban complex that makes it impossible to define exactly is the vagueness of its edges: unquestioned city grades outward through a transition zone into areas that are indubitably country or rural. The transition zone is the subject of this chapter. Again we shall be dealing with concepts and definitions. But the terms involved will not be so broad and basic as urban versus rural, or as city, urbanized area, and metropolitan area.

It should be emphasized, however, that the transition zone is of more than casual or secondary interest to urban geographers. It is a rapidly changing area. In the great metropolitan growth of recent years, it is in the transition zone, rather than the central city, that population has been burgeoning.[1] The population of central cities has tended to mark time or even to decline. The rapid population growth of the transition zone has brought with it painful problems of readjustment—problems that involve the central city as well as the various minor civil divisions of the outlying areas. These problems will come up here and there throughout this book. They are discussed to some degree in this chapter, but the chief purpose of the chapter is to lay a foundation of concepts applicable to the transition zone, concepts that will supplement those of the preceding chapter in which the city as a whole was the focus.

[1] Policies of the Federal government can be credited with much of this expansion. The Federal Housing Administration (FHA), for example, has increased the ease of financing home construction. There is little room left for such construction in the central cities; instead, the real growth is in the transition zone.

Preliminary View

Urban clusters with names and identities An overall view of the transition zone is first in order (see Figure 3.1). It was pointed out in the preceding chapter that there may be one or even two smaller central cities bordering the main central city or set at some distance from it. There may be also small cities that do not qualify as central cities, and small built-up areas of less than city status which, nevertheless, are administrative units with distinct names. Still other built-up areas, though not legal entities, may have distinct names by which they are known.

Nameless extensions of the city In addition to the named urban clusters lying near the central city, there may be still other built-up areas, essentially urban, which are continuations of the city, but have neither separate names nor separate administrative identities. In some places the central city seems almost to have spilled over the city limits into the adjoining countryside. Often these nameless extensions of urban development are particularly prominent along the most traveled routes, forming urban ribbons or streamers extending out from the central city.

Remainder of the transition zone There are, moreover, several other possibilities in the transition zone. For instance, there are scattered, individual suburban homes. Or such houses may be agglomerated in varying degrees. There may be a pair of houses, or three or four in close proximity. And there may even be a group of houses, sometimes surrounding or adjacent to a factory, all together forming a small urban cluster without administrative identity or even a name. In between these individual houses and small groups of houses, and between the major projections of urban growth and the named urban clusters, lie rural areas that have been affected in various ways by the presence of the nearby city and the incipient threat of residential expansion.

The zone of transition usually encircles the city. Its inner edge ordinarily is defined as the corporate boundary of the central city (or cities). Though its outer boundary is vague, the zone extends far enough out to include the several types of urban clusters that lie within the city's orbit as well as an area known as the *rural-urban fringe*.

Suburban Agglomerations

First, let us consider the clustered urban settlements that characterize the transition zone which customarily surrounds a city. Here the concepts of *suburb* and *satellite* are involved. For these terms there are no pat definitions furnished by the Census Bureau. Instead, we shall have to steer our course as best we may, guided in part by previous usage.

The terms *suburb* and *suburban* are popularly used to refer to all agglomerations in the transition zone that surrounds a city. According to popular usage the terms may refer not only to places that are administratively distinct, such as cities, boroughs, towns, villages, or other similar units, but also to urban clusters that have no names or administrative identities. People living in any of these urban clusters are regarded as suburban dwellers and are likely to think of themselves as living in the suburbs. In fact, the terms are commonly stretched even more, so that people living in essentially isolated houses in the transition zone are considered suburban and may say that they live in the suburbs, and so too may dwellers in some of the outer districts of the chief central city.[2] But the term suburb is better used in a more restricted sense.

Suburbs

An urban cluster with a name and administrative identity It is here contended

[2] An even more general term, *suburbia*, is now popularly used to refer to the transition zone.

that not all suburban agglomerations are suburbs. A person may live in the suburbs or in a suburban area without living in *a* suburb. For example, he may live in an area where the city seems simply to spill over the city line, or he may live in one of the scattered individual homes in the transition zone (Figure 3.1). Obviously, from the word itself, to be a suburb an urban agglomeration must be a unit area of some sort. The minimum requirements, except in New England, usually are that it be a built-up cluster in the transition zone, one that has a commonly accepted name and is to some degree separated administratively from its surroundings. It should not be a township or a county.[3]

Why restrict suburbs to administrative units? The practice of restricting the term suburb to an administrative unit is partly a concession to practicality, since published census data are available only by administrative units, but it is fairly realistic, too, since outside of New England most named places are separate administratively to some degree. Where a built-up cluster in an otherwise rural township area has a name but no separate administrative identity, and this is rare, it is probably best to think of the place as an embryo suburb on the path toward minor civil division status.

General characteristics of suburbs Outside of New England, the suburb has certain general characteristics. It may be contiguous to the city of which it is a suburb, or it may be 10, 20, or 30 miles away, the maximum tending to increase with city size. In any event, it is near enough to permit frequent travel back and forth as well as to have close economic and cultural ties with the city. The extent of the travel varies, we shall find, with the type of suburb.

Often a suburb, whether or not it is ad-

jacent to the city, is physically indistinguishable from adjacent areas, which themselves may be largely built up. Where a suburb is contiguous to a city, the line between city and suburb generally marks a change in administration rather than in land use. Originally standing out by itself and self-contained, the suburb may have been engulfed by the expanding metropolis, although it has managed to resist annexation, and thus retains administrative autonomy. But such close association with the main urban mass or with other suburbs is not necessarily typical. The urban unit may be surrounded by rural areas of its encompassing township or county but still be a suburb of the nearby city.

Harris's study of suburbs

The best way to arrive at worthwhile generalizations about a phenomenon such as the suburb is to delimit many examples, using the same definition, and then to find out what characteristics they have in common and into what subclasses they may be divided. Chauncy Harris followed this plan in a study which resulted in an article published in 1943.[4] He used the metropolitan district as his urban statistical unit, and regarded all minor civil divisions collectively as suburbs if they lay within such a district and yet outside the central city or cities of the district.[5] On this basis he arrived at some interesting generalizations about the high degree of suburbanization in the Northeastern states and the relation between functional type of city and extent of suburban development. Among the functional types, manufacturing cities were found to show the greatest development of suburbs.[6]

But Harris went further in classifying

[4] Chauncy D. Harris, "Suburbs," *American Journal of Sociology,* vol. 49, pp. 1–13, 1943.
[5] To get a more realistic picture of the suburbs Harris made other data adjustments which are described in his article.
[6] Harris's method of classifying cities functionally is discussed in Chap. 8.

[3] For the special case of the New England town see page 41.

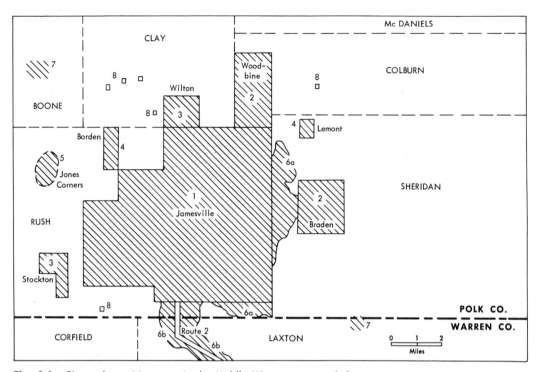

Fig. 3.1 City and transition zone in the Middle West, represented diagrammatically. The shaded areas on the map are built up, at least to some degree.
Numbers refer as follows: 1, main central city; 2, other central city; 3, small
city that does not qualify as a central city; 4, village, borough, or other built-up
unit with fixed boundaries, separate government, and separate name but not
incorporated as a city; 5, built-up area with name but no distinct administrative status or fixed boundaries; 6, spilled-over, built-up area without name or
distinct administrative status (a, area of overflow along city boundary; b, extension along highway); 7, isolated built-up area with no name or administrative status or fixed boundaries—may have grown up around factory; 8,
scattered suburban homes.

individual suburbs. He restricted his study
to cities of 10,000 or more population, lying
within metropolitan districts but outside
the central city or cities. This size was used
since it was the minimum for which data
were available in the 1935 Biennial Censuses of Trade and Manufactures. Using
these data, Harris differentiated housing or
dormitory suburbs; manufacturing or industrial suburbs; diversified suburbs (having both important trade and important
manufacturing); suburbs in which retail
trade appeared to be the chief function;
suburbs based on assembly wholesaling;
and several other types. Smaller unit areas,
though they might equally well be consid-

ered suburbs, could not be included due to
lack of data. Nor, of course, were any suburbs included that lay outside metropolitan
districts.

*Comparable studies using present census
areas*

As was pointed out in Chapter 2, the
metropolitan district was replaced in the
1950 Census by the standard metropolitan
area, which has now become the standard
metropolitan statistical area. To what extent could a study of suburbs comparable
to Harris's work be based on standard metropolitan statistical areas? Or upon urbanized areas?

Two principal functional types

Harris points out that the two most common types of individual suburbs are housing or dormitory suburbs and manufacturing or industrial suburbs.[7] The dominance of these two types has been emphasized by other writers as well. Though it has been realized that there are other types of suburbs, the fact remains that the fundamental contrast is twofold.

Residential versus employing suburbs

A slight variant of this contrast is that between residential (dormitory) suburbs and employing suburbs, the latter including centers of employment concentrating on manufacturing, mining, education, recreation, or possibly some other function or combination of functions.[8] The basis for the distinction is whether there are more people working in the suburb by day than the number of working people who sleep there at night, that is, whether it has a net excess of jobs.

Dormitory, balanced, and employing suburbs Victor Jones developed a three-fold differentiation of suburbs along essentially these same lines, and, with two co-workers, presented the information for 1958.[9] As a first step he classified each urban center of 10,000 population or more as independent, if it was located outside a standard metropolitan statistical area; as a central city, if it was designated by the Bureau of the Census as a central city of a

standard metropolitan statistical area; and as a suburb, if it was located in a standard metropolitan statistical area but was not a central city. Our concern here is with the third of these classes, the suburb.

Jones used an *employment-residence ratio* to separate the suburbs into three categories: dormitory, balanced, and employing. Ideally, the ratio is arrived at by dividing the total number employed in all activities within a given suburb by the total resident labor force of that suburb and multiplying the quotient by 100. If the ratio for a suburb turns out to be exactly 100, it means that the number of persons working in the suburb exactly equals the number in the resident labor force of the suburb. In other words, exactly as many workers work in the suburb in the daytime as sleep there at night. The suburb has neither an excess nor a deficiency of jobs.

But it is impracticable to obtain data on employment for all lines of activity. For example, such data are not readily available for the professions, transportation, communications, utilities, government, or mining. Therefore, in determining employment-residence ratios for places of 10,000 or more population for 1958, Jones used a ratio of total employment in manufacturing, retail trade, wholesale trade, and selected services to total resident labor force engaged in these activities. The employment data were obtained from the Censuses of Manufactures, Retail Trade, Wholesale Trade, and Selected Services; the resident labor-force data were industry-group data from the Census of Population (manufacturing; wholesale trade; retail trade [food and dairy products stores, eating and drinking places, and other retail trade]; and business services, repair services, entertainment and recreation services, and other personal services [which do not include private households]). In calculating the ratio, one has to take account of the fact that the Censuses of Manufactures and Business are for a different year from that of the de-

[7] Harris, *op. cit.*, p. 6. Note, again, that Harris was working only with suburbs of 10,000 or more population. Although he found that dormitory suburbs predominated, this predominance would probably have been much greater had he included the smaller suburbs as well.

[8] Leo F. Schnore, "The Growth of Metropolitan Suburbs," *American Sociological Review*, vol. 22, pp. 165–173, 1957.

[9] Victor Jones, Richard L. Forstall, and Andrew Collver, "Economic and Social Characteristics of Urban Places," *The Municipal Year Book*, International City Managers Association, Chicago, 1963, pp. 85–157.

cennial Census of Population. The 1958 estimate of resident labor force was obtained by straight-line interpolation between the 1950 and 1960 census labor-force totals except where the difference between the totals for 1950 and 1960 appeared negligible.

The ratios obtained give a basis for differentiating between three levels of suburbs. If a place is closely related to, and dominated by, a neighboring central city and has an employment-residence ratio of 116 or more, it is an employing suburb; if its ratio lies between 85 and 115 it is a balanced suburb; and if its ratio is 84 or less, a dormitory or residential suburb.

The way in which the ratios work can be made clearer with a few examples for 1958. For instance, in the Chicago area, Oak Park, with a ratio of 63, is clearly a dormitory suburb; and Elgin, with 93, is a balanced suburb. In the Buffalo area, Lackawanna, known for its steel mills and with a ratio of 218, is overwhelmingly an employing suburb. Burlington, New Jersey, just outside Philadelphia and with a ratio of 111, is a balanced suburb.

But Jones points out that for a number of reasons the ratios cannot be taken as exact indicators of commuting patterns. For one thing, many activities could not be included in arriving at the ratios because data were not available for them. A city might have an unduly low ratio because a substantial share of its labor force was employed in establishments just outside the corporate limits. A suburban city might contain large plants and draw workers from other suburbs or from the central city itself and thus have an unduly high ratio. Still another difficulty is that employment and labor-force data are not for the same years and therefore difficult adjustments are necessary. And, of course, no account at all is taken of places with less than 10,000 population. Nevertheless, Jones's results are interesting and should form a good basis for further work.

Satellites and suburbs

But dormitory suburb and employing suburb are cumbersome terms. There is much to be said for restricting the word suburb to those places that are predominantly residential and using the word satellite for employing suburbs.

Some opinions regarding satellites The term *satellite* as applied to a suburban community has entered the literature in varying degrees and with widely different meanings. Some writers never use it, and others tend to apply it to essentially all of the incorporated communities that surround a city. Harland Bartholomew, head of a planning firm that has studied many American cities, refers to "the satellite city" as "a community adjacent to a larger municipality." [10] It may, he says, be a dormitory suburb, with many of its people working in the central city, or an industrial suburb, which draws workers from the central city and other areas. In effect, he makes no real distinction between satellite and suburb. Chauncy Harris and Edward Ullman, on the other hand, speak of both residential and industrial suburbs, but regard satellites as distinct from suburbs:

> Satellites differ from suburbs in that they are separated from the central city by many miles and in general have little daily commuting to or from the central city, although economic activities of the satellite are closely geared to those of the central city.[11]

Recommended usage It is the opinion of the author of this book that a distinction can and should be made between *suburb* and *satellite*, even though the latter is, in a

[10] Harland Bartholomew, *Land Uses in American Cities,* Harvard University Press, Cambridge, Mass., 1955, p. 8.
[11] Chauncy D. Harris and Edward L. Ullman, "The Nature of Cities," *The Annals of the American Academy of Political and Social Science,* vol. 242, p. 16, 1945.

sense, a type of suburb rather than a completely distinct form. But the distinction should be an economic one rather than a matter of distance from the central city. Victor Jones's work furnishes a good start in this direction if we call his employing suburb a satellite and his dormitory suburb simply a suburb.

The satellite   What are the characteristics of a satellite? For one thing, it has, to a considerable degree, an independent economic base, which means that it has, within its borders, activities that support most of its own people and probably a number of workers from nearby areas as well. It is an employing suburb, as this term was defined earlier. It is almost always an industrial center. But the very fact that it is called a satellite indicates a secondary role. The satellite does not stand alone; it has ties with a larger city and, to a certain degree, operates within the orbit of the larger city. Although its activities are closely geared to those of the city and generate much travel back and forth, the satellite is not so dependent as the suburb upon daily commuting to other areas. The movement tends to be inward at the beginning of the working day and outward at its close.

The suburb   In contrast, the suburb is chiefly a sleeping place for people who work in the nearby city or its satellites. Though a suburb has some economic activities—usually a small commercial center of its own and perhaps some supporting industry—total employment in the community is less than the number of employed workers who sleep there at night. Thus it is characterized by greater per capita commuting than is the satellite: a greater movement out of the community at the beginning of the working day and into the community at its close.[12] The distinction can be made that

suburbs are suppliers of labor and consumers of commodities whereas satellites are consumers of labor and suppliers of commodities.[13]

The situation in New England   In New England the problem of satellite and suburb is complicated by the special pattern of administrative divisions (Appendix A). The built-up areas or villages, even though they have names, can hardly be regarded as satellites and suburbs since they have no boundaries or administrative identities. Instead, the towns and cities—which are areas rather like the civil townships of the Middle West—are the satellites or suburbs since they are the minor civil divisions. They are the areas for which we have data and which are governed and thought of as units.

An interesting contrast with most other sections of the country results. In most of the United States, suburbs and satellites are scattered around the city in a matrix of township land that may be largely rural. But, in Massachusetts, as in most of the remainder of New England, all the land around the city is divided into areas known as towns (see Figure A.1). Near the city, these are commonly suburbs or satellites, depending on their economic activities and their relationships to the city. Thus the suburbs and satellites tend to form a sort of belt around the city, the belt extending outward to such a distance that the town or city no longer shows close enough relationships to the central city to be regarded as either a suburb or a satellite.

Satellite, suburb, and balanced suburb   By way of summary, a threefold classification is recommended, based on an adaptation of Jones's employment-residence ratio,

[12] Theoretically, a satellite might have all of its workers coming in from the city or from adjacent suburbs and might thus have as much commuting as any suburb, but this is probably a rare situation.

[13] Adapted from comments regarding residential suburbs and employing suburbs by Leo F. Schnore in William M. Dobriner (ed.), *The Suburban Community*, G. P. Putnam's Sons, New York, 1958, p. 111.

a classification to be applied to places that are surburban in location. The designation satellite is used where the employment-residence ratio is 116 or more (see page 40). Following the same system, a suburb has a ratio of 84 or less, and places with ratios of 85 to 115 are called balanced suburbs. Of course, to set up any exact limits for satellites, suburbs, and balanced suburbs implies a fictitious exactness, whereas there is obviously no sanctity in the precise numbers Jones suggested as boundaries. Nevertheless, the method seems to be a reasonably rational first step toward straightening out terms that too often are used haphazardly.

Status not permanent Status as a satellite, suburb, or somewhere in between is not permanent. The positions of many places on the continuum have been changing and will continue to change. Some places that long were satellites have lost their industries, and, more and more, exhibit the characteristics of suburbs. It is possible, though probably not so common, for suburbs to acquire sufficient industry to become satellites. Moreover, a growing city may extend its influence so that places formerly economically independent of it become suburbs and satellites.

One should not, however, think of suburbs and satellites as embryo cities, even though occasionally one of them becomes large enough to gain the status of incorporated city. Ordinarily, they are simply parts of the geographic city. In the average agglomeration the central city is losing population relatively and often absolutely. Both manufacturers and people seeking places to live are on the march toward suburban locations, contributing to the growth of satellites and suburbs, respectively, and thus to the expansion of the urban agglomeration. The real city is expanding, with the suburbs and satellites representing footsteps outward.

Possible research The discussion of suburbs and satellites is by no means a record of finished business. On the contrary, there are many challenges to further research. The possibility was mentioned earlier of a follow-up study along the lines of Harris's work but using standard metropolitan statistical areas or urbanized areas instead of metropolitan districts. What characteristics of satellites and suburbs could be determined by field study of some of the more definite examples? How can small suburbs and satellites be differentiated? Research thus far has been based on places of 10,000 population or more, but it goes without saying that there is a vast number of smaller suburban places in the transition zones of cities which we should be able to place on the suburb-satellite continuum. In some places, local data may make this possible, but a method based on data from the Census Bureau or other country-wide source would be far preferable.

For an increasing number of places, commuting data are available, often collected by the state in collaboration with the U.S. Bureau of Public Roads. Such data present possibilities for a differentiation of suburbs and satellites that would include the small communities not considered individually in the studies described above. The details of such a method remain to be worked out, but certainly a large movement out of a place at the beginning of the working day and in again at night normally should be the telltale of the suburb in contrast to the satellite.

The Rural-Urban Fringe

So far we have been focusing on the urban agglomerations of the transition zone. Now let us consider a broader phenomenon of the zone, a phenomenon to which the name rural-urban fringe has been applied.[14]

[14] The rural-urban fringe should not be confused with urban fringe, a United States Census term re-

Definition

The term *rural-urban fringe* might hardly seem to merit a definition. One visualizes a circumferential belt surrounding the average central city (or central cities) and separating it from agricultural lands in which the city and the rural-urban fringe are analogous to an island with a bordering beach. To a lesser degree the phenomenon is repeated around satellites and suburbs. Unfortunately, however, the picture is not that simple.

Wehrwein, a land economist, who wrote one of the earliest and certainly one of the best-known papers on the rural-urban fringe, refers to it as "the area of transition between well recognized urban land uses and the area devoted to agriculture." [15] It would be hard to take serious exception to this definition, but how could it be applied in the field? Suppose you wished to generalize about the rural-urban fringe. The recommended procedure would be first to define the rural-urban fringe of a number of cities on exactly the same basis. But how could this be done?

Delimiting the rural-urban fringe

The rural-urban fringe of Detroit Myers and Beegle in a study of the rural-urban fringe of Detroit worked out a method based on only one factor: the concentration of non-village–rural non-farm (NV–RNF) population.[16] They used 36-square-mile townships and obtained the NV-RNF value for each township by sub-

tracting the sum of farm population and the population of incorporated places from the total population. The rural-urban fringe for Detroit was taken to include those townships having 50 per cent or more NV-RNF population and occurring in an essentially contiguous area outside the city, whereas townships with values of 25 to 50 per cent, normally farther from the city, were called "partial fringe" areas (Figure 3.2). All incorporated territory was excluded.

Though this is a rapid method of delimiting the rural-urban fringe and is based directly on census data it has certain disadvantages. One difficulty is that the necessary data are not available by townships unless special counts have been made. Also, townships are not always square. If they are irregular in size and shape, as they are in the Eastern and Northeastern states, should the small and large townships be given equal weight? Important, too, is the fact that the use of townships as unit areas results in a very coarse-textured delimitation. It could amount to little more than a rough approximation of the extent of the fringe.

The rural-urban fringe of Williamsport, Pennsylvania Blizzard and Anderson worked with the rural-urban fringe of Williamsport, Pennsylvania, a city with a population of about 45,000 in 1960.[17] The area around Williamsport lacks the regular townships of southeastern Michigan, so Blizzard and Anderson would have had difficulty using the method just described if they had desired to do so. Moreover, with a city as small as Williamsport, it may be assumed that the rural-urban fringe would be a fairly narrow belt, and hence the use

---

ferring to the urbanized area minus the central city or cities. Sometimes, too, the term fringe or suburban fringe is used more loosely to refer to all of the suburban belt surrounding a central city or central urban area regardless of the extent of the urbanized area.

[15] George S. Wehrwein, "The Rural-Urban Fringe," *Economic Geography,* vol. 18, pp. 217–228, 1942.

[16] Richard R. Myers and J. Allen Beegle, "Delineation and Analysis of the Rural-Urban Fringe," *Applied Anthropology,* vol. 6, no. 2, pp. 14–22, 1947.

[17] Samuel W. Blizzard and William F. Anderson, II, *Problems in Rural-Urban Fringe Research: Conceptualization and Delineation,* Progress Report no. 89, The Pennsylvania State College Agricultural Experiment Station, State College, Pa., 1952.

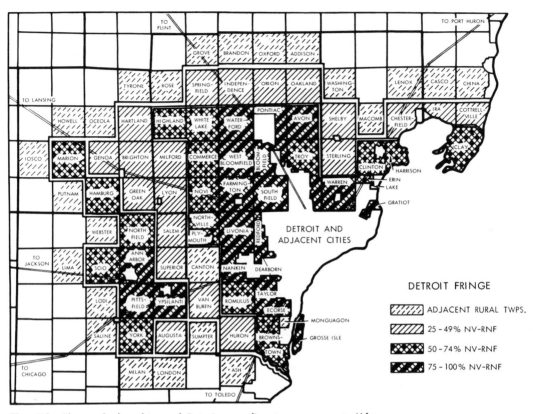

Fig. 3.2 The rural-urban fringe of Detroit according to one concept. (After Richard E. Myers and J. Allen Beegle, "Delineation and Analysis of the Rural-Urban Fringe," *Applied Anthropology*, vol. 6, no. 2, p. 20, 1947.)

of whole townships as unit areas would have been particularly undesirable. Blizzard and Anderson developed the following definition for their work in the Williamsport area: "The rural-urban fringe is that area of mixed urban and rural land uses between the point where full city services cease to be available and the point where agricultural land uses predominate (which includes waste lands and wooded areas)."

The inner boundary The work of Blizzard and Anderson is of particular interest in connection with the inner or cityward boundary of the rural-urban fringe. They visualize it as a series of points or a line reached in leaving the city beyond which city services are incomplete.[18] Normally,

[18] *Ibid.*, p. 11.

this is the corporate boundary of the central city or cities.

Occasionally, however, the inner boundary of the rural-urban fringe, when thus defined, actually extends a short distance into the city. Some characteristics associated with this phenomenon are lack of "town" water, no public sewage disposal system, lack of curbs or sidewalks, unpaved and "unaccepted" streets, and lack of city carrier service as evidenced by the presence of rural-type mail boxes. Where several of these manifestations are present there seems to be sufficient reason to consider an area an extension into the city of the rural-urban fringe. Conversely, a built-up area just outside the central city's boundaries is not regarded as rural-urban fringe if full city services are available.

The outer boundary Fixing the outer boundary of the rural-urban fringe presents more difficult problems. It is generally taken to be the limit of active urban-agricultural competition for the land. Inside this boundary, prices of farm land are inflated by the demand for urban-type residences. Sometimes the urban demand has actually spread a sort of shadow ahead: for example, in some parts of California, English walnut orchards lying near the city are not replanted since it is considered more profitable to hold the land for future sale for urban use. But how can the approximate limit of active urban-rural competition for the land be fixed objectively?

In this matter, Blizzard and Anderson are of little help. They speak of "the predominance of commercial farming, waste lands, or wooded areas" as marking the outer boundary; and, more exactly, they say that in their study, "the outer fringe boundary was placed at the approximate point where an urban pattern of living of some concentration yielded to a pattern of widely scattered acreage lots with nonfarm type houses among farms, or to 'pure' farming or forest land use." They emphasize training of the observer for field reconnaissance, thus underscoring the importance of subjective judgments in fixing the boundary in applying their method.

Can a really objective method be developed for establishing an approximation of this outer edge? If profiles of land values could be constructed radiating out from the city, would a "leveling off" mark the approximate boundary, the point beyond which farms were valued for their agricultural worth rather than for potential urban-type residences? Would a decrease in the number of sales of farms tend to mark the outer boundary? It would appear that there should be a more rapid turnover on the cityward side.

Irregularities of the rural-urban fringe

Undoubtedly, the highly irregular width of the rural-urban fringe and the frayed character of its edges complicate the attempt to define the boundary line. The rural-urban fringe is likely to extend farthest from the city along major highways, where not only residences but places of business and other urban-type uses can be located far out and yet maintain easy access to the central city. Such urban ribbons or extensions of residences and businesses along highways are a particularly characteristic development of recent years. Between such major routes, undisturbed rural land may extend cityward; in such places the rural-urban fringe belt may narrow until it is little more than a line. Frequently, too, patches of purely agricultural land lie inside the general rural-urban fringe boundary and islands of fringe occur in the agricultural areas. Such irregularities, of course, are typical of the rural-urban fringe and multiply the difficulties of fixing any suitable outer boundary.

Rural-urban fringe sequence

Sequence for the area around Flint, Michigan Even though we have not perfected methods for delimiting the rural-urban fringe, its general existence is a matter of common observation. It is useful to think of the conditions which distinguish the rural-urban fringe as changing in a regular sequence. In the following paragraphs this sequence is summed up vividly for the area around Flint, Michigan: [19]

> The development of local government in a typical fringe area appears to follow a cycle. This cycle begins with low taxes and a low level of services and concludes with the citizens demanding regular municipal services regardless of the governmental structure existing there to serve them.
>
> The settlement of population in the fringe area usually begins with prospective builders deciding to purchase land in

[19] Victor Roterus and I. Harding Hughes, Jr., "Governmental Problems of Fringe Areas," *Public Management*, vol. 30, pp. 94–97, 1948.

the outlying area where 'a cheaper lot' or 'a better place for the price' can be obtained, where there is 'plenty of elbow room,' 'no building restrictions,' and 'lower taxes.' The lack of appropriate low-cost rental units in the city may be a factor in this decision as fringe families are usually young, are often just beginning an urban occupation, and have no stake with which to buy a city home. Although the present suitability of the fringe locality for raising children is a prime factor in the sales talk addressed to the prospective settler, no mention is made of the locality's probable condition a few years hence.

Typically, the new fringe dweller finds himself under two units of government, the county and the school district. In certain parts of the country he is under a third unit, the township. The direct line services these governments are prepared to render him do not go far beyond welfare and medical assistance, dirt streets, police protection by the sheriff, and a rural school house for the children. Fire protection, refuse collection, public health sanitation, building inspection, libraries, recreation, storm sewers, and the protections of zoning are apt to be lacking completely. With few other houses around, the new home builder can drill his own well, construct a septic tank, and tell himself that his utilities problem is solved. That he does not always do this is indicated by the example of Flint, Michigan, where in 1940 half of the fringe homes had no running water and three-fourths had no inside flush toilets.

The second phase of the cycle is a large influx of population. Soon the early builders find less and less elbow room. Absence of building inspection, sanitary inspection, and zoning begin to pay unexpected dividends in the form of defective construction, a congested neighborhood, water pollution, cluttered lots, and unsightly structures. Residents who care for protection discover for the first time that deed restrictions, where employed, do not automatically enforce themselves.

The disadvantages of living in an urban environment without services of urban government become harshly apparent when a house down the street burns to the ground without a gallon of water being thrown on the flames. In less spectacular fashion, families with children begin to long for modern schools with trained teachers.

Growth of the locality and the accompanying realization of certain specific needs bring a natural third step in the cycle: demand for satisfaction of these needs. The burden falls on county and township governments and the school districts all geared physically and psychologically for serving rural areas. The inevitable result is slowly increasing services at relatively high unit costs. The disorderly pattern of fringe settlement with alternately scattered and crowded development is ill able to support city services at the same costs as the more compact and orderly settlement pattern of the city.

The territory around Flint has reached this stage of development. Public pressure was exerted first for city-style schools. As soon as new schools were built the tax rate soared. Today school operating and debt service costs are so high that already approximately half (47 per cent) of the fringe dwellers pay a higher total tax rate (county, township, and school district) than the citizen of Flint pays. Except for volunteer fire brigades, direct services performed by the townships are almost nonexistent, while the county has gradually stepped up only its health, library, and road programs—the last completely with state funds. The growing demand for city-type services resulted in a township water department and a special district water department in 1939, each serving a very limited part of the total fringe area and at rates now higher than those in Flint city. Today the most crowded sections of the fringe areas remain without paved streets, sanitary sewers, police patrol, building inspection, and zoning. Already demands are being made for sidewalks in the vicinity of schools, and the county government is being abjured to perform functions they are not in a position to perform.

The final step in the fringe cycle of governmental services is incorporation. If it doesn't come as a result of annexation, it comes in the form of new towns, villages, and cities. Some cities provide temporary expedients for their fringe areas by selling services outside the corporate limits, but otherwise citizens eventually demand some medium for providing the urban services which rural governments cannot effectively supply.

Some limitations The picture presented has certain limitations. For one thing it is based on conditions prevailing in the early 1940s; in the intervening years living standards have tended to rise, even in fringe areas. It should be noted, too, that use of the term "cycle" is questionable; instead there is a progressive development, a sequence of stages. Nevertheless, the quotation brings out with a vividness rarely achieved by geographers the qualities associated with the rural-urban fringe.

Farms, forests, and wastelands In the foregoing discussion it has been assumed that the rural-urban fringe lies between agricultural land and the city. Can rural-urban fringe exist where forests or wastelands rather than agricultural land surround the city? Wehrwein seemed to assume that the transition was urban-agricultural only; but Blizzard and Anderson speak also of wastelands and forest lands. Such areas may not present the phenomenon of active competition for land, but otherwise rural-urban fringe conditions seem to prevail.

High-grade developments in the rural-urban fringe The picture of rural-urban fringe conditions is generally a rather dismal one. Yet one does find occasional high-grade developments with deed restrictions as to house value, with their own schools, and with other aspects of model communities. While such better-than-average areas do occur, as Roterus and Hughes implied it is sometimes hard to enforce deed restrictions and, besides, such restrictions ordinarily have definite time limits. In short, such model communities tend eventually to suffer some of the same problems as other sections of the rural-urban fringe.

The rural-urban fringe and the edge of the central business district Firey has called attention to an interesting similarity between the rural-urban fringe and the edge of the central business district of the city (Figure 3.3).[20] Both are marginal areas

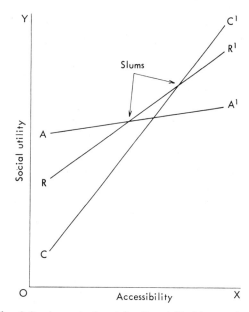

Fig. 3.3 Amount of social utility yielded by specified land uses at varying degrees of accessibility to a population center: AA', agriculturally used land; RR', residentially used land; CC', commercially used land. (After fig. 1 in Walter Firey, "Ecological Considerations in Planning for Rurban Fringes," *American Sociological Review*, vol. 11, p. 411, 1946.)

between two types of land use—agriculture and residences in the rural-urban fringe, and residences and business at the edge of the central business district. This marginality, he says, is based on accessibility (relative to that of other land uses) to some central transportation point. Broadly speaking, there is a tendency for slum conditions to occur in these areas.

Both the rural-urban fringe and the edge of the central business district, it may be added, exhibit to a high degree the dynamic qualities of the modern city. Con-

[20] Walter Firey, "Ecological Considerations in Planning for Rurban Fringes," *American Sociological Review*, vol. 11, pp. 411–423, 1946.

stant change is typical of the metropolis as a whole, but in these two belts it is likely to be particularly manifest.

Is the rural-urban fringe problem disappearing?

Typically, the rural-urban fringe has presented many problems, both for the individuals who have moved in and for the rural townships and counties unable to furnish the urban services demanded.

But the problems of the fringe are being mitigated in various ways. It has not been by chance that the fringe has been the subject of fewer magazine articles in recent years. Metropolitan planning boards, county zoning, laws permitting cities to supervise zoning within a certain distance of their borders, special-purpose utility districts, and the like—all have helped to alleviate the problems. The rural-urban fringe has not disappeared from the American scene, but it is now more controlled, more orderly.

Of course, annexation of areas adjacent to the city, where this is possible, helps to solve rural-urban fringe problems. As two students of the rural-urban fringe put it:[21]

> One key to the understanding of the fringe is political in nature. Although fringe phenomena occur spatially without regard to political boundaries, there is a political aspect in the origin of the fringe. That is, if the political organization of cities had kept abreast of the social and economic organization of the expanding urban population, the rural-urban fringe would be less of a hybrid area and might be less evident. Extensions of the political boundaries of cities tend to reduce and bring under control the types of disorganization which are typical of the fringe.

The rural-urban fringe in New England

In most of the United States small incorporated urban units are found outside the central city. Such an urban unit may

furnish most of the essential services to its residents, but it is likely to be something like an island. All around it is the rural-urban fringe area of the city, little affected by the island, since this surrounding area is under the jurisdiction of a township or county.

In New England, however, essentially all the land is divided into cities and towns with distinct governments (Appendix A). Most of the cities, or at least the larger ones, are almost completely built up, though some sections of the city near the edge may approach fringe conditions. Crossing the city boundary line, one does not reach open township or county areas as in most other parts of the United States. Instead, he finds himself in the jurisdiction of the next city or town (Figure 3.4).

In the small cities and towns of New England the picture is somewhat different from that of the larger cities. Normally, in each small town there is a central built-up area, often referred to as the *center*. At the center, most of the services, such as fire protection, water supply, sewage disposal, and the like, are available; but some, the water service possibly, may extend only a limited distance outward from the center. Schools, electricity, and police and fire protection usually cover the whole area of the town or small city. Since most of the people who live in outer portions of the town work in the center or in some nearby city rather than at rural pursuits, these outer areas of the towns may be regarded as approximating rural-urban fringe conditions, at least in certain respects. Of course, as always within the fringe, we are dealing with a gradation—in this case from reasonably full municipal services at the town's center to relatively primitive conditions in the outer regions. It follows that the edge of a town bordering a city will often have many of the attributes of a rural-urban fringe. There is likely to be a spillover of settlement from the city into the very portion of the town where services are at a minimum. And the new residents

---

[21] Blizzard and Anderson, *op. cit.*, pp. 2–3.

soon start appealing to the officials at the town's center for services.

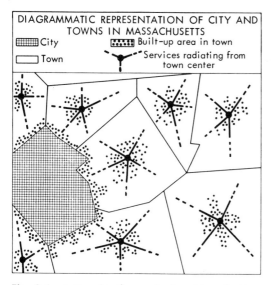

Fig. 3.4   Setting for the rural-urban fringe in New England, represented diagrammatically. The average town has a center from which services radiate—water, sewerage, schooling, fire protection, and such intangible services as zoning. In general, the town has a maximum built-up development near its center with services declining outward. Therefore, there is likely to be a mild manifestation of rural-urban fringe some distance outward from the center of the town, since services are more meagerly furnished there than nearer the center. Still farther out, at the edges of the town, more completely rural conditions generally prevail, except where the town borders a city of substantial size.

In going outward across the boundary line of a city of 100,000, for example, one passes directly into the jurisdiction of such a town. Normally, there is a spilling over of settlement from the city, but, since this is the outer portion of the adjacent town, available services are limited. This is the chief situation in which rural-urban fringe occurs in New England.

In many of the small New England cities and towns, the situation is confused by the presence of two or three built-up areas, each perhaps providing some municipal services, instead of just a single center. And the picture is complicated still further by the ribbon developments along major highways which now characterize New England just as they do so much of the rest of the country.

For some reason no studies of the rural-urban fringe pattern of New England have appeared in the literature. And yet it is a particularly challenging topic in view of the way in which the administrative structure has affected the pattern of the fringe.

Conclusions

This chapter, dealing with the transition zone that surrounds the city, has been concerned chiefly with definitions. The concepts of suburb and satellite have been considered, and also the rural-urban fringe. There is a great deal of vagueness in the use of these terms; hence certain usages are recommended on the basis of the state of our knowledge to date.

Even though it deals chiefly with problems of terminology, a chapter of this sort implies various lines of research that might be followed. For example, suburbs and satellites and the intermediate types referred to should be differentiated in various areas, and detailed studies should be made of their characteristics. For that matter, the whole problem of distinguishing suburbs from satellites needs further attention. How can we make the distinction for small urban centers for which employment data are not available from the United States Census?

The rural-urban fringe, too, needs further study. Certainly, it should be possible to find some more objective method for delimiting and hence studying the area. This is true for the country in general. New England has been pointed out as presenting a unique challenge because of the seeming effects of its governmental structure on the rural-urban fringe.

Selected References

Andrews, Richard B.: "Elements of the Urban Fringe Problem," *Journal of Land and Public Utility Economics,* vol. 18, pp. 169–183, 1942.

Blizzard, Samuel M.: "Research on the Rural-Urban Fringe: A Case Study," *Sociology and Social Research*, vol. 38, pp. 143–149, 1954.

———— and William F. Anderson, II: *Problems in Rural-Urban Fringe Research: Conceptualization and Delineation*, Progress Report no. 89, The Pennsylvania State College Agricultural Experiment Station, State College, Pa., 1952.

Dobriner, William M. (ed.): *The Suburban Community*, G. P. Putnam's Sons, New York, 1958.

Firey, Walter I.: "Ecological Considerations in Planning for Rurban Fringes," *American Sociological Review*, vol. 11, pp. 411–423, 1946.

Harris, Chauncy D.: "Suburbs," *American Journal of Sociology*, vol. 49, pp. 1–13, 1943.

———— and Edward L. Ullman: "The Nature of Cities," *Annals of the American Academy of Political and Social Science*, vol. 242, pp. 7–17, 1945.

Jones, Victor, Richard L. Forstall, and Andrew Collver: "Economic and Social Characteristics of Urban Places," *The Municipal Year Book*, International City Managers Association, Chicago, 1963, pp. 85–157.

McKain, Walter C., and Robert G. Burnight: "The Sociological Significance of the Rural-Urban Fringe from the Rural Point of View," *Rural Sociology*, vol. 18, pp. 108–117, 1953.

Murphy, Raymond E.: "Town Structure and Urban Concepts in New England," *The Professional Geographer*, vol. 16, pp. 1–6, 1964.

Myers, Richard R., and J. A. Beegle: "Delineation and Analysis of the Rural-Urban Fringe," *Applied Anthropology*, vol. 6, no. 2, pp. 14–22, 1947.

Schnore, Leo F.: "The Growth of Metropolitan Suburbs," *American Sociological Review*, vol. 22, pp. 165–173, 1957.

Wehrwein, G. S.: "Rural-Urban Fringe," *Economic Geography*, vol. 18, pp. 217–228, 1942.

4

The city's spheres of influence

NORMALLY, each city forms the core of a larger area which it dominates. With distance outward from the core, the domination tends to weaken, and eventually the influence of some competing urban center exceeds that of the city under consideration. It is with the area which the city dominates in a general way and with more specialized spheres of influence that this chapter deals.

When the area of dominance is analyzed it is found to consist of a number of single-feature nodal regions: the commuting area, the city newspaper circulation area, retail and wholesale trading areas, and many others—even such areas as those from which people come to the city's annual music festival. Some of these regions extend far beyond the boundary of the city's overall area of dominance; others fall short of that boundary. Some represent a daily movement; others, a much less frequent interaction between a city and its surrounding areas. The combination of influences diminishes with distance from the city until a divide is reached beyond which the combined influences of the various services operating from some competing urban center are greater than the waning aggregate of which the first city is the core.

Contiguous and non-contiguous regions
The single-feature regional boundaries that may be drawn around a city outline a series of contiguous areas, and the area of dominance of the city, too, is a contiguous area. In addition to these contiguous areas, the city has more limited and spotty connections that may be countrywide or even worldwide. For example, manufactured products may reach worldwide markets, and raw materials needed for the city's factories may come from half way round the globe. Similarly, a port may import goods for several widely separated urban centers far in the interior of the country and may export

goods originating in cities hundreds of miles inland. Though these non-contiguous points of connection are by no means unimportant to a city, and though they, themselves, form nodal regions with the city as the core, they do not greatly concern us here. Instead, we shall in this chapter focus on the contiguous areas that include the city and the surrounding territory that serves and is served by the city.

Terminology   There is no generally accepted terminology for discussing the types of contiguous regions we have described. Even the general term, *spheres of influence,* has been questioned on the ground that it sounds as though it implied political control.

Before going further, therefore, we must make several decisions in regard to terms. The area in which the influence of a city is dominant over that of competing cities has been variously called the city's tributary area, its supporting and tributary area, its market area, its sphere of influence, its hinterland, its umland, and its urban field; and the city's single-feature regions have been called tributary areas, hinterlands, urban fields or just fields, catchment areas, spheres of influence, and service areas. It is well to be aware of these different usages, each of which has certain advantages and certain disadvantages. Here we shall speak of the single-feature regions as *service areas* and the area of city dominance as a whole as the city's *tributary area.* Spheres of influence will be used in the more general sense of including both the city's service areas and its tributary area.

Geographers, sociologists, and others have studied spheres of influence   The study of a city's spheres of influence is by no means the exclusive province of geographers. Over the years, sociologists have been interested in these areas, too, and so have workers in several other disciplines. Nor is the idea a new one. Such delimitations, usually as parts of more general urban studies,

began to appear in the literature shortly after World War I.

Service Areas

In this chapter, service areas and tributary areas are analyzed. The former can be outlined with considerable definiteness for a number of different items. Because of this relative simplicity, service areas are discussed first.

Reasons for analyzing service areas   There are several good reasons for analyzing the service areas of a city. An analysis of the city's relations to its surrounding area brings a better understanding of the city itself. And broadly, the outlining of service areas can be a step toward delimiting the area of dominance: the city's tributary area. Moreover, detailed study of any particular service area may lead, through advertising and other active steps, to an extension of that service. Other values accruing to service area studies will be referred to later in this chapter.

Choice of criteria   A great variety of criteria may be used to delimit service areas. The number tends to increase with city size and the resulting complexity of services. Some of the more common criteria are shown in Table 4.1, but any reader can easily think of many others.

The choice of criteria on which to base service areas for studying a particular city depends on several factors. One is the nature of the city and its region. Thus for a small city in a farming district, the areas from which people come to buy farm machinery or to market their livestock or from which they truck wheat to the local elevator may be of special interest. Yet for many cities these criteria are of little significance.

For the average city there are several other considerations. The interest may be in just one type of activity, such as newspaper circulation, or in one group of activities, such as wholesaling. In such cases, the choice of criteria is obvious. But often the objective is more general: to present as best one may the major facets of a city's influence over or interconnections with the countryside. Then one must ask: Is this activity important, and is it a good indicator of the interrelationships between the city and its tributary area? A second and very practical consideration is: Can I get the necessary information to outline such a service area?

Table 4.1   Some of the bases on which service areas are commonly delimited

Bakery deliveries	Mail deliveries
Banks with deposits in the city banks	Meats (wholesale)
	Milk shed
Clients of city dentists	Motion pictures (wholesale)
Clients of city lawyers	
Clients of city physicians	Newspaper circulation
Commuting	Port collecting area
Dairy products (wholesale)	Radio
	Residence of people using various recreational and cultural facilities of the city
Drugs (wholesale)	
Furniture deliveries	
Gasoline and oil (wholesale)	
	Retail trade
Grain elevator customers	Telephone service
	Television
Groceries (wholesale)	United delivery service
Hardware (wholesale)	

Note: Some of the criteria involve areas from which people or products come to the city; others, the area reached by some service or type of merchandise emanating from the city.

There is no universal answer to such questions, since the most important indicator of the extent of influence of one type of city is not necessarily the most important for a city of a different type, and since the information readily available in one city may not be obtainable in another. At best, then, the selection of criteria remains a subjective problem. But it is well to know what boundaries and techniques have been found feasible and effective by other workers.

Sources and techniques in determining service area boundaries

To anyone interested in delimiting the service areas of a city, the methods of obtaining the necessary information and of actually locating the boundaries are matters of prime importance. For a small urban center it may be assumed that only a few service areas will be delimited and that most of the information necessary for locating the boundaries can be obtained from businessmen and other local people by direct consultation. For larger cities, however, the problems of selecting and delimiting service areas become progressively more complicated.

Harris's methods for Salt Lake City, Utah   Chauncy Harris, in a study of Salt Lake City, delimited the areas for twelve selected services or functions (Figure 4.1).[1] Five of these boundaries—those for retail trade, wholesale grocery trade, wholesale drug trade, radio broadcasting, and generalized trade—were taken from published sources. Thus, Harris was able to obtain his retail trade boundary from published maps and books dealing with retail trade of American cities; his wholesale grocery boundary from an atlas of wholesale grocery trading areas issued by the Bureau of Foreign and Domestic Commerce; his wholesale drug trade area from a distribution map of the United States issued by the National Wholesale Druggists' Association; his radio broadcasting area from a publication of the Columbia Broadcasting System; and his generalized trade area boundary from government publications.

In his monograph he explains, also, how the other seven boundaries were located. Two, the state boundary and the area served by the Salt Lake City branch of the Federal Reserve Bank of San Francisco,

[1] Chauncy D. Harris, *Salt Lake City: A Regional Capital,* doctoral dissertation, University of Chicago Libraries, Chicago, 1940.

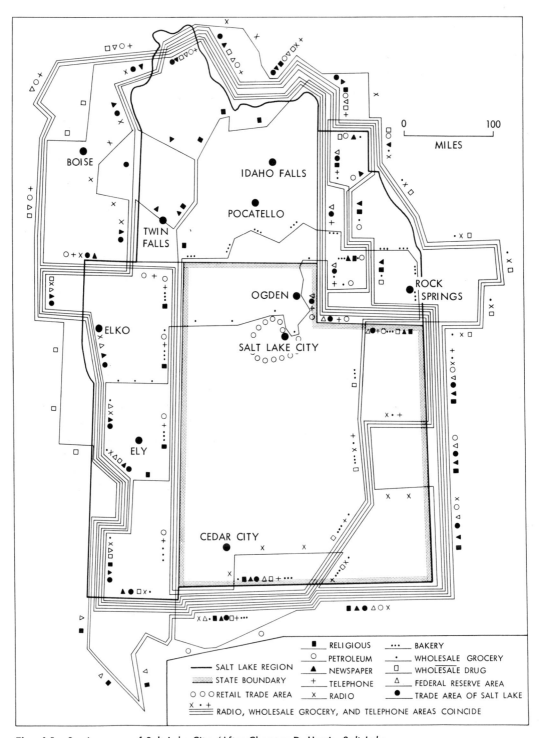

Fig. 4.1 Service areas of Salt Lake City. (After Chauncy D. Harris, *Salt Lake City: A Regional Capital*, doctoral dissertation, University of Chicago Libraries, Chicago, 1939, fig. 10.)

were legally established areas. The newspaper circulation area was based on his compilation from data of the Audit Bureau of Circulations (ABC).[2] The information was presented on a map on which the percentage of families receiving the leading Salt Lake City newspaper was shown for each county. The religious boundary was based on statistics derived from governmental and church sources. Harris included in his religious hinterland all counties in which 20 per cent or more of the population was Mormon.

Three of the service areas—the telephone area and the bakery and petroleum products areas—were based on interviews. Information regarding the telephone area came from the Mountain States Telephone and Telegraph Company, the bakery distribution area was generalized from the distribution areas of several different brands of bread, and the Utah Oil Refining Company furnished the information for the petroleum distribution area.

Ullman's work on Mobile, Alabama Edward Ullman used a somewhat different technique in delimiting the Mobile wholesale distribution areas for groceries, meats, and drugs (Figure 4.2).[3] Saying that he doubted the value of boundaries obtained directly from the wholesalers themselves, he based his work, instead, on a field procedure: questioning retailers in the country surrounding Mobile and drawing his boundary so as to enclose all places where 50 per cent or more of the wholesale business was with Mobile firms.

Ullman did not stop with wholesaling;

[2] ABC reports are issued by all major newspapers. Each lists the towns and cities covered by its retail trading area (the area where residents regularly trade with retail merchants in the city in a volume sufficient to justify advertising expenditures by merchants) and commonly gives newspaper circulation data for each urban center included.

[3] Edward L. Ullman, *Mobile: Industrial Seaport and Trade Center,* Department of Geography, University of Chicago, Chicago, 1943, p. 57, fn. 1.

he also determined the retail trade boundary and newspaper circulation boundaries. On another map in his monograph on Mobile he showed by means of proportional circles and dots the distribution of out-of-town charge accounts for Mobile's largest department store and, on still another map, the distribution of banks having deposits in Mobile banks. For establishing such service areas as charge accounts and bank deposits, the research worker must obtain a high degree of local cooperation.

Boundary problems Different types of service areas may be plotted on maps in different ways. Each method presents certain problems of establishing boundaries.

Distribution may be shown by means of proportional circles—as in Ullman's maps of the out-of-town charge accounts of the Mobile department store and of the banks with deposits in Mobile banks. But service areas so depicted have definite limitations. For instance, with such a map there is virtually no way to determine service area boundaries. Hence, comparisons with other service areas are difficult.

A single-line service area boundary is more commonly used. This may represent an administrative boundary such as the state line on Harris's map (Figure 4.1). Or it may result from a company decision, e.g., the edge of the area that a telephone company decides should belong in one exchange, or an agreement as to the limits of the area in which the united parcel delivery organization of a certain city will make deliveries. A single-line boundary might be used, too, to outline the extreme area from which customers of a department store come.

Ordinarily, however, the edge of a service area is gradational and can best be conceived of as marked by isopleths of descending value. Ullman used two newspaper boundaries—one in which Mobile papers accounted for 50 per cent or more

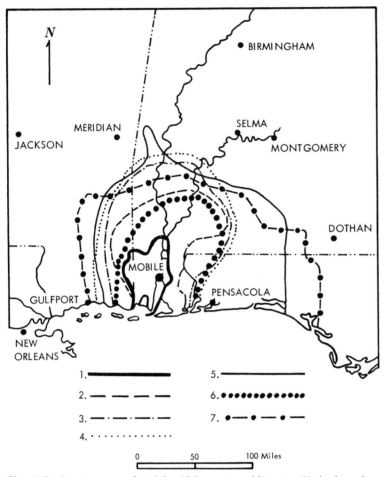

Fig. 4.2 Service areas of Mobile, Alabama. In addition to (1) the boundary of the area within which 50 per cent or more of the retail business is done in Mobile, the map shows the areas within which Mobile secures 50 per cent or more of (2) the wholesale grocery, (3) the wholesale meat, (4) the wholesale produce, and (5) the wholesale drug business. Two newspaper boundaries are shown: the first (6) enclosing the area within which Mobile newspapers have 50 per cent or more of the out-of-town newspaper circulation; and the second (7) enclosing the area within which Mobile newspapers have at least 15 to 20 per cent of the out-of-town circulation. (After Edward L. Ullman, *Mobile: Industrial Seaport and Trade Center*, Department of Geography, University of Chicago, 1943, fig. 7.)

of the out-of-town newspaper circulation and a second in which Mobile papers had at least 15 to 20 per cent of the out-of-town circulation (Figure 4.2). More often, however, some one isopleth is chosen as the boundary. Thus Harris based his religious area on counties in which 20 per cent or more of the people were Mormons, and

each of Ullman's several wholesale boundaries was based on the 50 per cent line which marked the outer limit of the area in which Mobile firms do 50 per cent or more of the wholesale business.

The use of the 50 per cent line suggests a limitation to the value of some service area boundaries. Where a value such as 50 per cent—say, for example, 50 per cent of all newspaper circulation—is used as the service area boundary, it is obvious that the entire service area is not represented: theoretically, the service area continues outward to a line beyond which no newspapers from the city are received. But for many types of services, the determination of such an extreme line would be difficult as well as impractical. One may assume that by far the most intense and significant part of the service area is enclosed by the 50 per cent line.

Such isopleth boundaries are not necessarily based upon percentages. For example, in delimiting the areas of newspaper circulation for Worcester, Massachusetts, one might use the ratio of Worcester newspapers received to total population of each of the nearby towns. Similarly, ratios may be based on clients of city physicians to town population, or of daily commuters to town population. Some one ratio value, however, would probably be selected to limit the city's service area for each individual service.

Ratios to town populations work particularly well in New England, since there, typically, all the land is divided into towns and cities, and isopleths can be used satisfactorily. Elsewhere, ordinarily, data are given for cities, villages, and the like, and, in each case, can be related to the population, but there are open spaces between places. A ratio can be indicated for each place, but isopleths are hardly feasible.

In summary, there is no one perfect way in which service area limits should be depicted. But it is important always to indicate the exact method of delimitation and the value on which each service area boundary is based.

Relative positions of service area boundaries

If a substantial number of service areas is outlined for a city, it will be seen that there is a great range in the positions of the boundaries, a range which tends to increase with the size of the city. Wholesaling boundaries, for example, lie much farther out from the city than those associated with retailing (Figures 4.1 and 4.2); and the larger the city, the greater these differences are likely to be.

Wholesaling boundaries According to Harris, Ullman, and others who have studied service areas, there are interesting differences even between the several wholesale types.[4] Wholesale grocery distribution, according to Harris, generally is somewhat more restricted by distance than other wholesale trade since the relatively great bulk of wholesale groceries in proportion to their value favors additional distribution centers in smaller towns. Some types of bakery products, he says, particularly bread, show this same tendency; and the tendency is reinforced by the perishability of the product. Cakes, with a higher value per unit of weight than bread, are distributed over a wider area. According to Ullman, in the Mobile area, wholesale meat and produce have slightly larger distribution areas than wholesale groceries, chiefly because the former are difficult to handle and ship, and the special equipment required rules out the small distributor. Wholesale drugs have an extensive service area, since they have such a high value in proportion to their weight. The service area for petroleum products tends to be particularly extensive because the advantages of refinery concentration more than offset transportation costs.

Hardware distribution presents a rather complicated picture. Ullman points out that even within the area served from Mobile, the larger urban centers buy most of their hardware direct from such cities as Louisville and St. Louis. Electrical appliances are often sold on an installment basis,

[4] The generalizations that follow are based largely on the studies of Salt Lake City by Harris and of Mobile by Ullman.

so that merchandising them requires a considerable investment. Therefore, manufacturers select the wholesalers carefully and give each one an exclusive franchise to a territory.

Retailing The retail trade area of the city ordinarily tends to be small. People will not travel far for frequently recurring shopping needs. On the other hand, they will come considerable distances to shop at a large department store, and the out-of-town charge accounts for such a store often have a distribution more like that of wholesaling than of retailing. Another characteristic of the retail trade area is based on quality. Customers interested in high-quality goods will travel farther than those interested only in low-quality goods.

Newspaper and other boundaries The newspaper area boundary usually occupies a position intermediate between those of wholesaling and retailing. Radio, television, banking, and telephone administration involve little transportation cost and hence are like the wholesaling types in penetrating wide areas.

Park and Newcomb's work with newspaper circulation areas

In the preceding pages some of the service areas (single-feature regions) that can be outlined for a city were discussed as well as the problems of outlining such regions. But a different scale of study is possible. Any one of the various types of services can be made the subject of a special, more comprehensive study that will involve not just one city, but several cities, or a large city and its satellites and suburbs. It is possible in this way to see the relations among urban centers with respect to this one type of service.

A notable example of such a study is an analysis of newspaper circulation by R. E. Park and Charles Newcomb, two sociolo-

gists formerly at the University of Chicago.[5] Though Park and Newcomb did not discuss the sources of data used for their study, it was pointed out earlier in this chapter that the Audit Bureau of Circulations issues data for most newspapers, giving number of copies going to each city and smaller urban centers. Since Park and Newcomb's work was done several decades ago, it is probable that details of the picture have changed a great deal, but the principles developed should still be sound and hence are summarized here.[6]

News as a commodity In America the newspaper has gradually assumed the nature of a commodity, that is, something to be sold and distributed. Nevertheless, there are special considerations which determine and limit the extent of its circulation. Larger operations are economical. On the other hand, time is an essential element of news; hence, rapid distribution is necessary. Moreover, newspapers operate on the basis of local news. Also, closely related to distance is advertising income. This tends to restrict circulation to areas where readers are potential buyers.

Circulation and the trade area The size of the trade area within which a paper circulates is determined primarily by (1) the size of the town, city, or metropolitan center in which it is published, and (2) the proximity of other competing centers of publication. Thus, Boston papers circulate widely over New England, whereas the circulation limits of competing centers such as Philadelphia, Baltimore, and New York are restricted by the proximity of these

[5] Robert E. Park and Charles Newcomb, "Newspaper Circulation and Metropolitan Regions," in R. D. McKenzie, *The Metropolitan Community*, McGraw-Hill Book Company, Inc., New York, 1933, chap. VIII.

[6] For convenience the present tense is used in this summary, even though the work was done in the late 1920s.

cities to each other. The very size of New York City,[7] however, assures its newspapers a wide circulation in the three other cities, and the smaller sizes of the other cities operate to restrict the circulation of their papers in New York City. For reasons similar to the foregoing, Minneapolis–St. Paul papers have a circulation area to the northwest that is limited only by factors of time and space, while to the south and east it is narrowed by competition with Chicago papers.

Metropolitan and local papers   Similar influences are dominant in explaining the areas of circulation of metropolitan and local newspapers within a given region. Metropolitan newspapers are defined as those published in the central city, and local papers as those published in the metropolitan region but outside the central city, that is, in the suburban towns, the satellite cities, and the larger area around the metropolis which Park and Newcomb call the "metropolitan hinterland."

New York City papers circulate widely through the territory adjacent to the city— in New England, New York State, Pennsylvania, and New Jersey—but Connecticut and New Jersey papers do not circulate in New York City; and Chicago papers circulate in Gary, Indiana, but Gary papers do not circulate in Chicago, though they compete with Chicago papers in territory suburban to Gary. The extent to which a metropolitan paper circulates outside of the corporate limits of the metropolis in competition with a locally published paper is an index of the metropolitan paper's dominance in that area and likewise of the dominance of the metropolis. Conversely, the number of copies published and circulated by a local paper in competition with a metropolitan paper is an index of the local

paper's (and the local community's) degree of economic and cultural independence.

Sometimes a local paper is published within the limits of a larger city. Such a paper may appeal to a particular element of the population, a foreign language group for example. There are also local weekly papers published in various quarters of large cities chiefly to carry advertising for the local merchants.

According to Park and Newcomb, it is difficult to maintain a daily newspaper in competition with the more important metropolitan dailies within 50 miles of a metropolis, and the difficulty increases as the means of transportation and communication integrate the metropolis with its suburban territory.

Papers of small cities versus metropolitan papers in the Chicago area   Examination of the newspaper circulation pattern for the Chicago area brings out some interesting points (Figure 4.3). The area in general is dominated by the Chicago papers, but there are seven local trade centers or "satellite centers" [8]—Joliet, Aurora, Elgin, Waukegan, Evanston, Hammond, and Gary —each of which publishes a daily paper of its own. In all of these except Evanston, the local paper is sold in greater numbers than the Chicago papers, and in the towns immediately surrounding each of them this dominance continues, some of the smaller villages receiving no papers at all except those from the satellite center.

With distance outward from the satellite center in any direction, the towns receive smaller and smaller proportions of their papers from the satellite center, until a line is reached marking the boundary of the area receiving 50 per cent or more of its papers from that source (see Figure 4.3). In towns beyond this line, metropolitan papers amount to more than 50 per cent of

---

[7] Not to mention, of course, the quality of its leading newspapers, the city's prestige, and other factors.

[8] Park and Newcomb use the term satellite center for any large suburban community.

the total. Thus each small city and its surrounding towns form a sort of island in a sea over which the metropolitan papers predominate.

Somewhat beyond the 50 per cent line around each of the satellite centers (see Figure 4.3) is a broken line marking the limits of the circulation of the local paper. This is essentially the limits of the local trade area. The ratio between metropolitan and local papers distributed in each of the satellite centers is one measure of the degree to which the satellite center is integrated with and dominated by the metropolis.

Varying degrees of independence Among the satellite centers there are wide differences in the extent of domination by metropolitan newspapers. Those satellite centers that are nearest the city and are most completely dormitory in character (therefore, true suburbs as defined in Chapter 3) receive the highest proportions of metropolitan papers. Evanston, nearest the city of all the satellite centers and most nearly a dormitory suburb, uses the highest proportion of metropolitan papers. At the other extreme are places such as Aurora, with substantial economic bases, thus justifying the designation of satellites, as defined in Chapter 3. Commuters to the city are likely to buy metropolitan papers, but the person who lives and works in the satellite more commonly buys a local paper. Aurora has a much larger proportion of its population working in the satellite center than does Evanston, and thus a much larger proportion of local papers is purchased. Moreover, in the trade areas of the industrial satellites, such as Aurora, are towns taking no papers at all from the metropolis; there are no such towns in the Evanston trade area.

The suburban belt nearer to Chicago Between the city limits of Chicago and the first towns taking any daily newspapers

from the satellite centers is an open belt on the map (Figure 4.3). This area consists of an essentially contiguous mass of communities such as Des Plaines, Maywood, Oak Park, Elmhurst, Melrose Park, and Cicero. These densely peopled communities are almost entirely dependent on Chicago for their daily papers. Since the interests of the people in these places are centered in Chicago, it is only natural that Chicago papers would circulate in this belt to the exclusion of those from the satellite centers.

Newspaper circulation in the Chicago area in summary Within 50 miles of the center of Chicago at State and Madison Streets, Chicago metropolitan papers make up by far the bulk of all circulation. Though each local publishing center has its trade area, dominated by its own circulation, these areas consume a relatively small proportion of the circulation consumed in the area in general. Another interesting point is that in each of the satellite trade areas the towns are limited in importance and size by their relation to the satellite centers, just as the latter in turn are limited in their development by their proximity to Chicago. According to Park and Newcomb, as communication and transportation develop in the metropolitan area, the importance of the satellite centers should diminish even more.

Market areas according to Reilly's law of retail gravitation

About the same time that Park and Newcomb were doing their work on newspaper circulation areas, William J. Reilly, an economist at the University of Texas, was making a special study of another type of service area—that of retail trade. However, his primary concern was not in outlining service areas so as to work out the degree of interdependence between a central city and subsidiary centers, as was the case with Park and Newcomb, but rather in

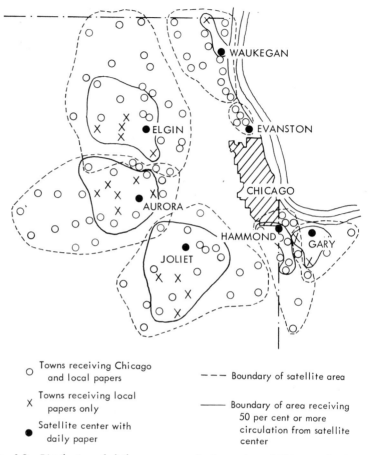

○   Towns receiving Chicago and local papers

X   Towns receiving local papers only

●   Satellite center with daily paper

---   Boundary of satellite area

———   Boundary of area receiving 50 per cent or more circulation from satellite center

Fig. 4.3 Distribution of daily newspapers in the region of Chicago, showing all towns receiving copies from Chicago and satellite centers in 1928. (After R. E. Park and Charles Newcomb, "Newspaper Circulation in Metropolitan Regions," in R. D. McKenzie, *The Metropolitan Community*, McGraw-Hill Book Company, Inc., New York, 1933, fig. 5.)

enunciating and attempting to verify his "Law of Retail Gravitation." [9]

Outline of method In its simplest form, the law states that under normal conditions two cities attract retail trade from a smaller intermediate city or town approxi-

[9] William J. Reilly, *The Law of Retail Gravitation*, Pillsbury Publishers, Inc., New York, 1931, 2d ed., 1953; William J. Reilly, *Methods for the Study of Retail Relationships*, University of Texas, Austin, Studies in Marketing no. 4, Bureau of Business Research, 1959. (Reprint of research monograph first published in 1929.)

mately in direct proportion to the populations of the two cities, and in inverse proportion to the squares of the distances from these two cities to the intermediate city or town. It is assumed that the distances are measured along the most direct improved highway.

The formula The general formula for the law of retail gravitation, as defined in the previous paragraph, is expressed as follows: $Ba/Bb = (Pa/Pb)(Db/Da)^2$ where Ba is the business which City A draws from intermediate Town T; Bb is the business which City B draws from intermediate Town T; *Pa* is the population of City A; *Pb* is the population of City B; *Da* is the distance of City A from intermediate Town T; and *Db* is the distance of City B from intermediate Town T. In this book we are not concerned with trade for its own sake, but the formula does tell us something about the location of the *breaking point* between any two cities. The breaking point is defined as "a point up to which one city exercises the dominating retail trade influence and beyond which the other city dominates." At the breaking point, $Ba/Bb = 1/1$. It follows that we might estimate the position of the breaking point between two cities and then check it with the formula.

Restatement of the law   But there is a simpler method of determining the position of the breaking point. This method is made possible through a restatement of Reilly's law to read as follows: [10] The number of miles from trading center A to the breaking point or outer limit of its retail trading area, computed along a major paved road running

$$\text{from A to B} = \cfrac{\text{miles between A and B}}{1 + \sqrt{\cfrac{\text{population of City B}}{\text{population of City A}}}}$$

An example of the application of Reilly's law   An example should make the use of Reilly's law and of the restated version clearer. The distance between Oklahoma City and Amarillo, Texas, is 266 miles as given in a road atlas. This is measured along a main highway between the two cities. The Oklahoma City Urbanized Area had a population of 429,188 in 1960 and the Amarillo Urbanized Area, 137,969.[11]

[10] Frank Strohkarck and Katherine Phelps, "The Mechanics of Constructing a Market Area Map," *Journal of Marketing*, vol. 12, pp. 493–496, 1948.
[11] Urbanized areas are used here since they are considered to represent the best expression of the city for which data are available. Of course, when Reilly developed his law the urbanized area idea was not yet in use. But since he refers in his book

Under the second or restated formula, the distance of the breaking point from Oklahoma City is $\cfrac{266}{1 + \sqrt{\cfrac{137,969}{429,188}}} = 169.7$ miles. Naturally, the point is nearer to Amarillo, the smaller city, than to Oklahoma City. It lies 96.3 miles east of Amarillo, very near Shamrock, a town in the Texas Panhandle. We can use Reilly's original law to check our calculations. Oklahoma City and Amarillo should share equally in the trade of Shamrock. The distances determined can be substituted in Reilly's original law (page 61) as follows:

$$\frac{\text{business Oklahoma City draws from Shamrock}}{\text{business Amarillo draws from Shamrock}}$$
$$= \left(\frac{429,188}{137,969}\right)\left(\frac{96.3}{169.7}\right)^2 = \frac{1}{1}$$

The fact that the formula works out as a 1:1 ratio shows that the breaking point has been correctly located.

Outlining the area   Only one point was determined between Oklahoma City and Amarillo, but if similar breaking points in various directions from the city were found, its retail trade area could be approximately outlined. Commonly, in doing this, one would consider only cities that compete in furnishing similar goods. Thus, Reilly described how the trade territory of Pittsburgh, Pennsylvania, was approximated.[12] The first step, he said, was to determine the cities around Pittsburgh that would compete in similar levels of "style and specialty goods." The following cities were selected: Cleveland, Youngstown,

(*The Law of Retail Gravitation*) to "Metropolitan St. Louis," "Greater Kansas City," and "Pittsburgh including immediate suburbs," it may be assumed that he used metropolitan district population totals or their equivalents, where these were available, and incorporated city data for smaller places. The latter still is necessary if we are working with cities too small to have urbanized areas.
[12] Reilly, *The Law of Retail Gravitation*, pp. 36–37.

Canton, and Steubenville, Ohio; Wheeling and Clarksburg, West Virginia; Cumberland, Maryland; Erie, New Castle, Johnstown, and Altoona, Pennsylvania; and Buffalo, New York. It would have been illogical to include in this list an urban center of, say, 5,000 population, since it would not be able to support stores with adequate selections of goods to compete with Pittsburgh. The breaking point between Pittsburgh and each of the listed cities was determined. The resulting trade area outline was based on a point on each of the various major highways leading away from Pittsburgh. Of course, the use of Reilly's law is by no means restricted to the determination of trade areas of cities the size of Pittsburgh. One can equally well separate from one another the trade areas of a group of smaller competing centers.

Modifying factors Reilly realized that the trade territories outlined by his technique were theoretical, so could be considered to apply only in a very general way. He mentioned relief, toll bridges, highway congestion, and conditions of highways as among the most important factors that modify the movement of trade.

Substitutions Some users of Reilly's law have substituted driving time for highway mileage and square feet of retail floor space for population.[13] For example, Town O has 50,000 square feet of food store selling area and Town N has 25,000 square feet. The time-distance from Town N to Town O is 70 minutes (7 units). Then the formula for determining the breaking point in trade between Town N and Town O is as follows:

$$x \text{ equals } \frac{\text{total units of driving time from Town N to Town O}}{1 + \sqrt{\dfrac{\text{sales area of Town O}}{\text{sales area of Town N}}}}$$

[13] See discussion of this point in Saul B. Cohen and William Applebaum, "Evaluating Store Sites and Determining Store Rents," *Economic Geography,* vol. 36, pp. 1–35, 1960.

In this case x represents the units of driving time from Town N toward Town O. By similar means the distance in total units of driving time from Town N toward other competing towns may be determined, thus outlining the retail trade area of Town N in units of driving time. However, at best, Reilly's law is only an approximation technique. In metropolitan areas, competition is to be found in so many different directions and at so many different scales that researchers often find it preferable to determine trading areas directly, using customer addresses from store interviews or automobile registrations.[14]

The law of retail gravitation and newspaper circulation Reilly pointed out that, because of the importance of local advertising, a close relationship exists between trade areas and areas of newspaper circulation. The publishers of a newspaper, he claimed, could use the law of retail gravitation to outline the retail trade territory of their city, and then use this trade territory as a basis for judging the adequacy of the newspaper's circulation pattern.

Research opportunities

The discussion of service areas in this chapter is based largely on studies done a number of years ago. Park and Newcomb and Reilly worked about 1930, and the studies by Harris and Ullman are now more than two decades old. Increased use of the automobile, changing methods of merchandise packaging and distributing (with a progressive decline of wholesaling),[15] the rise of television—these and other factors must be greatly altering the service area picture. It appears to be getting vastly more complex, especially in densely settled areas.

[14] See, for example, the work of Applebaum and Spears described on pp. 279–281.
[15] Much of the traditional wholesaler's function is being taken over by manufacturers and groups of retailers.

The subject of service areas, therefore, presents some real research challenges. The tentative generalizations presented here suggest that there is much of interest to be found out, but it is a changing picture and one for which data are often hard to get. Individual types of services, particularly, appear to merit investigation. Commuting patterns are already being studied wherever data are available, and work might be done, too, with respect to other service areas. The possibilities of newspaper service areas remain particularly challenging since Audit Bureau of Circulations data are available. Yet the interesting work of Park and Newcomb has not been followed up. A study of the newspaper circulation areas of the several competing cities in a relatively large and complex region—for example, in New England—should be well worth while, though difficult.

Tributary Areas

Thus far in this chapter, we have discussed individual or groups of individual service areas. Even the areas defined by Reilly's law represent only one general service: retailing. We are now ready to consider the problem of delimiting the area of combined influence of the various services: the city's tributary area.

The general situation

The situation in its simplest form may be stated like this: City A and City B, each with a population of 150,000, lie 100 miles apart. A series of service areas can be delimited for each, with the city as a focus. Outward from each city, the total influence of the city, as represented by an aggregate of all services, becomes smaller and smaller. In a zone about half way between the two cities a number of the service areas of the two cities may overlap; in fact it is even possible for some of the service areas of A to include B and for some of those for which B is the focus to include A. For some distance from A toward B there is no question regarding which city is dominant: A clearly dominates, attracting most of the people who wish to visit a city of this size and furnishing a variety of services to the countryside. In like fashion, for some distance from B toward A, B clearly dominates. But there is a belt in some intermediate position where the dominance is in doubt—for some purposes people may go to B; for others, to A. Or the decision may be based on habit or personal preference. This belt or transition zone, broad and vague though it may be, represents the boundary between the tributary areas of the two cities.

Of course, this is the situation in only one direction. In some other directions, the lack of a comparable city may result in the tributary area of A or that of B extending much farther; certainly the tributary area of a city is likely to be far from symmetrical.

Tributary areas of small urban centers

Delimiting tributary areas of very small urban centers is relatively simple, though even here the divides can be located only approximately. Field work consisting of simple inquiry along major connecting roads can often yield reasonably good approximations of such divides, or questionnaires may be substituted for field work.

Tributary areas of cities

What we are in effect doing is approximating a sort of median of various intercity service area boundaries. The range of such boundaries is relatively small for small urban centers, so the approximation is correspondingly simple. But with larger cities the range is greater, and the problem of arriving at an approximate line is correspondingly difficult. At the same time, greater interest attaches to such a possible delimitation.

Approximations based on single factors or combinations of factors One approach to the problem is to assume that some one factor or a simple combination of factors does a fairly good job of delimiting the city's tributary area. Park and Newcomb, for example, in a continuation of their newspaper circulation study described earlier, were able to draw a line connecting the outermost places taking 50 per cent or more of their metropolitan newspapers from Chicago as opposed to competing centers.[16] They had thus outlined an area of dominance of Chicago based on metropolitan newspaper circulation. Similarly, Reilly's law outlines areas of city dominance on the basis of retail trade. Some of the other types of criteria on which service areas are based might be similarly used to outline discrete city tributary areas, though of necessity they would have to represent goods or services for which people depend on all cities of comparable size.[17]

Which criteria are best for the purpose? Obviously, no one measure or combination of two or three measures can be completely satisfactory in outlining areas of dominance, since too many factors are involved. But Park and Newcomb pointed out that newspaper distribution areas are likely to be closely related to retail trade areas, and hence newspaper distribution areas, they felt, might well be the best single measure of city dominance.

The simplest and most definite procedure for determining the territory directly dominated by a particular city is to map the area surrounding the city wherein its communications, especially its daily newspapers, show more intensive coverage than do those from competing metropolitan centers.[18]

A good case can be made, too, for trade areas outlined according to Reilly's law, which are believed to show a fair degree of relationship to the areas of newspaper circulation.

Metropolitan newspaper circulation as a basis for metropolitan regions Park and Newcomb carried their ideas to the point of developing a system of metropolitan regions of the United States, based on metropolitan newspaper circulation.[19] One of their first problems was the selection of metropolitan centers. They decided to use primarily Federal Reserve cities, since these had already been chosen to perform one type of regional service. To these cities, Sioux City, Iowa, Des Moines, Iowa, Albuquerque, New Mexico, Charlotte, North Carolina, and Louisville, Kentucky, were later added, making a total of forty-one. The morning newspaper having the most extensive circulation was selected for each metropolitan center, and statistics were taken from the records of the Audit Bureau of Circulations.

The method involved study of the newspaper circulation data for the many small cities and towns throughout the country that received papers from more than one of the forty-one metropolitan centers. The final product was a map of the United States with the area divided among the forty-one centers. For each, the area outlined included nearly all cities and towns receiving 50 per cent or more of their metropolitan papers from the metropolitan center. In short, these were areas of dominance of each center as measured by the circulation of the selected morning metropolitan newspapers. There were some cases of overlap-

[16] Park and Newcomb, in McKenzie, *The Metropolitan Community*, pp. 105–106.
[17] One might outline the area around a city from which people came to the local music festival, but if no neighboring city of comparable size had such a festival, this criterion would not be of much value in separating the tributary areas of the cities.

[18] Park and Newcomb, in McKenzie, *The Metropolitan Community*, p. 96.
[19] *Ibid.*, pp. 106–110.

ping territory, however, and some excluded territory.

Generalized metropolitan regions
Whereas Park and Newcomb based their metropolitan regions on a single factor, the circulation of metropolitan newspapers, Dickinson published in 1934 a metropolitan regions map based on a generalization of several factors and preexisting maps (Figure 4.4).[20] In making his map, Dickinson had wholesale trade area and newspaper circulation area maps to work with, but he also took into account the retail and industrial distribution areas of the various cities. In effect, his map represents an attempt to delimit comparable tributary areas for the major cities through generalizing boundaries from several different factors.

[20] Robert E. Dickinson, "The Metropolitan Regions of the United States," *Geographical Review,* vol. 24, pp. 278–291, 1934.

Medians of single-factor boundaries
Another approach to the problem of outlining at least a portion of the area that a city dominates is through establishing a number of divides between it and a competing city, and then arriving at a median line. This amounts to looking at a portion of one of Dickinson's boundaries on a much larger scale. Howard L. Green used this method in a study of the dividing line between the "hinterlands" of New York City and Boston.[21]

Green depended upon seven "functional indicators":

(1) railroad coach ticket purchases, (2) an estimate of truck freight movement to New York and Boston, (3) metropolitan newspaper circulation, (4) long-distance telephone calls, (5) metropolitan origin

[21] Howard L. Green, "Hinterland Boundaries of New York City and Boston in Southern New England," *Economic Geography,* vol. 31, pp. 283–300, 1955.

Fig. 4.4 Metropolitan regions of the United States. (After Robert E. Dickinson, "The Metropolitan Regions of the United States," *Geographical Review,* vol. 24, 1934, fig. 8.)

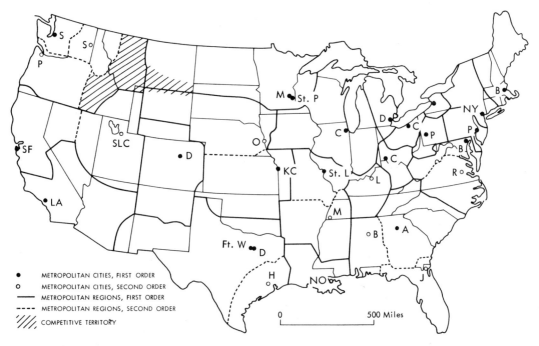

of vacationers, (6) business addresses of directors for major industrial firms, and (7) metropolitan correspondents for hinterland banks.

He used a map to present each of the seven. Two of these, the maps showing metropolitan newspaper circulation and long-distance telephone calls,[22] are reproduced here (Figures 4.5 and 4.6). And the map showing the median line based on the seven

hinterland measures, too, is shown (Figure 4.7).[23]

Such a median line has certain natural limitations. The use of additional indicators, for example, might have changed considerably the position of the line, and some of the factors used might well have been given more weight than others. But these are not major criticisms. Green's study is an outstanding contribution to our urban geography methodology.

[22] For a later study involving the use of intercity telephone calls see John D. Nystuen and Michael F. Dacey, "A Graph Theory Interpretation of Nodal Regions," *Papers and Proceedings of the Regional Science Association*, 1961, vol. 7, pp. 29–42.

[23] It is noteworthy that Green's median line occupies a position very similar to that of the same boundary on Dickinson's map (compare Figs. 4.7 and 4.4).

Fig. 4.5 Percentage of southern New England circulation for all New York and Boston daily newspapers, 1949. (After Howard L. Green, "Hinterland Boundaries of New York City and Boston in Southern New England," *Economic Geography*, vol. 31, 1955, fig. 4.)

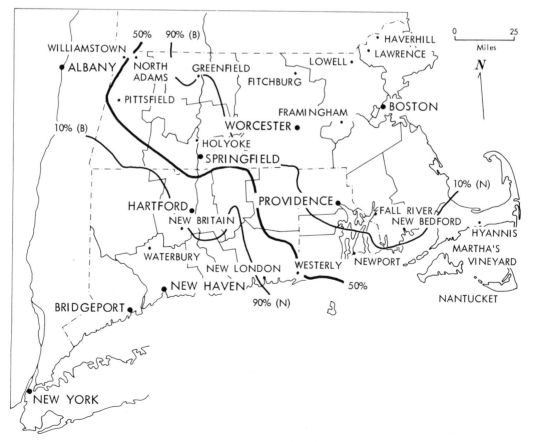

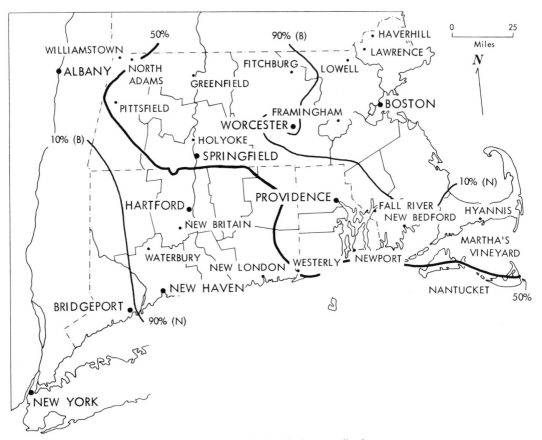

Fig. 4.6 Percentage of all southern New England telephone calls from hinterland points to New York and Boston. (After Howard L. Green, "Hinterland Boundaries of New York City and Boston in Southern New England," *Economic Geography*, vol. 31, 1955, fig. 5.)

Some General Considerations

Whether tributary areas or service areas are the chief concern, certain relevant factors should be considered at this point. For instance, all of these types of areas vary in shape and size from city to city, and all of them vary with time. There is, moreover, a practical side to the study of service areas and tributary areas.

Shape

Though brief references to shape and size have already been made, these qualities should be looked at a little more closely. Consider the matter of shape.

Tributary areas and service areas typically are far from symmetrical. An obvious basis for irregularity of shape is relations with other cities. The adjacency in a certain direction of a larger city, or of any seriously competing city, will have the effect of limiting the extent of the tributary area and of individual service areas. On the other hand, the absence of competing centers in another direction may explain the tributary area's great extent in that direction.

But competition is only one of many things that may affect the shapes of such areas. For example, a port city must of necessity have an asymmetrical tributary area; and relief features, variations in pro-

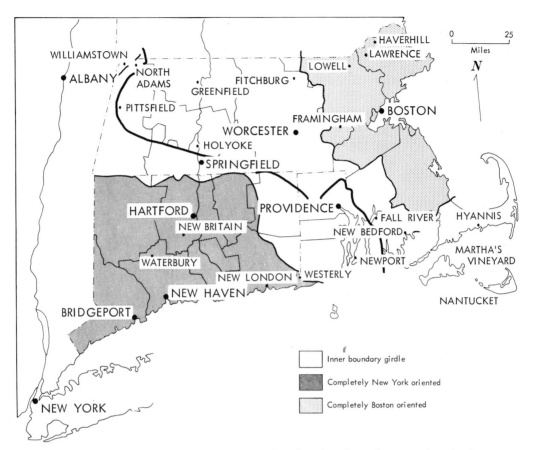

Fig. 4.7 Median boundary line based on the seven hinterland measures. (After Howard L. Green, "Hinterland Boundaries of New York City and Boston in Southern New England," *Economic Geography*, vol. 31, 1955, fig. 9.)

ductivity, administrative boundaries, highways, and a variety of other factors affect the shapes of tributary areas.

Service area shapes versus tributary area shapes The assumption here has been that service area boundaries reflect the shape of the tributary area. They often do; but they are individuals, too, and the trends of some service area boundaries differ greatly from those of others. This is to be expected, since the furnishing of each different service presents its own problems. But it may be assumed that tributary areas, representing as they do averages of service areas, would tend to be smoother in outline than service areas.

Size

Many of the factors that affect the shapes of tributary areas and service areas affect their sizes also. Other things being equal, the larger the city the larger the area. But there is another basis for differences in the size of service areas and the tributary area that needs to be emphasized: the nature of the city. It should be remembered that the tributary area is based not on the countrywide or worldwide connections of a city, but on relations to contiguous areas. It follows that, in an area of uniform population density and productivity, a city which is important chiefly as a trading center, serving the country around it, will tend to have a larger tributary area in proportion to the city's population than a city which depends mostly on the manufacture of products for non-local markets.

And there is another interesting basis for differences in extent of tributary areas. A city in a poor, sparsely settled area may have to reach farther with its services than one in a rich, densely populated area simply because the poor area can support fewer cities. For this reason, in proportion to city size, tributary areas tend to be rather large in regions of low population density, though, of course, they are of relatively low intensity.

Changes through time

From their very nature, the boundaries of service areas and tributary areas are impermanent. There are some fixed service area boundaries, e.g., state lines, but these are the exception. Through the endless competition between cities, most service areas and tributary areas constantly are changing in extent. In the study of current service patterns it should always be realized that we are obtaining only a cross section of the moment, that an understanding of how these service patterns are changing would be of great significance, but much more difficult to achieve.

Practical aspects

Practicality of delimitations of tributary areas and service areas Like so many phases of urban geography, the study of tributary areas and service areas has definite practical aspects. Perhaps the most striking example of this has to do with market areas. The merchants of a city usually want to know the extent of the city's retail trade area as contrasted with neighboring cities. This may be approximated through using Reilly's law or some modification of it. Newspaper circulation areas may be used for much the same purpose, since such circulation is closely related to the advertising carried on by merchants of the central city.

Service areas But the delimitations of individual service areas for their own sake have practical value, too. It is interesting to see just how far a particular service extends or over what area the goods are sold and to speculate regarding possible areal expansion. For example, if the wholesaling of groceries does not extend very far in a certain direction from a city that makes a considerable business of such wholesaling, the apparent anomaly might be worth investigating. Perhaps the leading department store of a city has relatively few charge accounts in a certain direction from the city. Why? Or if the location pattern of membership in a city's art museum shows some nearby areas to be largely unserved, an effort might be made to find out why.

Practical uses in the United Kingdom For some time, the British have recognized a type of practical value that might be derived from tributary area study, which thus far has not been much considered in this country.[24] They feel that their local government structure is badly in need of reform, chiefly because the pattern of local administrative areas was developed long ago and does a poor job of expressing the current situation. The study of tributary areas (called "urban fields" by the British) might well yield information useful in coping with this problem.

The potential value of studies of the tributary area and service areas to the professional planner has been pointed out by Smailes.[25] In the United States, relatively little work on tributary areas or service areas of individual cities has been done by planners, probably in part because most planners have been forced by time and

[24] A. E. Smailes, "Analysis and Delimitation of Urban Fields," *Geography*, vol. 32, pp. 151–161, 1947.
[25] A. E. Smailes, *The Geography of Towns*, Hutchinson University Library, London, 1953, pp. 153–156.

budget limitations to confine their activities to the interiors of cities. However, there are indications that city administrations are becoming increasingly aware of tributary areas and that these contiguous areas will be considered more in the city planning of the future.

Fields within Fields

It is perhaps best in concluding this discussion to emphasize complexity. The urban center with its tributary area and service areas does not exist in a vacuum. Instead, there is competition between urban centers, and the tributary areas of the larger cities characteristically contain smaller cities and their tributary areas, which in turn may contain still smaller centers and tributary areas.

Even this represents a gross oversimplification. In the present chapter, the concepts of tributary areas and service areas were considered largely for their own sake and for what they tell us about individual cities. In the two chapters that follow, the attempt will be made to fit these concepts into prevalent theories dealing with the location of urban centers and their interrelationships.

Selected References

Bogue, Donald J.: *The Structure of the Metropolitan Community: A Study of Dominance and Subdominance,* Horace H. Rackham School of Graduate Studies, University of Michigan, Ann Arbor, Mich., 1949.

Dickinson, Robert E.: *City and Region: A Geographical Interpretation,* Routledge & Kegan Paul, Ltd., London, 1964.

————: "The Metropolitan Regions of the United States," *Geographical Review,* vol. 24, pp. 278–291, 1934.

Fielding, Gordon J.: "The Los Angeles Milkshed: A Study of the Political Factor in Agriculture," *Geographical Review,* vol. 54, pp. 1–12, 1964.

Green, Howard L.: "Hinterland Boundaries of New York City and Boston in Southern New England," *Economic Geography,* vol. 31, pp. 283–300, 1955.

Harris, Chauncy D.: *Salt Lake City: A Regional Capital,* doctoral dissertation, University of Chicago Libraries, Chicago, 1941.

Huff, David L.: "A Probabilistic Analysis of Shopping Center Trade Areas," *Land Economics,* vol. 39, pp. 81–90, 1963.

McKenzie, R. D.: *The Metropolitan Community,* McGraw-Hill Book Company, Inc., New York, 1933. (Out of print but can be ordered in xeroxed form from a library that has a copy.)

Nelson, Howard J.: *The Livelihood Structure of Des Moines, Iowa,* doctoral dissertation, Department of Geography, University of Chicago, Chicago, 1949.

Nystuen, John D., and Michael F. Dacey: "A Graph Theory Interpretation of Nodal Regions," *Papers and Proceedings of the Regional Science Association,* 1961, vol. 7, pp. 29–42.

Park, Robert E.: "Urbanization as Measured by Newspaper Circulation," *American Journal of Sociology,* vol. 35, pp. 60–79, 1929–1930.

Reilly, William J.: *Methods for the Study of Retail Relationships,* University of Texas, Austin, Studies in Marketing no. 4, Bureau of Business Research, 1959. (Reprint of research monograph first published in 1929.)

Smailes, A. E.: "The Analysis and Delimitation of Urban Fields," *Geography,* vol. 32, pp. 151–161, 1947.

————: *The Geography of Towns,* Hutchinson University Library, London, 1953.

Ullman, Edward L.: *Mobile: Industrial Seaport and Trade Center,* doctoral dissertation, Department of Geography, University of Chicago, Chicago, 1943.

CHAPTER 5

Location of central places

THOUGH the study of service areas and tributary areas of cities is of value for its own sake, it has a broader value in laying the groundwork for a more sophisticated view of the distribution of urban centers and the relationships they have with each other and with surrounding territory. In the present chapter a theory of location of urban centers will be presented, based on their services to the surrounding regions. And in Chapter 6 methods of ranking urban centers in hierarchies are considered, based on functions they perform for tributary areas.

Background

Urban centers in a rural area

Suppose you were to make a population map of a section of the United States that is largely rural—a farming area with only local industries, where considerable uniformity of physical conditions prevails. You would find many small urban centers only a few miles apart, a smaller number of somewhat larger urban agglomerations at wider intervals, and, still more widely spaced, urban centers large enough to be classed as small cities.

You might discover several other interesting facts about these places and their distribution. Field observation would show that the various classes differ in their commercial functions, at least to the degree that the smallest places offer only limited goods and services, that places in the next largest size class offer these same goods and services and more specialized ones as well, and so on up the scale. In fact, you might base your ranking entirely on number and complexity of goods and services offered. The order of places you would arrive at in this way would not necessarily agree with that based on population totals, though no doubt there would be a general correspondence.

And there is something else worth considering. Looking at the map, you might note, or think that you noted, a certain regularity of spacing, at least for places of the smallest size, those offering the most limited range of goods and services.

Early networks of market centers

This regularity of spacing appears to have had its roots in conditions that prevailed in most of the country at the time of settlement, when there was a farming economy. Need for simple centralized services was then especially important in determining the size and spacing of urban centers. Rapid, easy transportation was still far in the future, and a network of small market or service centers was necessary to serve adequately the farms of the countryside. The radius of the tributary area of each of these service centers was limited chiefly by the distance one could travel conveniently on foot or with horse and wagon. Since, to a large degree, a subsistence economy prevailed, such trips were infrequent. And larger centers, more widely spaced and with more complex services, were visited even less frequently by the average individuals scattered over the countryside.

Relative decline of small centers

This was long ago. The simple picture has changed. Better roads and improved means of travel have put the small market centers at a disadvantage, a disadvantage which has been accentuated by the increasing complexity of goods and services that people demand. Particularly in farming areas, the net of small service centers remains, but many of the centers have tended to stand still or even to decline in size, since people can so easily travel to larger places which have been growing and becoming more complex in the services they offer.

How larger centers have changed

As the larger centers have grown, they have, in many instances, attracted factories. Some of these serve only the local area, but in the large city, raw materials may come from long distances and manufactured products reach countrywide or even worldwide markets. Chicago, for example, has grown immensely as a great service center for the productive Middle West, but it performs functions far beyond this role.

Three categories of cities

Though service centers or *central places,* large or small, are, in a sense, the norm, cities have developed in other ways, too. Harris and Ullman say that, on the basis of support, cities can be summarized in three categories: (1) central-place cities, which perform centralized services for adjacent areas; (2) transport cities, such as railroad centers and ports, which owe their importance to their situation with respect to the transport network; and (3) specialized-function cities, such as specialized manufacturing centers, resort and retirement cities, mining towns, lumbering centers, military bases, and the like.[1] Most cities represent a combination of the three categories. Providing goods and services for a surrounding area may be a minor concern of many specialized-function and transport cities, and the central-service function may have had little to do with the locations of these cities. Nevertheless, the performance of central services characterizes all cities to some degree and, therefore, is the common denominator for a theory of location of urban centers that will be described in this chapter.

Background in summary

The present pattern of urban centers of the United States (as well as that of other countries) seems to have developed on a base of early service centers or central places. Specialized-function cities (including transport centers) are numerous in some localities, and in others improved

[1] Chauncy D. Harris and Edward L. Ullman, "The Nature of Cities," *Annals of the American Academy of Political and Social Science,* vol. 242, pp. 7–17, 1945.

transportation and the growth of industry in some of the original service centers have distorted the simple, central-place pattern. Nevertheless, the basic framework of service centers, dating to horse-and-buggy days, seems to underlie the pattern of today.

A Theoretical Location Pattern

Since the regularity of spacing is assumed to be particularly characteristic of places that concentrate largely on serving the areas around them, it follows that the theory might be most applicable to agricultural areas. And it should be possible in such areas to work out a theoretical system of spacing of urban centers of various sizes.

This was the opinion of Walter Christaller, who developed his central-place theory on the basis of conditions in southern Germany several decades ago.[2] His model has attracted wide attention as the most acceptable theoretical basis which has been advanced for explaining the distribution of urban centers.[3]

Central places

Christaller's work was based on the premise that a certain amount of productive

land supports an urban center or central place,[4] which exists because of the necessity of providing goods and services for a *complementary area*. The basic element of a central place, according to Christaller, is that such a place be a source of goods and services for an area larger than itself.[5] The whole scheme involves relations with immediately surrounding areas. An industry using raw materials from outside the local area, for example, and shipping all its products to another locality is not classed as a central service, and an urban center dominated by such an industry or industries might have very little importance as a central place. It follows that though one city may be considerably larger than another it may be less important as a central place. This chapter deals with the location of urban centers only to the extent that they serve as central places.

Central-place functions and size of center

The central-place functions that a center performs tend to be more complex the larger the center. With minor exceptions, each higher level of central place performs all functions available in smaller central places, and additional, more centralized functions as well. Thus the city normally provides, in addition to all the types of services available in the various levels of smaller

[2] Walter Christaller, *Die zentralen Orte in Süddeutschland*, Gustav Fischer Verlag, Jena, Germany, 1933. See also Walter Christaller, *Central Places in Southern Germany* (trans. from "Die zentralen Orte in Süddeutschland" by Carlisle W. Baskin), Prentice-Hall, Inc., Englewood Cliffs, N.J., 1966; and the critique section of Carlisle W. Baskin, "A Critique and Translation of Walter Christaller's Die zentralen Orte in Süddeutschland," doctoral dissertation, University of Virginia, Charlottesville, Va., 1957.

[3] This discussion of Christaller's work is based largely on Edward Ullman, "A Theory of Location for Cities," *American Journal of Sociology*, vol. 46, pp. 853–864, 1941; Robert E. Dickinson, *City and Region: A Geographical Interpretation*, Routledge & Kegan Paul, Ltd., London, 1964; and Baskin's critique and translation of Christaller's book. These sources, including footnote references, should be consulted for details regarding the work of American rural sociologists along similar lines. See, also, John E. Brush, "The Hierarchy of Central Places in Southwestern Wisconsin," *Geographical Review*, vol. 43, pp. 380–402, 1953.

[4] Hans Carol says that the central place can be either the location of a single central function, such as the supply of consumer goods or medical care, or, as the term is generally interpreted, the location of a group of central functions. See Hans Carol, "The Hierarchy of Central Functions within the City," *Annals of the Association of American Geographers*, vol. 50, p. 420, 1960.

[5] Christaller defined the "centrality" of a place as the excess of central services over the needs of the central settlement, but it has been argued that centrality should be based on services for the center itself as well as for the surrounding area. In following out this idea, the terms *internal service area* and *external service area* have been used in referring to services to the city itself and to the surrounding area respectively. See *ibid.*, pp. 420–421.

centers, such relatively complex services as wholesaling, specialized retailing, large-scale banking, and specialized medical services. In each case it is the complexity of the services rather than the population of a center that determines its rank as a central place.

Threshold population and the range of a good

In central-place studies, the concepts of *threshold population* and *range* of a good are useful.[6] Threshold population has been defined as the minimum population size of an urban center which will support an urban function. Thus in a certain locality barber shops may be rare in villages with less than 300 inhabitants. This, therefore, marks the approximate threshold population for barber shops in the locality.

The range of a good marks out the zone or tributary area around a central place from which persons travel to the center to purchase the good (service or merchandise) offered at the place. Theoretically, the upper limit of this range is the maximum possible radius of sales. Beyond this limit the price of the good is too high for it to be sold, either because the distance results in too high a price, or because of the greater proximity of consumers to an alternate center (the *real* limit). The lower limit of the range is the radius that encloses the minimum number of consumers necessary to provide a sales volume adequate for the good to be supplied profitably from the central place. In the case mentioned, the population of the serving urban center is the threshold population for barber shops.

How a hierarchy of centers results

The lowest level of center performs certain functions (or furnishes certain central goods) that are limited in number and kind by the limited population within usual range of the center. A center of the next higher order performs all the functions (or furnishes all the goods) of the lower-order center plus a group of additional central functions (or goods) that this higher-order center can furnish by virtue of the considerably greater number of buyers available within its greater range. In other words the new goods have greater ranges; they will draw people from a considerably greater distance than the goods of the smaller center were able to do. It is this group of goods with ranges greater than those of the preceding group that differentiates this higher-order center from one of the next lower order. The next higher order of center will offer all the goods offered by the first two levels, but will be differentiated from the order just beneath it by a group of goods with greater ranges than those possessed by any of the goods of the next smaller center. Thus a sort of hierarchy of centers evolves.

Shapes of complementary areas

Ideally, the complementary area (or trade area) for each central place, whatever its level, should approximate a circle with radial traffic routes converging at the center.[7] Smaller circles, arranged radially, would fall within a larger circle that formed the service area of a larger central place at the center of this assemblage; and this larger circle would in turn be one of the

---

[6] Brian J. L. Berry and William L. Garrison, "A Note on Central Place Theory and the Range of a Good," *Economic Geography*, vol. 34, pp. 304–311, 1958.

[7] This is in accord with the idea of J. H. von Thünen, who, in his *Der isolierte Staat*, first published in 1826, theorized regarding the way in which a single city should develop on an entirely uniform plain on which nothing that might affect utilization of the land varied and a purely agricultural economy prevailed. Given only wagon transportation and no well-defined highways, the cost of bringing farm products to the city would be equal for all points equally distant from the market. The result, von Thünen said, would be a system of concentric belts or zones of land use around the central city. For a summary of von Thünen's theory, see Andreas Grotewold, "Von Thünen in Retrospect," *Economic Geography*, vol. 35, pp. 346–355, 1959.

radially arranged group surrounding a much larger central place.

But circles do not use space efficiently. Tangent circles would leave unserved space, and overlapping circles would mean competition in the overlapping areas. Christaller eliminated this difficulty, theoretically, by using a <u>pattern of hexagons</u> instead of circles. <u>Hexagons are the figures most nearly approximating circles that will use all the space without overlapping</u> (see Figure 5.1).

Christaller's hierarchy

Christaller developed his theoretical system to <u>include various levels or orders</u> of <u>central places</u>. He computed the populations of these places, their distances apart, and the sizes and populations of their tributary areas in accordance with his hexagonal theory (Figure 5.2 and Table 5.1).

The market town The smallest unit which Christaller included in his scheme, the market town,[8] had a population of

[8] Christaller assumed that the market town was the smallest complete service center, though he recognized the existence of smaller auxiliary centers.

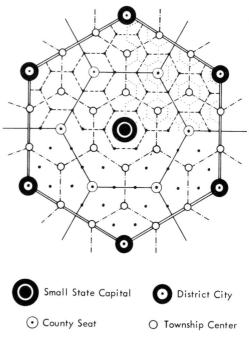

Small State Capital • District City
County Seat • Township Center
• Market Town

Fig. 5.2 The pattern of service centers and the hexagonal areas they serve according to Christaller's market principle. Five levels of centers are represented in the diagram, though Christaller considered two still higher orders of centers (Table 5.1). The market town, with a population of 1,000 and at a distance of 4.5 miles from its nearest neighbors and serving an area of 17 square miles, is the basis for the system. (After Christaller.)

Fig. 5.1 Ideally, each central place would have a circular tributary area as in von Thünen's model (see footnote 7, p. 75). But tangent circles (A) would leave unserved spaces, and overlapping circles (B) would mean competition in the overlapping areas. Hexagons (C) use all the space without overlapping.

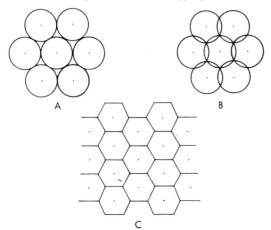

1,000 and was assumed to lie 4.5 miles from its nearest neighbors. This distance was, by design, calculated so that from any part of its service area the market town could be reached in approximately a one-hour walk. In other words, the costs of reaching a central place increased outward in all directions up to an economic limit set by transport costs and travel time; beyond that point it cost less to travel to another center of equal or higher rank. The market town, according to Christaller's estimates for southern Germany, had a tributary area of 17 square miles, and this tributary area had a population of approximately 3,000.

Seven levels of central places Though

the market town was his basic element, Christaller considered that in all there were seven levels of central places (Table 5.1). Ideally, places that performed only the market-center function would occur at 4.5-mile intervals. But some of the places performing the market-center function were also township centers, in a hexagon of the next largest size order, and such township centers were spaced at intervals of about 7.5 miles. County seats, centered in still larger hexagons, averaged a spacing of about 13 miles; and so on up through the several grades of urban centers. Each place performed the functions characteristic of its grade or rank and all those of lower-order centers as well.[9] Throughout, the distance between adjacent similar centers amounted to the distance between those of the preceding category times $\sqrt{3}$. For instance, $4.5 \times \sqrt{3} =$ approximately 7.5; $7.5 \times \sqrt{3} =$ approximately 13; etc. According to Christaller, the numbers of representatives of the seven levels of central places tend to follow a theoretical norm from the largest to the smallest as follows: 1:2:6:18:54:162:486.

Measures of centralized services

Centralized services Population alone is not a good measure of centrality. A large mining, industrial, or other type of special-

[9] This is referred to as a "nesting" pattern of lower-order trade areas within the trade areas of higher-order centers. A hierarchy of routes joining the centers is also involved.

ized-function town, for example, may have only a small tributary area and an importance as a central place far less than would be expected for its size. Christaller based his scheme, instead, on the centralized services which, he said, were concerned with administration, culture, health, social service, organization of economic and social life, finance, trade, service industries, the labor market, and traffic.

Telephones as a measure of centrality But Christaller felt that he needed a more practical and convenient method of classification than that of compiling data on kinds and number of central services in each place. He decided that telephones best represented the tie between a central place and its complementary region—in short, the centrality of the place. According to his method, the centrality of a place (the services it performs over and above the local needs of its inhabitants) is measured by the formula $Tz - Ez(Tg/Eg)$, where Tz is the number of telephones in the place; Ez, the number of inhabitants of the place; and Tg and Eg the number of telephones and inhabitants, respectively, in the surrounding region (Table 5.2).[10] This amounts to subtracting from the actual number of telephones in the place the number that it should have, in proportion to its population, according to the average of the area. Note that if two towns have the same number of

[10] Tg/Eg is the telephone density for the area.

Table 5.1   Some data for the various sizes of urban centers according to Christaller's hierarchy

Grades of urban centers	Towns		Tributary areas	
	Population	Distance apart (mi.)	Population	sq. mi.
I Market town	1,000	4.5	3,000	17
II Township center	2,000	7.5	11,000	51
III County seat	4,000	13.0	35,000	154
IV District city	10,000	22.5	100,000	463
V Small state capital	30,000	39.0	350,000	1,390
VI Provincial head city	100,000	67.5	1,000,000	4,170
VII Regional capital city	500,000	116.0	3,500,000	12,500

Table 5.2   Telephones and centrality for seven grades of centers according to Christaller

	Approximate population	Number of telephones	Centrality
Market town	1,000	10–20	0.5– 2
Township center	2,000	20–50	2 – 4
County seat	4,000	50–150	4 – 12
District city	10,000	150–500	12 – 30
Small state capital	30,000	500–2,500	30 – 150
Provincial head city	100,000	2,500–25,000	150 –1,200
Regional capital city	500,000	25,000–60,000	1,200 –3,000

SOURCE: Based largely on table in Walter Christaller, *Central Places in Southern Germany*, page 158.

telephones, and if one is in a richer area that supports more telephones in proportion to its population, then the centrality of that place will be less.

Objections to Christaller's telephone index   The value of telephones as a measure of centrality has been questioned by people who have tried to use the method elsewhere. Christaller claimed that telephones were a reliable index of centrality since they were used for business. This may have been true of southern Germany when Christaller did his work, but it is no longer valid even there. Telephones in homes have become the normal situation, and rural homes are even more likely to have telephones than homes in urban centers where more direct communication is possible. Certainly, in the United States, telephones are as common in homes as in business establishments and such an index would be of little value.

Other measures of centrality   Ullman points out that out-of-town telephone calls should be of some value in the United States in measuring centrality,[11] but he says

[11] Ullman, "A Theory of Location for Cities," p. 858. In connection with use of telephone data see also John D. Nystuen and Michael F. Dacey, "A Graph Theory Interpretation of Nodal Regions," *Papers and Proceedings of the Regional Science Association*, vol. 7, pp. 29–42, 1961.

that certain other measures might be better. He suggests, for instance, an evaluation of actual central services performed over and above those for the town itself. If one knew the average number of customers necessary to support certain specialized functions, then the excess of these functions in a place over what would be required for the people living there should give a measure of the place's centrality.[12] Among other

[12] Two recent studies are worth noting in this connection. One is based upon trade data from the U.S. Census Bureau. Cities which are above average in their proportions of wholesale (as compared with wholesale plus retail) trade are serving the needs of outside areas. Such extracity sales are accompanied by increased services rendered by the city and thus a correspondingly high degree of centrality. See William R. Siddall, "Wholesale-Retail Trade Ratios as Indices of Urban Centrality," *Economic Geography*, vol. 37, pp. 124–132, 1961. The second study deals with centrality in the Boston area. The method may be briefly summarized as follows: for each city and town in the 1950 Boston Standard Metropolitan Area the percentage contribution to the metropolitan area's total of the population served by a specific low-order function was calculated. Next, for the city or town the proportion of the metropolitan total of the function itself was determined. Then the town's percentage of the served population was subtracted from its percentage of the function. The resulting number measured the town's centrality or lack of centrality for that function. This procedure was followed for total employment, a selection of retail functions, and a combination of employment

possibilities for measuring centrality is the use of data on the number of automobiles entering a town.

Centralized services of various levels of centers

Christaller described his various levels of places on the basis of the centralized services offered.[13] For each category of central place, he listed the specific services and institutions.

The lowest level, the market town, was primarily characterized by:

> . . . its weekly markets, and still further by other institutions of the lowest rank: a vital statistics office, a police station, a physician; and, sometimes, a veterinary, a dentist, an inn (not just the restaurant); and, perhaps, a cooperative, a loan office branch, a greater selection of artisans larger repair shops, breweries, or mills.[14]

The market town nearly always had a railroad station, a post office, and a telephone exchange; and there were almost always important crossroads or terminals of bus lines. The number of telephones normally was between ten and twenty, and the telephone density was 0.5 to 2 (see Table 5.2).

The township center, the next highest order of central place, was the lowest administrative center. It was characterized by the lowest court, the elementary school, the public library, the museum, the apothecary, the veterinary, the cinema, the local newspaper, local clubs and cooperatives, special shops, savings and loan offices; and, frequently, railway crossroads. It was a seat of offices and was sometimes called an office town. The number of telephones averaged twenty to fifty and the centrality 2 to 4.

Baskin gives similar information for

each of Christaller's higher classes of centers. The next highest level, a seat of lower administrative authority, was essentially the county seat, with institutions consisting of the lower administrative offices together with county doctors, county newspapers, county savings offices, and a variety of other types of county organizations and functions at the county level. The successively higher levels, shown in Table 5.1, had increasingly more complex administrative and other activities. It should be kept in mind, however, that the characteristic services and institutions were those for southern Germany in about 1930.

Criticisms of the central-place theory

Many people have criticized Christaller's theory. Some have questioned the adequacy of his evidence and his methods; others have claimed that field tests fail to give confirming results.

Distortions due to local factors Critics have noted that the central-place scheme may be disrupted by various local factors. Among these are presence of important transportation routes, nature of relief, soil productivity, type of agriculture and intensity of cultivation, administrative organization, history of development, and extent of industrialization.

Transportation routes do not, in fact, simply radiate out from centers as is implied in the idea of a central place serving the area around it. Not infrequently, the central places may be strung out at short intervals along an important transportation route, in which case instead of forming hexagons the service areas may be elongated at right angles to the route.[15] On the other hand,

---

and retail trade. See Lane J. Johnson, "Centrality within a Metropolis," *Economic Geography*, vol. 40, pp. 324–336, 1964.

[13] The information given here is taken almost entirely from Baskin, *op. cit.*, pp. 345–346.

[14] *Ibid.*, p. 345.

[15] Christaller's central-place system is based on the "marketing or supply" principle. In order to explain why the expected number of places of various sizes was not always obtained by the marketing principle, Christaller formulated two other principles: the "traffic" principle and the "administrative" principle. According to the traffic principle the distribution of central places is the

Ullman points out that competitive railroads in Illinois, running nearly parallel and not far apart in an area of rather uniform land, have resulted in service areas that stretch out along the railroads instead of extending at right angles to them.[16]

The operation of some of the other factors is more obvious. Certainly this is true of relief. A region of parallel ridges and valleys, for example, could hardly have the symmetrical arrangement of centers that might occur in an area that is nearly flat. The location of routes and river crossings, soil productivity, type of agriculture, and intensity of cultivation—all must have modified the pattern;[17] and governmental organization may have had the effect of directing trade from its normal channels. The section-township-range system of land survey, which is in use in much of the United States, must have affected the local pattern of central places and service areas. And, certainly, the history of early development in a locality must have had a good deal to do with variations in the symmetry of the central-place pattern, especially if

the pattern took form over some time and under changing transportation influences.

Perhaps more than any other factor, though, industrialization has affected the pattern. Industrial development in some older centers has gone so far that industries have become dominant and centralized services secondary; in other cases industrial centers (and mining, resort, and certain other types of special-function centers, too, for that matter) were planted in the countryside. In areas with a high degree of industrialization the central-place pattern often has little significance in explaining the present distribution of urban centers.

General criticisms of the theory Although distortions due to a variety of local factors are to be expected, other objections to the theory have been advanced. For instance, Christaller has been criticized for insistence upon the hexagonal pattern of service areas. Although he notes the linear arrangement of centers along long-distance transport routes, and although he recognizes the effect of large-scale manufacturing in creating population concentrations, he discounts such controls in favor of his service-area principle and has based his conclusion on assumptions rather than upon empirical evidence. Of course, the whole idea was designed as a deductive theory.

According to Ullman, there are several respects in which the theory has been found not to work out well. For instance, it has been pointed out that most of the cities of Germany are not real central places but, instead, industrial centers or villages of farmers. And actual counts and measurements in fairly uniform agricultural areas in other parts of the world, especially in the United States, do not check with Christaller's findings as well as might be expected. Indeed, it has not been established that central places of the same rank are not randomly distributed.

---

most favorable one where as many important places as possible lie on one traffic route between two important towns. Railroad traffic is assumed. The administrative principle is based upon the need for administrative areas with administrative centers. According to this principle, the ideal areal unit is one with a capital at its center with a group of tributary centers of lower order, and a peripheral area of sparse population separating the administrative unit from its neighbors. But the marketing or supply principle is so much the most important in Christaller's scheme that the traffic and administrative principles are not considered further in this book.

[16] Ullman, "A Theory of Location for Cities," p. 860.

[17] Hans Carol points out that in the Karoo of South Africa, with its very low population density, one physician covers a service area of about 2,700 square miles. This supports the idea that the size of a service area (complementary area) is dependent chiefly on its density of population or, more precisely, on the density of purchasing power. See Carol, *op. cit.*, p. 420.

The system not static

It need hardly be mentioned that the system of central places is by no means static. It is constantly changing with changing conditions.

One of the most striking examples of this is the effect of changing transportation. With the relative increase of highway use, railroads have lost much of their local traffic, being replaced by trucks and automobiles. Since good roads are spread more uniformly over the landscape than railways, the change, theoretically, should result in a more perfect pattern of central-place distribution. But the good highways have had another effect. More people go longer distances to the larger centers for services that they formerly received in the local market towns, and, as a result, the smaller centers are getting smaller and the larger centers larger.

Various other developments also help to alter the system of central places through time. Undoubtedly, local booms, droughts, and the like have affected the pattern.

Central-place theory operative even in highly developed areas

Even in highly developed areas in the United States there are strong forces at work, according to Ullman, to produce a central-place distribution of settlements.[18] Goods brought into an area characteristically are handled through brokers, wholesale houses, and retail channels in central cities. This seems to support a central-place framework of settlements, though not necessarily with the spacing of Christaller's system.

General applicability

Ullman concludes that the great growth of industry and world trade in the last hundred years has often obscured the true relation of the city to the countryside. There is evidence that the rapid growth of some of our larger cities is not as industrial centers but as commercial and service centers for large tributary areas,[19] thus reflecting to some measure a central-place pattern. Some sort of central-place theory, Ullman feels, is the best explanation for the locations of cities, especially in agricultural areas, and the system may well have value, he claims, for all areas as a theoretical norm. He suggests the possible value, too, in planning new areas.[20]

Conclusion

Christaller's central-place theory has its critics, but the truth is that theories always awaken opposition. We shall find later in this book that several theories have been advanced to account for the arrangement of land uses in the city (see Chapter 12). They, too, have their attackers and their defenders. At a minimum assessment, Christaller's scheme seems to have value in explaining the distribution of urban centers in certain localities, and with modifications it may eventually be much more widely applicable. In the meanwhile, no one has put forward a better theory for the distribution of central places, and certainly the whole idea has inspired a great deal of research. Some knowledge of Christaller's central-place theory should be part of the background of anyone who is seriously interested in urban geography.[21]

[18] Ullman, "A Theory of Location for Cities," pp. 862–863.

[19] United States National Resource Committee, *Our Cities: Their Role in the National Economy: Report of the Urbanism Committee*, Washington, D.C., 1937, p. 37.

[20] The central-place scheme *has* been used in locating market centers in some of the new polder lands in the Netherlands.

[21] Only a very simplified version of Christaller's central-place theory has been presented here. References in the bibliographies of this chapter and the one that follows, however, make it possible to pursue the topic further.

Selected References

Baskin, Carlisle W.: "A Critique and Translation of Walter Christaller's *Die zentralen Orte in Süddeutschland,*" unpublished doctoral dissertation, University of Virginia, Charlottesville, Va., 1957. (Available in microfilm or xerox from University Microfilms, Inc., Ann Arbor, Mich.)

Berry, Brian J. L., and William L. Garrison. "A Note on Central Place Theory and the Range of a Good," *Economic Geography,* vol. 34, pp. 304–311, 1958.

——— and Allen Pred: *Central Place Studies: A Bibliography of Theory and Applications,* Bibliography Series, no. 1, Regional Science Research Institute, Philadelphia, 1961; reprinted 1965 (with supplement through 1964 by H. G. Barnum, R. Kasperson, and S. Kiuchi).

Carol, Hans: "The Hierarchy of Central Functions within the City," *Annals of the Association of American Geographers,* vol. 50, pp. 419–438, 1960.

Christaller, Walter: *Central Places in Southern Germany* (translated from "Die zentralen Orte in Süddeutschland" by Carlisle W. Baskin), Prentice-Hall, Inc., Englewood Cliffs, N.J., 1966.

———: *Die zentralen Orte in Süddeutschland,* Gustav Fischer Verlag, Jena, Germany, 1933.

Dacey, Michael F.: "Analysis of Central Place and Point Patterns by a Nearest Neighbor Method," Proceedings of the IGU Symposium in Urban Geography, Lund 1960, *Lund Studies in Geography,* ser. B, Human Geography, No. 24, Royal University of Lund, Sweden, pp. 55–75.

Dickinson, Robert E.: *City and Region: A Geographical Interpretation,* Routledge & Kegan Paul, Ltd., London, 1964.

Harris, Chauncy D., and Edward L. Ullman, "The Nature of Cities," *Annals of the American Academy of Political and Social Science,* vol. 242, pp. 7–17, 1945.

Johnson, Lane J.: "Centrality within a Metropolis," *Economic Geography,* vol. 40, pp. 324–336, 1964.

Lösch, August: *The Economics of Location,* Yale University Press, New Haven, Conn., 1954 (translated from the German).

Mayfield, Robert C.: "The Range of a Central Good in the Indian Punjab," *Annals of the Association of American Geographers,* vol. 53, pp. 38–49, 1963.

Siddall, William R.: "Wholesale-Retail Trade Ratios as Indices of Urban Centrality," *Economic Geography,* vol. 37, pp. 124–132, 1961.

Ullman, Edward: "A Theory of Location of Cities," *American Journal of Sociology,* vol. 46, pp. 853–864, 1941.

6

The urban
hierarchy

IN THE preceding chapter Christaller's work was presented chiefly as a theoretical scheme for explaining the distribution pattern of urban centers. An inherent part of his study, however, was the setting up of a hierarchy of central places (Table 5.1). The hierarchy concept will be more fully developed in the present chapter.

Hierarchy versus continuum The term *urban hierarchy* might be used to refer to a ranking of cities into successive groups on the basis of size or on various other bases. But in urban geography the concept has acquired a special meaning. The idea of an urban hierarchy is that there exist discrete classes of central places and associated groups of functions organized together in a nesting pattern (see page 77). Such a hierarchy is implicit in Christaller's deductive model. But the question remains whether it can be identified empirically, or whether only continuous functional relations exist.

Empirical work on hierarchies In contrast to Christaller's theoretical approach to the urban hierarchy, there has been a great deal of empirical work done on the subject. Some of this work was designed to check Christaller's results or in one way or another impinges on his theory; much of it, however, consists simply of investigations of the urban hierarchy in various areas. Such studies seem generally to have had as their goals the setting up of widely acceptable systems of dividing urban centers into vertical groups or orders on the basis of services they perform and the development of generalizations about the several orders.

Central services as the basis for ranking Most of these studies, like Christaller's theoretical one, are based on the idea that the services a city performs for the surrounding area [1]—its central services—rather than its size or governmental status should determine its position in the hierarchy. In arriving at the hierarchy, one must take account of the essential functions of urban centers and of the institutions concerned with performing them.

> . . . Urban centres act as collecting and marketing points for the products of their surrounding territories, and as distributing centres for goods from outside; as centres for provision of educational, health, recreational, and cultural services; and as crystallising points of local and regional feeling and thought, as well as transmitters and disseminators of external influences. Logically, these several functions must be reflected in the indices that are chosen to measure urban rank.[2]

Order of discussion People have attacked the problem of the urban hierarchy in various ways. No one study necessarily represents the right way. Each has added to the total picture. The method of this chapter will be to discuss representative contributions, more or less in chronological order, and then to try to sum up the accomplishments they represent. The urban hierarchy is an aspect of urban geography in which American geographers, at first at least, followed the lead of British geographers, a fact that is reflected in the large amount of space devoted here to discussions of British studies.

Two major approaches in hierarchy research The rank of a place as a service center generally has been determined in either of two ways. One of these involves assessment of the goods and services available in centers. In an early study to be described, this was done rather elaborately

for England and Wales. The other general method of approach focuses on measurement of the area dependent on each center for goods and services. Some work done in southern England on the places to which people travel for various services is a good example of this second approach. Both types of studies are presented in this chapter as well as some others that use slightly different methods in determining hierarchical status.

Smailes's Urban Hierarchy in England and Wales

One of the earliest and most comprehensive of the attempts to arrive at an urban hierarchy was Smailes's ranking of the urban centers of England and Wales (Figure 6.1).[3] It was based upon an assessment of business and services available.

Smailes first set himself the task of deciding on those indices that are most significant in grading urban centers and yet are widely applicable. He did not contend that he could achieve sharply defined grades or levels of towns since, he said, the urban scale is essentially a continuous one. Moreover, urban centers are constantly rising and slipping back in the urban scale, so that any system of ranking is for a particular period of time only. Smailes's study was based on conditions just before World War II and on the British scene, facts that should be kept in mind when considering his work.

Towns Among the index features, Smailes places banks as the most important hallmark of the true town,[4] since they are the best index of the importance of retail services. One or two banks are hardly sufficient for full urban stature; three or four are necessary, and their presence generally

---

[1] In practice, centrality is generally measured by the services a settlement performs for its own population as well as for the surrounding area. See discussion of this point in footnote 5, Chapter 5.

[2] Arthur E. Smailes, "The Urban Hierarchy in England and Wales," *Geography*, vol. 29, p. 41, 1944.

[3] *Ibid.*, pp. 41–51.

[4] Smailes follows the British practice of using town as more or less synonymous with city. Certainly, Smailes's "major towns" would be classed in the United States as small cities.

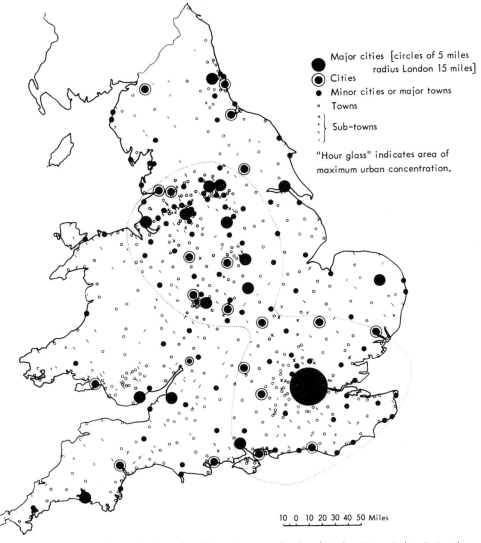

Major cities [circles of 5 miles radius London 15 miles]

Cities

Minor cities or major towns

Towns

Sub-towns

"Hour glass" indicates area of maximum urban concentration.

10 0 10 20 30 40 50 Miles

Fig. 6.1 The urban hierarchy in England and Wales. (From Arthur E. Smailes, "The Urban Hierarchy in England and Wales," *Geography*, vol. 29, p. 43, 1944.)

means, he says, that several large multiple retail businesses are present, such as drugstores, and that there is a Woolworth store. The last, Smailes regards as an extremely valuable measure of shopping importance.

Places that have attained this economic status, Smailes claims, are usually important as district centers for education and health services as well as for entertainment and a variety of social organizations. These are reflected in secondary schools, hospitals, cinemas, and newspapers—which hang together, he says, as members of a "trait-complex." When this assemblage is present, full-fledged town status is unquestioned. He represents the complex by the formula *ABCD: A,* standing for the economic status described; *B,* for both a secondary school and a hospital; *C,* for more than one cinema;

and *D*, for the publication of a weekly newspaper.

This standard for full-fledged towns requires some modification. At the time Smailes made his study, Woolworth stores had not expanded into all localities where they would naturally be expected. Likewise, Smailes says, neither hospitals nor secondary schools are invariably present in places which possess the other key services. For example, the hospital is frequently lacking for the reason that hospital facilities are available nearby and duplication is unnecessary. Similarly, especially in a crowded mining area, secondary schools may not correspond closely to the other services. The true town usually has more than one cinema. And, almost always, where there are three banks, a local weekly newspaper is published. Nevertheless, as Smailes applies his trait-complex, there is some give and take. A place that does not have the full economic status (perhaps is lacking in a Woolworth store) is indicated as A' rather than A; B' rather than B indicates that either the hospital or the secondary school is absent; C' indicates the presence of only one cinema, and so forth. The formulas $A'B'C'D$ and $A'BC'$ represent the minimum qualifications for town ranking.

But there are other characteristic, though perhaps less significant, features of British towns: for instance, a range of professional people, branch insurance offices, the more highly specialized retail businesses, the headquarters of a local cooperative society, and a wide range of church denominations. Towns are also likely to contain, Smailes says, various government offices such as the employment exchange, inland revenue offices, and, generally, a head post office. In fact he regards the presence of a head post office as the most satisfactory rough indicator of town status. Most places with full rank as towns have, he adds, attained government status as urban districts. Agricultural markets, formerly considered essential to town status, are no longer found in every town and often are associated with places of low urban status that would definitely not be ranked as towns.

Sub-towns Beneath the minimum qualifications for town ranking are places that are deficient either in community services or in shopping facilities and are classed by Smailes as sub-towns. Often a place of considerable importance as a shopping and entertainment center lacks both a secondary school and a hospital. Such sub-towns are usually essentially suburban to fully equipped urban centers.

But there are other possibilities for sub-towns. A few places, usually in thinly peopled rural districts, may have all other requirements but have inferior shopping facilities. And there are other sub-towns that are less specialized but that in one way or another lack the full town requirements.

Urban villages and villages Smailes does not go into detail about any order beneath the sub-town, but he does mention the "urban village" and the "village." The former has some combination of the key features mentioned for sub-town status, but not enough for it to rate as a sub-town. Still more limited in services is the village.

Towns versus cities Smailes contends that from the bottom of the urban scale up through towns there is a steady gradient. It is between the town and the city that he would make more of a break. All the towns, he says, are integrated into larger communities, the centers of which he recognizes as cities. The city offers a greater range of services than the town, as well as services of more specialized character, e.g., higher education, specialized medical services, and many types of entertainment. The inhabitant of a town, village, or isolated homestead must look directly to the city for these services.

Major cities In his consideration of

the ranks above towns, Smailes begins at the top. London, of course, is in a class by itself, and Smailes believes Manchester to be second in metropolitan character. But he treats both as members of a group of sixteen "major cities." The inclusion of London needs no explanation; the chief criterion for selecting the others is regional importance. Eight—Birmingham, Bristol, Cardiff, Leeds, Liverpool, Manchester, Newcastle, and Nottingham—are unquestionably regional capitals. They are headquarters of divisions of the country for a variety of purposes, including branches of the national administration. The other seven —Bradford, Hull, Leicester, Norwich, Plymouth, Sheffield, and Southampton—are of less outstanding regional importance, but merit inclusion in the group of major cities because of importance in one way or another: some because of distance from other major cities (e.g., Plymouth) and others because of their size and their eminence in commercial and industrial activities.

The sixteen major cities taken together include, he says, the culminating points of regional organization for the national government as well as for private organizations operating on a national or regional scale. They include the greatest ports, the great banking centers, the insurance centers, the centers of wholesale distribution, the centers of specialized industrial areas. They are the centers of the regional universities with their associated medical schools. And with three exceptions, they have morning newspapers; only four cities outside the group have these.

Cities Next below the major cities in Smailes's classification is a group of twenty-one "cities." They include, he says, some of the greatest market centers, and all have large department stores and are important, too, in wholesale distribution. But they do not exercise these functions for such large areas as do the regional capitals. They have post office headquarters and large general hospitals with specialized services. All have daily newspapers, though with only two exceptions these are evening papers.

Minor cities or major towns Lastly, Smailes considers a heterogeneous class, "minor cities or major towns," intermediate between cities and towns. Here he has three types: industrial, "county," and resort towns —although there is some overlap.

The industrial centers owe their size largely to important manufacturing. Many are industrial satellites of larger metropolitan centers. Because of their size these industrial centers have attained various functions, but, generally speaking, their services and influence are "narrowly local." In other words, they have only small tributary areas, so their roles as central places are usually much less than would be expected from their sizes.

The county towns are, in contrast, of long-standing importance. Added to their local administrative importance is an active role as market centers. Their services for surrounding areas are likely greatly to exceed what would be expected.

The larger seaside resorts and a few inland resorts form Smailes's third class of minor cities or major towns. As a class they tend to have numerous banks and excellent shopping and entertainment facilities; a few have evening newspapers. But they do not have important markets and often do not have much association with the surrounding rural life.

Along with cities, the minor city or major town group stands out as including the principal theater centers and centers of sporting events; they contain most of the technical colleges, art schools, and teachers' training colleges; and they generally have at least medium-sized hospitals and specialized medical services. They are also important traffic centers. But according to Smailes, the industrial centers, county towns, and seaside resorts are being invaded by multiple commercial concerns and so are tending to be less and less distinct in appearance.

Some further details In later comments, Smailes says that he has made no attempt to identify and categorize the subcenters of the great conurbations. He concludes with a statement about the numerical relationship between the three principal categories distinguished. Cities (including his major cities and cities), minor cities or major towns, and towns, in descending order, were found to increase in number roughly in the ratio 1:3:9.

Comments on Smailes's study Certain points with respect to Smailes's method are worth calling attention to. He does not discuss his sources of data, though it is fairly clear from a table included in his article that he relied on a wide variety of published sources. Nowhere does he give population figures for his various ranks of urban centers, but this is probably by design, since the idea of the study was to base the hierarchy on central services rather than on size or governmental status. It need hardly be pointed out that many subjective decisions must have been involved in separating the several categories or grades of urban centers. Smailes's maps showing the location and spacing of his five grades of centers do not appear to reflect Christaller's hexagonal scheme.

Smailes's work is summarized here, not for information about the levels of British cities, but for the method involved, since it represents a rather elaborate attempt to arrive empirically at a classification of urban centers. Much the same reasoning would have to be used by anyone attempting to arrive empirically at a ranking of urban centers for any considerable area in the United States, though, of course, different data and data sources would be involved. Whether the final product of Smailes's work was a hierarchy or a classification is largely a matter of definition. No doubt he attempted

to arrive at classes separated by actual breaks, but the urban hierarchy-continuum argument was not then under way.

Developing Terminology

Smailes used rather general descriptive terms for his several levels of urban centers: major cities, cities, minor cities or major towns, towns, and sub-towns.[5] In later studies, there has been an increasing tendency to number the several levels or orders.

Numbering of orders of urban centers Here are several examples of such numbering. In an article published in 1950, F. H. W. Green says, "Five such orders are postulated: First Order, Metropolitan Centre; Second Order, Provincial Centre; Third Order, Major Regional Centre; Fourth Order, Ordinary Regional Centre; and Fifth Order, Service Village."[6] Carol, ten years later, considered that there were seven orders.[7] These are first, lowest order, hamlet; second, low order, village; third, middle order, town; fourth, high order, city; fifth, higher order, metropolis; sixth, highest order, super metropolis (New York is his example); and a seventh order or world capital, of which there is no example as yet. Each of his main orders, except the seventh, has three subdivisions, resulting in eighteen suborders in the hierarchy.

[5] Robert E. Dickinson, several years earlier, employed some of the same criteria as Smailes in differentiating four levels of central places in a rural section of southeastern England. See Robert E. Dickinson, "The Distribution and Functions of the Smaller Urban Settlements of East Anglia," *Geography*, vol. 17, pp. 19–31, 1932.
[6] F. H. W. Green, "Urban Hinterlands in England and Wales: An Analysis of Bus Services," *Geographical Journal*, vol. 116, p. 64, 1950.
[7] Hans Carol, "The Hierarchy of Central Functions within the City," *Annals of the Association of American Geographers*, vol. 50, pp. 421–422, 1960. The words hamlet, village, etc., are given by Carol as an approximate basis for correlating with United States terminology. The several orders are based on central services rather than on size of the urban center.

Philbrick, in a study in which he speaks of "orders of areal organization" rather than orders in the urban hierarchy, has seven levels.[8] His first order is focused on the individual establishment; his second order, on a small rural village; his third order, on a small city performing a wholesaling function for second-order places around it (Kankakee, Illinois, is given as an example); his fourth order, on a specialized center of transshipment (South Bend, Indiana, is his example); and his fifth, sixth, and seventh orders are focused on increasingly complex cities, with New York as the only example of the seventh order.

There is no sanctity either in the particular numbers used or in whether numbering should begin at the top, as Green has done it, or with the lowest order, as Carol and Philbrick prefer. But it is clear that confusion can result from this variation in practices. In the rather considerable amount of American research on the urban hierarchy that has been carried on in the last decade the practice has been to begin numbering with the lowest order.

The Urban Hierarchy in Wisconsin

Brush's study of the urban hierarchy in southwestern Wisconsin,[9] like Smailes's work on England and Wales, is primarily based on an assessment of the business and services existing in centers. Retail and wholesale establishments, banks and financial agencies, trades and personal services, amusements, and various other services, including the professions and government, are considered in determining each center's status. With data from Dun and Bradstreet's *Reference Book for Wisconsin, 1949*, Brush uses star-shaped graphs to represent the central services of each trade center (Figure 6.2). The limits of service areas of centers are determined from traffic divides, using state highway commission data. Brush works chiefly with small urban centers, relating the functions to a size classification—hamlets, villages, and towns.

Orders of urban centers represented Brush designed his study in part to check Christaller's ideas, but he also comments on the relation of his work to the findings of Smailes and Carol. The farmstead, he says, possesses the lowest degree of centrality and, in Wisconsin, should hardly be regarded as a level in the hierarchy. The lowest level of agglomeration in the area in which Brush worked is the hamlet or single-service center, spaced at 2.5 to 5.5 miles but with fewer than 100 inhabitants.

He describes three higher hierarchical levels. The lowest well-developed center in Wisconsin, according to Brush, is the village or semicomplete center, spaced at 8 to 10 miles and with 500 to 900 inhabitants. This he regards as equivalent to Smailes's subtown. The complete, partially specialized centers designated as towns in Wisconsin average 3,000 to 3,500 in population and are 20 to 25 miles apart. A further step upward in the hierarchy is represented by centers with highly specialized urban services. These occur at 30- to 40-mile intervals in Wisconsin. Brush claims that this order of centers and two higher ones postulated by Smailes and Carol are not clearly understood.

Bus Services and the Urban Hierarchy

As early as 1944, Smailes referred to the desirability of using quantitative data on bus travel as a measure of urban rank.[10] It was not until some six years later, however, that the first study appeared in which

[8] Allen K. Philbrick, "Principles of Areal Functional Organization in Regional Human Geography," *Economic Geography*, vol. 33, pp. 299–336, 1957.
[9] John E. Brush, "The Hierarchy of Central Places in Southwestern Wisconsin," *Geographical Review*, vol. 43, pp. 380–402, 1953; see also John E. Brush and Howard E. Bracey, "Rural Service Centers in Southwestern Wisconsin and Southern England," *Geographical Review*, vol. 45, pp. 559–569, 1955.
[10] Smailes, *op. cit.*, p. 49.

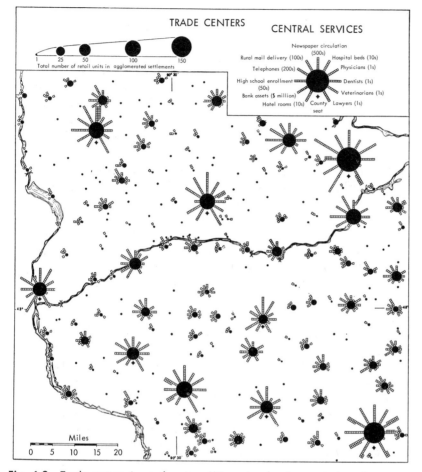

Fig. 6.2 Trade centers in southwestern Wisconsin, showing central services provided. (From John E. Brush, "The Hierarchy of Central Places in Southwestern Wisconsin," *Geographical Review*, vol. 43, 1953, fig. 4.)

bus services were used as a key to hierarchical status.

Bus services in delimiting hinterlands

The name of F. H. W. Green is associated especially with the use of bus services in the delimitation of the hinterlands of what he regards as fourth-order centers in the urban hierarchy.[11]

Green's definition of fourth order Green considers a place to be a fourth-order center if it has operating from it a bus line which serves only places smaller than itself.

[11] Green, *op. cit.*, pp. 64–88.

If at least one local route emanates from it serving only a neighboring village, then the place of origin qualifies as a fourth-order center.

The method in detail The method Green used may be briefly described. He obtained timetables for the ordinary local buses which run on schedule picking up passengers at recognized stops, and from the timetables he determined the towns from which at least some buses operate that serve no place larger than themselves. For each of these he drew a diagram on tracing paper showing bus lines radiating from the center. Then, placing the diagrams in their relative positions on a map, he drew the hinterland boundaries.[12] The boundaries thus drawn were somewhat subjective, but Green thought of them as transitions rather than clean breaks and compared them to watersheds.

Comparison with Smailes's work It is interesting to note that Green's bus technique results in about the same number of centers in England and Wales as the total of sub-towns and higher in Smailes's earlier study. But not all centers qualify according to both systems. Thus some of Green's fourth-order centers in sparsely inhabited areas do not possess the minimum number of facilities to qualify as a sub-town or higher according to Smailes's method; and some of Smailes's centers are industrial towns or seaside resorts that have little connection with surrounding areas.

Many of Green's fourth-order centers also of higher order Of course, many of the centers for which the bus hinterlands are determined are also higher-order centers. It is implicit in the whole hierarchy idea that each center performs central-place functions of the highest order to which it belongs for a correspondingly large service area, and also those of all lower levels for progressively smaller areas.

Bus services and second- and third-order centers in England and Wales Another British geographer, Carruthers, has discussed more fully the use of bus services in defining the higher orders of centers and their hinterlands.[13] Carruthers's method involves, first, determining for each place the number of bus journeys made into or through the town, and, second, calculating the number of these journeys that serve no place larger than the town itself. This information, plotted on maps, together with more subjective information about the various urban centers of England and Wales, forms the basis for Carruthers's definition of second- and third-order centers and their hinterlands. His chief contribution appears to be in connection with the third-order centers which he subdivides into 3A, 3B, 3C, and general. But he also divides the fourth-order centers into three subclasses and the second-order centers into two, and discusses possible correlations between his several levels of centers and those arrived at by Smailes.[14]

Applicability of bus-service techniques in the United States

The question might well be raised whether bus-service techniques can be used to determine service areas and orders of central places in the United States as they have been in Northwestern Europe. Mechanically, there is no reason why the idea could not be applied. Almost any city, in addition to having buses linking it to larger cities, would be likely to have buses going out in several directions to places all of which are smaller than the city itself; and some of the smaller places thus served would be found, in turn, to have buses going out from them to still smaller places.

But in the United States the private automobile is so important that bus travel has been relegated to a minor role. Though some people commute to work by bus, normally they form an extremely small proportion of the commuters of a city, and buses

---

[12] The average population of these tributary areas (not including the centers themselves) was 16,000 for England and Wales.

[13] W. I. Carruthers, "A Classification of Service Centres in England and Wales," *Geographical Journal*, vol. 123, pp. 371–385, 1957.

[14] Sven Godlund's studies of bus service and urban centrality in Sweden should also be noted. See Bus Service in Sweden, *Lund Studies in Geography*, ser. B, Human Geography, No. 17, Royal University of Lund, Sweden, 1956; and The Function and Growth of Bus Traffic within the Sphere of Urban Influence, *Lund Studies in Geography*, ser. B, Human Geography, No. 18, Royal University of Lund, Sweden, 1956.

are of little significance as far as shopping is concerned. What Green really measured was essentially the journey-to-shop. Buses are used a good deal for this purpose in Northwestern Europe, so bus service gives a good measure of the degree to which the originating urban center dominates surrounding areas and, therefore, is a good measure of its rank as a central place. But it is obvious that a grading of centers and a determination of hinterlands based on bus services, though possible in the United States, would have very little meaning in terms of journey-to-shop.

Bracey's Index of Centrality

A study by Bracey,[15] like those dealing with bus services, focused on the area served by a place rather than on an assessment of goods and services available, which was the basis for Smailes's work. Bracey claims that a direct count of shops, services, and professions in an urban center as a method of measuring its centrality is all right for places not exceeding 2,000 in population, but that for towns and larger villages it is more satisfactory to work from small villages and find out what larger centers they use for what services.

Questionnaires To obtain this information from parishes (small villages) in a county in southwestern England, Bracey used questionnaires which listed a number of services and asked for the names of larger places commonly visited for their satisfaction. The fifteen services listed are as follows: clothing stores: men's outfitting, ladies' outfitting, boots and shoes; household goods stores: hardware, electrical, radio, furniture; medical services: doctor, dentist, optician, druggist; other professional services: bank,

solicitor, public accountant, auctioneer. The questionnaires were sent to the head teachers of schools, chairmen of parish councils, clergymen, and other responsible persons. The index is based on ordinary shopping and professional services, ignoring the unusual.

Each service is allotted 1 point. Where two towns are indicated as places visited, for example, as the places commonly visited for hardware, then each receives ½ point; if three towns, ⅓ point; and so on. For each parish there is a total of fifteen points which may be credited to one town or distributed among several. The total of all the village scores attained by a city is its "index of centrality."

Results For Somerset, which is the area in which Bracey worked, the indices for the thirty-eight centers listed run from 815 for Taunton to 11 for Nailsea. Though in general the indices vary with the population of the centers, this is only roughly true. For example, the largest center, Bath, ranks fourth in centrality, with an index of 409; the second largest, a resort center, ranks only eighth in centrality. Although six towns stand out above all others as rural service centers, having the six highest indices, throughout most of the list the decline from one center to the next is small.

District centers Bracey calls attention to two other towns that should be added to the first six, making a total of eight which he says have certain common distinctive features and which may be called "district centers." Each has a rural service area of at least 100 square miles, with a population of approximately 20,000. The intensive area,[16] where there is little or no competition from nearby centers, forms a substantial part of the total service area of each of the eight towns (Figure 6.3).

[15] H. E. Bracey, "Towns as Rural Service Centers: An Index of Centrality with Special Reference to Somerset," *Institute of British Geographers: Transactions and Papers*, 1953, Publication no. 19, 1954, pp. 95–105.

[16] Bracey suggests that for each sizable town it is possible to outline an intensive area, an extensive area, and a fringe area. *Ibid.*, pp. 99–100.

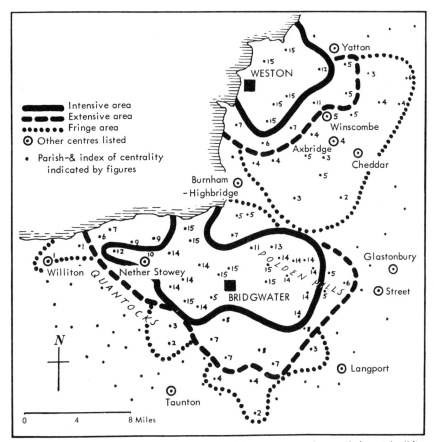

Fig. 6.3 The intensive, extensive and fringe areas of two of the eight "district centers." (After H. E. Bracey, "Towns as Rural Service Centers: An Index of Centrality with Special Reference to Somerset," *Institute of British Geographers: Transactions and Papers*, Publication no. 19, fig. 1, 1954.)

Other grades In his second grade, Bracey includes the next eight towns in the order of their indices of centrality. These indices range from 169 through 85. In these, the intensive areas are smaller and yet the scores are high enough to suggest important service functions. Bracey says that centers of this grade might be considered "local centers." He does not attempt to subdivide the remaining towns, though he thinks they all have sufficient of the service function to be described as centers.

Comparison with Smailes's results Bracey points out that Smailes, in his study of the urban hierarchy in England and Wales, classifies as minor cities or major towns several places that he, Bracey, classes as district centers. Four of Smailes's towns appear as district centers and the others, with one exception, are local centers according to Bracey's classification. But differences of this sort are to be expected, since Smailes's study was essentially an urban classification and that of Bracey grades places for their rural service only.

The Hierarchy of Central Functions in the City

Carol has carried the hierarchy idea a step further, applying it to the business

areas within cities.[17] He says that by studying the distribution of the various central
services in Zurich, Switzerland, a city of
some 500,000 persons, he and his students
were able to distinguish four distinct levels:
local business district (lowest order), neighborhood business district (low order), regional business district (middle order), and
central business district (high order).
Though the terminology is similar to that
of various other studies of city business
areas, the results, according to Carol, were
arrived at independently in the Zurich research. Each higher order of district was
found to have represented all services represented in the lower orders as well as special services of its own.

The Urban Hierarchy and Historical Geography

In studies of central places and the
urban hierarchy it is implicit that hierarchical status is not static. Though most centers
maintain, over the years, a certain level as
compared with neighboring centers, some
rise in relative importance and others decline. Harold Carter, reporting on his work
in Wales, emphasizes the value of historical
geography in hierarchy studies, and especially the value of developing urban hierarchies for past periods and of outlining the
areas served by the various centers for each
period.[18] A graph showing the changing
status of towns from period to period, he
says, should be of great value in understanding the present hierarchy (Figure 6.4).

Relation to Smailes's hierarchy study
Then Carter discusses the difficulties of such
a scheme. It is hard enough to distinguish

[17] Carol, *op. cit.*, pp. 419–438.
[18] Harold Carter, "Urban Grades and Spheres of
Influence in South West Wales: An Historical Consideration," *Scottish Geographical Magazine,* vol.
71, pp. 43–58, 1955; Harold Carter, "The Urban
Hierarchy and Historical Geography: A Consideration with Reference to North-East Wales," *Geographical Studies,* vol. 3, no. 2, pp. 85–101, 1956.

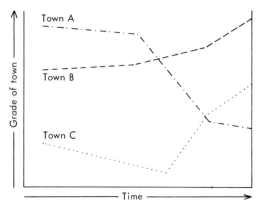

Fig. 6.4 Hypothetical graph of town grade
against time. (After fig. 1 in Harold Carter, "The
Urban Hierarchy and Historical Geography: A
Consideration with Reference to North-East Wales,"
Geographical Studies, vol. 3, no. 2, 1956.)

between levels of central places at the
present time, but think of the problems
faced when working with a past period.
Obviously, questionnaires cannot be used.
Smailes's method—an assessment of goods
and services available in a center as reflected in establishments (or what Smailes
calls institutions)—appears to be the only
practical technique. Smailes selected for
each level of his hierarchy not just an arbitrary collection of criteria, but criteria that
tended to occur in characteristic association
in what he called a trait-complex. It is much
more difficult to achieve this for a past
period than for the present.

*Difficulties in applying scheme in
Northeastern Wales* Carter goes on to discuss the difficulties he encountered in
attempting to set up hierarchies for northeastern Wales in 1835 and in 1600 comparable to those he had established for 1950.
For each historical period a distinctive set
of criteria had to be chosen and an entirely
new grading scheme constructed. Comparison of the three hierarchies brings out some
interesting changes in the relative ranks of
centers. But Carter emphasizes that the
hierarchy for each period should be regarded as an end in itself, and that it must

be examined for its own sake and no identity assumed between similar grades at different periods. There is no good reason, for example, to link a Grade 2 town of the 1830–1835 period with a Grade 2 town of 1950, since, of necessity, they have been based on different criteria.

The Work of Berry and Garrison

Outstanding in central-place research in the United States have been the names of Berry and Garrison. Writing in 1958 they pointed out that there were several reasons for wishing to produce evidence of a system of classes of central places (a hierarchical class system).[19] A considerable body of theory relating to city size, function, and arrangement had accumulated, and one of the implications of this theory was that a hierarchical class system existed. There was ample evidence that other implications of the theory were valid, namely, that larger centers are functionally more complex than smaller centers, with this increasing functional complexity being accompanied by increasing size of the urban complementary region. There was evidence, too, that by virtue of the differential provision of central functions there was interdependence between urban centers in the provision of central goods and services. On the other hand, no satisfactory evidence had been provided that a hierarchical class system of centers did indeed exist. The results of a study of Snohomish County, Washington, were presented by Berry and Garrison as evidence of the existence of a hierarchy.

Briefly, in the study of Snohomish County and, later, in southwestern Iowa,[20] the field work amounted, first of all, to an inventory of establishments performing central functions. In the work in southwestern Iowa every such building was located on a map and the functions indicated. Maps of trade areas were constructed for selected establishments in a sample of twenty central places, and interviews were conducted with customers at central places and with individuals at their homes. In this way as complete data as possible were obtained regarding the central functions performed by each place.

These data were ranked and, with the use of various statistical techniques, the data were analyzed to see to what extent there were steplike breaks and to what extent only continuous functional relations existed. The authors point out that their empirical evidence does, in fact, identify hierarchies but, on the other hand, does not disprove the existence of a continuum. "It all depends," they say, "upon the level of the inquiry, elemental or aggregative, and whether the observations are kept in an explicit spatial framework or abstracted from that framework."[21]

The Hierarchy Problem in Summary

People who have been working with the urban hierarchy have been attempting to demonstrate that broad ranks or classes of urban centers can be differentiated on the basis of characteristic central-place functions as distinct from population or administrative status. But do the several classes that are differentiated actually exist as discrete entities?

It may be, say the skeptics, that the classes exist only in arbitrary form; that the number of classes in the average hierarchical study is the result of an arbitrary decision, conscious or unconscious; and that there could be more classes or fewer classes at the will of the researcher. Also, the decision as to where the dividing line comes between one class and the next may be, and no doubt often is, an arbitrary one.

[19] Brian J. L. Berry and William L. Garrison, "The Functional Bases of the Central Place Hierarchy," *Economic Geography,* vol. 34, pp. 145–154, 1958.
[20] Brian J. L. Berry, H. Gardiner Barnum, and Robert J. Tennant, "Retail Location and Consumer Behavior," *Papers and Proceedings of the Regional Science Association,* 1962, vol. 9, pp. 65–106.

[21] *Ibid.,* p. 102.

Actually, the idea of distinct classes with real breaks between them is rooted in Christaller's work and is in fact inherent in his theory. The discrete population levels of the central places of each class are considered to arise because the income which supports the population of a central place is brought into the center by the activities which provide goods and services for surrounding consumers. Since central places of each class possess discrete groups of activities, they should also tend to have discrete population levels and have service areas of different sizes. But, in spite of the logic of Christaller's system, the question remains, do such discrete classes actually exist? Or are they arbitrarily delimited along what is in reality a continuum?

Universality of the Hierarchy

If a hierarchy of urban centers can be differentiated for one area, does it follow that it is a universal hierarchy? Will the fourth order as determined in Western Europe correspond closely to the fourth order as determined in the United States? This hardly seems probable. To the degree that hierarchies can be differentiated, they may vary by culture areas, by countries, or even by regions within a single country.

A Broader View

The hierarchy question, however, is only one aspect of research dealing with central-place theory. People whose interests lie in this general field are at work examining various implications of the central-place system. Unquestionably, Christaller's spatial model of central places has given rise to the most active research cluster in American urban geography.

Selected References

Berry, Brian J. L.: "The Impact of Expanding Metropolitan Communities upon the Central Place Hierarchy," *Annals of the Association of American Geographers,* vol. 50, pp. 112–116, 1960.

———— and William L. Garrison: "Recent Developments of Central Place Theory," *Papers and Proceedings of the Regional Science Association,* 1958, vol. 4, pp. 107–120.

————: "The Functional Bases of the Central Place Hierarchy," *Economic Geography,* vol. 34, pp. 145–154, 1958.

————, H. Gardiner Barnum, and Robert J. Tennant: "Retail Location and Consumer Behavior," *Papers and Proceedings of the Regional Science Association,* 1962, vol. 9, pp. 65–106.

Bracey, H. E.: "A Rural Component of Centrality Applied to Six Southern Counties in the United Kingdom," *Economic Geography,* vol. 32, pp. 38–50, 1956.

————: *Social Provision in Rural Wiltshire,* Methuen & Co., Ltd., London, 1952.

————: "Towns as Rural Service Centers: An Index of Centrality with Special Reference to ·Somerset," *Institute of British Geographers: Transactions and Papers,* 1953, Publication no. 19, 1954, pp. 95–105.

Brush, John E.: "The Hierarchy of Central Places in Southwestern Wisconsin," *Geographical Review,* vol. 43, pp. 380–402, 1953.

———— and H. E. Bracey: "Rural Service Centers in Southwestern Wisconsin and Southern England," *Geographical Review,* vol. 45, pp. 559–569, 1955.

Carol, Hans: "The Hierarchy of Central Functions within the City," *Annals of the Association of American Geographers,* vol. 50, pp. 419–438, 1960.

Carruthers, W. I.: "A Classification of Service Centres in England and Wales," *Geographical Journal,* vol. 123, pp. 371–385, 1957.

————: "Service Centres in Greater London," *The Town Planning Review,* vol. 33, pp. 5–31, 1962.

Carter, Harold: *The Towns of Wales,* University of Wales Press, Cardiff, 1965.

————: "Urban Grades and Spheres of Influence in South West Wales: An Historical Consideration," *Scottish Geographical Magazine,* vol. 71, pp. 43–58, 1955.

————: "The Urban Hierarchy and Historical Geography: A Consideration with Reference to North-East Wales," *Geographical Studies,* vol. 3, no. 2, pp. 85–101, 1956.

Dickinson, Robert E.: *City and Region: A*

Geographical Interpretation, Routledge & Kegan Paul, Ltd., London, 1964.

————: "The Distribution and Functions of the Smaller Urban Settlements of East Anglia," *Geography*, vol. 17, pp. 19–31, 1932.

Godlund, Sven: Bus Service in Sweden, *Lund Studies in Geography*, ser. B, Human Geography, No. 17, Royal University of Lund, Sweden, 1956.

————: The Function and Growth of Bus Traffic within the sphere of Urban Influence, *Lund Studies in Geography*, ser. B, Human Geography, No. 18, Royal University of Lund, Sweden, 1956.

Green, F. H. W.: "Community of Interest Areas: Notes on the Hierarchy of Central Places and Their Hinterlands," *Economic Geography*, vol. 34, pp. 210–226, 1958.

————: "Community of Interest Areas in Western Europe: Some Geographical Aspects of Local Passenger Traffic," *Economic Geography*, vol. 29, pp. 283–298, 1953.

————: "Urban Hinterlands in England and Wales: An Analysis of Bus Services," *Geographical Journal*, vol. 116, pp. 64–88, 1950.

———— and Robert F. A. Edwards: "A Commercial Application of Urban Hinterland Studies," Proceedings of the IGU Symposium in Urban Geography, Lund 1960, *Lund Studies in Geography*, ser. B, Human Geography, No. 24, Royal University of Lund, Sweden, 1962, pp. 191–195.

Philbrick, Allen K.: "Principles of Areal Functional Organization in Regional Human Geography," *Economic Geography*, vol. 33, pp. 299–336, 1957.

Smailes, Arthur E.: "The Urban Hierarchy in England and Wales," *Geography*, vol. 29, pp. 41–51, 1944.

————: "The Urban Mesh of England and Wales," *Transactions and Papers*, Institute of British Geographers, 1946, pp. 85–101.

Taaffe, Edward J.: "The Urban Hierarchy: An Air Passenger Definition," *Economic Geography*, vol. 38, pp. 1–14, 1962.

See also reference list for Chap. 5.

CHAPTER 7

The urban economic base

THE last three chapters have been concerned with relations of the urban center to a contiguous area that surrounds it. This contiguous belt, it was found, is made up of individual service areas, not only service areas based on economic criteria, but cultural service areas as well; and there is an overall area of dominance, referred to as the center's tributary area. But it was pointed out that an urban center's activities do not stop with the contiguous area. There are more limited and spotty connections that may be countrywide or even worldwide.

In the present chapter the concern is only with economic relations, but note that we are interested in all economic relations, not just those with the contiguous area but also those with the rest of the world. The concept discussed, the *urban economic base,* involves a distinctive way of looking at the exterior relations of a place. The concept will first be presented in popular terms and later examined more critically.

The urban economic base defined
The urban economic base, as commonly defined, consists of all activities that export goods and services to points outside the community or that market their goods and services to persons who come from outside. All the activities referred to are considered *basic* in that they bring money into the community. They have been referred to as the community's "breadwinners." In contrast are those activities whose goods and services are consumed within the confines of the urban area and, consequently, do not bring outside money into the community. They are supported by the basic activities, but are themselves referred to as *nonbasic.*

Examples The contrast may be made clear by some examples. At one extreme is the type of factory that ships all of its products out of the urban area. According to the theory being discussed, it is 100 per cent basic. So, too, is a mail-order establishment that has no local sales. At the other extreme is a neighborhood grocery, a small barber shop, or a local laundry. Such places do essentially all of their business with the townspeople. No money comes into the city from these activities; they merely serve people of the community. Thus they are 100 per cent nonbasic.

Establishments rarely completely basic or nonbasic Needless to say, such extremes are rare. Though an establishment may be predominantly basic or predominantly nonbasic, it is unlikely to be entirely one or the other. Economic base theory attempts to separate the two types, even to the extent of dividing the activities of a single establishment.

The ratio The situation for a community may be stated more succinctly by means of a ratio, which often is expressed in terms of employees. Thus we may say that the basic-nonbasic ratio (B/N ratio) of a certain city is 1:1, which means that the urban area has just about as many workers in basic activities as in nonbasic activities. In another city the ratio is 1:2, meaning that there are twice as many people engaged in nonbasic activities as in basic activities.

The employment multiplier It follows from the foregoing, according to extreme advocates of the base ratio theory, that if a new basic enterprise is added to a city the new activity should bring, in the long run, an increase in nonbasic employment, its extent depending on the ratio for the city.[1] For example, the addition of 1,000 basic workers to the first city mentioned above should, if the ratio is correct, result in 1,000 more jobs in the nonbasic activities; addi-

tion of the same number of basic workers to the second city should mean the addition of 2,000 nonbasic workers. This multiplier effect, as it is called, is part of the urban economic base concept. It was the addition to the basic employment that started the multiplying. According to the theory, therefore, if cities are to grow and prosper, attention should be paid especially to the industries that are entirely or predominantly basic. This has been the reasoning of the most literal advocates of the theory.

Further evaluation needed The foregoing has been little more than a preliminary, popular view of the urban economic base. In the pages that follow, the concept will be considered in more detail, and its possibilities and limitations in the field of urban geography assessed.

Problems of Terminology

We may well begin our more detailed consideration of the urban economic base with a brief look at some of the problems of terminology that have arisen.

Economic base In the first place, the general term for the concept, *economic base*, is loosely used. It is considered by some writers as synonymous with the tax base of the city; others have used it to refer to those activities of the city that furnish the major volume of employment. To avoid confusion, the term should best be restricted to those activities that bring money into a community, and only a study whose major objective is to distinguish between basic activities and their nonbasic complements should be referred to as an *economic base study*. On the other hand, a general study of the economy of a city without special emphasis on the economic base can better be called simply an *economic survey*.

Basic versus nonbasic There are problems of terminology, too, with respect to the

---

[1] Richard B. Andrews, "Mechanics of the Urban Economic Base: The Concept of Base Ratios," *Land Economics*, vol. 31, pp. 47–53, 1955.

two types of activity with which the concept deals. The term *basic activities* has been rather generally applied to the activities that bring in net earnings, but there are various other descriptive terms that are sometimes substituted for basic. Among them are active, city-building, export, urban growth, external, primary, and supporting.

In contrast the activities that are completely local and involve no export beyond predetermined limits of the community have been referred to as nonbasic, service, ancillary, secondary, internal, city-serving, passive, and by various other names. In this chapter the most commonly accepted term, nonbasic, is used.

Evolution of the Concept

Early statements of the idea The urban economic base concept seems to have first been given expression in the early 1920s. Frederick L. Olmstead wrote in a letter of February 21, 1921:

> . . . productive occupations may be roughly divided into those which can be called primary, such as . . . manufacturing goods for general use (i.e., not confined to use within the community itself), and those occupations which may be called ancillary, such as are devoted directly or indirectly to the service and convenience of the people engaged in the primary occupations.[2]

In the same year, M. Aurousseau wrote:

> It is well known that towns have an extraordinary power of growth. This appears to be due to the relationship between the primary occupations and the secondary occupations of the townsfolk. The primary occupations are those directly concerned with the functions of the town. The secondary occupations are those concerned with the maintenance of the well-being of

the people engaged in those of primary nature.[3]

Homer Hoyt and the urban economic base concept An economist, Homer Hoyt, is most closely associated with the development of the economic base idea. Though he outlined the concept in 1936, his first complete statement of it did not appear until three years later.[4] In 1939, Hoyt advanced the idea of a mathematical relationship between basic and nonbasic employment, pointing out that the ratio varied from city to city and suggesting the value of the basic-nonbasic ratio in analyzing the economic condition of a city and of discerning economic trends in the city. He described a technique of analysis consisting essentially of: (1) calculation of total employment in each basic activity in the community as a whole, (2) estimation of the proportion of basic employment to nonbasic employment, (3) estimation of ratio of population to employment, (4) estimation of the future trend in each segment of the base, (5) calculation of total employment and total future population on the basis of trends in basic employment.

Later work In the years that followed, there appeared a flood of planning reports and articles that refined the original urban economic base concept and added significantly to the techniques for applying it, though, at the same time, pointing out some of its limitations. Certainly the most comprehensive study was a series by Richard B. Andrews which appeared between 1953 and 1955.[5] But work on the economic base con-

[2] Quoted in Robert Murray Haig and Roswell C. McCrea, *Major Economic Factors in Metropolitan Growth and Arrangement,* vol. 1 of *Regional Survey of New York and Its Environs,* New York, 1927, p. 43, footnote 1.

[3] M. Aurousseau, "The Distribution of Population: A Constructive Problem," *Geographical Review,* vol. 11, pp. 563–592; reference, p. 574, 1921.
[4] According to Richard B. Andrews, "Mechanics of the Urban Economic Base: Historical Development of the Base Concept," *Land Economics,* vol. 29, pp. 161–167, 1953.
[5] Richard B. Andrews, "Mechanics of the Urban Economic Base," *Land Economics,* vol. 29, pp.

cept by no means ended with this thorough analysis. Every year there have been additional applications of the concept, and economists, planners, and geographers have continued to argue various aspects of the idea. In all this, Hoyt, through his economic base studies of various communities and his talks and magazine articles, has continued to play a prominent role.

Application of the Concept

On the preceding pages the urban economic base was introduced in general terms and its evolution briefly summarized. Next a general overview of the application of the concept will be presented.

Units of measurement

One of the first problems that faces people applying the urban economic base concept is the question of units of measurement. Among the measures that have been considered are employment, payrolls, community income and expenditures, value added by manufacture, dollar sales volume, and physical production.

Employment   The most widely used measure has been employment. Employment data in general are likely to be easier to get and available for more and different unit areas than data for any other possible economic base measure.

But employment is not a perfect measure. For example, workers' salaries in the basic activities may increase markedly, bringing a corresponding increase in the income of a community. This important development is not directly reflected in basic employment, but is likely to result in expansion of nonbasic employment. The picture is further complicated by the fact

that the salary increases may be much greater in some activities than in others. Seasonal employment, part-time employment, and fluctuating monthly employment present other difficulties in the use of employment data; nor of course does employment take any account of outside investments which bring money into the community.

Payrolls as a measure   In view of these limitations of employment as a measure of the economic base, some people have advocated a different though somewhat related measure: payrolls. But some interesting and perplexing questions arise. For example, does one job at $10,000 have the same economic weight as two at $5,000? How would local service spending and service employment differ in the two cases? Or, to carry the problem to more extreme ends, are 10 positions in the community, each paying $50,000, the economic equivalent of 100 positions paying $5,000 each? Payroll data, moreover, require price-change adjustments if there are to be comparisons of several years. And payroll information is not so readily available as employment data or so easy to split where an enterprise is only partly basic.

Income and expenditure accounts for the community   Dollar income, outgo, and internal circulation measurements for a community should really be involved in a study of the economic base. The results of such a study of Oskaloosa, Iowa, a city of some 10,000 to 12,000 population, were published in 1938.[6] The study embraced all monetary transactions of the community, both basic and nonbasic. The greatest single advantage of the approach is considered the inclusion of returns on capital invested outside the community. These are neglected when other measures are used. By measur-

_____

161–167, 263–268, and 343–350, 1953; vol. 30, pp. 52–60, 164–172, 260–269, and 309–319, 1954; vol. 31, pp. 47–53, 144–155, 245–256, and 361–371, 1955.

[6] "Oskaloosa versus the United States," *Fortune*, April, 1938, pp. 55–62 ff.

ing the balance of payments between Oskaloosa and the "rest of the world" a
distinction was arrived at between payments to local creditors and to non-local
creditors.

Though the balance-of-payments technique has much to recommend it philosophi-
cally, it is, unfortunately, impracticable.
In the Oskaloosa study, the work was done
by the research staff of *Fortune* magazine
and underwritten by the magazine. It is
believed that ordinarily the expense of such
a study would be close to prohibitive. For
a city of any great size, not only would the
cost be great, but it would be virtually impossible to get at all the relevant data and
to unravel the maze of internal transactions.[7]

Other measures   Three other units of
measurement sometimes considered in
studying the urban economic base are value
added by manufacture, dollar sales volume,
and physical production. "Value added"
applies to manufacturing alone and is
broken down by industries only for the
more highly industrialized standard metropolitan statistical areas. Dollar sales volume
has the advantage that it can be applied to
trade in general, but it shares with "value
added" the difficulty of being affected by
complex price movements. On the other
hand, dollar sales volume data are useful in
the process of segregating basic from nonbasic activity within an enterprise. In this
process the sales volume is ordinarily converted into employment. Physical production appears to be of little help except
possibly in analyzing the comparative positions of base activities engaged in manufacturing. And none of these three units

measures such activities as a university or
a medical center, yet obviously such establishments may represent important basic activities in a community.

Units of measure in summary   No one
of the units discussed is perfect for base
identification. Income and expenditure accounts for the community may well be the
best measure, but this possibility is virtually
ruled out by cost and the difficulties of applying the method. Payroll data correct
some of the inequities of employment figures, but the latter are easier to obtain and
use. In fact, employment has been by far
the most popular unit of measure to date,
certainly the most practicable, and it seems
likely that this preference will continue.
Hence, throughout the remainder of this
chapter, the unit of measurement is employment unless otherwise specified.

Techniques of determining the basic-nonbasic ratio

Two principal methods are used to determine the proportion of employment that
brings money into the community.

An approximation technique [8]   One of
these methods is an approximation technique which has grown out of the work of
Homer Hoyt and is applied principally to
large urban areas where detailed techniques
would be too time-consuming. It makes use
of United States Census data or other data
available on a national basis.[9] The technique compares the employment pattern of
the area under study with that of the nation,
and assumes that the population of a par-

---

[7] This is essentially the measure employed in input-
output techniques of analysis. See, for example,
Walter Isard and Robert Kavesh, "Economic Structural Interrelations of Metropolitan Regions,"
American Journal of Sociology, vol. 60, pp. 152–
162, 1954.

[8] The manipulation involved is essentially that
used in calculating the location quotient, which is
discussed on pp. 324–327. Hence, this technique
for determining the ratio is sometimes called the
"location quotients method."
[9] Estimates of a city's share of the total United
States purchasing power can be obtained from
Sales Management magazine's "Survey of Buying
Power" issue, published in the spring of each year.

ticular urban area consumes its proportionate share of the national totals of goods and services, and that production beyond this amount is basic.

Here is something of the way it works: basic employment in manufacturing, for example, is determined for a certain city by first finding the percentage that the city's [10] workers in each line of activity (as shown in the Census of Population) makes up of the total number in this line in the country as a whole. This figure is then compared with the city's proportion of the country's population determined from the Census of Population. For each specific line of manufacturing in which the local proportion exceeds the city's proportion of the national purchasing power or population, the activity is considered to be basic to that degree. For each line, the basic increment is converted into employment, and these employment figures are totaled to give the total basic employment in manufacturing.

The example of one manufacturing group, chemicals and allied products, will illustrate the method. A simple equation can be used: The number of basic employees in chemicals and allied products in City A = number of employees in chemicals and allied products residing in the city −

$$\left(\frac{\text{total population of City A}}{\text{national population total}} \times \text{number employed in chemicals and allied products in nation} \right).$$

Obviously, if the result is zero or a negative number the city has no basic employees in chemicals and allied products.

A similar approach is used for wholesale and retail trade, transportation, finance, the professions, government, and other lines of economic activity. In each instance the percentage of the area's total workers in the specific line of activity is compared with what might be expected from the city's proportion of United States purchasing

power or population. Any line that is in excess of these United States proportions is considered basic to that degree, and this proportion is converted into employment figures. These figures are added to the basic employment in manufacturing to give total basic employment which, of course, is compared with all employment in arriving at the basic-nonbasic ratio for the area.

Economic survey and base study Another method of determining the urban economic base is through a local economic survey and base study. Interviews or questionnaires (sometimes partly on a sampling basis), or some combination of the two, are used to determine the percentage of sales or other business that brings money into the city and the proportion that is local. This information is obtained for manufactured goods sold; for wholesale and retail sales; for receipts from hotels, theaters, tourist homes, garages, gas stations, and other services; for units of government and for educational institutions; and even for the business represented by bank deposits, loans, and insurance policies. In each instance these percentages are applied to total employment figures for each line of activity so as to obtain a separation of basic and nonbasic employment.[11]

The two methods compared The faults of the approximation method are obvious. For instance, why should a community be expected to perform in the same proportions as the country as a whole, especially in view of the fact that the national totals are based on rural as well as urban areas? The question has been asked, too,

---

[10] Corporate city, standard metropolitan statistical area, urbanized area, or any other area selected.

[11] For example, if the management of a department store with 80 employees estimates that 50 per cent of its sales are to people from outside the city and the other 50 per cent to people from inside the city, then 40 employees are listed as basic and 40 nonbasic.

what if the community is more productive than the national average in terms of output per employee? And there are various other objections.[12]

On the other hand, although the local economic survey and base study approach may seem more precise, it, too, presents some serious problems. Individual firms may be loath to cooperate; or their records may not be kept in accordance with the base area used in the survey, in which case they can only make estimates which may be far from accurate. Finally, the economic survey method involves a good deal of time and expense and, therefore, is probably not feasible for large metropolitan centers. For these, the approximation technique appears to be more practicable.

Special problems Whichever method of determining the urban economic base is employed, various special problems arise. Here are a few that are discussed by Andrews.[13] If you were analyzing a suburb how would you count commuters? Obviously, they are part of the community's economic base as they bring money in. Universities, too, present certain identification problems. Ordinarily, the proportion of students supported by parents living outside the community is taken as the basis for dividing the university employees into basic and nonbasic, but what of local stores, selling almost exclusively to students? They probably should be considered basic in the same proportion as the university itself. The division of local government employees into basic and nonbasic components presents problems; and transportation and communication and absentee ownership raise some interesting questions.

Linked activities sometimes give rise to problems in connection with base identification. Andrews gives the example of a starter factory selling all of its product to an automobile factory in the same community. The general conclusion is that it should be classed as basic to the same degree that the automobile factory is basic, since only a formal organizational boundary separates the two plants that are engaged in making the same final product. But what of a plant that sells its entire product to the starter plant? How long can such a chain of connections be? And must a plant sell all of its products to another plant in order to be considered linked to it for purposes of base identification? The complexities are readily apparent.

Other techniques Though the methods described are the chief ones that have been used, they are not the only possibilities.

SIGNIFICANT ENTERPRISES APPROACH One variation that has been suggested holds that it is unnecessary to survey the complete base, that there are a few "significant enterprises," an adequate study of which tells what is happening to the community's economic base as a whole. Through concentrating on these, one could greatly reduce the work of a survey. But the subjective aspects of this approach are obvious. What, for instance, is the test for significance? Should the significant basic activities be single firms or whole activity groups? And since the significant enterprise approach does not deal with all economic activities, it cannot result in ratios of basic activity to nonbasic activity and to population.

THE MINIMUM REQUIREMENTS APPROACH Another technique that has been suggested is the minimum requirements approach.[14]

[12] For a fuller criticism of the method see Charles M. Tiebout, *The Community Economic Base Study*, Committee for Economic Development, New York, 1962, pp. 47–49.

[13] See Andrews, "Mechanics of the Urban Economic Base," *Land Economics*, vol. 30, pp. 260–269, 1954.

[14] Cf. Edward L. Ullman and Michael F. Dacey, "The Minimum Requirements Approach to the Urban Economic Base," *The Regional Science Association: Papers and Proceedings*, 1960, vol. 6, pp. 175–194; also published in Proceedings of the IGU Symposium in Urban Geography, Lund 1960,

Like the approximation technique, it is based on United States Census data. A minimum percentage of the labor force of an urban area is required in each sector of the area's economy to maintain the viability of the urban area. Employment beyond this minimum requirement is called "excess employment." The minimum requirement closely approximates the nonbasic needs of the urban area, and the excess employment is essentially export or basic.

Charles Tiebout has given a simple summary of the method together with a hypothetical example.[15] One might base such a study on, say, 100 communities. For each, the percentage of the total labor force in each industry is calculated. For example, a community might be found to have 4.2 per cent of its total employment in the baking industry. This might be the highest proportion in this particular activity for any one of the communities. The lowest proportion for any one of them might be 0.7 per cent. According to the minimum requirements technique the presumption is that 0.7 per cent of the total labor force in baking is the minimum required by any community to satisfy its own needs and that all employment in baking in excess of this amount in any other of the communities is basic or export employment. It follows that 3.5 per cent of the total employment in the first community mentioned is basic employment in the baking industry. For another industry, some other community might be found to have the minimum, and this minimum would be the base for determining the basic employment for that industry for each of the other communities. Repeating this process would yield a basic total for each industry for each community and, by combining, the total basic employment for any particular community could be determined and, of course, the basic-nonbasic ratio.

But Tiebout points out several difficulties with this approach. For instance, it has been contended that some "oddballs" may be involved, e.g., communities whose economic bases are atypical for one reason or another. To avoid this situation, one might, it has been suggested, drop the five communities at the bottom of the list in each industry. This avoids, supposedly, some spurious cases. But such a procedure has its disadvantages. Why drop five communities? Why not four? Or six? Or eight? Obviously, the higher the cutoff point the less the basic or export activity for each community.

The choice of a base area

But choice of a unit of measurement and of a technique is only part of the story. An important decision remains: What base area should be used in an urban economic base study?

The legal city   The legal or corporate city has been used in a number of such studies. It is admittedly a highly artificial area, since built-up sections often continue across the city line without interruption. However, the legal city has some advantages as a base area. For one thing, in a number of important respects the legal city operates as a unit. It must, for example, operate as a financial unit, and hence, to the administration of the city, identification of those activities that bring money in may be of prime importance. Moreover, the legal city is the most convenient unit to refer to if an interview technique is being used. Thus the manager of a large department store might well be able to make an intelligent estimate of the proportion of the store's customers that come from within the city limits, since charge accounts are often kept on this basis. Lastly, for cities of less than 50,000 population, urbanized areas and

Lund Studies in Geography, ser. B, Human Geography, No. 24, Royal University of Lund, Sweden, 1962, pp. 121–143. See the latter source for reference to authors who presented essentially similar concepts prior to Ullman and Dacey.
[15] Tiebout, *op. cit.,* pp. 49–50.

standard metropolitan statistical areas have ordinarily not been established,[16] so it is difficult to work with anything except the legal city.

The urbanized area The urbanized area represents a much better approximation of the real city than the corporate city does and, where it has been delineated, might logically be used as the base area for an economic base study. But it is not an economic unit as is the legal city. And an obvious disadvantage of the urbanized area is that its boundaries are generally not well known locally. If interviews and questionnaires are used, therefore, estimates of the proportions of business carried on with firms or people from outside the area can hardly be very reliable.[17]

Metropolitan areas More popular as a base area has been some form of metropolitan area: the metropolitan district before 1950; the standard metropolitan area in the 1950s; or, at present, the standard metropolitan statistical area. We can speak in terms of the last of these, since it is practically the same as the standard metropolitan area.

There are several reasons for the popularity of the standard metropolitan statistical area as a base area. Its activities, according to the Bureau of the Census, form an integrated economic and social system. It is a better approximation of the economic city than is the legal city or the urbanized area, and its boundaries, since ordinarily they are county boundaries, are much better

known than those of the urbanized area. Thus not only is the standard metropolitan statistical area suitable for application of the approximation technique, but it is also much better adapted to the interviews and questionnaires of the economic survey and base study than is the urbanized area.

Other possibilities Though, in nearly every economic base study, the legal city, some type of metropolitan area, or the urbanized area has formed the base area, there are still other possibilities. Some people advocate using special market areas—e.g., local trade areas outlined by the Audit Bureau of Circulations or market areas outlined by Reilly's law. In spite of their theoretical appeal, however, the use of such areas seems unrealistic, since there are no census data available for them and since it would be difficult to describe their extent sufficiently for an interview-questionnaire type of approach.

Base area for study of suburb or satellite A special problem arises when an economic base study is to be made of a suburb or a satellite. Here it is necessary, ordinarily, to rely on the legal unit as a base area. In New England, of course, this would be the area known as the town or city (see Appendix A).

Specifying the base area If comparisons of basic-nonbasic ratios of different cities are to be made, it is desirable that the studies use similar base areas. But in any event it is absolutely essential that ratios never be given without defining the base area for which they are determined.

Ratios differ from city to city

When Hoyt first elaborated his urban economic base concept in the 1930s it was assumed that the ratio of basic to nonbasic activities in every city was approximately 1:1. A few years later, however, Hoyt realized that this was not so. It is now gener-

---

[16] For special treatment of twin central cities see Chap. 2.

[17] In an economic base study of Madison, Wis., John Alexander used the city's urbanized area as his base and obtained his information from interviews and questionnaires. However, Madison is widely separated from other cities of comparable size, and its urbanized area is such a good approximation of the real city that probably no serious problem arose in distinguishing between business with people and firms from inside and from outside the city.

ally believed that ratios vary from city to city, but that, for the most part, they will be found to lie between 1:0.5 and 1:2 (Table 7.1). Why should these variations occur?

This is a question that cannot be answered at all definitely. It is rather generally accepted that the nonbasic component tends to increase with size of the city (Table 7.1). Empirical studies indicate this, and it is to be expected, since large cities are known to perform functions for themselves that smaller cities do not perform for themselves. A larger city naturally has a greater proportion of its employed persons furnishing goods and services needed in the local urban area.

But in addition to city size, there are a number of other possible bases for variations in the ratio from city to city. Among these are age of city (the nonbasic propor-

tion is presumed to increase with city age), stage in economic cycle, functional character of the city, and probably various others.[18]

It is interesting to speculate about the reasons for ratio variations, but it is apparent that small differences may have very little if any significance. Different types of base areas often are involved, and, in any event, the techniques used may have been sufficiently different in detail to account for minor ratio differences.

Differing ratios for same city

Even for the same city the results of two economic base studies may differ. There

[18] For further discussion of some of these reasons for ratio differences, see Richard B. Andrews, "Mechanics of the Urban Economic Base: The Concept of Base Ratios," *Land Economics*, vol. 31, pp. 47–53, 1955.

Table 7.1   Some estimates of basic-nonbasic employment ratios by size of city

Town	Date	Population	Basic	Nonbasic
Auburn, Wash.	1953	6,500	1	0.8
Ajo, Ariz.	1954	7,500	1	0.35
Oskaloosa, Iowa	1937	10,000	1	0.8
Streator, Ill.	1939	17,000	1	0.9
Medford, Ore.	1952	20,000	1	0.8
Oshkosh, Wis.	1950	42,000	1	0.6
Albuquerque, N. M.	1948	100,000	1	0.9
Madison, Wis.	1952	110,000	1	0.8
Brockton Area, Mass.	1946	120,000	1	0.8
Tucson, Ariz., SMA	1952	175,000	1	0.99
Albuquerque, N. M., SMA	1956	210,000	1	0.82
Wichita, Kans., MA	1950	241,000	1	1.47
Denver, Colo., SMA	1950	564,000	1	1.54
Cincinnati, Ohio, MA	1940	787,000	1	1.1
Washington, D.C.*	1947	1,000,000	1	1.1
Detroit, Mich., MA	1940	2,337,000	1	1.1
New York, N.Y., MA	1940	12,000,000	1	2.1

Note: SMA = standard metropolitan area; MA = metropolitan area; * probably the equivalent of the metropolitan area.
SOURCE: Based on table I in Andrew H. Wilson, *Albuquerque Economic Support Analysis*, General Plan Monograph, City of Albuquerque Planning Department, 1948, with modifications. The author of the bulletin gives credit for most of the ratios in the table to Edward L. Ullman.

are several possible reasons for such variations.

Ratio in relation to the base area   One of the most important factors in explaining such differences in the ratio that may be determined for a city is the selection of the base area. The importance of this point is brought out vividly by Victor Roterus and Wesley Calef.[19]

They begin by considering a crossroads hamlet, consisting of a tavern, a filling station, and a grocery store. The township in which the hamlet lies is the market area. It is further assumed that none of the store owners or their employees trade at any of the other hamlet stores. Obviously, the hamlet's employment is 100 per cent basic, since the stores export all of their goods and services.

Suppose it is further assumed that all other employed people in the township are dairy farmers whose product is sold entirely outside the township. If the township is taken as the base area and the basic-nonbasic ratio is again calculated, the farmers are found to represent basic employment, but the hamlet businessmen have become nonbasic workers since they furnish goods and services to the farmers but do not, themselves, bring any money into the area.

But suppose that there is a large city in the county and that all the farmers in the township are dairy farmers who sell fluid milk in the city. If the county is taken as the area for study and the basic-nonbasic employment ratio calculated for that area, then the dairy farmers are nonbasic employees since they bring no money into the county.

To elaborate their point still further, Roterus and Calef suggest that the United States as a whole be considered as the area for which the basic-nonbasic ratio is being

[19] Victor Roterus and Wesley Calef, "Notes on the Basic-Nonbasic Employment Ratio," *Economic Geography,* vol. 31, pp. 17–20, 1955.

calculated. The ratio of basically employed to nonbasic workers is then very small since only workers producing for export out of the country would be considered basic.[20]

The foregoing deals with extremes in order to make a point. But certainly the choice of base area has a good deal to do with the resulting basic-nonbasic ratio. Surveys of the same community are likely to give substantially different results depending upon whether the corporate city, the urbanized area, or the standard metropolitan statistical area is taken as the base. And if the city's market area is used instead, the ratio will be different still.[21]

Ratio in relation to the technique used   A second factor that probably affects the ratio is the technique used. For example, although we have no direct evidence on this point, it is quite possible that the ratio for an urban center would be substantially different depending upon whether a local economic survey and base study (with interviews and questionnaires) or the approximation technique or some other method were used.

How the ratio changes with time   There is reason to think, too, that the same person, using the same city base area and the same method, might get a different ratio if he studied the city again after an interval of a few years. Cities do not stand still economically. Instead, the decline of old enterprises and the starting of new ones are

[20] The basic-nonbasic ratio for the United States has been estimated at about 1:20. See Hans Blumenfeld, "The Economic Base of the Metropolis," *Journal of the American Institute of Planners,* vol. 21, no. 4, p. 117, Fall, 1955.
[21] A suburb would be likely to have a basic-nonbasic ratio very different from that of a central city. It would, for example, tend to have a low nonbasic component, since most of the residents are employed elsewhere and bring money into the community, whereas much of the nonbasic activity may be furnished by the neighboring city.

constantly changing the picture and the ratio must change accordingly.

The basic-nonbasic ratio in population predictions

Just as there is a basic-nonbasic ratio, so too a ratio can be calculated between basic employment and total population (see page 100). Through a study of the trends in the basic industries it is possible to project basic employment, and, using a ratio of basic employment to total population, to estimate the future population of a community. This can clearly be only the roughest sort of estimate, since there are so many variables in modern life that can seriously affect the health of an existing basic industry or bring a new industry to a community. Nevertheless, it appears that economic base calculations may be of some value as a check against other methods of population prediction.

The urban economic base as a guide to economic expansion

Where the urban economic base is worked out for a community by comparison with averages for the country as a whole, it is only natural to carry the matter a step further by asking whether there are neglected opportunities in some of the activities which do not find average representation. Of course, common-sense checks and balances have to be applied. Nevertheless, if the necessary resources are available and the local market is large enough, it may be possible through this sort of analysis to arrive at some practicable ideas for economic expansion.

Geographic Qualities of the Basic-Nonbasic Concept

We are now ready to assess the economic base concept in more general terms. Alexander contends that the basic-nonbasic concept of classifying economic activities has four qualities which recommend it to geographers.[22]

In the first place, he says, the concept provides a view of economic ties which bind a city to other areas. By way of example, Alexander refers to the contrast between Oshkosh and Madison, two Wisconsin cities for which he made economic base studies (Table 7.2 and Figure 7.1). Total employment as shown in the table is not very revealing, but when basic employment alone is considered, the differences in the employment structures of the two cities become much clearer. Oshkosh is dominated by manufacturing, whereas government and manufacturing are near rivals in the support

[22] John W. Alexander, "The Basic-Nonbasic Concept of Urban Economic Functions," *Economic Geography*, vol. 30, pp. 251–255, 1954.

Fig. 7.1 A comparison of the economic structures of Oshkosh and Madison, two Wisconsin cities. Letters refer as follows: S, services; T, trade; G, government; M, manufacturing; O, others. (After fig. 1 in John W. Alexander, "The Basic-Nonbasic Concept of Urban Economic Functions," *Economic Geography*, vol. 30, p. 250, 1954.)

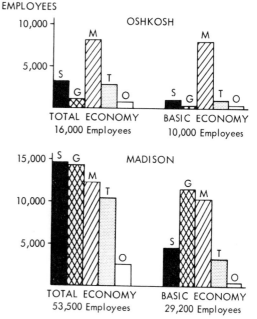

Table 7.2   Employment in Oshkosh and Madison, Wisconsin

	Oshkosh	Madison
1950 population	42,000	110,000
1940–1950 population growth	5%	28%
Total employment	16,000	53,500
Basic employment	10,000	29,000
Leading basic activity	Manufacturing	Government
Nonbasic employment	5,900	24,300
B/N ratio	100:60	100:82
A. Total employment		
1 Services	3,100	14,500
2 Government	1,200	14,300
3 Manufacturing	8,200	12,100
4 Trade	2,700	10,200
5 Others	800	2,400
Number of employees	16,000	53,500
B. Basic employment		
1 Services	900	4,500
2 Government	120	11,300
3 Manufacturing	7,880	10,100
4 Trade	950	300
5 Others	250	3,000
Number of employees	10,100	29,200

SOURCE: From John W. Alexander, "The Basic-Nonbasic Concept of Urban Economic Functions," *Economic Geography*, vol. 30, 1954, table I, based on Alexander's economic base studies of Oshkosh, 1951, and Madison, 1953.

picture of Madison. Thus the components of the urban economy connecting the city with other areas are brought into clear focus.

Another geographic value of the economic base concept, according to Alexander, is that it permits a better classification of cities in terms of regional function. The structure of nonbasic activities seems to be substantially the same for every city. It is through concentrating on the basic activities alone that we can get an unobstructed view of those activities that connect a city with its supporting territory.

The basic-nonbasic concept may have value also, he says, in differentiating types of cities. This is hardly possible as yet, how-

ever, since not enough ratios based on comparable methods are available.

Finally, according to Alexander, the basic-nonbasic ratio represents a new method of measuring the role of an individual business firm in a city's economic life. Knowing whether an enterprise is predominantly basic or nonbasic may be more important than knowing whether its dominant function is manufacturing or trade.

Questions for Further Research

Alexander poses several questions regarding the B/N ratio which he feels can be adequately answered only by further research.[23] Most of them have already been implied in this chapter, but they are summarized here. Is the B/N ratio truly a meaningful characteristic for distinguishing between cities? Does the ratio vary with size of settlement? With type of settlement? With location of settlement? Does the ratio vary from time to time? Does a vigorously growing city characteristically have a different ratio from a stagnant city of the same size? Are nonbasic activities similar from city to city? What is the ideal area that should be delimited for application of the basic-nonbasic concept? What is the best method for applying the basic-nonbasic concept after the area has been delimited?

Blumenfeld's Criticisms

Adverse criticisms of the urban economic base idea by Hans Blumenfeld have attracted wide attention.[24] Though he questions many aspects of the concept, a point of particular interest is his skepticism regarding the relative importance of the basic and nonbasic activity groups.

Blumenfeld maintains that large metropolitan areas exist, survive, and grow because their highly developed "business and consumer services" and other "secondary

[23] *Ibid.*, pp. 259–260.
[24] Blumenfeld, *op. cit.*, pp. 114–132.

industries," together with the availability of labor of all kinds, enable them to substitute new export industries for those that decline. Blumenfeld says:

> It is thus the "secondary," "nonbasic" industries, both business and personal services, as well as "ancillary" manufacturing, which constitute the real and lasting strength of the metropolitan economy. As long as they continue to function efficiently, the metropolis will always be able to substitute new "export" industries for any which may be destroyed by the vicissitudes of economic life.[25]

Conclusions

Since the economic base concept seems to rest on such uncertain ground, why has it attained such popularity?

A thoughtful examination of the ratios listed in Table 7.1 is sufficient evidence of the lack of exactness in the application of the concept thus far. Anyone knowing the background of some of the studies must realize that the base areas and techniques used vary so widely that ratio comparisons are of significance only in the roughest way. It has been suggested that a procedural guide might be worthwhile so that the results of future studies would be more comparable. But perhaps, as Roterus and Calef point out, it would be a mistake to expend too much time and effort on developing precision in something that is best utilized as a crude general measure. "Elaborate precautions to establish the ratio with great accuracy will lead to false notions concerning the stability of the findings; . . ."[26]

But the question regarding the popularity of the concept remains. There is, probably, no better answer than the following from an article by Hoyt, the chief protagonist of economic base studies: "The most important contribution of the economic base theory, in my opinion, is its function in furnishing a sound method of analyzing the economic structure of an urban region."[27]

Finally, the question might be asked: Is the urban economic base concept a concern of the urban geographer, or should it be left to the economist and the urban planner? All three have played important roles in studies of the idea and it would appear to be one of those natural meeting grounds between disciplines. It is here contended that, since the concept measures the interaction between the community and outside areas, whether in terms of employment or of income accruing to residents, it represents one of those aspects of the city which the geographer should not overlook. In the long run, judgment of the intrinsic value of this much-discussed idea is as much the concern of the urban geographer as it is that of members of the other interested disciplines.

[27] Homer Hoyt, "The Utility of the Economic Base Method in Calculating Urban Growth," *Land Economics,* vol. 37, p. 58, 1961.

Selected References

Alexander, John W.: "The Basic-Nonbasic Concept of Urban Economic Functions," *Economic Geography,* vol. 30, pp. 246–261, 1954.

————: *Oshkosh, Wisconsin, An Economic Base Study,* Bureau of Business Research, School of Commerce, University of Wisconsin, 1951.

————: *An Economic Base Study of Madison, Wisconsin,* Bureau of Business Research, School of Commerce, University of Wisconsin, 1953.

Andrews, Richard B.: "Mechanics of the Urban Economic Base," *Land Economics,* vol. 29, pp. 161–167, 263–268, and 343–350, 1953; vol. 30, pp. 52–60, 164–172, 260–269, and 309–319, 1954; vol. 31, pp. 47–53, 144–155, 245–256, and 361–371, 1955.

Blumenfeld, Hans: "The Economic Base of the Metropolis," *Journal of the American Institute of Planners,* vol. 21, no. 4, pp. 114–132, Fall, 1955.

Hoyt, Homer: "Homer Hoyt on Development

[25] *Ibid.,* p. 131.
[26] Roterus and Calef, *op. cit.,* p. 19.

of Economic Base Concept," *Land Economics,* vol. 30, pp. 182–186, 1954.

————: "The Utility of the Economic Base Method in Calculating Urban Growth," *Land Economics,* vol. 37, pp. 51–58, 1961.

Homer Hoyt Associates: *The Economic Base of the Brockton, Massachusetts, Area,* Brockton, Mass., 1949.

McCarty, H. H.: "A Functional Analysis of Population Distribution," *Geographical Review,* vol. 32, pp. 282–293, 1942.

Mattila, J. M., and Wilbur R. Thompson: "Measurement of the Economic Base of the Metropolitan Area," *Land Economics,* vol. 31, pp. 215–228, 1955.

"Oskaloosa versus the United States," *Fortune,* April, 1938, pp. 55–62ff.

Pfouts, Ralph W. (ed.): *The Techniques of Urban Economic Analysis,* Chandler-Davis Publishing Company, West Trenton, N.J., 1960.

Roterus, Victor, and Wesley Calef: "Notes on the Basic-Nonbasic Employment Ratio," *Economic Geography,* vol. 31, pp. 17–20, 1955.

Thomas, Morgan: "The 'Economic Base' and a Region's Economy," *Journal of American Institute of Planners,* vol. 23, no. 2, pp. 86–92, 1957.

Tiebout, Charles M.: *The Community Economic Base Study,* Supplementary Paper 16, Committee for Economic Development, New York, 1962.

Ullman, Edward L., and Michael F. Dacey: "The Minimum Requirements Approach to the Urban Economic Base," *The Regional Science Association: Papers and Proceedings,* 1960, vol. 6, pp. 175–194.

8

Functional classifications of cities

FACED with an array of thousands of urban centers, people have naturally attempted to classify them. When a man refers to one urban center as a village, to another as a small city, and to still a third as a metropolis, he is, though perhaps unconsciously, classifying these places according to size. Or he may know that the city in which he lives is older than certain neighboring cities. If so, he is classifying cities according to age. Undoubtedly, too, he thinks of some cities as superior to others, thus rating them according to a subjective, intangible factor called quality. Size, age, quality—these are but a start. The urban hierarchy, too, amounts to a classification—one based upon services. In fact, the number of possible ways of classifying urban centers is essentially without limit.

In this chapter we shall be concerned with a type of classification that has long proved intriguing to urban geographers and others interested in cities: a classification on the basis of function. How can cities best be grouped on the basis of the economic activities they perform?

We may begin by saying that every city worthy of the name is multifunctional. Trade is ubiquitous to urban centers, every city is to some degree a focus of transportation, and it is hard to conceive of a city so small and specialized that it would not have at least a minor development of manufacturing. Universities, hospitals, recreational facilities, government buildings, and other specialized establishments give evidence of an even greater complexity in the functional makeup of some cities.

Classifications Based on Single Functions

In spite of the admittedly multifunctional character of cities, however, some single function usually dominates, and many a city has acquired a distinction for the real or reputed dominance of one or another function. As a result, writers frequently have referred to commercial, industrial, mining, educational, and resort cities, usually citing some examples. The exact terminology has varied, and categories have been added or dropped at the discretion of each writer.

But these functional classifications have suffered from certain limitations. The specific cities to which they have been applied usually were restricted to a few well-known examples, their choice representing, for the most part, subjective, common-sense judgments. Therefore, it was impossible either to evaluate the selections or to apply the same method of selection with any precision to other urban centers. In an attempt to remedy these deficiencies, Chauncy Harris developed specific criteria for classifying cities functionally, and in an article published in 1943 suggested quantified limits for each class.[1]

Harris's classification based on dominant function   Harris based his classification on the activity of greatest importance in each city. Recognizing that all cities are more or less multifunctional, he attempted, nevertheless, to set up quantitative definitions that would permit him to assign each city to one class or category.

Harris's sources of data   To do this, Harris depended chiefly upon two somewhat different types of United States Census data then available: employment figures and occupation figures. Employment figures were obtained through reports from each industrial and trading establishment; the resulting data were available in the Census of Manufactures and Census of Business volumes. Occupation data, on the other hand, were published in the Census of Pop-

ulation volumes; they were obtained by the Bureau of the Census through asking each person what he did for a living.[2] Harris used employment as the major basis for his classification (Table 8.1). But occupation data, too, were considered; and they formed the basis for distinguishing two of the functional types: transportation centers and mining towns. To simplify comparisons, Harris reduced all figures to percentages: occupations to percentages of all gainful workers, and employment to percentages of workers in manufacturing, wholesaling, and retailing combined. For two classes, university towns and resort and retirement towns, Harris depended upon non-census sources.

Bases for classification   Harris based his classification upon cities of well-recognized types. From analyses of the statistical data for these cities, he was able to set up limits for each of his types.

How urban activities vary in importance   Harris recognized that some activity groups employ many more persons than others do. For example, of the employed urban population in the nation, 27 per cent are engaged in manufacturing and only about 4 per cent in wholesale trade.[3] It is obvious, therefore, that different standards have to be applied for different functions. A city with 25 per cent of its wage earners engaged in manufacturing would certainly not stand out as a manufacturing center; but no city, no matter how specialized in wholesaling, could be expected to have 25 per cent of its wage earners employed in wholesaling. Harris overcame this difficulty by assigning higher percentages to some functions than to others.

---

[1] Chauncy D. Harris, "A Functional Classification of Cities in the United States," *Geographical Review*, vol. 33, pp. 86–99, 1943.

[2] Harris's study was carried out in the 1930s. Industry-group data, such as are now published as part of the Census of Population, were not then available.

[3] At least this was true in 1960 according to industry-group data in the 1960 Census of Population.

Table 8.1   Criteria used by Harris in classifying cities on a functional basis

Manufacturing Cities M′ Subtype Principal criterion: Employment in manufacturing equals at least 74% of total employment in manufacturing, retailing, and wholesaling (employment figures). Secondary criterion: Manufacturing and mechanical industries contain at least 45% of gainful workers (occupation figures). **Note:** A few cities with industries in suburbs for which no figures were available were placed in this class if the percentage in the secondary criterion reached 50.

Manufacturing Cities M Subtype Principal criterion: Employment in manufacturing equals at least 60% of total employment in manufacturing, retailing, and wholesaling.
Secondary criterion: Manufacturing and mechanical industries usually contain between 30% and 45% of gainful workers.

Retail Centers (R) Employment in retailing is at least 50% of the total employment in manufacturing, wholesaling, and retailing and at least 2.2 times that in wholesaling alone.

Diversified Cities (D) Employment in manufacturing, wholesaling, and retailing is less than 60%, 20%, and 50%, respectively, of the total employment in these activities, and no other special criteria apply. Manufacturing and mechanical industries with a few exceptions contain between 25% and 35% of the gainful workers. *many of the larger US cities come under this category*

Wholesale Centers (W) Employment in wholesaling is at least 20% of the total employment in

manufacturing, wholesaling, and retailing and at least 45% as much as in retailing alone. *Today consider 10% - has char of christaller's central place usually high relationship between W+T.*

Transportation Centers (T) Transportation and communication contain at least 11% of the gainful workers, and workers in transportation and communication equal at least one-third the number in manufacturing and mechanical industries and at least two-thirds the number in trade (occupation figures). (Applies only to cities of more than 25,000, for which such figures are available.)

Mining Towns (S) Extraction of minerals accounts for more than 15% of the gainful workers (applies only to cities of more than 25,000, for which such figures are available). For cities between 10,000 and 25,000 a comparison was made of mining employment available by counties only with employment in cities within such mining counties. Published sources were consulted to differentiate actual mining towns from commercial and industrial centers in mining areas.

University Towns (E) Enrollment in schools of collegiate rank (universities, technical schools, liberal arts colleges, and teachers' colleges) equaled at least 25% of the population of the city (1940). Enrollment figures from *School and Society*, vol. 52, pp. 601–619, 1940.

Resort and Retirement Towns (X) No satisfactory statistical criterion was found. Cities with a low percentage of the population employed were checked in the literature for this function.

SOURCE: From *Geographical Review*, vol. 33, 1943, table 1. *as move out from med. sized city (200,000) to larger metropolitan area · usually goes into the class of diversified. Diversification one of the char. of a metropolitan area.*

Metropolitan districts used wherever possible In addition, Harris faced the problem, so common in urban geography, of just which urban statistical units to use. He was restricted, of course, to the census areas in use at the time he did his research, which was in the late 1930s. Not even 1940 census data were yet available. But metropolitan districts had been in use for several decades. They made better functional units than incorporated cities did, he decided. So he used metropolitan districts wherever possible, treating Minneapolis–St. Paul, Albany–Schenectady–Troy, Fall River–New

Bedford, and other multiple metropolitan districts, as well as districts with single central cities, as units for classification.

But many cities were too small to have metropolitan districts. Therefore, in actual fact, the functional units that he classified consisted of 140 metropolitan districts; 9 small clusters of urban centers which he treated as single units (for example, Lewiston–Auburn, Maine; Champaign–Urbana, Illinois; and Manitowoc–Two Rivers, Wisconsin); and 456 other urban units, each with only one city of more than 10,000 population. In some of the latter, industrial suburbs were known to be important and were considered along with their urban centers in the classifications. The smallest urban center classified by Harris had a population of 10,000 or more, but in at least one category, transportation, only places of 25,000 or more could be differentiated, since the necessary data were not available for smaller places.

Harris's results Harris did not include in his article a list of urban centers and the categories to which they belonged, but he did refer to the fact that a full mimeographed list was obtainable from the American Geographical Society. The distribution of the cities classified and the type to which each belongs are shown in Figure 8.1.

Modifications of Harris's classification

A few years later Grace M. Kneedler

Ohlson [4] published a classification covering each American city having a population of 10,000 or more. Though Mrs. Ohlson's technique was based on Harris's classification, there were several differences. For one thing, Mrs. Ohlson in all cases used incorporated units rather than metropolitan districts, and she had later and better census data available and was able to improve upon Harris's method in several respects. Thus, she differentiated government centers, defined resort or retirement towns more precisely, and refined some of the other class definitions.

Classification by Victor Jones Victor Jones, in *The Municipal Year Book* of 1953,

[4] Grace M. Kneedler Ohlson, "Economic Classification of Cities," *The Municipal Year Book,* International City Managers Association, Chicago, 1945, pp. 32–40 and table IV. (Reprinted in the several following editions of the *Year Book.*)

Fig. 8.1 Distribution of principal functional types of cities in the United States as classified by Harris. For identification of types see Table 8.1. (From Chauncy D. Harris, "A Functional Classification of Cities in the United States," *Geographical Review,* vol. 33, 1943, fig. 1.)

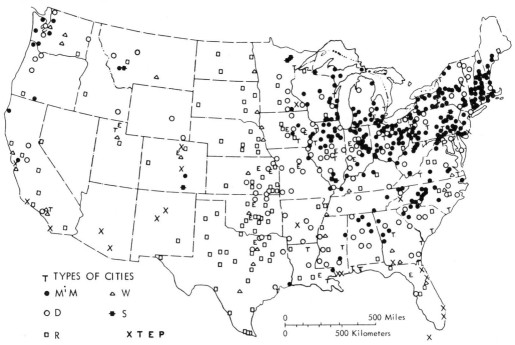

T TYPES OF CITIES

● M¹M   △ W

○ D   ✦ S

□ R   X T E P

used the same statistical limits as did Mrs. Ohlson for classifying cities. Like her, he based his classification on political units, but Jones was able to use later census data and hence give a more recent picture of the cities and other incorporated places included.

Later, Jones and some of his associates, working with 1958 and 1960 data, revised the classification (Table 8.2).[5] They used the same general technique that Jones had used in his earlier work. Thus, incorporated units were the areas classified (1,679 in all),[6] and chief dependence was placed on the Censuses of Manufacturing and Business. For a few special classes of urban places, however, labor-force data from the Census of Population were used.

A Multifunctional Classification

Howard Nelson pointed out that the classifications just discussed—those of Harris, of Ohlson, and of Jones in 1953— had two serious handicaps.[7] In the first place, how does one know whether or not the type cities were chosen wisely? We are not informed which specific cities were used as types or how they were chosen. Secondly, we have to rely upon the author's judgment as to the significance of the limiting figures that are used for the various classes of cities. Nelson developed a classification that he felt avoided these difficulties by using a stated procedure that he said could be checked and understood by other workers.

Selected industry groups as bases for classification Claiming that the proportion of the labor force of a city engaged in performing a service is the best means of measuring the distribution of that activity, Nelson decided to base his classification entirely upon major industry groups as listed in the 1950 *Census of Population* for standard metropolitan areas, urbanized areas, and urban places of 10,000 population or more.[8] However, some of the groups, for example, agriculture and construction, are obviously of little significance in differentiating types of cities. Therefore, Nelson omitted and condensed until he arrived at the nine activity groups shown in Table 8.3.

Urbanized areas used where possible Nelson, like earlier workers, faced the problem of what unit areas to use. The Census Bureau gave industry-group data for 1950 by standard metropolitan areas and by urbanized areas as well as by urban places of 10,000 population or more. Nelson decided to use urbanized areas where possible and to supplement these with urban places. To avoid duplication, all urban places inside urbanized areas were dropped, since they were covered in each case by an urbanized area classification. A total of some 897 individual urban concentrations (urbanized areas and separate places), each with a population of 10,000 or more, remained.[9]

How activity groups differ in proportions employed The percentage of the total labor force in each of the nine activity

[5] Victor Jones, Richard L. Forstall, and Andrew Collver, "Economic and Social Characteristics of Urban Places," *The Municipal Year Book*, International City Managers Association, Chicago, 1963, pp. 85–157.
[6] In the 1963 issue of the *Year Book*, pp. 31–44, there is also an article by Victor Jones and Richard L. Forstall on "Economic and Social Classification of Metropolitan Areas."
[7] Howard J. Nelson, "A Service Classification of American Cities," *Economic Geography*, vol. 31, pp. 189–210, 1955.

[8] Comparable statistics appear as table 75 in each of the state sections of *Census of Population: 1960*, vol. I, *Characteristics of the Population*, 1961.
[9] Working with urban centers of less than 10,000 population would present several serious disadvantages. It would vastly increase the calculations and the possibility of results being affected by the greater size range of urban centers (see the section below on "Variations with Size of City"). Besides, for cities of less than 10,000, the Census Bureau combines wholesale and retail trade, so wholesale and retail centers could not be separated.

Table 8.2   Classes and definitions followed by Victor Jones, Richard L. Forstall, and Andrew Collver in *The Municipal Year Book*, pp. 112–113, 1963, modified from Harris's and Ohlson's earlier work.

Mm   **Manufacturing:** 50% or more of aggregate employment is in manufacturing, and less than 30% is in retail trade.

M   **Industrial:** 50% or more of aggregate employment is in manufacturing, and over 30% is in retail trade.

Mr   **Diversified-manufacturing:** employment in manufacturing is greater than retail employment, but less than 50% of aggregate employment.

Rm   **Diversified-retailing:** greater employment in retailing than in manufacturing, but manufacturing is at least 20% of aggregate employment.

Rr   **Retailing:** retail employment is greater than manufacturing or any other component of aggregate employment, and manufacturing is less than 20% of aggregate employment.

W   **Wholesaling:** employment in wholesale trade is at least 25% of aggregate employment.

Mg   **Mining:** resident labor force employed in mining is greater than either manufacturing or retail employment.

T   **Transportation:** resident labor force in transportation is greater than either manufacturing or retail employment.

X   **Resort:** resident labor force in en-tertainment, recreation, and personal services employment, other than private households, totals more than either manufacturing or retail employment.

G and AF   **Government and armed forces:** for G cities, resident labor force in public administration, plus the armed forces, is greater than manufacturing and retail employment combined and greater than any other category, and the public administration labor force exceeds the armed forces. For AF cities, the resident armed forces constitute more than 50% of the significant resident labor force, *or* they exceed combined employment in manufacturing and retailing *and* are more than 20% of the city's total population.

Pr   **Professional:** resident labor force in professional activities (other than health and education) exceeds either manufacturing or retail employment.

H   **Hospital:** resident labor force employed in hospitals exceeds that in either manufacturing or retailing.

Ed   **Education:** resident labor force employed in education is greater than either manufacturing or retailing employment.

S   **Service:** employment in selected services is at least 30% of aggregate employment, but the city does not qualify for any other category.

Note: Total number of persons employed in manufacturing, retail trade, wholesale trade, and selected services is referred to as "aggregate employment." This does not include employment within the city in mining, transportation, public administration, and other activities not reported in the Censuses of Manufactures and Business.
SOURCE: The functional definitions above are quoted with permission of the International City Managers' Association.

groups for each of the 897 urban concentrations was calculated, and an arithmetic average was determined for each activity group for all the cities together. These averages are shown in the first line of Table 8.4. The several activity groups obviously differ

Table 8.3   Census items making up Nelson's nine activity groups

Selected major industry groups from table 35 of *U.S. Census of Population: 1950*, vol. II, *Characteristics of the Population* (state volumes)	Activity groups used by Nelson	Abbreviations *
Mining	Mining	Mi
Manufacturing	Manufacturing	Mf
Railroads and railway express service Trucking service and warehousing Other transportation Telecommunications	Transportation and communication	T
Wholesale trade	Wholesale trade	W
Food and dairy prod. stores, and milk retail Eating and drinking places Other retail trade	Retail trade	R
Finance, insurance, and real estate	Finance, insurance, and real estate	F
Hotels and lodging places Other personal services Entertainment and recreational services	Personal service	Ps
Medical and other health services Educational services, government Educational services, private Other professional and related services	Professional service	Pf
Public administration	Public administration	Pb

* In his classification Nelson also used the abbreviation D for diversified.

greatly in this respect, ranging from 27.07 per cent for manufacturing to only 1.62 for mining.

Variations with size of city The question arose whether these percentages would not vary so much by size of city as to invalidate any study that did not take city size into consideration. Nelson did find a definite tendency for the percentages employed in some activities to vary with city size. For example, he found that the proportions of the labor force in retail trade, professional services, and mining generally declined with increase in city size; most of the other activities seemed, if anything, to increase in relative importance. However, there were exceptions, and the trends did not appear marked enough, in any event, to require different treatment of cities in different size classes.[10]

Departures from averages vary by activities Another matter considered by Nelson was that some cities departed considerably from the averages shown in Table 8.4 and these departures varied by activities (Figure 8.2 and Table 8.5). Thus, although the mean employed in manufacturing was 27.07 per cent of the labor force, a few cities had less than 5 per cent in this activity. On the other hand, ninety-one cities had over 50 per cent of their labor force in manufacturing, and some had more than 65

[10] For a brief summary of a classification in which city size plays an important role, see pp. 126–127.

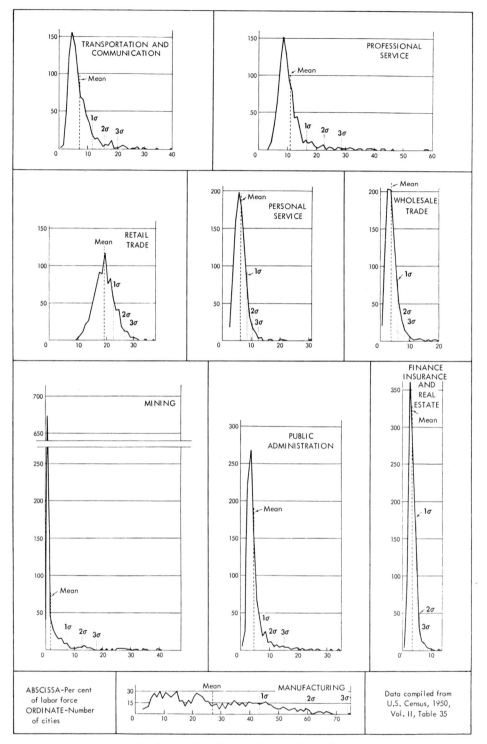

Fig. 8.2 Frequency graphs showing distribution of economic services among American cities. (From Howard J. Nelson, "A Service Classification of American Cities," *Economic Geography*, vol. 31, 1955, fig. 1.)

Table 8.4   Averages and standard deviation in percentages for selected activity groups in 1950 as developed by Nelson

	Manufac- turing	Retail trade	Profes- sional service	Transporta- tion and commu- nication	Personal service	Public adminis- tration	Whole- sale trade	Finance, insurance, and real estate	Mining
Average	27.07	19.23	11.09	7.12	6.20	4.58	3.85	3.19	1.62
Standard deviation	16.04	3.63	5.89	4.58	2.07	3.48	2.14	1.25	5.01
Average plus 1 SD	43.11	22.86	16.98	11.70	8.27	8.06	5.99	4.44	6.63
Average plus 2 SD	59.15	26.49	22.87	16.28	10.34	11.54	8.13	5.69	11.64
Average plus 3 SD	75.19	30.12	28.76	20.86	12.41	15.02	10.27	6.94	16.65

SOURCE: From Howard J. Nelson, "A Service Classification of American Cities," *Economic Geography,* vol. 31, p. 195, 1955.

per cent. In fact, cities depart so far from the mean for manufacturing that this figure alone tells us very little about the importance of manufacturing in the American city.

The situation was considerably different for retail trade. On the average, for the group of cities considered, 19.23 per cent of the labor force was engaged in serving the retail needs of the people, but in no city was less than 6 per cent of the working force so employed, and the extreme in the other direction was only 36.22 per cent. Thus for retail trade the average is fairly representative.

Nelson pointed out that the seven remaining activities fell into a third general type of frequency distribution. Typically, most of the cities had a fairly common, rather low percentage of their labor force in the given activity, but in each activity there were a few cities in which the service was performed in outstanding amounts.

When is a city specialized? All this leads up to the question: How much should

Table 8.5   Proportion of labor force in selected activities, sample cities, 1950

	New York, N.Y. In 000's	%	Detroit, Mich. In 000's	%	Kearney, Neb. In 000's	%	Rochester, Minn. In 000's	%	Average of 897 cities
Population	12,296	—	2,659	—	12.11	—	29.88	—	—
Labor force	6,099	—	1,068	—	3.28	—	13.0	—	—
Manufacturing	1,573	25.8	501	46.9	0.27	8.3	0.81	6.1	27.07
Retail trade	822	13.5	164	15.3	1.18	36.2	2.72	20.7	19.23
Professional service	448	7.3	73	6.9	0.84	25.6	4.39	33.3	11.09
Transportation and communications	475	7.8	71	6.7	0.32	9.7	0.73	6.3	7.12
Personal service	361	5.9	59	5.5	0.36	11.0	1.40	10.6	6.20
Public administration	227	3.7	36	3.4	0.20	6.1	0.41	3.1	4.58
Wholesale trade	274	4.5	33	3.1	0.22	6.6	0.42	3.1	3.85
Finance, insurance, and real estate	353	5.8	36	3.4	0.13	3.9	0.39	2.9	3.19
Mining	3	0.05	0.3	0.01	0.005	0.15	0.01	0.09	1.62

SOURCE: After Howard J. Nelson, "A Service Classification of American Cities," *Economic Geography,* vol. 31, p. 191, 1955.

a city score above the average, or mean, for it to be classed as outstanding or specialized in a given activity? It would certainly have to exhibit a percentage considerably above the average to be considered outstanding as a manufacturing city, but with a much smaller amount in excess of the mean a city might be regarded as specialized in retail trade. The same problem must be faced for each of the other activities. How much deviation from the average, or mean, marks a city as specialized? It will be recalled that Harris met this problem by assigning different percentages to different functions (see page 114).

Standard deviation as basis for classification Nelson decided that a better answer was the use of a statistical technique, the standard deviation (SD).[11] He reasoned that the SD was the simplest and most widely understood of all statistical measures of variation, and that the *degree* of variation could be compared by use of the SD even if, in some cases, we were dealing with large numbers, as in manufacturing, and in others with small numbers, as in mining or wholesale trade. Standard deviations from the mean as calculated by Nelson for each of the nine activity groups are shown in Table 8.4.

[11] Though the author believes statistical methods can contribute much to urban geography, no attempt is made in this book to present such methods or to criticize their application except as parts of research studies being discussed.

Perhaps it should be pointed out, however, that a major criticism has been leveled at Nelson's classification. The critics claim that it represents an inappropriate use of the standard deviation. The standard deviation plus or minus the mean defines known portions of a normal or approximately normal frequency distribution. The frequency distributions with which Nelson worked are all skewed to the right. In some cases, therefore, the mean plus 3 SDs would not cover the full range of the percentage values. And, conversely, if one were to examine the standard deviation below the mean for these data he would be dealing with negative percentages of the working force.

Several specializations and three degrees of specialization possible According to Nelson's classification, a city can be specialized in more than one activity and to varying degrees. Thus he showed for each city all activities that qualified by scores of plus 1, plus 2, or plus 3 SDs above the mean, indicating for the city the nature of each such activity and the appropriate value for each. For example, Fort Collins, Colorado, received a classification of Pf2F, meaning that it had 22.87 or more but less than 28.76 per cent of its labor force employed in professional service and 4.44 or more but less than 5.69 per cent employed in finance, insurance, and real estate (see Tables 8.3 and 8.4). The Allentown–Bethlehem Urbanized Area, on the other hand, was classed as Mf because it had 43.11 or more but less than 59.15 per cent of its labor force in manufacturing activities and did not have an outstanding proportion of its workers employed in any other activity. In short, the number of SDs indicates the degree to which an urban center stands out for the activity in question. A city that was not as much as 1 SD above average in any activity appeared as diversified, D, in Nelson's classification.[12]

The Classification Methods Compared

It may be of value to compare, briefly, the classification methods that have been discussed here.

Areal units used For instance, we might compare them on the basis of the areal units classified. Harris used metropolitan districts for the larger urban centers, and, with a few exceptions, corporate units for smaller urban centers where metro-

[12] A classification of the 897 urban concentrations Nelson worked with forms an appendix to his article, *op. cit.*, pp. 205–210. Nelson also constructed maps showing the distributions of various types of functional cities. These appear in Chap. 9 of this book.

politan districts were not established. In classifications stemming from Harris's work, Ohlson, and later Jones, used the corporate city as the primary unit. Nelson, on the other hand, used urbanized areas wherever possible. Using the incorporated urban unit, as Ohlson and Jones have done, has certain practical advantages. Whether we like it or not, people still think in terms of these units, and we operate within their governmental boundaries. Moreover, use of the same type of unit for all sizes of urban centers has the advantage of consistency. On the other hand, the urbanized area is unquestionably a much better expression of the real city, and use of the urbanized area by Nelson (and, earlier, of the metropolitan district by Harris) avoided the necessity of considering the innumerable and irrational political units into which a large urban area is so typically divided. For example, the Los Angeles–Long Beach Urbanized Area, in 1960, included between eighty and eighty-five separate incorporated cities.

This last statement serves to introduce a serious disadvantage of Jones's classification, at least from a geographer's point of view. The classification does not lend itself to presentation on maps at any practicable scale. In the Los Angeles–Long Beach Urbanized Area there are, according to Jones's classification, nineteen Mm cities, fourteen Rr cities, twelve Rm cities, ten Mr cities, one Mr(AF) city, and one S city.[13] Suppose you wished to show United States manufacturing cities on a scale such as those of Figures 8.1 and 9.1 in this book. Distinct, separate dots for the nineteen manufacturing cities of the area would be impossible, and there would be other, similarly difficult situations elsewhere on the map.

Contrasts in sources of data A second difference in the classification systems has to do with the data used. Harris and his

followers depended principally upon employment figures from the Censuses of Business and Manufactures, whereas Nelson based his technique entirely upon industry-group data from the Census of Population. The latter has the advantage of being available for the urbanized area, which, in many respects, is the most realistic Census Bureau expression of the city. But the industry groups have disadvantages, too. A person may live outside the urbanized area in which he works. Although the proportion of workers who do this is probably not great, nevertheless, employment data, obtained as they are directly from firms, undoubtedly do a better job of localizing activities.

Classification technique used Another way in which the techniques of classification vary is in the handling of the data. Harris based his classification on a type of city or type cities for each functional class, and then set up arbitrary limits for the type. Ohlson and Jones followed Harris in this procedure. Nelson, on the other hand, used a statistical technique, the standard deviation. He recognized three degrees of specialization measured in terms of standard deviations above the mean. Though he did not have to decide upon a different boundary value for each of his classes, as Harris did, Nelson did not avoid the problem of arbitrariness of boundaries, since, after all, the dividing line between 1 SD and 2 SDs or between 2 SDs and 3 represents an arbitrary break. Nevertheless, he used a widely known, standardized approach, the mechanics of which avoid subjectivity.

Unifunctional versus multifunctional classifications Still another contrast, a particularly critical one, is in the number of lines of specialization shown for a city. Harris's classification is unifunctional. A metropolitan district or an urban place is classified as a manufacturing city (M' sub-

[13] Only cities of 10,000 or more population are classified.

type), a manufacturing city (M subtype), a wholesale center, a university town, or some other single functional type, but never as more than one at once, except as this is implied by the "diversified city" designation. Ohlson and Jones, in their work, adhere largely to this same unifunctional standard, although occasionally they use combinations such as the following: Rm(AF): diversified-retailing with Armed Forces important, with El Paso, Texas, and Bangor, Maine, as examples; Mr(Mg): diversified-manufacturing with mining, with Duncan, Oklahoma, as an example; and Mm(Ed): manufacturing and education, with Cambridge, Massachusetts, as an example.

According to Nelson's classification, on the other hand, a city may show several types of functional specialization. Though this is realistic, it has disadvantages. For instance, Harris was able to show his entire classification on a single map (Figure 8.1); this is not practicable under Nelson's system. Moreover, correlations of functional type of city with other characteristics, such as education or income, are simpler when the classification is based on the single activity of greatest importance in each city.

Contrasts in types of specialization The two systems of classification, that of Harris-Ohlson-Jones and that of Nelson, result in about the same number of types of specialization, though the exact designations of the classes are slightly different. In a few instances, a secondary type as well as the primary one is shown in the lists of cities according to Jones's system, but Harris did not arrive at any combinations. Another particularly significant contrast is that Nelson has a type of specialization—finance, insurance, and real estate—not differentiated under the other systems. And, of course, the classes arrived at by the several systems are defined differently. Some of these differences will be made clearer in the discussion

of the individual functional classes of cities in the next chapter.

Comparison of results An obvious way of comparing methods of classification is through a comparison of results. This has been done in Table 8.6 for thirty-five American cities chosen largely at random. It will be seen that in some cases the same classes are arrived at by all three techniques, but that in others there are substantial differences in results. Nelson's classification tends frequently to vary from the other two, presumably because the others are related in origin. Moreover, Nelson used some functional classes that were different from those used by the others, and his technique permitted a city to be specialized in several different classes at once.

Other Functional Classifications

The classification techniques of Harris and Nelson have been described in considerable detail in order to make clear the problems that must be faced in classifying cities. Ohlson and Jones, it was pointed out, based their classifications upon Harris's technique, and his method has been used, too, with modifications, in classifying cities of more limited areas.[14]

Several studies have appeared in print in which a classification of American cities is involved without the classification being the primary purpose of the work. In view of the secondary roles of the classifications in these works, and since most of the principles of city functional classification have already been discussed, these further studies will be summarized only briefly here. Any-

[14] See, for example, John E. Brush, "Economic Classification of Urban Places," *The Population of New Jersey*, Rutgers University Press, New Brunswick, N.J., 1956, pp. 60–72; John Fraser Hart, "Functions and Occupational Structures of Cities of the American South," *Annals of the Association of American Geographers*, vol. 45, pp. 269–286, 1955.

Table 8.6   Classifications of selected cities according to three different techniques

City	Harris *	Jones †	Nelson ‡
Altoona, Pa.	T	T	T3
Ann Arbor, Mich.	E	Ed	Pf3
Austin, Tex.	R	Rr	Pb3
Boston, Mass.	D	Mr	F
Buffalo, N.Y.	M	Mr	D
Butte, Mont.	S	Rr (Mg)	Mi3
Chicago, Ill.	D	Mr	F
Columbus, Ohio	D	Mr	F
Denver, Colo.	W	Rm	WF
Detroit, Mich.	M'	Mr	Mf
Harrisburg, Pa.	T	Rm (G)	Pb3T
Hibbing, Minn.	S	Mg	Mi3
Indianapolis, Ind.	D	Mr	F
Iowa City, Iowa	E	Ed	Pf3
Los Angeles, Calif.	D	Mr	F
Lowell–Lawrence, Mass.	M'	Mm	Mf
Memphis, Tenn.	W	Mr	W
Miami, Fla.	X	Rm (X)	Ps3RF
Minneapolis–St. Paul, Minn.	D	Mr	F2W
Nashville, Tenn.	D	Mr	F
New Orleans, La.	T	Rm	TWF
New York–NE N.J.	D	Mr	F2
Phoenix, Ariz.	X	Rm	PsWF
Pittsburgh, Pa.	M	Mr	D
Reading, Pa.	M	Mm	Mf
Rochester, N.Y.	M	Mm	Mf
Sacramento, Calif.	D	Rr (G)	Pb3
St. Louis, Mo.	D	Mr	D
Salt Lake City, Utah	W	Rm	F
San Antonio, Tex.	W	Rm (G)	Ps3Pb2F
San Francisco, Calif.	W	Rm	F2
Seattle, Wash.	W	Mr	F2
Suffolk, Va.	W	Mr	W3
Tulsa, Okla.	R	Rm	F
Yakima, Wash.	W	Rm	W2RF

* Classification based on metropolitan districts wherever possible.

† Classification applies only to incorporated city first named. Classification is really that of Jones, Forstall, and Collver (Ohlson classification not shown here).

‡ Classification where possible based on urbanized area of which the city first named is part.

one interested in following up the subject of classification should consult the original sources.

Alexandersson's method

General outline of method The first of the studies that will be summarized is by Gunnar Alexandersson of the Department of Geography, Stockholm School of Economics.[15] In an analysis of the urban economy of the United States, he determined what he called the "chief city forming industries" for 864 urban areas with 10,000 inhabitants or more. In arriving at these 864 urban areas, Alexandersson used urbanized areas wherever possible, but, in a few instances, where urbanized area data were not given, he used standard metropolitan areas; for smaller urban centers, he used incorporated units or even clusters of incorporated units that seemed to him to approximate urbanized areas as they would have been if these census areas had been developed for cities of less than 50,000 inhabitants. Like Nelson, he based his work on industry-group data from the 1950 *Census of Population*.

Treatment of ubiquitous activities A feature of special interest is Alexandersson's method of treating the ubiquitous activities of cities. He said that most activities present in a city are to some degree city serving or nonbasic and to some degree city forming or basic. As a first step in his classification system he developed a technique for focusing on the city-forming or basic employment. He used the letter k to designate the percentage of employment devoted to city-serving production within each of 36 manufacturing and service industries. Let us take, for example, wholesale trade. For each of the 864 urban areas, Alexandersson calculated the percentage of the gainfully em-

[15] Gunnar Alexandersson, *The Industrial Structure of American Cities*, University of Nebraska Press, Lincoln, Nebr., 1956.

ployed persons engaged in wholesale trade. Then he listed all of the urban areas in order, based on these percentages, the one with the smallest percentage being placed at the bottom of the list. The value separating the lowest 5 per cent or 43 of the urban areas from the remainder was 1.4 per cent. This was the k value for wholesale trade.

He used it in this manner: for each urban area 1.4 per cent of *all* of the gainfully employed persons in the urban area is subtracted from the total gainfully employed persons in that area who are *engaged in wholesaling*. If the remainder is equal to 5 to 10 per cent of the total employment in all industries in the urban area, then the urban area qualifies as a C town in wholesaling; 10 to 20 per cent makes it a B town; and more than 20 per cent puts it in the category of an A town in this activity.

The same technique was applied for each of the other manufacturing and service industries that Alexandersson investigated. Naturally, the k value is different for each of the various activities, though in each case it is the value dividing the lowest 43 (or 5 per cent) of the 864 areas from the remainder in a ranking for the given industry.

Some characteristics of the resulting classification According to the classification here described, many cities achieve A, B, or C status in several industries, but some do not attain sufficiently high employment in any line to merit classification as economically specialized cities. Thus Hartford, Connecticut, ranks as a B city in finance and in machinery production and as a C city in the manufacture of transportation equipment. Pittsburgh, Pennsylvania, ranks as a B city in construction and in administration and as a C city in retailing. Los Angeles, on the other hand, does not attain sufficiently high employment in any single activity to merit classification as an economically specialized city.[16]

[16] A reviewer points out that it would have been better to classify such cities as diversified.

Thirty-six industry groups used It will be remembered that Nelson condensed the major industry groups shown in table 35, *Census of Population: 1950*, Volume II, into nine activity groups. In contrast, Alexandersson, though using the same source of data, worked with thirty-six groups, essentially all of those for which separate data were given by the Bureau of the Census. The only groups he omitted were agriculture, forestry and fisheries, and the "not specified" and "not reported" categories.

Wide range of maps resulting Thus Alexandersson studied city specialization for many more different urban activities than Harris, Ohlson and Jones, or Nelson. Though he did not make a distribution map for every one of these activities, he did produce a great many maps. In addition to maps showing cities with more than average specialization in wholesaling, retailing, education, and the like, he shows, for example, the distribution of cities that are above average in construction, as railroad centers, and in household service. Moreover, he presents maps of urban centers specialized in each of a number of different types of manufacturing: primary metal towns, furniture and lumber towns, textile towns, etc. These maps of manufacturing specialization go further than would normally be expected in a study devoted to classifying cities on a functional basis.

The Duncan and Reiss classification

Two sociologists, Duncan and Reiss, considered the problem of functional classification of cities as part of an attempt to discover the "demographic, economic, and socio-economic" characteristics associated with various types of functional specialization.[17] Even more than in Alexandersson's

[17] Otis D. Duncan and Albert J. Reiss, Jr., *Social Characteristics of Urban and Rural Communities, 1950*, John Wiley & Sons, Inc., New York, 1956, esp. part IV and pp. 387–409.

work, therefore, their actual classification method is incidental to another purpose.

How the classification differs from earlier ones As the authors themselves point out, their procedures for classifying communities differ from those of Harris and of Ohlson and Jones in two principal respects: (1) The criteria of functional specialization are varied according to community size and metropolitan location. (2) It is possible for a given community to appear in more than one functional classification, for example, to be both a trade center and a center of higher education. The latter was true, also, of Nelson's classification and of that developed by Alexandersson, but these had not been published at the time Duncan and Reiss did their work. In the classification by Jones and his associates, appearing in 1953 and discussed earlier in this chapter, a secondary activity is shown in a few cases.

Some idea of the method used by Duncan and Reiss may be obtained from the fact that, for manufacturing specialization, the percentage of resident labor force employed in manufacturing is used, and quintile limits are established for each of four metropolitan status groups—standard metropolitan areas, central cities, suburbs, and independent cities—and for two population size classes within each group. For "high" manufacturing rating, a place must be in the uppermost quintile for its group in the percentage of its labor force in manufacturing. "Low" rating means that it lies in the bottom quintile. Most urban centers are not shown with any manufacturing specialization, however, since they fall within the other three quintiles.

Through a somewhat complicated procedure, per capita retail sales and per capita wholesale sales, along with metropolitan status and size, are used to arrive at a ninefold division based on trade: Ww, wholesale trade center; Rr, retail trade center; TC, trade center; TCw, trade center, wholesale; TCr, trade center, retail; MTC,

maintenance trade center; NT, non-trade center; NTw, non-trade center, wholesale; and NTr, non-trade center, retail.

Finally, various types of "minor specialization" are identified, chiefly on the basis of quintile and decile limits applied to census data for metropolitan status and size groups, as in the case of manufacturing. The minor specializations identified include education (Ed), public administration (PA), transportation (Tr), military (My), and entertainment and recreation (ER).

Austin, Texas, as an example An example based on 1950 census data may help to make the classification system clearer. According to Duncan and Reiss, the Austin, Texas, Standard Metropolitan Area had low specialization in manufacturing; Rr for trade; and the following minor specializations: Ed, PA, My, and ER. As a central city in the Austin Standard Metropolitan Area, Austin had low specialization in manufacturing; NT for trade; and two minor specializations: Ed and ER.

The occupational profile and types of cities

Occupational data and profiles Another research worker, Paul Bates Gillen of Teachers College, Columbia University, approached the problem of city classification through occupational profiles or patterns of occupation distribution.[18] These he based on data for major occupation groups as shown in the 1940 *Census of Population*. Gillen simplified the list by eliminating farming activities and the "occupation not reported" group.

From the remaining data, he pointed out, it is a simple matter to make an occupational distribution profile for a city. This is done by calculating the percentage of workers in each broad occupational category, using the total number of employed workers as a base. With these results, bar

[18] Paul Bates Gillen, *The Distribution of Occupations as a City Yardstick*, King's Crown Press, Columbia University, New York, 1951.

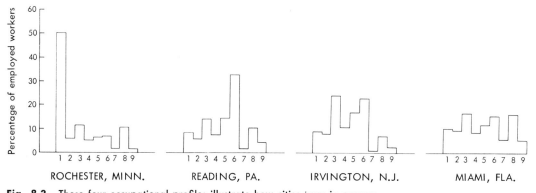

Fig. 8.3 These four occupational profiles illustrate how cities vary in occupational characteristics. The numbers refer as follows: (1) professional, technical, and kindred workers; (2) managers, officials, and proprietors, excluding farm; (3) clerical and kindred workers; (4) sales workers; (5) craftsmen, foremen, and kindred workers; (6) operatives and kindred workers; (7) private household workers; (8) service workers, except private household; and (9) laborers, except farm and mine.

Note the importance of professional, technical, and kindred workers in Rochester, Minn., a medical center, and of service workers both in Rochester and in Miami, Fla., the latter known chiefly as a winter resort. From the profiles, it is easy to infer that Reading, Pennsylvania, and Irvington, New Jersey, are industrial cities, but why, one wonders, are operatives strikingly predominant in Reading whereas in Irvington they are slightly less important than clerical workers?

The profiles are based on "major occupation group" data from table 74 of state volumes of the *Census of Population: 1960,* vol. I, *Characteristics of the Population.* These are 1960 data instead of 1940 figures such as were used by Gillen, but Gillen's method is followed in that the items related to farming activities and "occupation not reported" are eliminated.

diagrams may be constructed like those shown in Figure 8.3.

Composite scores and typing of cities
The profiles are of value in themselves, bringing out, as they do, interesting differences between cities, but they were only incidental to Gillen's purpose. He wanted to translate the occupational patterns into composite scores that would, he said, "reflect comprehensively the relative levels of city functions." To arrive at an occupational score, he calculated for each city the deviation of each occupational group from the mean for cities of the same size group and applied weights based upon income. The resulting typing of cities, he claimed, was of more value than a functional classification in indicating levels of education, health,

overcrowding, and the like. But Gillen's occupational indices, valuable though they may be, are not discussed in detail here since they do not amount to a functional classification.

Conclusions

This chapter has dealt with various attempts to classify cities on a functional basis. The results thus far are interesting and useful, but they show considerable variation for individual cities.

This is not surprising in view of problems of methodology that are involved. For instance, what unit areas should be classified? The several methods described in this chapter have differed on this point. How many and which classes is it possible and desirable to differentiate? Should the classification be so constructed that each city can fall into only one class? Should the criteria differ with metropolitan status? In answering these and similar questions, one must keep in mind the possibilities and limitations of United States Census data.

Of course, it is hardly to be expected that any one technique will serve the purposes of workers in all fields. What special qualities of a classification recommend it to the urban geographer? Perhaps most important is that the method lends itself to the making of distribution maps so that the patterns may be studied and relationships to other area distributions worked out. The next chapter is an attempt to show in a preliminary way how the results of a functional classification can be used.

Selected References

Alexandersson, Gunnar: *The Industrial Structure of American Cities,* University of Nebraska Press, Lincoln, Nebr., 1956.

Aurousseau, M.: "The Distribution of Population: A Constructive Problem," *Geographical Review,* vol. 11, pp. 567 ff., 1921.

Brush, John E.: "Economic Classification of Urban Places," *The Population of New Jersey,* Rutgers University Press, New Brunswick, N.J., 1956, pp. 60–72.

Duncan, Otis D., and Albert J. Reiss, Jr.: *Social Characteristics of Urban and Rural Communities,* 1950, John Wiley & Sons, Inc., New York, 1956, esp. part IV and pp. 387–409.

Gillen, Paul Bates: *The Distribution of Occupations as a City Yardstick,* King's Crown Press, Columbia University, New York, 1951.

Harris, Chauncy D.: "A Functional Classification of Cities in thé United States," *Geographical Review,* vol. 33, pp. 86–99, 1943.

Hart, John Fraser: "Functions and Occupational Structures of Cities of the American South," *Annals of the Association of American Geographers,* vol. 45, pp. 269–286, 1955.

Hoyt, Homer: "Economic Backgrounds of Cities," *Journal of Land and Public Utility Economics,* vol. 17, pp. 188–195, 1941.

Jones, Victor, and Richard L. Forstall: "Economic and Social Classification of Metropolitan Areas," *The Municipal Year Book,* International City Managers Association, Chicago, 1963, pp. 31–44.

———, ———, and Andrew Collver: "Economic and Social Characteristics of Urban Places," *The Municipal Year Book,* International City Managers Association, Chicago, 1963, pp. 85–157.

Moser, C. A., and Wolf Scott: *British Towns: A Statistical Study of Their Social and Economic Differences,* Oliver & Boyd, Ltd., Edinburgh and London, 1961.

Nelson, Howard J.: "A Service Classification of American Cities," *Economic Geography,* vol. 31, pp. 189–210, 1955.

Ohlson, Grace M. Kneedler: "Economic Classification of Cities," *The Municipal Year Book,* International City Managers Association, Chicago, 1945, pp. 30–38 and table IV. (Reprinted in the several following editions of the *Year Book.*)

CHAPTER **9**

Distribution patterns and characteristics of functional classes[1]

IN THIS chapter the story of the functional classes of cities is carried further. The distribution of cities of each functional class is described and an attempt made to explain the pattern. Also, distinctive features and other attributes that appear to be associated with each class are considered. Finally, some general questions are raised about possible regional variations in the characteristics of the city classes.

Certain limitations are inherent in these lines of inquiry. In the first place, the results of the several methods of classification were far from identical. Nevertheless, certain broad distributional patterns resulted, on which there is a fair measure of agreement.

In the discussion that follows, Nelson's maps are used, chiefly because they show each service (or function) separately. It should be remembered, however, that according to Nelson's classification system many places have more than one form of functional specialization.

The problem of finding distinctive traits associated with each of the several classes presents even more serious difficulties. We cannot expect the different classes of cities to stand out very strikingly from one another since all cities are to some degree multifunctional. But there are characteristics that are found to be associated with specialization in certain activities even though, in each case, the city may actually be specialized in other activities at the same time.

With these questions and limitations in mind, we shall consider each of the func-

[1] This chapter is based largely on the works of Harris and Nelson cited in Chap. 8. Chief dependence has been placed on Nelson, however, since his study is less subjective and is based on more recent data than were available to Harris. Part of the foundation for the chapter is also provided by a later study by Nelson (see Howard J. Nelson, "Some Characteristics of the Population of Cities in Similar Service Classifications," *Economic Geography*, vol. 33, pp. 95–108, 1957).

tional classes in more or less random order.

Manufacturing Cities

The largest specialized class Manufacturing cities are more numerous than those of any other specialized category. Harris [2] found that 44 per cent of the metropolitan districts and 43 per cent of the smaller centers which he classified were in one or the other of his two manufacturing classes; and more than one-fifth of the 897 urban areas Nelson [3] considered were specialized to some degree in manufacturing.

Range in intensity of specialization Since manufacturing cities are so numerous,

[2] Chauncy D. Harris, "A Functional Classification of Cities in the United States," *Geographical Review*, vol. 33, pp. 86–99, 1943.
[3] Howard J. Nelson, "A Service Classification of American Cities," *Economic Geography*, vol. 31, pp. 189–210, 1955.

it is not surprising to find that they show a considerable range in the intensity of specialization. Harris, in his classification, used two subtypes for manufacturing (see Table 8.1), the first overwhelmingly manufacturing and the second with other functions of considerably greater importance than in the first subtype, but still secondary to manufacturing. Harris used M′ and M for these two subtypes; Jones used the terms "manufacturing city" and "industrial city" to indicate the two levels (see Table 8.2); and Nelson judged differences in intensity of manufacturing by the number of SDs the various urban areas were above the mean for all urban areas. According to Nelson's classification a place might be specialized in manufacturing to the extent of 3 SDs.

Areal concentration Manufacturing cities also exhibit a more marked areal concentration than any other type of city (Figures 8.1 and 9.1). As might be expected, the

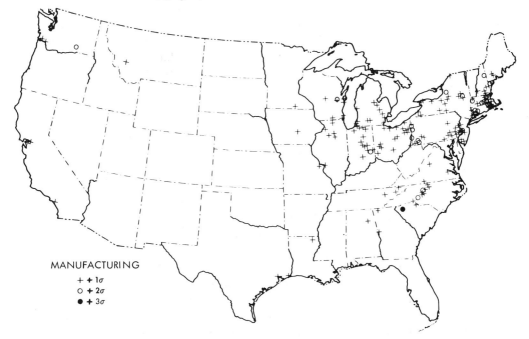

Fig. 9.1 Cities specialized in manufacturing, 1950. (From Howard J. Nelson, "A Service Classification of American Cities," *Economic Geography*, vol. 31, 1955, fig. 2.)

MANUFACTURING
+ +1σ
o +2σ
● +3σ

principal area of concentration corresponds to the "manufacturing belt," more than 80 per cent of the manufacturing centers lying east of the Mississippi River and north of the Ohio River. There are extensions south-westward along the eastern and western edges of the Appalachian Highlands, how-ever. Elsewhere in the country, cities with manufacturing specialization are rare, though there seems to be some tendency for such centers to develop along the Gulf Coast and in a few places on the Pacific Coast. Later censuses will probably show more centers specialized in manufacturing in these areas.

Few manufacturing cities with high degree of specialization There are few manufacturing cities of great intensity. The only urban center which Nelson found to have a large enough proportion of its labor force in manufacturing to fall in the Mf3 category (that is, at least 3 SDs above the mean) is Brandon-Judson, a small, unin-corporated textile center in western South Carolina. Of the 183 manufacturing cities he differentiated, only 29 lie in his Mf2 category, and most of these are small indus-trial towns rather than large cities. Only 1 lies west of the Mississippi: this is Richland, Washington, an atomic energy center cre-ated during World War II. The remaining 153 manufacturing centers fall into the Mf class.

Few great cities exhibit specialization in manufacturing Manufacturing special-ization is more characteristic of our me-dium- and small-sized urban centers than of the large cities. The Detroit and Provi-dence Urbanized Areas are the only ones with populations of half a million or more that are sufficiently specialized in manu-facturing to be classed with the Mf cities. This does not mean, of course, that manu-facturing is unimportant in our large cities. But they have so much development of other activities, particularly in the finance-insurance-real estate group, that the per-centage of persons occupied in manufactur-ing ordinarily is not great enough to bring them into the manufacturing category as Nelson defines it. As was pointed out in an earlier chapter, the nonbasic proportion of employment tends to increase with city size (see page 107). The Chicago (F) and New York–Northeastern New Jersey (F2) areas are prime examples of this situation. No one would question the importance of manufacturing in these cities; yet neither has manufacturing as a specialty according to Nelson's classification. Moreover, a num-ber of his diversified cities—e.g., Cleveland, Cincinnati, Pittsburgh, and Milwaukee—are well-known industrial centers. In these, too, other activities keep the percentage em-ployed in manufacturing below the level at which the city would be recognized as specialized in manufacturing.

This may seem to be a serious limitation of Nelson's classification technique, but it must be remembered that we are not study-ing the distribution of manufacturing; in-stead, we are interested in discovering which cities are specialized in manufactur-ing. And boundary lines are arbitrary by nature; a number of the large cities shown as diversified or with 1 SD in finance-insur-ance-real estate may have percentages of occupied persons in manufacturing that are only slightly less than those for Detroit and Providence.

Are manufacturing cities distinctive in appearance? But we are concerned in this chapter with more than the distribution of the various classes of cities; we are inter-ested, too, in the characteristics that may be associated with each class of city. For in-stance, are manufacturing cities distinctive in appearance? And are there other less obvious properties associated with this class of city?

It might be expected that manufactur-ing, more perhaps than any other line of specialization, would result in a distinctive landscape; that it would be simple, therefore, to describe the typical features of the manufacturing city. The very word "manufacturing" conjures up a picture of large factory buildings, great smokestacks, a maze of railroads, rows of workers' houses. But this is somewhat of a caricature of an industrial city.

In reality, such a concentration of industrial landmarks is rare, since variations in types of manufacturing, size of urban center, degree of manufacturing specialization, age of factories, and similar factors affect the appearances of manufacturing cities.

TYPE OF MANUFACTURING AS A FACTOR The type of manufacturing present is an important consideration. Primary metals manufacture and the industries commonly associated with it may be reflected locally in the sort of picture described above, and so too may certain other of the so-called "primary" industries. But metal *products* plants are likely to result in a somewhat different-looking city, with less smoke and dirt and fewer of the other disagreeable aspects of industry. Textile mills have their own associated features; and so have a number of other lines of specialization. Mixtures of types add to the complexity. Textile mills, blast furnaces, refineries, and the like are easily recognized evidences of manufacturing, but no one or no combination of such features is typical of all manufacturing centers.

SIZE OF URBAN CENTER The size of the urban center must be considered, too, in any attempt to characterize cities of manufacturing specialization. In a large city, though certain areas may be mazes of factories and related landscape elements, such telltales are partly obscured by the ubiquitous features of cities. It is likely to be the small industrial city or the industrial satellite that presents the most striking aspects resulting from manufacturing dominance.

DEGREE OF SPECIALIZATION Degree of specialization is likely to be reflected in the picture that an industrial center presents. An Mf city could hardly be expected to reveal manufacturing features as markedly as an Mf2 or an Mf3 city. But it will be remembered that these higher concentrations are found only in smaller urban centers. We shall have to look to these smaller places for really striking concentrations of manufacturing features.

AGE OF FACTORIES Still another factor affecting the picture presented by a city of manufacturing specialization is the age of the city or, more precisely, of its factories. Some types of modern factories are attractive-looking buildings on landscaped grounds with few of the disagreeable features that commonly have been associated with such land use, except perhaps the large parking lots and the periodic influx and exodus of workers.

FEW DISTINCTIVE OBSERVABLE FEATURES It is clear, then, that there is little which we can unhesitatingly say regarding features common to manufacturing cities.[4] Nevertheless, some small cities that are more or less specialized in manufacturing have been described in the literature and so, too, have some manufacturing areas of larger cities. A few such studies are included in the list of references at the end of this chapter.

Other characteristics associated with manufacturing specialization But visible aspects of the city are only part of the story. Howard Nelson studied variations in the social and economic characteristics by class of city, basing his work on his own classifica-

[4] The proportion of land devoted to manufacturing might be of some value. Some data of this sort have been assembled (see, for example, Harland Bartholomew, *Land Uses in American Cities*, Harvard University Press, Cambridge, Mass., 1955), but such information on a really standardized basis is not available for most American cities. Manufacturing ordinarily uses little land, a fact that helps to explain the lack of a distinctive appearance, even where an urban center is definitely specialized in manufacturing.

tion and on data from the 1950 *Census of Population.*[5]

The resulting table permits some generalizations regarding manufacturing cities (Table 9.1). On the average these cities seem to be growing more slowly than cities of any other class. Participation in the labor force tends to be high for manufacturing cities, and median income is high. On the other hand, the educational level tends to be lower than for other classes of cities. Such statements must be regarded as highly

[5] Nelson, "Some Characteristics of the Population of Cities in Similar Service Classifications." For a more statistical consideration of these factors see Otis D. Duncan and Albert J. Reiss, Jr., *Social Characteristics of Urban and Rural Communities, 1950,* John Wiley & Sons, Inc., New York, 1956, esp. part IV and pp. 387–409.

tentative. Nevertheless, they add something to our picture of American manufacturing cities.

Retail Centers

Retailing, of necessity, is a function of all urban centers, but some cities stand out for specialization in this activity. According to Nelson's classification, Miami, Florida, is the only really large city with a sufficient proportion of its employment in retailing to justify a retail classification, and in Miami retailing is combined with two other lines—personal service and finance-insurance-real estate (Ps3RF). No other city of over 100,000 inhabitants has a sufficient proportion of its employment in retailing to qualify; in fact most retailing centers are

Table 9.1   Averages of selected criteria for all cities and for all SD3 and SD2 cities according to Nelson

	All cities	Mf3 & Mf2	R3 & R2	Pf3 & Pf2	T3 & T2	Mi3 & Mi2	Pb3 & Pb2	Ps3 & Ps2	W3 & W2	F3 & F2
% increase in population, 1940–1950	27.9	2.2	39.4	65.0	17.5	31.1	40.0	61.0	30.4	35.6
% 65 years old or older	8.6	7.6	9.0	7.6	9.7	7.4	7.3	9.2	7.7	10.0
Average years of school completed	10.0	8.9	10.5	12.3	10.4	9.7	10.8	11.0	9.9	11.1
Participation in labor force (% of males over 14 years of age)	77.8	82.8	77.1	55.8	78.0	79.2	77.8	73.2	80.0	75.6
Participation in labor force (% of females over 14 years of age)	32.8	35.9	30.3	34.1	29.2	27.1	33.0	33.3	33.0	34.6
% unemployed	5.1	5.4	6.7	3.6	4.7	5.5	4.7	5.8	6.9	4.1
Median income	$2,643	$3,134	$2,560	$1,674	$2,733	$2,822	$2,658	$2,227	$2,566	$2,780
Number of cities	897	30	27	39	50	34	41	36	36	35

SOURCE: From Howard J. Nelson, "Some Characteristics of the Population of Cities in Similar Service Classifications," *Economic Geography,* vol. 33, p. 97, 1957.

under 50,000 in population, and many are much smaller.

Not so concentrated areally as manufacturing Retail centers are less sharply concentrated areally than manufacturing centers (Figure 9.2), yet their distribution, too, shows some interesting aspects. For instance, they are largely absent from the Northeast and from the Southern Appalachians. In those areas, manufacturing and in some cases other activities have tended to eclipse retailing. The most striking positive feature of the distribution pattern is a broad north-south band of retail cities in the central part of the United States. Many of these are county seats with substantial trade areas. California and Florida also have important concentrations of retailing centers.

Retail cities often have other specializations, too Unlike cities with manufac-turing specialization, which usually occurs by itself, many retailing cities specialize in several other activities as well. Interesting examples of this are Uniontown, Pennsylvania (R2Mi2), and Middlesborough, Kentucky (MiR), both coal mining centers; and three Texas cities—Lamesa (MiR), Wichita Falls (RMiPs), and Gainesville (RMi)—where the oil industry shares the economic scene with retailing. A number of resort centers, too, occur as combinations with retailing: for example, Miami (Ps3RF) and Daytona Beach (PsF2R), Florida, and Monterey (Ps2R), California, though Monterey may be more important as a garrison town (Fort Ord) than as a resort and retirement center.

Characteristics of retail centers It is hardly to be expected that retail trade centers as a class would exhibit any very distinctive observable features or that they would be found to have well-defined social

Fig. 9.2   Cities specialized in retail trade, 1950. (From Howard J. Nelson, "A Service Classification of American Cities," *Economic Geography*, vol. 31, 1955, fig. 3.)

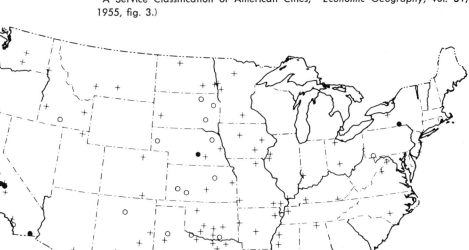

RETAIL TRADE

+ +1σ
o +2σ
● +3σ

or economic characteristics (Table 9.1). This is partly because retail trade is ubiquitous to cities of all kinds, so that retail trade centers come close to approximating the national mean for American cities. But there is the added fact, brought out in the last paragraph, that retail specialization is often combined with one or more other specialties.

Wholesale Centers

Cities that have a high proportion of their labor force in wholesaling are less numerous than retail centers.

Wholesaling often combined with other specialties Like retailing, wholesaling is often combined with other specialties. For instance, in some of the larger cities it is associated with finance-insurance-real estate. In a number of cities it is associated with transportation—sometimes with railroads and, in New Orleans, with the port function—but most often of all, wholesaling is associated with retailing.

Two types of wholesale centers There are two rather different types of urban centers that may exhibit specialization in wholesaling. In one the emphasis is on the sale of commodities in large quantities to retailers. The other is the type of community which specializes in the assembly and sale of commodities to jobbers. "Wholesale trade" as given under industry groups in the Census of Population includes both of these types.

The first of the two types consists of wholesale centers in the traditional sense, typified by firms that sell groceries, hardware, or drugs in bulk to retailers in the city and in the surrounding smaller cities and towns. These wholesale centers may be fairly large cities; at least they are likely to be larger than any neighboring urban centers. According to Nelson's classification, New Orleans, Denver, Minneapolis–St.

Paul, Portland (Oregon), Memphis, and Omaha are examples of cities with more than average development of wholesaling of this sort; and Memphis is the largest city in the United States that rates exclusively as a wholesale center. No one of these large cities, however, reaches the degree of specialization represented by the W2 class.

In the other category of wholesale centers are small agricultural assembling towns, such as Suffolk, Virginia, center for a peanut producing region; Yakima, Washington, apples; Sanford, Florida, celery; and El Centro, California, vegetables. Most of the W3 and W2 places are collecting centers of this sort. A very few places, e.g., a few Great Plains cities, attain their rank in wholesaling through a combination of collecting and shipping of grain and livestock with distribution of commodities to the smaller towns around.

Patterns of distribution Since wholesaling consists of two somewhat different types, we should not attempt to read too much into the general distribution pattern of wholesale trade centers (Figure 9.3). Nevertheless, some aspects are worth noting. For one thing, wholesale centers are like retail centers in being generally absent from the manufacturing belt. It is not surprising that the agricultural assembling type of wholesale center is rare in this belt. Though in considerable part the manufacturing belt coincides with important agricultural areas, there are few localities within it where the picking and sorting of agricultural products are important.

We might expect to find at least the distribution type of wholesale center. Of course, many of the larger urban centers in the belt do have an important wholesaling function of this sort, but because manufacturing is so important the proportion of wholesaling employees is too low to show specialization in this line. New York and Chicago are prime examples of this condi-

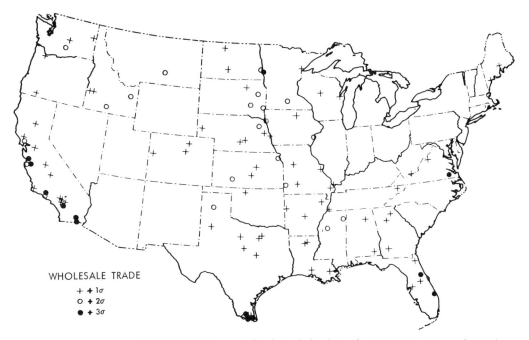

Fig. 9.3 Cities specialized in wholesale trade, 1950. (From Howard J. Nelson, "A Service Classification of American Cities," *Economic Geography*, vol. 31, 1955, fig. 8.)

tion. Though they are the principal wholesale distribution centers of the United States, the percentage of total employment in wholesaling in neither city is great enough for it to be specialized in wholesaling according to Nelson's classification. Instead, both fall in the finance-insurance-real estate category.

A second characteristic of the overall distribution of the cities with wholesaling specialization is a tendency for concentration in the same central north-south belt as the retailing centers. This does not mean that either function is of unusual absolute importance, but rather that the area is a populous one without any other activity, such as manufacturing, present in sufficient amount to overshadow retailing and wholesaling. The association of the two is rather to be expected, since retailing and wholesaling are closely related activities. In fact, a city that is engaged in both retailing and wholesaling is often referred to as a "trade

center" without regard to the proportions of the two activities. It may be assumed that this central belt includes many wholesale centers of the traditional type—distributing centers serving smaller cities around them.

But there are concentrations of wholesale centers also in California and Florida. Here, though the larger cities may do a good deal of distributing, the most specialized wholesale centers conform to the assembly type: they are small cities located in regions of intensive vegetable and citrus fruit production and engaged in the assembly and sale of commodities to jobbers.

Distinctive features of wholesale centers When most people think of wholesale centers they are thinking of wholesaling in the distribution sense. Other than limited sections devoted to wholesale establishments, with display rooms and storage warehouses, and located near railroads, near water, or near an important highway intersection, such cities generally have no very distinctive assemblage of features.[6] The actual wholesale business is often conducted through offices in the central business district.

The assembly type of wholesale center, though smaller and less commonly associated with wholesaling in the public mind, has more distinctive features, or perhaps it is just that these features are likely to be more visible because of the characteristically small size of this type of city. Probably the most important index feature is some sort of packing or assembling plant associated with railroad tracks or trucking platforms. In some places, cotton gins, grain elevators, or other similar features may replace the packing plant, thus reflecting differences in the dominant agriculture.

Economic and social characteristics
Like retail trade centers, wholesale centers

[6] See discussion of wholesaling in Chap. 14.

do not exhibit any very distinctive social or economic characteristics (Table 9.1). This seems to be due, in large degree, to the fact that wholesaling is so often combined with other specialties; but there is the added fact, pointed out earlier, that wholesale centers are of two fairly distinct subtypes. After all there is no reason to expect wholesale centers of the distributive type to have social and economic characteristics similar to those of the assembly type of wholesale center.

Transportation and Communication Cities

Transportation and communication[7] centers are about equal to wholesale cities in number. Nelson found that, in ninety-six cities, transportation was carried on in sig-

[7] Communication was included by Nelson, but it is not a factor in classifying the cities, so it will not enter into our discussion.

Fig. 9.4 Cities specialized in transportation and communications, 1950. (From Howard J. Nelson, "A Service Classification of American Cities," *Economic Geography*, vol. 31, 1955, fig. 5.)

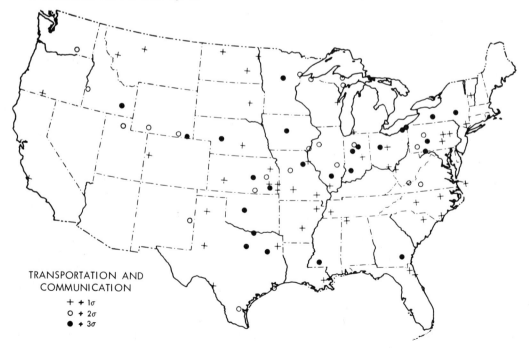

TRANSPORTATION AND
COMMUNICATION

+ + 1σ
o + 2σ
● + 3σ

nificantly above-average proportions (Figure 9.4).

Railroad centers predominate   A considerable proportion of these places—seven-eighths of them, according to Nelson—are railroad centers, reflecting the fact that transportation in the United States is chiefly land transportation and, until recently at least, land transportation has been predominantly railroad transportation. These railroad centers are usually small cities, division and junction points along main railway lines. Altoona, Pennsylvania; Hornell, New York; North Platte, Nebraska; and Cleburn, Texas, are outstanding examples of T3 cities, but there are a number of others. It is of interest that more than half of the ninety-six cities show T3 or T2 rating, thus balancing the many urban centers of the country that are strikingly low in their proportions of this specialty.

Distribution pattern   Since so many of the transportation and communication cities are railroad centers, it is clear that railroads must play an important role in explaining the distribution pattern. At first glance, the distribution seems countrywide, but after a closer look, certain broad elements of variation become clear. Unlike the retail and wholesale cities, transportation and communication centers are relatively numerous in the manufacturing belt, a fact which is related to the concentration of railroad lines in that locality. Cities with this specialty are fairly common, too, throughout central United States. Farther West they seem to fan out along the major transcontinental railroad lines. The route of the Union Pacific is especially noticeable in this regard. On the other hand, the Far West is strikingly deficient in transportation and communication centers.

Ports as second type of transportation center   Though railroads explain the distribution of most transportation and com-

munication cities, water transportation is represented, too. The movement of iron ore by water accounts for the importance of Duluth and several other Great Lakes ports; and five cities along the Atlantic and Gulf Coasts—New Orleans, Galveston, St. Augustine, Jacksonville, and Newport News—have larger than average proportions of their labor forces in transportation. New Orleans is the largest of these ocean ports, but only Galveston reaches the T2 class. In fact, Galveston is the only ocean port in the United States that has 16.28 per cent or more of its labor force (that is, 2 SDs or more above the mean) employed in transportation, and some of the major ports of the country are not listed in the transportation category at all. The New York–Northeastern New Jersey Urbanized Area is classified as F2 and the Philadelphia Urbanized Area as F. Chicago, certainly the country's greatest railroad center, also has an F classification. In very large cities, we have found, employment is so varied that it is often difficult for an important activity to stand out. Finance-insurance-real estate, on the other hand, is peculiarly concentrated in great cities.

Trucking centers   Truck transportation has grown so much in recent years that one might expect to find some trucking centers among the transportation and communications cities. But trucking is more widespread than railroad transportation and tends to be concentrated in large cities where it is difficult for any single activity to achieve a high enough relative concentration to show even 1 SD of specialization.

Social and economic characteristics   In his study of the social and economic characteristics of various classes of cities, Nelson did not find much that was distinctive regarding transportation and communication centers (Table 9.1). It appears, however, that they are growing more slowly than most other types of cities. A possible explanation for this slow growth is not hard to find. Most of the transportation and communication cities are railroad centers, and railroads, especially in the eastern half of the country, have not been prosperous in recent years.

Landscape features of railroad centers

It is hardly feasible to generalize about the features of all transportation centers, since, as was pointed out earlier, two types are represented. However, the railroad center, by far the most common type of transportation center, has certain rather distinctive features.[8] Switching yards, railroad shops, classification yards, tie treating plants, and other railroad facilities are likely to be associated in varying proportions. They may characterize only limited sections of very large cities, but in the smaller cities in the T3 and T2 categories they stand out strikingly. (For further discussion of railroads in the city, see Chapter 13.)

Distinctive features of port cities

Though port cities have not been differentiated from other transportation centers in any of the functional classifications, the actual port sections of large cities are likely to show unusually distinctive landscape features. For instance, there are extensive terminal facilities for loading and unloading ships. One thinks immediately of piers (wharfs or quays) jutting out from the shore like irregularly spaced teeth, with docks between for the ships. Often the piers are covered over so that they are essentially long sheds. On the piers are cranes, storage facilities for freight, tracks for railroad cars that are being loaded or unloaded, accommodations for trucks, and facilities for taking on fuel and other necessities. There are passenger line docking facilities, general cargo piers, and piers designed particularly for

[8] For a discussion of an urban place exhibiting such features, see Robert Wrigley, Jr., "Pocatello, Idaho, as a Railroad Center," *Economic Geography*, vol. 19, pp. 325–336, 1943.

the handling of bulk cargo, such as iron ore and coal, which require special equipment. If the port is an active one, ships are tied up at the piers, loading and unloading, and there is an endless coming and going of ships. The ubiquitous tug is an important part of the picture. The emphasis on things maritime may carry over to adjacent business streets of the city where marine specialization may be much in evidence. And the availability of local water transportation combined with the possibility of importing and exporting have made the waterfront an attractive site for factories. In fact, the whole waterfront district is likely to be a particularly active area in the port city.

The degree to which this sort of picture dominates a city varies from port city to port city, depending upon several factors. If the city is small and the port is a very active one, the port function may be so outstanding as to impress almost any visitor to the city. Indeed, the activity may be of sufficient relative importance to give the city a T1 or T2 rating according to Nelson's classification. But one might spend some time in Manhattan without seeing much evidence of New York's great port function. Nor is it reflected in the city's classification. Other activities are too outstanding for transportation to appear. (For further discussion of water transportation in relation to the city see Chapter 13.)

Mining Centers

There are too few cities classified as mining centers to justify much discussion of their pattern of distribution (Figure 9.5). An obvious fact is that they tend to cluster, frequently reflecting coal fields, areas of ore production, or oil fields. Some of the anthracite mining centers of eastern Pennsylvania; a few bituminous coal towns in Pennsylvania, in West Virginia, and in the Middle West; iron mining centers near the head of Lake Superior; some oil towns in

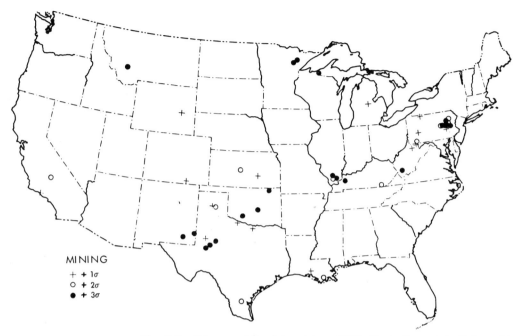

Fig. 9.5 Cities specialized in mining, 1950. (From Howard J. Nelson, "A Service Classification of American Cities," *Economic Geography*, vol. 31, 1955, Fig. 10.)

Texas and Oklahoma; and Butte, Montana, a famous metal mining city, make up the list.

Coal and metal mining centers The features associated with mining centers vary so greatly as to make it impracticable to generalize about the class as a whole. Thus headframes, breakers, and waste piles may be said to characterize the anthracite towns; headframes, loading tipples, and waste piles frequently mark the bituminous coal town; drift mouths replace the headframes in many small coal centers in West Virginia; strip pits are a common landscape feature around some of the coal towns; and many of these same features and others characterize metal mining centers. Railroads are ubiquitous in the coal and metal mining towns, and, typically, low-quality housing prevails. Most of these centers have been in existence for a long time, and the smoke and dirt that often accompany mining and related activities have led to rapid deterioration of the housing.

Oil centers The oil centers of Texas present a very different picture. Often the derricks, storage tanks, and other features that we associate with the oil industry lie outside the town itself, but oil well supply houses, oil company offices, establishments dealing in oil leases, and, above all, a new and "boom" appearance are likely to give this type of urban center a special flavor. Such urban places are generally of recent origin. This fact, together with the sudden wealth so often associated with petroleum production, militate against the old, low-quality housing and the other decadent aspects of many coal and metal towns. In fact, the oil centers hardly seem to be mining towns at all in the usual sense of the word, but they are so classified here since oil and gas extraction is included by the Census Bureau in the occupation of mining.

Social and economic characteristics
Just as mining towns vary in appearance, depending on the particular type of mineral commodity, so do they vary greatly socially and economically. As a result, generalizations of this kind for mining centers as a class are of little value. But there are some interesting differences that can be correlated with the mineral produced. When Nelson contrasted coal mining centers of Mi3 specialization with oil centers of similar intensity, he found that eleven of the seventeen coal centers, including all eight of those in the anthracite region of Pennsylvania, had lost in population in the 1940–1950 period (Table 9.1).[9] In contrast, all twelve of the oil centers had gained, the gain averaging 88 per cent.

Several other somewhat related contrasts are of interest. For one thing, the coal mining centers were found to have higher proportions of old people. The coal mining industry in many places has been declining, owing to the exhaustion of local coal seams and to a general decline in the markets for coal. Under these circumstances the young men migrate to other areas where they can get more steady work, but the older men find it too late in life to change and so stay on, working short shifts in coal mining or taking what other jobs they can get in the vicinity or, in some cases, going on relief. The coal mining centers also have a higher proportion of women in the labor force than the oil centers. With the marginal living conditions that have long prevailed in the coal fields there has been a demand for supplementary income and, therefore, a tendency for types of manufacturing that employ the wives and daughters of the coal miners to locate in these centers. For obvious reasons, the coal mining centers also have substantially lower average incomes and higher percentages of unemployment than the oil centers.

[9] Nelson, "Some Characteristics of the Population of Cities in Similar Service Classifications," pp. 99–100.

Most mining centers small As was pointed out earlier in this chapter, the urban centers that invite study as examples of the various functional types of cities are likely to be places where the activity is strikingly represented. Certainly this is true of mining. But the most highly specialized mining centers, though numerous and though they account for the bulk of our mining activity, generally fall short of a population of 10,000, and hence are not included among the urban centers with mining specialization shown by either Nelson or Harris. This explains why some well-known mining towns are not represented in Figure 9.5. But the fact remains that these small centers have the greatest relative concentrations of mineral production features. Studies of several such mining communities, places that are too small to be differentiated in the classifications, appear in the reading list at the end of this chapter.

The centers of mining specialization that are large enough to be classed as small cities and hence to appear in Figure 9.5 have been less commonly described, and then most often the discussion has been incidental to studies of mining areas. In these larger centers many of the landscape features earlier described are present, but more diluted by normal city activities than they would be in a mining camp. These cities of mining specialization (in contrast to mining camps) might well merit special study. What features, in the cities, most clearly reflect the mining activity? And what means can be devised objectively to measure the economic importance of mining activity to these urban centers?

The names of several larger cities are associated with mineral products—for example, Pittsburgh with coal, Denver with metals, Oklahoma City with petroleum—because they serve mining areas. But even where some mines or oil wells occur inside such cities, commercial, industrial, and other functions are likely to outweigh mining so that the city falls into another classification.

Professional Service Cities

Professional and related services, according to the Bureau of the Census, include medical and other health services; educational services, government; educational services, private; and other professional and related services. Nelson found that in eighty-one cities of the country outstanding proportions of the labor force were engaged in the performance of such professional services (Figure 9.6). These cities are rather widely scattered, though with some tendency to concentrate in the Middle West.

Professional service cities small Since medical and educational services are needed by all, we might expect to find professional

service centers closely reflecting the distribution of the country's population, but none of the large cities is represented in this category. In the larger cities professional service is lost among other activities.

For this reason, professional service cities average small. Madison, Wisconsin (Pf2PbF), with a population of 126,706 in 1960, is the largest, and here the professional rating is shared with public administration and finance. This is because Madison serves as the state capital as well as the site of the state university. But this is not a common practice in the United States; state legislatures have usually made a determined attempt to separate the two functions.

College towns and medical centers Three-fourths of the professional service cities are college towns, and most of the remainder are medical centers. The medical centers stand out because they are often the

Fig. 9.6 Cities specialized in professional services, 1950. (From Howard J. Nelson, "A Service Classification of American Cities," *Economic Geography*, vol. 31, 1955, fig. 4.)

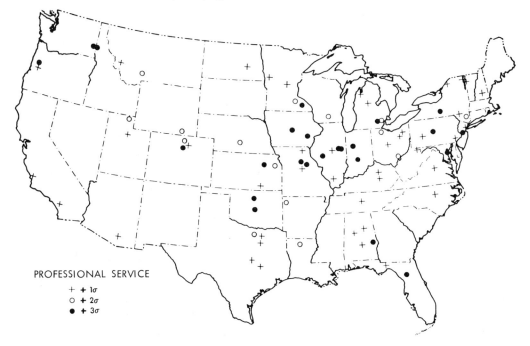

PROFESSIONAL SERVICE

+ + 1σ
○ + 2σ
● + 3σ

sites of mental institutions, veterans' hospitals, sanitoriums, and the like. Rochester, Minnesota, with a population of 40,663 in 1960, is noted for the presence of the Mayo Clinic, but this is an exceptional case; most clinics are found in larger cities. It should be pointed out, too, that many of the university and college towns are also medical centers. Madison, Wisconsin, and Ann Arbor, Michigan, are good examples of this. Combining the two professional activities is logical; in fact, the medical school of a large university could not function without an affiliated hospital.

Social and economic characteristics Professional service towns as a class have some rather interesting social and economic characteristics, most of which reflect the fact that so many of them are the sites of colleges or universities (Table 9.1). For instance, most professional service centers are growing rapidly, a result, chiefly, of the way in which college education has been booming. Since college students are counted as residents of the community where they go to school, it is not surprising that professional service towns rate higher than any other class in average number of years of school completed. Two other related characteristics are the remarkably low proportion of men who are in the labor force and the low median income. Men outnumber women two to one in colleges and universities, and the large student component reduces the proportion of males participating in the labor force. It also helps to account for the low median income, since college students commonly are either supported entirely by money from home, and hence are recorded as having no income, or else have only part-time jobs. But balancing this low median income is the considerable flow of money into the community for student support.

Observable characteristics Most professional service towns have distinctive appearances. The buildings which house the universities and medical centers are likely to be large and imposing. More than that, the grounds that surround the buildings are often extensive, giving a parklike atmosphere to the community. Closer inspection usually brings out the presence of one or more shopping areas nearby, where food, clothing, books, and supplies are sold. In university towns these shops often have features in keeping with the collegiate atmosphere, and the merchandise itself shows the presence of a special clientele.

Blighted areas near universities Attractive as many university campuses are, their presence often seems to have a blighting effect upon the housing in the vicinity. This is largely because rooms are in great demand near the campus, and houses which may at one time have been occupied by faculty families have long since gone over to a rooming-house function. Places of this type take on a battered appearance. As the need for office space, laboratories, and classrooms expands, the university buys adjacent property, thereby pushing the blighted rooming-house district farther and farther into the better residential areas. Even the small commercial centers near the larger universities suffer from the encroaching campus. Often when the university has not acquired the land outright, it is held under option, thus giving a temporary and somewhat shoddy character to the business activities. As these enterprises are forced out, they are likely to find new locations by edging into the surrounding residential areas, pushing the rooming-house district ahead of them.

Public Administration Cities

Though Harris in his classification of cities referred to political capitals and to army garrison towns and naval bases, he did not attempt to delimit a type of city that would include them. But Ohlson and

Jones delimited a "government center" class (see Table 8.2); and Nelson differentiated public administration cities, basing his class on the proportion of the labor force in public administration (Table 8.4). Nelson says that such cities are almost exclusively of two general types—either capital cities or cities near large military installations; but Alexandersson [10] suggests another explanation for some of the public administration centers of the West: that they are headquarters of large irrigation projects being administered by the Federal Bureau of Reclamation.

Distribution pattern Public administration cities, according to Nelson, total eighty-five, only slightly more numerous than professional towns, and they are even more widely scattered (Fig. 9.7). This is

[10] Gunnar Alexandersson, *The Industrial Structure of American Cities,* University of Nebraska Press, Lincoln, Nebr., 1956, p. 116.

partly due to the role politics plays in determining the location of the capitals. To begin with, Washington, D.C., as might be expected, stands out strongly as a public administration city (Pb3F); and we might expect to find that the forty-eight state capitals (Alaska and Hawaii were not included in Nelson's study) would all show some specialization in this category. But in fact, only half of them do so.

Let us examine the twenty-four capital cities that are not classified as public administration centers. Four—Carson City, Dover, Montpelier, and Pierre—are too small to be classified, and the other twenty are too specialized along other lines for public administration to show up as a specialty. Finance-insurance-real estate, either alone or in combination with other activities, characterizes sixteen of the twenty. Some of the sixteen are large cities—Boston, Atlanta, Columbus, Minneapolis–St. Paul, Indianapolis, Denver—and we have found that

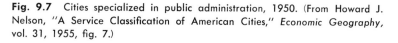

Fig. 9.7 Cities specialized in public administration, 1950. (From Howard J. Nelson, "A Service Classification of American Cities," *Economic Geography,* vol. 31, 1955, fig. 7.)

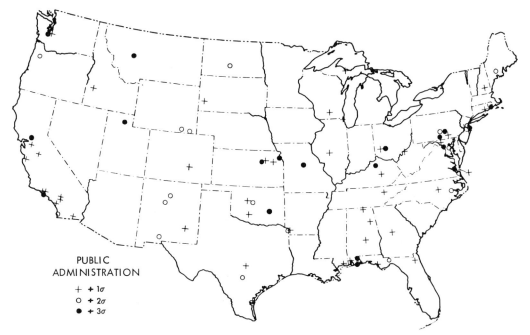

PUBLIC
ADMINISTRATION

+ $+ 1\sigma$
o $+ 2\sigma$
● $+ 3\sigma$

in cities of this size the finance-insurance-real estate group is likely to be so important that other possible specialties are submerged. A few small capitals—e.g., Des Moines, Hartford, and Lincoln—are specialized in the finance-insurance-real estate group by virtue of having important concentrations of insurance offices. And some of the others (e.g., Richmond, Virginia) are important enough as regional centers to be outstanding financial cities. Of the four other capitals that did not qualify as public administration centers, one, Providence, is classified as a manufacturing city. The other three are diversified.

Military towns   In addition to Washington, D.C., and twenty-four state capitals, sixty other cities qualified as public administration centers at the time Nelson carried out his classification. It may be assumed that most of the sixty are near military installations. Such cities are somewhat new to the American scene, though long recognized as garrison towns in Europe. They are located near important airfields, naval or army bases, or ordnance depots. Nelson gives Warrington and Key West, Florida; Newport, Rhode Island; Riverview, Virginia; and Junction City, Kansas, as examples of this group.[11]

It might be supposed that such cities would be distributed at least roughly in proportion to population. But other considerations have been important, too. Naval bases obviously require good harbors, preferably away from important seaports. Airfields need space for large runways and they need clear skies. Cold weather and excessive rain or snow may seriously handicap military operations of any sort. Such factors are no doubt important in explaining the location of so many of these bases in the southern half of the country and especially in the Southwest. And, unquestionably, po-

[11] Nelson, "A Service Classification of American Cities," p. 200.

litical pressures are important in bringing bases to some localities.

Observable characteristics   Capital cities are readily recognizable by the capitol buildings and their attendant office buildings, often set in parklike surroundings. Hotels are numerous in capital cities, for transient needs are great. The presence of large hotels tends to make capital cities attractive convention places. And no doubt the central location and general attractiveness of many capital cities also contribute to the desirability of these towns for conventions.

Cities near military installations, in contrast to capital cities, have few exclusive distinguishing characteristics within the cities themselves. The nearby military establishment, with its barracks, its administration buildings, its airfields, and the like, is distinctive enough, but it generally lies several miles from the city. Bars, poolrooms, and pawnshops are likely to be abundant in the city, and bars and drive-in restaurants frequently line the public roads leading to the post limits. Transient housing accommodations—apartments, rooming houses, motels, and trailer parks—typically are numerous, but this is likely to be true of capital cities also.

Social and economic characteristics   Possibly because of the somewhat diverse bedfellows which the class includes, public administration cities can hardly be said to have any very distinctive social and economic characteristics (Table 9.1).

Finance-Insurance-Real Estate Cities

In 123 cities, according to Nelson, the services of finance, insurance, and real estate are performed in outstanding proportions (Figure 9.8). It is significant that these cities include most of the country's largest cities. Four of the five largest cities

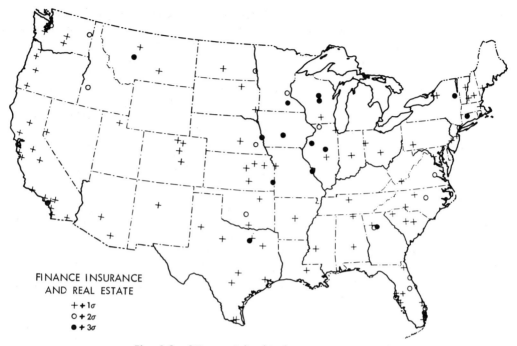

Fig. 9.8 Cities specialized in finance, insurance, and real estate, 1950. (From Howard J. Nelson, "A Service Classification of American Cities," *Economic Geography,* vol. 31, 1955, fig. 9.)

in the United States and seventeen of the twenty-five largest are specialized to some degree in this category (Table 9.2). Most of them are Federal Reserve Bank cities or else have branches of such banks. Large cities seem to attract financial and related activities. The fact that these great cities have enough concentration of such services to show up as specialized in finance, insurance, and real estate is remarkable, nevertheless, when it is remembered that the diversity of occupations in a large city makes it difficult for the city to have an outstanding proportion of its work force in any one activity.

Importance of finance, insurance, and real estate Actually, this category is made up of three related services—finance, insurance, and real estate—services which, in some combination, are a necessary complement to every line of economic activity.

This helps to explain why cities in this category are so numerous and so widespread (Figure 9.8). Though most of the large cities of the country show some specialization in the finance-insurance-real estate category, such specialization is by no means limited to the great cities and few great cities attain the F2 class. Dallas is the largest city with an F3 rating.

The three services in relation to city size The three lines of service show interesting relationships to city size. Though banking is the chief activity in this category in very large cities, insurance companies are often drawn to them, too. But insurance is more concentrated in certain smaller cities, such as Hartford, Connecticut (F3), and Des Moines, Iowa (F3), which are only moderately important as banking centers. In fact, most of the F3 cities are insurance centers. Finally, as Nelson points out, some

Table 9.2   Functional classifications of twenty-five largest urbanized areas ranked in order of size (size is based on population of urbanized areas in 1960; classifications according to Nelson, who based his work on 1950 data)

Urbanized areas	1960 population	Classification	Urbanized areas	1960 population	Classification
New York–Northeastern N.J.	14,114,927	F2	Baltimore, Md.	1,418,948	D
Los Angeles–Long Beach, Calif.	6,488,791	F	Minneapolis–St. Paul, Minn.	1,377,143	F2W
Chicago–Northwestern Ind.	5,959,213	F	Milwaukee, Wis.	1,149,997	D
Philadelphia, Pa.	3,635,228	F	Houston, Tex.	1,139,678	F
Detroit, Mich.	3,537,709	Mf	Buffalo, N.Y.	1,054,370	D
San Francisco–Oakland, Calif.	2,430,663	F2	Cincinnati, Ohio	993,568	D
Boston, Mass.	2,413,236	F	Dallas, Tex.	932,349	F3W
Washington, D.C.	1,808,423	Pb3F	Kansas City, Mo.	921,121	F
Pittsburgh, Pa.	1,804,400	D	Seattle, Wash.	864,109	F2
Cleveland, Ohio	1,784,991	D	Miami, Fla.	852,705	Ps3RF
St. Louis, Mo.	1,667,693	D	New Orleans, La.	845,237	TWF
			San Diego, Calif.	836,175	Pb2PsF
			Denver, Colo.	803,624	WF
			Atlanta, Ga.	768,125	F2

of the smallest F3 cities, like Newport Beach, California, and Fort Lauderdale and Hollywood, Florida, are real estate centers.[12]

Distinctive features Are there distinctive ways in which the appearance of finance-insurance-real estate centers reflects their specialization? This is hardly to be expected for the class as a whole because of the range in size from great cities to small and the somewhat different activities included in the category. But three variants do suggest themselves. First, one sees the great banks and associated offices of the large city, culminating in such famous financial districts as Wall Street. Second, are the office buildings of insurance companies that give character to Hartford and certain other moderate- to small-sized cities; they may be present in the great cities, too, but do not stand out since they are among many tall buildings. And, third, one gets the picture of a small, rapidly growing urban center in Florida or California with a multiplicity of real estate offices. But these are only

[12] Nelson, "A Service Classification of American Cities," p. 203.

glimpses, obviously representing extremes. The finance-insurance-real estate group is far too diverse to produce any landscape features that can be said to differentiate this service class from all others.

Social and economic characteristics For much the same reason one could hardly expect to find typical social and economic features among all finance-insurance-real estate cities. But study of the social and economic characteristics of the subtypes—of insurance cities, for example, or of real estate centers—might prove rewarding.

Personal Service Cities

Mostly resort and retirement towns Ninety-two cities in the United States are specialized to some degree in "personal service," a category under which Nelson includes the following industry groups listed in Table 35 of state volumes of the *United States Census of Population: 1950*, Volume II: hotels and lodging places, other personal services, and entertainment and recreational services. Generally, according to Nelson, personal service cities are urban centers that for one reason or another attract a transient or at least a semitransient population, and thus, in the Ps3 and Ps2 range, they consist mostly of resort and retirement towns.[13]

Size Personal service cities tend to be small. San Diego, Miami, and San Antonio are the only ones that can be regarded as really substantial in size.

Associated with other functions The personal service specialty rarely occurs alone. Professional service and public administration are common associates of personal service, and retailing even more so. The association of retailing with personal service is particularly common in resort and retirement cities, often with some speciali-

[13] Ps1 is not considered to represent a sufficient concentration to justify calling such a place a resort or retirement town.

zation in the finance-insurance-real estate category as well. Note, for example, the following Florida cities: Miami (Ps3RF), Fort Lauderdale (F3Ps2R), Daytona Beach (Ps3F2R), and Hollywood (Ps3F3). No doubt in these cities it is the real estate branch of the finance-insurance-real estate category that is most important as an associate of personal service specialization.

Locational characteristics The fact that so many personal service cities are resort and retirement centers accounts for a peculiarity of distribution. Though they are widely scattered, two-thirds of the personal service centers are in the southern half of the country, with a particularly great concentration in Florida and a lesser one in California (Figure 9.9). Thus it is clear that winter resorts predominate, though Northern resort cities like Saratoga Springs and Atlantic City also are represented.

Fig. 9.9 Cities specialized in personal service, 1950. (From Howard J. Nelson, "A Service Classification of American Cities," *Economic Geography*, vol. 31, 1955, fig. 6.)

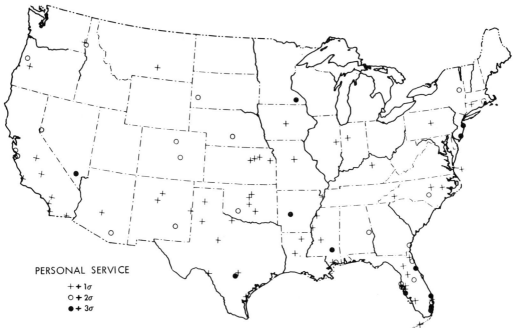

PERSONAL SERVICE

+ + 1σ
○ + 2σ
● + 3σ

Florida versus California The map shows nearly twice as many towns with personal service specialization in Florida as in California. One wonders why. Of course, Florida can draw on the great urban concentrations of the Northeast, from which it is not too far to be easily reached for stays of a few days up to several months. So Florida has a better basis for resort development than California does, as well as much the same opportunities for a retirement business. But there is another reason for the contrast. California has a better basis for a diversified economy in which the resort and retirement industries are submerged.

Many resort centers are too small to be shown Nelson's personal service category fails to include a number of well-known resort centers which are less than 10,000 in population. One looks in vain for such places as White Sulphur Springs, West Virginia; Bar Harbor, Maine; Estes Park, Colorado; and various others. This is a difficulty inherent partly in the nature of resort centers: many of them are small. The same problem was found, it will be recalled, with mining centers (see page 142). To work with smaller urban centers in the classification, however, would have been impracticable (see footnote 9, page 117).

Not all personal service cities are resort centers The personal service classification has another disadvantage as far as distinguishing resort and retirement centers is concerned. Not all of the places showing personal service specialization are resort towns, though it may be assumed that if not they are in some degree retirement places. Some small college towns and other professional towns are included; and a number of garrison towns, too, have some specialization in personal service.

Social and economic characteristics Since personal service so often occurs in combination with other specializations, it is difficult to generalize about the social and economic characteristics of the class. On the whole, cities showing Ps3 and Ps2 ranking seem to be gaining in population more rapidly than cities in other categories, the proportion of people sixty-five years old or over tends to be higher, and there is a lower average percentage of the men of these communities in the labor force. In view of the retirement element, we might expect, too, to find a fairly high death rate.

Distinctive features Resort towns have distinctive features that can be pointed out. Local natural advantages of beaches, mountains, and the like are combined in such places with the more standardized resort features. The commercial aspect of these towns is likely to be strongly developed. The shops have a cosmopolitan atmosphere, and hotels and motels are numerous. Swimming pools, riding stables, tennis courts, golf courses, and, in some areas, gambling casinos are common. Manufacturing is usually not a welcome addition to these towns, and it is never prevalent in a sufficient amount to cause a city to be specialized in both personal service and manufacturing. Wholesaling, transportation, and mining rarely mix with personal service, but some lines of financial interest do, and real estate offices are ubiquitous in most resort cities.

The emphasis in the foregoing paragraph was on resort towns because they are likely to be particularly striking in appearance. Where there is less of the resort function, but more retired people, towns tend to be more nearly like the average American urban center.

Diversified Cities

Nelson showed some cities as diversified; so, too, did Harris. And the patterns of distribution of diversified cities in the two studies are similar: such places are largely concentrated in the eastern half of the country except in Florida; and there are a few in the Far West, particularly in the Northwest (Figure 9.10). This similarity of distribution is remarkable in view of the different definitions of diversified that were used in the two classifications.

Harris's concept of diversified cities Harris classed as diversified those cities in which "employment in manufacturing, wholesaling, and retailing is less than 60 per cent, 20 per cent, and 50 per cent respectively of the total employment in these activities" (see Table 8.1). In such cities, though both trade and manufacturing are well developed, neither is clearly dominant. In short, for Harris, diversified cities were likely to be cities that had considerable manufacturing but had developed a large amount of trade also, or retailing centers that had developed local industries to the point where retailing was no longer clearly

dominant. In other words, diversity represented various stages between manufacturing cities and trade centers.

Nelson's concept of diversified cities Nelson, on the other hand, in his definition of diversity, gives no special place to manufacturing or to trade. Instead, he restricts the diversity category to places that do not have a sufficiently high proportion of the labor force in any activity to be considered specialized. It follows that in Nelson's classification there can be no degrees of diversity, as there are for his other classes, nor can it occur in combination with any other category. The same is true of Harris's diversity category, of course, since all of his classes are mutually exclusive.

Nelson found a total of 246 diversified cities, more than for any line of specialization he studied. The cities ran the gamut from large to small. Pittsburgh, St. Louis, Cleveland, Baltimore, Milwaukee, and Cincinnati are among the large ones.

Fig. 9.10 Diversified cities, 1950. (From Howard J. Nelson, "A Service Classification of American Cities," *Economic Geography*, vol. 31, 1955, fig. 11.)

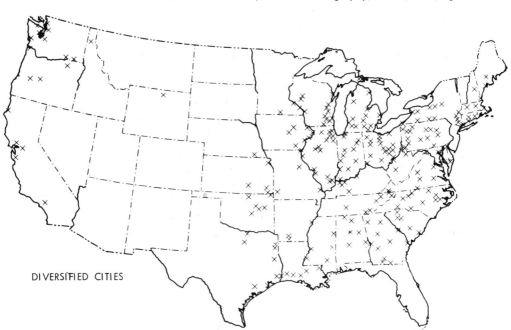

DIVERSIFIED CITIES

Average American cities? It is interesting to speculate about the significance of the diversified city. At first glance it might appear to be just a sort of "all others" category, a receptacle for cities that did not qualify for any one of the special ratings. But in reality the diversified city, as Nelson defines it, represents a city close to the country average.

Other Classes of Cities

In this chapter, ten more or less distinct classes of cities have been discussed. They are the ones differentiated by Nelson. Harris had nine classes, and Ohlson and Jones each distinguished eleven. This does not mean, however, that there are just ten functional classes of cities, or nine or eleven.

Within the limits of census data a great many more "classes" could be distinguished. Alexandersson studied thirty-six industry groups (see pp. 125–126), thus, in a sense, differentiating many more classes of urban centers or classes and subclasses than did the others. For instance, instead of having a transportation and communications class, as Nelson did, Alexandersson studied cities in terms of each of the following: railroads and railway express service; trucking service and warehousing; other transportation; and telecommunications. This high degree of detail served very well Alexandersson's purpose of examining the industrial structure of American cities. It should be kept in mind, in any event, that the number of distinct classes discussed in this chapter is by no means the extreme. Many more could have been differentiated and discussed.

Recently, another class of city has been suggested: the management center.[14] It is closely related to financial specialization and yet cannot adequately be measured in terms of employment. Instead, it has been defined as a concentration of headquarters

offices of nationally important companies. The concept involves the presence of a considerable number of such offices and of very substantial gross assets. Naturally, New York leads, with Chicago second, but beyond this the order of cities varies, depending upon the exact criteria used.

Regional Contrasts

A subject that has a good deal of interest for the geographer is the degree to which city classes vary regionally. This topic ranges from contrasts in distribution of classes of cities to the question of whether or not class characteristics vary with the section of the country.

Regional variations in distribution A fact that has been emphasized throughout the chapter is that there are marked regional variations in the classes of cities that predominate. The Northeast has a particularly striking concentration of manufacturing cities. There is a disproportionate concentration of cities classified as retail trade centers and wholesale trade centers in a north-south belt between the Rockies and the Mississippi River. Balancing this belt of concentration of retail and wholesale cities is the virtual absence of cities with these specializations in the Northeast. Still another peculiarity of distribution, though not a surprising one, is the location of at least two-thirds of the cities with personal service specialization in the southern half of the country. Other, more subtle, anomalies in the regional predominance of city types have already been indicated. It is interesting to note that, in the instances mentioned at least, the maps of both Harris and Nelson show these regional variations in spite of differences in the techniques and data used.

Regional variations in social and economic characteristics Nelson produced evidence to show that the classes of cities

---

[14] William Goodwin, "The Management Center in the United States," *Geographical Review*, vol. 55, 1965, pp. 1–16.

he differentiated tend to reflect the regions in which they occur. For example, for the most part, the cities in the West have been growing faster than the national mean, and, in most service classes, the average growth of cities in the West has been more rapid than the class mean.[15] This is true, too, for other social and economic characteristics—years of school completed, median income, etc. There is a tendency for each Western city to show its own class features but to reflect, also, those of its region: higher or lower than the average for its class depending on whether the regional tendency is higher or lower.

Nelson found the regional effect to be particularly strong for the West. The fact that it is a relatively young area within the nation is repeatedly reflected. The South, too, has strong regional characteristics which tend to be carried over to the cities of each service group. On the other hand, Nelson points out that the Northeast and North Central sections of the country do not have as strong regional qualities as the West and South, so neither region is as strongly reflected in the individual city classes in these areas.

Regional variations in observable characteristics An attempt has been made to generalize about the appearance of each class of city. It would be logical to carry the inquiry one step further and to ask, Do the distinctive features of different classes of cities vary region by region? For example, do manufacturing centers in the Northeast differ in appearance from manufacturing centers in the South or the West? No doubt they do, but it seems likely that such observable contrasts are slight compared with those between classes, and we can hardly hope to point them out very successfully until we can do a better job of characterizing cities of each class.

[15] Nelson, "Some Characteristics of the Population of Cities in Similar Service Classifications," pp. 103–107.

Conclusions

In this chapter and the preceding one, certain tentative generalizations have been presented. A classification itself is a generalization, and as we attempt to explain the distribution patterns and to associate various characteristics with the functional types, we are generalizing still more. Consideration of how the city classes may vary regionally carries the process still further.

Emphasis should be placed on the tentative nature of the generalizations. Since there is no general agreement on the best method of classifying cities functionally, it follows that generalizations based on such classifications can at best be little more than beginnings. But our concern in this book is not so much with facts as with methods of inquiry and with the sorts of things that can be investigated. In a sense, what has been presented is the current state of the inquiry regarding functional classes of cities and the characteristics of these classes.

Selected References

Alexander, John W.: "Rockford, Illinois: A Medium-sized Manufacturing City," *Annals of the Association of American Geographers*, vol. 42, pp. 1–23, 1952.

Alexandersson, Gunnar: *The Industrial Structure of American Cities*, University of Nebraska Press, Lincoln, Nebr., 1956.

Camu, Pierre: "Notes on Port Studies," *The Canadian Geographer*, no. 6, pp. 51–59, 1955.

Chambers, William T.: "Kilgore, Texas: An Oil Boom Town," *Economic Geography*, vol. 9, pp. 72–84, 1933.

Cramer, Robert E.: *Manufacturing Structure of the Cicero District, Metropolitan Chicago*, doctoral dissertation, Research Paper 27, Department of Geography, University of Chicago, Chicago, 1952.

De Merlier, Mercel J.: *Manufactural Occupance in the West Central Area of Chicago*, doctoral dissertation, Research Paper 11, Department of Geography, University of Chicago, Chicago, 1950.

Fletcher, Merna Irene: "Rochester, Minnesota:

A Professional Town," *Economic Geography*, vol. 23, pp. 143–151, 1947.

Gold, Robert N.: *Manufacturing Structure and Pattern of the South Bend–Mishawaka Area*, Research Paper 36, Department of Geography, University of Chicago, Chicago, 1954.

Goodwin, William: "The Management Center in the United States," *Geographical Review*, vol. 55, 1965, pp. 1–16.

Harris, Chauncy D.: "A Functional Classification of Cities in the United States," *Geographical Review*, vol. 33, pp. 86–99, 1943.

Murphy, Raymond E.: "A Southern West Virginia Mining Community," *Economic Geography*, vol. 9, pp. 51–59, 1933.

———: "Johnstown and York: A Comparative Study of Two Industrial Cities," *Annals of the Association of American Geographers*, vol. 25, pp. 175–196, 1935.

——— and Marion Murphy: "Anthracite Region of Pennsylvania," *Economic Geography*, vol. 14, pp. 338–348, 1938.

Nelson, Howard J.: "A Service Classification of American Cities," *Economic Geography*, vol. 31, pp. 189–210, 1955.

———: "Some Characteristics of the Population of Cities in Similar Service Classifications," *Economic Geography*, vol. 33, pp. 95–108, 1957.

Parker, Margaret Terrell: *Lowell: A Study of Industrial Development*, The Macmillan Company, New York, 1940.

———: "Tucson: City of Sunshine," *Economic Geography*, vol. 24, pp. 79–113, 1948.

Weaver, John C.: "Silver Peak and Blair: Desert Mining Communities," *Economic Geography*, vol. 15, pp. 80–84, 1939.

Weigend, Guido G.: "Some Elements in the Study of Port Geography," *Geographical Review*, vol. 48, pp. 185–200, 1958.

Wrigley, Robert, Jr.: "Pocatello, Idaho, as a Railroad Center," *Economic Geography*, vol. 19, pp. 325–336, 1943.

CHAPTER 10

People in
the city

MAN is important in all branches of urban geography, since the city is, after all, man's creation and, nowadays, in large sections of the world, the principal home of man. But there are some portions of the field that deal more directly than others with people. In the present chapter we shall focus particularly on these human phases of urban geography.

The human and social aspects of urban geography can be considered as they characterize the city as a whole, thus tending to differentiate cities from one another and to give a basis for regional contrasts; and they can be dealt with for the interior of the urban area, where they form various patterns. Both levels of approach can lead to interesting generalizations about cities; both will concern us in this chapter.

City Size

City size means city population Size is a fundamental aspect of a city, one that is likely to be thought of first, and city size normally is expressed in terms of people. To a certain degree, size can be inferred from the city's area,[1] the heights of buildings near the center, the density of traffic, and the number of people on the streets. But these indicators furnish only rough, rule-of-thumb methods of estimating size. We are likely to use, instead, the population total for the city as given on a road map or in an atlas, and this total in turn usually is based upon United States Census sources.

City size in relation to city concept The size of a particular city varies, of

[1] The unreliability of this relationship was emphasized in 1963 when, through a process of widespread annexation, Oklahoma City became by far the largest city in the United States in *area*. But it was still only a moderate-sized city according to the normal measure of city size, population.

course, depending upon the way the city is defined. Traditionally, the incorporated or legal city has been the area for which population is given. Though it leaves much to be desired as an expression of the urban agglomeration, it must be remembered that the corporate city is a definite legal entity and that, for a variety of purposes, knowing its exact population is important.

There are, however, two other "cities" for which population totals are given by the Census Bureau (Table 10.1): the urbanized area, or physical city, and the standard metropolitan statistical area, or metropolitan community. These were discussed in some detail in Chapter 2. Either one is often more expressive of the urban agglomeration as a whole than is the legal city. Perhaps some day population of the urbanized area or of the standard metropolitan statistical area will supplant that of the incorporated city as the popular basis for giving the size of an urban agglomeration, but, if so, totals for corporate units will still be needed. In the meanwhile, city size is nearly always expressed as population of the corporate city, though locally the people of a city may recognize the inadequacy of the total and may even be able to give a rough population estimate for their "metropolitan area" or their "greater city."

Distribution of cities as a basic pattern

A possible theoretical basis for explaining patterns of distribution of urban centers was discussed in Chapter 5. Regardless of the causes of distributions, however, the way cities of varying sizes are distributed forms one of the basic patterns of urban geography. It is important for its own sake, but even more as an aid to understanding patterns of city distribution based on other social and economic factors.

Population Densities of Cities

Density of population as a city measure

Closely related to city size is the popu- lation density of the city. Ordinarily, this is expressed as persons per square mile of city land area rather than of total city area, thus excluding lakes or other water bodies. Since it combines two important attributes of the city—population and area—urban density might appear, at first glance, to furnish an ideal basis for city comparisons. But it is a comparative measure that has distinct limitations and one that must be used with caution.

Factors accounting for variations in density

What factors are involved in the variations in population density from one city to another? They include city definition, city size, site, original layout (e.g., street width), age, history, dominant housing types, state annexation laws, city policy in setting boundaries, possible nearness of a larger urban center and relations with it, architectural type of city, urban function, and probably a number of others.

City population density in relation to city definition

In considering city population densities one must always inquire, first, about the city definitions on which the density figures are based. Normally, population density is given for the corporate city, but it was pointed out earlier in this book that the corporate boundary does a poor job of outlining the real population agglomeration. The density for the corporate city is usually the density of the older portion of the urban agglomeration; suburban areas are not included. Whereas some cities have been able to expand their areas through annexation and to keep up fairly well with the geographic or real city, others, particularly in older sections of the country, in effect have had their legal boundaries frozen for many years. Density based on the urbanized area of the city is more realistic than density based on the corporate city, but we have found that even the urbanized area is often a poor areal expression of the geographic city (see Chapter 2). In practice, it is more

Table 10.1   The twenty-five largest urban agglomerations in the United States in 1960 according to three different "city" definitions

Corporate cities		Urbanized areas		SMSAs	
City	Population	Area name	Population	Area name	Population
1 New York, N.Y.	7,781,984	1 New York–North-eastern N.J.	14,114,927	1 New York, N.Y.	10,694,633
2 Chicago, Ill.	3,550,404	2 Los Angeles–Long Beach, Calif.	6,488,791	2 Los Angeles–Long Beach, Calif.	6,742,696
3 Los Angeles, Calif.	2,479,015	3 Chicago–North-western Ind.	5,959,213	3 Chicago, Ill.	6,220,913
4 Philadelphia, Pa.	2,002,512	4 Philadelphia, Pa.–N.J.	3,635,228	4 Philadelphia, Pa.–N.J.	4,342,897
5 Detroit, Mich.	1,670,144	5 Detroit, Mich.	3,537,709	5 Detroit, Mich.	3,762,360
6 Baltimore, Md.	939,024	6 San Francisco–Oakland, Calif.	2,430,663	6 San Francisco–Oakland, Calif.	2,783,359
7 Houston, Tex.	938,219	7 Boston, Mass.	2,413,236	7 Boston, Mass.	2,589,301
8 Cleveland, Ohio	876,050	8 Washington, D.C.–Md.–Va.	1,808,423	8 Pittsburgh, Pa.	2,405,435
9 Washington, D.C.	763,956	9 Pittsburgh, Pa.	1,804,400	9 St. Louis, Mo.–Ill.	2,060,103
10 St. Louis, Mo.	750,026	10 Cleveland, Ohio	1,784,991	10 Washington, D.C.–Md.–Va.	2,001,897
11 San Francisco, Calif.	742,855	11 St. Louis, Mo.–Ill.	1,667,693	11 Cleveland, Ohio	1,796,595
12 Milwaukee, Wis.	741,324	12 Baltimore, Md.	1,418,948	12 Baltimore, Md.	1,727,023
13 Boston, Mass.	697,197	13 Minneapolis–St. Paul, Minn.	1,377,143	13 Newark, N.J.	1,689,420
14 Dallas, Tex.	679,684	14 Milwaukee, Wis.	1,149,997	14 Minneapolis–St. Paul, Minn.	1,482,030
15 New Orleans, La.	627,525	15 Houston, Tex.	1,139,678	15 Buffalo, N.Y.	1,306,957
16 Pittsburgh, Pa.	604,332	16 Buffalo, N.Y.	1,054,370	16 Houston, Tex.	1,243,158
17 San Antonio, Tex.	587,718	17 Cincinnati, Ohio–Ky.	993,568	17 Milwaukee, Wis.	1,194,290
18 San Diego, Calif.	573,224	18 Dallas, Tex.	932,349	18 Paterson–Clifton–Passaic, N.J.	1,186,873
19 Seattle, Wash.	557,087	19 Kansas City, Mo.–Kans.	921,121	19 Seattle, Wash.	1,107,213
20 Buffalo, N.Y.	532,759	20 Seattle, Wash.	864,109	20 Dallas, Tex.	1,083,601
21 Cincinnati, Ohio	502,550	21 Miami, Fla.	852,705	21 Cincinnati, Ohio–Ky.	1,071,624
22 Memphis, Tenn.	497,524	22 New Orleans, La.	845,237	22 Kansas City, Mo.–Kans.	1,039,493
23 Denver, Colo.	493,887	23 San Diego, Calif.	836,175	23 San Diego, Calif.	1,033,011
24 Atlanta, Ga.	487,455	24 Denver, Colo.	803,624	24 Atlanta, Ga.	1,017,188
25 Minneapolis, Minn.	482,872	25 Atlanta, Ga.	768,125	25 Miami, Fla.	935,047

SOURCE: Data from 1960 *Census of Population.*

common to speak of the density of the corporate city since the latter is much better known than the urbanized area and, in many ways, operates as a unit.

City population density and relief

Population density as a basis for comparing either corporate cities or urbanized areas has a disadvantage that is sometimes overlooked. It takes no account of the nature of the site. If a city is located on rugged terrain, the number of persons per unit of area may be comparatively low and yet the usable land may be seriously overcrowded. Anyone familiar with Pittsburgh's rugged site, for example, must realize that residential crowding in that city is considerably more serious than would be expected from the city's population density of 11,171 persons per square mile in 1960. In other words, the city's *real* density is substantially greater than the simple man-land ratio indicates. Unfortunately, however, comparable real densities of cities would be extremely difficult to determine, so we have to be content with ordinary population density ratios.

Great cities and great density

The significance of population density as an expression of the city seems to be borne out if we look at the densities of some of the world's great cities. New York City, for instance, had a density of 24,697 per square mile within its city limits in 1960. Though customs among countries differ with respect to city boundaries, making exact comparisons with other world cities impossible, this density for New York City is apparently of about the same order of magnitude as the comparable figures for other giant cities. According to Harris, Paris had a density of 27,000 per square mile in 1936; London, 28,600 in 1951 (county of London); and Tokyo, 30,000 in 1940.[2]

[2] Chauncy D. Harris, "The Pressure of Residential-Industrial Land Use," in William L. Thomas, Jr. (ed.), *Man's Role in Changing the Face of the*

The fact that these giant cities all have comparatively great population densities seems reasonable enough. After all, a great city represents a sort of massing or piling up of people, reflected in a high proportion of high-density housing types (Figure 10.1). Though dwelling density normally declines toward the city's edge, the average density for the city as a whole is likely to be high.

Population density and city size

With smaller and smaller cities it would seem that there would be less and less of the agglomerative effect and therefore lower and lower densities.

THE URBAN PLACES LIST If one turns to the list of urban places as given by the U.S. Census Bureau, however,[3] he will find it difficult to discern any relationship between size of urban place and population density. But the list for 1960 is a long one: the Census Bureau included 4,699 incorporated places and 620 that were unincorporated. In such an extensive list it is only to be expected that some urban places would depart far from any regular size-density relationship and that any limited section of the list might show little evidence of density varying with size, even though, when the places were all averaged together by size groups, the relationship might hold.

POPULATION AND DENSITY IN GROUPS OF PLACES Average population density may be calculated for groups of urban places classified as to size. When this was done by the Census Bureau for 1960, it was found that population per square mile was less for each successively smaller size class (Table 10.2). "Among urban places, the number of inhabitants per square mile decreased as the size of place decreased."[4]

Earth, University of Chicago Press, Chicago, 1956, p. 887.
[3] U.S. Bureau of the Census, *Census of Population: 1960*, vol. I, part A, *Number of Inhabitants*, 1961, *United States Summary*, table 30.
[4] *Ibid.*, Introduction, p. xiii.

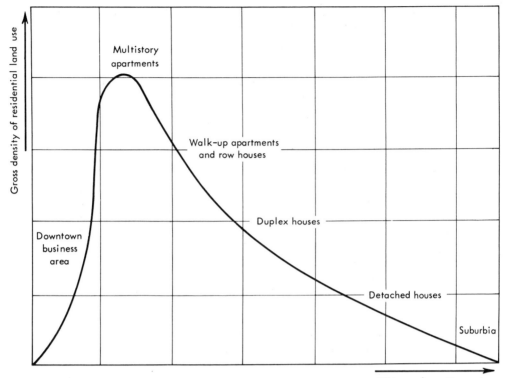

Fig. 10.1 Schematic relationship of population density to distance from city center in relation to type of housing. (After Marion Clawson, R. Burnell Held, and Charles H. Stoddard, *Land for the Future*, Baltimore, 1960, fig. 6.)

Table 10.2 **Population and density in groups of places classified according to size, the United States, 1960**

Places with population of	Population per sq mi of land area for group
1,000,000 or more	13,865
500,000–1,000,000	5,885
250,000– 500,000	4,484
100,000– 250,000	4,271
50,000– 100,000	3,910
25,000– 50,000	2,811
10,000– 25,000	2,532
5,000– 10,000	1,954
2,500– 5,000	1,446

SOURCE: Based on U.S. Bureau of the Census, *Census of Population: 1960*, vol. 1, part A, *Number of Inhabitants, Introduction*, table E, p. xiii.

MANY URBAN PLACES WITH HIGH DENSITIES ARE SUBURBS OR SATELLITES A ranked list of the twenty-five most densely populated incorporated urban places in the United States, together with the population total of each, is presented here as Table 10.3. No correlation is apparent between densities and sizes of urban places, but this is not surprising in view of the small number of places included. However, the table is of interest in another respect: it shows that a number of urban places of less than 100,000 population have high densities. This fact might appear to contradict the idea of density decreasing with city size. But most of the small urban places of high density that appear on the list border great cities and partake of the great city densities. Nearly half are suburbs or satellites of New York City, and some of the others bear similar re-

Table 10.3   The twenty-five most densely populated incorporated urban places in the United States in 1960

Rank in density	Name of urban place	Population per sq mi of land area	Population	Area, sq mi
1	Union City, N.J.	40,138	52,180	1.3
2	Lakeview, Tex.	38,490	3,849	0.1
3	Hoboken, N.J.	37,262	48,441	1.3
4	West New York, N.J.	32,315	35,547	1.1
5	Guttenberg, N.J.	25,590	5,118	0.2
6	New York, N.Y.	24,697	7,781,984	315.1
7	Braddock, Pa.	24,674	12,337	0.5
8	Somerville, Mass.	23,097	94,697	4.1
9	Jersey City, N.J.	21,239	276,101	13.0
10	Central Falls, R.I.	19,858	19,858	1.0
11	Cliffside Park, N.J.	19,602	17,642	0.9
12	East Orange, N.J.	19,315	77,259	4.0
13	Irvington, N.J.	19,155	59,379	3.1
14	Mount Vernon, N.Y.	18,539	76,010	4.1
15	Passaic, N.J.	17,407	53,963	3.1
16	Newark, N.J.	17,170	405,220	23.6
17	Paterson, N.J.	17,103	143,663	8.4
18	Cambridge, Mass.	17,098	107,716	6.3
19	Shamokin, Pa.	17,093	13,674	0.8
20	Mahanoy City, Pa.	17,072	8,536	0.5
21	Mount Rainier, Md.	16,425	9,855	0.6
22	Dormont, Pa.	16,373	13,098	0.8
23	Orange, N.J.	16,268	35,789	2.2
24	Hamtramck, Mich.	16,256	34,137	2.1
25	East Lansdowne, Pa.	16,120	3,224	0.2

SOURCE: Data from U.S. Bureau of the Census, *Census of Population, 1960,* vol. I, part A, *Number of Inhabitants, United States Summary,* table 30.

lationships to other large cities, especially old eastern cities. Some of them tend to be almost entirely residential, which helps to account for the high densities.

DENSELY POPULATED CENTRAL CITIES Few such high-density suburbs and satellites appear in Table 10.4, chiefly because the table is not based on all urban places but on the central cities of urbanized areas. Jersey City, Passaic, Newark, and Paterson, besides being central cities of the New York–Northeastern New Jersey Urbanized Area, are also essentially satellites of New York City, but there are few other places on the list that are at all suburban in character.

The high densities of such small central cities as Trenton, York, and Reading require some explanation. Small original lot sizes and narrow streets, the presence of "continuous row" houses or other types of housing conducive to high densities, corporate boundaries virtually impossible to change because of incorporation of all adjacent areas, site limitations—these and doubtless various other factors enter into the explanations of the high densities of these small Eastern central cities.

LOW DENSITIES CHARACTERISTIC OF WESTERN CITIES Los Angeles and Houston are particularly interesting exceptions to the

Table 10.4 The fifty most densely peopled central cities of urbanized areas in the United States in 1960

Density rank	City	Population per sq mi of land area	Area, sq mi	City size	Density rank	City	Population per sq mi of land area	Area sq mi	City size
1	New York, N.Y.	24,697	315.1	7,781,984	26	Pawtucket, R.I.	9,419	8.6	81,001
2	Jersey City, N.J.	21,239	13.0	276,101	27	Hartford, Conn.	9,321	17.4	162,178
3	Passaic, N.J.	17,407	3.1	53,963	28	Wilkes-Barre, Pa.	9,210	6.9	63,551
4	Newark, N.J.	17,170	23.6	405,220	29	Bridgeport, Conn.	8,757	15.1	156,748
5	Paterson, N.J.	17,103	8.4	143,663	30	Rochester, N.Y.	8,753	36.4	318,611
6	San Francisco, Calif.	16,599	44.6	740,316	31	Syracuse, N.Y.	8,642	25.0	216,038
7	Chicago, Ill.	15,836	224.2	3,550,404	32	Minneapolis, Minn.	8,546	56.5	482,872
8	Philadelphia, Pa.	15,743	127.2	2,002,512	33	Miami, Fla.	8,529	34.2	291,688
9	Trenton, N.J.	15,428	7.4	114,167	34	New Haven, Conn.	8,494	17.9	152,048
10	Boston, Mass.	14,586	47.8	697,197	35	Lancaster, Pa.	8,364	7.3	61,055
11	Buffalo, N.Y.	13,522	39.4	532,759	36	Milwaukee, Wis.	8,137	91.1	741,324
12	Charleston, S.C.	12,926	5.1	65,925	37	Racine, Wis.	7,959	11.2	89,144
13	Washington, D.C.	12,442	61.4	763,956	38	Canton, Ohio	7,946	14.3	113,631
14	St. Louis, Mo.	12,296	61.0	750,026	39	Schenectady, N.Y.	7,930	10.3	81,682
15	Detroit, Mich.	11,964	139.6	1,670,144	40	Dayton, Ohio	7,808	33.6	262,332
16	Baltimore, Md.	11,886	79.0	1,418,948	41	Champaign, Ill.	7,747	6.4	49,583
17	York, Pa.	11,597	4.7	54,504	42	Altoona, Pa.	7,712	9.0	69,407
18	Providence, R.I.	11,592	17.9	207,498	43	Long Beach, Calif.	7,498	45.9	344,168
19	Pittsburgh, Pa.	11,171	54.1	604,332	44	Erie, Pa.	7,364	18.8	138,440
20	Cleveland, Ohio	10,789	81.0	876,050	45	Grand Rapids, Mich.	7,267	24.4	177,313
21	Harrisburg, Pa.	10,486	7.6	79,697	46	Troy, N.Y.	7,257	9.3	67,492
22	Huntington, W.Va.	10,453	14.0	83,627	47	Lowell, Mass.	7,031	13.1	92,107
23	Reading, Pa.	10,227	9.6	98,177	48	Clifton, N.J.	7,016	11.7	82,084
24	Lawrence, Mass.	9,852	7.2	70,933	49	Binghamton, N.Y.	6,967	10.9	75,941
25	Johnstown, Pa.	9,634	5.6	53,949	50	Denver, Colo.	6,956	71.0	493,887

SOURCE: Data from U.S. Bureau of the Census, Census of Population, 1960, vol. 1, part A, Number of Inhabitants, United States Summary, table 22.

rule of large cities having great densities. Los Angeles, though third in size among United States cities, had a density in 1960 of only 5,451, much less than the densities of many substantially smaller cities (Table 10.5). The corporate city of Los Angeles is peculiarly spread out, with its boundary so drawn that Los Angeles had in 1960 the largest area of any city in the United States.[5] Houston, likewise, had a relatively low density, 2,860 in 1960, related to a liberal placing of its boundary.[6]

[5] For developments since 1960 see footnote 1 of this chapter.

[6] Houston's population density was only moderate, 3,726, even in 1950. From 1950 to 1960 the population increased 58 per cent, but since the area of

The fact that Los Angeles and Houston are missing from Table 10.4 focuses attention on a related point of interest: the table includes only five central cities west of the Mississippi River. This seems to give support to the idea that there is a new, low-density type of city which is in contrast to the old, high-density city. The latter is found chiefly in the East but San Francisco is a Western representative of the type. However, the contrast seems chiefly to result from the relatively liberal annexation laws that prevail in many of our Western and Southwestern states.

the city doubled through annexations the net effect was a decline in density.

Table 10.5   Population densities of fifty largest cities in the United States, 1960

Rank in size	City	Population density	Area, sq mi	Rank in size	City	Population density	Area, sq mi
1	New York, N.Y.	24,697	315.1	26	Indianapolis, Ind.	6,689	71.2
2	Chicago, Ill.	15,836	224.2	27	Kansas City, Mo.	3,664	129.8
3	Los Angeles, Calif.	5,451	454.8	28	Columbus, Ohio	4,423	89.0
4	Philadelphia, Pa.	15,743	127.2	29	Phoenix, Ariz.	2,343	187.4
5	Detroit, Mich.	11,964	139.6	30	Newark, N.J.	17,170	23.6
6	Baltimore, Md.	11,886	79.0	31	Louisville, Ky.	6,841	57.1
7	Houston, Tex.	2,860	328.1	32	Portland, Ore.	5,546	67.2
8	Cleveland, Ohio	10,789	81.0	33	Oakland, Calif.	6,935	53.0
9	Washington, D.C.	12,442	61.4	34	Fort Worth, Tex.	2,536	140.5
10	St. Louis, Mo.	12,296	61.0	35	Long Beach, Calif.	7,498	45.9
11	San Francisco, Calif.	15,553	44.6	36	Birmingham, Ala.	4,576	74.5
12	Milwaukee, Wis.	8,137	91.1	37	Oklahoma City, Okla.	1,009	321.5
13	Boston, Mass.	14,586	47.8	38	Rochester, N.Y.	8,753	36.4
14	Dallas, Tex.	2,428	279.9	39	Toledo, Ohio	6,598	48.2
15	New Orleans, La.	3,157	198.8	40	St. Paul, Minn.	6,004	52.2
16	Pittsburgh, Pa.	11,171	54.1	41	Norfolk, Va.	6,117	50.0
17	San Antonio, Tex.	3,662	160.5	42	Omaha, Nebr.	5,891	51.2
18	San Diego, Calif.	2,979	192.4	43	Honolulu, Hawaii	3,506	83.9
19	Seattle, Wash.	6,295	88.5	44	Miami, Fla.	8,529	34.2
20	Buffalo, N.Y.	13,522	39.4	45	Akron, Ohio	5,387	53.9
21	Cincinnati, Ohio	6,501	77.3	46	El Paso, Tex.	2,414	114.6
22	Memphis, Tenn.	3,881	128.2	47	Jersey City, N.J.	21,239	13.0
23	Denver, Colo.	6,956	71.0	48	Tampa, Fla.	3,235	85.0
24	Atlanta, Ga.	3,802	128.2	49	Dayton, Ohio	7,808	33.6
25	Minneapolis, Minn.	8,546	56.5	50	Tulsa, Okla.	5,475	47.8

SOURCE: U.S. Bureau of the Census, *Census of Population, 1960.*

Densities of urbanized areas This discussion of urban density in relation to size of urban center has been based on corporate units. It might be expected that urbanized areas, since they are more realistic than corporate units, would show a closer relationship between population and density. The urbanized areas of a number of our largest cities do, indeed, rank high in density (Table 10.6), with the New York–Northeastern New Jersey Urbanized Area highest of all, but there are some strange anomalies. For instance, the Racine Urbanized Area, the Champaign–Urbana Urbanized Area, and the urbanized area of

Kenosha, Wisconsin, are among the first ten in density. It is obvious that a number of factors other than city size must enter into explanations of these density differences. About all that can be said is that the urbanized areas of the very great cities tend to have high densities, probably for many of the same reasons that the great corporate cities themselves tend to rank high in this respect (see page 158).

Variations in density within the city Average city density, whether for corporate city or for the urbanized area, masks wide variations. Chauncy Harris points out that

Table 10.6   **The twenty-five most densely populated urbanized areas of the United States in 1960**

Rank in density	Area name	Population per sq mi of land area	Area, sq mi	Total population
1	New York–Northeastern N.J.	7,462	1,891.5	14,114,927
2	Buffalo, N.Y.	6,582	160.2	1,054,370
3	Racine, Wis.	6,566	14.6	95,862
4	Baltimore, Md.	6,441	220.3	1,418,948
5	Champaign–Urbana, Ill.	6,291	12.4	78,014
6	Chicago–Northwestern Ind.	6,209	959.8	5,959,213
7	Philadelphia, Pa.–N.J.	6,092	596.7	3,635,228
8	Kenosha, Wis.	5,519	13.2	72,852
9	Washington, D.C., Md.–Va.	5,308	340.7	1,808,423
10	Charleston, S.C.	5,198	30.8	160,113
11	St. Louis, Mo.–Ill.	5,160	323.2	1,667,693
12	Binghamton, N.Y.	5,101	31.0	158,141
13	Syracuse, N.Y.	4,923	67.7	333,286
14	Reading, Pa.	4,843	33.1	160,297
15	Detroit, Mich.	4,834	731.9	3,537,709
16	Denver, Colo.	4,824	166.6	803,624
17	Lima, Ohio	4,806	13.1	62,963
18	Los Angeles–Long Beach, Calif.	4,736	1,370.0	6,488,791
19	Lawton, Okla.	4,693	13.2	61,941
20	Boston, Mass.	4,679	515.8	2,413,236
21	Norfolk–Portsmouth, Va.	4,676	108.6	507,825
22	Miami, Fla.	4,657	183.1	852,705
23	Altoona, Pa.	4,614	18.0	83,058
24	Johnstown, Pa.	4,594	21.0	96,474
25	Laredo, Tex.	4,495	13.5	60,678

SOURCE: Data from U.S. Bureau of the Census, *Census of Population: 1960,* vol. I, part A, *Number of Inhabitants, United States Summary,* table 22.

in Chicago in 1950 the "community area" with the highest density had four times the average of the city of Chicago as a whole, and that two small census tracts had seven times the city average.[7] New York City has similar contrasts. For example, though the corporate city had a population density of 24,697 in 1960, Manhattan Borough's density was three times that great.

But any comparisons of cities on the basis of interior density patterns are questionable, since there are no areal units that are very satisfactory for the purpose. Suppose, for example, that we wished to compare density patterns of Cleveland with those of some other large city. Census tracts would hardly serve the purpose, since the corporate city of Cleveland is divided into more than two hundred tracts. We need a system of areal units considerably larger than census tracts that would be logical divisions for comparing interior density patterns. Community areas might come closer (see page 442), but perhaps an areal unit could be developed that would be really satisfactory for the purpose.

The Population Map

The discussion of variations in density in the interior of the city leads logically to the population map that can be made for a city. Though such a map normally is too fine-textured for the sorts of city comparisons just referred to, it does give a picture of the population distribution and densities for an individual city. In so doing it shows variations which, when explained, tell us much of the complete urban geography of the city. And it is through similar maps for a number of urban areas that generalizations are arrived at regarding population distribution within the American city. Here we are concerned with the problems involved in the making of a population distribution map of a city for the most recent decennial census year.

[7] Harris, *op. cit.*

Data and unit areas   Data for a population map of the city normally are obtained from the U.S. Bureau of the Census. Population data by enumeration districts are not published, but may be purchased for any city and are sometimes available at the local city planning office. Totals by city blocks are published for those cities for which block housing surveys have been conducted, and by census tracts for all tracted cities (for descriptions of tracts, enumeration districts, and city blocks, as well as various types of administrative divisions of the city, see Appendix B).

Availability of data varies with city size   For cities of 50,000 or more population, there are block housing data, enumeration district data, and normally data by census tracts, though not all cities of 50,000 population have been tracted. For a city of 25,000, only enumeration district data are likely to be available. Block housing data have not been published for cities of less than 50,000 population, except where a special arrangement was made in advance by the community to pay for such a survey. If the city of 25,000 population lies close to a large city, the tract system of the standard metropolitan statistical area may have been extended to include the small city; otherwise, it would not have census tracts.

Necessary decisions   Given the availability of data by the several types of areas mentioned, there are two principal decisions to be made before construction of the population map begins: how large an area should the map cover and what type of map should it be? The population map generally is based on the corporate city only, but it may cover a larger area. Often, census tracts have been laid out for the corporate city and a considerable adjacent area as well, and enumeration districts have been established for all areas. If block housing data are to be used, however, one is more restricted, since block housing surveys normally cover the corporate city only. As to the type of map to be made, there are two principal alternatives: the dot map and the choropleth map.[8]

The dot map of city population The dot map is usually considered the most effective method of showing population distribution in the city (Figure 10.2). Just how exact and detailed the map is depends on the exactness of the data used.

BLOCK DATA AND THE DOT MAP The most exact population distribution data now available for American cities are population totals by city blocks, given in city block bulletins of the Census of Housing for the first time in 1960. Each report includes a base map for the city at a scale of about 1 inch to 2,000 feet. Use of this scale and a dot value of ten or twenty persons permits considerable precision in the placing of dots. For large blocks, however, there is room for some variation. Here a land-use map or air-photo coverage is needed to guide the placing of the dots.[9]

VARYING SCALES AND DOT VALUES The map scale and dot value can be varied, depending upon the size of the city and the purpose of the dot map. For a small city (or for a small portion of a large city) it may be desirable, in order to avoid crowding, to reproduce the base map at a larger scale than it appears in the city blocks bulletin.

For a larger city, on the other hand, or for a substantial section of any city, it may be desirable to have the base map photographed down to a smaller scale and perhaps to use a larger dot value—say fifty or even more persons per dot. Enumeration districts or census tracts can be outlined on the map and enumeration district or tract populations used. The block totals can then serve as guides in locating the dots.

CITIES WITHOUT BLOCK HOUSING DATA For cities that do not have block housing data, and this includes most cities of less than 50,000 population, the use of Sanborn Atlas maps and a city directory in conjunction with enumeration district data has been recommended.[10] First, the boundaries of all enumeration districts are laid off on the base map, which presumably already shows block outlines. The number of dwelling units in each block is obtained with fair accuracy by counting the family dwelling units on the Sanborn maps (see discussion of Sanborn maps, page 189). A city directory is used to ascertain the number of apartments in each multiple-family building, since the Sanborn maps do not give this information but do give the address of each building. Because Sanborn maps usually do not cover the very sparsely populated fringes of cities, a small amount of supplementary field work may be necessary to complete the information regarding dwelling units. If there is any institutional population or if there are other persons in "group quarters" [11] this number is subtracted from the enumeration district total, and the remainder is divided by the number of dwelling units (as shown on the Sanborn maps) to get a population index per dwelling unit. This figure is used to calculate the population per block. As in making a dot map of a larger city, a land-use map is a desirable adjunct in placing the dots in the larger blocks. Though for most of the city much of this information can be obtained from the Sanborn maps, a general land-use map

---

[8] An isopleth map based on persons per square mile might be another possibility, but the values do not vary gradationally as they should for effective use of this technique.

[9] Use of these auxiliary sources may be of help in another respect. In the discussion of block housing data in Appendix B it is pointed out that there is a serious chance of error in statistics for individual blocks. Land-use maps, air photos, topographic sheets, or even a rough field check will help to catch such errors.

[10] William Applebaum, "A Technique for Constructing a Population and Urban Land Use Map," *Economic Geography*, vol. 28, p. 241, 1952.

[11] Each such concentration can be shown by a proportional symbol of some sort or possibly just a solid mass of dots.

ONE DOT EQUALS TEN PERSONS

PLANNING BOARD
WORCESTER, MASS

Fig. 10.2 Dot map of distribution of population in Worcester, Massachusetts. The map shows nighttime distribution since that is the way in which the data are collected by the Census Bureau. (Map from Worcester City Planning Department and based on United States Census, 1960. Data by enumeration districts.)

greatly facilitates the final placing of the dots.[12]

[12] In the article referred to, Applebaum describes the preparation of a map on which both population and land use are shown (see Fig. 11.1). In the present instance we are concerned only with population.

The choropleth map Though it is generally agreed that the dot map is the most effective method of painting a picture of population distribution throughout the city, choropleth maps are worth consideration, too. The choropleth map, normally, is based on persons per unit of area, and usually line patterns of varying intensity or possibly colors are used to achieve its effects. Such a map has the advantage that one can read approximate density values directly from it. The chief problem involved is the matter of what unit areas to use. City blocks, census enumeration districts, and census tracts—all are possibilities, but none is entirely suitable.

CITY BLOCK DATA AND THE CHOROPLETH MAP City blocks may be considered first. Population data by blocks from the Census of Housing represent the most detailed city population data now available. But this very degree of detail is a handicap for a choropleth map. The resulting map would be very fine-grained, consisting of such small unit areas as to present a confusing picture that would obscure the broad general elements of the pattern.

CENSUS ENUMERATION DISTRICTS AND CHOROPLETH MAPS Census enumeration districts represent a somewhat coarser-textured base, which is more suitable than city blocks for a choropleth map of population distribution. But census enumeration districts have certain disadvantages, too. The data are not published, but must be purchased from the Census Bureau. Though an attempt is made to keep all census enumeration districts approximately equal in population, with about 1,000 inhabitants each in urban areas, this sometimes cannot be achieved. Rules regarding the boundaries result in some districts being abnormally small or sparsely populated (see discussion of census enumeration districts in Appendix B). Such abnormal districts make incongruous units for a population map. Still another difficulty is that no attempt is made to keep census enumeration district boundaries the same from one census to the next. This means that maps made for one census period are not very comparable with those based on the previous census. Nevertheless, census enumeration districts are reasonably satisfactory if an ordinary choropleth map (persons per unit of area) is the objective.

But such a choropleth map does not present a very accurate picture of population distribution unless land use can be taken into consideration. In some sections of a city, the enumeration districts may consist of fairly uniform residential areas; in others the enumeration districts may include factory areas, stores, and areas of railroad tracks, along with small clusters of residences. If a good land-use map were available one might, in each case, subtract the areas of the principal pieces of land devoted to factories, parks, railroad tracks, and major non-residential buildings from the calculated area of each enumeration district, or even do a more careful job of determining strictly residential space, in order to achieve a fairly realistic ratio. But the calculations and adjustments involved would represent a substantial amount of work and would require some difficult and subjective judgments.

CENSUS TRACTS AND CHOROPLETH MAPS Census tracts are in several respects the most suitable of the available statistical areas on which to base an urban population choropleth map. For one thing, census tract data are published and readily available. A second advantage is that census tracts are more or less permanent, so that the resulting maps may be compared with those of earlier or later periods to see what shifts have taken place. A third advantage is that there is available by tracts a variety of other data, both from the Census Bureau and from local sources. Patterns that result when these data are plotted may show some interesting relationships to the pattern of population distribution. A fourth advantage is that census tracts are larger than census enumeration districts (and far larger than city blocks); hence, the resulting pattern is coarser than one based on census enumeration districts. On the whole this is good. For a large city there may be 100 to 200 or even more tracts, which gives as detailed a map as can be readily used.

On the other hand, census tracts have the same disadvantage as census enumeration districts when it comes to constructing a choropleth map of population distribution. A simple population-to-area map is not very realistic since it takes no account of land use. Yet there is no practicable way of doing this on a choropleth map.

GENERAL DISADVANTAGES OF CHOROPLETH TECHNIQUE Regardless of the unit areas with which one chooses to work, there are disadvantages inherent in the choropleth map. For one thing, areas are not published for city blocks, enumeration districts, or tracts. This means extensive and time-consuming measurements. The population-to-area ratio takes no account of the presence of manufacturing land or other non-residential areas, and it is difficult if not impossible to adjust for this land-use factor. Yet in making a dot map it is easy to do this (see pages 165 to 166).

Another difficulty in making choropleth maps is that, in order to maintain approximately equal populations, both tracts and enumeration districts have to be considerably larger near the edges of the city than near the center. Obviously, divisions that are essentially uniform in size all over the city would result in a better choropleth map. But data are not available for any such ideal units except possibly blocks, and these, as was pointed out earlier, are too small to be very effectively used.

Other ways of representing urban population distribution Choropleth maps require calculations—of the areas of tracts, enumeration districts, or blocks—and then of the ratio for each. A simpler method of attaining much the same effect is to use proportional circles or some other proportional symbols. Or population distribution might be represented by regular rows of dots in each tract or other area chosen. This is not a dot map, since no attempt is made to show even approximate distribution within the tract. The map merely represents the distribution quantitatively by tracts. The method is often used for census tracts

when a simple display map is needed. But use of proportional circles, rows of dots, and the like can yield only rough results, crude diagrams rather than maps.

Interpreting the population map The population map, whether on a dot or on a choropleth basis, and regardless of the unit areas used, is not an end in itself. Instead, we are concerned with interpreting the map, with accounting for the variations in the pattern. Why is the population dense here? Why is it sparse there? For this local and detailed understanding, information regarding site factors, land use, and history of development must be depended upon.

Generalizations Though no two cities are exactly alike in these respects or in their patterns of population distribution, we try to see some features of the pattern that may hold good for cities in general. For instance, a largely vacant area on the population map corresponds in most cities to the central business district (Figures 10.1 and 10.2). This tends to be encircled by a belt that has the city's lowest quality of housing and its greatest density of population. Nowadays, parts of this belt are likely to be undergoing redevelopment, and in many cities multistoried apartments are appearing. From this belt, density tends to grade away toward the edges of the city, where housing is more spread out and where it averages higher in quality. But the outward gradation is by no means uniform: for example, the population often is more highly concentrated along or near certain major radial transportation routes than in sections that are less accessible. Of course, this paragraph by no means tells the whole story, but it shows the sorts of generalizations that can result from studying the population distribution patterns of cities.

Intercensal Population Maps

In the preceding discussion it has been

assumed that the population distribution map is made shortly after the data from a regular United States Census have become available. Census data become less and less valuable through the ten-year period following the publication of the decennial census. Suppose it is late in the ten-year period between censuses. In a rapidly growing urban area the data for the last regular census are pitifully out of date. The problem is not so much one of estimating population of the city; estimates usually are available for the corporate city—if not for every year, then at least for the year half way between regular censuses.

Local data for intercensal years However, such estimates involve no areal breakdown within the corporate city or at least no very satisfactory one. But sometimes local sources may prove useful. Thus an annual record of voters by precincts or of school children by school districts may be available for a city. These data can be the basis for figuring approximate population totals for the precincts or school districts, and the estimates thus obtained might be used for making a population distribution map of the city. The result may be a fair picture of population distribution, though perhaps not exact enough for close comparison with a map based on regular data for the last decennial United States Census.

A British attempt to make an intercensal population map Hunt and Moisley, two British geographers who faced the problem of making an intercensal population map, worked with "registered electors" to good advantage.[13] Registers, giving the full address, street by street, of every person entitled to a parliamentary vote, are revised annually. The ratio of total population to registered electors for the latest decennial census year, the T/E factor, was worked out

for each ward.[14] It was assumed to have remained constant. For the desired year the T/E factor for each ward was applied to the known number of electors in the ward in order to obtain a population figure. From street addresses the number of electors in each block in the ward was obtained and converted to total population by using the T/E factor for that particular ward. Presumably, the total for the blocks was made to equal the ward total. Actually, Hunt and Moisley carried their research into considerably greater detail, but this brief outline of the work will suffice for our purposes.

Could such a method be applied in the United States? For instance, does total population bear a reasonably constant ratio to registered voters in the American city? The general plan of the British study is described here since it is felt that, through some such method, data obtained locally each year in the city might be used as a basis for an intercensal population map.

People in the City at Various Hours of the Day

Maps of daytime population distribution The maps that we have been discussing show where people reside, since that is the way population is counted by the Census Bureau. The fact that this is not the whole story, however, has impressed people for some time. In a report issued several decades ago that has become a classic in the study of urban areas, it was stated: "the dot map of Manhattan appears pale in those portions of the city which, from the number of persons seen on the streets, one ordinarily thinks of as most congested."[15] A few years after this report was published, Mark Jefferson pointed out the need for a new type of

[13] A. J. Hunt and H. A. Moisley, "Population Mapping in Urban Areas," *Geography*, vol. 45, pp. 79–89, 1960.

[14] For details regarding wards in American cities, see Appendix B.

[15] Regional Survey of New York and Its Environs, *Population, Land Values and Government*, New York, N.Y., 1929, vol. 2, p. 75.

census count.[16] With the increasing mobility of population, he argued, it is no longer sufficient to base our census on where people sleep. Censuses of cities awake are needed, he said.

The Census Bureau still bases its population count on the places where people sleep. However, maps of *daytime population* have been made for most large cities. Daytime population has been defined by the Bureau of the Census as follows:

> For any given standard location the daytime population at the selected hour represents the sum of the number of persons physically present in the area working, attending school, shopping, conducting personal business, enroute from one place to another, or engaging in other activities away from their homes, and the number of resident persons remaining in home at the location.[17]

The potential values of a knowledge of daytime population are coming to be recognized. Two relevant studies are discussed here.

The daytime population of Winnipeg

T. R. Weir made a daytime population survey of Winnipeg.[18] In the resulting article, the methodology is discussed in considerable detail.

Weir points out that the population of an urban area during the working hours of a typical day may be divided into four groups: (1) residential, (2) institutional, (3) gainfully employed, (4) transient and mobile. The first of these groups consists of housewives, preschool children, and domestic help; the second, people in hospitals, homes for the infirm, reformatories, schools and colleges, etc. The third group is made up of those actually at work in buildings or other specific locations, chiefly in the commercial and industrial zones of the city. The fourth group consists of shoppers in stores; people in theaters, offices, etc., who do not work in these establishments; pedestrians on the streets; and passengers in public and private vehicles. The transient and mobile group would include some people who are gainfully employed, as we normally use the term, but in Weir's study the latter term included only those actually at places of work. To determine exactly the number and location of people in each of the groups for a particular day and hour, Weir thinks, is virtually impossible. But a reasonable approximation of the numbers and distribution of people during a mid-morning or mid-afternoon period of a typical working day is possible.

Obviously, statistics for the institutional population presented no great difficulty. They could be obtained by telephone contact or by personal visits. Similarly, the gainfully employed (on premises) were a matter of record and presented no problem. The chief difficulties were encountered in obtaining data for the residential and the transient and mobile groups.

Residential estimates were based on the latest Canadian Federal Census data, modified through field observations. The Canadian census gives nighttime population by census tracts just as does the United States Census. Within each census tract, blocks that appeared to be typical were checked in the field to discover the numbers usually at home during the daytime. A simple ratio was thus obtained which was applied to the nighttime population of the entire tract.

As might be expected, the transient and mobile element of the daytime population presented the greatest problems. Using the city directory, Weir's group of investigators made a survey of business and industrial establishments on a block-by-block basis, and obtained estimates from superintendents of large office buildings, businesses, and

[16] Mark Jefferson, "The World's City Folks," *Geographical Review*, vol. 21, pp. 446–465, 1931.

[17] U.S. Bureau of the Census, *Population Estimates for Survival Planning*, prepared for the Federal Civil Defense Administration Department of Commerce, 1956, vol. 1, p. 9.

[18] Thomas R. Weir, "A Survey of the Daytime Population of Winnipeg," *Queen's Quarterly*, vol. 67, no. 4, Winter, 1961.

industrial concerns as to the numbers found on their premises during a typical working day. Actual counts were made in the smaller stores. Counts were made of pedestrians on streets and in vehicles for the central business district. Transport companies made available estimates of numbers of passengers carried, and the traffic department provided vehicle counts for specified hours.

By the use of these various methods, a daytime population picture was obtained that Weir claimed was accurate enough to be of real practical value.[19]

"Population Densities around the Clock" In a study of Flint, Michigan, Chapin and Stewart, though dealing with the same general topic, considered the distribution of population for several different periods within the twenty-four hours of the day.[20] Their paper was based on a special traffic study of the city's metropolitan area conducted by the State Highway Commission of Michigan in cooperation with the U.S. Bureau of Public Roads. Home interviews with approximately 5 per cent of the population of the built-up area of Flint were conducted, and roadside interviews gave coverage of areas outside the central city. Although the surveys were designed primarily for traffic analyses, they included enough information on basic population characteristics and individual trips of household members to be of use in determining and explaining daytime-nighttime variations in population distribution. The University of North Carolina's Institute for Research in Social Science studied the data under a research contract.

Chapin and Stewart did not discuss

[19] Weir's group conducted a detailed land-use classification at the same time as the population survey, and in his paper Weir discusses the distribution of the daytime population by land-use areas.
[20] F. Stuart Chapin, Jr., and Pearson H. Stewart, "Population Densities around the Clock," *The American City*, vol. 68, no. 10, pp. 98–99, October, 1953.

their methods of working with the traffic-study data, but they did present some interesting generalizations (Figure 10.3). As might be expected, the number of people increased in manufacturing areas and in central business areas during working hours, and the population in residential areas decreased. The greatest changes in population density occurred in the work areas of the city. For example, the central business district had a density ranging from approximately nine persons per acre at 6 A.M. to about fifty-five at 3 P.M.

Residential areas experience less variation in density throughout the twenty-four hours than work areas. The variation in residential areas adjacent to the central business district is small in spite of a spilling over of commercial and small industrial uses from the central area. Apparently, it is common for the people of these residential areas to work near where they live. On the other hand, variations in density are greater in suburban residential areas than in any other residential areas because, on the average, suburban residents live farthest from their work places.

The time schedule of variations is of interest, too. During daytime working hours about 25 to 30 per cent of the people of the Flint urban area are concentrated in the small work areas. At night about 97 per cent of the people are widely dispersed in residential areas. The time of greatest dispersal is 4 A.M. Then most people are in their homes, and the population pattern comes closest to the facts of distribution based on where people sleep, as given by the Census Bureau.

Value of studies of urban population distribution at various hours of the day It is hardly necessary to point out the practical value of studies such as the two just described. In traffic and transportation analyses, for example, channels of movement must be planned as much on a detailed knowledge of daytime population distribu-

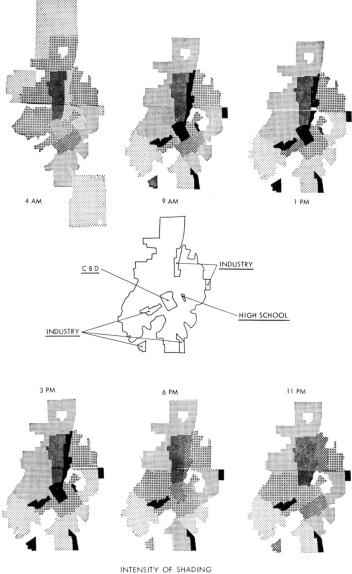

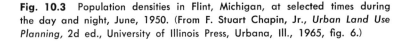

Fig. 10.3 Population densities in Flint, Michigan, at selected times during the day and night, June, 1950. (From F. Stuart Chapin, Jr., *Urban Land Use Planning*, 2d ed., University of Illinois Press, Urbana, Ill., 1965, fig. 6.)

tion as upon knowledge of where people sleep. Distribution of parking, location of shopping facilities, and public utility needs are closely related to the picture of where people spend their daytime hours. This daytime pattern is of potential value, too, in zoning, for setting up more realistic density standards, and in local programs for industrial dispersion and for defense and disaster planning. In fact, any plans for the future of the city must be based in part upon such information.

Nor should the value of the work be judged only by possible practical benefits. Tentative generalizations, such as those arrived at by Chapin and Stewart, can add substantially to our understanding of the American city.

Help needed from Census Bureau It should be noted, however, that the study by Chapin and Stewart involved the cooperative efforts of government agencies in collecting the data and the work of a research organization in reaching final conclusions, and that the Winnipeg study was backed by the Geographical Branch of the Canadian government. Though they demonstrate what can be done, the methods have not been reduced to a practical possibility for the individual worker. Thus far, for this country, the decennial census gives little information that is of value in such an analysis.

The Changing Intracity Population Pattern

The intercensal population map may be compared with the population map for the last regular census period and certain changes discerned. But it is particularly when new decennial census data become available that tempting possibilities arise for studying changes in population distribution within the city—changes since the last census period or changes over several census periods. Various sections of the city are gaining population at varying rates, and others are losing in population.

Unit areas for studying change For studying intracity changes of this sort, city blocks are too small unless great detail is desired. The census tract is the unit area generally depended upon. It is a much more suitable areal unit than the enumeration district, since enumeration district boundaries are likely to change from one census to the next whereas census tract boundaries

ordinarily remain fixed. Sometimes it is convenient to work with units coarser than census tracts, with, for instance, the administrative units that make up the urban agglomeration.

The dot method To show the population change by census tracts from one census year to another, a common method is to use different-colored dots. Each red dot placed in a census tract shows, let us say, a decrease of ten persons; each black dot, an increase of ten. Of course, no one census tract would have both; it is an area of decline or of increase—or it may have experienced no change at all, and, therefore, would have no dots. In any event, the dots, ordinarily, should be placed in regular rows to avoid any implication that the map shows exactly where within a tract the change took place.

Much the same type of study could be based on city blocks, but it would require a much larger-scale map. Moreover, it will hardly be feasible until 1970 census data are available, since the Census Bureau gave population totals by blocks for the first time in the 1960 census.

How a city loses or gains population The dot method by tracts (or other areal units) could be used to investigate population decline in a city. For example, Detroit, Michigan, had a population of 1,849,568 in 1950 but only 1,670,144 in 1960. Thus it suffered a net loss of 179,424 or 9.7 per cent. Which of the city's 400 to 500 census tracts sustained the greatest losses? And exactly how did such losses take place? The same question could be posed for Reading, Pennsylvania, which lost 10.2 per cent in population, or Pittsburgh, where the loss was 10.7 per cent. In a similar manner the mechanics of population gain might be studied for cities where the population increased.

Relative-change map based on administrative units A slightly different sort of population change could be measured by means of a relative change map. Such a map could be based on the administrative units of an urban area. For instance, we might consider Worcester, Massachusetts, and the ring of towns that surrounds it (Figure 10.4). They can be compared for 1950 and 1960. What percentage of the population total of the group did Worcester and each of the towns have in 1950? In 1960? The difference is an index of the change in relative importance of that one administrative area. It will be read as a plus number (relative gain) or a minus number (relative loss), depending on whether the area gained or lost relatively. The number is not

Fig. 10.4　Relative population change map of Worcester, Massachusetts, and the ring of towns that surrounds it, 1950 versus 1960. In 1950, of the population living in Worcester and the adjacent ring of towns, the city contained 79.2 per cent. In 1960, it had only 70.1 per cent, thus sustaining a substantial relative loss of nearly 10, and an absolute loss as well. In contrast, every town in the ring around Worcester gained relatively, with Shrewsbury gaining most and Boylston least. Just why did Worcester lose relatively? And why did some of the towns gain more than others? Field investigation is needed in answering such questions.

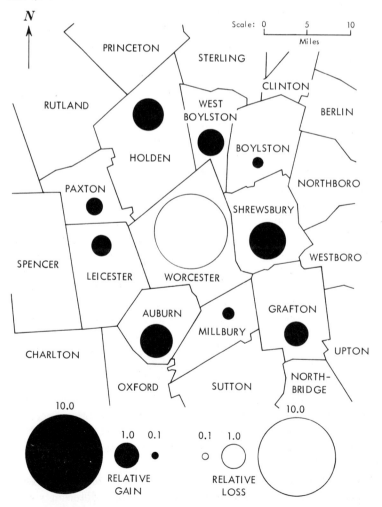

a percentage change, but a change in the percentage contribution to the total. The same determination is made for each of the towns that surround Worcester. Worcester will be found to have lost relatively, just as did the central cities of most large urban agglomerations of the country.

A similar study might be applied to the Boston Standard Metropolitan Statistical Area. Here seventeen cities and fifty-nine towns would be involved, but the same technique could be used as for the Worcester area.

The relative-change idea based on administrative units is particularly applicable in New England since in New England the standard metropolitan statistical area or other convenient area chosen is made up of a compact group of cities and towns. But the study need not be restricted to standard metropolitan statistical areas. Indeed, in the study of Worcester, only the immediate bordering towns were considered. In areas outside of New England it might be better to disregard the standard metropolitan statistical area and to use, instead, the group of cities, villages, etc., that seem to make up the real city. It is now commonly realized that most large urban areas represent clusters of political units with common problems. Hence, changes in the pattern of population distribution within such an agglomeration from one census period to the next are of obvious importance. A limitation is that exactly the same units must be used for the current and for the earlier year being studied and that the units should not change in area. Where cities are growing by annexation, adjustments have to be made in order to apply the relative-change idea.

Relative-change map based on census tracts Not infrequently, nowadays, most census tracts will be found to have gained from one decennial census to the next, but some more rapidly than others. This, too, can be investigated by means of the relative-change map. For example, some tracts

had larger proportions of the city's total population in 1960 than they had in 1950; that is, they gained relatively. Others had a smaller proportion of the total than they had in 1950; they lost relatively. This will be true even if every census tract in the urban area has gained in population. The changes measured are not absolute gains or losses, comparable to those measured by the dot method earlier described but, instead, relative changes.

Centers of gravity Where it is suspected that there has been a pronounced shift of the urban population in a certain direction, this can be checked by calculating *centers of gravity* or *mean centers* of population for each of the periods involved. Such a center is comparable to the center of population calculated for the United States by the Census Bureau. The calculations of the center of gravity may be based on population by minor civil divisions in a large urban area such as Greater Boston or any other urban area where there are minor civil divisions or administrative areas. Or they can be based on census tracts where the city and adjacent areas are tracted.[21]

[21] A simple method for finding the center of gravity is as follows: The approximate center of population of each minor civil division or census tract or other unit area is marked with an X. If no special knowledge is available regarding population distribution within the unit area, the geographic center, which can be approximated, is used. A north-south axis is drawn just to the left of the unit areas and an east-west axis is drawn at right angles to it, just south of the unit areas. Each unit area is then listed by name or by number in a table, together with its population total. For each, the distance from its center to the north-south axis is measured and recorded. Total population times distance is calculated for each of the unit areas, and the product is recorded. The products are then added and the total is divided by the total population of the unit areas. The resulting quotient is the distance the north-south axis must be shifted to the east. In similar fashion, measurements are made from each individual center to the east-west line. Calculations are made as before with the resulting quotient being the distance that the east-west axis

There are limitations to the mean center or center of gravity for studying the direction of expansion of an urban area. For instance, urban growth is often largely radial. It would be possible for a city to have a large population increase and yet for the growth to be approximately equal in all directions and hence not be reflected in any appreciable movement of the mean center.[22]

Explaining the changes The foregoing are only a few of the possible methods of studying changes in the pattern of population distribution within urban ,agglomerations. But whatever the method of analyzing population shifts in the urban area, the geographer is interested in explaining these shifts. Here the concern is as much with areas of decrease as with those of increase, and we are particularly interested in attempting to detect and explain shifts that may be true of cities in general, such as the tendency for the central cities to lose popu-

lation compared with other units of the urban area.

Other Intracity Social Patterns

Though population distribution is unquestionably the most important social pattern of the city, there are many other social aspects that may be investigated. Types of social information available by census tracts for tracted cities include, in addition to population numbers, such interesting aspects as age structure of the population, the sex ratio, educational level, marital status, race, nativity, country of birth of foreign-born population and of foreign-born parents, mobility of residence, employment status, occupation group, industry group, median family income, means of travel to work and place of work, and several others. Housing data from the Census of Housing, many of which have considerable social significance, are also available by census tracts and, in less detail, by blocks from the Census of Housing. Various items of social information, too, are assembled locally by census tracts—health data, vital statistics, juvenile delinquency records, number of relief cases, etc.

Beginnings of generalizations Any of the items mentioned may, by itself, show an interesting distribution pattern for a city, but of more concern to the geographer are the possibilities of these social patterns being correlated with others or with such additional patterns as those of land use and land values. It is through discovering such patterns and relationships in successive cities that reliable generalizations may eventually be achieved.

Variety of problems The problems that may be investigated are almost limitless. Only a few are suggested here and these only to give some idea of the range. They may be based on census tract or block housing data or on data collected by the

---

must be moved to the north. The intersection of the two new axes is the mean center or the center of gravity of the population. One center is of little significance, but if such a center is calculated for 1950 and another for 1960 one can see in what direction and how far the mean center has shifted, and thus in what general direction the city's population has been expanding or intensifying. For further details regarding centrographic analysis, see E. E. Sviatlovsky and W. C. Eels, "The Centrographic Method and Regional Analysis," *Geographical Review*, vol. 27, pp. 240–254, 1937. John F. Hart, in "Central Tendency in Areal Distributions," *Economic Geography*, vol. 30, pp. 48–59, 1954, suggests a slightly different method of calculating center of gravity from the one recommended here, and also presents a simple method for approximating the position of the "center of minimum travel."

[22] The mean center concept has a number of other possible uses in urban geography. For instance, the writer has had occasion in studying central business districts to calculate the center of area of the outlined central business district and also to calculate the mean centers for various types of establishments in the district. The utility of such centers becomes much greater, of course, where they can be determined for several successive periods.

minor civil divisions that make up the urban agglomeration. For instance, do the areas of poorest health conditions in the city coincide with areas of the greatest proportions of foreign-born? Do distributions of people of white and non-white races in a particular city show that there is pronounced segregation? Is there a correlation between the areas with highest educational levels and those with highest median family income? Do the suburban areas of the city have a higher proportion of young people than the older-established sections? Is there a much higher proportion of Negroes in the central city than in the suburbs? How does the pattern of age structure correspond to the income pattern in the urban area? How is the sixty-five-year-and-older age group distributed in the average city and with what factors is this distribution associated? Certain of the block housing data that are available also by tracts have been generally considered "blight factors"—inadequate plumbing facilities, dilapidation, low contract rent, high proportion of renter occupancy, a high ratio of persons per room. The patterns they exhibit are particularly interesting to study in relation to other tract data.[23]

And, of course, the locally assembled tract data mentioned earlier suggest various other problems. How, for example, does the distribution of juvenile delinquency cases compare with patterns of educational levels? To what extent is the pattern of incidence of crime coincident with the distributions of different ethnic groups?

Voting behavior There is social information, too, not available by tracts that is interesting to compare with the patterns that have been described. For instance, the voting pattern of a city may be plotted by precincts and these compared with patterns by tracts or other unit areas. Do the suburbs tend to vote Democratic? Are high-income areas of the city predominantly Republican? Can relationships to racial or religious groups be demonstrated? To employment patterns? There are many other possible problems for investigation. And the study of the vote on local issues has great practical possibilities.[24] An attempt to relate voting patterns to other patterns, however, runs into difficulties, because different areal

---

[23] Some interesting work of this sort was done by Howard Whipple Green of Cleveland, who, for a number of years, was Director of the Cleveland Real Property Inventory, a sort of annual land-use inventory of the Cleveland Standard Metropolitan Area. As a Census Bureau adviser Green had a great deal to do with promoting the census tract idea, and the entire Cleveland area has been tracted for a number of years.

In addition to its work for the city, the firm which Green headed did various studies under contract. For example, Green did consulting work for the publishers of a national weekly news magazine. Using a census tract street directory and a list of the magazine's subscribers for a certain large city, he plotted the locations of these subscribers by tracts (see Appendix B). Through also plotting by tracts a variety of housing data, he was able to demonstrate that the magazine went chiefly to those census tracts in which the people had better than average buying power. To the publishers of

the magazine this information was of value in appealing to prospective advertisers.

Another line of work that Green and his assistants did under contract had to do with the homes of workers of various firms. Here the argument was that difficulties with workers often stemmed from poor conditions in the home neighborhood. Green's staff plotted worker residences by census tracts from the company's address files and a census tract street directory, and presumably the firm for which the work was done received also maps of various relevant items of social data shown by tracts in the census volumes. The latter information was necessary, Green said, so that the firm would have a basis for evaluating the areas in which its employees lived.

[24] Some years ago the head of the planning board in one of the larger Texas cities told the author of this book of work he had done in that city in which he plotted the vote on Plan E government and could demonstrate that the greatest opposition came from those sections of the city that had the highest proportions of voters of Mexican descent, the very people who were being exploited under the existing governmental system. This is just one instance of the possible practical value of study of the social geography of the city.

units are involved. Voting patterns are by precincts, whereas most of the other patterns are based on data available by tracts. Sometimes, indeed, some of the data involved are by still other unit areas.

Contrasting Socioeconomic Status of Cities and Suburbs

It has generally been assumed that, characteristically, the socioeconomic status of suburbia is higher than that of the city, but this appears to be too simple a generalization, according to a study by Leo Schnore.[25] He bases his study on 200 urbanized areas in each of which he regards all portions outside the central city or cities as suburban.[26] He uses three measures of socioeconomic status: (1) median family income, (2) percentage of the population aged twenty-five years or over with at least four years of high school, and (3) proportion of the total employed labor force in white-collar occupations. In his statistical work, age [27] and size of settlement are considered, and allowance is made for what Schnore called the annexation factor—the extent to which the politically defined city is coextensive with the urbanized area.

Schnore's chief conclusion is that the traditional relationship is more likely to hold good for old settlements than for more recent ones. Older urbanized areas tend strongly to possess peripheral populations of higher socioeconomic standing than the populations of the central cities themselves exhibit. In contrast, in newer urban agglomerations, the central cities tend to rank higher in education, occupation, and income than their respective suburbs. To a lesser degree the contrast can be expressed in terms of size, since in general the older settlements are the larger ones.

An explanation of this contrast seems to lie in the following: the central cities of the older urbanized areas suffer from obsolescence in spite of the slum clearance and urban renewal under way in such areas. In contrast, in newer urbanized areas the housing of the central city is not as old or unattractive. At the same time, with the availability of the automobile and the truck, factories and commercial land use in newer urbanized areas are likely to have leap-frogged central residential areas because of the attractiveness of peripheral shopping centers and industrial parks. In consequence, central residential zones in newer cities are more likely to compare favorably with peripheral zones in socioeconomic status.

Census Tract Data and Ethnic Studies

The distribution of ethnic groups in urban areas is an attractive topic for investigation since many practical problems arise out of the presence of distinctive, concentrated minorities. For this type of work the census tract appears, at least at first glance, to be the ideal unit. It is small enough to give a reasonably fine-grained coverage of the city. At the same time, data for census tracts are published.

Ethnic data by tracts In order to work effectively with ethnic group patterns in the city, however, it is necessary to understand just what is and is not available. This has varied from one census to the next. What information of this sort is available in the 1960 census? Data on white, Negro, and other races are given by census tracts. For five Southwestern states (Arizona, California, Colorado, New Mexico, and Texas) separate data are given by tracts regarding white persons with Spanish surnames. In all

[25] Leo F. Schnore, "The Socio-economic Status of Cities and Suburbs," *American Sociological Review,* vol. 28, pp. 76–85, 1963.
[26] Note that the area Schnore calls suburban is the area designated by the Census Bureau as urban fringe (see Chap. 2).
[27] Age of an urbanized area was measured by counting the number of decades that had passed since its central city or cities first contained 50,000 inhabitants.

states except these five, Puerto Ricans are enumerated by tracts. Finally, there is a breakdown by tracts of foreign-born people as to country of origin, and of natives of foreign or mixed parentage as to country of origin of their parents. These data, we shall find, do not give the complete ethnic picture of a city, but they are helpful, and it is surprising that more use is not being made of them.

Puerto Ricans in Manhattan Occasionally some ethnic data for small areas are collected by the Census Bureau, but for reasons of economy cannot be issued through the regular channels. In the 1950s, before data on Puerto Ricans were being published by census tracts, a study of the distribution of Puerto Ricans on Manhattan Island was carried out by Robert Novak.[28] The Census Bureau published a separate report on "Puerto Ricans in Continental United States" for 1950, but this did not include any census tract data. However, a special tabulation was made by enumeration districts in New York State of persons born in Puerto Rico or of Puerto Rican parentage (hereafter referred to as Puerto Ricans), and the percentage of these people in the total population of each census tract was made available in the New York City Welfare and Health Council's publication *Population of Puerto Ricans (Birth or Parentage) for New York City*, 1952.

Much of Novak's article consists of a study by census tracts of just where Puerto Ricans live in New York City. The study is confined to Manhattan Borough which, Novak points out, contained 56 per cent of the Puerto Ricans in the entire city in 1950.

Though Puerto Ricans live in practically all sections of Manhattan, there are several noticeable areas of concentration (Figure 10.5). The main area consists of a group of thirty-three census tracts adjoin-

ing Central Park on the northeast. Novak also points out two much smaller areas lying northeast of the main concentration. These three areas are within approximately half a mile of one another. In addition, there are three minor areas of concentration in Manhattan that do not stand out clearly on the map—one in the southeast, one in the southwest, and one in the north—and several small clusters.

Novak suggests two explanations for the concentrations. Puerto Ricans locate in areas of low-cost housing where they can live with previously established families that preceded them to the United States, even though living conditions are poor and housing substandard in such areas. They tend to locate near express stops or terminals on major subway or bus lines. The common employment of these people is in the service trades—hotels, restaurants, nightclubs, etc.—and accessibility to cheap transportation is considered essential.

Patterns of Cultural Groups in Worcester, Massachusetts

Research based on social factors need not be confined to tracted data, nor must it always be based on statistics collected by the Census Bureau or by other agencies. In a study of patterns of cultural groups in Worcester, Massachusetts, Creveling obtained all of his information in the field.[29]

A city characterized by cultural variety Worcester has a remarkable variety of peoples. This is, of course, not unusual among the cities of Northeastern United States. In spite of the melting-pot effect of a number of decades of living in the same community, many of the diverse peoples of Worcester

[28] Robert T. Novak, "Distribution of Puerto Ricans on Manhattan Island," *Geographical Review*, vol. 46, pp. 182–186, 1956.

[29] Harold F. Creveling, *Patterns of Cultural Groups in Worcester*, unpublished doctoral dissertation, Clark University, Worcester, Mass., 1951. Published in condensed form as "Mapping Cultural Groups in an American Industrial City," *Economic Geography*, vol. 31, pp. 364–371, 1955.

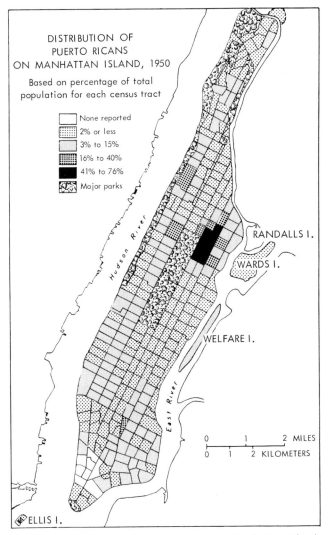

Fig. 10.5 Distribution of Puerto Ricans on Manhattan Island, 1950, based on percentage of total population for each census tract. (Redrawn from Robert T. Novak, "Distribution of Puerto Ricans on Manhattan Island," *Geographical Review*, vol. 46, 1956, fig. 1.)

still think of themselves as belonging to distinct groups. There are many churches and clubs for particular linguistic and religious groups, and there are stores that specialize in the needs of these individual groups. The group consciousness may be based upon a common racial or national origin or upon a common religion. But the fact of importance is that there are such well-defined groups. Since they are not ex-

clusively racial, or religious, or national, Creveling decided to call them "cultural groups." His problem was to map and explain the distribution of cultural groups in the city.

Limitations of Census Bureau publications For making a map of these cultural groups, publications of the Census Bureau were of little help. Census tracts had not been set up in Worcester in time for the 1950 census, but, even if they had been, they would not have brought out the information wanted. The ethnic information available by tracts does not go beyond race and country of birth of foreign-born persons and foreign-born parents of native Americans, whereas it was found in Worcester that many individuals continued to be closely identified with a cultural group through members of families residing in the United States through several generations. Moreover, census data do not make it possible to differentiate between religious groups from the same country, such as Jews and Catholics from Poland, though they constitute distinct social groups in Worcester. In addition, it was apparent that the variations in the patterns of cultural groups could not be worked out in real detail with areal units as large as tracts or even enumeration districts.

Systematic sampling Creveling used an interview method. He superimposed a grid pattern on the city street map for interview control. East-west lines ¼ mile apart were drawn on the map; then north-south lines were drawn with similar spacing. Where the presence of any resident population made it possible, two interviews were conducted at each intersection and at the center of each square.

Wording of the interview The wording of the interview was very important. A typical question was: "Do most (that is, over half) of the people in this neighborhood belong to any one group?" "Group" was explained to apply to Negroes, Yankees, and Jews as well as to nationalities. If the answer was "Yes," then the question "What group?" followed. If the answer was "No, they are mixed," then questions were asked as to which groups and in what proportions. A notebook was used to record the data, with the notes keyed to numbers on the field map.

The predominant cultural groups map From the field notes a map of predominant cultural groups was constructed (Figure 10.6). The cultural groups map was checked with mail carriers, with the pastors of churches that served some of the special groups, with members of the District Nursing Society, and with various others who were considered to have special knowledge of the city's cultural groups. There was general agreement on the accuracy of the map.

How the map was put to use The cultural groups map took on more meaning when compared with physical, social, and economic distributions in the city, and it was found to be of practical value. In Worcester, social agencies were interested in it in connection with planning services for the various neighborhoods. It was welcomed, too, by the leading newspaper and by the Chamber of Commerce, since it was of value in answering questions that arose regarding where to locate specialized stores so as to reach certain of the cultural groups.

Do other cities have similar distributions? Though most American cities, if mapped by this technique, would probably show interesting cultural group patterns, it is doubtful if many outside the Northeast and the northern Middle West would appear so variegated as Worcester. More studies of this sort might bring out some interesting regional differences among cities in the United States.

Other values of the technique Of course, a technique such as the one Creveling used may have value beyond its original purpose. Are there other aspects of the social geography of the city that could be mapped through a systematic field sampling such as the one he used? A coarser or finer grid might be desirable, depending on the nature of the distribution being mapped and the size of the city.

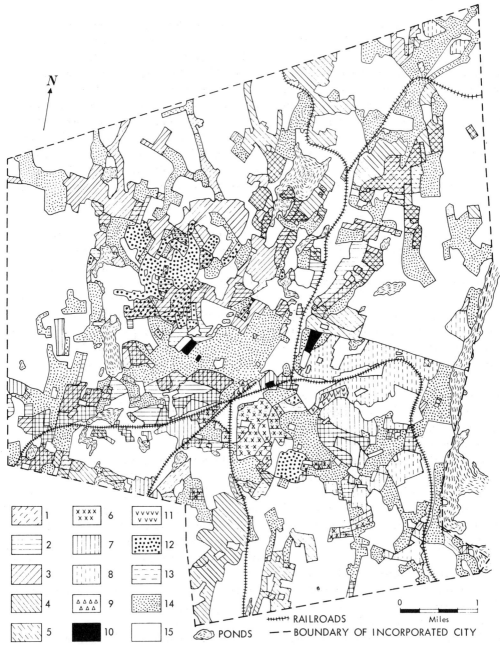

Fig. 10.6 Predominant cultural groups in Worcester, Massachusetts. Numbers refer as follows: 1, English; 2, Irish; 3, Yankee; 4, Swedish; 5, Finnish; 6, Polish; 7, French; 8, Italian; 9, Albanian; 10, Negro; 11, Syrian; 12, Jewish; 13, Lithuanian; 14, very mixed; 15, non-residential. A single pattern indicates that at least one-half of the population belongs to that particular group. One pattern overlying another means that the two groups together equal at least one-half of the population within the area. Three patterns indicate that the three groups together similarly predominate. (From Harold F. Creveling, "Mapping Cultural Groups in an American Industrial City," *Economic Geography*, vol. 31, 1955, fig. 2.)

How Intracity Social Patterns Vary through Time

The way in which the pattern of population distribution within the urban area changes through time was discussed earlier in this chapter. The other social factors, too, present interesting problems of change. Instead of concentrating on the current age pattern of the population, for example, we can go further and see how the age pattern of the city has changed since the last census period, and attempt to determine how this pattern of change is related to other patterns.

But this is only one possibility; essentially all of the intracity social patterns mentioned earlier can be studied through working with data from successive censuses or other information for two or more periods of time. Problems such as those listed can be given much greater depth through introducing the time factor. The original list of problems summarized on pages 176 to 177 was based on static distributions; we can ask, also, how is this or that situation changing? And we can attempt to explain the changes.

Cultural group changes in Worcester

Creveling, in his study of the pattern of cultural groups in Worcester, faced a more complicated problem. He found that certain of the cultural group areas were relatively static, whereas others were shifting position rapidly. The changes involved dilution of the concentrations in some areas, and in others the actual advance of some boundaries and the retreat of others. But, as will be recalled, no statistics were available for studying even the static patterns. A serious investigation of the dynamic characteristics of the cultural group areas would have to be done largely by field interviews. Though this would have been a logical follow-up of Creveling's study, the time required necessitated deferring the project until some later date.

Social Characteristics of Cities

In the early pages of this chapter, we spoke of size and density as they could be expressed for the city as a whole. Thus the distribution of cities by size over the country was referred to as one of the basic patterns of urban geography, and there was some discussion of the way cities contrasted regionally as to population density. For instance, it was pointed out that the Eastern cities tended to have greater densities than those of Western United States. Now the question is asked, how do cities differ with respect to the various other social factors discussed in this chapter? And do they differ regionally, or only as individuals? What patterns of distribution result? And to what other patterns of distribution are they related? Such intercity studies may be based on any one of the three city areas—corporate city, urbanized area, or standard metropolitan statistical area.

Nelson's study of social and economic characteristics of city populations

There is little in the geographic literature making use of social characterizations of cities. One interesting exception, however, was mentioned earlier in this book. Nelson followed his classification of American cities with an attempt to determine the social and economic characteristics of the population of cities in various service groups which he had differentiated in an earlier study.[30] Thus for each of the SD3 and SD2 cities of each service class, and using the Census of Population as his source, he considered these seven categories: percentage increase in population; proportion of population sixty-five years old or older; average years of school completed; percentage of males in labor force; percentage of females in labor force; percentage unemployed; and

[30] Howard J. Nelson, "Some Characteristics of the Population of Cities in Similar Service Classifications," *Economic Geography*, vol. 33, pp. 95–108, 1957.

median income (see Table 9.1). This was further broken down to show how the value of each of these categories in each service group varied for the four census regions of the country.

City social differences as basis for regions If we consider cities in general, as they have been taken up in this chapter, here are some of the types of questions that might be raised: Do the cities of some sections of the country average younger populations than those of other sections? Are there marked regional differences in the ages of cities? In educational level of population? In sex ratio? In marital status? Similar questions could, of course, be based on most of the other social characteristics—on race, ethnic characteristics, employment status, income, religion, voting behavior, etc.

Another way of stating what is being asked is this: Suppose we were to plot on a United States map the median age of the people for each city of the country. Would we be able to outline fairly distinct regions on this basis? Or would one city vary from the next seemingly without order or reason? Or we might plot the sex ratio, the percentage of foreign-born in the population, the median school years completed, the median income, or the percentage of Negroes for each city. In each case, could fairly definite regions of high or low or intermediate value be outlined? And there are some housing factors that might form regions on a social basis (see Chapter 18). Could information be had to characterize cities on such items as voting behavior? Religion? How would these cities be found to regionalize? And insofar as cities were found to regionalize on the basis of each of these characteristics, how could the resulting patterns be related to other patterns?

Variations in city social differences through time Of course, regions based upon city social differences are subject to change through time, just as are intracity patterns. For example, the patterns of cities based upon median age may change from one census period to the next. So, too, can patterns of cities based on any of the other social factors. The reasons for such changes make interesting problems for investigation.

Summary

This chapter has dealt with people. It is a long chapter, as it should be, since people must be the first concern of any urban study. First, population was considered: city size and population densities of cities were followed by a detailed consideration of population distribution within the city, of the possibilities of an intercensal map showing this distribution, and of population distribution at various hours of the day. These static phases of population study were in turn followed by a discussion of the changing population pattern of the city.

Other types of social patterns were then considered as they vary within the city—variations in population age structure, sex ratio, voting behavior, income, and a host of other factors. Studies of ethnic and cultural groups were emphasized, as well as changes in intracity social patterns through time.

Finally, social characterizations of the city as a whole were considered. How do cities vary one from another in social characteristics and what distribution patterns result from these differences? Lastly, the variations in city social differences through time were considered.

Selected References

Applebaum, William: "A Technique for Constructing a Population and Urban Land Use Map," *Economic Geography*, vol. 28, pp. 240–243, 1952.

Berry, Brian J. L., James W. Simmons, and Robert J. Tennant: "Urban Population Densities: Structure and Change," *Geo-*

graphical Review, vol. 53, pp. 389–405, 1963.

Borchert, John R.: "The Twin Cities Urbanized Area: Past, Present, Future," *Geographical Review*, vol. 51, pp. 47–70, 1961.

Chapin, F. Stuart, Jr.: *Urban Land Use Planning*, 2d ed., University of Illinois Press, Urbana, Ill., 1965, chap. 5.

——— and Pearson H. Stewart: "Population Densities around the Clock," *The American City*, vol. 68, no. 10, pp. 98–99, October, 1953.

Clawson, Marion, R. Burnell Held, and Charles H. Stoddard: *Land for the Future*, Johns Hopkins Press, Baltimore, 1960.

Creveling, Harold F.: "Mapping Cultural Groups in an American Industrial City," *Economic Geography*, vol. 31, pp. 364–371, 1955.

Foley, Donald L.: "Urban Daytime Population: A Field for Demographic-Ecological Analysis," *Social Forces*, vol. 32, pp. 323–330, 1954.

Future Development of the San Francisco Bay Area, 1960–2020, Office of Area Development, U.S. Department of Commerce, 1959.

Grytzell, Karl Gustave: "The Demarcation of Comparable City Areas by Means of Population Density," *Lund Studies in Geography*, ser. B, no. 25, Lund, Sweden, 1963.

Haughton, Joseph P.: "The Social Geography of Dublin," *Geographical Review*, vol. 39, pp. 257–277, 1949.

Hunt, A. J.: "Urban Population Maps," *Town Planning Review*, vol. 23, no. 3, pp. 239–248, October, 1953.

——— and H. A. Moisley: "Population Mapping in Urban Areas," *Geography*, vol. 45, pp. 79–89, 1960.

Jones, Emrys: "Delimitation of Some Urban Landscape Features in Belfast," *Scottish Geographical Magazine*, vol. 74, pp. 150–162, 1958.

———: "The Distribution and Segregation of Roman Catholics in Belfast," *The Sociological Review*, vol. 4, no. 2, pp. 167–189, 1956.

Laing, Jean: "The Pattern of Population Trends in Massachusetts," *Economic Geography*, vol. 31, pp. 265–271, 1955.

Lewis, Pierce F.: "Impact of Negro Migration on the Electoral Geography of Flint, Michigan, 1932–1962: A Cartographic Analysis," *Annals of the Association of American Geographers*, vol. 55, pp. 1–25, 1965.

Murphy, Raymond E.: "The Relative Change Map," *The Professional Geographer*, vol. 5, no. 2, pp. 4–5, March, 1953.

Nelson, Howard J.: "Some Characteristics of the Population of Cities in Similar Service Classifications," *Economic Geography*, vol. 33, pp. 95–108, 1957.

Novak, Robert T.: "Distribution of Puerto Ricans in Manhattan Island," *Geographical Review*, vol. 46, pp. 182–186, 1956.

Sviatlovsky, E. E., and W. C. Eels: "The Centrographic Method and Regional Analysis," *Geographical Review*, vol. 27, pp. 240–254, 1937.

Thomas, Edwin N.: "Areal Associations between Population Growth and Selected Factors," *Economic Geography*, vol. 36, pp. 158–170, 1960.

Weir, Thomas R.: "Land Use and Population Characteristics of Central Winnipeg," *Geographical Bulletin* no. 9, Ottawa, pp. 5–21, 1956.

———: "A Survey of the Daytime Population of Winnipeg," *Queen's Quarterly*, vol. 67, no. 4, Winter, 1961.

11

Urban land-use maps and patterns

A KNOWLEDGE of the arrangement of land uses in the city and of the relative proportions of land devoted to the several uses is basic to geographic research and to planning. The traditional way of gaining this knowledge is through the preparation of a general land-use map.

Every city is characterized by variations in land use. There are areas devoted to stores and offices and commercial parking lots, and others used primarily for residences. Factories represent a third type of land use; and streets, railroad tracks, railroad stations, bus stations, and air terminals a fourth. Land devoted to schools, churches, parks, and playgrounds is a fifth type. The land uses described are referred to by definite names—business or commercial; residential; manufacturing; transportation; public and semipublic—or their equivalents. And there are still other types of use, depending upon the particular classification followed and the degree of detail attempted. Vacant land within the city (including land used for non-urban purposes, such as a relict farm) can be considered a class of urban land, too, a class that is particularly important because of its potential for the future. How are these land uses arranged and what spatial relationships do they represent and generate? The present chapter and a number of those that follow it deal with this question.

The chapter is focused on the construction and values of the general land-use map and on the patterns it presents. Urban land uses are considered as they exist together in the city; and land economics, zoning, urban renewal, and other factors are introduced that help to explain urban land-use patterns.

The General Land-use Map

When a city planning department began active operations in Worcester, Massachusetts, several decades ago, the first large job undertaken was the construction of a land-use map of the city. This map was at a scale of only 1 inch to 1,600 feet; later it was followed by a much more detailed land-use map of the city at 1 inch to 400 feet which had to be prepared in several sheets.

But the planner is not the only one interested in land use in the city. The urban geographer, wishing to take advantage of the laboratory near at hand, is likely to be equally concerned with a land-use map, since it can be a starting point for his research. He may find such a map ready-made at the city planning office, but it is unlikely that it will serve his purpose precisely, for there is a certain individuality in land-use maps.[1] For the urban geographer, making such a map serves several purposes. One is a matter of understanding. It is hardly possible to get the most from any urban land-use map without having had the experience of constructing such a map or at least having made a general land-use map of a portion of a city. More immediately, making the map brings a firsthand familiarity with the general layout of the city. And, finally, the map itself is useful in a number of ways. In the present instance we are most concerned with the construction of an urban land-use map as one step in a broad research program. More will be said later regarding the value of the map. Let us turn, now, to the problems that must be faced in its construction.

Land-use Map for a Moderate-sized City

It is obvious that the land-use map will vary greatly with the size of the city. Consider, first, the map that might be made for

[1] Unfortunately for the geographer, the land-use map most readily available for a city is likely to be one published as part of a zoning ordinance and showing land uses prescribed rather than existing. Normally, this is backed up by a detailed but unpublished map available in the planning office that shows actual land uses.

a city with a population of 100,000 to 200,000 within its corporate limits and with a moderate amount of urban overflow around its edges.

The area to be mapped

One of the first questions to be answered is, Should the general land-use map deal with the incorporated city only, or should it include adjacent areas with urban density? The latter alternative obviously comes closer to reality, but practicality may dictate another course. For instance, the city planning department owes its first obligation to the government of the city, and this consideration may result in a land-use map restricted to the corporate city. But the geographer, too, may find it expedient to restrict his map to the corporate city. There is much more likely to be a suitable base map available for the corporate city alone than for the corporate city plus adjacent overflow areas, and, besides, to show adjacent urban areas along with the incorporated city at a reasonable scale may result in a map of unwieldy size. Of course the latter point does not apply to a very small city; and for a very large city a single-sheet map ordinarily is not feasible. But size of the map may well be important in mapping a moderate-sized city.

Consider Salt Lake City, with a population of 189,000 in 1960. The incorporated city is nearly square, approximately 9 miles on a side, but the urbanized area, though only about 9 miles in width, extends between 25 and 26 miles from north to south. To represent the corporate city at a scale of 1 inch to 1,000 feet would require a map 4 feet on a side. This is awkwardly large. At the same scale, the urbanized area would need only a slightly wider east-west dimension, but a north-south extent of 11 or 12 feet would be required, which, of course, is impossibly large for a single-sheet map.

The scale

The matter of scale deserves further

consideration. In general, the larger the city the smaller the scale that can be used if a single-sheet map is desired, but this will vary somewhat from city to city with population density. For instance, the corporate city of Roanoke, Virginia, population 97,110 in 1960, has an area of 26 square miles; whereas the area of Hartford, Connecticut, population 162,178, is only 17.4 square miles. The same degree of detail requires a larger map for Roanoke, which is the smaller city. Another factor is the degree of generalization planned. If one expects to generalize all land uses into five or six types and does not plan to use a base map with lot lines, then a very large scale is not necessary.

It is, therefore, hard to be specific about the scale needed for the base map. In general, 1 inch to 500 or 600 feet is desirable. With cities at the upper end of the size range here being considered, and for smaller cities such as Roanoke where the city area is particularly great in proportion to population, a scale of perhaps 1 inch to 800 or 1,000 feet may have to be used. Smaller scales than this would be too small to show the desired information except in an extremely generalized form. Ordinarily, for the general land-use map, one uses as large a scale as is possible, limiting one's self to a single sheet, which will be easy to reproduce and work with. If the mapping is to be done in greater detail, a larger-scale map may be needed even though this requires several sheets.

The base map

The foregoing discussion to a considerable degree has dealt with ideals. It is all very well to speculate on what area should be covered and what scale would be best for a certain size of city. In the last analysis, however, for the geographer, the area to be included and the scale of the map are often controlled chiefly by expediency: to save time and expense, he may decide to use a base map which the city has in stock.

Fortunately, for the moderate-sized city, a base map is usually available at a reasonably acceptable scale. It is less common to find maps of adjacent areas at exactly the same scale. To make a map of the entire built-up area may require enlargement or reduction of existing maps of areas outside the city's corporate limits, and even where maps at the same scale are to be had, they may fit together poorly and require splicing. For suburban areas it may be necessary, as it frequently is for the New England town, to construct the base map from enlargements of United States Geological Survey topographic sheets, with corrections where the sheets are out of date. An excellent base map can be made in this way. Ordinarily, no attempt is made to reproduce the contours, since it is desired to achieve a base map that is as simple and uncluttered as possible. For some cities there is another source for the map. If the municipality has tax maps, they usually are numbered and indexed on a key map which is likely to be up to date and fairly accurate. With some minor redrafting this key map makes a reasonably good base map.

Lot lines are desirable on the base map but ordinarily are not practicable. Even at the largest scale possible for a single-sheet map of a moderate-sized city, lots near the city center would be too small to map as separate units. More often than not, the geographer must use a map on which the streets form the only guides to location.

Available base maps are rarely ideally suited to the purpose at hand. Almost invariably they include streets that have been planned but have not yet materialized; or some of the most recent side streets may not be shown. For these reasons and since most base maps carry extraneous information or are otherwise not perfectly suited to the making of the land-use map, it is desirable, where practicable, to correct the base map and then prepare a tracing from which prints of the new base can be made.

There is, it may be added, a practical

limit on the sizes of base maps. Tracing linen, blueprint paper, etc., seldom come in rolls that are over 42 inches wide. If the map exceeds 42 inches in width, the cost of blueprinting or other reproduction is exorbitant.

Making the land-use map

The base map is just the beginning. The information for a land-use map, itself, may be obtained entirely through field work; or Sanborn maps may be used, supplemented, ordinarily, by field work and possibly by the use of air photos. Another possible source for land-use information is assessors' records.

Sanborn maps Sanborn maps show streets, railroad tracks, lot lines, the dimensions of buildings, the nature of building materials, the number of stories, the uses of buildings, and certain other information. They are plotted on uniformly sized sheets, and since they are at a scale of 1 inch to either 50 or 100 feet, a large number of sheets is necessary for each city. These are bound together in a loose-leaf atlas and are kept up to date by the Sanborn Map Company through periodic surveys and pasting in on the maps of pieces showing new and revised information. Since the Sanborn maps are intended primarily for fire insurance purposes, some of the outer portions of the city, if consisting of considerable vacant land and widely scattered buildings, may not be mapped at all. An atlas of Sanborn maps for the local city is likely to be available in a realtor's office, in any office dealing with fire insurance rating, in the city planning office, or at the county courthouse.

Much of the information needed for a land-use map can be obtained directly from the Sanborn maps; in fact, unless a very detailed map is being prepared, the information available from these maps is so voluminous that it will have to be generalized considerably. But the Sanborn maps must be supplemented by field work for the outer sections of the city. Also, since the declared purpose of the Sanborn maps is to show buildings, it will be necessary to check the use of land that, from the Sanborn sheets, appears to be vacant. A field check of the final map is desirable, anyhow, to catch any current changes in land use. Also, field checking allows one to gain first-hand familiarity with the city.

Air-photo interpretation Air photos are valuable in supplementing the Sanborn maps. Particularly in outlying portions of the city, it is often possible to map residential land use directly from the air photos, and they may be especially valuable in allocating the amount of space actually used, as, for example, where a single house is the only occupant of a 10-acre parcel.

This brings up the intriguing question of how far one can go with air-photo interpretation in differentiating urban land uses. Apparently, the major land-use classes can be distinguished with fair accuracy except in the more crowded commercial areas where, on upper floors, residences and even factories may alternate with business use. Field work, or the use of Sanborn maps, will probably continue to be necessary for a really precise knowledge of the extent of even the major land-use classes in these more complex portions of the city.

On the other hand, building heights can be determined from air photos, and air-photo interpretation seems to have great possibilities in comparative studies of urban morphology.

Classifications of land use

In the construction of a land-use map, the classification of land uses as they are to appear on the map and in the legend is of primary importance. It is by no means a cut-and-dried matter, as might be supposed. Though many planners use roughly similar classifications in their urban land-use mapping, there is no universally accepted system.

An interesting approach to a standardized classification is that presented in the *Standard Industrial Classification Manual* in which both manufacturing and non-manufacturing industries are classified at 2-digit, 3-digit, and 4-digit levels. The material in city directories can be retabulated on this basis to get details about the number of different activity or functional types represented. However, such classification methods are of little value in making a general land-use map, since for such a map the emphasis is not on individual establishments but, instead, on land occupied as observed in the field or transferred from Sanborn maps. And the residential function is not represented at all in the standard industrial classification.

Classifications used by geographers Most urban land-use maps by geographers have shown approximately the following major classes: business (or commercial); industrial (generally somewhat broader than manufacturing); residential; public and semipublic; vacant (including agricultural) (Figures 11.1 and 11.2). The exact wording and order may differ from one study to another, but the major classes remain about the same. Railroads and railroad property may be included as a division under industrial land use or may be given a separate heading, or they may be shown as transportation, which includes also air and bus terminals and airports. But streets, which certainly are used for transportation,

Fig. 11.1 A combined population and urban land-use map of a hypothetical city or section of a city. (From William Applebaum, "A Technique for Constructing a Population and Urban Land Use Map," *Economic Geography*, vol. 28, 1952, fig. 1.)

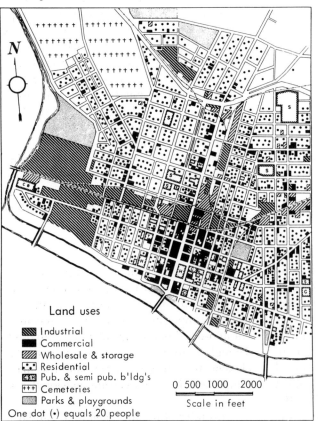

Land uses

▨ Industrial
■ Commercial
▨ Wholesale & storage
⁙ Residential
▦ Pub. & semi pub. b'ldg's
+++ Cemeteries
▨ Parks & playgrounds
One dot (•) equals 20 people

0   500 1000   2000

Scale in feet

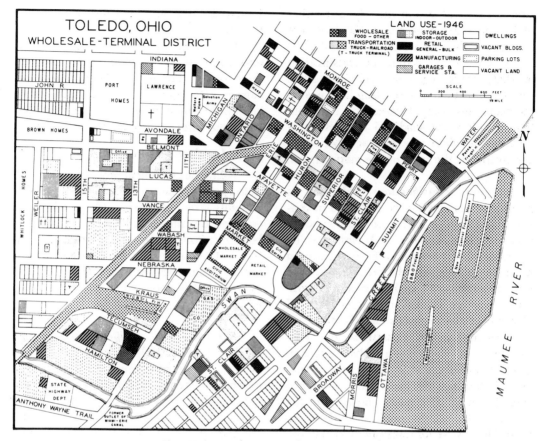

Fig. 11.2 Land-use map of a section of Toledo, Ohio. (From Albert G. Ballert, *The Primary Functions of Toledo, Ohio,* doctoral dissertation, The University of Chicago, Chicago, 1947, fig. 20.)

are always left blank on the land-use map.

Further breakdowns on geographers' maps have usually depended upon the type of city and the objective of the particular study. A few examples may make the situation clearer. Business or commercial land may be subdivided into retail, wholesale and storage, and financial and administrative, or even subdivided still more. Residential land use may be broken down on the basis of single-family, two-family, and multifamily, or it may even be subdivided in still other ways. Industrial land use may be subdivided into manufacturing and nonmanufacturing; into light versus heavy manufacturing; into basic and nonbasic; or on

the basis of various types of products such as textiles, food products, etc.

Some of the problems of subdividing will be discussed later in connection with the individual land uses. Obviously, however, it is impossible to show detail for all classes on a single map even at a scale of 1 inch to 400 or 500 feet. The decision as to which, if any, classes to subdivide depends upon whether manufacturing, commercial activities, residences, or some other land-use type is the principal subject of interest in the particular city study. Scale, too, may play a part in the decision. Thus, on a city map at a scale of 1 inch to 500 feet it would be extremely difficult, if not impossible, successfully to subdivide the commercial

land of a central area of the city, but a simplified breakdown of residential land use
throughout the city would be feasible.[2]

Whatever the system of classification
or whatever the degree of subdivision, some
shorthand method of indicating land use on
the map is necessary. Generally, a combination of colors (or shading) and letters is
used, but numbers or even fractional codes
are possible if the scale of the map permits.

Planners' classifications   Where it is
possible to map on a large scale and in considerable detail, a fairly complete subdivision of land uses under each class may be
desirable. This is generally necessary in
planning, and some of the breakdowns used
by planners may be of help to the geographer, although he may not agree with all
elements of the planner's classification.

BARTHOLOMEW'S CLASSIFICATION   Bartholomew, a well-known urban planner,
gives an alphabetical index of urban land
uses, indicating the main class to which
each belongs.[3] His main classes are R-1
and R-2, for single-family and two-family residences; M for multifamily dwellings;
C for commercial areas; P for parks and
playgrounds; SP for public and semipublic;
LI for light industry; HI for heavy industry;
and RR for railroad property. Nuisance
value of the use plays an important role in
Bartholomew's method, as it does in most
planners' classifications. Wholesaling does
not appear as commercial but, instead, is
classed as light industry; and the less desirable types of manufacturing are classed
as heavy industry, chiefly, apparently, because they are considered bad neighbors.[4]

[2] Planners sometimes use maps at different scales
for different parts of the city. Thus a scale of 1
inch to 50 feet might be used for the central area
and 1 inch to 400 or 600 feet for the outlying
areas.
[3] Harland Bartholomew, *Land Uses in American
Cities,* Harvard University Press, Cambridge, Mass.,
1955, esp. appendix B.
[4] Some planners object to the arbitrary assumption
that certain lines of manufacturing necessarily make

Junkyards, too, are classified with heavy
industry.

VARIATIONS IN PRACTICE   Other planners might arrive at different decisions on
these points. There is a general tendency,
moreover, to separate commercial land uses
into those oriented toward motor vehicles
and those oriented toward the pedestrian.

Special problems of mapping

Numerous technical problems are faced
in the actual making of a land-use map. The
difficulty of showing adequately the
crowded downtown section of the city has
been mentioned. One must either be content with a high degree of generalization
for the entire city, or else make a general
map and, also, a special map of the downtown area.

Several stories of differing uses   A related and particularly difficult problem involves what to do about buildings with a
number of stories of differing uses. What
can be done when the first floor of the
major structure is devoted to stores, and
the second and third floors to apartments?
There is no completely satisfactory answer,
although sometimes a diagonal line is used
to divide the parcel of land in half. One half
then is used to show ground-floor use, the
other to show use of the second floor. The
diagonal is drawn so as to leave the ground-
floor half fronting on the street (*A* in Figure
11.3). When it is necessary to show third-
floor use, the right angle indicating the
second-story use may be divided, and third-
floor use indicated in the triangle which
has the rear lot line as its hypotenuse (*B* in
Figure 11.3). For tall buildings, it may be desirable to represent in the third triangle the
dominant use of all floors above the second.
But such devices are not very satisfactory.
For special studies of the downtown area,
a profile field method is sometimes used to

bad neighbors. See discussion of this point under
"Obsolete Classification," p. 366.

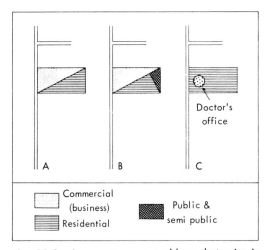

Fig. 11.3 Answers to some problems that arise in making an urban land-use map. In A, the ground floor is in stores and the second floor consists of apartments; in B, the ground floor consists of stores, the second floor is divided into apartments, and the third floor is a Masonic hall; in C, a doctor maintains an office in his home. (Based on E. B. Wilkins, *Mapping for Planning*, Public Administration Service, Chicago, 1948, to which the reader is referred for further suggested solutions.)

record the details of land use (see pages 292 to 294), but there is still the problem of showing the different uses on the final map. Sometimes separate maps of ground-floor use, second-floor use, and other upper-floor uses are resorted to.

Probably the most common method of handling the problem, however, is to base the mapping entirely on ground-floor use, a procedure that finds some justification in the fact that ground-floor use is usually more intensive than that of any higher floor. Some mappers attempt to classify each parcel of land according to its predominant use, but the subjectivity of determining predominant use is obvious.

Vacant space around building Another problem involves what to do about a building that covers only part of a lot. Normally, this need not unduly trouble the geographer even if he is working with a map that shows lot lines, since he is inter-

ested primarily in the overall use of the land. The generally accepted procedure is to map the entire lot as having the type of land use represented by the building.

Office or factory in home Still another practical problem encountered in mapping is that of a factory or an office or a commercial establishment, such as a beauty parlor, in a private home. One way in which this may be solved is to show the lot as residential, but use a circle in the appropriate color or pattern to represent the non-residential use (*C* in Figure 11.3).

Other problems Other special mapping decisions are sure to be required, and there are always difficult problems of classification. For instance, when a firm engages in both wholesaling and retailing from a single store, which designation should be used? Because of the necessity of decisions such as these, it is unlikely that any two persons, even if similarly trained, would produce identical maps of an area although starting with the same legend. Land-use mapping remains a far from cut-and-dried, objective procedure. Much reliance must be placed upon the judgment of the mapper as he meets various problems in the field.

Land-use Maps for Larger and Smaller Cities

The discussion thus far has been based on cities of moderate size. But what of larger cities and smaller ones?

Larger cities As one works with larger and larger cities, smaller and smaller scales are necessary to keep within the bounds of a single-sheet map, and generalizations of land-use detail reach a point where the map is of little value. To maintain a reasonable scale so that worthwhile information about land use can be shown, it becomes necessary to make the map in several sheets.

Smaller cities With decreasing city size, the construction of a land-use map becomes progressively simpler. Larger and larger scales can be used and more and more detailed breakdowns of the general land-use types are possible. In a sense the small city has its compensations in the matter of urban studies. For a city of 40,000, for example, no urbanized area has been outlined, there is no standard metropolitan statistical area, and no census tracts or block data ordinarily are available. On the other hand, it is more feasible for a person to do his own mapping and collect his own data in a small city.

The Final Map and Its Use

The chief product of the process that has been described is a general land-use map. A field map is usually prepared in color, but the final map may be in colors or in black and white, depending largely upon the purpose for which it is to be used. If the map is intended as a wall map, or otherwise for display purposes, it is customary to use colors. If it is to be reproduced in a book or magazine, however, it will have to be prepared with this in mind. The use of color in reproductions ordinarily is prohibited by cost, so a sufficient number of distinctive black and white patterns must be selected, patterns that will stand the reduction to the final, desired map size.

Common uses by geographers and planners

The completed land-use map serves many purposes. For the geographer, it is valuable in classroom instruction since it gives an overall picture of the patterns of land uses in a city as they exist in interrelation. It also gives him and his students a natural foundation for planning research dealing with the American city and for testing various research ideas. In the planning office, the general land-use map is in constant demand, since it is the foundation for the planner's work. Not only is it con-

sulted in daily planning activities, but it serves a useful purpose, too, as a wall map for public talks and talks with city officials —a necessary part of the planner's work if he is to see his plans bear fruit.

Proportions of land uses

The general land-use map, when used in still another way, can lead to conclusions that are extremely important to students of the city. The areas devoted to various purposes can be measured with the use of a polar planimeter or a dot planimeter or some other measuring device, and these areas can be converted into percentages of total city area. As such information becomes available for more and more cities, we are increasingly in a position to generalize about land use in the American city and to investigate the factors accounting for variations from the norm.

Bartholomew's study of land uses in American cities Harland Bartholomew made what is probably the chief contribution to our knowledge of land-use proportions in the American city, basing his averages on measurements from land-use maps which he and his associates had prepared over a period of years in zoning surveys of fifty-three central cities, thirty-three "satellite cities" and eleven urban areas.[5] Since we are concerned here chiefly with Bartholomew's methods, we shall consider in detail only his central cities. Twenty-eight of these had less than 50,000 population each; thirteen, 50,000 to 100,000; seven, 100,000 to 250,000; and five, 250,000 and over. He used the term "developed area" in contrast to "city area" to refer to all land used for purposes that are characteristically urban. City area is the total area of the corporate city. Developed area is city area minus vacant land (including farmland) and minus water areas that are not embraced within a park or recreational area. In his summary for the fifty-three cit-

[5] Bartholomew, *op. cit.*

ies, Bartholomew found the proportions of land uses indicated in Table 11.1.[6]

Table 11.1   **Summary of land uses in fifty-three central cities as determined by Bartholomew**

Use	Per cent of developed area	Per cent of city area
Single-family dwellings	31.81	17.76
Two-family dwellings	4.79	2.68
Multifamily dwellings	3.01	1.68
Commercial areas	3.32	1.85
Light industry	2.84	1.59
Heavy industry	3.60	2.01
Railroad property	4.86	2.71
Parks and playgrounds	6.74	3.77
Public and semipublic property	10.93	6.11
Streets	28.10	15.69
Total developed area	100.00	55.85
Vacant areas (including land used for agriculture)		30.10
Water areas		14.05
Total surveyed area		100.00

SOURCE: After table 3 in Harland Bartholomew, *Land Uses in American Cities*, Harvard University Press, Cambridge, Mass., 1955.

GENERALIZATIONS   The percentages given in Table 11.1 represent averages. Some types of use are of increasing relative importance and some of decreasing relative importance with increasing city size, and the proportions of some do not seem to vary with city size. Chiefly through the use of tables and scatter diagrams, Bartholomew

[6] Bartholomew worked with occupied ground area. This does not take account of upper-story space, which is considerable in a large city. But, to include such space, one would have to use total floor area at all levels rather than ground area, and the calculations would be more complicated. Besides, there is logic in restricting the measurements as Bartholomew did, since ground-floor use normally represents the most intensive use of a site and reflects best the competition for space.

worked out a number of such relationships and tendencies. Here are a few of his many conclusions and inferences with respect to central cities.

Developed area per capita decreases with increase in size of city until, in the larger cities, a sort of equilibrium appears to be reached.

The amount of land used for all residential purposes is proportional to the total developed area of the city, and the ratio of land to population varies inversely with the size of the city (Figure 11.4).

The area in single-family dwellings tends toward a constant proportion of total developed area regardless of the size of the city.

Though two-family structures are traditionally associated wtih the larger cities, conversions of single-family dwellings in small cities are tending to change this condition and there now seems to be little relation between population of city and percentage of total developed area devoted to two-family dwellings.

The larger the city the greater is the proportion of the developed land used for multifamily houses.

The percentage of the developed area devoted to commerce (business) increases as size of city increases.

In cities of more than 50,000 population there seems to be a tendency for the proportion of land devoted to light industry to increase with city size. For smaller cities no such relationship is apparent.

The percentage of total developed area in parks and playgrounds usually increases with size of the city.

There is a tendency for the proportion of land that is public and semipublic property to decrease with city size.

In general, smaller cities have higher percentages of vacant land than larger cities.

The foregoing are given here in summary form. Bartholomew quite properly qualifies many of his conclusions, since, in most instances, some cities stand out in apparent contradiction to the general rules. Nevertheless, the conclusions mentioned and many others included in the book represent a good start on a body of generaliza-

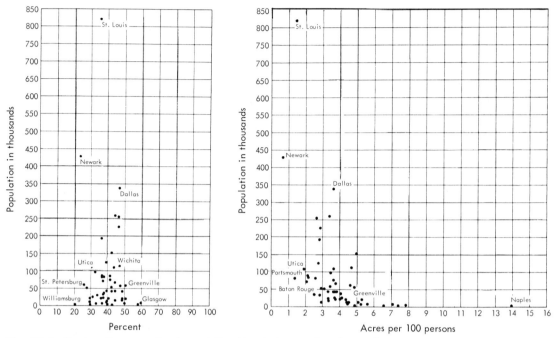

Fig. 11.4 Scatter diagrams showing relationships between city size and area used for residential purposes in fifty-three central cities studied by Bartholomew. In the first graph, city size is plotted against residential area as a percentage of total developed area. In the second graph, city size is plotted against acres of residential land per 100 persons. It is apparent that residential areas make up about the same proportion of the total developed area regardless of city size, but that residential land per 100 persons tends to decrease with increase in city size. It should be noted, however, that few very large cities were included in the fifty-three central cities. Only one, St. Louis, exceeded 500,000 in population, and only twelve exceeded 100,000. (After Harland Bartholomew, *Land Uses in American Cities,* Harvard University Press, Cambridge, Mass., 1955, figs. 2 and 3.)

tions regarding land uses in the American city. If similar data for enough cities were available, interesting by-products might result. For instance, Bartholomew discusses some variations in land use by city size, but the geographer would like to know to what degree the land-use proportions vary regionally and by functional types of cities.

Need for standardized mapping To arrive at the best possible generalizations we should have land-use maps of all cities in the country, based on exactly the same land-use categories and on otherwise standardized procedures. But this would be a difficult goal to attain. It may be assumed

that the maps prepared by one organization, such as Bartholomew and his associates, are reasonably standardized in these respects, but what of other urban land-use maps? There seems to be an increasing tendency for planners to settle on a standardized legend. The State Development Commission of Connecticut, for example, in its regional planning program at the state level, requires a generalized land-use map of each municipality, prepared according to a standardized legend; and the idea of standardized land-use mapping is gaining popularity in other states as well.

But geographers' classifications are likely to differ from those of planners in several respects. For instance, the geographer would probably not use nuisance value as a determinant in his classification of land uses. To the planner, a wholesale grocery establishment may be classed with light industry; to the geographer it is wholesaling, a subdivision of business or commercial. Moreover, geographers are more likely to work as individuals and therefore to differ from one another in the details of their maps.

Would a completely standardized system be desirable? Its value as a basis for generalizations is obvious. But even if agreement could be reached on the details of such a system there might be the objection, by some geographers, that a rigid system would make it impossible, in any particular study, to emphasize adequately land-use characteristics that are of special local importance. But geographers more and more are tending to follow, in their mapping as well as in all their research, procedures that give promise of leading to generalizations.

Criticisms of the general land-use map

The general land-use map has been criticized on the grounds that it is static, that what we should be mapping is motion—the flow of goods, the movement of people on the streets.[7] Also, it is subject to the

[7] P. R. Crowe, "On Progress in Geography," *Scottish Geographical Magazine*, vol. 54, pp. 1–19, reference, p. 14, 1938.
A dynamic way of looking at the urban land-use picture, an approach that might to some degree meet Crowe's criticism, is represented by some research carried on by the Institute for Urban Land Use and Housing Studies at Columbia University. Land use, in the research mentioned, refers to the activities customarily engaged in by an *establishment*, the latter being conceived of as an individual or group of individuals occupying a definite recognizable place of business, residence, government, or assembly. The activities of each establishment take the form of repeated relationships with other establishments and individuals. Establishments vary greatly in the volume of traffic in persons and goods that they generate. The relationships between establishments, characterized by recurrent interactions requiring the movement

criticism that the map is old almost as soon as it is made. Some system is needed for keeping the information up to date, but the problem is not a simple one. Moreover, it seems to be more a matter for the planner than for the geographer who is not, ordinarily, concerned with the minute continuous elements of change. He is likely to be more interested in the patterns of a particular time or as they existed at widely separated times.

IBM cards Some people feel that International Business Machine cards (or their equivalents) are the answer, and that they may even replace the general land-use map entirely. According to this plan, a card, keyed to a numbering system on a map, is punched for each lot, indicating the nature of the use of the ground and buildings in as much detail as is desired. The card method has the advantage that much more information can be recorded than on a map; also, any change in the use of a lot is easily recorded since only a single card is involved. And it is possible with such cards quickly to obtain various facts and desired correlations. The system, however, is probably practicable chiefly for large cities. Moreover, in either a large city or a small one, punched cards are not a complete substitute for the general land-use map, since, after all, the latter shows the patterns of land use that are so important to an understanding of the city.

Machine mapping Even the use of punched cards threatens to be rendered obsolete by machine mapping in which data

of persons or goods or the exchange of information, are referred to as *linkages*. The analysis of land use may be approached by setting up schematic patterns reflecting these linkages. See Robert B. Mitchell and Chester Rapkin, *Urban Traffic: A Function of Land Use*, Columbia University Press, New York, 1954, and John Rannells, *The Core of the City*, Columbia University Press, New York, 1956.

are fed into a computer and a land-use map produced.[8]

Separate Maps for Major Use Classes

Although there is unquestionably much to be gained by seeing the several urban land uses on a single map, it is sometimes worthwhile examining each land use separately. From the general land-use map separate tracings can be made to show the distribution of land used for manufacturing, for residences, or for business. Just seeing each of these uses by itself often brings out elements of the pattern that might be overlooked on the general map.

The advantage of showing one class of land use by itself is illustrated by a map of manufacturing in York, Pennsylvania, that the writer prepared several decades ago (see Figure 16.2). The city was a small one and could be mapped in considerable detail. In the field mapping, which was really a combination of the use of Sanborn maps and field work, it was decided to obtain more information about manufacturing than for the other classes of land use. The general land-use map proved satisfactory for showing the patterns of the major land uses in the city, but the separate map showing areas devoted to manufacturing proved of much greater value. The locations and outlines of the manufacturing properties were traced from the general map. Patterns and numbers were used to indicate types and subtypes, details regarding which were obtained partly through the original mapping and partly from a directory. Railroads were shown on the manufacturing map since they appeared to be closely related to the manufacturing pattern.

Several features of manufacturing land

use became readily apparent. Most of the manufacturing areas, for instance, were strung out along the railroads. On the other hand, certain types of manufacturing were largely independent of rail transportation. These were chiefly in the textiles and textile products class; but food products plants (local bakeries, ice-cream plants, etc.) showed this same independence, and so too did the production of hand-made cigars, an activity that has long since ceased.

Of course, it is entirely possible to focus upon a single land-use class in field mapping, and thus to obtain more detail than would be possible in a more general project. But this involves special problems of mapping and of classification that will be discussed more fully in the chapters dealing with the several individual land uses.

Understanding the Urban Land-use Map

Several factors should be considered that contribute to an understanding of the urban land-use pattern as a whole. In any particular city, of course, such unique factors as the nature of the site and the city's history are important, but these do not concern us here. We are interested in urban land-use patterns of cities in general rather than the patterns of individual cities. What are the major land-use determinants that operate in every city?

It need hardly be pointed out that economics plays a major role. National, regional, and local economic forces are involved, though in explaining intracity patterns, the last of these is by far the most important. In the next few pages some of the economic bases of the patterns are discussed. Then a study by Charles Colby that brings out the idea of the centrifugal and centripetal forces that are constantly affecting land uses in the city is summarized. Since land values and valuation data are important in explaining land-use patterns, they too are considered. So, also, are zoning

[8] In this connection see "Geographic Ordering of Information: New Opportunities" (report of the Geographic Coding Subcommittee, Census Advisory Committee, Association of American Geographers), *The Professional Geographer,* vol. 16, no. 4, pp. 39–43, July, 1964.

and urban renewal, as well as the effects of limited-access highways.[9] In Chapter 12 the several theoretical explanations of city structure are discussed, and in successive chapters, the patterns of the various individual land uses are considered.

Economics and urban land use

First we may look at the urban land-use map from the point of view of the land economist. The present urban pattern can be thought of as resulting from a struggle for the most efficient use of the land.

> . . . The determination of urban land use is a market process. The use that is made of each parcel is the result of economic competition among alternative uses. Thus the processes of city growth are economic processes and the pattern of land use is the product of the urban land market.[10] . . .
>
> Because in every community there exists a variety of land uses, each parcel is the focus of a complex but singular set of space relationships with the social and economic activities that are centered on all other parcels. To each combination of space relationships, the market attaches a special evaluation, which largely determines the amount of the bid for that site which is the focus of the combination. Thus certain locations are more highly valued for residential use than other sites because of the greater convenience to shops, schools, centers of employment, and recreation facilities. Corner locations command a higher price for certain types of retail use because of greater convenience to streams of pedestrian traffic. . . .[11]
>
> It is the competition of land uses in the market that distributes the use types in an arrangement that approaches the most efficient pattern.[12]

The land-use pattern of an urban area

is far more than a current phenomenon. It is a reflection of the cumulative needs over a period of years, and is not the same pattern that would result if a new community of the same size and character were being planned at the moment.[13] The fixity of investment of land improvements has resulted in a lag in adjusting to social and economic needs. In most cities the skeleton of the street and utility systems is a relic of earlier times and a majority of the buildings are representative of generations past.

But it is far beyond the scope of this book to deal with urban land economics in any detail. For fuller treatment the reader is referred to the work of Ratcliff and other economists who have specialized in this field.

Dynamic character of the urban land-use pattern

The dynamic character of the urban land-use pattern was emphasized by Charles Colby several decades ago.[14] He said that the pattern is constantly in a process of evolution through modification of established functions and the addition of new ones. This calls for new functional forms, for modifications of previously established forms, and for extensions and realignments of the urban pattern. These developments, he claimed, are governed by forces, among which two groups stand out. One group consists of the centrifugal forces, which impel functions to migrate from the central areas of the city toward the periphery; the second group consists of centripetal forces, which hold certain functions in the central zone and attract others to it. The centrifugal forces are made up of a combination of uprooting impulses in the central zone and attractive qualities of the periphery; while the centripetal forces focus on

---

[9] Various other factors also help to explain the land-use pattern, but they are not so general in their effects, and thus are not discussed here.

[10] Richard U. Ratcliff, *Urban Land Economics*, McGraw-Hill Book Company, Inc., New York, 1949, p. vi.

[11] *Ibid.*, pp. 283–284.

[12] *Ibid.*, p. 289.

[13] *Ibid.*, p. 386.

[14] Charles C. Colby, "Centrifugal and Centripetal Forces in Urban Geography," *Annals of the Association of American Geographers*, vol. 23, pp. 1–20, 1933.

the central zone of the city, making that the center of attraction for the entire urban area.

In carrying his discussion further, Colby used three divisions of the urban area—an innermost or nuclear zone, a second or middle zone, and an outermost or peripheral zone—and he gave examples of shifts involving these zones. Examples of centrifugal migrations are numerous. Many manufacturers, for instance, facing rising taxes and other handicaps, have abandoned their downtown plants and located in the suburbs. The high-quality residential function in most cities has moved outward over the years; and branches of department stores in outlying shopping centers are competing seriously with downtown stores, which amounts in effect to a centrifugal movement of the department store function. In contrast, the centripetal forces are evidenced by the increased growth of regional offices in central areas of great cities such as Chicago and of multistoried apartment houses in or near the central zone.

Centrifugal forces Colby goes on to analyze each group of forces more carefully. For instance, concentrating on the centrifugal forces, he analyzes the uprooting conditions of the central zone of the city: high land and property values and high tax rates; traffic congestion and high cost of transportation; difficulty of securing adequate space for expansion; desire of factory owners to avoid nuisance complaints; inability to obtain sites with special qualities needed; and miscellaneous handicaps such as irksome legal restrictions, outgrown laws, and decline in the social importance of certain areas.

Complementing these uprooting conditions of the central zone are attractive qualities of the peripheral zone of the city. These include the availability of large parcels of land at relatively low cost; transportation services suited to the migrating function;

attractive site qualities such as level land, good drainage, and water frontage; and possibly previously established control of a sizable area.

Centrifugal forces in summary The two sets of centrifugal forces—uprooting on the one hand, attracting on the other—can be expressed, according to Colby, as six combined forces: (1) the *spatial force*, under which congestion in the central zone uproots and vacant spaces of the outermost zone attract; (2) the *site force*, involving the disadvantages of the intensively used central zone in contrast to the relatively unused natural landscape of the city's periphery; (3) the *situational force*, which arises from unsatisfactory functional spacing and alignment in the central zone and the prospect of satisfactory conditions in these respects in the outermost zone; (4) the *force of social evaluation*, under which high land values, high taxes, and inhibitions growing out of past difficulties in the long-established central zone create the urge to move, and low values, low taxes, and freedom from restrictions imposed by previous occupance in the newly developing peripheral zone represent the attractions of this particular zone; (5) the *status and organization of occupance* in which obsolete functional forms, inertia of pattern, traffic congestion, and unsatisfactory transportation facilities of the central zone are balanced against modern forms, a dynamic pattern, freedom from traffic congestion, and highly satisfactory transportation facilities in the outermost zone; and (6) the *human equation*, a vague category that includes a variety of other migratory impulses such as those arising from religion, personal whims, real estate booms, and manipulated politics.

Centripetal forces The centripetal forces in urban development focus on the central zone of the city. This area is characterized by the great number and complexity of its urban functions, and, in the larger cities, by multiple levels of use, extending from the lowest basements to the highest floors of skyscrapers. What are the attractive qualities of this central area?

Colby suggests five groups. One is *site attraction*, owing to a river crossing, an accessible waterfront, or some other natural advantage. *Functional convenience* is a second attractive quality of the central zone. The area is not only the natural focal point for the city, but also for the region and possibly for a group of regions. A third attraction is *functional magnetism:* for example, the attraction of several branches of an industry for each other, or of one class of shop for others of similar type. *Functional prestige* is a fourth, slightly different force: a section of a street may become famous for fashions; doctors often cluster for reasons of functional prestige. Lastly, Colby suggests the *human equation* as a centripetal force. Some people wish to live close to the theaters and various conveniences of the downtown.

The ever-increasing effects of the automobile and the airplane in weakening the centripetal pull of the city center should be noted. Commercial establishments can draw customers as well or even better from a location on the city's periphery as from a downtown store; and the truck has freed many factories from their ties to the railroads. Airports, which must of necessity have peripheral locations, similarly work against the attraction of the city's center. Such developments were under way even when Colby made his study but they have accelerated at a pace that he could hardly have anticipated.

Balance of forces The two sets of forces—centrifugal and centripetal—are constantly in conflict. In some cases one set is obviously dominant; in others, the matter is uncertain. In still others the effect is to divide the function into two parts, one remaining in the downtown zone and the other seeking a location near the periphery of the city. Sometimes, only an office remains downtown while a plant moves to the suburbs. (See, in this connection, Foley's study, "Suburbanization of Administrative Offices in the San Francisco Bay Area," summarized in Chapter 14.) In the matter of residences, some people are drawn to the outer areas whereas others, for good reasons, prefer apartments at the edge of the central business district.

Conclusions In any city it is possible to decipher shifts that can be definitely attributed to the operation of centrifugal forces and others that reflect centripetal forces. The locations of most functions, it may be assumed, result from a balance or compromise between the two sets of forces.

Of course, the city is by no means a closed system. Some functions move into the urban area from outside the city and some new ones originate inside the urban area. But all of these, too, presumably tend to be located in accordance with centrifugal and centripetal forces. Thus a new multi-story office building, built to serve not only the metropolitan area but the entire region as well, may logically be located in the focal downtown area of the city. And a new, modern, single-story factory, serving a similar area, seeks a location at the edge of the city. The whole concept is an interesting one. It will arise again in connection with the theoretical explanations of city structure in Chapter 12. But several factors that help to explain the urban land-use pattern remain to be discussed.

Property value and valuation data

The locational attributes of a site are reflected in its monetary value, and this value, in turn, is a strong determinant of land use. Property must be valued (appraised) for any buying and selling, but information of this sort normally is not available on any standardized basis.

Three forms of valuation data Valuation data are available to the research worker chiefly because the accumulation of such information is a necessary step in the taxation process. Valuation data take three forms: the value of land, the value of buildings on the land (technically referred to as "improvements"), and the value of land and buildings combined.

Assessed value Although it would be desirable to use market value appraisals for both the value of land and the value of buildings, the only data ordinarily available are assessed values prepared by city and county (or town in New England) tax offices. Assessed value is some percentage of appraised value. This percentage may be fixed by law, but it varies from city to city and region to region and may differ with the major type of land use. The fact that the assessed value is only a percentage of the real value does not matter a great deal to a geographer concerned only with a single city, since he is more interested in the differential pattern within the city than in absolute values. Unfortunately, however, in some cities, the relationship between assessed values and real values is said to vary considerably even from one part of the city to another.

Front-foot values Ordinarily, the data on downtown commercial land values (not including buildings) are expressed as front-foot values reduced to a standard depth from the front of the lot. This is done because the frontage on the street, particularly in business sections, is of considerably greater value than the land farther to the rear of the lot. Other areas of the city are generally assessed on an acreage basis.

Maps based on valuation data The urban geographer's concern with valuation

data is chiefly with their relationships to land use. Therefore, maps based on valuation data are compared with the land-use map.

VALUE OF LAND AND BUILDINGS Building values vary in relation to size, age, location, use of the buildings, and possibly some other factors. The map of value of land and buildings combined tends to be something of a hotchpotch. Though useful for other purposes and though the pattern it presents is worth studying for its own sake, it is of little help in interpreting the land-use map.

LAND-VALUES MAP The land-values map is considered more fundamental than the land-and-buildings-values map for a study of the relationships between valuation data and land use. Assessed values of land (and, of course, appraised values where these are available) are supposed to reflect location, thus representing, in a sense, the potential of the land; at the same time they are affected somewhat by the present use of the land in the vicinity. The nature or size of the building on a lot affects the valuation of the lot, and the fact that the lot is in an outlying shopping section or other city area where land is much in demand certainly affects its valuation.

The land-values map of a city is likely to show the highest values around the busiest intersection, a fact that holds good whether a lot is occupied by a department store or is empty. From this peak point, values, on the average, decline outward, though extensions of higher-than-average values continue from the center out along the main thoroughfares (see Figure 15.1). Other areas of high valuation will be found to coincide with high-grade residential sections, with shopping centers, and with industrial tracts. Thus, the valuation pattern seems in fact to be based primarily on location and secondarily on general use of each area.

Valuations and land use Valuations unquestionably affect land use. For example, lots near the main street intersection of the city are likely to have such high assessments (and therefore have such high taxes levied against them) that the only feasible land uses are ones that will yield very large returns; and lots bordering major radial streets are likely to be assessed at so high a figure that residences must give way to businesses. Businessmen of the central business district sometimes complain that the high assessed values of the downtown area are ruining them (through high taxes) while encouraging the development of outlying shopping centers where assessments are lower.

Limitations of valuation data and valuation maps Valuation data have several serious limitations from the geographer's point of view. The most serious of these is that the data for different cities are not comparable. This is chiefly because the bases for valuation differ so much from city to city. Indeed, in some instances they may differ significantly within a single city.

A second problem is that of availability of maps based on valuation data, or, where such maps are not available, of data for making the maps. Though maps of land values and of land-plus-building values of the downtown area of the city have been constructed by many planning departments, it is unlikely that these maps have been extended to cover the entire city. Ordinarily, it is possible to assemble from the assessor's office the data necessary for making such maps, but it is at best a laborious procedure.

Nevertheless, it is the author's belief that geographers have not done enough work with land values. It is generally agreed that land values are of prime importance in urban land-use studies since they both determine and reflect the character and intensity of land use.

How taxes may vary by corporate units
As was pointed out earlier, valuation data

form the basis for taxation. Actually, two factors are involved: valuation and tax rate. The valuation pattern is likely to be significant in explaining the varied land-use pattern within a city. Tax rate does not enter into the story since it is ordinarily the same throughout the corporate unit.

In the city's competition with its satellites and suburbs and with other cities, however, tax rates must be considered.[15] There are a number of cases of factories being located just outside a city and annexation being resisted because of the higher taxes on the other side of the boundary line.[16] Moreover, a manufacturer planning to establish a branch plant will give serious attention to the tax rates of the cities he is considering.

Tax-exempt property Even when the data are assembled it will be found that a number of properties are tax exempt, thus leaving vacant spots on a map showing assessed values.[17] Generally, state legislatures have exempted from taxation all public, education, religious, cultural, and charitable non-profit institutions and cemeteries. The reasons for such exceptions are obvious, but as the amount of property in these categories increases, the tax base diminishes accordingly.

Perhaps the problem can best be pointed up by calling attention to a news item that appeared in April, 1957, in which the Boston Finance Commission declared that one-third of the property in its city was tax exempt. Boston, it was pointed out, is

[15] Actually, both valuation and tax rate must be taken into account. In one city the tax rate may be low but property may be appraised at nearly its full market value. In a second city the tax rate may be higher but the appraisal practice such that actual taxes paid on comparable property are no higher than in the first city.

[16] In some states, an area cannot be annexed without the consent of owners of at least 50 per cent of the valuation in the area under consideration.

[17] Appraisal values are sometimes available for tax-exempt land but not assessed values.

helpless as more and more of the city's best property moves into the tax-exempt column. Most large cities of the country, according to the report, average about 23 per cent tax-exempt property. The proportion is growing in nearly all cities, but Boston is in a particularly serious predicament. Massachusetts cities and towns depend very largely upon real estate taxes for their support. Boston is small in area and, as with other New England cities, there is little or no chance for it to add to its area through annexation. Thus it is difficult for the city to increase its gross valuation which is the basis for tax revenue. This makes the growing proportion of tax-exempt land a particularly serious matter.

Here is an interesting and practical topic for research. As studied for an individual city, the tax-exempt property could be indicated on a map and classified. This should yield the answers to some intriguing questions. What proportion of the tax-exempt property is owned by the city? How much is held by churches? By each of the principal denominations? How much is owned by schools of various types? How much is Federally owned? How much, state owned? What other types of owners are represented? If similar data for an earlier period are assembled, then a further question can be asked and answered: How are the amount and proportion held in each of the various categories changing?

And there are various related questions for which answers might be found. What is the typical distribution within the city of the tax-exempt property? To what extent does such property serve the whole metropolitan region or even a larger area as contrasted with the corporate city only? How does the amount of tax-exempt property vary with city size? With type of city? From region to region?

Investigation of the problems of tax-exempt urban land, like the study of most urban research topics, would be most productive if carried out in a number of cities, so that we could learn what is happening in the American city rather than in just one city. But study of the problem even in a single city should be a step toward the general answers that are needed.

Zoning and urban land use

Another urban pattern closely related to land use is that of zoning districts. Nearly all American cities (and many smaller communities) have adopted zoning ordinances, and in the average city a zoning map and ordinance are available. Zoning laws tend to limit the ideal market competition described earlier in this chapter, since the individual is free to exploit the revenue potential of his parcel of land only within the limits set by such laws.

However, in most cities, zoning was initiated only a few decades ago and is not retroactive, so the observable effects are correspondingly limited. This is particularly true since, to a large degree, zoning ordinances tend to reflect the previously existing land-use pattern. Central areas usually exhibit a mixture of uses developed before the advent of zoning, and the regulations established for zoning districts in these areas have only a long-run effect, that of working toward less congestion when buildings are replaced.

It is in areas that were vacant at the time zoning was adopted that regulations have made the most observable impression. A former student now working as an urban planner reports that the effects of zoning are particularly striking in some suburban towns contiguous to central cities. These towns adopted zoning in the mid-twenties, before the period of rapid suburbanization. Hence, to a large degree, they have developed according to their original zoning plans.

And the effects of zoning can be analyzed more exactly. To some degree, at least, zoning must be credited with the absence of business development in the newer, high-quality residential areas. It may help in explaining the concentration of industry in some outer sections of the city that have been zoned for industry for a number of years. Zoning accounts for the wide spacing of houses in some suburban communities where a large minimum lot size has been adopted deliberately to keep down the population density. And it has had various other effects.

The implication here is that zoning is wise zoning. Unfortunately this is not always so. For instance, too much land may be zoned for business or for manufacturing, or too little land or land of too poor quality.

It is not always easy to decipher the relationships between zoning and the urban land-use pattern. One basis for difficulty is a peculiar characteristic that most past zoning has exhibited. On land zoned for industry, that or any "higher" use (business, residential) was permitted; and land zoned for business could be used either for businesses or residences. Only residentially zoned land has been restricted to that use alone. But this element of confusion seems to be passing; single-purpose zoning is now more generally favored (see in this connection pages 365 to 367). Another basis for confusion is introduced whenever an appeals board grants a variance, which permits use of a lot for a different purpose from that prescribed for the zone in which it is situated.

As a geographic factor, zoning is destined to become more and more important as the years go by. It may be assumed that fifty years from now the land-use map of the average city will show the molding effect of such regulations much more than it does today. Zoning will be discussed in more detail in connection with some of the individual land uses in the chapters that follow.

Limited-access highways

Though not a matter of zoning, the construction in the city of a limited-access highway (generally referred to as a freeway or an expressway) is somewhat similar locally to zoning in affecting land use. The building of such a highway may require broad changes in the zoning map. It may eliminate poor areas or seriously reduce the quality of others. Particularly, too, it is likely to exert a strong influence on the location of supermarkets and controlled shopping centers, which can hardly exist without ready access to the main flows of traffic. The exit points, therefore, often become sites for such developments, just as they are likely to prove attractive to manufacturers looking for plant sites.

Urban land use and urban renewal

Control of land use by the government, whatever the level, is, therefore, an important land-use determinant. Zoning amounts to regulation by the city government of future land use in the city, and we have found that it must be reckoned with as affecting the land-use pattern even though this effect is pronounced only in newer sections of the city. Limited-access highways represent a combination of state and Federal efforts. There is another way, too, in which the local government, in cooperation with the Federal government, is changing the land-use pattern of the city. This is through *urban renewal*, undertaken, normally, by a redevelopment agency.

Three different levels of urban renewal are recognized. Reconditioning is used in an area as a temporary measure, but it itself is hardly to be classed as urban renewal. *Conservation*, the first of the three levels, is a more permanent measure. It is a type of renewal treatment aimed at restoring the economic and social values of deteriorating areas. Some structures are classified as standard, some as conservable (requiring certain improvements), and some as requiring demolition. *Rehabilitation* implies even stronger measures; it is the second level of urban renewal. The third and most drastic level is *clearance and redevelopment*. Property is purchased by the local public agency, structures are cleared, utilities are installed, and other site improvements are made. The property is then sold or leased to redevelopers, who build new structures on these sites according to an urban renewal plan prepared by the local public agency.

In its effect upon the urban land-use pattern, urban renewal is in rather interesting contrast to zoning. Zoning is in a sense passive and permissive, establishing regulations as to what may and may not be done with the land hereafter. Urban renewal, on the other hand, is dynamic. Through it, blight is arrested in some areas, and restoration effected in others. But urban renewal is most dynamic in the case of clearance and redevelopment since an area can then be completely rebuilt in a few years.[18] A second contrast is that the most observable effects of zoning are likely to be in the newer, undeveloped sections of the city, whereas urban renewal has its chief effects in the older sections.

Urban renewal projects have often been concerned with blighted residential areas. The methods used for delimiting such residential areas will be discussed further in connection with residential land use.

Selected References

Applebaum, William: "A Technique for Constructing a Population and Urban Land Use Map," *Economic Geography*, vol. 28, pp. 240–245, 1952.

Bartholomew, Harland: *Land Uses in American Cities*, Harvard University Press, Cambridge, Mass., 1955.

Chapin, F. Stuart, Jr.: *Urban Land Use Planning*, 2d ed., University of Illinois Press, Urbana, Ill., 1965.

Colby, Charles C.: "Centrifugal and Centripetal Forces in Urban Geography," *Annals of the Association of American Geographers*, vol. 23, pp. 1–20, 1933.

Fisher, Ernest M., and Robert M. Fisher: *Urban Real Estate*, Holt, Rinehart and Winston, Inc., New York, 1954, esp. chap. 13.

Ratcliff, Richard U.: "Efficiency and the Location of Urban Activities," in Robert Moore Fisher (ed.), *The Metropolis in Modern Life*, Doubleday & Company, Inc., Garden City, N.Y., 1955, pp. 125–148.

————: *Urban Land Economics*, McGraw-Hill Book Company, Inc., New York, 1949, esp. chap. 13.

Standard Industrial Classification Manual, U.S. Bureau of the Budget, 1957.

Weimer, Arthur M., and Homer Hoyt: *Principles of Real Estate*, 4th ed., The Ronald Press, New York, 1960, esp. chap. 18.

Wilkens, E. B.: *Mapping for Planning*, Publication no. 101, Public Administration Service, Chicago, 1948.

Wrigley, Robert L., Jr.: "The Sanborn Map as a Source of Land Use Information for City Planning," *Land Economics*, vol. 25, pp. 216–219, 1949.

---

[18] Admittedly, however, the change is not always rapid. There are often delays due to court action. Generally, too, three levels of government are involved—Federal, state, and local—each zealous in guarding its own powers, and this results in further delays. Moreover, the problem of relocating displaced people often consumes still more time, and it is not always easy to sell or lease the land resulting from clearance and redevelopment.

12

Theoretical explanations of city structure

IN ADDITION to its value as a basis for urban research and planning, the general land-use map is a graphic presentation of a challenge: Is there to some degree a common pattern or order which carries over from city to city and which implies similar processes of origin? Many students of the city have claimed that there is and have tended to follow one or another of three ideas that have been advanced. These have commonly been referred to as the *concentric zone* theory, the *sector* theory, and the *multiple nuclei* theory.[1]

In this chapter the three theories are considered as they were originally conceived and as they have stood the test of time. Each of the three is presented first largely in its traditional form. Then an attempt is made to assess the effects on the theory of the tremendous changes in cities that have taken place in recent decades.

The Concentric Zone Theory

The first of these proposals to attract wide attention was the concentric zone theory advanced by Ernest W. Burgess, a sociologist, in the 1920s. Though he developed his scheme particularly with respect to Chicago, it has been regarded as applicable to cities in general.

Statement of the theory

According to Burgess, "in the absence of counteracting factors" the American city should take the form of five concentric zones.[2] The characteristics of these zones

[1] It has been argued by some that these might better be referred to as generalizations or graphical descriptions, but throughout this chapter, largely for convenience, they will be called theories.

[2] Burgess' concentric zone theory may be considered an adaptation of von Thünen's theory, but von Thünen's scheme is applied to the area around the city and Burgess' theory to the city itself. More-

are summarized in essentially their original form in the following paragraphs (Figure 12.1).[3]

Zone 1. The central business district
At the center of the city is the central business district, the focus of the city's commercial, social, and civic life, and of transportation. Burgess considered this district to consist of two parts. The heart of the area is the downtown retail district with its department stores, smart shops, office buildings, clubs, banks, hotels, theaters, and headquarters of economic, social, civic, and political life. In small communities these various activities intermingle; in large cities there are likely to be subdistricts—a financial area, a theater area, and others. Encircling the downtown retail district, according to Burgess, is the wholesale business district with its market, warehouses, and storage buildings. When the city is situated on a waterfront, its port functions may be interspersed with the wholesaling functions.

Zone 2. Zone in transition
Surrounding the central business district is a zone of residential deterioration. Here business and light manufacturing from Zone 1 have encroached upon residential areas. Though there may be residual islands of "first citizen" homes, rooming houses represent the most typical residential use. In portions of this zone are likely to be found the city's principal slums—areas of poverty, degradation, and crime. A few decades ago, in many

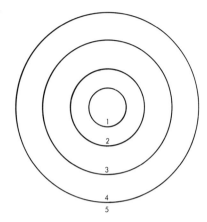

Fig. 12.1 Generalized zones according to Burgess' concentric zone theory. The zones are supposedly applicable to all cities. Numbers refer as follows: (1) the central business district; (2) zone in transition; (3) zone of independent workingmen's homes; (4) zone of better residences; (5) commuters' zone.

over, von Thünen does not imply an outward progression of the zones as Burgess does. See footnote 7 on page 75.

[3] Based on Ernest W. Burgess, "Urban Areas," in T. V. Smith and L. D. White (eds.), *Chicago: An Experiment in Social Science Research*, The University of Chicago Press, Chicago, 1929, pp. 113–138. The theory was first presented in its simplest form in the *Proceedings of the American Sociological Society*, 1923, vol. 18, and reprinted as "Growth of the City," Chap. 2 in Robert E. Park, Ernest W. Burgess, and Roderick D. McKenzie (eds.), *The City*, The University of Chicago Press, Chicago, 1925, pp. 47–62.

American cities, this belt was largely composed of colonies of recent immigrants. The inner belt of the zone is likely to be a business and light manufacturing district, and the outer boundary, a ring of retrogressing neighborhoods from which, as people become more prosperous, they escape into Zone 3.

Zone 3. Zone of independent workingmen's homes
The third urban ring is made up largely of the houses of workingmen—factory workers, laborers, etc. These are often people who have moved out of Zone 2, but desire to live within easy access of their work. In many American cities, second-generation immigrants are important elements of the population in this zone.

Zone 4. Zone of better residences
Next is the zone in which the great middle classes of native-born Americans live. These people are likely to be proprietors of small businesses, professional people, clerks, and salesmen. Locally, single-family dwellings have tended to give way to apartment houses and residential hotels. At strategic

spots are business subcenters of growing importance.

Zone 5. Commuters' zone

Zone 5. Commuters' zone Beyond the city limits a ring of small cities, towns, and the like, mostly dormitory areas, makes up the commuters' zone. There is a spotty development of fairly high-quality residences along lines of rapid travel. Most of the people in this zone are supported by work in the central business district.

Shifting of zonal boundaries

Several other points should be made in order to complete the picture of Burgess' statement of the theory. A particularly critical aspect of the scheme is that the five zones are by no means static. Each, under conditions of normal city growth, tends to extend its area by invading the next outer zone. The process has been likened to the outward movement of ripples when one tosses a stone into a still pond.[4]

Vulnerability of new idea

It is not surprising that Burgess' theory should have found its vigorous opponents and its ardent supporters. Generalization along such lines was a new venture at the time the theory was presented. Hence it attracted much attention. Moreover, the very nature of the theory is such that evidence both for and against was easy to find.

Criticisms of the theory

In judging the theory, critics raised several questions. For example, how literally should we expect it to apply? Are we concerned only with demonstrating that a concentric zonation exists in the city? Or does the ultimate test involve whether or not the particular land uses Burgess mentioned as typifying each zone actually do predominate there? Burgess, himself, in his main

statement of the theory, published in 1929, pointed out the distortions in the zones that may result from variations in relief features and from the checkerboard pattern found in so many American cities.

One of the most active critics of the theory was M. R. Davie of Yale University, who mapped the land uses of New Haven and also studied the distribution of various social classes in the city.[5] Neither in New Haven, he claimed, nor in various other cities for which he had the information, did the concentric zone idea apply. Instead, according to Davie, the cities generally exhibited the following pattern: (1) a central business district, irregular in size and often more square or rectangular than circular; (2) areas of commercial land use extending out the radial streets from the central business district and concentrating at strategic points elsewhere; (3) industry located near lines of transportation by water or rail; (4) low-grade housing near industrial and transportation areas; and (5) second- and first-class housing almost anywhere else. Low-grade economic areas were somewhat concentrated near the center of the city, but in reality were found in every zone, generally adjacent to industrial and railroad property. Davie concluded that there was no universal pattern, in fact not even an "ideal" type.

Several more specific criticisms have been leveled at Burgess' theory. It has been contended, for example, that Burgess did not take due account of historical inertia. Buildings, streets, and railroads cannot be easily moved, and a cultural area that has gained a foothold may cling tenaciously to its old location.

Another criticism deals with Burgess' treatment of wholesaling. Though wholesaling may be found to some degree around the edge of the central business district,

---

[4] Conversely, it is claimed that when an urban area decreases in population the transition zone tends to expand into the central business district, but the outer zones remain essentially stationary.

[5] Maurice R. Davie, "The Pattern of Urban Growth," in G. P. Murdock (ed.), *Studies in the Science of Society,* Yale University Press, New Haven, Conn., 1937, pp. 133–161.

most often it lies adjacent to the district on only one side, the side with maximum railroad availability.

Burgess' failure to consider heavy industry, too, has been criticized. Though he refers to a "factory district" in his description of the zone in transition, it has generally been assumed that he is referring to light industry. His followers admitted this and regarded heavy industry as one of the several distorting factors, but Davie contended that it should have been included as a normal part of the urban organization. Heavy industry is especially significant in accounting for the distribution of low-grade economic areas. And it certainly does not, in the modern city, take the form of a concentric belt just outside the central business district. Instead, it tends to form wedgelike areas along transportation lines which follow river valleys or lake or ocean fronts, or other easy routes across the city. In fact, all the non-residential uses tend to be near transport routes and to reach their greatest extents along such routes.

In defense of Burgess

Supporters of the Burgess theory, on the other hand, point out the substantial number of cities in which the theory was tested and seemed to apply. Also, various other confirming arguments are advanced. As Quinn, one of the chief supporters, says, common-sense observations tend to confirm the theory.[6] A retail business district constitutes the heart of the city. Deteriorated areas develop near this business area, and, in general, poorer homes are located closer to the business center and better homes farther out. Moreover, studies of urban gradients indicate the probability of a concentric urban structure centered around the dominant retail area, and maps of social data in various cities have tended to support the same idea. Local irregularities frequently violate the symmetry of concentric zones, yet, Quinn says, most cities tend to conform at least roughly to the Burgess pattern.

Opponents of the Burgess theory have pointed out that the ideal circular pattern rarely can be found, that, more often, rectangular or irregular shapes prevail. But Quinn says that it is incorrect to use simple linear distance from the center as a basis for outlining the concentric zones, and that better results would be obtained if the concentric zones were based on travel time.

The concentric zone theory and modern conditions

It must be remembered that Burgess' theory was based on conditions in the 1920s and that certain details of the picture have changed. The rise of the automobile has been by far the most important development. Basically it has allowed all uses greater locational flexibility. But what other changes have come about, especially in land uses, that might affect the applicability of the theory?[7]

The central business district   First we can focus on the central business district. In most cities it is still the largest shopping district, but it has lost relatively through the huge growth of planned shopping districts in the city's periphery and in the suburbs, a development that can be traced in large part to the automobile. In a few cities access to the downtown has been improved through the building of expressways to the extent that there has been some construction of new stores, but this has been the exception. Offices have multiplied in the downtown centers of a few of the largest cities, owing to an increase in their significance as international or regional centers. Such office construction often has been as-

[6] James A. Quinn, "The Burgess Zonal Hypothesis and Its Critics," *American Sociological Review*, vol. 5, pp. 210–218, 1940.

[7] The following notes regarding the theory are based largely on Homer Hoyt, "Recent Distortions of the Classical Models of Urban Structure," *Land Economics*, vol. 40, pp. 199–212, 1964.

sociated with redevelopment. In other cities new offices have grown up outside the central business district and even at the outlying shopping centers. And in many cities of growing population, few new office buildings are being erected. Thus generalizations can no longer be made about office-building location in the central business district. Central hotels have declined in importance, owing to the rapid growth of new motels and motor hotels (with parking) on the periphery of the central business district and on the outskirts of the city. These are changes that could hardly have been anticipated when Burgess developed his ideas. Nor could the rise of apartment houses in or near the central business district, often in areas of redevelopment. Still another change affecting the district has been the decline of wholesaling due to increasing direct sales by manufacturers to merchants. Finally, redevelopment has done much to mitigate the slum conditions that Burgess described as characterizing the outer portions of the zone.

To sum up:

> Thus, in view of the shifting of uses in the central business districts, the overall decline in the predominance of central retail areas, the rapid growth of office centers in a few cities compared to a static condition in others, the emergence of redeveloped areas, and intown motels, the former descriptions of patterns in American cities must be revised to conform to the realities of 1964.[8]

Changes in other zones No attempt will be made to consider in detail the changes in other sections of the city that might affect the present applicability of the concentric zone theory. Clearance and redevelopment have certainly been operating to change the picture. But far more than any other influence has been the fluidity of residences, business establishments, and factories resulting from the rise of the passenger automobile and the truck.

[8] *Ibid.*, p. 205.

As a result, it would appear impossible for any such system of concentric zones as conceived by Burgess to be applicable now in the American city except in an extremely general way.

The Sector Theory

The sector theory, advanced by Homer Hoyt several decades ago, holds that residential land uses tend to be arranged in wedges or sectors radiating from the center of the city along the lines of transportation. In contrast to Burgess' theory, where business and light manufacturing land uses, too, are considered, Hoyt's theory deals only with residential land use.

Origin of the theory The origin of the sector theory can be traced in part to the work of Hurd,[9] but Hoyt's development of the theory is based much more on a vast amount of empirical work. In 1934, data were collected for individual blocks in sixty-four American cities by the Works Progress Administration. These were the data available to Hoyt, who was then Principal Housing Economist of the Division of Economics and Statistics, Federal Housing Administration. The sixty-four cities were small and medium sized, but Hoyt supplemented the data for these cities with surveys of New York, Chicago, Detroit, Washington, and Philadelphia. Average rent and various other data were plotted on work maps. It was from these maps that Hoyt derived the details of his theory. Thus it amounts in large part to an empirical generalization.

Hoyt found that a single element, rent, closely reflected a series of other housing

[9] Hurd discussed "axial growth, pushing out from the center along transportation lines, and central growth." The latter consists of growth around the major center and from various subcenters. The normal result, he said, is a star-shaped city. See R. M. Hurd, *Principles of City Land Values*, The Record and Guide, New York, 1924, pp. 58ff. Hurd's book was first published in 1903, preceding by two decades the work of Burgess.

characteristics. He claimed that the patterns of rent could be relied upon as a guide to the structure of residential areas.

Statement of the theory

According to Hoyt:

> . . . Rent areas in American cities tend to conform to a pattern of sectors rather than of concentric circles. The highest rent areas of a city tend to be located in one or more sectors of the city [Figure 12.2]. There is a gradation of rentals downward from these high rental areas in all directions. Intermediate rental areas, or those ranking next to the highest rental areas, adjoin the high rent area on one or more sides, and tend to be located in the same sectors as the high rental areas. Low rent areas occupy other entire sectors of the city from the center to the periphery.[10]

The various rent areas are by no means static. Thus a high-quality residential area in a certain sector tends to migrate outward

[10] *The Structure and Growth of Residential Neighborhoods in American Cities*, U.S. Federal Housing Administration, Washington, D.C., 1939, p. 76.

Fig. 12.2 Theoretical pattern of distribution of rent areas in six American cities. (Based on fig. 28 in *The Structure and Growth of Residential Neighborhoods in American Cities*, U.S. Federal Housing Administration, Washington, D.C., 1939.)

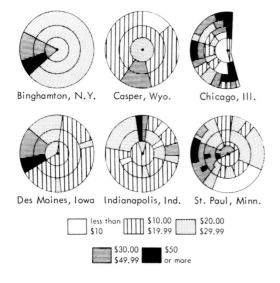

Binghamton, N.Y.   Casper, Wyo.   Chicago, Ill.

Des Moines, Iowa   Indianapolis, Ind.   St. Paul, Minn.

less than $10 ⎸ $10.00 $19.99 ⎸ $20.00 $29.99

$30.00 $49.99 ⎸ $50 or more

in the sector, and the area of older houses remaining behind becomes a medium-quality area. Expansion of high-grade neighborhoods is toward the periphery. Wealthy people do not reverse their steps and move into the obsolete sections,[11] and on each side of the existing high-quality neighborhood there is usually an intermediate-rental area, so expansion toward the periphery of the city is the only possibility. Where a low-rent residential area develops in a sector, residential development, as it extends outward in the sector toward the city's periphery, will tend to retain this low quality.

In considering a city's growth, one finds that the movement of the high-rent area is, in a sense, the most important, since it tends to pull the growth of the entire city in the same direction (Figure 12.3). The high-grade residential area, according to Hoyt, had its point of origin near the retail and office center. This is where the higher-income groups work and it is the point that is farthest removed from the side of the city that has industries and warehouses.

Movement of high-rent areas

Hoyt listed a number of factors which, he said, tended to determine the part of the city in which the high-grade residential areas would grow: [12]

> 1. High-grade residential growth tends to proceed from the given point of origin, along established lines of travel or toward another existing nucleus of buildings or trading centers.
> 2. The zone of high-rent areas tends to progress toward high ground which is free from the risk of floods and to spread along lake, bay, river, and ocean fronts, where such water fronts are not used for industry.
> 3. High-rent residential districts tend

[11] The high-quality apartment houses now arising at the borders of some central business districts appear to represent a partial reversal of this trend.
[12] The first nine factors are quoted from *The Structure and Growth of Residential Neighborhoods in American Cities*, pp. 117–119. The tenth factor is given by Hoyt on p. 114 of the same volume, but is unnumbered.

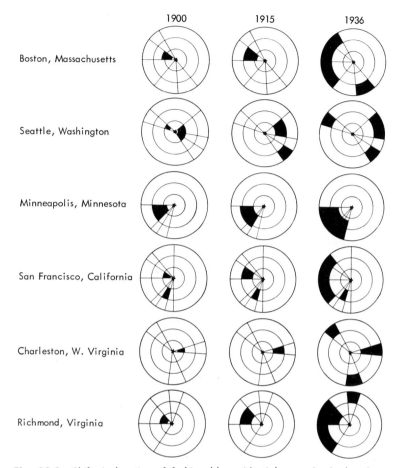

Fig. 12.3 Shifts in location of fashionable residential areas in six American cities, 1900–1936. Fashionable residential areas indicated by solid black. (After fig. 40 in *The Structure and Growth of Residential Neighborhoods in American Cities*, U.S. Federal Housing Administration, Washington, D.C., 1939.)

to grow toward the section of the city which has free, open country beyond the edges and away from "dead end" sections which are limited by natural or artificial barriers to expansion.

4. The higher priced residential neighborhood tends to grow toward the homes of the leaders of the community.

5. Trends of movement of office buildings, banks, and stores pull the higher priced residential neighborhoods in the same general direction.

6. High-grade residential areas tend to develop along the fastest existing transportation lines.

7. The growth of high-rent neighborhoods continues in the same direction for a long period of time.

8. De luxe high-rent apartment areas tend to be established near the business center in old residential areas.

9. Real estate promoters may bend the direction of high-grade residential growth.

10. The high-rent neighborhoods of a city do not skip about at random in the process of movement—they follow a definite path in one or more sectors of the city.

From the foregoing factors it is apparent that the outward migration of high-class residential areas along established lines of travel is likely to be persistent and is particularly pronounced along lines of fastest transportation; along waterfronts not used for industry; and toward high ground, open country, the homes of community leaders, and existing nuclei of buildings or trading centers.

A criticism of Hoyt's theory It will be recalled that Burgess' theory was tested by workers in a number of cities, and that some of the results seemed to confirm and others to refute the theory. Hoyt's theory has been subjected to relatively little testing of this sort, probably because it was based on so much empirical work. The wealth of data he had available for his studies could hardly be equaled. Nevertheless, the theory has not gone unchallenged. Walter Firey carried out a land-use study of central Boston,[13] which, he claimed, seemed to contradict various aspects of Hoyt's theory.

Firey advanced a number of objections to the sector theory. For instance, he questioned the validity of comparing the results of work in a number of cities when relief, location on a waterfront, and other factors affected the sector pattern of some cities so markedly. He questioned, too, the whole cartographic approach to land-use theories, claiming that at best maps can give only clues to theories that need to be worked out in terms of abstract concepts. Also, Firey maintained that Hoyt had not sufficiently considered the roles of cultural and social systems in conditioning land use.[14]

Hoyt's 1964 evaluation In an article published in 1964, Hoyt takes a later look at his sector theory.[15] Is it still true, he asks, that high-rent areas are located in one or more sectors of the city and do not form a circle completely around it? This was, in effect, what he claimed in 1939 when he formulated the sector theory.

Hoyt's answer is that in general the high-income families are still definitely concentrated in certain sectors. But the automobile has opened up large regions beyond existing settled areas. There is greater flexibility in urban growth patterns resulting from radial expressways and belt highways. As a result, some higher-income communities have developed beyond low-income sectors, though, Hoyt says, they usually do not enjoy so high a social rating as new neighborhoods located in the high-income sector.

The Multiple Nuclei Concept

Two basic classes of nuclei Chauncy D. Harris and Edward L. Ullman, in their multiple nuclei concept, have combined the concentric zone and sector theories and added certain other ingredients in explaining the pattern of land uses. They suggest that frequently the land-use pattern of a city is built around several discrete nuclei rather than around a single center such as is postulated in the concentric zone and sector theories (Figure 12.4).[16] The term nucleus, as here used, refers to any attracting element around which growth—residential, business, industrial, or other—takes place. In some cities, Harris and Ullman point out, the nuclei have been in existence from the time of origin of the city, persist-

[13] Walter Firey, *Land Use in Central Boston,* Harvard University Press, Cambridge, Mass., 1947.
[14] For a discussion of the pros and cons of the sector theory see Llyod Rodwin, "The Theory of Residential Growth and Structure," *The Appraisal Journal,* vol. 18, pp. 295–317, 1950; in the same volume, see Homer Hoyt, "Residential Sectors Revisited," pp. 445–450, Walter Firey, "Residential Sectors Re-examined," pp. 451–453, and Lloyd Rodwin, "Rejoinder to Dr. Firey and Dr. Hoyt," pp. 454–457.

[15] Hoyt, "Recent Distortions of the Classical Models of Urban Structure," pp. 208–209.
[16] The idea of multinucleation was suggested in the early 1930s by R. D. McKenzie in *The Metropolitan Community,* McGraw-Hill Book Company, Inc., New York, 1933, p. 198. Details presented here are based largely on C. D. Harris and E. L. Ullman, "The Nature of Cities," *The Annals of the American Academy of Political and Social Science,* vol. 242, pp. 14–15, November, 1945.

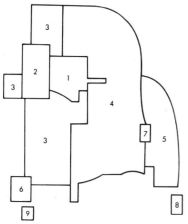

Fig. 12.4 Generalizations of city structure according to multiple nuclei theory. The diagram represents one possible pattern among innumerable variations. Numbers refer as follows: (1) central business district; (2) whole-sale light manufacturing; (3) low-class residential; (4) medium-class residential; (5) high-class residential; (6) heavy manufacturing; (7) outlying business district; (8) residential suburb; (9) industrial suburb. (After C. D. Harris and E. L. Ullman, "The Nature of Cities," *The Annals of the American Academy of Political and Social Science,* vol. 242, November, 1945, fig. 5.)

of the city. But other nuclei have played roles as the city has grown.

The rise of separate nuclei and differentiated districts reflects a combination of four factors:

1. Certain activities require specialized facilities. The retail district, for example, is attached to the point of greatest intracity accessibility, the port district to suitable water front, manufacturing districts to large blocks of land and water or rail connection, and so on.

2. Certain like activities group together because they profit from cohesion ° . . . Retail districts benefit from grouping which increases the concentration of potential customers and makes possible comparison shopping. Financial and office-building districts depend upon facility of communication among offices within the district. The Merchandise Mart of Chicago is an example of wholesale clustering.

3. Certain unlike activities are detrimental to each other. The antagonism between factory development and high-class residential development is well known. The heavy concentration of pedestrians, automobiles, and streetcars in the retail district is antagonistic both to the railroad facilities and the street loading required in the wholesale district and to the rail facilities and space needed by large industrial districts, and vice versa.

4. Certain activities are unable to afford the high rents of the most desirable sites. This factor works in conjunction with the foregoing. Examples are bulk wholesaling and storage activities requiring much room, or low-class housing unable to afford the luxury of high land with a view.

The number of nuclei which results from historical development and the operation of localization forces varies greatly from city to city. The larger the city, the more numerous and specialized are the nuclei.[17]

Types of districts developed around nuclei Harris and Ullman describe several

ing as urban growth has filled in around them. Metropolitan London is given as an example, with "The City" and Westminster originating at separate points in open country, one as a center of finance and commerce and the other as a political center.

In other cities, Harris and Ullman say, nuclei developed as city growth stimulated migration and specialization. An example of this second type is furnished by heavy industry in Chicago. At first, heavy industry was localized along the Chicago River in the heart of the city, but it migrated to the Calumet district where it formed the nucleus for new urban development. Many cities can be traced back to a single initial nucleus: the retail district, the port, rail facilities, a factory, a mine, or some other localizing point, depending upon the nature

---

° Exceptions are service-type establishments such as some grocery stores, dry cleaners, and gasoline stations.

[17] Harris and Ullman, *op. cit.,* pp. 14–15.

types of districts that they say have developed around nuclei in most large American cities. The central business district, at the focus of transportation facilities, serves as a nucleus or, on another scale, as several nuclei—the retail district, the financial district, the theater district, etc.—each with its own special requirements. Government buildings often cluster not far from the center of the retail district. "Automobile row" is a particularly good example of nucleation of establishments of a certain type. It is likely to be located at the edge of the central business district, extending out along one or two major highways.

Various other districts may be cited as resulting from the attraction of nuclei. Wholesale establishments are likely to be concentrated along railroads, usually adjacent to the central business district but not surrounding it, although recently highway availability has been setting up a counter-attraction for wholesaling. Light manufacturing is somewhat like wholesaling in its requirements: good transportation, available floor space, and nearness to the markets and labor of the city. Heavy industrial districts are likely to be near the present or former outer edge of the city. Transportation needs, combined with the nuisance problems likely to be associated with heavy industry, have resulted in its clustering in areas away from the center of the city.

Residential areas have their own special requirements. High-class residential districts are likely to be on well-drained, high land as far as possible from railroad lines and heavy industry. Low-class neighborhoods are often localized near factories and railroad districts. Areas with ethnically segregated groups will show in the extreme the cohesiveness of residential neighborhoods.

Other nuclei include the university, which may form the attraction for a quasi-independent community; parks and recreational areas, which may serve to attract high-class or middle-class residential de-

velopment; and outlying business districts, which have obvious effects in attracting additional growth. Suburbs and satellites form other centers of nucleation that are essentially part of the city.

In further support of the multiple nuclei theory In a recent article, Ullman discusses the multiple nuclei theory further.[18] He points out, first, that there is now a general feeling that the central business district may lose its uniqueness, that it may become just one of the many centers in the city. It may still be the most important center, but of much less relative importance than in the past. According to this idea it may be the shopping center for the large, low-income area around it and an office center on a reduced scale for older activities or smaller concerns that can use poor, vacant space or large amounts of cheap labor. The high-grade activities now attracted to the central business district because of its top hierarchical position will abandon it for centers better located to serve the high-income areas. In this manner the dominant nuclei are proliferating.

Other centers will develop on a regional or specialized basis, Ullman predicts, thus strengthening the multiple nuclei generalization. He points out the nuclear function of airports, which must, of necessity, be near the city's edge and which increasingly will draw conventions and out-of-town visitors; outlying shopping centers that will handle retail trade;[19] the new large factories and other employment centers which will be on the city outskirts on large

[18] Edward L. Ullman, "Presidential Address: The Nature of Cities Reconsidered," *The Regional Science Association: Papers and Proceedings,* 1962, vol. 9, pp. 7–23.
[19] A large integrated shopping center, it may be noted, is a sort of ready-made nucleation. Instead of consisting of one large store which draws others to it, the integrated shopping center anticipates the attraction of the nucleus by the inclusion of a cluster of other establishments that would naturally be drawn by the initial store.

tracts of land; and the specialized entertainment, educational, cultural, and recreational centers that will be scattered over the city to serve the whole population.

Some Differences and Similarities

In any consideration of the three schemes described in this chapter certain differences and similarities should be kept in mind. For instance, the concentric zone theory and the multiple nuclei theory deal with the entire urban pattern; in contrast, the sector theory is concerned mostly with residential land use. Secondly, the concentric zone and sector theories consider primarily only one center, whereas the multiple nuclei theory takes account of various centers or nuclei in the city. And all three of the ideas have been criticized on the grounds that they represent only predominant land use at any given location, which amounts, generally, to the use of space at street level, and fail to take into account the rise of multistoried buildings now so typical of portions of almost every city.[20]

Conclusions

Is it possible to draw any conclusions regarding the relative merits of the three schemes? No one can deny, for instance, that the concentric zone theory applies in a very general way in the average city. We could hardly expect sharply defined zones, each of uniform width throughout; and distortions due to relief contrasts or the presence of heavy manufacturing along transportation lines cutting across the zones are to be expected. It seems likely, however, that the zonation might have been more in evidence before the widespread use of the automobile added so greatly to the mobility of labor.

Certainly, elements of the sector theory are evident in most growing communities. The past maintenance of residential quality throughout sectors was demonstrated by Hoyt, but the fluidity of automobile transportation is likely to lessen this conformance in the future in the growing outer portions of our cities.

The multiple nuclei theory is essentially a schematic representation. In a way it is simpler than the other two theories and adjusts more easily to current conditions. It is a theory that fits the highly flexible modern urban scene. Whereas the automobile has lessened the applicability of the concentric zone and sector theories, the multiple nuclei theory seems to fit even better as a result of transportation changes.

Selected References

Alonso, William: "The Historic and the Structural Theories of Urban Form: Their Implications for Urban Renewal," *Land Economics*, vol. 40, pp. 227–231, 1964.

Burgess, Ernest W.: "Growth of the City," in Robert E. Park, Ernest W. Burgess, and Roderick D. McKenzie (eds.), *The City*, The University of Chicago Press, Chicago, 1925, pp. 47–62.

———: "Urban Areas," in T. V. Smith and L. D. White (eds.), *Chicago: An Experiment in Social Science Research*, The University of Chicago Press, Chicago, 1929, pp. 113–138.

Davie, Maurice R.: "The Pattern of Urban Growth," in G. P. Murdock (ed.), *Studies in the Science of Society*, Yale University Press, New Haven, Conn., 1937, pp. 131–161.

Firey, Walter: *Land Use in Central Boston*, Harvard University Press, Cambridge, Mass., 1947.

——— "Residential Sectors Re-Examined," *Appraisal Journal*, vol. 18, pp. 451–453, 1950.

Harris, C. D., and E. L. Ullman: "The Nature of Cities," *The Annals of the American Academy of Political and Social Science*, vol. 242, pp. 7–17, November, 1945.

[20] See discussion of this point by Ernest M. Fisher and Robert M. Fisher, *Urban Real Estate*, Holt, Rinehart and Winston, Inc., New York, 1954, p. 313.

Hoyt, Homer: "Recent Distortions of the Classical Models of Urban Structure," *Land Economics*, vol. 40, pp. 199–212, 1964.

————: "Residential Sectors Revisited," *Appraisal Journal*, vol. 18, pp. 445–450, 1950.

Quinn, James A.: "The Burgess Zonal Hypothesis and Its Critics," *American Sociological Review*, vol. 5, pp. 210–218, 1940.

Rodwin, Lloyd: "The Theory of Residential Growth and Structure," *Appraisal Journal*, vol. 18, pp. 295–317, 1950.

Smith, P. J.: "Calgary: A Study in Urban Pattern," *Economic Geography*, vol. 38, pp. 315–329, 1962.

Structure and Growth of Residential Neighborhoods in American Cities, U.S. Federal Housing Administration, Washington, D.C., 1939.

Ullman, Edward L.: "Presidential Address: The Nature of Cities Reconsidered," *The Regional Science Association, Papers and Proceedings*, vol. 9, pp. 7–23, 1962.

CHAPTER **13**

Transportation in relation to the city

WITHOUT transportation, cities could never have developed. First of all, transportation forms the circulatory system that connects cities with each other and with the countryside. Cities are the culminating points in a system of overlapping and interconnected transportation nets: of railroads, highways, waterways, and air routes. And, of course, transportation is just as vital to the interior of the city. Lacking transportation, the goods and people needed for commercial activities could not be brought together; nor could the materials and labor needed for manufacturing. The specialized residential areas of the city would be impossible. In short, without transportation, the functional differentiation of the city into areas of specialized land uses could not have occurred. The modern city would not be in existence.

Transportation Patterns and the City

Several types of urban patterns are based on transportation. Thus there are the patterns of railroads, highways, waterways, and air routes in and near the city. The land used by the various kinds of transportation in the urban area also forms interesting patterns. Transportation is ubiquitous throughout the city; land used for this purpose is exceeded in total acreage only by land used for residences. When streets, railroad property, the airport, and the space occupied in some cities by a port and port facilities are considered, the total area devoted to transportation is found to amount to one-third or more of the built-up urban area, and it is increasing. Another form of land use, parking, is generated by transportation even though much of it normally is classed as commercial. For that matter all other forms of land use are so dependent on transportation as to make the one-third a ridiculously low figure.

The urban geographer, in his concern with transportation, by no means stops with the interior of the urban area. The sizes and locations of cities result in a pattern that is closely related to transportation, and the distribution of cities characterized by special kinds of transportation is of interest— for example, the pattern of distribution of ports, of railroad centers, and of cities with unusual intercity trucking activity.

The diverse patterns referred to are of particular interest since they relate to various other distributions and because of the movement or spatial interaction implicit in the complex. P. R. Crowe has pointed out that the real concern of the geographer should be with currents of men and things moving.[1] And Ullman appears to have this in mind in saying: "Transportation facilities are examined [by the geographer] primarily as indicators of the degree of connection and as patterns of spatial interchange."[2]

The Historical Factor

One cannot go far in the study of urban transportation geography without recognizing the significance of the historical factor. The story of transportation is one of evolution of the various types of transport. Moreover, many anomalies in the distribution of cities and in intracity patterns as well have their roots in the transportation patterns of the past. Waterways, railroads, highways, and streets have played important but constantly changing roles. Only air transportation is so recent that little history is involved.

Data Sources and Urban Transportation

One of the most significant aspects of

[1] P. R. Crowe, "On Progress in Geography," *Scottish Geographical Magazine*, vol. 54, pp. 1–19, 1938.
[2] Edward L. Ullman, "Transportation Geography," in Preston E. James and Clarence F. Jones (eds.), *American Geography: Inventory and Prospect*, Syracuse University Press, Syracuse, N.Y., 1954, chap. 13, p. 311.

the study of transportation is the meagerness of standardized statistics. This is true of transportation in general and certainly of transportation in or pertaining to the city.

United States Census data

The only United States Census data bearing on urban transportation are in the Census of Population volumes and these data are extremely limited. As with all Census of Population data they deal with place of residence rather than with place of employment. The data are of two general types.

Industry groups of employed persons
The first type is based on industry groups of employed persons and gives an overall view of those people who work at various transportation jobs.

For standard metropolitan statistical areas, urbanized areas, and urban places of 10,000 population or more, employment data are given for three categories: railroads and railway express service, trucking service and warehousing, and "other transportation."

A somewhat more detailed breakdown of people by industries is available for standard metropolitan statistical areas of 100,000 or more population. Here the transportation categories for which employment totals are given are railroads and railway express service, street railways and bus lines, taxicab service, trucking service, warehousing and storage, water transportation, air transportation, petroleum and gasoline pipelines, and services incidental to transportation.

Much more limited industry-group data are given by census tracts for tracted cities. Total employment in transportation is here broken down into two categories: railroads and railway express service, and other transportation.

Place of work and means of transportation to work
The second type of Census

of Population data directly relevant to transportation is represented for the first time in the 1960 *Census of Population*. For standard metropolitan statistical areas, urbanized areas, and urban places and selected towns of 10,000 population or more, the total for all workers is subdivided on two bases (see table 72, General Social and Economic Characteristics section of the Census of Population, state volumes). The first shows those who work in county of residence, those who work outside county of residence, and those for which place of work was not reported. The second method of subdivision is on the basis of means of transportation to work and involves the following categories: private automobile or car pool; railroad, subway, or elevated; bus or streetcar; walked to work; other means; worked at home; and "not reported."

For standard metropolitan statistical areas of 100,000 or more population (see table 131 of Detailed Characteristics, Census of Population, state volumes), workers are divided into "living in central city" and "living in SMSA ring" (that is, in the standard metropolitan statistical area but outside the central city or cities), and each of these is further subdivided into "working in central city," "working in SMSA ring," "working outside SMSA of residence," and "place of work not reported." The means of transportation data are the same as those described for smaller units.

Place of work and means of transportation data are given also for census tracts (see any tract bulletin for 1960). The means of transportation data require no special comment, since the categories are exactly the same as those already described. Instead of the places of work division being between those who work in county of residence and those who work outside county of residence, however, the division in the case of the census tract is between those who work inside the standard metropolitan statistical area and those who work outside. Only the former, those who work inside the standard

metropolitan statistical area, are subdivided further.

The details of this further breakdown by tracts differ somewhat with variations in standard metropolitan statistical areas. Where only one county is involved, the division of those who work inside the area normally is between those who work in the city and those who work in the remainder of the county. If there are several other counties in the standard metropolitan statistical area, then the number working in each is given, and where there is more than one central city similar information is given for each. Where cities are independent of counties, as in Virginia, data for both counties and cities in which people work outside the central city but inside the standard metropolitan statistical area are given; and in New England, where towns rather than counties make up the standard metropolitan statistical areas, "inside the standard metropolitan statistical area" may be broken into the city, the inner part of the remainder of the county, and the outer part of the remainder of the county.

Certainly, the place of work and means of transportation data form an interesting new basis for research on the journey-to-work, a topic that will be discussed further later in this chapter.

Other urban transportation data

Fortunately, urban transportation data sources do not end with census possibilities. For ports, annual tonnage figures from the Corps of Engineers of the Department of the Army are commonly used; railroads furnished data for a study of hinterlands that will be discussed; an airline traffic survey of the Civil Aeronautics Administration, Washington, D.C., is of value for a comparative study of cities on the basis of air passengers embarking or landing; and origin and destination data from the U.S. Bureau of Public Roads in cooperation with state highway departments, though they have not yet been much used by geographers, are considered an important source in urban traffic studies. These and various other sources that may be unearthed, though not so satisfactory as the United States Census for general comparability, help to make up for the statistical deficiencies that are an inherent difficulty in urban transportation research.

Importance of group research

It is not surprising in view of the difficulties of obtaining data that there has been little individual geographic research on the transportation function of cities, at least little research that is more than descriptive. Group research to a considerable extent replaces individual research in systematic studies in the transportation field. In the study of street traffic, for example, and of highway traffic in relation to cities, it is only through the cooperation of such groups as state highway departments and the Federal Bureau of Public Roads that the geographer can hope to collect data on the scale needed for most modern research studies. Though there is worthwhile work to be done by individuals in the study of urban transportation, they operate under a special handicap in this matter of data.

Branches of Urban Transportation

The general term, urban transportation, includes several branches that are distinct but, at the same time, interrelated. The railroad, for example, gives rise to problems in relation to the city that are very different from those arising from streetcars and automobiles; and water and air transportation present still other problems. Trains and trucks complement each other as well as competing in freight movement; and suburban trains and buses, locally still important in moving people to and from the city, have been supplemented, and in many cases overwhelmed, by a competitor, the private automobile.

Order of Discussion

The discussion of the various forms of urban transportation will follow, in a very general way, a chronological order. Thus water transportation will be discussed before railroads, and air transportation, the most recent member of the family, will be discussed last.

Each of the various types of transportation will be presented in turn as a framework for discussing problems and research that has been done or might be done. Throughout the entire discussion an attempt will be made to focus on patterns of transportation as they relate to the city.

Urban Patterns Based on Water Transportation

Though little has been written on urban patterns based on the actual dynamics of water transportation, there has been some interesting work on port geography. Chiefly for this reason, and because most available water transportation data deal with ports, port geography receives primary attention in this section on urban patterns and water transportation even though, admittedly, such a focus departs somewhat from the central theme of transportation.

Urban water transportation is more selective than other major forms of transportation serving the city. Railroads, highways, and air routes serve all cities to some degree, but water transportation is possible only where a city is located on the ocean, on a river or lake, or on a canal. Of course, it is not important in every city so situated. Where it is important, this is not due, ordinarily, to intracity activity in water transportation but to the port function of the city. The port possibilities may well have accounted for the original location of the city and may still account for much of the city's economic support.

What distinctive characteristics of a

city are associated with the port activity? This differs greatly from city to city. The actual port function may be minor in a city, or it may form the principal basis for the city's existence. And it will differ considerably depending upon whether the port is on the ocean, on a lake, or on a river or canal. The distinctive features that reflect port activity in a city were summed up earlier in this book (page 140). Here we are concerned more broadly with ports and studies of ports.

Statistics available

There are better statistics published for water transportation than for most other branches of urban transportation. As was pointed out earlier, the Census of Population carries data on persons engaged in water transportation. These are of some value in differentiating cities. Much more important, however, are the annual tonnage figures by ports published as "Waterborne Commerce of the United States" by the United States Army Corps of Engineers. These data include totals of exports and imports and of coastwise trade by ports, including breakdowns by commodities. There are also waterborne export and import data by customs districts and selected ports that are published by the U.S. Bureau of the Census in a quarterly summary. And in the *Port Series,* published jointly every few years by the Corps of Engineers and the Maritime Administration, facilities available in major ports are described in detail.

Research on ports

Many studies of ports have been purely descriptive accounts of individual ports. Fortunately, however, there has been some systematic work, too.

A comparative analysis of United States ports

In one study, Richard Carter showed various aspects of the traffic of United States ports on a series of maps in order to cast some light on the ways the ports differ.[3] The aspects shown were total tonnage, commodities handled (Figure 13.1), type of traffic (foreign, coastwise, lakewise, internal, local), balance of traffic (imports versus exports), variety of commerce, and value of foreign commerce.

From analysis of the maps, Carter inferred the following tentative generalizations: (1) When evaluated by tonnage the commodity structure of United States ports exhibits a strong tendency to be composed mainly of one class, such as iron ore, coal, or petroleum. (2) There are only a few ports whose leading commodity by tonnage is not petroleum, iron ore, or stone products. (3) Though one type of traffic often accounts for over 50 per cent of the tonnage moved at a port, usually at least one or two other types are represented. For example, though the greater part of Houston's tonnage is in the form of domestic coastwise movements, the port is also an important generator of both overseas and inland waterway traffic. (4) Most ports have marked imbalances of traffic flow; a minority have relatively equal amounts of inbound and outbound movements. (5) A wide range in the variety of commodities or commerce handled is a distinguishing characteristic of United States ports. Those with the greatest diversity are the general cargo ports, while the ones at the lower end of the scale are ports associated almost exclusively with mining activities or service mainly as mineral fuel terminals. (6) An apparent relationship exists between the value of foreign commerce at any given port and the variety of that commerce. (7) The distribution of foreign commerce as measured in dollars is highly concentrated in a few ports. This concentration is much

[3] Richard E. Carter, "A Comparative Analysis of United States Ports and Their Traffic Characteristics," *Economic Geography,* vol. 38, pp. 162–175, 1962.

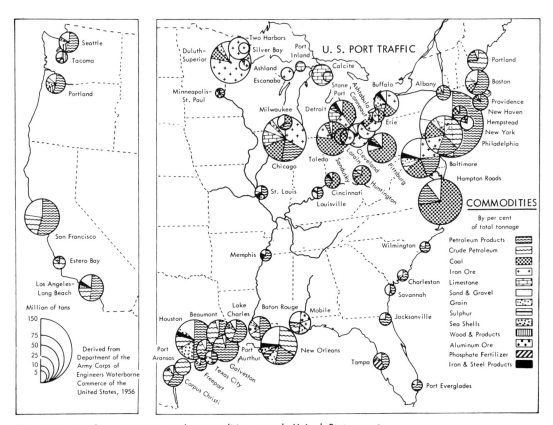

Fig. 13.1 Total port tonnage and commodities moved, United States ports, 1956. (After Richard E. Carter, "A Comparative Analysis of United States Ports and Their Traffic Characteristics," *Economic Geography*, vol. 38, 1962, fig. 2.)

greater than that of foreign commerce as measured in tons.

Lastly, on the basis of the six characteristics studied, the following types of ports were identified: (1) ports associated with the manufacture of steel, (2) ports associated with mining activity, (3) ports associated with petroleum refining, (4) ports which serve as petroleum terminals, (5) ports whose function is the transfer of bulk products, (6) general cargo ports, and (7) ports which embody two or more of the functions represented in the foregoing types. Study of additional characteristics, Carter points out, should lead to a more detailed typology.

Variations through time A time ele-

ment can be introduced in this sort of analysis through a relative-change study of ports. (See Figure 13.2. For details regarding the relative-change technique, see Chapter 10, pages 173 to 175.) Which United States ports have gained relatively and which have lost relatively over a specified period of years? The relative-change map can be based on total tonnage or on exports or imports. It can deal with all United States ports or with just one competitive group, such as Atlantic ports or Great Lakes ports.

Any really penetrating study of the changing port picture must be based on such changes through many decades or even a century or two. For example, a study of the relative growths of cities of Eastern

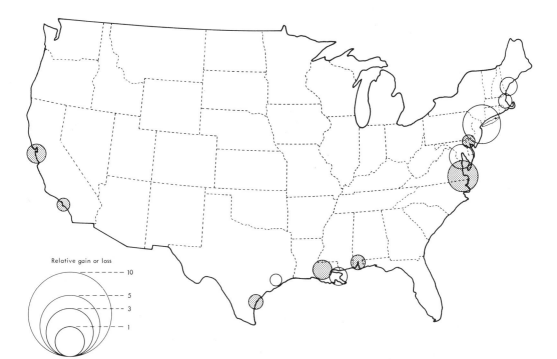

Relative gain or loss

Fig. 13.2 Relative-change map of foreign trade, United States ports, 1948–1950 to 1958–1960. Shaded circles represent relative gain; open circles, relative loss. Note that Hampton Roads experienced the greatest relative gain; New York harbor and Baltimore harbor and channels, the greatest relative losses. In fact, both New York and Baltimore gained in total tonnage. It was only in their proportions of total United States tonnage that they lost. (Data from "Waterborne Commerce of the United States," by the United States Army Corps of Engineers.)

United States could mean little without consideration of the strong competition among Atlantic seaboard ports during the nineteenth century.

A study of general cargo hinterlands
And there are various other possible lines of research based on port activities. Some years ago, Donald J. Patton published a study of the general cargo [4] hinterlands of New York, Philadelphia, Baltimore, and New Orleans. It represents another approach to port geography.[5]

[4] See discussion of "The Cargo" on p. 229.
[5] Donald J. Patton, "General Cargo Hinterlands of New York, Philadelphia, Baltimore, and New Orleans," *Annals of the Association of American Geographers,* vol. 48, pp. 436–455, 1958.

THE MAPS   The maps on which Patton's article is based show by proportional symbols the points of origin of railroad carloads of general cargo exported through each of the four ports for June, 1955, and, in similar fashion, the points of destination of carloads of imports through the same ports. This was an instance where no census or other Federal data were available. Patton got most of his information directly from the railroads involved.

GENERAL CONCLUSIONS   In the article, the extents of the various hinterlands are discussed and explanations advanced for some of the differences, and certain general conclusions are presented. Patton claims that port differentials—that is, favorable freight rates from interior areas—may be of con-

siderable help. For instance, the growing
strength of New Orleans in parts of the
Middle West, he says, is believed to be
based on rate advantages of this sort (Figure 13.3). But New York City, which has a
relatively scant rate advantage territory,
serves a much larger area and has the largest
total of general exports of all, so obviously

other factors are involved. The nature of
cargo liner services is of vital importance in
attracting traffic to a port. In this respect
lies much of New York's advantage. Patton
also states that a major railroad network
having a single outlet acts as a powerful
solicitor for a port. Other advantages he
mentions are the degree of efficiency

Fig. 13.3 Origins of carloads of general cargo exported through New Or-
leans during the month of June, 1955. (After Donald J. Patton, "General
Cargo Hinterlands of New York, Philadelphia, Baltimore, and New Orleans,"
Annals of the Association of American Geographers, vol. 48, 1958, fig. 4.)

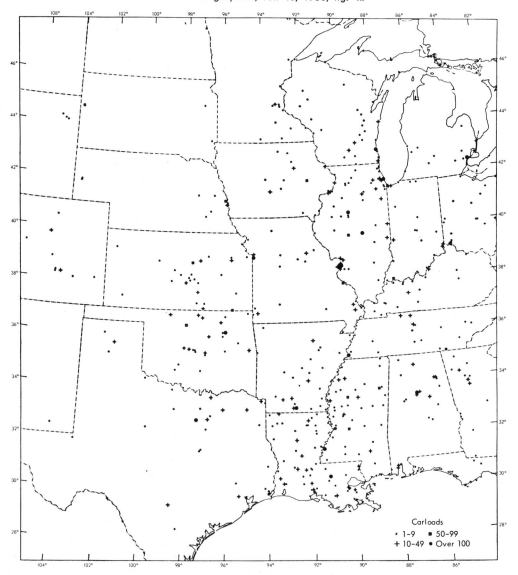

reached by port terminals, the structure of industry in the port, and, as in the case of New York, the magnitude and the articulation of the commercial and financial organization back of the port.

SOME FURTHER PROBLEMS Patton closes with some questions based on the sizes and shapes of the several cargo hinterlands. For instance, the symbols on the export maps show the continental points at which the final continuous export movements begin, rather than the real points of origin of the exports; those on the import maps show the initial inland point of consignment in each case, rather than the final destinations. How, he asks, would the patterns of the "ultimate" export and import hinterlands differ from those shown on his maps? These and other questions are raised by way of suggesting further hinterland research.

Elements of port geography

In a still broader study, Weigend has analyzed the elements of port geography as a step toward the formulation of general principles.[6] He lists the following as some of the basic elements of port geography: port, carrier, cargo, hinterland, foreland, and maritime space. These are certainly topics that should be considered by anyone studying the geography of a port city and wishing some understanding of the activities and features of ports.

The port

The first of the elements considered here is the port itself.

A WATER-LAND TERMINAL The port is a water-land terminal. Its primary function is the transfer of goods and people between ocean vessels, on the one hand, and land or inland carriers, on the other. Weigend refers to it as "a knot where ocean and inland transport lines meet and intertwine." Railroads, roads, rivers, canals, and coastal

[6] Guido G. Weigend, "Some Elements in the Study of Port Geography," *Geographical Review*, vol. 48, pp. 185–200, 1958.

shipping routes interfinger with the docks and piers of the waterfront. The activity of the various transportation types at this place of meeting is the traffic of the port; this determines to a considerable degree the prosperity of the port city and of the region around it.

DESIRABLE ATTRIBUTES The origin and growth of a port and its ability to attract traffic are based on a complex of physical and human factors. The desirable attributes of a port may be summed up briefly as a good harbor, easy access to a large producing and consuming hinterland, a good location relative to the world's main trade routes, and efficient terminal facilities. The resultant of these attributes is the ability of the port to attract trade: ports grow or fail to grow in proportion to this ability.

IMPORTANCE OF SITE Among the physical factors, site is of outstanding significance. The site of a port should furnish enough space for its operations; other features should be easy entrance to the harbor, deep water, small tidal range, and a climate that permits easy operation of the port throughout the year. It is not common for a port to meet all these requirements. Fortunately, sites can be modified in a number of respects by man if the need is great enough.

SITUATION Situation is a particularly important concept in the development of ports. Physically, a port may have an *interior situation*, away from the open ocean, often on an estuary; or an *exterior situation*, directly on the coast. Throughout history, most of the great ports of the world have been interior ports, but it is contended by some that the advantages of the interior situation have been decreasing. Modern navigation, they say, favors the seashore location. Ships are larger and shippers want fast and easy access to ports and a rapid turnaround. But the question of interior versus coastal location cannot be disposed of this simply. No two situations are identical, and there are places where interior locations are proving superior and others where the exterior situation seems to be better.

But situation is not always a matter of physical conditions; the major channels of world trade change, and the port that is in a good position to tap this trade today may be left to one side tomorrow.[7]

GOVERNMENTAL EFFECTS   Various types of administrative decisions may affect ports, too. A decision to "protect" our domestic oil industry by higher tariffs on crude petroleum, for example, may greatly lessen the significance of a petroleum importing port if it depends upon foreign sources. And favorable freight rates on coal shipped from the interior may encourage certain exporting ports at the expense of others.

PORT AUTHORITIES   In addition to Federal, state, and local governmental controls that may affect ports, the port may have its own administration, called the *port authority*. The port of Boston is governed by a port authority, and the Port of New York Authority governs the entire port which lies partly in New York and partly in New Jersey. Proper administration of a port is extremely important. Aggressiveness and imagination by both the port administration and commercial interests are considered vital to a successful port. Service facilities must be provided that will induce maritime interests and shippers in the hinterland to use the port in preference to competing ports.

CLASSIFICATION OF PORTS   Since analysis of a port can be approached from so many different angles, numerous classifications have been advanced. Thus we speak of river ports, coastal ports, and lake ports; international, national, regional, and local ports; petroleum ports, coal ports, ore ports, and others based on dominant merchandise

handled; ports based on disposition of cargo, such as industrial, commercial, transit, and transshipment ports; and ports based on type of carrier. Many other classifications are possible and the same port may be classified on several different bases. To the initiated, the various classes of ports suggest certain index features by which it is possible to identify the nature of the port at a glance.

TERMINAL AND ENTREPÔT PORTS   A simple and useful classification divides ports into terminal and entrepôt ports. The average port is largely a terminal port, and that is chiefly the type discussed throughout this section. Cargoes are discharged that are definitely assigned to that particular port and hinterland, and shipments, too, are from that particular port and hinterland. New York, for example, is primarily a terminal port. But there are also entrepôt ports serving as middlemen between other ports. Such ports receive goods, often from smaller ports; then after warehousing and possibly some processing, the goods are re-shipped. Singapore is an important entrepôt port in Southeastern Asia, and London gained much of its reputation as a world port on the basis of this type of activity.

FREE PORTS   The term *free port* implies another type of classification. In such ports an area is fenced off as a *free zone*. Within this area, goods may be sorted, processed, and stored without payment of duty to the country in which the port is situated. The port of New York has a free-port area, though the term *foreign-trade zone* is used because that was the wording in this country's enabling legislation.[8]

The carrier   The carrier may affect port operations. The division of carriers into

---

[7] Situation is a much more comprehensive concept than has been suggested here. Relation to land routes, size of hinterland, export and import potentials of the area in which a port is situated, location of competitors, and other factors are involved.

[8] Foreign-trade zones were opened, too, in New Orleans, San Francisco, Los Angeles, and Seattle; San Antonio had a foreign-trade zone at its municipal airport for a few years. For details regarding the free-port problem see Richard S. Thoman, *Free Ports and Foreign-Trade Zones*, Cornell Maritime Press, Cambridge, Md., 1956.

tramps, liners, passenger liners, etc., does not have the significance it once had, but size of carriers still is important. Ships are being constructed now that few ports can berth. Weigend points out that some of the largest oil tankers can be accommodated by only a handful of ports, one of which is San Francisco. Even there, they must unload part of their cargo into small tankers before they come alongside the oil jetty. If even through dredging and the installation of special equipment ports still cannot meet the needs of such large ships, they are likely to lose certain lines of business.

The cargo The volume of cargo, its nature, and the direction of flow all affect a port. Bulk cargoes, such as grain, ore, crude oil, and coal, are likely to represent the greatest tonnages handled in a port, but such activity is highly mechanized, so that no very great labor force is required. General cargo consists of a group of commodities that must be handled individually. It is considered much more valuable to a port than bulk cargo, since general cargo demands a greater and more diverse labor force and hence tends to bring greater port prosperity.

The origin and destination of cargoes are important to the port. A port that is a terminus for incoming merchandise is less likely to expand and develop than one where most goods move to and from interior areas. In the latter a larger and more diverse labor force is involved.

The hinterland The hinterland is of particular significance, since it is the real basis of the port. It has been described as "organized and developed land space which is connected with a port by means of transport lines, and which receives or ships goods through that port." [9] Hinterlands commonly are non-contiguous regions, as this term was defined in Chapter 4. A port usually has both a shipping and a receiving hinterland, as was brought out in Patton's study, and it may well differ in summer and winter.[10]

Maritime space and the forelands Maritime space and the forelands that lie beyond are vital elements to a port. But they are less directly and formally tied to the city than is the hinterland, so are of less interest to the urban geographer. Forelands have been described as "the land areas which lie on the seaward side of a port, beyond maritime space, and with which the port is connected by ocean carriers." [11] The foreland is the background of the port as viewed from the land.

Other aspects of water transportation in cities

Modifications of the ocean port picture It was pointed out earlier that in addition to great ports with many manifestations of the port function, there are various modified forms. Smaller foreign-trade ports, of course, present the picture in a correspondingly limited form. Moreover, in a large port such as New York there is a good deal of movement within the harbor that amounts to intracity water transportation and is not directly related to foreign or coastal trade. Then, away from the great ports, there are ports along the coast that have only coastwise shipping and that manifest in very limited degree the characteristics of a great ocean port. And there are Great Lakes ports, where freighters are the principal ships accommodated, and interior river cities, where only barges tied up at factories

[9] Weigend, *op. cit.*, pp. 192–193. Sometimes hinterland is used to denote the area serving a city even where the latter is not a port (see p. 52).

[10] A study of Saint John, New Brunswick, brings out the interesting difference between its winter and summer hinterlands. In summer the St. Lawrence River is ice-free and Saint John's effective hinterland is small. In winter, the port flourishes. At that time its hinterland is much of Canada. See Marion H. Matheson, "The Hinterlands of Saint John," *Geographical Bulletin*, no. 7, pp. 65–102, Ottawa, 1955.

[11] Weigend, *op. cit.*, p. 195.

along the riverfront or along a canal reflect the water transportation.

Minor elements of urban water transportation There are other, minor elements of water transportation in cities. In some cities, ferries still operate and may furnish a vital link in the mass-transportation system, but they have tended to be replaced. Private boats, unlike the private automobile, rarely are of any significance in urban transportation.

Railroads and the City

Most cities of the United States predated railroads. They originated on good harbors, or, more often, at intersections, river crossings, mountain gaps, and the like on early highways. The railroads accounted for much of the differential growth that came later. Thus the railroad served as a centripetal factor pulling more and more people to small areas, the growing cities. You may think immediately of a few small American cities that are without substantial railroad connections, and you may think also of the way in which motor-driven vehicles on the highways have eclipsed the railroads in recent years. But the fact remains that nearly every American city of substantial size owed a large part of its nineteenth-century growth to the railroad and still depends considerably upon railroads.

Sources in the study of railroads and the city

Though railroads have been of immense importance in connecting cities and in the growth of cities, our concern here is chiefly with studying railroads in the city and with characterizing cities as to their railroad activities. Thus a general map of United States railroads is of secondary interest except for those parts of the pattern formed by the railroads around the various cities, and many sources of information that are of value in studying the railroad pattern

for the country as a whole are not of much help when the focus is on the city.[12]

United States Census data The possibilities of United States Census sources for studying transportation in relation to the city were summed up on pages 220 to 222. Industry-group data in the Census of Population give some measure of the importance of railroading activities for cities of 10,000 or more population and make it possible to compare cities on several bases. Total employment by the railroads and railway express service group is one possible comparative measure. Another is the proportion of total employed persons in this activity group.

It should be kept in mind, however, that the proportion of total employed persons in an activity such as this cannot be very large even for a very large city. For example, Chicago has eight times as many persons engaged in the railroads and railway express service group as Altoona, Pennsylvania, population 69,407, and it is generally recognized that Chicago is the greatest railroad center in the country. Yet the proportion of employed persons so engaged amounts to only 4 per cent for Chicago, compared with 50 per cent for Altoona. Though the activity is a dominant one in Altoona, it is dwarfed to a minor position in Chicago by the presence of so many other activities that employ large numbers of people.

Industry-group data might be used, too, for comparing railroads and railway express service with other transportation groups. For example, in both the Fall River and New Bedford, Massachusetts, Urbanized Areas six times as many people are engaged in trucking service and warehousing as in railroads and railway express, whereas in the Springfield-Chicopee-Holyoke, Massa-

---

[12] See, for example, the sources referred to in Edward L. Ullman, "The Railroad Pattern of the United States," *Geographical Review*, vol. 39, pp. 242–256, 1949.

chusetts, Urbanized Area trucking service and warehousing employ only 1½ times as many people. In the Pittsburgh, Pennsylvania, Urbanized Area twice as many are employed by the railroads and railway express service as by trucking service and warehousing, and in the Altoona, Pennsylvania, Urbanized Area ten times as many. Investigation of such variations should prove interesting and might result in the discovery of significant spatial patterns.

Railroad companies as sources of data It might be thought that data on people and freight moving into and out of cities could be obtained directly from the railroads, and actually, Patton, in his study of general cargo hinterlands, described on pages 225 to 227, did get his data in this way. But such statistics generally are not divulged, since the data for any one railroad may be of direct value to the road's competitors.

Railroad patterns in and near the city

There are certain standard features and broad elements of pattern associated with railroads in cities. These were briefly summarized in Chapter 9 in the discussion of transportation and communication cities (pages 138 to 140) but are considered here in somewhat greater detail.

Railroads in small and medium-sized cities Primarily, we are interested here in the patterns or courses of the railroads—a simple matter in a small city but much more complicated in a city where a number of lines are represented. But we shall look first at the railroad features of small and medium-sized cities. Grade crossings, once an unfortunate accompaniment of the railroad as it passed through a city, are now less common; more often tracks pass under or over the streets. Other reflections of the railroad include railroad shops, switching yard, coach yards, passenger terminals, freight terminals, and offices associated with the railroads. To these features are added

more extensive freight yards, repair shops, and the like in cities that are more specialized in railroad activities.

Features associated with railroads of large cities The features associated with small and medium-sized cities are duplicated in large cities but in far greater numbers. In general, each railroad is represented by multiple trackage. In some of the more intensively used areas of the city, as in parts of Chicago, the tracks may be covered over, thus creating additional industrial and commercial space. For each line represented, there may be a passenger terminal near the city center, with possibly several secondary stations as the line enters the city. A single, union passenger station is the ambition of most large cities, but it is an ambition that is not always achieved.

The arrangement of radial and belt lines is likely to be particularly distinctive in a large city. The radial lines of the various railroads of necessity are concentrated into a few trunk lines in approaching the city center. The pattern of radial or trunk lines, fairly symmetrical where relief obstacles do not intervene, may be complemented by one or more successive belt lines girdling the city. Referring to the situation in Chicago, Mayer says: "Typically the spider-web pattern of radial trunk lines and intersecting belt lines, and the bands of land occupied by factories for which the railroads constitute the axes, produce a series of cells within which residential communities develop." [13] The belt lines make possible the shifting of freight from one radial or trunk line to the others. Though passengers are carried to the center of the city, more and more of the freight handling has been shifted to the periphery. Here, outside the outermost belt line, each of the trunk

[13] Harold M. Mayer, "Urban Geography," in Preston E. James and Clarence F. Jones (eds.), *American Geography: Inventory and Prospect,* Syracuse University Press, Syracuse, N.Y., 1954, chap. 6, p. 157.

lines is likely to have extensive classification yards where cars are sorted and reassembled into trains. But we should not generalize too much from the Chicago situation. Most cities do not have a sufficient number of belt lines to give rise to the pattern of radial lines, trunk lines, and cells that Mayer describes.

Density of rail net There are variations in density of the rail net in the vicinity of the city and also marked variations in the apparent freedom of directions from which the railroads approach the city. Variations in density of the net are based on several factors. One of these is city size: in general, the larger the city the greater the number of approaching and interconnecting rail lines. More important, though, is the presence or absence of physical features, such as mountains, lakes, bays, peninsulas, valleys, and the like. A very extensive rail net can hardly develop where approaches to the city are seriously limited, though it may be densely developed along the avenues of approach that are available. Still a third factor is situation. If the city is near the center of a large productive interior area, it is likely to have a dense rail net since the area, at least in the past, has been so completely dependent upon this form of transportation. It is obvious, too, that differences in developmental history must be important in explaining contrasts in rail net density.

Railroad patterns in relation to relief features The pattern of railroads as they reach the city and inside the city is closely related to relief and to physical features, since railroads are very sensitive to grades. Moreover, as railroads approach a city there is little choice of location, so tunnels or other adjustments to relief often are necessary. Hence, there has been of necessity a much greater acceptance of capital cost than for railroad construction elsewhere. The limiting effects of relief are particularly noticeable in a hilly region, as in the vicinity of Pittsburgh, where the railroads have had to follow the valleys.

Even more serious are the limiting effects of relief features such as coastal islands and peninsulas. The core of New York City is on Manhattan Island, and entrance from the west is barred by the Hudson River. As a result, a number of railroads have their termini on the Jersey side and rely on ferries to reach Manhattan Island. It was not until 1910 that the Pennsylvania Railroad managed to complete a tunnel to Manhattan, and even today only the Pennsylvania and New York Central lines (the latter from the north) reach the island.[14] San Francisco, on a peninsula, has had similar difficulties. On the other hand, in more level areas, where water bodies do not intervene, railroads have been able to enter cities from almost any direction, as in the case of Indianapolis.

Railroads versus highways: A contrast in development It is inevitable that railroad patterns should be contrasted with highway patterns since the railroad and the highway have so often been in competition. In any such contrast, differences in development history must be considered. Railroads are geared primarily to intercity movement and are a private enterprise system, although they are a public utility and hence subject to governmental control. Highways are a public facility designed both for local and regional movement and consist of a wide variety of forms ranging from local streets to arterials.

Inertia of railroad patterns Railroad patterns have tended to remain fixed. The

---

[14] There is a possible third. The New York, New Haven, and Hartford also enters Grand Central Station, Manhattan, though there is a legal argument as to whether or not the railroad owns part of the Park Avenue tunnel. Thus the company appears to have the physical ownership of a partial line into Grand Central Station.

railroads require roadbeds in which investments are too great for many changes to be made. Railroads are common carriers, and therefore railroad companies have the right to condemn land needed for constructing new lines or changing courses, but during much of the period of growth of the railroads, condemnation proceedings were politically unpopular and were avoided when possible. Also, railroads have tended to attract complementary land uses and settlement to such a degree as to discourage shifts in routes. And, no doubt, part of the seeming inertia of railroad patterns in recent years has been the result of the static or declining role of many railroads.

Of course, railroad patterns have changed in some degree. Spurs have been built to serve new factories, and even inside some cities, the courses of main lines have been shifted and lines have been duplicated. But such changes have been rare. In the average city it may be assumed that the path of the railroad through the city is much the same as the course originally laid out. The urban sprawl of today could hardly have taken place without a more flexible form of transportation.

Railroad patterns and suburban growth Around and before the turn of the century, when people were dependent upon railroads for commuting, the railroads had an interesting effect on the shapes of some of our larger cities. Suburbs, like beads on a string, reached out from the city along the principal commuting lines. Their outer limit was set by the reach of commuter trains. The so-called "Main Line" towns west of Philadelphia developed in this way. Similarly, towns just west of Boston, along the Boston and Albany Railroad, gained population through the growth of commuting; and commuter settlements developed on the St. Louis and San Francisco and the Missouri Pacific Railroads just west of St. Louis, and along some of the railroad lines radiating from Chicago. Not all of these places remained commuter towns. There has been an outward shift in the location of work places, and some of the towns developed into industrial satellites. In any event when we examine the extent of the modern city it is well to keep in mind that some of the towns reaching out from the main body of the city were generated by the railroad, just as other, more recent extensions have been associated with the automobile.

Railroad pattern and manufacturing and wholesale patterns The railroad pattern inside the city is likely to be closely related to the patterns of manufacturing and wholesaling. Railroads commonly form the axes of factory belts or connect manufacturing nodes. In part, the railroads form the axes for wholesale areas, too, wholesaling of the older, distributive type. This close relationship of railroads with manufacturing and wholesaling is now being undermined by the rise of trucking.

Competitors of railroads in the urban area

The competition of trucks and railroads by no means stops with service to factories and wholesale establishments. The truck is by far the railroad's chief competitor in general freight movements, except where availability of waterways brings an additional transportation form into the competition. Of course, the real competition with trucks is in movement of freight between cities; within the individual city, the truck's greater flexibility and lower cost of operation for short hauls give it an overwhelming advantage.

It is in the movements of people, however, that the greatest changes have taken place. The number of passengers carried by railroads has declined greatly. Though the airplane has become an extremely serious competitor of the railroad in intercity passenger movement, thus far it is of limited significance in travel within the urban area.

Elevated trains and subways compete with railroads in the larger cities, and buses play an important role in transporting people. But, above all, the private automobile has taken over the task of moving passengers. Railroads that formerly were depended upon for commuting to and from the city do little of this business now. It has become unprofitable and in most cases they would like to get out of it altogether.

Railroad decline

With their freight business undermined by trucks and with a passenger business that is losing money, railroads have faced hard times. The effects, especially where the railroads are mostly passenger carriers, have been lowered revenue, fewer trains, and an inability to keep ahead of a general creeping obsolescence. The effects in urban areas in such regions are particularly striking. Passenger stations have become dreary places indeed. As railroads threaten to go into bankruptcy there are likely to be demands for public aid, with the alternative of this type of transportation being cut off entirely at least as far as passenger service is concerned.[15] In New England, for example, abandoned lines and unused passenger stations may be found in a growing number of towns.

But a distinction should be made between short-haul and long-haul passenger movements. It is the short-haul movement that commonly must be carried on at a loss, whereas with long-haul passenger travel the railroads are said to make money or at least break even. Historically, in providing short-haul service, the railroad took on a job for which it was not suited but for which at the time there was no alternative. Long ago the business became unprofitable.

Geographic research dealing with railroads in relation to the city

Geographers have done surprisingly little work on rail transportation and railroad problems in relation to the city. What they have done has been largely descriptive—studies of the railroad facilities and problems of individual urban centers. But it is hardly fair to single out geographers. In a list of projects covering needed metropolitan and urban research, edited by a sociologist and published in 1953, not a single suggested project dealt directly with railroads or railroad land use.[16] This may reflect in part the lack of statistics, but certainly it is due in some measure to the fact that railroads attract less research interest than newer, more dynamic transportation types. Little money is available for studies dealing with railroads, but there are almost unlimited sums for highway research.

Patton's study of general cargo hinterlands One systematic study by a geographer, involving rail transportation, dealt with general cargo hinterlands of four Eastern United States ports. Though data from the railroads formed the chief source of information, the focus was on the ports. Therefore, the study was discussed under "Urban Patterns Based on Water Transportation" (see pages 222 to 230).

Other research possibilities Some of the most promising possibilities for urban geographic research dealing with railroads are in the realm of historical geography.

---

[15] It is common nowadays for a railroad company to ask legal permission to drop some or all of its passenger trains and maintain only the relatively profitable freight service. An instance was reported in the newspapers in 1963 in which the railroad carried its case to the people. The 200 commuters on the line from Butler, N.J., to North Bergen, N.J., were offered $1,000 each by the new chairman of the line if they would allow the railroad to abandon the service. Almost to a man the commuters refused.

[16] Donald J. Bogue (ed.), *Needed Urban and Metropolitan Research*, Scripps Foundation Studies in Population Distribution no. 7, Miami University, Oxford, Ohio, and University of Chicago, Chicago, 1953.

One possible research topic would be a careful study of the growth and subsequent contraction of the railroad patterns and railroad service of several cities in order to arrive at generalizations regarding the processes involved. Such a study might best be carried on in a long-settled area such as New England where the decline is far advanced. What happens to the railroad property in a city when the operation is terminated? How are the railroad land and buildings fitted into the existing land-use pattern? Not infrequently the land is valuable, and it is reported that the pricing of rail stocks takes this real estate value into account.

Some near relatives of the railroad

The ordinary surface railroad has several near relatives. They require fixed rights-of-way like the railroad, but unlike the railroad, they are very largely passenger carriers. Included in this list of relatives are the street railway, the interurban, the elevated, and the subway.

The electric streetcar or street railway was the earliest of these to be invented. It followed the horsecar, which had proved to be slow and expensive to operate. There was a marked difference between the street railway and the regular railroad, both in terms of ease of entry into the business and in ramifications of lines. Street railways could be started or expanded by simply securing a franchise from a city council or from the community through which the railway was to run. Also, because street railways had a much greater freedom with respect to grades, it was possible to expand them much more rapidly than railroads, and also to overinvest and overbuild. Nevertheless, the railroads lost much of their short-distance passenger business to the expanding street railways. The street railways were important in encouraging suburban development. Some of the suburbs west of Boston, for example, have been referred to as "streetcar suburbs."

An unfortunate characteristic of the street railway was that it literally got in the way of its more modern competitors. Its tracks occupied part of the regularly traveled street or were adjacent to the part of the street used by automobiles.

There was no sharp distinction between street railways and interurbans. In general the latter ran between urban centers, but in New England, where there was a good deal of business of this sort, the name interurban was never very generally applied. Nevertheless, throughout much of Eastern United States the interurban became a popular mode of transport though a somewhat short-lived one. For a time, interurban tracks radiated out from most cities. Indianapolis, for instance, was the center of the greatest development of this sort anywhere in the country.

But rising costs and motor competition spelled the doom of the street railways and the interurbans alike. The interurban is now chiefly of interest to the historian and the historical geographer.

In most American cities, the street railway or streetcar is now obsolete and the tracks have been pulled up or paved over. But streetcars are still operated successfully as an integral part of the mass-transportation system in Boston and San Francisco. In those cities special circumstances have dictated their continuance but it seems unlikely that even there they can long survive.

The elevated and the subway are sometimes regarded as types of railroads; in fact, they often extend outward at ground level as ordinary railroad operations. Both are restricted to urban areas, but the elevated railway has tended to blight the area through which it passes and hence is not so popular as the subway. The elevated has been declining while subway systems are expanding in various cities. Subways usually are focused on the central business district in response to the established function of the district as the heart of the city. Neither elevateds nor subways as such have been the subject of published geographic research.

A study of rail commuting

Another exception to the lack of systematic geographic studies of railroads in relation to the city involves subways as well as ordinary railroads. It is a study by David Neft of rail commuting in New York, London, and Paris.[17] Neft's stated purpose is to compare the rail commuting facilities of the three cities.

Method of approach Neft used a series of maps in comparing the facilities for commuting by rail for New York City, London, and Paris. These maps show distribution of passenger rail stations, distribution of passenger rail lines, and frequency of passenger service (Figure 13.4). Rail transportation is taken to include not only the regular railroads but also the subway systems in the three cities. On each map the center of the city, from which distances are measured, is the approximate center of commuter arrivals rather than the geographic center.

Contrasts in the facilities of the three cities Some interesting facts are brought out in comparing the three cities. Paris does not compare favorably with New York and London in density of stations and frequency of service. London provides the most frequent commuting service and has the greatest number of stations between 30 and 50 miles from the "center."[18] New York has the greatest number of stations close to the center of the city. A major factor in explaining these and related differences is the extent of the subway system in the three cities; the Paris system, though dense, serves

the smallest area of the three, and there are fewer people within 50 miles of the center of Paris than in corresponding areas around the centers of New York and London. In New York, railroad officials complain that increasing use of automobiles has seriously reduced the number of commuters, but it can be equally well maintained that inadequate rail facilities have encouraged the increased use of automobiles.

The adequacy of facilities, Neft points out, is determined partly by the number of stations and the frequency of service, but also by extent of the network of rail lines connecting stations. London is particularly well off in the number of intersecting lines with transfer points, which facilitates reaching specific destinations. The inefficiency of New York's system in carrying railroad passengers coming into the city to points near their destinations is emphasized.

Roads and Streets and Their Users

Roads and streets, though hardly as we know them today, were important long before railroads. While they continued to play a significant role during the era of railroad dominance, their real surge forward accompanied the rise of the automobile. Not only has the use of roads and streets increased relatively as compared with that of railroads, but people seem to have more faith in the future of automotive transportation. In the projection of intraurban needs, there is far more talk of automobile traffic in 1970 or 1980 or 2020 than of possible railroad activities. Ordinary railroads, as we have known them, seem marked for continued decline, especially in urban areas; the future is measured instead in potential use of roads and streets, possibly supplemented by some form of rapid transit.

Roads and streets in city transportation

The major roads of the original urban nucleus and their point of intersection or

[17] David Neft, "Some Aspects of Rail Commuting: New York, London, and Paris," *Geographical Review*, vol. 49, pp. 151–163, 1959.

[18] Such a comparison is of somewhat doubtful value, however, in view of the extent of water in New York City's 30- to 50-mile belt.

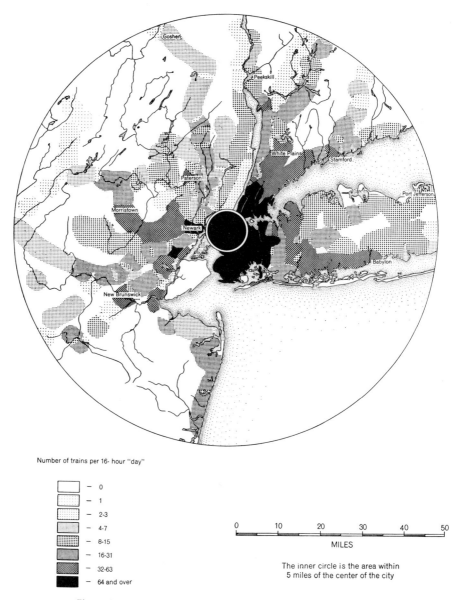

Number of trains per 16- hour "day"

- 0
- 1
- 2-3
- 4-7
- 8-15
- 16-31
- 32-63
- 64 and over

```
0        10       20       30       40       50
|————————|————————|————————|————————|————————|
                   MILES
```

The inner circle is the area within
5 miles of the center of the city

Fig. 13.4 Frequency of rail commuting service for New York City. (Reproduced from David Neft, "Some Aspects of Rail Commuting: New York, London, and Paris," *Geographical Review*, vol. 49, 1959, plate II. The plate, which showed similar information for New York, London, and Paris, is copyrighted by the American Geographical Society of New York.)

focus often are still important in the city of today. The street pattern by which the city was laid out or which evolved as the city grew is of enormous significance in explaining the present transportation complex. Important in many cities, too, are the express-

ways, which represent one phase of the current attempt to meet traffic needs.

The street pattern

Since urban patterns of movement of various types are guided in considerable degree by the street pattern, it is mentioned in some detail here. The concern of the urban geographer interested in transportation is less with street pattern as a form than as an explanation of current and possible future transportation patterns.

The grid or rectangular pattern By far the most common type of street pattern in United States cities is the *grid*, a pattern of rectangles which may or may not be squares. An examination of street-pattern maps of American cities reveals few cities of any size that show unmodified grids, however. Adjustments to rivers and other water bodies, relief, the original system of land subdivision, location with respect to neighboring cities, early relationships to railroads or roads, and the demands of modern transportation—these and other factors often are reflected in present modifications of the grid. In this connection a major fault of the grid system should be pointed out: if the city site has considerable relief, rigid application of the system may result in some streets with difficult or even impossible grades.

Sometimes the streets of the grid are oriented with the cardinal points of the compass. This is particularly likely to be true in those areas with the township and range system of land division (the region of the Great Lakes, the Mississippi Valley, and the Western states) since the grid plan fitted well into this system. In some cities in the township and range areas of the country, however, local conditions have resulted in the grid pattern departing, in limited areas, from this orientation. In downtown Tulsa, for example, the streets run northeast-southwest and northwest-southeast, parallel to and at right angles to the St. Louis and San Francisco Railway; and in Detroit, the grid of the downtown area, which happens to be similar in orientation to that of downtown Tulsa, is based on the course of Detroit River. In the remainder of both cities

the regular north-south and east-west street trends prevail.

But departures from the perfect grid are often much more involved than this. Several different sections of a city may show different grid orientations. Thus, suburbs frequently have developed their own grids without reference to that of the adjacent city. Nor is such variability restricted to contrasts between city and adjacent suburban areas; it is sometimes true within the incorporated city itself, reflecting separate real estate developments or the annexation of areas which already had grid patterns of their own. Philadelphia has several differently oriented grids within its corporate limits (which coincide with the boundary of Philadelphia County), and the suburban towns which lie to the northwest, outside the corporate area but part of the geographic city, show even greater variety. Los Angeles has a mosaic of grids reflecting separate real estate developments and annexations. Locally, in various cities and in their suburbs, occasional areas of curved streets form seemingly incongruous elements. They often are areas of recent origin and of higher-than-average housing values.

The radial or axial pattern Contrasted with the grid pattern is the *radial* or *axial* pattern. In the simplest form of this pattern, the streets radiate or diverge in straight lines from a common center or from several subcenters. Cross streets between each two radial streets may be arcs of circles or sides of polygons. No American city has a fully developed radial pattern. Washington, D.C., sometimes given as an example of the radial pattern, represents, in reality, a combination of the grid and radial patterns.

The radial pattern is reflected in at least a few radiating streets in most large cities. In some instances they are converging roads that preceded the grid plan. In others they have been imposed upon a preexisting grid pattern and represent an attempt to meet modern vehicular demands in a more efficient manner than the grid pattern allows. Expressways may be of this type.

Other street patterns It should be reemphasized that mixtures and modifications of patterns are the rule. In Worcester, Massachusetts, for example, a grid pattern is generally considered to prevail, yet even in the downtown area hardly a street meets another at exactly a right angle, and at some distance from the center, adjustments to relief have resulted in still greater modifications of the grid as well as varying street orientations. In fact, broadly viewed, the pattern for the city as a whole is almost radial. In the older sections of Boston the narrow, winding streets represent chiefly an adjustment to the original shape and slopes of Shawmut Peninsula.

Expressways and freeways The map of the American city of substantial size is likely to show one or more major routes that bear little relation to the remainder of the pattern of streets. Not infrequently these major routeways use, in part, overpasses and routes above the regular streets; loops and clover-leaf intersections are also common. These routeways are *expressways* and *freeways*. The American Association of State Highway Officials defines an expressway as "a divided arterial highway for through traffic with full or partial control of access and generally with grade separations at intersections," and a freeway as "an expressway with full control of access."

Freeways perform two main functions in the metropolitan area. They separate through traffic from local traffic, thereby relieving congestion, and they provide rapid and convenient accessibility between different parts of the area and between one metropolitan area and another. The automobile made it possible for the metropolitan area to spread out, but produced serious problems of traffic congestion; the freeway helps to solve these problems.[19] Circumferential expressways and inner-loop routes designed to encircle the central business district are special variants of the freeway and expressway systems in some urban areas.

The freeways that are now appearing in our larger metropolitan areas are part of the National System of Interstate and Defense Highways, which was authorized by Congress in 1956 and is scheduled for completion in 1972.[20] Of the 5,300 miles of freeways planned for urban areas, some 2,700 miles had been completed in January, 1964. In addition, 800 urban miles of non-interstate freeways had been completed. In the meanwhile, urban areas are continuing to spread out and the demand for freeways can be expected to grow accordingly.

Terminology in studies of road and street use

In studies of the use of roads and streets, certain special terms and devices have become standard.

Traffic counts and traffic-flow maps Traffic counts based on the number of vehicles passing certain checkpoints are often referred to, and flow maps of cities are commonly made, showing lines following streets and varying in width with total traffic volume. Such a traffic-flow map for the city as a whole or for a section of the city, such

[19] But the case is not all in favor of the freeways and expressways. Where the downtown area is bypassed by such a route, the merchants may complain that they have lost trade, and studies may be undertaken to establish the facts. When, on the other hand, the new highway is so constructed as chiefly to carry automobiles into the downtown area, congestion and its attendant problems are greatly increased.

[20] *What Freeways Mean to Your City,* Automotive Safety Foundation, Washington, D.C., January, 1964.

as the downtown, has become a standard item for anyone interested in transportation planning.

Origin and destination surveys   In recent years, the traffic of many cities has been analyzed through what are known as origin and destination surveys, often referred to as O & D surveys. The origin and destination survey obtains information on intra- and intercity movements. Ordinarily, it is based on home interviews (on a sampling basis), supplemented by information obtained by stopping and interviewing a sample of the motorists passing through a "cordon line" drawn around the urban interview area. In fact the city often is divided into a number of zones by such lines, and movements from each zone to each of the others are tabulated. Information on commercial movements is obtained from truck and taxicab operators.

Origin and destination surveys are expensive and specialized operations, requiring a substantial staff not only for the actual survey but for tabulation and analysis of the results as well. In most instances such surveys have been conducted by state or city highway departments in cooperation with the U.S. Bureau of Public Roads. The results both in tabulated and graphic form often appear in planning reports, and are considered to be of great value in gaining an understanding of the movements of people and goods in the city.[21]

Desire lines   One of the chief graphic devices based on origin and destination surveys is the desire line. A desire line tells by means of its width the amount of traffic between two points. It does not show the detailed course of the traffic, but is just a straight line between the points. Desire lines can be based on each of various modes of transportation, and the relative impor-

[21] The study of Chapin and Stewart described in Chap. 10, p. 171, was based on an origin and destination survey.

tance of the several desire lines can be shown for different times of day and for each mode of travel.

The practical value of desire lines can hardly be questioned. For instance, desire lines of private automobile travel for a city may show that the chief movement to the central business district is from the northeast, which is obviously useful information if the building of a new expressway to serve the district is contemplated. Another map may show desire lines between various pairs of points throughout the city, thus focusing attention upon the heavy travel between certain points and bringing out the desirability of improving certain routes in the city to meet crosstown traffic needs.

Isochronal charts   Still another type of map that has come into common use in transportation studies is based on isochronal lines. Such a map may be focused, for example, on the principal intersection of the central business district of a city. A point can be marked on the map on each street leading away from the center of the district to represent ten minutes of travel based on normal driving speed of a passenger automobile. The same procedure may then be followed for points twenty minutes distant from the center, and so on. Normally, on such a map, the ten-minute points are connected with the corresponding ten-minute points on adjacent streets, the same thing is done for the twenty-minute points, etc. The connecting lines result in discrete areas which are sometimes in color. Of course, the connecting lines have no real significance, since the time-distance measurements are based only on street travel, but the map as a whole has value in showing at a glance approximate areas of similar driving-time accessibility.

Types of road and street users

In an American city the chief road and street user is the private automobile. But trucks and buses use the streets, too, and in some cities streetcars and trolley buses. There is some merit in taking up truck transportation first, since the other types all concentrate on the movement of people and lead, logically, to consideration of mass transportation and the journey-to-work.

Urban Truck Transportation Patterns

Varieties of trucking

Trucking has become commonplace on highways and streets. If we consider only that which appears in the average city, here are some of the varieties: private trucking of manufacturing and commercial concerns; commercial trucking where the trucks operate only in the particular city being studied; trucking involving business only in that city and neighboring urban centers; trucking that is restricted in its operations to one state; trucking that operates in a somewhat limited section of the country, as in New England or in Eastern United States; and trucking that operates over the entire country. There are other possible varieties, too. For example, some trucking concerns are common carriers but are restricted to the moving of petroleum products, and others specialize in the moving of heavy machinery. And there are milk trucks and moving vans and a huge variety of other trucks for special purposes. Ordinarily, however, the trucking industry is divided into three classes: (1) common carrier trucking, (2) contract carrier trucking, and (3) private trucking.

Obviously, such different types of trucking will tend to have different patterns of travel in the urban area. All these patterns are of interest and concern, since trucking in general is playing an ever-increasing role in keeping our economy going and, at the same time, is complicating city traffic. However, it is the intercity common carrier trucking that is of most significance and has brought the city its greatest problems.

The rise of intercity truck transportation

A study of intercity truck transportation patterns of Chicago by Jerome D. Fellmann furnishes some insight into this type of transportation.[22] Apparently, common carrier highway freight traffic throughout the country in general began in the late 1920s and early 1930s. It expanded rapidly until the early 1940s when wartime restrictions limited development for a time. In the years since World War II, however, highway carriers have competed so successfully with railroads that the highway carriers have outgrown their terminal facilities and have brought serious problems of traffic congestion and conflicts in land use to already congested urban areas.

Resulting problems

The larger cities have borne the brunt of this congestion since they are the principal origin, destination, and interchange points for this new form of freight handling. The construction of new terminals and the expansion of existing facilities have been concentrated chiefly within terminal zones already clogged by truck movements and extensive on-street parking of trucks. Where terminals are grouped in widely spaced clusters, uncoordinated freight interchange by individual companies has added to the number of trucks on the move, and hence to the congestion.

The trouble has not been restricted to terminal districts. Multiple-purpose streets throughout the metropolitan region also have suffered. Tractor-semitrailer units reach the centralized terminals along streets that were not designed for the flow of these ponderous vehicles. And independent pickups and deliveries of individual intercity trucking companies affect commercial streets and many residential streets as well, interfering with normal city traffic. Particu-

[22] Jerome D. Fellmann, "Emergent Urban Problems of Intercity Motor Transportation," *Land Economics*, vol. 27, pp. 91–101, 1951.

larly is this true near central business districts.

The specific case of Chicago

Intercity motor truck facilities in Chicago, according to Fellmann, developed, as in other cities, with little planning or coordination of action by the separate trucking companies. Localization of the terminals dates back to local cartage operations which centered around the light manufacturing and retailing of the central business district, and the downtown tracks and freight houses of the railroads.

The central business district focus
The central business district has been the major traffic source; and new, intercity common carrier terminals have grown up along its edges, especially to the south and southwest where vacant, low-priced land was available, though there are numerous secondary agglomerations of terminals as well. Highway freight movement is chiefly between the terminals to the south and southwest of the central business district and any one of the several points at which the intercity carriers enter the urban area.

Time of construction Modern freight interchange terminals began to appear in the early 1930s, but the greatest spurt in their construction came in the postwar period. The more than two hundred Class I intercity common carriers of general freight operating in the Chicago area were leaders in the development. Their terminals and other facilities formed the core around which the highway freight industry has developed.

Converted versus new buildings Terminals are held on several different bases. Some are converted, old buildings, but an increasing number are new terminals. To a much greater extent than converted buildings, new terminals provide for multiple occupancy of motor carriers.

Truck routes The tractor-semitrailer units follow channelized truck traffic patterns within the Chicago urban area. They may enter the metropolitan area at any one of several entrance points; then they proceed as directly as possible to their home terminals. Local truck movements occur on every unrestricted avenue of the city, with some concentration in the light manufacturing and commercial areas, but they do not so completely dominate the traffic movement of a few routes as do the intercity haulers. For the latter, some thirty approach arteries consolidate near the corporate limits of Chicago into twelve city trucking routes. Though routes enter the city from each of the several landward directions, the greatest volume of this traffic arrives from the southeast. Unfortunately, not all the established routes are designed for easy passage of such heavy vehicles. The multiple-purpose nature of most of the routes, numerous right-angle turns, and a variety of other handicaps multiply the congestion.

Planning for intercity common carriers in great cities

The problems generated in large cities by the operations of intercity trucking firms are serious and are of increasing concern to city planners. Fellmann points out that three basic needs are involved: first, uprooting of the intercity truck terminals from their present locations near the hearts of urban centers, thus lessening land-use conflicts and the present extreme traffic congestion; second, reducing the number of intercity common carrier local delivery vehicles performing duplicate services; and third, facilitating the movement of highway freight units to and from outlying entrance points to existing terminal areas.

A solution commonly suggested is the establishment of union trucking terminals. Community sponsorship is usually implied, with space leased to trucking companies, and pickup and delivery services by local carriers assigned to serve specific territories of the city in the interests of all trucking concerns housed in the union buildings. Unfortunately, much of the demand for terminal services comes from and will continue to come from the hearts of the cities, where crowding is already at a maximum. Nevertheless, the removal of numerous, scattered individual terminals should help in this respect, and it has been suggested that expressways might be opened to tractor-semitrailer traffic. In any event, it is much easier to plan revisions in the trucking patterns of a city than revisions in the patterns of its railroad routes and facilities.

Generalizations regarding interstate truck patterns of great cities

Fellmann's work in Chicago is an interesting start in the study of truck movement patterns in large cities. The central business district focus; the terminals at the edge of the central business district; the concentration along certain established routes of much of the traffic to and from the terminals from outside the city; the confusion added by pickups, deliveries, and transfers carried on by intercity trucks; the advantages presumed to accrue from union terminals—all these, at least in general, characterize great cities. Of course, the situation in the individual city will differ from this pattern in certain details, and knowledge of other specific cities will result in improvements in the generalizations that have been based chiefly on conditions in Chicago.

Intercity truck patterns of moderate-sized cities

What is the pattern of intercity motor transportation in cities of 200,000 to 300,000 population? Is the central business district the focus of the intercity movements in such urban centers? Are there truck terminals which lie just outside the central business district as in large cities?

The intercity trucking patterns of cities of intermediate size and of small cities

would appear to merit investigation. It is not an easy line of research, however, since little or no data are available, and the information would have to be obtained through field inquiries and observations.

Buses

Buses play an important role in moving people into, out of, and within the average American city, and the pattern of flow of bus passengers is often an important part of the transportation picture of the city. Unlike trucks, buses present no great terminal problem, since there are likely to be only one or two bus terminals. These ordinarily are in or near the central business district in response to the considerable flow of people to and from the district and the fact that, in any event, some central gathering and transfer point is necessary.

Trolley buses

In some cities, as street railways declined, trolley buses took their places. The trolley bus requires a double wire overhead, so it cannot merely use the overhead wiring of the former street railway. But for the most part trolley buses have now disappeared in favor of self-powered buses.

Two types of intercity buses

Two levels of intercity bus travel usually are represented. Some buses are engaged in moving people long distances; no particular urban area is more than one of a number of stops. Of more interest here is a second level of intercity bus: the kind that brings people to the city from neighboring, smaller urban centers, thus forming one type of contiguous sphere of influence, a bus service area. Many of these people are commuters, and such buses may compete with commuter trains although, of course, nowadays, private automobiles carry most commuters to their destinations or at least part of the way. Both this type of bus, and the long-distance bus, travel on the central city streets, but they commonly reach and leave the city center by the most convenient possible routes and usually do not pick up passengers for movement inside the central city.

City buses

In addition to the two levels of bus services mentioned, each city commonly has its own bus system, ordinarily operated as a public utility. Generally, the bus system is a corporate descendant of the trolley, so bus routes are likely to coincide with or at least follow closely the pattern of the streetcar system that preceded them.

Research on bus transportation

Geographers may be interested in studying the bus pattern in more detail, either for the corporate city or for a somewhat larger area. A map of bus availability in the city would be interesting. This might be made by blocking out all areas within a certain distance of an intracity bus route. The white sections remaining would be those areas of the city most poorly situated with respect to bus lines. Comparison with a population dot map would show in what areas the largest number of people are poorly served by buses. And comparison with a map of median family income by census tracts should answer, at least to some degree, the question of whether the higher-income or lower-income sections of the city are better served. But the original map as suggested is too simple. For instance, account should in some way be taken of bus stops and of bus frequency, both of which are relevant to such a study.

Other buses serve the whole urban area. In England, F. H. W. Green made interesting use of local intercity bus travel for delimiting the hinterlands of cities (see pages 90 to 92).

Private Automobiles

Of course, the private automobile is by far the greatest user of roads and streets at the present time. In going to work, in conducting business, in shopping, in visiting friends, in going out for recreation and entertainment, people use their own automobiles if they can. And it is in the urban area that this tendency reaches its climax.

Planning problems

Many problems are associated with this enormous use of private cars. Private automobiles account for much of the massive traffic flow into the city in the morning and out in the late afternoon and for similar movements from the residential parts of the city to the work areas—all with the concurrent problems of access and parking. Varying street widths and inadequacies of street pattern add to the problem. Planners spend much of their time contriving more efficient ways for the vast ebb and flow to take place. And in city after city the attempt is being made to project our knowledge into the next few decades. How many cars, it is asked, will be coming into the city in 1980? Or into the central business district?

The Private Automobile and Mass Transit

Important though they are, however, automobiles do not stand alone in handling the human transportation problems of the average large city. When people discuss the increasing pressure of private automobiles in cities, they are likely to refer also to *mass transit*, which includes commuter trains, buses, streetcars, elevated trains, subways—in fact any means of moving people in mass. The question arises in the average large city, How can we encourage more people to use our mass-transit system? And an interesting phenomenon is involved. In spite of ever-increasing numbers of people to be transported, the mass-transit systems of many cities are having trouble maintaining enough load to operate efficiently since more and more people are turning to the use of their own cars.

Is mass transit doomed?

It does not follow that mass transit is obsolete, and soon will be only a relic of the past. On the contrary, there is every evidence that it will continue to play an essential role in the average city as well as in large cities. Certainly, there is nothing to be gained by viewing the motorcar and mass transit as enemies locked in a death struggle. Rather, the concern should be with the ways and means by which individual and public transport can share most effectively the job of urban transportation.

Rapid transit in relation to mass transit

But the private automobile and ordinary mass transit together frequently seem unable to keep up with demands. It is for that reason that *rapid transit* comes into the picture. In its broadest sense it refers to a mass-transit system that is faster than average. The transit system is on a private right-of-way—subway, at grade, or elevated—so that the speed of operation can be controlled directly by the operator, and thus can be increased beyond that of the general movement of traffic.

Research by geographers

Strangely enough in view of the geographic challenge of the private-car–mass-transit complex, only a few geographers have done any research in this field. Certainly, they have been considerably outnumbered by persons from other disciplines. There seem to be several reasons for this. For one thing, geographers, at least those whose backgrounds might lead them to work in this area, are few in number. Then there is the added point that the situation is an extremely complex one. From such a maze, it is hard to carve out small workable problems, and it has been one of the characteristics of the geographic discipline in the past that much of the research has been

individual research with the limitations that this imposes. But the picture is changing. More and more geographers, either as individuals or as members of organizations, are tackling the problems of transportation of people on our city streets.

Characteristics of the research attack

It is probably because of the complexity referred to, combined with the practicality and immediacy of the problems, that so much of the research on street and road transportation in urban areas is being done by research organizations, rather than by individuals, and that mathematical models and other theoretical methods are being extensively employed. The *Chicago Area Transportation Study*,[23] for example, represented an organizational attack on this scale.

Bypass studies

One of the topics that has been the subject of a good deal of research, some of it by geographers, is the effect of the courses taken by certain new routes near or through urban centers. In some cases, cities have been bypassed; in others, the central business district of a city has been bypassed. The attempt has been made to determine the effects on the area bypassed.

Most studies of this sort have dealt with bypassing of small cities. The research is applied rather than pure research, since the studies are designed to answer specific practical questions. Various approaches have been used. One is to attempt to find out just what has happened to the volume of business of the urban area that was bypassed. This is feasible, particularly, in those states where there are sales taxes and the records of sales tax data are made avail-

[23] *Chicago Area Transportation Study*, Final Report, vol. I, *Survey Findings*, December, 1959; vol. II, *Data Projections*, July, 1960; vol. III, *Transportation Plan*, April, 1962. Sponsored by Illinois, Cook County, and Chicago in cooperation with the U.S. Department of Commerce, Bureau of Public Roads.

able to the research worker. A second approach is through study of the effects on land values. A third is through opinion sampling to find out what businessmen in the bypassed area consider the effects to have been. A fourth line of attack is the study of changes in activity as reflected in commercial and residential building permits.

The chief difficulty in such studies is to determine just how much of what has happened to the urban center is due to its having been bypassed and how much would have happened anyhow had previous trends continued. Some sort of standard is necessary in order to measure effects. For example, it may be possible to project the performances of certain activities that have been going on in the area for some time and to compare these projections with the actual trends in the same activities since the bypassing. The methods mentioned are not the only ways of attacking the problem, but they are the usual approaches.

An analog study

Another example of transportation research dealing with a specific practical situation is a case study by John R. Borchert and his staff at the University of Minnesota, supported by the Minnesota Highway Department and the U.S. Bureau of Public Roads.[24]

The problem can be briefly stated. A segment of Trunk Highway 100 (commonly called the "belt line") has served since the 1930s as a circumferential and urban distributor route through the western sections of the Minneapolis-St. Paul Urbanized Area. A segment of the proposed interstate freeway system, which was opened in 1965, provides a new "super" belt line approxi-

mately paralleling Highway 100 some 5 or 6 miles to the west. The two highways are roughly analogous in direction, and the new highway occupies about the same position in the urbanized area that Highway 100 did at the time of its construction. It is also intersected by about the same radial highways and railways.

The basic idea of the study was that the experience with Highway 100 should be of value in planning for development along this new route. Borchert and his associates used two assumptions: (1) that, as available industrial land is absorbed on the old belt line, demand for industrial land in western portions of the urbanized area will shift to the new belt line; and (2) that neighborhood-oriented and traffic-oriented commercial uses will develop much as they have along the old belt line. Using these two assumptions in conjunction with the growth rates and locational characteristics established from the study of the original belt line, commercial and industrial uses were projected for the new route. It is suggested in the study that projections of this type are of value in highway programming, land acquisition, and planning the fringes of large urban areas.

Urban Transportation and Dynamic Analysis

The discussion of transportation in this chapter has been largely systematic in approach, involving one after another of the principal elements of circulation in the urban area. It was pointed out earlier that trucks and railroads compete in bringing freight to the city and, to a much lesser degree, in intracity freight movements, and that the private automobile competes with mass-transit media—railroads (especially where commuter trains are in use), streetcars, buses, elevated trains, subways, and perhaps even some of the more modern forms of rapid transit—in moving people.

[24] John R. Borchert, *Belt Line Commercial-Industrial Development: A Case Study in the Minneapolis-St. Paul Metropolitan Area*, Department of Agricultural Economics and Department of Geography, University of Minnesota, Minneapolis, Minn., 1960.

It is with the movement of people that we are chiefly concerned here. Is the picture as complex as it seems, or is there some central unifying theme whereby the geographer can reach a better understanding of the city? James E. Vance, Jr., has suggested a system of dynamic analysis which is useful in bringing order to the story of urban population movements.[25] In the system, he combines analysis of current movements with evolution of the transportation pattern through time. Parts of Vance's study are drawn upon freely in the paragraphs that follow.

Nature of urban circulation

Circulation of people within the urban area results from the economic or social interests of individuals. The largest element of this circulation, according to Vance, is that of workers, the *journey-to-work*.[26] A second movement, the *journey-to-shop*, is neither so repetitive nor so predictable. Though in the past largely to and from the central business district (or in shorter movements to local shops within residential districts), the journey-to-shop now often terminates in outlying shopping areas. A third type of economic movement is *commercial circulation*. It includes both commercial contacts within a financial or other office area and sales and delivery of commodities and services. Along with the journey-to-shop, it is economically rational and provides a key to the location of economic activities. *Social visiting* in a large city is far more indiscriminate. Still another movement, *recreational circulation*, is dominated by institutionalized areas of recreation, either public or commercial, and is thus very similar to journey-to-shop, at times actually part of it.

Some of these types of city movements have collective termini; this is true of journey-to-work, journey-to-shop, and recreational circulation—all characterized by the assemblage of people from many geographical origins. In contrast, commercial circulation, in considerable part, involves dispersion, and social visiting is largely a matter of individual ties.

Journey-to-work as an indicator

Vance points out that the several types of urban movement have received contrasting degrees of attention. Journey-to-shop has been attracting great attention in recent years, chiefly because flexible individual transportation has been taking the place of inflexible mass transportation. But the data are so recent that no historical picture of this movement is possible. Much the same is true of the other urban circulations, with the exception of the journey-to-work.

Recent studies suggest the paramount importance of the journey-to-work in the picture of urban transportation. Because the trip home combines the return from a number of different types of journeys, it explains the greatest number of trips. But in terms of destinations other than home, the journey-to-work accounts for by far the largest percentage of the diurnal trips in the urban area.

Zones of conflux and dispersion

The tidelike movement to and from work obviously is essential to the functioning of the urban complex. It is impossible to conceive of a large factory, or of a central business district, or of a major wholesale district without the journey-to-work. Borrowing from Kate Liepmann,[27] Vance refers to the places of work as *zones of conflux*, and city residential areas and outlying suburbs as *zones of dispersion*.

Here a distinction should be drawn

[25] James E. Vance, Jr., "Labor-shed, Employment Field, and Dynamic Analysis in Urban Geography," *Economic Geography*, vol. 36, pp. 189–220, 1960.
[26] For a study of journey-to-work based on rail commuting see pp. 236–237.

[27] Kate K. Liepmann, *The Journey to Work*, Oxford University Press, Fair Lawn, N.J., 1944, pp. 4–5.

between city areas and suburban areas. Thus there are two types of zones of dispersion: city residential areas and suburban residential areas. And there are comparable distinctions in the zones of conflux. In the central city, the zones of conflux have an established terminology, such as business district, industrial area, and wholesale district. In suburban areas no such clear distinction has been made. However, in an earlier chapter it was pointed out that many suburban areas are largely residential, whereas others have industries that attract workers. All gradations are represented between the suburb, an area of dispersion, and the satellite, an area of conflux.

Areal selectivity of growth

If we assume that every city developed around an initial nucleus (zone of conflux), then we might also assume that further growth would tend to take the form of simple peripheral expansion. But there would be selectivity: in the outer sections, at first only the better land need be used. It would be superior in physical characteristics, and it might also be superior in terms of transportation. Of course, transportation is subject to continuing revision with technological advance, new economic thinking, changing social attitudes, and the like.

Time and technology

In his discussion of urban transportation and dynamic analysis, Vance emphasizes the importance of the time dimension. In the initial city, according to his generalization, a zone of conflux, localized by a factory or a railroad station or some other local influence, was surrounded by a residential area. The proximity of residence and employment was essential, since most people walked to work. Adjacent to the initial zone of conflux, a central business district tended to develop. The business district expanded into the surrounding residential area; in contrast, manufacturing, which ordinarily could not displace housing eco-

nomically, tended to develop new, outlying centers of conflux, often with their own residential areas near them. Satellites developed in this way.

Vance points out, also, the effects of changes in transportation technology. With the development of the railroad, it became possible for factories to reach farther for their help and for workers to travel farther to and from work. Suburbs as we know them came into being. Then câme the street railway. This brought no increased extent in distance traveled to work, since the street railway was slower than the railroad, but it did bring a more uniform filling in of space, since the street railway conformed more to the street and road pattern. Finally, the automobile freed the journey-to-work still more. The labor-shed tended to become more symmetrical again, with distance controlling the outer limit as it had when people walked to work, but with the outer limit greatly expanded over that of the walking period.

Air Transportation and Cities

Still another element of transportation which may be studied in relation to the American city is the airplane used for commercial purposes. Here one will find little in the way of intracity patterns. The average city has an airport located somewhere outside the city limits, where sufficient flat land can be purchased or leased, and a route established for limousines to and from a downtown terminal which may amount to little more than a counter in a hotel. In larger cities helicopter travel is a new but significant element of the pattern. On an intercity basis the distribution of air-travel centers is a matter of considerable interest and has been the subject of research.

Air transportation and urban distribution

Edward J. Taaffe used a series of maps as a basis for inferring the effects on air traffic of such urban characteristics as size, function, proximity of other cities, and railroad services.[28]

City population and air passengers His first two maps compared the sizes of United States urban centers with their air-passenger activity. The first showed by proportional circles the number of air passengers for each of the 106 air-passenger generating cities in 1951 (Figure 13.5). The circles on his second map were proportional in size to the population of the 106 largest standard metropolitan areas, and patterns were used to indicate whether each area had a high, medium, or low air-passenger index (Figure 13.6). As might be expected, there was an easily observable relationship between the belt of densest population and

[28] Edward J. Taaffe, "Air Transportation and United States Urban Distribution," *Geographical Review*, vol. 46, pp. 219–238, 1956.

the volume of air passengers. The American manufacturing belt stood out on both maps. Outside the manufacturing belt, the maps were similar in the prominence of the largest regional centers.

The traffic-shadow effect Closer examination of Figures 13.5 and 13.6 shows that where cities are grouped there is a tendency for the largest city to act as the traffic-receiving point for the entire cluster. The smaller cities suffer from what is known as the traffic-shadow effect. This is noticeable in the smaller cities around Chicago, and it is true of various other clusters in the manufacturing belt, especially in the New York City area. The large number of low-index cities in Eastern United States, particularly in the Northeast, is due to cities being too close together for effective air connections with each other to be maintained. It is interesting

Fig. 13.5 The 106 largest air-passenger generators in 1951 and the number of air passengers enplaned at each. Data from "Enplaned Airline Traffic by Community, Calendar Year, 1951," Civil Aeronautics Administration, Washington, D.C., 1952. (From Edward J. Taaffe, "Air Transportation and United States Urban Distribution," *Geographical Review*, vol. 46, 1956, fig. 1.)

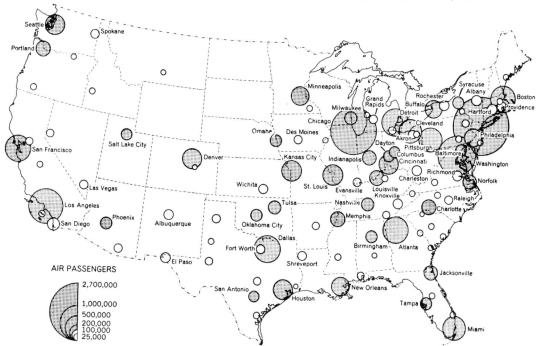

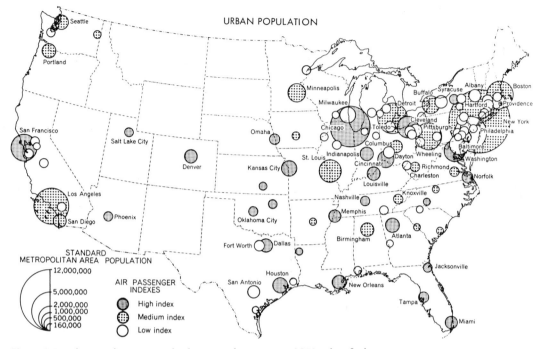

Fig. 13.6 The 106 largest standard metropolitan areas, 1950, classified as to air-passenger indexes. An open circle indicates that the area has fewer air passengers than the median figure of 201 passengers per 1,000 population. Population data from U.S. Census of Population, 1950, vol. I, Washington, D.C., 1952. (From Edward J. Taaffe, "Air Transportation and United States Urban Distribution," *Geographical Review*, vol. 46, 1956, fig. 2.)

that large cities, too, may suffer from the traffic-shadow effect. For example, neither Philadelphia nor Baltimore generates as many air passengers as would be expected from its population total. In each, this is a direct reflection of the city's position between the two great passenger-generating centers, New York and Washington.

There is, of course, competition among cities for air service. A relatively isolated city may be able to have service because it has no nearby possible rival for the building of an airport and the securing of services. But if another city of comparable size is located only 40 miles away, the right of the first city to have the airport may be seriously contested.

City function as a control Some of the differences between the air-passenger and population maps apparently result from city function. This is thought to explain the high indexes of Washington, D.C., and of such resort centers as Miami and Phoenix. Such regional commercial centers, too, as Denver, Dallas, and Atlanta have high indexes as compared with the low indexes of many Eastern manufacturing cities.

Overnight rail service as a factor Still another pertinent observation has to do with the relatively high air-passenger importance of cities scattered rather sparsely in a belt just west of the manufacturing belt. This is attributed partly to the absence of traffic shadow and partly to the fact that these cities are long-haul cities; that is, they are beyond the reach of overnight rail service from Chicago or New York. Air transportation has a definite advantage over land transportation under these circumstances.

Other factors Taaffe uses additional maps to reemphasize the importance of the four factors mentioned. To explain the high per capita air traffic of certain other specific cities he brings in such additional factors as poor surface connections, strategic route situations as at the intersection of streams of air traffic, and airline policy.

The future In conclusion, Taaffe points out that to predict changes in the air-passenger pattern amounts to attempting to predict the amount and direction of technological development. If the present trend toward air travel continues, then the airlines' share of the combined air-rail passenger traffic will increase still more and the circles on the air-passenger map will be larger without necessarily much alteration in the pattern. Development of an economical short-haul or local-service airplane or helicopter might modify the effects of traffic shadow by favoring smaller cities. On the other hand, a greatly increased emphasis upon speed seems more probable, and this should increase still more the primacy of the large centers.

Land Use for Parking

Thus far this chapter has dealt with the forces and flows of transportation. In addition to the land devoted to railroad tracks, streets and roads, airplane runways, and the like, however, a substantial area in the city, though unquestionably dominated by transportation, is less actively used for this purpose. One thinks immediately of railroad stations, bus depots, and the terminal of the airport, and such fixed features of transportation have indeed been mentioned briefly throughout the chapter. But they are dwarfed into insignificance by the use of land for parking, which in turn reflects the

enormous importance of the automobile in modern transportation.

Parking is difficult to place in a land-use classification, since it is so diverse. It is generated by transportation but in many respects belongs with other forms of land use. The commercial parking lot, operated by private interests, might well be discussed under commercial land use. It is comparable to a parking garage which would be so regarded. And city parking lots, though generally having parking meters or otherwise charging for parking, could be considered public and semipublic, a designation frequently used in classifications. Customer parking is normally mapped along with the land use of the particular business it serves; and employee parking, too, may well be shown simply as part of the land used by whatever concern does the employing.

But there are situations in which parking is less easily classified. For instance, some stores have arrangements for their customers to park without charge in commercial parking lots. And there is on-street parking. This is another special type of parking, but it is thought of more often as one element of a twofold classification, on-street versus off-street parking. All the other types of parking mentioned fall in the latter category.

What research can the geographer do with respect to parking? Like the planner, he may be interested in studies of the adequacy of parking in the city where he lives. And there have been many studies by planners, traffic departments, and the like with respect to the parking resources of downtown areas, since the downtown is normally the critical parking area of the city.[29] But when such a study is attempted, one runs into the diversity referred to earlier. How can all the different types of parking be added to give a meaningful total of parking space?

[29] See the discussion of business zoning, pp. 276–278.

The Changing Scene

Viewed in its entirety, the transportation picture of the city cries out for study of patterns changing through time. The first urban centers developed when only waterways and primitive roads were available. Chiefly, they were located on coastal or river harbors, at river junctions, at river crossings, and at road intersections. Then railroads appeared, supplementing the waterways and early highways. The new form of transportation brought rapid growth to many urban centers while others, less well situated, stagnated. Railroads were important, too, in determining the shapes and interior patterns of the growing cities, and, through commuter trains, in the beginnings of suburbanization. At the same time street patterns were expanding and streetcar systems evolving, further promoting the process of suburbanization. Then came the phenomenal rise of the passenger automobile and the decline of the streetcars and railroads. Truck transportation developed, and buses arose as a method of mass transportation. With the new means of journey-to-work, particularly the passenger automobile, suburbs and satellites burgeoned. The urban area as a whole increased in population while, as often as not, its center declined in population. Finally, and affecting intercity patterns more than intracity patterns, came the airplane.

These changing patterns might well be studied comparatively for a number of cities. How has the picture changed from period to period, and how have the various stages left their mark on the city of today? Present emphasis is on analyzing current data as a basis for predicting future needs, but generalizations would be interesting regarding past patterns and concerning the evolution of our urban transportation patterns. In a study described earlier in this chapter, Vance analyzed the evolution of urban transportation on a theoretical basis.

But comparative studies and case studies of specific cities are needed too.

Urban Transportation in Summary

The topics that have been covered in this chapter are extremely diverse, but they have one thing in common: they deal with one aspect or another of transportation in relation to the city. Transportation is a huge field, and many transportation problems reach their peaks in the city. At best, this chapter represents only a brief outline of the field, with little more than a casual mention of some of the research that has been done and remains to be done.

Selected References

Bird, James: *The Geography of the Port of London,* Hutchinson University Library, London, 1957.

Camu, Pierre: "Notes on Port Studies," *The Canadian Geographer,* vol. 6, pp. 51–59, 1955.

Carter, Richard E.: "A Comparative Analysis of United States Ports and Their Traffic Characteristics," *Economic Geography,* vol. 38, pp. 162–175, 1962.

Fellmann, Jerome D.: "Emergent Urban Problems of Intercity Motor Transportation," *Land Economics,* vol. 27, pp. 91–101, 1951.

Garrison, William L., and Marion E. Marts: *Influence of Highway Improvements on Urban Land: A Graphic Summary,* Department of Geography and Department of Civil Engineering, University of Washington, Seattle, Wash., 1958.

Garrison, William L., et al.: *Studies of Highway Development and Geographic Change,* University of Washington Press, Seattle, Wash., 1959.

Hilton, George W., and John F. Due: *The Electric Interurban Railways in America,* Stanford University Press, Stanford, Calif., 1960.

Liepmann, Kate K.: *The Journey to Work,* Oxford University Press, Fair Lawn, N.J., 1944.

McKenzie, R. D.: *The Metropolitan Community,* McGraw-Hill Book Company, Inc., New York, 1933.

Matheson, Marion H.: "The Hinterlands of Saint John," *Geographical Bulletin*, no. 7, pp. 65–102, Ottawa, 1955.

Mayer, Harold M.: "Cities, Transportation, and Technology," *Land: The Yearbook of Agriculture*, Washington, D.C., 1958, pp. 493–502.

———: "Localization of Railway Facilities in Metropolitan Centers as Typified by Chicago," *Journal of Land and Public Utility Economics*, vol. 20, pp. 299–315, 1944.

———: "The Railway Terminal Problem of Central Chicago," *Economic Geography*, vol. 21, pp. 62–76, 1945.

———: "Urban Geography," in Preston E. James and Clarence F. Jones (eds.), *American Geography: Inventory and Prospect*, Syracuse University Press, Syracuse, N.Y., 1954, chap. 6.

Morgan, F. W.: *Ports and Harbours*, Hutchinson University Library, London, 1952.

Neft, David: "Some Aspects of Rail Commuting: New York, London, and Paris," *Geographical Review*, vol. 49, pp. 151–163, 1959.

O'Dell, A. C.: *Railways and Geography*, Hutchinson University Library, London, 1956.

Patton, Donald J.: "General Cargo Hinterlands of New York, Philadelphia, Baltimore, and New Orelans," *Annals of the Association of American Geographers*, vol. 48, pp. 436–455, 1958.

Stanislawski, Dan: "The Origin and Spread of the Grid-Pattern Town," *Geographical Review*, vol. 36, pp. 105–120, 1946.

Taaffe, Edward J.: "Air Transportation and United States Urban Distribution," *Geographical Review*, vol. 46, pp. 219–238, 1956.

———: "The Urban Hierarchy: An Air Passenger Definition," *Economic Geography*, vol. 38, pp. 1–14, 1962.

———, Barry J. Garner, and Maurice H. Yeates: *The Peripheral Journey to Work: A Geographic Consideration*, Northwestern University Press, Evanston, Ill., 1963.

Thoman, Richard S.: *Free Ports and Foreign-Trade Zones*, Cornell Maritime Press, Cambridge, Md., 1956.

Ullman, Edward L.: *Mobile: Industrial Seaport and Trade Center*, Department of Geography, University of Chicago, Chicago, 1943.

———: "The Railroad Pattern of the United States," *Geographical Review*, vol. 39, pp. 242–256, 1949.

———: "Transportation Geography," in Preston E. James and Clarence F. Jones (eds.), *American Geography: Inventory and Prospect*, Syracuse University Press, Syracuse, N.Y., 1954, chap. 13.

Vance, James E., Jr.: "Labor-shed, Employment Field, and Dynamic Analysis in Urban Geography," *Economic Geography*, vol. 36, pp. 189–220, 1960.

Warner, Sam B.: *Streetcar Suburbs: The Process of Growth in Boston, 1870–1900*, Harvard University Press, Cambridge, Mass., 1962.

Weigend, Guido G.: "Some Elements in the Study of Port Geography," *Geographical Review*, vol. 48, pp. 185–200, 1958.

14

Commercial activities and the city

THE chief reason people live in cities is to carry on commercial or business activities. Although manufacturing employs the largest portion of the labor force in some cities, and still other activities are dominant in a few, when all American cities are averaged, commercial activities are found to account for 40 per cent or more of the urban labor force and thus to represent the principal source of urban employment. The land devoted to these purposes, though it takes up a relatively small segment of the city's area —usually somewhat less than 5 per cent— includes most of the city's tallest, most conspicuous urban structures.

Commercial Activities and Commercial Structure of the City

Insofar as any brief classification can cover the business activities present in the city they may be divided as follows: (1) retailing of goods; (2) handling of finance, insurance, and real estate; (3) rendering of services; and (4) wholesaling of goods. Possibly another division, (5) governmental business, might be added.

In this chapter we are concerned with the business or commercial activities of cities, and we are concerned with commercial land use. Whether activity or land use is emphasized, varying commercial patterns become apparent, patterns that serve to differentiate the interior of the city and to generate the frequent interactions between people that characterize urban areas. It is chiefly with these patterns that we are concerned, for they lead to an understanding of the structure and operation of the city. But commercial land use and commercial activities serve, too, to characterize cities, giving bases for city classifications and patterns of city distribution that are important in our inquiry.

Census Sources for the Study of Commerce and the City

United States Census data are of value in the study of urban commercial activities, though we shall find that they are of help chiefly in city comparisons and of less assistance in differentiating the interior of the city. The most significant census source for studying commerce and the city is the Census of Business, the latest issues of which, as this is being written, were for 1954 and 1958.[1]

Census of business and the commercial activities of cities

Three volumes of the regular Census of Business are of particular interest to the student of commercial activities of cities. The following details apply to the 1958 census.

Retail trade In *Volume II, Retail Trade, Area Statistics,* data are furnished for each kind of business on number of establishments, sales, payroll, personnel, and number of proprietors for each standard metropolitan statistical area, and for each county and city with 500 or more retail establishments. Less detailed kind-of-business groupings are shown for all counties, for each city of 2,500 or more inhabitants, and for the larger New England towns.

Wholesale trade In *Volume IV, Wholesale Trade, Area Statistics,* data for wholesaling are furnished for each kind of

business on number of establishments, sales, payroll, personnel, and number of proprietors for each standard metropolitan statistical area and for each county with 100 or more wholesale establishments. Less detailed wholesale trade data are given for "other counties," for each city of 5,000 or more inhabitants, and for the larger New England towns.

The Census Bureau recognizes five types of operations under wholesaling: merchant wholesalers, manufacturers' sales branches and sales offices, petroleum bulk plants and terminals, merchandise agents and brokers, and assemblers of farm products. But only a twofold separation is followed in the tabulations referred to in the preceding paragraph, a division into "merchant wholesalers" and "other operating types." The latter, presumably, include the other four types mentioned.[2]

Selected services In *Volume VI, Selected Services, Area Statistics,* data are furnished for hotels, motels, tourist courts, and camps; personal services; miscellaneous business services; repair services; motion pictures; and amusement and recreation services, except motion pictures. For each of these groups (and for subdivisions of the groups), number of establishments, receipts, payroll, personnel, and number of proprietors are given for each standard metropolitan statistical area and for each county and city with 200 or more establishments in the selected services group. Less detailed selected services data are given for all counties, for each city of 2,500 or more inhabitants, and for the larger New England towns.

Disclosure limitations Unfortunately, the data published in the three volumes just described suffer from several limitations.

---

[1] Final state reports for the 1963 *Census of Business* are *Retail Trade, Series BC63-RA; Wholesale Trade, Series BC63-WA; Selected Service, Series BC63-SA.* Separate reports for central business districts, issued in mid-1965, are known as *Major Retail Centers* reports, *Series BC63-MRC.* The bound volumes in which these data appear will be generally comparable to those for 1958 and are scheduled for publication by the end of 1966: vol. II, *Retail Trade, Area Statistics;* vol. III, *Major Retail Centers;* vol. V, *Wholesale Trade, Area Statistics;* vol. VII, *Selected Services, Area Statistics.*

[2] For more detail regarding the difference between merchant wholesalers and other types see pp. 267–268.

One such limitation follows from the fact that the Census Bureau is prohibited by law from publishing any statistics that would disclose information reported by individual concerns. Ordinarily, this disclosure rule does not affect the major kind-of-business groups, but frequently some of the data for the subdivisions of groups have to be omitted.

General limitations of Census of Business coverage In addition to problems rising out of the disclosure rule there are some general limitations. In the first place, by no means all business activity of the city is covered by the Census of Business. For example, the *Standard Industrial Classification Manual* lists several activities—finance, insurance, and real estate; medical and other health services; legal services; and some types of miscellaneous services—that are definitely elements of the business picture of the city but are not included in the Census of Business. It might be said that the Census of Business coverage is reasonably adequate for retail trade and for wholesale trade, but services are less completely covered, and the finance, insurance, and real estate group is not represented at all.

There also is the general limitation that no data are given in any of the three regular Census of Business volumes that in any way serve to bring out variations within the corporate city. However, where several central cities are clustered, data may be available for each and variations within the urban area worked out in this way, and where smaller urban centers border a central city or central cities, these smaller urban units may be large enough to have some independent data available within the limits mentioned in preceding paragraphs. One can also arrive at separate data for a central city and the remainder of a standard metropolitan statistical area and for the constituent counties of a standard metropolitan statistical area.

Central business district statistics But the Bureau of the Census does give us some help in differentiating the business picture of the interior of the city. For 1954, for 1958, and again for 1963, as part of the Census of Business, the Bureau delimited for each of selected cities of the country an area which it called the city's "central business district" (see Figure 14.1) and published a report for each.[3] The basis for the delimitation of these districts will be discussed in Chapter 15. It is sufficient for our purposes here to assume that each such area includes most of the important business blocks near the center of the city.

At this point we are concerned chiefly with the data made available in the bulletins. Data are given on number of establishments, sales, payroll, employees, etc., for retail stores in total and for some twenty to twenty-five separate kinds of retail stores; [4] data are also given for two types of selected services—hotels and motion-picture theaters. These data are for the central business district, and are summed up in companion tables for the corporate city and for the standard metropolitan statistical area. In additional tables the same data are analyzed on a percentage basis. The central business district data, like other Census of Business data, are subject to the disclosure rule, so some items have to be withheld.

Major retail centers For the 1958 *Census of Business*, the Bureau of the Census took another step toward differentiating

[3] Central business districts were outlined for standard metropolitan statistical areas in those cities of 100,000 or more inhabitants in which the local census tract committees recommended such areas in response to an inquiry from the Census Bureau. (See discussion of census tracts in Appendix B.) For a list of the selected standard metropolitan statistical areas included, see *Central Business District Statistics, Summary Report,* 1958 *Census of Business,* pp. 30–31; or, for 1963, vol. III, *Major Retail Centers.*

[4] Excluding non-store retailers.

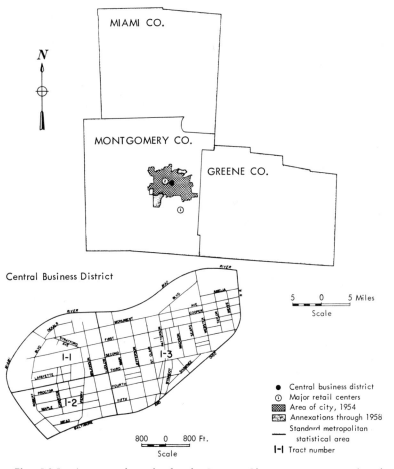

DAYTON, OHIO

STANDARD METROPOLITAN STATISTICAL AREA
AND CENTRAL BUSINESS DISTRICT

Fig. 14.1 A map such as this for the Dayton, Ohio, area was part of each 1958 central business district statistics report. Similar though slightly more elaborate maps are included in each of the major retail center reports of 1963.

the business pattern of the interior of the city. In the central business district statistics reports, in addition to depicting certain areas as central business districts and giving data for them, the Census Bureau defined major retail centers (MRCs) and presented limited information for those also (Figure 14.1).

Major retail centers were defined as those concentrations of retail stores (located inside the standard metropolitan statistical areas but outside the central business districts themselves) which included a major general merchandise store—usually a department store. Major retail centers were not delineated where the publication of data for them would result in violation of the census disclosure rule. The major retail centers include not only planned suburban shopping centers, but also the older string-street and neighborhood developments which meet the prerequisites described.[5] The number of major retail centers for which data are shown in a single standard metropolitan statistical area varied, apparently, according to the population of the area and the compactness of the urban development.

The data for each major retail center are somewhat less elaborate than those for the central business district, the corporate city, and the standard metropolitan statistical area that are published in the same reports. For each major retail center the following information is given except where the disclosure rule makes it impossible: total number of retail stores and total sales; total number and total sales of convenience goods stores, shopping goods stores, and all other stores making up the foregoing retail store totals; and number of establishments for each of about twenty-five kinds of retail business. The sales totals may be affected by the disclosure rule; the number of establishments is always given.

Each major retail center is represented only by a numbered circle on the map in the central business district statistics (or, for 1963, the major retail centers) report for a city. However, the location of each is described in detail in the report.

Census of Population and commercial patterns of the city

General characteristics Though less useful than the Census of Business for studying commercial activities in the city, the Census of Population adds some information of value in this line (Table 14.1). Thus there are industry-group data for finance, insurance, and real estate, and for some of the services for which the Census of Business gives no data.

The extent of detail differs somewhat with the type of area for which the data are

Table 14.1 Industry groups of commercial activities for which "employed persons" totals are given for standard metropolitan statistical areas, urbanized areas, and urban places of 10,000 or more population in the 1960 *Census of Population*

Wholesale trade
Food and dairy product stores
Eating and drinking places
Other retail trade
Finance, insurance, and real estate
Business services
Repair services
Other personal services (excluding private household)

SOURCE: *U.S. Census of Population: 1960, vol. I, Characteristics of the Population (state volumes), table 75.*

given. For urban places of 2,500 to 10,000 population, there is some grouping of items shown in the table, but they are given separately for standard metropolitan areas, urbanized areas, and urban places of 10,000 or more population. For standard metropolitan statistical areas of 250,000 population or more, some of the data are broken down in more detail than that shown in Table 14.1. Moreover, information regarding class of workers (private, government, self-employed, or unpaid family workers) and even on income is given by industry groups for each standard metropolitan statistical area with 250,000 or more population.[6]

All Census of Population data, of course, are by place of residence rather than by place of employment. This makes it difficult to localize the business activities, since employees listed for a city in a certain industry group may live in the city but work outside its boundaries. But Census of Popu-

[5] For further details regarding the delineation and characteristics of major retail centers see any central business district statistics report of the 1958 *Census of Business* or any one of the comparable 1963 reports, *Major Retail Centers.*

[6] Occupation data, especially for clerical and kindred workers and for sales workers in retail trade, also are available for the same types of areas and furnish an additional rough measure of commercial activities (see, for example, pp. 127–128).

lation data have a compensating virtue: they are not subject to the disclosure rule.

Data by census tracts The Census of Population also gives industry-group totals by census tracts for wholesale trade, eating and drinking places, other retail trade, and business and repair services; and for some other groups, such as "other personal services" and "other professional and related services," which are only partially commercial activities. In any case the data for each tract records only the industry groups for people residing within the tract. Since it is hardly to be expected that a large proportion of the population in a tract will work in the tract, such data can tell us little about the pattern of commercial activities within the city. Occupation data by census tracts are subject to this same limitation.

Census Sources versus Other Sources in Studying Commercial Activities and the City

The data sources that have been described serve fairly well for studies of commercial activities at the intercity level. Harris used Census of Business data in his functional classification of urban centers, and so too did Ohlson and Victor Jones, and Nelson and Alexandersson made use of Census of Population industry-group data involving commercial activities in their classifications (see Chapter 8). Other studies involving city comparisons might well be made, based, for instance, on regional contrasts in the extent and nature of commercial development by urban centers. It is surprising that geographers have not done more along these lines.

Single types of business at the intercity level

A slightly different problem is presented in studies involving particular kinds of business at the intercity level, e.g., hardware stores. By way of illustration the question might be asked, Do Great Plains urban centers tend to rank high in hardware store sales per capita of population? This or other studies of kinds of business would normally be based on the Census of Business. This is a satisfactory source except for the more detailed kinds of business where the Census Bureau's disclosure rule may limit the availability of data.

For some kinds of business the Census of Population is of more value than the Census of Business. For example, the Census of Business gives no data whatever on banking. The Census of Population, on the other hand, contains industry-group data for finance, insurance, and real estate, and, for standard metropolitan statistical areas of 250,000 or more, for "banking and other finance."

Often it is possible to supplement the United States Census data. For banking and certain other individual lines of business, some sorts of directories or other publications of national groups may be found that will add a great deal to the story. Regional groups or branches of national associations may have membership lists or directories. And many state governments through departments of commerce or labor or other divisions assemble data and other information that may prove useful. However, such sources are likely to lack countrywide comparability. This does not mean that they are not of value, but it is a fact that must be kept in mind when they are used.

Intracity studies

Use of census material Until the central business district bulletins appeared in 1954 there were no census data available regarding variations in commercial activity within any corporate city. As was pointed out earlier, it is now possible not only to get some differentiation among the census central business district, the corporate city, and the standard metropolitan statistical area, but also to focus on certain major retail centers outside the central business district.

Just how these data will be worked into studies that lead to a better understanding of the commercial structures of cities remains to be seen.

Field mapping of commercial land use
Most geographers interested in intracity studies have turned to non-census sources or to direct data collection through field mapping. Commercial land use is emphasized in the mapping—with such general classes mapped as retailing; wholesaling; and finance, insurance, and real estate. Or even more specific types may be mapped. The mapping can focus entirely on retailing, with appropriate divisions such as men's clothing, department stores, jewelry, furniture, food and drink, drugs, etc., or may be restricted to any single one of these use types that the investigator may be particularly interested in. Commercial land use is likely to be so congested near the center of the city that it will be desirable to map the central portion separately on a larger scale than that used for the outlying areas.

Mapping of commercial land use in the city is of value in several ways. Not only does one get a picture of all commercial uses in interrelation, but distribution maps of individual use types, too, may result—such as wholesaling or filling stations or department stores, or parking lots of various types—and any one of these patterns may itself give rise to geographic problems for investigation. Also, calculations can be made of the proportions of different types of commercial land use. More than anything else, though, the patterns of commercial use and of individual commercial uses in relation to other urban patterns are of interest.

Other bases for differentiating the commercial pattern of the city Another approach to the study of commercial structure of the city is through the construction of maps on which proportional symbols are used to show employment in each of various kinds of businesses. For example, the distribution of department stores or drugstores may be shown, or the distribution of grocery stores. The addresses of such commercial concerns can be obtained from a Polk's directory or other similar source. However, in the average American city it may be somewhat difficult to get even approximate employment data for commercial establishments, partly because many of the establishments are small, with a labor force that varies from week to week. There generally is a list available giving employment totals, either exact or approximate, for factories, but it is rare for such data to be so readily available for stores, banks, and other commercial concerns. Nevertheless, through the chamber of commerce or some similar source, it should be possible to get much of this information, though supplementary field work or telephoning may be necessary. If a study through time is being made it is usually possible through directories to get the addresses of establishments for earlier periods. But employment totals for past periods are much more difficult to obtain.

Various other bases for differentiation of internal commercial patterns are sometimes used. For instance, for mapping supermarkets, floor space has been used and so has number of cash registers. Volume of business by establishments or by firms would be particularly valuable if it were available.

City Commercial Structure

The commercial patterns of the city usually are considered on the basis of the broad types of business activity that are dominant (see page 254). Thus we are likely to speak of the city's retail areas, with full realization that the retailing of goods is only one function represented; that intimately associated with stores devoted to over-the-counter selling of goods are establishments engaged in finance, insurance, and real estate operations; others devoted to the rendering of services of varying sorts; and still others conducting local or national government business. Some of these myriad activities are carried on through offices, and there are offices with much broader, supervisory functions that seem to be a characteristic accompaniment of retailing and the other business types listed. Present also may be some wholesaling concerns, but wholesaling in the average city is likely to be sufficiently concentrated in one or two areas so that we think of wholesaling as a thing apart. Studies of city retail structure, therefore, often are in reality studies of areas characterized by a variety of classes of business and conceived of chiefly in contrast to other business areas of the city that are devoted largely to wholesaling.

In the pages that follow, city commer-

cial structure will be considered first in terms of these two chief phases—city retail structure and city wholesale structure (Figure 14.2). Then certain individual elements of the business structure will be discussed.

City retail structure

What patterns of land uses characterize the so-called "retail" areas of the American city, and what spatial interaction do they generate?

Proudfoot's concept of city retail structure In the middle 1930s Malcolm Proudfoot presented his classification of retail structure of the city. His work was based on studies in a number of the larger cities of the country and on reconnaissance observations in others. He differentiated five types of retail structure which accord fairly well with classifications that have appeared in

Fig. 14.2 Schematic diagram of commercial structure of an American urban area showing examples of the various type areas in which business establishments characteristically occur. Numbers and letters refer as follows: 1, central business district; 2, outlying business center; 2a, controlled outlying business center; 3, principal business thoroughfare; 4, neighborhood business street; 5, isolated store cluster; 6, controlled regional shopping center; 7, railroad-oriented wholesaling area; 8, newer, highway-oriented wholesale development.

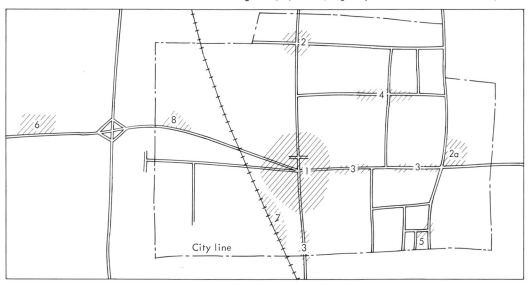

books on retailing and on real estate. Proudfoot summarized his five types as follows:[7]

The *central business district* represents the retail heart of each city. Here, individually and collectively, retail stores do a greater volume of business per unit area than elsewhere within the city. This areal concentration is manifested by the use of multistoried buildings of which retail stores, for the most part, occupy choice street level frontage, service establishments are concentrated into upper story offices, and residential occupance is restricted to scattered hotels. Here retail occupance is characterized by large department stores, numerous women's and men's clothing stores, furniture stores, shoe stores, jewelry stores, and similar outlets selling shopping goods. Added to these though of subordinate importance, are numerous drug stores, tobacco stores, restaurants, and other stores selling convenience goods.

The central business district draws customers from all parts of the city proper and from outlying suburbs and nearby incorporated towns. Many people, besides being customers, are likewise employed in the various commercial and service occupations which constitute the complex of human activity within this district. To serve this movement of purchasing and working population to and from residential areas, all modes of intra-city transportation are focused here. This district, therefore, experiences extreme traffic congestion during the work-day and more particularly during the morning and late afternoon "rush hours." The personal inconvenience of this congestion, and the commutation cost in time and money all have favored the development of the outlying business center, catering to the shopping goods wants of outlying population.

The *outlying business center* represents, in miniature, the same type of retail structure characterizing the central business district. The center possesses a marked areal concentration where closely spaced retail stores do a volume of business exceeded only by those of the cen-

tral district. Here, for the most part, are found shopping goods outlets such as women's and men's clothing stores, furniture stores, shoe stores, jewelry stores, one or more large department stores, and an admixture of convenience goods stores. Although individual outlying business centers do not draw customers from all parts of the city, they frequently attract them from long distances. Since these centers depend on customers drawn from wide areas, they all have developed at focal points of intra-city transportation where pedestrian traffic is increased by passengers of mass and vehicular conveyance.

The *principal business thoroughfare* is characterized by the co-existence of two related attributes. It is both a business street and a traffic artery. As a business street it possesses large, widely-spaced shopping and convenience goods stores. As a traffic artery it carries a heavy density of mass and vehicular traffic. This dense traffic primarily results from attractive forces exerted on residential population by the central business district or some outlying business center. Although stores of this structural type cater to, and are primarily dependent on, customers derived from this dense traffic, their presence has little counter effect on the density of the traffic. Offering the special inducement of ample curb-side parking space, these stores manage to thrive by attracting customers from a small fraction of the passengers of this inter-community traffic.

The *neighborhood business street* is primarily of neighborhood significance. It draws customers, almost without exception, from easy walking distances. This structural type consists of more or less continuous rows of grocery stores, meat markets, fruit and vegetable stores, drug stores, and other convenience goods outlets, interrupted by a minor admixture of shopping goods stores. These streets extend through residential portions of the city and take the form of a more or less regular network following the principal mass transportation and trucking routes which are undesirable for residential purposes; are extensions to outlying business centers; or are isolated from other retail structures.

The *isolated store cluster* is the final, and individually the least significant, type of retail structure. These clusters usually

[7] Malcolm J. Proudfoot, "City Retail Structure," *Economic Geography*, vol. 13, pp. 425–428, 1937. References to figures in the original article have been deleted, and italics have been supplied by the present author.

comprise two or more complementary rather than competitive convenience goods stores. Thus there may be a drug store, a grocery store, a meat market, a fruit and vegetable store, a delicatessen, and possibly a small lunch room grouped together at a minor street intersection. These stores usually supply a large portion of the immediate convenience goods wants of residential families located within easy walking distance. Frequently these store clusters develop in sparsely settled fringes of the urban area, but in many instances they are found within densely populated residential areas, restricted by the chance of occupance or by zoning regulations, to a scant block or even a city lot.

Although they do not constitute a distinct structural type, it is necessary for the sake of completeness, to mention that within any of the principal cities there are numerous instances of single isolated retail stores. Of these the corner drug store, the grocery store, and the delicatessen are the most numerous, although individually, they do a small volume of business. Other less numerous outlets, such as milk distributors, coal and lumber yards, mail order houses, and the retail stores of mail order houses, as a rule, do a large volume of business. It is the heterogeneous character of these stores, their relative unimportance when taken in aggregate, and, in many instances, their unusual function (such as milk distributor serving a wide area with house to house wagon delivery), which supports the conclusion that they should not be classified as a distinct structural type.

In reality a twofold division

Proudfoot's five types of retail structure can be viewed more simply as consisting of just two basic forms: the string-street or ribbon development and the nucleation.

STRING-STREET OR RIBBON DEVELOPMENT The string-street or ribbon development amounts to retail use of property along a traffic artery, with only minor extensions on intersecting streets. The principal business thoroughfare obviously follows this conformation; so, too, does the neighborhood business street. In the first case, use of the street as a traffic artery results in emphasis on retail shops for transients. In the second, the neighborhood business street, the proximity of residential areas encourages more convenience-type outlets.

Of course, the automobile plays a much more important role than it did when Proudfoot differentiated his types of city retail structure. For instance, a recent study of string-street or ribbon developments refers to urban arterial business districts, highway-oriented business districts, and automobile row.[8]

THE NUCLEATION The nucleation is a cluster of retail outlets. The central business district is, of course, the extreme of nucleation in the city. Often, nowadays, it is being rivaled by the regional shopping center, but this, in its fullest development, is normally outside the city limits. Inside the city, the outlying business center usually is second in the nucleation hierarchy. Located at an important intersection, often at the junction of two string-street developments, a major center of this sort may provide on a reduced scale most of the services available in a central business district. Nucleations grade from such centers down to isolated store clusters.

Controlled shopping centers

Proudfoot did his work in the 1930s, and there have been some striking changes in city retail structure in the intervening years. Probably the chief one has been the growth of controlled or planned retail shopping centers in and near cities. The controlled shopping center is situated on land owned by a single agency. This makes possible control of architecture and other features of the center by developers, including the provision of adequate parking. Efficiencies of operation result.

The trend toward controlled shopping centers has not been very noticeable in cen-

[8] Brian J. L. Berry, "Ribbon Developments in the Urban Business Pattern," *Annals of the Association of American Geographers*, vol. 49, pp. 145–155, 1959.

tral business districts, since most of these were developed a number of years ago. Typically, little room was left for such space-demanding developments as controlled shopping centers. But there are some marked exceptions. Through redevelopment projects it has been possible to change central business districts considerably. The pedestrian malls that have been established in the downtown areas of a few cities include many of the features of controlled shopping centers. Often the redeveloped land is owned by a single agency which leases sites to various concerns. Locally, a few controlled shopping centers may be found in such long-established business areas as outlying business centers, principal business thoroughfares, neighborhood business streets, and even isolated store clusters. But such controlled developments are likely to be only parts of larger business areas in which separate ownership of business lots is the rule.

On the other hand, a number of the newer shopping centers in cities are completely controlled or planned. This is sometimes true of the newer, larger outlying business centers. But the largest and most impressive type of controlled shopping center does not find its unplanned equivalent at all among Proudfoot's types. This is the controlled regional shopping center, typically located just outside a large city. Such centers depend on customers from extensive areas, so their development awaited the modern rise of the automobile and the tremendous highway expansion. Controlled regional shopping centers are much more impressive than the other controlled shopping areas, since each serves a much larger population than any planned outlying business center inside the city and each has a correspondingly extensive line of shopping and specialty goods. Such regional centers have been referred to as decentralized substitutes for central business districts. Vast parking areas reflect the major advantage of such centers over their downtown com-

petitors. Controlled shopping centers parallel planned developments for other functions such as the industrial park and the residential subdivision.

A special type of controlled shopping center is found in many of the largest recent subdivisions. The subdivision has its own shopping center which, with the housing, forms a single planned development.

Research on city retail structure   City retail structure has attracted a good deal of research attention. Three such projects are summarized here to illustrate objectives and methods.

FUTURE OF A STRING-TYPE SHOPPING STREET   The first of the studies to be described involved a string-type shopping street, Ventura Boulevard, which stretched 15 miles along the southern edge of the San Fernando Valley in suburban Los Angeles.[9] It was a busy shopping street but one that was shortly to be relieved of some of its traffic by a new, multilane, limited-access through highway which would roughly parallel the boulevard at a distance varying from several hundred feet to about a mile. The designed purpose of the freeway was to siphon off the through traffic from the heavily traveled boulevard. The idea of the research project here summarized was to study business land use along the street in detail, so that after the freeway is built it will be possible to determine with some exactitude just what effect it has had on the business of the boulevard.

The first steps involved land-use mapping and classification. A land-use map was made of the entire 15-mile length, using a detailed classification scheme. The authors found that there were four groups of business establishments along the boulevard: (1) those serving neighborhood needs, (2)

[9] Gerard J. Foster and Howard J. Nelson, *Ventura Boulevard: A String-type Shopping Street*, Real Estate Research Program, Bureau of Business and Economic Research, University of California, Los Angeles, Calif., 1958.

those serving a wider territory with customers deliberately coming to the establishments, (3) those serving a wider territory with only casual customers, and (4) those whose location on Ventura Boulevard reflect a peculiarity of the boulevard itself.

Looking into the future, the authors believed that the greatest effects of the new freeway would be at nodal concentrations. Associated as they are with major cross streets, these nodal concentrations will be provided with access points to the freeway. The vicinities of such points should become particularly attractive locations, and land values should rise. For internodal points, where most of the stores serving local needs are found, there may not be many changes. But the exact facts cannot be determined until sometime in the future.

In the meanwhile this is a rather unusual type of research: study of the current picture to furnish a base from which changes can be measured at a future date.

EMERGING PATTERNS OF COMMERCIAL STRUCTURE The second study to be described is the work of J. E. Vance, Jr. It dealt with city retail structure with particular reference to the San Francisco Bay area.[10] The purposes of the work as described in the resulting paper were: (1) to consider briefly what factors had in the past influenced the location and nature of American commercial districts, (2) to undertake to formulate the general location factors affecting commercial development today, and (3) to test this formulation against actual conditions in the highly diversified structure of the San Francisco Bay area.

Because of space limitations, only a few of Vance's more general findings and conclusions can be included here. He

[10] James E. Vance, Jr., "Emerging Patterns of Commercial Structure in American Cities," Proceedings of the IGU Symposium in Urban Geography Lund 1960, *Lund Studies in Geography,* ser. B, Human Geography, p. 24, Royal University of Lund, Sweden, 1962, pp. 485–518.

speaks, first, of several dynamic factors that have affected commercial structure in the American city. The most important of these has been the change from mass transportation to the automobile. This, he says, has less effect on the office quarter of the city than on the retail quarter, since retailing could change its location requirements more easily. A second dynamic factor has been the general increase in per capita expenditures. A third has been the increased distance of housing from the city core, which has favored the new mass integrated shopping center. A fourth dynamic factor is zoning. This has operated particularly against the isolated shop. Still a fifth dynamic factor Vance mentions is the fuzzing of lines of demarcation between types of shops, typified by the modern drugstore, which is essentially a variety store.

Next, Vance considers some elements in the evolution of the present commercial pattern: the general store, the department store, the five-and-ten, ready-made clothing sales, and the drugstore of today. The four mass selling establishment types—department stores, the five-and-ten, ready-made clothing, and drugstores—still account for 60 per cent of the business in the central business district, yet they have been in the van in developments outside the core.

Vance claims that throughout the history of commercial development in the United States there has been a constant effort to develop selling units as close to the customers as possible. There has been, in fact, a continuing reduction in the size of trading areas. With the regional shopping center we seem to have reached the minimum size of trade area for mass selling. Under conditions of automobile transportation, further reduction in size of tributary areas may result in unprofitable operations.

The central business district, Vance predicts, will continue to exist but shorn of much of its former purpose. Now it is more and more thought of as a place of offices rather than of large stores. The focus of metropolitan arteries plus convenience of geographic integration for offices tends to maintain the financial subdistrict at the core. In some cities this focus is being reinforced by introduction of rapid transit. But the retail subdistrict is less favored by mass transit. Shoppers at most visit the downtown infrequently and prefer the flexibility of driving to shop. The office district with its congestion and preempted parking is not a good location for specialty shops. Vance sees a trend toward two downtowns, possibly with a band of parking between. The single focus of the past may be lost and we may in the future, he thinks, have to limit the designation central business district to the office district and coin a new name, like "metropolitan specialty district," for the other downtown focus.

The central business district has become the mass seller to the inner part of the metropolis, the specialty seller to the geographic city, and the office area for the region. In contrast, the regional integrated shopping center has become the mass seller to the individual suburb.

The foregoing paragraphs cover only a few of the generalizations advanced in the paper. It has been impossible, for example, to include Vance's application of his ideas to the San Francisco Bay area. In a sense, the research consists of using a case study plus observations in various other localities as bases for generalizations.

COMMERCIAL STRUCTURE AND COMMERCIAL BLIGHT IN CHICAGO A study of the Chicago area by Brian Berry represented a broad attack on problems associated with city retail structure.[11] The purpose of the project, as described by Berry, was to determine the extent, location, nature, and trends

[11] Brian J. L. Berry, *Commercial Structure and Commercial Blight: Retail Patterns and Processes in the City of Chicago*, Research Paper 85, Department of Geography, University of Chicago, Chicago, 1963.

of commercial blight and deterioration. Outside the Loop (which is essentially Chicago's central business district) the 500 street miles occupied by 55,000 retail and service establishments, the author says, are not an undifferentiated whole but, as in other large American cities, are highly structured both locationally and functionally. The major structural elements include: (1) ribbons; (2) several kinds of specialized functional areas, such as automobile rows, furniture districts, and the like; and (3) a hierarchy of business centers both unplanned and planned. The business centers beneath the level of the Loop were classified as major regional centers, smaller shopping goods centers, community centers, and neighborhood centers.

Neighborhood differences were involved. For instance, the hierarchy of centers differed markedly in the higher- and lower-income neighborhoods of the city. The higher-income areas were found to have all four of the classes of business centers, but lower-income neighborhoods had neither regional centers nor community centers. The author found, too, that changes were constantly under way, changes in retailing on the one hand and changes in population and income on the other. These changes were of particular interest as they related to retailing, since that was the focus of the research.

Berry points out that the effects of changes can be measured. A 1 per cent change in population of an area, for example, was found to engender a 1 per cent change in the number of retail establishments in that area, and a 1 per cent change in real income to generate a 0.86 per cent change in retail establishments. The combined effects of increasing scale of retailing and increasing consumer mobility are causing a 5.87 per cent average annual loss in retail establishments. Declines were greater in stable lower-income communities of the city than in stable higher-income communities, and the rate of decline in areas in transition from higher-income to lower-income status was greater than in either of the others. When average annual increase in store size was combined with the information on rates of change it was found that changes in demands for space were negligible in higher-income areas, amounted to −2 per cent annually in lower-income areas, and equaled −3 per cent in areas undergoing socioeconomic change.

The story of commercial blight is at the heart of the study. In high-income areas, as they obtain in outer portions of the city, vacancy rates are relatively low both in centers and in ribbons. But low-income groups are expanding outward from the older areas of the central city, and higher-income areas are dropping to a lower-income status. The first development reflecting social change in a neighborhood is that demands drop, particularly for the more highly specialized stores. Such specialty stores are in the hearts of larger business centers, so vacancy rates increase rapidly in these centers. As the neighborhood declines, land values and rents drop in the business centers. Vacant stores are filled by uses from the adjacent ribbons and by types of business serving demands characteristic of lower-income groups. Vacancies rise in the ribbons, as businesses shift to centers and demands for services decline. These vacancies occur in the older, poorer, more deteriorated buildings, and owing to the structural deterioration the vacancies are not being replaced. It is the increase in quantity and expansion in areal coverage of this vacancy-plus-deterioration accompanying socioeconomic turnover that is Chicago's real problem of commercial blight.

The study that is here briefly summarized was group research. Detailed field mapping and field inquiry as well as statistical and other office work were involved. It is an inquiry that obviously is designed to be followed by remedial action through planning.

City wholesale structure

As was pointed out earlier, one type of business land use is largely excluded from a study of city retail structure: the use of land for wholesaling. Although wholesaling has been considered by geographers in various city studies, no systematic study of this activity has been published comparable to those on retailing and no such generalizations are available.

Definitions The first problem, or group of problems, facing anyone interested in studying wholesale land use in the city is that of definitions. At first glance the meaning of *wholesaling* is simple: the selling of goods to retailers in contrast to sales to consumers. But such a definition falls considerably short of telling the whole story.

STANDARD INDUSTRIAL CLASSIFICATION DEFINITION The *Standard Industrial Classification Manual* is helpful in this matter. Wholesale trade, according to the manual, is defined as follows: [12]

> This division includes establishments or places of business engaged in selling merchandise to retailers; to industrial, commercial, institutional, or professional users; or to other wholesalers; or acting as agents in buying merchandise for or selling merchandise to such persons or companies. The principal types of establishments included are: (1) merchant wholesalers—wholesalers who take title to the goods they sell such as wholesale merchants or jobbers, industrial distributors, voluntary group wholesalers, exporters, importers, cash-and-carry wholesalers, drop shippers, wagon distributors, retailer cooperative warehouses, terminal elevators, and cooperative buying associations; (2) sales branches and sales offices (but not retail stores) maintained by manufacturing or mining enterprises apart from their plants or mines for the purpose of marketing their products; (3) agents, merchan-

[12] *Standard Industrial Classification Manual*, U.S. Bureau of the Budget, p. 147.

dise or commodity brokers, and commission merchants; (4) petroleum bulk stations; and (5) assemblers, buyers, and associations engaged in the cooperative marketing of farm products.

The chief functions of establishments included in wholesale trade are selling goods to trading establishments, or to industrial, commercial, institutional, and professional users; and bringing buyer and seller together. In addition to selling, functions frequently performed by wholesale establishments include maintaining inventories of goods; extending credit; physically assembling, sorting, and grading goods in large lots; breaking bulk and redistribution in smaller lots; delivery; refrigeration; and various types of promotion, such as advertising and label designing.

Many wholesalers have large storage warehouses, and as a result warehousing is sometimes classified along with wholesaling. Here we consider storage and warehousing as parts of wholesaling only to the extent that they actually are part of the wholesaling operation. Other storage and warehousing, for example the storage of your furniture if you are to be away for a few years, are considered transportation land use, since for the most part the warehouses are maintained by trucking concerns.

DISTRIBUTIVE VERSUS COLLECTIVE WHOLESALING   In the discussion of wholesale centers (pages 136 to 138), a distinction was made between distributive and collective wholesaling. The former, covered by types 1 through 4 in the Standard Industrial Classification definition, is most relevant to the current discussion since it is the phase of wholesaling that competes for space in every large city. In the following paragraphs, therefore, only distributive wholesaling is considered.

OTHER PROBLEMS OF DEFINITION   But even if the field of inquiry is thus arbitrarily limited, it is not always easy to draw the line between what is and what is not wholesaling. The general picture, however, is well defined. A wholesale drugstore, for example,

may carry much the same pharmaceutical supplies as a retail drugstore, and the store's shelves may be stocked with standard pharmaceutical products. But the words "wholesale only" accompany the firm's name on the front of the building and no sales are made to individual consumers.

Unfortunately, deciding what is or is not wholesaling is seldom so simple as this, a fact that may have deterred would-be students of the geography of wholesaling. Though some establishments sell wholesale only, others may sell wholesale and retail, and the proportions of the two for any one establishment may be hard to determine. If you were mapping the pattern of wholesale establishments in a city, just where would you draw the line? Frequently, too, individual users, if they buy in quantity, may be able to buy at wholesale prices from a firm that sells "wholesale only."

Another problem is, What types of establishments should be included in wholesaling? The wholesale drug concern mentioned was a simple case. Is a sales office maintained by a manufacturing concern wholesaling if it sells only to retailers? And what about brokers who maintain no stock at all but, instead, buy and sell goods wholesale without ever seeing the goods?

Some preliminary generalizations   The character and extent of wholesaling vary a great deal with city size. In a very large city, the picture is correspondingly complicated, with more activity of agents and brokers than one would expect in a city of 100,000 to 200,000. Also, the extent and character of wholesaling can be expected to vary with the type of city.

One would expect to find in the average American city of moderate size a concentration of wholesale establishments just outside the central business district at a location where railroad facilities are available (Figure 14.2). Many of the buildings housing the wholesaling in this area are likely to be old.

In contrast, throughout the city other wholesale establishments may occur that are, on the average, somewhat newer and are highway-oriented. There may even be a concentration of such establishments at a point some distance away from the older district, perhaps at a location where a highway junction gives exceptionally good access. Trucking terminals, too, may characterize this new wholesale cluster.

And it is to be expected that some wholesale establishments will have been localized by the particular demands of certain city areas. Thus some types of wholesale establishments may be located within the central business district because of particularly close relations with retail outlets in the area.

But this description of wholesaling is largely hypothetical. Only research can give such a picture reality or disprove it. Even more than in the case of retailing, field study is required, since the United States Census gives little that is of help in localizing wholesaling within the city.

The wholesale structure of Columbus, Ohio

An investigation of the patterns of wholesale establishments in Columbus, Ohio, provides a start in this direction.[13] In the study, the yellow pages of the July, 1960, issue of the Columbus telephone directory were the primary source of information. All firms and establishments located inside the Columbus Urbanized Area which were indicated as wholesale or were suspected of being so were listed according to street addresses. Establishments were then visited and, through interviews, the exact kinds of businesses and numbers of employees were determined. This field work revealed few additional wholesale establishments, thus confirming the reliability of the directory approach. The data were

[13] Richard W. Reseska, "The Locational Structure of Wholesale Establishments in Columbus, Ohio: A Case Study," unpublished master's thesis, Clark University, Worcester, Mass., 1962.

mapped on United States Geological Survey topographic sheets of the Columbus Urbanized Area. The distribution of wholesale establishments was then analyzed.

Wholesale activity is scattered rather generally throughout the Columbus Urbanized Area, but strong concentrations occur near the center of the city and to the northwest of the center (Figure 14.3). In the definition and classification of types of wholesaling, four criteria were used: (1) other land uses associated with the wholesale establishment, (2) transportation available within 1,000 feet, (3) shape of concentration of establishments to which individual establishment belongs, and (4) straight-line distance from center of city (measured from peak land value intersection in central business district).

Chiefly through analysis of these criteria and from field data on kind of business and number of employees, six types of wholesale structure were differentiated.

1. The central wholesale complex of Columbus takes its character chiefly from nearness to the center of the city, its maximum extent being approximately 1¼ miles from the peak land value intersection. This area, which accounts for 38 per cent of all wholesale establishments and employment in the Columbus Urbanized Area, includes and surrounds the city's central business district. The central wholesale complex is considered to include four subtypes: the primary wholesale district, secondary wholesale districts, special wholesale clusters, and small clusters and individual establishments. In general, the kinds of business represented are those that benefit by location near the city center.

2. The secondary wholesale complex lies just northwest of the central wholesale complex in Columbus. Railroad spurs, factories, and contracting establishments are prominent in the area. The wholesaling involves chiefly distributors of construction and industrial machinery, metals, building supplies, and electronic equipment.

3. Wholesale strings or ribbons occur along some of the principal thoroughfares, especially those emanating from the central business district on the north and south. They occur both within and outside of the central

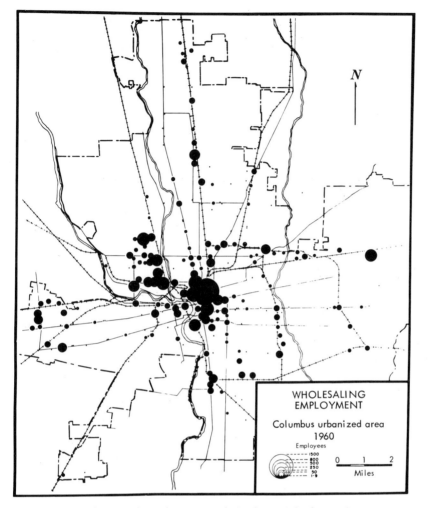

Fig. 14.3 Distribution of employees in wholesaling, Columbus, Ohio, Urbanized Area, 1960. (After Richard W. Reseska, "The Locational Structure of Wholesale Establishments in Columbus, Ohio: A Case Study," unpublished master's thesis, Clark University, Worcester, Mass., 1962, fig. 4.)

wholesale complex. Small in terms of average number of employees, the establishments are engaged in supplying such concerns as beauty parlors and barber shops, restaurants, hotels, and upholsterers.

4. Railroad-highway clusters constitute the most common type of locational structure beyond the central area. Some of these clusters are at intersections and others are within industrial areas. With about one-fifth of the wholesale establishments of the Columbus Urbanized Area, this type is second only to the central wholesale complex in number of establishments and total employees.

5. Commercial-highway clusters represent

a minor type. They occur chiefly among the neighborhood business streets. Mostly they distribute products of low bulk to a small sector of the city.

6. Outlying warehouse complexes consist of clusters of large warehouses and petroleum bulk terminals dispersed toward the perimeter of the urbanized area in the north, northwest, and west.

The foregoing represents one man's conclusions regarding the wholesale structure in one particular city, Columbus, Ohio. But it is through successive studies of this sort that widely applicable generalizations regarding the wholesale structure of the American city may be perfected.

The changing pattern It should be noted that the study of the wholesale structure of Columbus dealt with a cross section of the moment and only that. If the study described could be supplemented by a similar study of the wholesale structure of Columbus for 1950, it would give us some basis for saying how the wholesale structure has been changing. Would it show the shift toward highway orientation postulated earlier in this chapter? The geographer is concerned with such changes as well as with the current picture. How are the wholesale patterns of the American city changing and how are they likely to change in the future?

A study might also reveal a change in total number and in kinds of wholesale establishments. It has been recognized for some time that distributive wholesaling has been declining in importance. To a measurable degree, functions in which the wholesaler specializes are being taken over by the manufacturers and by retailers or groups of retailers.

Wholesale service areas Still another aspect of the wholesale picture involves the extent of the city's wholesale territories. How far does the city reach out in distributing various lines of goods wholesale? Wholesale areas as well as a variety of other types of service areas were discussed in Chapter 4, "The City's Spheres of Influence." It would be particularly interesting if the wholesale areas of a city could be outlined for different periods of the past.

Studies of Components of Total Business Structure

Urban retail structure and urban wholesale structure have been discussed for the city as a whole. It is feasible, too, to single out individual sections for more detailed study. In fact one city retail area, the central business district, is considered so important that it is made the subject of the next chapter of this book.

Studies of Individual Elements of City Business Structure

In like fashion individual types of establishments within the business structure of the city may be investigated.

Location requirements and associations of establishments

A considerable body of generalizations is being built up regarding the locational demands of different kinds of commercial outlets. For example, drugstore sites are based chiefly on accessibility to large numbers of people. Corner locations for drugstores are not essential where pedestrian traffic is sufficiently heavy, but they are considered highly desirable. Since restaurants and lunchrooms vary widely in the quality of the food offered and correspondingly in price levels, each must be located near the economic group it is designed to serve. Women's shoe stores require sites in the women's shopping zone and seek the vicinity of apparel shops, department stores, and variety chains. Men's clothing stores of the better class tend to be in either of two types of locations: near banks and office buildings, where they depend upon the men who work in these places, or near large department stores, where they are accessible to women shoppers who buy for the family.

Some of the locational requirements amount more to associations. Certain types of establishments complement each other, and others are normal associates because they appeal to the same economic level of the population. Men's shoe stores, men's clothing stores, sporting-goods stores, and cigar stores are considered good neighbors. Low-priced theaters are likely to be associated with kindred establishments such as pawnshops, cheap restaurants, and stores handling low-priced jewelry or clothing. And there is the well-known tendency of department stores to locate near each other. Each department store also is likely to have its coterie of smaller stores—clothing stores, drugstores, five-and-ten stores—located close at hand. Similar rationalizations can be applied to a number of other types of retail outlets.[14] For that matter, types of wholesale establishments, if similarly studied, might be found to have some interesting associations and interrelationships.

Research possibilities

The patterns of individual establishment types form interesting topics for research, especially when the time factor is taken into consideration.

Grocery stores   For instance, the evolution of the present pattern of grocery stores in the city would be an interesting subject for study. One can imagine that for many cities such an investigation would reveal the disappearance over the years of many scattered individual stores as modern patterns developed. When did supermarkets enter the picture and what shifts in their location within the city can be traced? One geographer, writing in 1953, said:

> In the past, location in intensely-used areas of larger secondary shopping centers has been characteristic; but in recent years, as growth has taken place in peripheral areas, supermarkets are being located primarily in centers where adequate parking facilities can be provided.[15]

[14] See Ratcliff, *op. cit.*, chap. 5, and also Richard U. Ratcliff, *The Problem of Retail Site Selection*, Michigan Business Studies, vol. 9, no. 1, Bureau of Business Administration, University of Michigan, Ann Arbor, Mich., 1939.

[15] Howard L. Green, "The Super Market in Relation to the Retail Pattern of Greater Boston," unpublished paper delivered at a meeting of the American Association for the Advancement of Science, Boston, Dec. 20, 1953.

Other aspects of city business structure

But grocery stores are only one of a number of possibilities. What is the pattern of drugstores in the city and how has it changed in recent decades? Through the use of city directories it should be possible to work out an interesting story, the main elements of which would be found to hold good for other cities. The changing distribution of doctors' offices is another topic that might be investigated, or, for that matter, any type of business establishment in which one is interested can be made the subject of a geographic study. There is a practical element in such studies, since an understanding of patterns of locational change is necessary to locate new units properly.

The geography of offices

The changing pattern of doctors' offices was referred to in the preceding paragraph as a possible topic for research. Other types of offices, too, might be studied. In fact, offices represent such a distinctive form of city landscape that they are here looked at collectively. Considered in this way, their study represents more of a morphological than a functional investigation.

Normally, offices reach their peak in the busiest part of the urban area, their concentration marked by the skyscrapers that characterize the great American city. But what is an office? Let us begin with an absurdly simple definition: an office is a place for the transaction of certain kinds of business. Among the economic activities centered in urban areas there are a number of business activities that require office space.

Classifications of offices   The picture becomes clearer if one considers some of the ways in which offices are classified. Thus on a simple physical basis they may be divided into offices attached to stores or factories, single offices, suites of offices, and office buildings. Or on a locational basis, they may be classified into downtown offices and outlying offices, with various subcategories of the two.

Probably the most critical division is into *general* offices and *headquarters* offices. General offices occupy the average office building and upper stories of many downtown buildings. Usually they are diverse, with no direct relations between adjacent offices on the same floor, though sometimes they are specialized, as in a medical arts building or in a building devoted largely to lawyers' quarters.

Headquarters offices represent a generally more specialized type of office use, since one concern normally uses most or all of the space in a building or on a floor. Though the headquarters function for a small concern may be carried on on one floor of a general office building or even in a single office, the designation usually is associated with larger developments. Headquarters offices usually are *home* or *regional* offices of an oil company, an insurance company, or the like. The regional offices that have become so important in recent years are headquarters offices in a regional metropolis. A headquarters offices unit or suite of offices may serve more or less than the region dominated by the metropolis, depending upon the policy of the parent company.

The term *administrative offices* usually is used synonymously with headquarters and regional offices, though perhaps with more of a local connotation. Within a single city, there may be administrative offices located at each of a company's several plants, but a top administrative office, coordinating the work of the regular administrative offices and located by itself, need not necessarily be near the plants. A likely location would be in the central business district. Depending upon the magnitude and nature of a concern, the administration of a company's activities may be carried on from a room or two attached to a store or a factory, or from a suite of offices in an office building or a building of mixed uses, or from a specialized office building devoted entirely to the affairs of that particular company.

Functions of offices The nature of an office is still more illuminated if the various possible functions of offices are considered. For instance, the direct handling of merchandise—over-the-counter sales—ordinarily is not involved. Certain direct personal service establishments, too, are eliminated, such as barber shops and beauty parlors; but, on the other hand, some personal services, such as those of the doctor and the dentist, are typically included.

And the functional enumeration can be carried much further. Many offices are devoted to the administration of a company. Many others carry on businesses in the finance-insurance-real estate group. Others are used as the headquarters for selling operations. Brokerage firms and manufacturers' representatives occupy offices. Some offices conduct government business—Federal, state, or local. A considerable number of offices are occupied by lawyers. But no list is complete. The range of activities carried on through offices is large indeed.

Locational factors The problems of office location may be examined both from the standpoint of choosing the city and of deciding upon a location within the city. The proportion of space needed for offices seems to vary with size of city and type of city. Small urban centers need relatively little office space, and cities that are industrial centers require less than financial centers and distribution centers. There are some cities in which the predominant activity requires unusual office facilities. This is true of Hartford, Connecticut, with its development of headquarters offices of casualty insurance companies, and of Washington, D.C., with its innumerable government agencies.

Within the individual city, the locational factor is not so important in the case of offices as in the selection of retail space.[16] However, convenience of access is important where offices are to serve consumers from all over the city. Another locational consideration sometimes affecting selection of office space is convenience for employees in getting to and from work. Important, too, in guiding the choice of an office location, is the appeal of new office buildings with good elevator service.

The pattern of office distribution   The urban geographer is interested both in the pattern of offices by cities and the pattern within the city. It was suggested that offices are often concentrated in the central area of the city where the tallest buildings prevail.[17] To what extent are great headquarters offices and regional offices concentrating in the largest cities? Certainly this is occurring in Chicago. While the Chicago central business district has declined in some functions in recent years, regional offices have been increasing in importance in the district. And New York has been witnessing a similar development. In a news item appearing in February, 1963, it was pointed out that offices, especially headquarters offices, are occupying more and more space in Manhattan. Headquarters and regional offices are rather stable in terms of employment and, at the same time, are not likely to present as many problems to surrounding areas as factories do.[18] These

qualities make such offices particularly desirable in the modern city, and the administrators of cities are happy to encourage office expansion. But not all cities are acquiring regional and headquarters offices (see pp. 210–211). In what sizes of cities is this concentration taking place?

In some cities certain types of offices appear to be decentralizing. This has happened in some of the insurance cities. And decentralization or suburbanization of administrative offices in the San Francisco Bay Area was the subject of a research project carried on by a sociologist, Donald Foley, in the 1950s.[19] His methods were essentially those of the urban geographer.

Suburbanization of administrative offices in the San Francisco Bay Area   Foley posed four questions. To what degree, he asked, have top administrative offices in the Bay Area been suburbanized during recent years? Which types of administrative offices have shown the greatest tendency in this direction? What factors are taken into account in deciding whether an office should be relocated? What locational trends may we expect offices to show during coming years?

DEFINITIONS   Early in the project, the problem of definitions arose. "Large firm or organization," "top administrative office," "special administrative office," "an office move," "detached office," and "attached office" were terms for which definitions seemed essential.

THE RESEARCH   Foley described his re-

[16] Ratcliff, *Urban Land Economics*, pp. 133–136.
[17] This suggests a possible related intercity study: the geography of skyscrapers. Suppose one were to obtain data on square feet of floor space above a certain number of stories for each American city and then determine the ratio of this floor space to city size. From there on it would be a matter of explaining the anomalies presented by various cities. How many can be explained by physical factors such as underlying rock structure? How much do limiting laws enter in? How much is due to local pride? And many other factors are involved.
[18] The experience of London, however, is interest-

ing in this regard. Factories were discouraged in the downtown area in order to prevent a heavy ebb and flow of workers. But offices have concentrated there to an unforeseen degree so that today the movement of white-collar workers to and from their jobs means enormous crowding of mass-transportation media and private automobiles.
[19] Donald L. Foley, *The Suburbanization of Administrative Offices in the San Francisco Bay Area*, Research Report 10, Real Estate Research Program, Bureau of Business and Economic Research, University of California, Berkeley, Calif., 1957.

search as consisting of three major elements: (1) a telephone survey of approximately 1,100 San Francisco Bay Area firms; (2) personal interviews with about sixty executives, consultants, and real estate specialists in the Bay Area; and (3) a review of reports on other metropolitan areas and of discussions of the general problem of suburbanization of administrative offices.

THE FINDINGS The findings in summary form are as follows: (1) For the quarter century preceding 1954, the proportion of top administrative offices of the Bay Area concentrated in central San Francisco dropped steadily. (2) Suburban top administrative offices relocated or initially established during the period were almost all attached to manufacturing plants, warehouses, or transportation terminals. (3) Large firms showed an increasing tendency to establish one or more offices in suburban or subcenter locations to supplement their downtown offices. (4) The movement of top detached [20] offices to the suburbs was negligible. (5) The central portion of the Bay Area (namely, central San Francisco, central and northwestern Oakland, Berkeley, and Emeryville) retained a striking concentration of administrative offices,[21] and the proportion would undoubtedly have been even greater if the offices were weighted for size.

COMPETING FORCES Foley goes on to enumerate reasons for the shift to the suburbs or, as in other cases, for the countertendency, the locating of administrative offices in a central district of the metropolitan area. Among the principal reasons for the suburban shift are the following: to locate in association with a manufacturing plant or other non-office operating facility; to permit office workers and executives to live in a nearby suburban area involving a minimum of transportation; to gain flexible and expandable office space with suburban-type amenities; to escape downtown congestion; to locate near establishments of other firms to which accessibility is advantageous. On the other hand, reasons for locating in the central district include maximum accessibility to the central district and to the whole metropolitan area; the presence of superior office space; the nearness of the main office-worker labor market; ready accessibility to business and professional services of the central district; association with a type of operative establishment that functions best in a central district; advantages of function and prestige; greater availability to out-of-town visitors.[22]

OFFICE-LOCATIONAL DECISIONS Office-locational decisions are numerous, according to Foley. At least a fourth of all main-office locations in the Bay Area are being reconsidered during each ten-year period. Inability to find additional space at the present location may force a firm to restudy its office location. Also, the creation of a completely new office, reflecting business growth, reorganization, or urban expansion, requires an office-location decision. Another facet of the situation is that some of the suburban communities are trying to attract offices, and others, largely residential, are trying to keep them out.

EFFECT ON CENTRAL CITY The real problem underlying this study of suburbanization is the possible effect of suburbanization of administrative offices on the central city. As Foley sums up the situation: "From the downtown point of view, it is not what has happened, but the question whether recent trends are but initial accelerations in a more violent future series of changes in

---

[20] "Detached" is defined as not located within a city block of an important non-office type of establishment operated by the same firm or organization.

[21] About 65 per cent of all Bay Area top administrative offices lie in the central area—49 per cent in central San Francisco—and the remainder in what Foley refers to as the "San Francisco financial-office-district core."

[22] Compare this discussion with the summary of centrifugal and centripetal forces in urban geography, pp. 199–201.

which the central city might suffer, that warrants close observation." [23]

Other office studies needed Is the story of what is happening with respect to top administrative offices in the San Francisco Bay Area unique to that urban area? Is it unique to certain sizes of urban areas? These are questions that only the study of additional urban areas can answer. Foley's study included only administrative offices. As was pointed out earlier, there are various other office types. Moreover, each administrative office was treated as a unit without any attempt at weighting for size of office force or amount of office space. The need is apparent for similar studies of office-location trends in other cities and for the development of supplementary approaches to the problem.

Changing Patterns of Commercial Land Use

Urban commercial patterns are constantly changing. This was referred to in connection with possible studies of supermarkets, drugstores, and doctors' offices, and in the next chapter some research is described in which directories were used in a study of functional changes in patterns of commercial activity in the central area of Madison, Wisconsin.

Information in issues of the Census of Business would make possible a study of changes in intercity patterns of commercial land use. A wealth of data is available for the city as a whole, and through the use of these data, various intercity patterns could be arrived at for the successive periods.

But until recently the Census Bureau was of little help in studying business patterns or changes in such patterns in the interior of the city. With the appearance of the Census Bureau's central business district statistics reports, however, it has become possible to investigate some intracity

[23] Foley, *op. cit.*, p. 5.

movements. Since data in these reports are given for the central business district, the city, and the standard metropolitan statistical area, it is possible to study relative shifts from 1954 to 1963. And to some degree one can go back to 1948, since the 1954 reports include estimates for the earlier year.

Business Zoning

Commercial land use, whether it takes the form of offices, or stores, or other uses, does not develop without control in the American city. Almost all cities nowadays have zoning (see pages 204 to 205), and zoning affects business land use in a number of ways.

Nature of business zoning Zoning commonly restricts the location of business development to certain areas. If a city does not have zoning, and a few still do not, a store or a wholesale concern or a nightclub might be established anywhere in the city where it was believed the function would prosper. A hot-dog stand might be located in the midst of a high-quality residential section. Through zoning, such incompatibility is avoided. It is a corollary of the foregoing that business zoning can be used to control the patterns of business development. For instance, it can be used to prevent string developments of business along various traffic arteries, a distribution that is now generally frowned upon by planners.

But business zoning goes much further than this. Areas where business developments are allowed are subdivided into districts, for each of which definite use regulations are set up. The zoning regulations proposed for the central area of Worcester, Massachusetts, several years ago will illustrate the point (Figure 14.4). In a general business district, for example, establishments for the retail sale of merchandise are permitted without special limitations; in a limited business district such

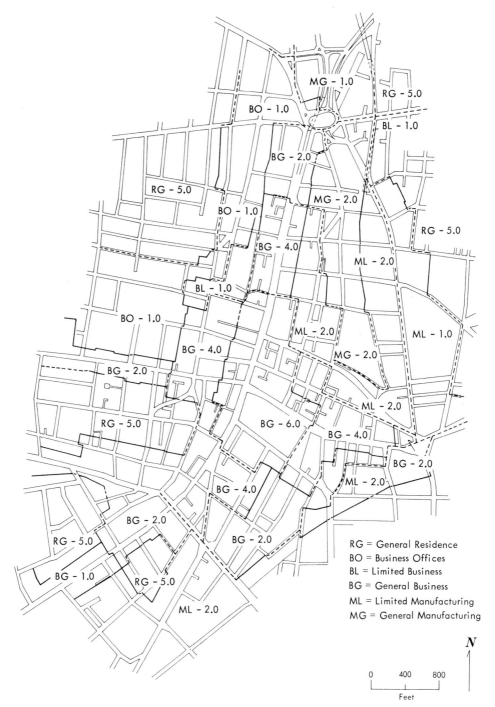

Fig. 14.4 Zoning districts proposed for downtown Worcester in 1951. The original zoning ordinance for the city was adopted in 1924; the revision, of which the downtown section is shown here, was presented in 1951. But, as is often the case with such proposals, the rezoning plan was subject to numerous hearings and many revisions before finally being adopted on July 1, 1963.

establishments are allowed only with a permit from the board of appeals; in a business offices district they are not permitted at all. A motion-picture theater is allowed in a general business district, but not in a limited business district or a business office district without the permission of the board of appeals. A bowling alley is allowed in a general business district but is not allowed, even with a permit, in either of the other two types of districts. In like manner the allowed activities, those that are allowed upon permission of the board of appeals, and those that are not allowed at all are established for each type of district.

The floor area ratio On the map of central Worcester a number follows each letter combination. This is the floor area ratio, or FAR, the ratio of gross floor area to total lot area. In general business districts the maximum allowable floor area ratio for any lot is 6, as shown by the district's designation, BG-6, at the center of the map near the city hall. That is, a six-story building may cover an entire lot; or a twelve-story building might be built on half the lot. In a BG-4 district the maximum floor area ratio is 4. In a BO-1 district the maximum floor area ratio is 1. The map indicates clearly that more intensive building is allowed at the center of the city than away from the center. In a sense, these imposed floor area ratios are intended to maintain the peak of the central business district where it now is, through allowing higher buildings per unit of lot area than are allowed in districts farther away from the center, that is, through allowing more intensive land use in the central area.

Other controls In addition to the floor area ratio maximum, business districts may be controlled in several other ways. For instance, the height of buildings may be directly limited, and off-street parking and loading requirements may be set. The off-street parking and loading requirements are commonly based on one car space to a certain number of feet of floor area in the building, varying with the type and use of the building. In Worcester, no parking facilities are required for districts BG-6 and BG-4. This is because these areas are already built up so solidly that parking requirements for new buildings are out of the question. Parking lots established in and at the edge of these districts are presumed to meet the requirements, besides which this is a focus of mass transportation and many people come and go from these areas by buses. The other commercial districts have parking requirements varying with the types and uses of buildings.

Variations in business zoning Though basically similar in many cities, such business zoning requirements must be adjusted to local needs. Regulations differ somewhat from city to city, and those for an outlying business center differ from those for the central business district.

Marketing Geography

Discussion of commercial activities in the city leads naturally into a consideration of direct applications of geography in business. The possible applications are numerous, but there has developed, most outstandingly of all, a type of applied geography which is generally closely related to the city. This is marketing geography.[24] Most of the initial work was for supermarket chains and had to do with locating stores and evaluating markets. But, today, geographers are employed in many lines of business as well as in consulting work along similar lines.

[24] See William Applebaum, "Marketing Geography," in Preston E. James and Clarence F. Jones (eds.), *American Geography: Inventory and Prospect*, Syracuse University Press, Syracuse, N.Y., 1954, pp. 245–251.

Application of urban geography in work for supermarket chains: An example

Since marketing geography has grown up chiefly inside individual business firms it could hardly be expected to have a profuse published literature. The exact details of locating a store, for example, or of evaluating its market area are the private business of the firm that pays for the work. However, a study by Applebaum and Spears, which appeared some years ago, gives details regarding some phases of marketing geography.[25] Generally speaking the urban geographer's methods of studying the city give him a good foundation for this sort of activity.

The problem A major problem, as Applebaum and Spears describe it, is to delimit precisely on a map the boundary of a supermarket's trading area. Collecting data for this has been attempted in several ways. One method, they point out, is through addresses derived from car registrations, but this method takes no account of customers who walk or come by bus. Another method is for the supermarket to run a cooking school and obtain the addresses of customers, but men, an increasingly important fraction of the supermarket trade, are omitted by this method. Addresses obtained in connection with contests, prize drawings, or other promotions have the disadvantage that the names are only of persons attracted by the prizes and not necessarily of regular customers. Interviews at check-out stands, described in a later paragraph, are still another source of data for delimiting the trading area.

Information wanted Just what infor-

[25] William Applebaum and Richard F. Spears, "How to Measure the Value of a Trading Area," *Chain Store Age,* January, 1951. See also the series of articles on store location and development that appeared in the January, 1961, issue of *Economic Geography.*

mation would the average supermarket operator like to have about the store's trading area? The following list of items, according to Applebaum and Spears, is little more than a minimum:

1. Where the store's customers live
2. How often these customers visit the store
3. How long they have been customers of the store
4. The ratio of the customers who walk to the store to those that come by car
5. Breakdown of customers in terms of men, women, couples, and children
6. Income groups represented
7. How much various customers spend in the store per visit or per week
8. The more significant shopping habit characteristics of customers who live a considerable distance from the store contrasted with those of customers who live near the store

Of course, not all of this information needs to be obtained about every customer; sampling can be used to advantage.

Interviews The interviews by which this information is obtained are carried on, normally, by girls stationed at the exit end of check-out stands. Applebaum and Spears explain the details of conducting the interviews in their article, but these need not concern us here. A specially designed card is used by the interviewer to record the facts; these are later punched in and tabulated.

Use of the data What is done with the information collected? This depends on research ingenuity and on how much money the concern is willing to spend, but a good deal of valuable information can be obtained with a relatively small expenditure of time and money. To determine the store's trading area, for example, a city base map and a city directory are obtained, and the interview cards are arranged by streets in alphabetical order and in numerical sequence for each street. The location of the store is used as the center, and concentric circles are drawn on the map establishing a series of zones at progressively greater distances from the store. The intervals suggested by Applebaum and Spears are: (1) 0 to ¼ mile; (2) ¼ to ½ mile; (3) ½ to ¾ mile; (4) ¾ to 1 mile; (5) greater than 1 mile; and (6) outside the city. The authors also suggest that because of the increasing importance of highway supermarkets and suburban shopping centers it may be desirable to subdivide further the area beyond the mile radius from the store. Plotting each customer's location as a dot on the map and, at the same time, recording on the card the zone in which the dot falls accomplishes a double purpose: the map shows at a glance the distribution of the store's customers; and the cards, with the distance zone and other information for each customer recorded, are available for statistical analysis.

The map shows variations. Dots for customers will be very closely spaced in some sections of the trading area, less dense in others, and extremely scattered or even absent in other sections. This pattern should be studied in relation to such factors as population distribution and income.

If certain other information is recorded on the cards, it is possible to find out more about the store's customers. For instance, an income map of the city gives valuable information. Such maps are sometimes available from private sources; or where the city has been divided into census tracts, an income map can be constructed from United States Census data which are based on a 25 per cent sample. If such a map is available or can be constructed, the income classification can be recorded on each card as the customer's location is spotted on the distribution map. Average monthly rent, based on block housing data, can be substituted where income information is not available.

Through tabulation and statistical analysis it is now possible to arrive at some

useful breakdowns; e.g., into customers by sex, by adults and children, by single shoppers and couples. Other breakdowns can be based on mode of travel to store, frequency of visits to store, length of store patronage, size of purchase, departments of the store patronized, distance of customers from store, and income groups; and various cross tabulations are possible as well. Applebaum and Spears go on to point out ways in which the resulting information can be put to practical use, especially in conjunction with a population dot map of the city and with some knowledge of the land-use pattern.[26]

Competition from other stores Studying a store's trading area, the authors suggest, is all right as far as it goes, but more is needed. Competition from other stores must be considered, both those of competing firms and those owned by the operator himself. For this purpose, construction of a map showing the location of all food outlets in the city is recommended. Often the information for such a map can be obtained from the advertising department of a local newspaper with some checking in the field; or, if necessary, the map can be constructed entirely by field work.

Trading areas not static As Applebaum and Spears point out, trading areas are not static, and it is important to interpret correctly changes in the store's trading area and in the store's per capita sales performance throughout the area. Competition is the most important factor bringing about such changes.

Practical applications The authors conclude by discussing various ways in which knowledge of a store's trading area and of the distribution of competing food outlets is of practical value. The operator,

[26] In this connection see William Applebaum, "A Technique for Constructing a Population and Urban Land Use Map," *Economic Geography*, vol. 28, pp. 240–243, 1952. See also summary of the article on pp. 165–166 and 190 of this book.

they say, can now direct his attention to specific problems. Should he find that he is not covering certain sections of the city with his established stores he can consider the advisability of installing additional units in the least-served territory. He can avoid the mistake of establishing a new store in a location where it might draw customers chiefly from his existing stores.[27] And a knowledge of the store's trading area is valuable in any intelligent advertising program.

Other aspects of the work of the geographer for supermarket chains By no means all the work described by Applebaum and Spears is urban geography. Rather, it represents a blend of the urban geographer's knowledge with that of the marketing specialist. Moreover, the activities described are not the only ones which the urban geographer working in marketing geography for chain stores may be called upon to perform.

He may be asked to locate a site for a warehouse in such a position that it will most efficiently serve all of the company's stores in one locality. Here the ideas of centrography, widely used by geographers (see pages 175 to 176), might serve to give an initial indication of the best spot, although this first step would have to be followed by the study of other factors such as accessibility and availability of a suitable piece of land.

In his marketing work, the geographer may need to know a good deal more about variations within the city than the average income by tracts or the average rent by blocks referred to by Applebaum and Spears. For instance, the age structure of the population is considered important in assessing a marketing area, and so, too, is

the educational level. Both of these items of information can be obtained by tracts. Race may be important, and also country of birth for the foreign-born, the latter since it gives a quick clue to specific ethnic market areas in the city.[28] And dwelling unit characteristics by census tracts or blocks, plotted on city maps, give information regarding variations in the economic level of the market throughout the city. Also, the study of these factors for several successive census periods may be of real value in marketing. Some tracts will be found to be actively growing in population or changing in race or ethnic composition.

Marketing geography and other urban commercial activities

In spite of the importance of the work that geographers have done for the supermarket chains there is no reason for their efforts to be restricted to these enterprises. An increasing number are doing marketing and location work for other businesses, and undoubtedly demands of this sort will increase.

Sometimes the requests for assistance are with respect to a single development. Not long ago the writer was asked about determining the best site for a new bank. Many of the same basic spatial principles apply whether the proposed establishment is to be a store or an office or a bank, though in each case there are added considerations related to the nature of the particular business.

Related Topics

Since every city is a business center, at least to some degree, certain aspects of the city's commercial activities are discussed in other chapters of this book. Thus many of the service areas of the city are related to commercial land use; the urban hierarchy has to do in large part with busi-

[27] For a good discussion of the problem of store location see Saul B. Cohen and William Applebaum, "Evaluating Store Sites and Determining Store Rents," *Economic Geography*, vol. 36, pp. 1–35, 1960.

[28] For a method of making a more complete assessment of a city's ethnic groups see pp. 179–181.

ness activity; commercial land use plays a role in the urban economic base; and in the classification of cities, retail and whole-sale centers are important types. Land use for parking, though in many respects commercial, is generated by transportation, and hence is discussed in the chapter dealing with transportation.

Selected References

Applebaum, William: "Marketing Geography," in Preston E. James and Clarence F. Jones (eds.), *American Geography: Inventory and Prospect,* Syracuse University Press, Syracuse, N.Y., pp. 245–251, 1954.

Berry, Brian J. L.: *Commercial Structure and Commercial Blight: Retail Patterns and Processes in the City of Chicago,* Research Paper 85, Department of Geography, University of Chicago, Chicago, 1963.

————: "Ribbon Developments in the Urban Business Pattern," *Annals of the Association of American Geographers,* vol. 49, pp. 145–155, 1959.

The Boston Globe Map of Metropolitan Boston, prepared under the direction of Robert L. M. Ahern by George K. Lewis and Saul B. Cohen, Boston, 1962.

Cohen, Saul B., and William Applebaum: "Evaluating Store Sites and Determining Store Rents," *Economic Geography,* vol. 36, pp. 1–35, 1960.

Foley, Donald L.: *The Suburbanization of Administrative Offices in the San Francisco Bay Area,* Research Report 10, Real Estate Research Program, Bureau of Business and Economic Research, University of California, Berkeley, Calif., 1957.

Foster, Gerard J., and Howard J. Nelson: *Ventura Boulevard: A String-type Shopping Street,* Real Estate Research Program, Bureau of Business and Economic Research, University of California, Los Angeles, Calif., 1958.

Getis, Arthur: "The Determination of the Location of Retail Activities with the Use of a Map Transformation," *Economic Geography,* vol. 39, pp. 14–22, 1963.

Kelley, Eugene J.: "Retail Structure of Urban Economy," *Traffic Quarterly,* vol. 9, pp. 411–430, 1955.

Mayer, Harold: "Patterns and Recent Trends of Chicago's Outlying Business Centers," *Journal of Land and Public Utility Economics,* vol. 18, pp. 4–16, 1942.

Proudfoot, Malcolm J.: "City Retail Structure," *Economic Geography,* vol. 13, pp. 425–428, 1937.

————: "Outlying Business Centers of Chicago," *Journal of Land and Public Utility Economics,* vol. 13, pp. 57–70, 1937.

Ratcliff, Richard U.: *Urban Land Economics,* McGraw-Hill Book Company, Inc., New York, 1949, chap. 5.

————: *The Problem of Retail Site Selection,* Michigan Business Studies, vol. 9, no. 1, Bureau of Business Research, School of Business Administration, University of Michigan, Ann Arbor, Mich., 1939.

U.S. Bureau of the Budget, *Standard Industrial Classification Manual,* 1957.

U.S. Bureau of the Census, *Census of Business: 1958; 1963;* area statistics for retail trade, wholesale trade, and selected services. Also, central business statistics reports, 1958, and major retail centers reports, 1963.

Vance, James E., Jr.: "Emerging Patterns of Commercial Structure in American Cities," Proceedings of the IGU Symposium in Urban Geography Lund 1960, *Lund Studies in Geography,* Human Geography, ser. B, no. 24, Lund, 1962, pp. 485–518.

15

The central business district

PROUDFOOT, in his description of city retail structure, emphasized the importance of the central business district (see pages 262 to 263). Much of what he had to say in 1937 regarding the district holds true several decades later. The central business district is still the retail heart of the city and normally has the tallest buildings. It may actually be far from centrally located, especially in a seaport or a city located on a substantial river. But it remains unique in drawing its customers from all parts of the city and areas bordering the city rather than from limited sections of the urban area.

Interest in the central business district has been increasing over the years. But though still in many respects the peak area of the city, the district has also become a problem area. In many cities the area is being strangled by difficulties of access and parking; and businessmen, who have seen their large investments in the district threatened by the growth of outlying shopping centers, are striving mightily to maintain its supremacy. While they battle on this practical front, the area has become more and more the subject of research studies by geographers and other social scientists. In this chapter the central business district is examined in the light of this work, and some of the more promising lines for further research are pointed out.

Variations within the Central Business District

Even a cursory examination of the central business district brings out the fact that it is far from homogeneous. First of all is a variation in what might be called commercial intensity. This is reflected in the tendency of some writers to use the designation "commercial core" for the more highly concentrated central portion of the central business district. The term "hard core," too, has been used to distinguish this central area.

It should not be inferred, however, that sharply defined intensity areas are normal to the district. There is a point of maximum intensity which usually is well known locally: the street intersection around which front-foot land values average highest. This *peak land value intersection* normally stands out because it is the locality with the maximum pedestrian concentration, and, not infrequently, the point of greatest vehicular congestion.[1] From this center, various measures of intensity ordinarily decline in value toward the edges of the city, though more sharply in some directions than in others.

On the other hand, there is an observable regionalization within the central business district. Financial, theater, nightclub, intensive shopping, and other specialized areas often may be differentiated. Such regionalization of the central business district varies greatly with individual cities and ordinarily is more striking the larger the city. In addition there is a vertical zonation, retail stores tending to occupy the choice ground-floor positions, and offices or sometimes merchandise storage, the higher floors. In large cities "loft" industries may occupy some of the upper floor space in outer parts of the district; in small cities the upper floors except at the very center of the district are likely to be shared with dwelling units. But over all is the tendency for intensity of use to decline with distance from the peak value point, though often with tongues of more than average intensity extending outward along major traffic arteries.

Edge of the Central Business District

From the fact that intensity values decline with distance from a point of maxi-

mum concentration it follows that the edge of the district is itself gradational. Such obstacles to expansion as a park or, in a state capital, a group of government buildings, may give the central business district some line boundaries, but such sharp edges are exceptional. Much more often the edge is a belt or zone.

The zonal character of the central business district border has been recognized by various students of the city, partly because this border area tends to be decadent and hence to present social problems. In Dickinson's words, "The combination of high land values and obsolescent buildings, ripe for demolition, accounts for the dingy-looking 'zone of deterioration' that surrounds the business center of almost every city."[2] Firey refers to the border area as "the blighted zone which generally lies between a city's central business district and the surrounding residential districts. . . ."[3] (see Figure 3.3). The supposed commercial potential has resulted in high land values, but in fact the zone is not well enough located to support prosperous commercial activities. As a result, aging multifamily houses and rooming houses are often intermingled with marginal commercial establishments. It is this zone that has furnished the sites for many of the urban renewal projects.

The Problem of Delimitation

In view of the importance of the central business district it is indeed remarkable that until recently no standardized method of delimiting the district had been developed. For each city the limits of the central business district had been a matter of local judgment, and most geographers, sociologists, planners, and other writers who had focused upon the central business dis-

---

[1] In the average city the peak land value intersection is known to policemen, to downtown businessmen, and to others who know the center of the city well.

[2] Robert E. Dickinson, *City Region and Regionalism,* Routledge & Kegan Paul, Ltd., London, 1947, p. 96.

[3] Walter Firey, "Ecological Considerations in Planning Rurban Fringes," *American Sociological Review,* vol. 11, p. 411, 1946.

trict or had dealt with it incidentally had relied upon this judgment. This is all very well for the planner in an individual city, working on local problems, but it is only through the use of a standardized method of delimitation that significant comparisons of central business districts are possible. And it is only through such comparisons that a really sound knowledge of the content and functioning of this critical area can be attained.

Many possibilities for delimiting the central business district may occur to the reader, but most of them, when considered in some detail, are found not to yield practicable delimitation techniques. The author of this book feels that it is worthwhile, however, to consider the pros and cons of the possible delimitation bases, largely as background for the discussion of the Central Business Index Method. This method, it is believed, is the most satisfactory one thus far advanced for outlining comparable areas that approximate the central business district.

A Case Study in Geographic Research

The development and application of the method can be regarded as a case study illustrating the sequence of steps that may be required in geographic research. Previous relevant studies are first summarized. Then various possible approaches to delimitation are discussed. Next the Central Business Index Method is presented in detail. With this background, the broader application of the method to a number of cities is described, together with a considerable number of tentative generalizations about the central business district that resulted from the studies. Finally, some examples are given of use of the method by urban planners and geographers.

A Survey of Early Methods

Until the 1950s, publications that dealt directly with delimitations of the central business district were few. Some work done in Sweden and Norway, however, and one study carried on in this country seemed to bear sufficiently upon the problem to be worth looking into.

Scandinavian studies

We may consider first the Scandinavian studies. In outlining the "central shopping district" of Stockholm, W. William-Olsson used a technique that seemed promising.[4] For retail trade, which he defined as trade not only in goods but in meals, amusements, and lodgings, he used a *shop rent index* which he described as the total of shop rents of a building divided by the length of its frontage. This was indicated graphically on William-Olsson's maps by rectangles, the base of each being a building frontage, and the vertical, reaching away from the street, the shop rent index in kroner. Sund and Isachsen in a study of dwelling and working places in Oslo pointed out that they were unable to obtain shop rent data for the city and hence used total turnover or trade instead.[5] Their *trade index* was plotted on a map in much the same manner as William-Olsson's index except that the vertical dimension of the rectangle (that at a right angle to the street frontage) was proportional to the value of total trade. It might appear at first glance that some minimum shop rent index or trade index value could be used to delimit the central business district of the American city. However, both methods require data difficult if not impossible to assemble for United States cities.

Proudfoot's Philadelphia study

Sometimes, however, a research worker has access to data not normally available. Thus, trade was used in a study of Philadel-

[4] W. William-Olsson, "Stockholm: Its Structure and Development," *Geographical Review*, vol. 30, pp. 420–438, 1940.
[5] Tore Sund and Fridtjov Isachsen, *Bosteder og arbeidssteder i Oslo*, Oslo kommune, Oslo, 1942.

phia supervised by Malcolm J. Proudfoot.[6] In setting up intracity business areas, Proudfoot used *block-frontage-volume-of-sales*. This term refers to the total annual volume of sales, for each side of a block, of all stores whose addresses indicate that they front on that side. Thus any block would have four such totals, though the figure might be zero for one or more sides if no establishments fronted on those sides. "For the outer zone of the central business district . . . a block frontage lower limit of $75,000 was used. . . ." An inner zone of the central business district also was delimited; this had a block frontage lower limit of $300,000. It would be possible in any city, Proudfoot said, to have the Census Bureau prepare at cost a map showing total volume, not only of retail trade but of services and wholesale trade as well, for each side of each block in the central portion of the city. But aside from the time and cost involved, a fundamental objection to this delimitation method is that it fails to take account of the activities of offices and banks, both extremely important in the central business district.

Other Possible Approaches

Other possible approaches to delimitation deal in turn with building heights, population distribution and related phenomena, traffic and pedestrian flows, valuation data, and land use.

Building heights

A method that the casual observer almost instinctively applies is based on building height. Certainly it is true that the central business district has, on the average, higher buildings than any other part of the city. Then why not use some building height on a lot basis as the boundary of

the district? For one thing it would be difficult to outline the edge of the district on this basis, since building height rarely grades away at all evenly. The resulting boundary would be very irregular, but could be smoothed out by basing the map on blocks rather than on lots.[7] In either case, however, a building-heights map takes no account of land use. Apartment houses, factories, and other obviously non-central business uses may rank with office buildings and department stores in terms of height.

Population distribution and related phenomena

Use of population data, either directly as such or through the location of dwelling units, is based on the fact that the central business district is essentially lacking in permanent residents. Visualize, if you will, the population dot map of a city of 200,000 or 300,000 (see, for example, Figure 10.2). There should be an essentially dotless area corresponding to the central business district and bordered by a belt of particularly dense population. In similar fashion a map of dwelling units based on block housing data should show a relatively open area corresponding to the district. The chief objection to either of these methods is that open areas on such maps, though they may be due chiefly to the presence of central business activities, are subject to other explanations as well. Blocks of factories, a large public school with its grounds, or a park would produce the same effect. Though the larger units of this sort would be easy to eliminate in the field, nevertheless the blank area surrounding the peak land value intersection on the map is likely to give an exaggerated impression of the extent of the central business district.

If it were possible to obtain, and to localize on a map, data on the number of

---

[6] U.S. Bureau of the Census, *Intra-City Business Census Statistics for Philadelphia, Pa.* (Prepared under supervision of Malcolm J. Proudfoot, Research Geographer) May, 1937.

[7] A figure representing the height in stories for each block is obtained by dividing the total of floor space at all levels by the ground-floor area of the block.

persons employed in offices, in retail stores, and in service establishments, this might form the basis for a suitable delimitation technique. Scandinavian geographers in their studies often have used such employment data not only for factories but also for commercial establishments, presenting them in the form of proportional circles. But in the United States, at least, employment data for commercial establishments are not, ordinarily, a matter of record. To assemble such data through field inquiry would be too laborious a procedure to lend itself to a reasonably rapid, standardized delimitation technique.

Traffic flow and pedestrian counts

Traffic flow and pedestrian counts, reflecting as they do the activity on the streets, represent additional possible approaches to central business district delimitation. The edge of the district on each street leading away from the peak intersection might, conceivably, be fixed where certain minimum counts are reached. Traffic flow must be dismissed as a possibility, however, since the modern tendency is to route traffic around the peak intersection and to prohibit parking in downtown areas during the busier hours of the day. Moreover, cities vary in these traffic-routing policies, which would make it impossible to use traffic flow to delimit districts that would be at all comparable for different cities.

Pedestrian counts are considered more promising. It is true that pedestrian counts, like the blank areas on the population and dwelling-unit maps, may reflect the presence of factory workers from an adjacent district or of students from a downtown high school, but these difficulties can be partially offset by proper timing of counts. Although the same limiting pedestrian count could hardly be expected to prevail in one city as in another, if all counts in a city were expressed as percentages of the maximum count, a limiting percentage might be found that would be consistent from city to city.

But the technique described could result only in a point on each street leading away from the peak land value intersection.

Valuation data

Valuation data appear to have some possibilities for delimiting the district (for a general consideration of valuation data see pages 201 to 204). Land values, it is apparent, furnish a more promising basis for delimitation than land and building values combined. Building values do not grade regularly from any peak point and, besides, a large, new apartment house or a factory might result in a marked area of high land and building values, though the uses were obviously not central business in type. There is the added practical point that, though most city planning agencies have assembled land values for the central part of the city, land and building values are not so readily available.

It may be assumed that the land value data for any one city are derived in a reasonably consistent manner. Therefore, as far as reliability of data is concerned, land values could form an adequate basis for a central business district delimitation for that city. Thus the director of the Worcester Department of Planning early in the 1950s delimited the central business district of Worcester on front-foot assessed land values of lots, reduced to a uniform 100-foot depth (Figure 15.1). He drew his boundary at the outer limit of the lots with values of $300 or more, and the boundary of a hard core at the outer limit of lots with values of $2,000 or more. This was a satisfactory delimitation for one city, but since valuation methods differ markedly from city to city the direct use of land values can hardly be expected to yield comparable central business districts for different cities.

Another possibility based on valuation data seems more broadly applicable. This, like the method applied in Worcester, is based on front-foot assessed land values, but involves the use of percentages. Thus

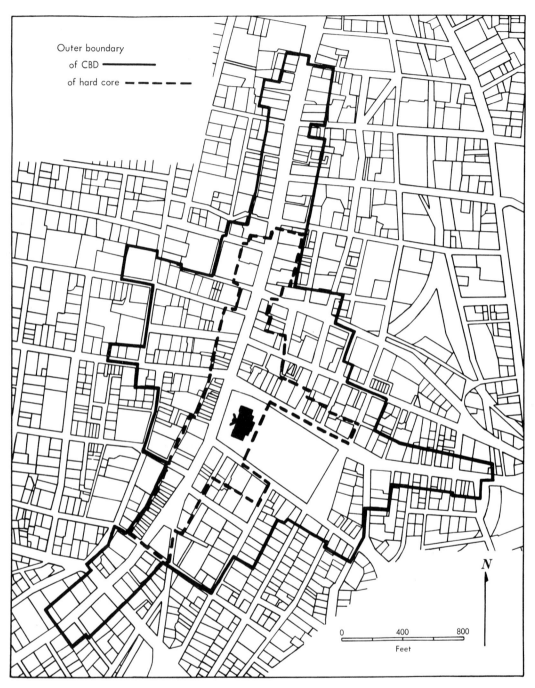

Fig. 15.1 Worcester's central business district and hard core as delimited by Charles M. Downe, Worcester planner, about 1950. He worked with lots, basing his boundaries on front-foot land values reduced to a uniform 100-foot depth.

the front-foot land value at 100-foot depth for the highest-valued lot is 100 per cent, and the value of each other lot is calculated as a percentage of the value of this peak value lot. The line enclosing the lots with percentages of 5 or higher seems best to represent the edge of the district. Since this technique is based on the percentage that each lot value makes up of the highest lot value, it makes no difference whether the land value data are given as assessed values or appraised values. Moreover, such an index system allows comparability from city to city.

The land-valuation technique just described requires no field work, other than visits to official offices to obtain the data, and since the values are on a lot basis, the delimitation is a fine-textured one.[8] But balanced against these advantages are disadvantages that are true of any method based on land values. In some cities the data, though on the assessor's books, have not been assembled. Sometimes, too, for one reason or another, city authorities are unwilling to make valuation information public. Another difficulty is that tax-exempt property, which may represent a considerable number of lots, is commonly not assigned a valuation.

And there is another shortcoming of land values, one that land-value techniques share with some of the delimitation methods mentioned earlier: they do not discriminate among land uses. It is entirely possible for a factory block or a block of apartment houses to occur in an area of high land values and hence appear to belong in the central business district even though the types of land occupance are non-central business in character. This problem is not so likely to arise near the center of the district; it is near the district's edge that these other uses may compete successfully for the land with central business uses and where the difficulty of discriminating arises. In

[8] It may be too fine-textured. See comments regarding lots versus blocks on p. 295.

other places along the edge of the district, central business uses may be of low quality and hence extend into areas of generally low land values. Under these circumstances, too, land values make a poor basis for a boundary.

Some methods based on land use

Land values are, after all, only a reflection of the uses to which land can be put. Therefore, land use should furnish a more direct and realistic approach to delimitation of the central business district than land values. There are several possible delimitation methods which, though based on land use, do not require complete land-use mapping of the central portion of the city.

A break in land use The simplest of these methods involves a break in continuity. At some point on every street leading away from the peak land value intersection of the city, the shops and office buildings that characterize the central business district give way to residences or factories or some other non-central business uses. On a map, this point can be plotted for each street. This is a simple, observational method but involves a good deal of subjectivity. For instance, how much of a break must there be in order for it to be significant? And is there any good reason for supposing that a certain extent of break marks the edge of the central business district?

Identification of types of establishments marking edge Another observational method of delimitation is based upon the hypothesis that certain types of establishments, characteristically absent from the central business district, begin to occur at the district's edge. Among the types that are often said to appear in this position are supermarkets, large furniture stores, filling stations, and rooming houses. However, field tests of this method suggest that identification of types of establishments at the edge of the district has value only for a preliminary rough spotting of the boundary on the principal streets leading away from the peak intersection.

Central business use of block frontage
Still another possible land-use method is based on the percentage of block frontage occupied by central business uses. Frontage is admittedly realistic; the tendency for land use to differ by streets is a matter of common observation. However, since one side of a block may reach the required percentage and another not, a problem is presented when it comes to outlining a contiguous central business district area. As ordinarily applied, too, this method is unrealistic in considering only ground-floor uses.

The Central Business Index Method

None of the land-use methods discussed involves complete land-use mapping of the central area of the city. Yet it would appear that detailed land-use mapping should furnish the most practicable basis for the delimitation of comparable central business districts. The district is best thought of as a functional area containing an assemblage of land uses, some of which are especially distinctive and typical. Moreover, land-use maps are relatively easy to construct since they do not depend upon the availability of any unusual data or require interviews. The Central Business Index Method, which will now be described, is based entirely upon land-use mapping and is believed to be sufficiently objective to provide comparable central business districts in various cities.[9]

Preview of the method

First, we may consider briefly the method as a whole. Basically, it requires a

[9] For details regarding the original research on which the method is based, see Raymond E. Murphy and J. E. Vance, Jr., "Delimiting the CBD," *Economic Geography*, vol. 30, pp. 189–222, 1954.

distinction between central business uses and other forms of land use that are considered not to be central business in character though often found in downtown areas. The real foundation of the delimitation method is field work. This involves detailed mapping of what might be called the obvious central business district—the area around the peak land value intersection, with department stores, offices, and other unquestionably central business, uses—plus enough additional land to encompass any area that could possibly be thought of as included in the district. The final calculations are by blocks, and involve the amounts of space used for central business purposes. An index is determined for each block, and the central business district is considered to consist of those blocks that meet certain index values and are part of a contiguous group surrounding the peak land value intersection. These are the major points, but each phase of the technique will now be discussed in detail.

Central business uses

By no means are all of the land uses represented in the central business district equally at home. There is a considerable difference in this respect between a church or a downtown high school, engulfed by central business district development, and a department store, which depends directly upon the advantages that a location in the central business district has to offer.

The more essential central business functions appear to be the retailing of goods and services for a profit and the performing of various financial and office functions. Stores of all sorts that retail merchandise, shops that offer services, banks, and the whole miscellany of offices so often found near the center of a city are considered characteristic central business uses. Similar establishments occur elsewhere in the city, but their area of maximum concentration is the central business district, where they are oriented around the peak land value intersection and where they tend to serve the city as a whole rather than any one section or any one group of people. These establishments are the ones upon which delimitation of the district is based in the Central Business Index Method.

On the other hand, various types of land use, though found in the central business district, are considered not to be real central business uses. Wholesaling is one of these. As a type it is not primarily a central business function, since in its major developments it is localized more by the presence of railroads or major highway routes through the city than by the pull of centrality. Even more obviously, factories and residential units (private dwellings, apartment houses, and rooming houses), though represented in the central business district, are not characteristic elements.

Absence of the normal profit motive excludes from the central business list municipal and other governmental buildings and parks, churches and other religious establishments, public and other non-profit-making schools, organizational establishments such as the quarters of fraternal orders, and several other types of space occupance. The establishments included in this group perform necessary functions, and they add to the crowding, and hence to the problems, of the central business district. But they are not the businesses that give the area its essential character.

It may be argued that certain forms of retailing are non-central business in character, and it is undoubtedly true that supermarkets, filling stations, and automobile sales agencies are rare within the central business district of a city of any size. But if these specific types of retailing are non-central business, there are others that are only a little less so; and although wholesaling is considered non-central business, there are certain specific types of wholesaling that profit considerably from a central location.

In short a whole series of centrality judgments would arise that are unnecessary for the delimitation of realistic and comparable central business districts.[10] Hence, in the method being described, all retailing is classified as central business just as all wholesaling is regarded as non-central business.

An exception to the general rule regarding the non-central business nature of factories is made in the case of a city newspaper. Since the same concern often prints the newspaper, sells it, and sells advertising in the newspaper, and since the whole operation is closely identified with other central business activities, newspapers are considered a part of the central business district assemblage, though they do have many aspects of manufacturing.

Large, specialized office buildings, such as the home or regional office of an insurance company, present a problem, since often they might be located equally well almost anywhere in the city. But since they derive benefits from association with banks, lawyers' offices, restaurants, and the like that do belong in the district, and because they are so similar to other central business office establishments in type, they are included in the group of central business establishments.

In line with the foregoing, certain uses are considered non-central business in character (Table 15.1). All of them are found to some degree in central business districts, but they are considered either antagonistic to true central business uses (e.g., permanent residences and industrial establishments) or neutral (e.g., governmental establishments).

The mapping procedure

For the central area of the average American city, a lot-line map on a scale of 1

[10] The need for a scale of centrality which would rate various specific functions as to their need to be located near the peak land value intersection has long been recognized.

Table 15.1   Types of land occupance considered non-central business

Permanent residences (including apartment houses and rooming houses)

Government and public (parks and public schools as well as establishments carrying out city, county, state, and Federal government functions)

Organizational institutions (churches, colleges, fraternal orders, etc.)

Industrial establishments (except newspapers)

Wholesaling

Vacant buildings or stores

Vacant lots

Commercial storage

Railroad tracks and switching yards

inch to 200 feet is available.[11] This is the normal map equipment for the field mapping. The desired results are three land-use maps: one for the ground floor, one for the second floor, and a third, an upper-floors map, that represents a generalization of the remaining floors.

Profile method   Though maps for each floor can be constructed directly in the field, a profile method was found to be more efficient for recording the desired information. The profiles are constructed on ordinary lined tablets. The horizontal scale is the same as the scale on the base map, and the space between each two lines on the tablet is considered one story. On these profiles each non-central business unit on each floor (as shown in Figure 15.2) is indicated by an *X*.[12] Each other space unit is marked

[11] This is the recommended scale. An inch to 100 feet or even an inch to 50 feet can be used, but mapping at these larger scales is unnecessary and subsequent analysis of the maps takes more time than if working at the recommended scale.

[12] In some central business districts, many basements house central business units—grocery stores, shoeshine parlors, bookstores, and the like—but such basement stores and shops usually occur only intermittently. Moreover, they would be difficult to cover in a rapid reconnaissance survey such as the one on which the delimitation technique is based. They can be disregarded in applying the

with the letter *C*, which indicates the presence of a central business use. To discriminate between the individual central business or non-central business uses requires much more mapping time and is unnecessary if the purpose is merely one of delimitation.[13]

technique if only a delimitation of the district is desired. On the other hand, if a complete inventory of floor-space use in the central business district is being attempted, basement use should be included.

[13] In the original field work on which the Central Business Index Method was based, more detail was wanted and a classification was developed accordingly. It is given here for the benefit of anyone who may wish to record more information about land use while he is mapping than is possible through classifying everything directly as *C* or *X*. This same detail can be carried through the measurements described on the following pages. Eventually, however, each item is listed under *C* or *X*, and the extent of the delimited district is exactly the same as if the simpler mapping procedure had been used.

The detailed classification includes three major groups. These in turn are subdivided into use types, most of which are broken down still further into specific land uses. The details of the classification are as follows:

RETAIL BUSINESS USES *Food:* FA, restaurant; FB, supermarket; FC, general food; FD, food specialty; FE, delicatessen and ice-cream parlor; FF, package store; FG, bar. *Clothing:* CA, women's clothing; CB, men's clothing; CC, family clothing; CD, clothing specialty; CE, general shoestore; CF, men's and women's clothing. *Household:* HA, furniture; HB, hardware and appliances; HC, dry goods, rugs, curtains, etc.; HD, coal, oil, ice, and heating sales; HE, used furniture and antiques. *Automotive:* AA, sales of motor vehicles, new and used; AB, service station or garage; AC, accessory, tire, and battery sales; AD, automotive rental. *Variety:* VA, department store; VB, five-and-ten; VC, drugstore; VD, cigar and news. *Miscellaneous:* MA, sport, photo, hobby, toy, etc.; MB, jewelry and gift; MC, florist shop; MD, bookstore; ME, office machines and furniture; MF, office supply and stationery; MG, pawnshop; MH, amusement establishment.

SERVICE, FINANCIAL, AND OFFICE USES *Financial:* BA, bank; BB, personal loan; BC, insurance agencies and real estate offices; BD, brokers, stock, etc. *Service Trades:* TA, personal service; TB, clothing service; TC, household service; TD, business service; TF, newspaper publishing. *Head-*

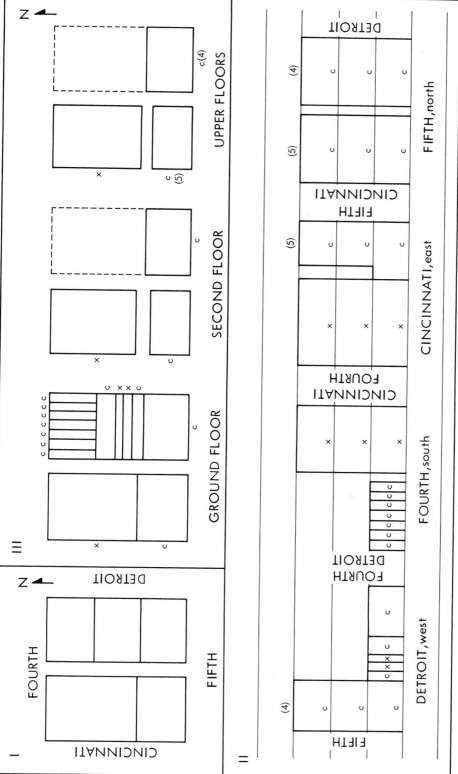

Fig. 15.2 A block of downtown Tulsa on a scale of 1 inch to 200 feet. A lot-line map of the block (I) is followed by profiles (II) and the three resulting land-use maps (III). Each profile is drawn from left to right as the observer faces the block. "Detroit, west" refers to the west side of Detroit Ave.; "FOURTH, south," to the south side of Fourth St.; and so on around the block. (From Raymond E. Murphy and J. E. Vance, Jr., "Delimiting the CBD," *Economic Geography*, vol. 30, 1954, fig. 5.)

Several other points regarding the profiles need to be emphasized. Every floor of use is thought of as one story in vertical dimension. A commercial parking lot (or the customer parking lot of a store) is mapped as one story of *C*, and a vacant lot as one story of *X*. Each building is mapped as if occupying its entire lot, unless the departure from this situation is extreme. In general throughout the central business district such deviations are slight, and to map separately the small scraps of land that may be left over around buildings would require more time than the slightly increased accuracy of the results would justify. On the other hand, where the second floor or upper floors occupy substantially less than the total area of the lot, an attempt is made to record the facts so as to approximate the true extent of the buildings at these higher levels. The completed profiles show at a glance the number of floors for each space unit as well as the use classification, *C* or *X*.

The example of one block In order to make the method clear, the details of profiling for one block in downtown Tulsa are shown in Figure 15.2. Section I shows a plan view of the block as it would appear on a typical lot-line map of the downtown area of any city. Section II shows the profiles of the four sides of the block, and Section III shows the three resulting land-use maps of the block. The land uses do not, necessarily, correspond exactly to lot lines, though

quarters *Office:* OA. *General Office:* EA. *Transportation:* RA, railroad uses; RB, bus uses; RC, air transport; RD, trucking. *Parking:* PA, customer parking; PB, commercial parking. *Transient Residence:* LA, hotels and other transient lodging.

NON-CENTRAL BUSINESS USES *Residential:* DA, permanent dwelling units. *Public and Organizational:* GA, public building space and public ground space; GB, organizational and charitable institutions. *Industrial:* IA. *Wholesale* (not including wholesale offices separate from wholesale establishment): WA. *Vacancy:* XA, vacant building or store; XB, vacant lot; XC, commercial storage

the lot lines are useful as guides. Note that in the present instance the ground-floor map departs considerably from the original lot lines. The lot at the corner of Fourth Street and Detroit Avenue, for example, is divided among seven establishments.

The third or upper-floors map is a generalized representation of the third and higher floors. Floors above the second normally are so uniform in use that such a generalization is practicable. On this upper-floors map, the letters represent third-floor use only, unless a number is given. If there are more than three stories, then a number is shown. This tells the number of floors of the particular use above the second. Thus, on the upper-floors map the letter *X* standing alone shows that the building at the corner of Cincinnati Avenue and Fourth Street is three stories high, with the top floor in non-central business use. And the letter *C* accompanied by the number 5 indicates that, at the corner of Cincinnati Avenue and Fifth Street, central business uses prevail, or at least predominate, on the third to seventh floors of a seven-story building.

Ground-floor, second-floor, and upper-floors maps Although a single block is used here in order to make the method of profiling and map construction clear, in practice the profile may be made for the same side of a street for a series of blocks. And the end product is not a number of maps of individual blocks but three maps (ground floor, second floor, and upper floors) for the entire central section of the city.

Government establishments More detail is shown regarding one group of non-central business uses, government establishments, although none chanced to occur in the block shown in Figure 15.2. Government establishments are shown with the *X* designation just as are other non-central business establishments, but they are also labeled in some manner on the maps. This is done because in the delimitation method a special rule is applied to such structures.

A short-cut mapping method for smaller cities

Although the profile method described is recommended for cities of 100,000 to 150,000 population or larger, a simpler procedure may suffice in a city of 50,000 to 100,000. To begin with, for such a small city, a scale of 1 inch to 100 feet is recommended. There may be few buildings over three stories high even in the downtown area, and profiles are hardly necessary, particularly at this scale. Instead, in each lot or separate use area on the field map the land uses of the several floors are indicated almost in fraction form. For instance, for a two-story building with a store on the ground floor and apartments on the second floor, a C, with a short line over it and an X above that, tells the story; in an area occupied by a five-story building with central business uses on the ground floor and apartments on all other floors a C is shown with a line over it, an X above that to represent the second floor, a line over that and above this second line an $X(3)$ is shown. In some instances, however, in such a small city, only one floor is represented, so a single letter can be used; or if there are two floors, a two-letter "fraction" will be sufficient. The method described merely does away with the necessity for profiles. The three final maps are prepared just as they would be if profiles had been constructed.

Office calculations and resulting ratios

The three land-use maps are by no means end products. The office calculations that follow involve, first of all, finding the total floor area, the central business floor area, and the non-central business floor area for each block that might conceivably be part of the contiguous group making up the central business district.[14] Why are blocks rather than lots used in the calculations, since lot lines were used in mapping wherever possible and since lots would appear to permit a finer-textured delimitation? Working with lots would give a highly irregular effect and present great difficulties in drawing a boundary. Moreover, calculation of the index by any division smaller than a block implies precision of mapping whereas the method is essentially an approximate one. For these reasons all calculations are summed up by block and the central business district is considered a group of blocks. Incidentally, it is sometimes hard to decide what constitutes a block. In general, the practice is recommended of considering that a block ends only where a named street occurs.

All measurements are based on floor areas. A vacant lot or a parking lot is considered one floor in height just as is a one-story building, so that the total ground-floor space in the block is the total of all ground-floor area minus alleys. Second-floor space is the total floor area at the second-floor level of all buildings that are two stories or greater in height; and upper-floor space is the total of all floor areas above the second floor. The system of tabulating the data resulting from the area measurements will be clear from a comparison of Table 15.2 with Figure 15.2. To simplify later checking, all measurements begin at the southeast corner of the block and proceed clockwise around the block.

We are now in a position to calculate for each block two ratios that are fundamental in the Central Business Index Method for delimiting the central business district. The Central Business Height Index (CBHI) is the number of floors of central business uses if these are thought of as spread evenly over the block. It is obtained

[14] For these measurements a pattern of squares .1 inch on a side ruled on transparent paper is recommended.

by dividing the total floor area of all central business uses (the C space) by the total ground-floor area of the block. The Central Business Intensity Index (CBII) is the percentage that the floor area of all central business uses in the block makes up of the total floor area at all levels. In summary, note that the block shown in Figure 15.2 and Table 15.2 has a CBHI of 2.4 and a CBII of 69.8 per cent.

Why two indices are needed

Why is it necessary to use both of these indices? Why would it not be sufficient to include in the central business district only those blocks that exceeded a certain CBHI value? A block might, for instance, have a CBHI of 2. This would mean that floor space used for central business in the block

totaled the equivalent of a two-story building devoted exclusively to central business uses and covering the entire block. This would seem at first glance to qualify the block adequately for the central business district.

But the CBHI has a serious limitation: it fails to show the proportion of space in central business uses. Though the CBHI is 2 for the block just mentioned, this could result from two stories of central business uses overlain by four stories of apartments or four stories of manufacturing, and it seemed inappropriate to include in the central business district a block in which more space was used for non-central business purposes than for central business uses. Use of the CBII corrects this difficulty since it requires that at least one-half of all the floor

Table 15.2   **Measurements and calculations for Tulsa block shown in Figure 15.2 (all measurements are in sq in. at a scale of 1 in. to 200 ft; measurements begin with the first land-use unit at the southeast corner of the block and proceed clockwise around the block)**

Ground floor		Second floor		Upper floors			Block inventory	
Use	Space	Use	Space	Use	Space	Adjusted value	Use	Space
C	0.350	C	0.350	C	0.350x4	1.400	C	4.935
C	0.385	C	0.315	C	0.315x5	1.575	X	2.135
X	0.665	X	0.665	X	0.665	0.665	Total	7.070
C	0.050							
C	0.050							
C	0.050							
C	0.050							
C	0.050							
C	0.050							
C	0.050							
C	0.140							
X	0.070							
X	0.070							
C	0.070							
Total	2.100		1.330			3.640	Total space = 7.070	

Central Business Height Index = C space ÷ ground floor area = 4.935 ÷ 2.100 = 2.4.
Central Business Intensity Index = (C space ÷ total space) × 100 = (4.935 ÷ 7.070) × 100 = 69.8%.

space in the block be in central business uses.

The method in detail

The Central Business Index Method for delimiting a central business district involves fixed values for each of the indices and requires the application of certain rules. They may be summed up as follows:

1. To be considered part of the central business district a block must have a CBHI of 1 or more and a CBII of 50 per cent or more.

2. The block must be part of a contiguous group surrounding the peak land value intersection. Even though a block touches the others only at one corner it is considered contiguous.

3. A block that does not reach the required index values, but is surrounded by blocks that do, is considered part of the central business district.

4. A block completely occupied by the buildings and grounds of a city hall or other municipal office building, a municipal auditorium, city police or fire department headquarters, or a central post office is included within the central business district if it is adjacent to (or contiguous with) blocks meeting the standard requirements. In some cities it will be necessary to add to this list the buildings and grounds of certain other government buildings: the courthouse in a county seat; the capitol building of a state capital; and occasionally certain Federal buildings in addition to the post office, e.g., a Federal court building or other Federal office building the activities of which are closely integrated with those of the city and the region. In no instance should such government buildings as those described in this paragraph result in the extension of the central business district for more than one block beyond normal central business district blocks. A group of such government buildings cannot be split. Thus where there is a group of state buildings occupying several blocks that border the central business district, as in some state capitals, the whole group is considered to lie outside the central business district.

5. If the structures mentioned in rule 4 occupy only part of a block which is contiguous with other central business district blocks and if the inclusion of these establishments as central business would bring the two indices of the block to the required totals, then the block is considered part of the central business district.

Central business district of Worcester

The Central Business Index Method may be made clearer by application to a specific city, Worcester, Massachusetts (Figure 15.3).

In Worcester a block far to the south and a cluster of three small blocks to the east, even though they satisfy both indices, are omitted from the central business district because of non-contiguity. Special cases of included blocks that do not reach the required indices are the post office block, near the southern end of the district; the block occupied by the city hall and common just southeast of the peak land value intersection; and, farther north, two blocks that are essentially surrounded by blocks with the specified index values. A county courthouse and a municipal building just north of the district are excluded because they are separated from the main central business area by several blocks that do not meet the required index values. (For delimitation of another central business district using the same technique, see Figure 15.4.)

Evaluation of the method

It may be well at this stage to evaluate the Central Business Index Method. What are the method's good points and how does it fall short?

It should be emphasized, first of all, that the boundary which results from application of the method in a city is not *the* boundary of the central business district for that city. To think that it is would be naïve, indeed, since the edge of the central business district is a zone. But the area delimited undoubtedly does include the major part of the central business district for that

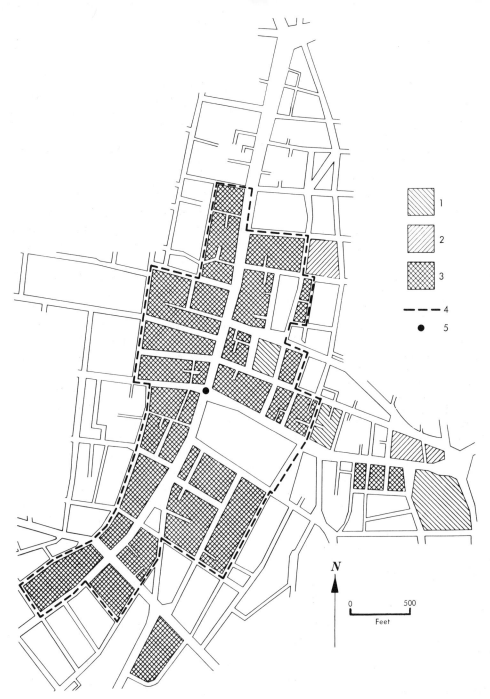

Fig. 15.3 Worcester's central business district is elongated in a roughly north-south direction along its axis, Main Street. A relatively steep upward slope to the west, particularly north of the center, and the presence of railroad tracks to the east help to account for its shape. The peak land value intersection is at the point where Pleasant Street reaches Main Street from the west and continues southeastward as Front Street. The delimitation problem was complicated by a great range of block sizes in central Worcester. Key to legend: 1, Central Business Height Index of 1 or more; 2, Central Business Intensity Index of 50 or more; 3, Central Business Height Index of 1 or more and Central Business Intensity Index of 50 or more; 4, Central business district boundary as determined by Central Business Index Method; 5, Peak land value intersection. Field work for this and following map done in 1952–1953. (From Raymond E. Murphy and J. E. Vance, Jr., "Delimiting the CBD," *Economic Geography*, vol. 30, 1954, fig. 6.)

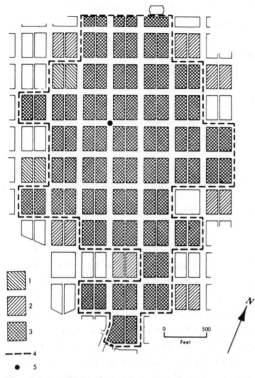

Fig. 15.4 Tulsa's central business district has a rolling site. The peak land value intersection, at the crossing of Fourth Street (trending ENE–WSW) and Main Street, is on a minor rise of land from which there is a slope outward in all directions. Railroad tracks occur at the northern edge of the district and also just to the east of the central business district. Key to legend: 1, Central Business Height Index of 1 or more; 2, Central Business Intensity Index of 50 or more; 3, Central Business Height Index of 1 or more and Central Business Intensity Index of 50 or more; 4, Central business district boundary as determined by Central Business Index Method; 5, Peak land value intersection. A block in the northwest, partly occupied by the post office, was included under Rule 5. (From Raymond E. Murphy and J. E. Vance, Jr., "Delimiting the CBD," *Economic Geography*, vol. 30, 1954, fig. 12.)

by block units, and block shape and block size differ from city to city and even within cities. Also, the indices are based on a subjective classification of certain establishments as central business and others as noncentral business. It is hardly to be expected that everyone will agree with the decisions involved in such a classification. For example, it will be argued that the central post office, the city hall and other city buildings, and even the courthouse (in a county seat) should be considered central businesses. But are such establishments fundamentally different from other government buildings?

There is also a factor of quality which the method fails to take into account. Thus, there may be two blocks with identical indices, but one block may be characterized by a much lower grade of establishments than the other. This is well brought out by hotels. A fifteen-story hotel may be the best hotel in the city or it may be of obviously low quality. Perhaps differences such as this should be considered in delimiting the central business district.

The method was based on cities of a limited size range. Will it work for a city of 25,000 population? Attempts to apply it to cities of this size and smaller suggest serious limitations. In such a small city only a few blocks could possibly meet the required index values, and the inclusion or exclusion of a single one of these would mean a considerable difference in the size and character of the central business district. The factor of block shape, too, is more serious in small cities. If blocks are long and narrow, extending at right angles back from the main street into a residential area, the indices may not quite reach the values necessary for inclusion of blocks in the central business district, whereas if the blocks are small and square a larger district may result.

On the other hand, the method works well in moderately large cities. In very large cities it might serve to bring out not only the central business district but secondary business districts as well. For the latter

city, and the boundary is believed to be as fair an approximation of the zone as any single line can be. Moreover, since in each city in which the method is applied the boundaries are drawn according to the same indices and the same rules, the areas delimited in the various cities are comparable.

There are certain obvious shortcomings of the method. For instance, delimitation is purpose, of course, one would outline clusters separated from the group centered at the peak land value intersection. But a thorough testing in very large cities remains to be carried out.

Balanced against any shortcomings of the method is the fact that the delimitation is realistic except in very small cities. It works and can be completed rapidly. It is admittedly a reconaissance method. In fact, after some experience, it is possible for the field man to determine almost at a glance the blocks that unquestionably belong to the central business district and those that unquestionably do not, leaving only a fringe of doubtful blocks to be mapped. And the method is sufficiently objective that the areas delimited by workers in different cities should be comparable enough for generalizations about the district to carry some weight.

This factor of comparability is important and should not be lost sight of. For workers concerned entirely with their own city such a method of delimitation as the one described serves less purpose. A delimitation agreed upon locally may be adequate. But seldom does such complete isolation prevail. The desire to compare the local central business district with that of some other city will arise, thus favoring the use of a standardized technique of delimitation. And when comparison of central business districts of several cities is a major objective, then a standardized method of outlining central business districts is essential. It may also be desirable here to use the detailed classification described on page 292, footnote 13.

Tentative Generalizations Regarding Central Business Districts

The use of a standardized delimitation technique such as the one just described is justified particularly if the central business district delimited is to be compared with others similarly delimited, because, in this way, we can begin to build up a body of generalizations. For instance, in the project in which the Central Business Index Method was developed, the same delimitation technique was applied to nine cities of moderate size: Grand Rapids, Michigan; Mobile, Alabama; Phoenix, Arizona; Roanoke, Virginia; Sacramento, California; Salt Lake City, Utah; Tacoma, Washington; Tulsa, Oklahoma; and Worcester, Massachusetts.[15] Some of the tentative generalizations resulting from this study are presented here.

Generalizations regarding size

We may begin with central business district size. The popular concept of central business district size is a two-dimensional one. But size obviously includes height also. So it is the volume of the central business district rather than its area with which we are properly concerned. This can be based on total floor space in the central business district, but as was pointed out, many buildings in the district have uses that do not belong there. They are non-central business in character as the term was defined earlier. It is more realistic, therefore, to base size on floor space used for central business activities. On this basis the nine central business districts mentioned were found to vary in size from 75.5 acres for Mobile to 207.7 acres for Tulsa. One might wonder whether this size tends to vary most closely with corporate city population, with population of the urbanized area, or with standard metropolitan statistical area population. But the study on which this discussion is based did not result in much information along these lines since cities were deliberately chosen that did not have a great size range.

[15] Murphy and Vance, op. cit. See also, Raymond E. Murphy and J. E. Vance, Jr., "A Comparative Study of Nine Central Business Districts," Economic Geography, vol. 30, pp. 301–336, 1954; and Raymond E. Murphy, J. E. Vance, Jr., and Bart J. Epstein, "Internal Structure of the CBD," Economic Geography, vol. 31, pp. 21–46, 1955.

Shape of the central business district

The shape of the central business district is interesting. Obviously, the two-dimensional shape or outline varies greatly from city to city (Figure 15.5). However, if a number of central business districts are delimited and compared it is found that the shape tends to resemble that of a quadrate cross (Figure 15.6). This is because the central business district frequently has developed at a major road or street intersection. It expands outward along the two intersecting streets and, at the same time, tends to fill in between them for a short distance from the intersection.

But this is shape in map view only, and it was pointed out earlier that the central business district is really three-dimensional. It is probably best visualized as a pyramid-like figure, with an irregularly shaped base that approximates a quadrate cross in shape, and a height that varies in proportion to total central business floor space.[16] Among the cities listed, the pyramid for Tulsa's central business district has the greatest height, reflecting the highly concentrated character of that city's central area. At the other extreme, with the lowest pyramid, is Phoenix, which seems to represent a new, low type of city.

Outline of the central business district in relation to barriers

To what extent is the outline of the central business district related to the barriers that border the district? That there are barriers to the expansion of the central business district is obvious. Railroads, areas devoted to public buildings, water bodies, steep slopes, and possibly other, similar features and conditions act as barriers (Figure 15.5). The central business district may approach the barrier closely. This sometimes happens in the case of public buildings, where the central business district may be adjacent to them or occasionally surrounds them. It happens also with parks. But, where there are railroad and water barriers, the central business district does not usually abut directly upon these barriers. Instead, there is commonly a cushion of non-central business uses between the central business district and the barrier. Relief as a barrier deserves special mention. There is no doubt that steep slopes serve as an obstacle to central business district expansion; if it is at all possible, steep slopes are avoided.

There appears also to be a limiting distance from the peak land value intersection beyond which the central business district tends not to expand because of the inconvenience of traveling farther, either on foot or by other means.

Sooner or later, the central business district comes to a boundary where other uses take over and the combination of floors of central business use and intensity of such use does not warrant including a block under consideration in the central business district. This will happen in central business districts that are uninhibited by tangible barriers as well as in those that are more restricted. But when barriers are involved, the breaking point comes sooner in a direction in which the central business district has to overcome these barriers than in other directions.

Land values in the central business district

Study of the central business districts also yielded some information on typical land-value variations in the district. With distance from the peak land value intersection, values normally drop off rapidly at first, then less and less rapidly. That is, they decrease at a decreasing rate with distance from the peak intersection.

[16] The base corresponds to the ground-floor area of the central business district; the volume amounts to the central business floor space in the central business district; the height may be calculated by using the formula $V = 1/3\ Bh$. When this formula was applied to the nine central business districts, the pyramid heights were found to range from 7.8 stories for Tulsa to 4.4 stories for Phoenix.

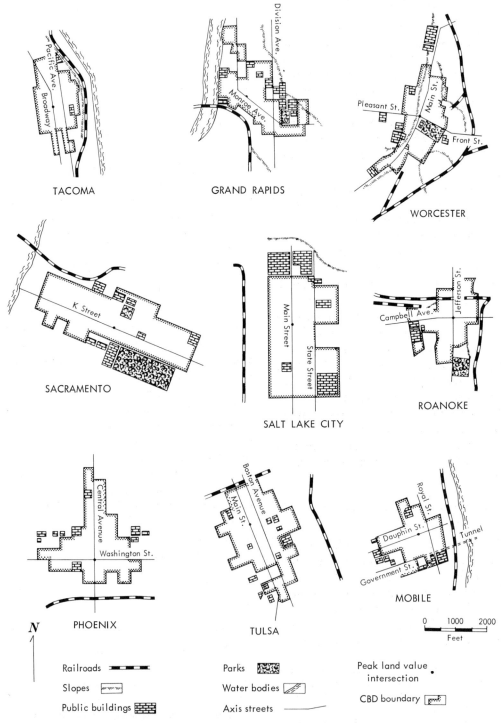

Fig. 15.5 Barriers have affected the shape of the central business district through limiting expansion in certain directions. (From Raymond E. Murphy and J. E. Vance, Jr., "A Comparative Study of Nine Central Business Districts," *Economic Geography*, vol. 30, 1954, fig. 23.)

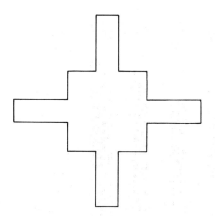

Fig. 15.6 If the outlines of many central business districts are generalized the result seems best to approximate a quadrate cross such as is shown here. (From Raymond E. Murphy and J. E. Vance, Jr., "A Comparative Study of Nine Central Business Districts," *Economic Geography*, vol. 30, 1954, fig. 24.)

But symmetry does not always prevail. In an elongated central business district, the rate of decline tends to be much lower along the axis of the district than at right angles to it.

Land use in the central business district

In the study of the nine central business districts, delimitation was only one of the objectives. Another aim was to gain more information about the exact land-use variations than a simple classification into central business uses and non-central uses permitted. Hence, a detailed classification was used.[17] Because of this, it was possible to show variations in land use in the several districts (Figure 15.7). Some of the information shown is to be expected: thus, by definition of the central business district, two groups of land uses—service-financial-office uses and retail business uses—predominate over non-central business uses.

But of interest, too, are the details for each central business district and for an average of the nine. As additional central

business districts are delimited according to the Central Business Index Method, it is interesting to compare their averages with the average for the nine districts, just as it is interesting in this series to see how the various individual central business districts stand out from the average. Note, for example, the much greater relative importance of offices in the central business district of Tulsa than in the other central business districts of the group.

Arrangement of land uses

Other results of the study of the nine central business districts included certain generalizations regarding the arrangement of business activities within the district in the average American city of moderate size. The key point is the peak land value intersection, which is never more than a few hundred feet from the geographic or areal center of the city's central business district. With distance outward through the central business district from this intersection, retailing tends to decline in the proportion of space occupied; offices and financial activities first increase and then begin to decrease; and non-central business increases in relative importance. With distance upward from the ground floor, through successive stories, retailing and certain of the service and financial uses decline in space occupied, and offices increase.

But it is of interest to look in more detail at the changes in land use with increasing distance outward through the central business district. In the inner zone, around the peak point, there are likely to be one or more department stores (with such closely related establishments as women's clothing stores), drugstores, five-and-ten stores, restaurants, and miscellaneous specialty stores of one kind or another. In a few cities, a city hall and a park or common may occur near the peak value intersection. One thing is true of most stores in the inner zone: for their kind, they are likely to be large. Here one finds the district's

[17] See footnote 13.

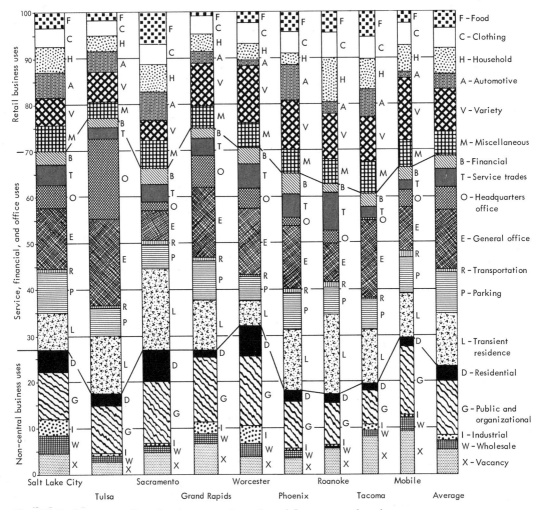

Fig. 15.7 Percentage chart showing proportions of total floor space of each central business district (and of an average of the nine central business districts) devoted to various uses in 1952–1953. The bars are proportional in width to total floor space in the central business district. It is important to keep in mind that the picture presented by each bar on the chart is one of land use in the central business district, not in the city. For example, a smaller proportion of automotive sales is shown for Worcester than for any of the other eight cities. This does not mean that in the city of Worcester automotive sales are less important than in the other cities. It merely means that less of this business is carried on within the Worcester central business district. Automotive sales in Worcester happen to be concentrated in several areas that are well outside the central business district. (From Raymond E. Murphy and J. E. Vance, Jr., "A Comparative Study of Nine Central Business Districts," *Economic Geography*, vol. 30, 1954, fig. 25.)

largest department stores, the largest drug-stores, the largest five-and-ten stores. Department stores frequently occupy several floors of a building, but most of the other retail users remain on the ground floor or at most make use also of a basement and the second floor.

Though substantial buildings often occur around the peak land value intersection, a little farther from this point even taller buildings are likely to be found, with retail services and financial activities occupying the ground floor and offices dominating the floors above. Some of the city's tallest buildings have been built to house the central or regional offices of single companies, and use from top to bottom may be by one concern. More often, though, office buildings contain a number of individual units, and frequently these units do a considerable amount of business with one another. Banks and hotels are likely to be located in the belt 200 or 300 yards from the peak point, but hotels are even more important at slightly greater distances from the center.

Typically, near the edge of the district such establishments as furniture stores and automotive stores occur, and, still farther out, often spilling over the edge, one finds auto sales (with associated garages, filling stations, and the like) and supermarkets, both land uses that require not only cheap land but much parking space. This area, close to the boundary of the central business district, is often, in a sense, automobile-oriented, especially where it occurs near the ends of an elongated district.

Zones of assimilation versus zones of discard

It must be remembered that the edge of the district is gradational, the gradation varying with the nature of adjacent areas. Along the contact with sections dominated by industry and wholesaling these activities as well as low-grade residences may extend into the district, often on the second and third floors of buildings whose ground-floor levels are occupied by low-grade commercial establishments. Beyond the district's edge, of course, these land uses become more important than commercial activities, even at the ground level.

Higher-quality sections of the central business district, on the other hand, tend to grade into strings of commercial develop-

ment that extend into better-class residential areas. Here, too, upper-floor residences may characterize the fringe of the district, but new apartment houses and better-class rooming houses are more likely to be found in these areas, along with new commercial development, whereas wholesaling and industry generally are not present at all.

All this leads to the idea that different parts of the central business district edge are likely to vary considerably in dynamic qualities. The central business district seems to be growing in some directions and declining in others, while still other sections of the district's border seem to be essentially static (Figure 15.8). In the zones of growth or assimilation, shopping goods outlets are typical. Specialty shops, automobile showrooms, drive-in banks, headquarters offices, professional offices, and the newer

Fig. 15.8 Approximate positions of zone of assimilation and zone of discard for the Tulsa central business district. It may be assumed that the white areas are essentially static or balanced. (From Raymond E. Murphy, J. E. Vance, Jr., and Bart J. Epstein, "Internal Structure of the CBD," *Economic Geography*, vol. 31, 1955, fig. 16.)

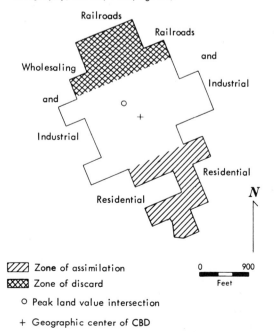

hotels are found. Other portions of a district's border may be regarded as constituting a zone of discard. Here one finds pawnshops, family clothing stores, bars, low-grade restaurants, bus stations, and cheap movies, and credit jewelry, clothing, and furniture stores. These low-grade establishments gain through being together since they appeal to a similar economic level. In the whole picture the factor of prestige enters. The van is the zone of the future, whereas the zone of discard lacks prestige and fosters commercial types that make no pretense to more than a place to sell goods and services.

Movements of the centers

As the central business district shifts, so too do the areal or geographic center of the district and the peak land value intersection. Normally, the movement of these centers will be toward the zone of assimilation. Though the geographic center appears to progress slowly and more or less steadily, the peak land value intersection seems to leapfrog. But it is a very slow process. An intersection several blocks from the present peak value point may gain in importance until, eventually, it becomes the peak intersection. It is hard to get the details regarding shifts of this sort since careful study of the central areas of cities for past periods is involved.

Development of generalizations

The foregoing is by no means a complete summary of the tentative generalizations that resulted from the study of the nine central business districts. However, most of the more important findings have been discussed, and they should suffice to illustrate the possible results of such research.

The generalizations were based on the study of only nine central business districts and these in cities that 'did not differ much in size. As more central business districts are studied, particularly those of cities of a greater size range, it should be possible to check the tentative generalizations and to advance many new ones. For any significant results, however, it is essential that some standardized delimitation technique be used for outlining the central business districts of the various cities. But important as comparative studies are—of central business districts or of other urban areas—they are by no means the only possibility. Case studies of individual central business districts and of other urban areas are not to be disparaged since they often suggest possible generalizations that can be checked through further research.

Later Applications of the Central Business Index Method

The Central Business Index Method of delimiting the central business district has become widely known and has been used in a number of planning studies and in research by geographers.

Use by planners

In many cities, large and small, the method has been used by planners in defining their central business districts. In some cases it has been applied without modification; more often it has been modified to meet presumed local needs or special conditions. For example, in Albuquerque, New Mexico, the buildings tended to be so low that the indices rigidly applied gave a smaller central business district than was locally regarded as realistic. Therefore, some blocks were included that did not quite reach the specified index values. Such departures from the defined technique are unfortunate, since the chief value of the method—for outlining central business districts on comparable bases—has been sacrificed.

Use by geographers

The Central Business Index Method has been used, also, by several geographers.

Peter Scott used the idea in his study of central business districts in Australia; D. H. Davies found that it worked out satisfactorily in his study of the central business district of Cape Town, South Africa; and D. R. Diamond tested it in a study of Glasgow. Articles describing these studies are listed at the end of this chapter.

Hard Core of the Central Business District

It has long been realized that within the central business district there tends to be a hard core, an area that stands out for the quintessence of qualities which we associate with the district. Charles Downe outlined such an area for Worcester in his map based on front-foot land value of lots (Figure 15.1). But it remained for D. H. Davies to suggest a technique of hard-core delimitation based chiefly on land use.[18]

Central Business Index Method as foundation

Davies reasoned that differences between the central business district as a whole and the part of it known as the hard core are really differences in degree, not in kind; that the kinds of characteristics which set off the central business district from other areas of the city should also serve to outline its hard core. He had already used the Central Business Index Method to delimit Cape Town's central business district, and he decided to use the same kinds of indices to determine the district's hard core, but to use higher values.

Frequency graphs and limiting values

But what values should he use? To determine which values were most significant, Davies plotted the values of the two

[18] D. Hywel Davies, "The Hard Core of Cape Town's Central Business District: An Attempt at Delimitation," *Economic Geography*, vol. 36, pp. 53–69, 1960. See also Davies's more general study of Cape Town's central business district listed at the end of this chapter.

indices—height and intensity—against the numbers of blocks having these values. He noted where the most marked break in slope occurred on each graph. Tentatively, Davies decided that a Central Business Height Index of four stories should be used to delimit the hard core. This is a considerable increase over the one story required to outline the central business district as a whole. In similar fashion, he decided to use a Central Business Intensity Index of 80 per cent for the hard core rather than the 50 per cent used to delimit the larger area.

Traffic and land valuation

Davies decided to test his hard-core land-use boundary by plotting two more hard-core boundaries. One was based on a recent traffic survey carried out in Cape Town. The number of traffic visits to each block was compared with the number of such visits to the peak block. The 30 per cent isopleth seemed to come close to the probable edge of the hard core. A second boundary was based on land valuation. A block was considered to lie in the hard core if its land valuation was 30 per cent or more of that of the peak block.

Analysis of discrepancies

Davies now had three boundaries to compare: one based on the combined height and intensity indices, the second based on traffic count, and a third on land valuation. Blocks that were not enclosed by all three boundaries were checked in the field and it was found that most of the discrepancies occurred in blocks that were dominated by land uses atypical of the hard core on theoretical grounds. For instance, cinemas, hotels, headquarters offices, and newspaper publishing and printing establishments do not appear to require the extreme centrality of the hard-core area. Government offices dominated some of the other blocks where the boundaries did not agree. They represent a form of land use that is probably best considered atypical of the hard core. The same judgment applies to certain department stores that lie some distance away from those near the peak land value intersection and are definitely lower-grade establishments.

Recalculation of indices and outlining of hard core

Considering the foregoing uses as non-central business, or at least as non-hard-core business, Davies recalculated the CBHI and the CBII for each block of the entire central business district. On the basis of these revised values the hard core was drawn to enclose all contiguous blocks around the peak land value intersection having CBHIs of 4 or more and CBIIs of 80 per cent or more.

A step toward hard-core delimitation

Davies does not suggest that his method of delimiting the hard core is a precise or final method. Rather, he refers to it as a first step that may prove useful in subsequent studies.

Suppose we wished to apply the technique to any one of the nine cities for which central business districts were delimited in the research project described earlier. If we used Davies's method, we would consider that cinemas, hotels, headquarters offices, newspaper publishing and printing establishments, government offices (municipal, state, or Federal), and "second-grade" department stores are X uses; and would then recalculate all block indices. Using these revised values, we would draw the hard core to include all contiguous blocks with the higher index values Davies prescribes.

However, there would be some difficulties. For example, as Davies himself points out, one would need to develop some sort of scale for measuring the quality of department stores. And there might be other types of establishments to which a quality judgment should be applied. In fact, we might find that there were some central business land uses not mentioned by Davies that were equally atypical of the hard core and which we would, therefore, wish to add to the list. Finally, it should be kept in mind that Cape Town is a considerably larger city than the nine for which central business districts were outlined in the research project in which the Central Business Index Method was worked out. It may be unrealistic to expect a hard core to stand out distinctly in the central business district of a city of 200,000 population.[19]

But problems such as those enumerated add to the interest of research. Certainly, Davies's approach to hard-core delimitation is a promising start and should be tested in application to American cities.

The Census Bureau's Central Business Districts

A new element was injected into the picture of research on the American central business district when the U.S. Bureau of the Census issued central business district statistics reports for ninety-five American cities as part of its 1954 *Census of Business* (see pages 256 to 258). In the 1958 census similar bulletins were issued for 109 cities; in the 1963 census, reports for 116 cities were planned. What purpose do these area delimitations serve? As the Director of the Census Bureau put it, "The primary objective of this operation is to provide a basis for comparing changes in business activity in the Central Business District with those in the remainder of the metropolitan area or of the central city."[20] Has this objective been accomplished? And are the newly delimited areas of value in other respects?

[19] Downe's hard core for Worcester, Mass. (see Fig. 15.1), indicates that central business districts in moderate-sized cities do have this feature, but his hard core was based exclusively on land values.
[20] The nature and value of the data available in the central business district statistics report were discussed in Chap. 14. For an example of the map appearing in each report, see Fig. 14.1.

Basis for delimitation

The Census Bureau did not have the time or the funds to enter upon a serious program of central business district delimitation. Instead, the Bureau's approach to the problem was that of enlisting the cooperation of the census tract committee of each city concerned. The Bureau did not give rigid specifications for defining the central business district, but it:

(1) provided a general characterization of the CBD, describing it as "an area of very high land valuation, an area characterized by a high concentration of retail businesses, offices, theaters, hotels, and 'service' businesses, and an area of high traffic flow"; and (2) required that the CBD ordinarily should be defined to follow existing tract lines, i.e., to consist of one or more whole census tracts.[21]

The details of deciding upon the tract or tracts that most nearly approximated the district for each city were left to the local census tract committee, which, in turn, was supposed to enlist the help of representatives from a variety of local interests such as "business firms and associations, newspapers, planning agencies, welfare organizations, local governmental bodies, etc." Thus the final outline of each central business district amounted more to an expression of local opinion than to the result of the application of any real method of delimitation.

The Census Bureau points out that it is realized that the use of tracts means there may be some land "not properly within a strictly defined" central business district included in a particular census central business district, and that some small portions of such a strictly defined district may be excluded. But it was not believed that such variations significantly altered the magnitudes which the census central business

districts are designed to measure.[22] Also, the relative permanence of tracts and the fact that so many other data are available by tracts argued in favor of tract boundaries.

It is of interest to compare the Census Bureau's central business districts with some of those outlined according to the Central Business Index Method (Figure 15.9). As might be expected, the census central business districts tend to be considerably larger.

Evaluation of the Census Bureau's central business district

The Census Bureau's central business district is a convenient unit, but it can hardly be regarded as representing a serious attempt to delimit the district. By definition, no census tracts or group of such tracts can approximate the central business district very satisfactorily. Ideally, each census tract is supposed to have a population of approximately 4,000,[23] whereas the central business district by any reasonable definition is characterized by an almost complete lack of resident population. Any system of delimitation of the district that brings in some blocks that are largely residential must be recognized as having serious limitations.

The Census Bureau's adoption of a tract or several tracts as the central business district of a city has given a certain sanction to the designated area so that people are likely to refer to it as *the* central business district of the city. This is unfortunate. To have separate business statistics for one or

[21] See any 1958 central business district statistics report, p. 3, or any major retail centers report for 1963.

[22] The Census Bureau's central business districts are something like standard metropolitan statistical areas in that, while they may be satisfactory for comparing absolute data, they should never be used for comparisons on the basis of data per unit of area. See p. 22.

[23] Existing census tracts were used in defining most central business districts. Where new tracts are being laid out, a central business district may be designated which has a much smaller population total than the ordinary tract. See Appendix B, p. 441.

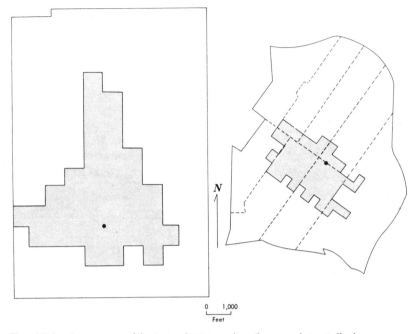

Fig. 15.9 Census central business districts ordinarily are substantially larger than central business districts outlined according to the Central Business Index Method. Here the Census central business districts of Phoenix, Arizona, and Richmond, Virginia, are contrasted with the districts resulting for these cities when the Central Business Index Method is used. The latter are shaded on the chart with the dot in each case marking the peak land value intersection. The contrast varies a great deal from city to city. The "fit" is not bad for Phoenix but is very bad for Richmond. Eight census tracts are combined in the Census Bureau's central business district for Richmond; for Phoenix, a larger city, only one census tract is used. The outer boundary in each case is that of the Census Bureau's central business district.

more of the central census tracts of the city is helpful. Nevertheless, the central business district as the Census Bureau has delimited it must be recognized as an extremely rough approximation and one that gives little basis for comparing the districts of various cities and arriving at sound generalizations.

Other Examples of Census Business District Research

There have been a number of research attacks upon the central business district and its problems in addition to those described earlier in this chapter. For example, Breese and Foley concerned themselves with daytime population of the district and the daily flow of population to and from the district; Ratcliff studied functional change in the central portion of Madison, Wisconsin, as a case study of what was happening generally in the central areas of cities; Rannels used an establishments approach in studying central business districts (see footnote 7, p. 197); and Horwood and Boyce discussed the central business district "core-frame" concept. Two of these studies, those of Ratcliff and of Horwood and Boyce, are sufficiently relevant to the geographer's approach to be summarized here.

Functional change in the central business area of Madison, Wisconsin

Early in the 1950s, Ratcliff investigated

the competition between downtown areas and urban borders as illustrated by Madison, Wisconsin.[24] Growth of commercial facilities on the outskirts of cities was a matter of common observation. Were the "downtowns" declining accordingly? Ratcliff wanted to know what really was happening.

He found that two hypotheses were being advanced. The most widely credited of these was that a literal decentralization, a dispersal of retail activities from the center of the city to the outskirts, had gone on around the city and was still under way, and that a decline in volume of business and in land values in the center of the city would ultimately follow. The alternative hypothesis was that the peripheral growth of retail facilities is consistent with and proportionate to population increase and spatial expansion of the urban area. According to this second hypothesis, the central area of the city may be expected to continue to grow in productivity; business volume and property values will continue to rise as total population of the urban area increases, though probably at a slower rate than population.

A case study of functional change Ratcliff's work was a case study of functional change in the central portion of Madison. He reasoned that a recording of the types and numbers of retail outlets in the central area of a city at varying intervals over a period of years should bring out some interesting trends. One would expect to find a decline in the number of representatives of certain types of retailing, the disappearance of some types, and increases in the numbers of still others. Though such findings might not justify a definite judgment between the two hypotheses mentioned, they should throw light on the questions of what is happening and what is likely to happen to the central business district.

The study area The study area, which Ratcliff called "the central Madison business area," consisted of the city's "retail core" and a broader surrounding area which had no well-defined outer edges. The retail core, as he defined it, might come close to coinciding with Davies's idea of the hard core.

The method For the study area, land uses were recorded for the years 1921, 1925, 1931, 1935, 1941, 1946, and 1950.[25] From city directories for these years non-residential occupancies were recorded by street address. Using between 150 and 160 categories, Ratcliff determined the number of representatives of each category for each of the seven years. Only ground-floor occupancies were recorded. Ratcliff justified this on the grounds that the study was focused on the more intensive central land uses, particularly retail services, which, he contended, were closest to the concern of the property owner, the merchant, and the tax collector. It should be noted, too, that the entire study was based on the number of outlets, and, secondarily, on front feet of land use, both based on information available from the directories.

In the course of his research, Ratcliff reclassified the 150-odd categories into fourteen groups on the basis of their varying tendencies to change in importance and to shift during the thirty-year period represented. Presentation of these group classifications in tabular form and analyses of the tables occupied most of the body of Ratcliff's report.

[24] Richard U. Ratcliff, *The Madison Central Business Area: A Case Study of Functional Change,* Wisconsin Commerce Papers, vol. I, no. 5, Bureau of Business Research and Service, University of Wisconsin, Madison, Wis., 1953.

[25] Actually, the data were recorded separately for Area A, the retail core, and Area B, the broader surrounding area, but no further attention will be paid here to this twofold breakdown, since our concern is with the general research plan.

Some findings The central area of Madison was found not to have expanded in the last twenty years, at least as measured by number of non-residential establishments, but this was not considered serious, since analysis revealed that there had been changes in the direction of more intensive uses. An adequate test, it was pointed out, must take full account of changes in the proportionate land use by outlets of varying degrees of productivity or rent-paying ability. And data on front footage by groups showed that there had been a steady increase in space devoted to shopping goods outlets in the retail core area. There was a continuing replacement of less intensive uses with more intensive uses, of types with lower rent-paying capacity with types of higher ability in this respect. This should mean a steady increase of land values. There was other evidence, too, that Madison's central area was far from dead, but space does not permit going into more detail regarding the research and its results.

It is hardly to be expected that a research study of this sort would result in a definitive decision between the two hypotheses advanced (see pages 310 to 311). Nevertheless, the sum total of the evidence seems to favor the second hypothesis: that the central area of the city will continue to grow in productivity and that business volume and property values will continue to rise as total population of the urban area increases, though probably at a slower rate than population.

General applicability of findings The study dealt with only one city, Madison, Wisconsin, and, as Ratcliff points out, the findings of no one case study can be expected to apply to cities in general. But there is so much uniformity in structure among American cities that some of the findings should be generally applicable. "The cause of central areas," he says, "is far from hopeless."

Value of the technique Ratcliff's work has been presented here partly as a study of central business district problems and partly to portray a method—directory analysis—for studying changing patterns in the central business district. Obviously, the technique has other applications as well. For instance, it should be of value in studying the zones of assimilation and discard in the central business district.

The core-frame concept

The core-frame concept of Horwood and Boyce is another contribution to understanding of the central business district of the American city.[26]

According to this concept the central business district *core* is described as "the central part of the central business district." It is the area of most intensive land use and highest concentration of social and economic activities within the metropolitan complex. Land use is characterized by offices, retail sales, consumer services, banks, hotels, and theaters. The area has the city's highest buildings, the highest retail productivity per unit of ground area, and the greatest daytime population concentration. It is the focus of headquarters offices for business, industrial activities, and government, and the chief area of convergence of the city's mass-transit system. Growth tends to be vertical rather than horizontal. Horizontal movement is minor; in fact the boundaries of the area commonly are fixed by walking distances except where stopped short of this by natural barriers.

Surrounding the core is the central business district *frame*. It is characterized by "nodes" of off-street parking, automobile sales and services, special services (e.g., medical), wholesaling with stocks, warehousing, intercity transportation terminals and facilities, light manufacturing, and

[26] Edgar M. Horwood and Ronald R. Boyce, *Studies of the Central Business District and Urban Freeway Development*, University of Washington, Press, Seattle, Wash., 1959, esp. sec. I.

multifamily residences. Lines of "goods flow" connect the nodes with each other, with the core, and with areas beyond the frame. Natural barriers, heavy industry, and residential neighborhoods form most of the outer boundary of the frame.

The core-frame idea is of interest as a way of viewing the central business district, but it has definite limitations. In the first place, the core and frame together, as they are described by Horwood and Boyce, include considerably more of the city than it seems reasonable to include in the central business district. A more serious objection to the idea, however, is that Horwood and Boyce have suggested no practicable method for locating the boundaries of the core and the frame. In outlining such areas on a map in the field a great deal of subjectivity would be involved. Hence, there could be little comparability of the areas as they might be outlined in several cities.

Other Lines of Central Business District Research

Several unsolved questions regarding the central business district have been referred to throughout this chapter. In this section these will be summed up, together with several other ideas regarding possible research dealing with the central business district.

Some general questions

How does the central business district vary with type of city specialization? Does the central business district of a highly industrialized city, for example, tend to have characteristics that are measurably different from those of a city that is predominantly a regional trade center?

How do central business districts vary regionally throughout the United States? For instance, does there tend to be a new type of central business district, characterized by low, rather than high, buildings? The Southern city, in addition to a normal central business district, often has a Negro business district which tends to have some of the central business district features. These "Negro central business districts" would make an interesting subject for study even though the necessity for them may be disappearing. Or, perhaps, the areas referred to are not really central business districts. This suggests another possible topic for research: ethnically oriented business areas in American cities.

How do central business districts vary with city size? We certainly do not have enough studies of central business districts of cities of sufficient size range to speak with assurance on this point. Does central business district size (as measured by floor space) vary in direct proportion to city size? And if so, is the relationship closest to size of the legal city, of the standard metropolitan statistical area, or of the urbanized area? How do central business district land uses vary with city size? And at what size level does the central business district tend to be regionalized functionally with a well-defined financial district, a theater district, and the like?

The zone that borders the central business district

A particularly challenging topic for research is the zone that borders the central business district. This zone is of special interest since it is so often a problem area. It lies, in a sense, in the shadow of the central business district. Much of the land is not needed for central business district expansion and yet neither its location nor its high valuation favors other use. Not infrequently land in the area is being held for speculation and in the meanwhile is put to whatever use will best pay the taxes. Slums are common in this border zone, since, unfortunately, slum residences may pay a good return to a landlord. Nevertheless, for social reasons, the zone is the target of much of the redevelopment activity going on in our cities.

The uniformity of the zone could easily be exaggerated, however. For one thing, it varies greatly in width. In some places the central business district blends slowly into the land uses of neighboring areas, whereas in other places the district abuts against some barrier so the transition zone is essentially absent. There is variation in quality in the zone, too. In sections of it, the central business district is expanding outward, resulting in new buildings and a prosperous look to the area. In other sections, development is at a standstill or the area may be actually deteriorating. Such areas border the zones of discard discussed earlier in this chapter.

At any rate, this is a belt or zone the existence of which has been widely recognized and which the geographer should be able to delimit and study. Perhaps it could be delimited on the basis of block housing data from the Census of Housing, but it may be that the block unit is too coarse. The occurrence of certain types of land use may best mark the zone, or perhaps valuation data would form a better basis for delimiting it. Another possibility is that the zone may be found to be bordered on the outside by an almost continuous series of blocks, each of which is essentially homogeneous in land use, in contrast to the mixture of land uses characterizing blocks in the border zone. But whatever method may ultimately be used, the delimitation and study of the zone of transition that borders the central business district present a challenge to the urban geographer. It is surprising that thus far it has given rise to no published literature.

Freeways in relation to the central business district

A problem that is arising in many central business districts has to do with the effects of freeways. The problem is focused on central business districts that are reached by freeways or at least have freeways coming close enough to them to give fairly direct access to the district. Where such freeways have been completed for several years what, if any, changes in the central business district can be attributed to them? And what is the best way to measure these effects? [27] Closely related is an evaluation of the effects of a freeway that bypasses the central business district.

One possibility is that of a change in land use. Land use in the central business district could be mapped as it is today and a similar land-use map reconstructed for a period before the coming of the freeway. Here the factor of time enters in. Would an interval of ten years be long enough for substantial land-use changes to have occurred? Would twenty years be necessary? And even if measurable and substantial changes in land use have taken place how much of such change is due to the freeway?

Another possibility is that the presence of the freeway might result in a measurable change in land values in the downtown area. Unfortunately, however, real estate transactions in downtown areas usually are few during any reasonable length of time, and land values adjust slowly to changing price levels.

No doubt there are other, entirely different ways of attacking the problem. In a broad sense the question is, How can trends in the central business district be compared with those that would have held good without the freeway? But, however the question is attacked, the effects of freeways on central business districts remain a practical and interesting topic for research.[28]

[27] In this connection see Robert J. Huhtanen, Paul J. Mika, Richard E. Preston, and Raymond E. Murphy, *A Study of the Effects of Freeways on Central Business Districts*, report submitted to U.S. Department of Commerce, Bureau of Public Roads, February, 1961.

[28] There is a voluminous literature dealing with bypass studies in general, but little has been done on the relationships between central business districts and freeways.

Outlook for the District

This chapter has dealt with an important functional area of the city: the central business district. It is in a sense a regional chapter in a book that is predominantly systematic, but this variation is justified by the importance of the area and its problems. Moreover, the singling out of the central business district for special discussion is sanctioned by general usage; no other area of the city has been studied and written about so much.

The question that will occur to many readers of this book is, What is likely to be the future of the central business district of the American city? To answer questions such as this is not the function of this book or of this chapter, which has dealt, instead, with central business district research. Nevertheless, the possible future of the central business district has been discussed in several places throughout the book, though largely incidentally. In Chapter 14, for example, Vance foresees the central business district of the great city developing two downtowns—one an office district and the other a metropolitan specialty shopping district (page 266). In Chapter 12, Ullman suggests that the central business district may lose its uniqueness and become just one of a number of centers in the city (pages 216 to 217). In the same chapter, Hoyt emphasizes the overall decline in the predominance of central retail areas (pages 210 to 211). He stresses the growth of offices in downtown centers, but says that such growth has been occurring in only a few of the largest cities. Thus there are differences of opinion about details of what is happening to the central business district but general agreement that it is changing markedly and is destined to change still more.

Selected References

Breese, Gerald W.: *The Daytime Population of the Central Business District of Chicago, with Particular Reference to the Factor of Transportation,* University of Chicago Press, Chicago, 1949.

Davies, D. Hywel: "Boundary Study as a Tool in CBD Analysis: An Interpretation of Certain Aspects of the Boundary of Cape Town's Central Business District," *Economic Geography,* vol. 35, pp. 322–345, 1959.

————: "The Hard Core of Cape Town's Central Business District: An Attempt at Delimitation, *Economic Geography,* vol. 36, pp. 53–69, 1960.

Diamond, D. R.: "The Central Business District of Glasgow," in Proceedings of the IGU Symposium in Urban Geography Lund 1960, *Lund Studies in Geography,* ser. B, Human Geography, no. 24, Royal University of Lund, Sweden, 1962, pp. 525–534.

Firey, Walter: "Ecological Considerations in Planning for Rurban Fringes," *American Sociological Review,* vol. 11, pp. 411–423, 1946.

Foley, Donald L.: "The Daily Movements of Population into Central Business Districts," *American Sociological Review,* vol. 17, pp. 538–543, 1952.

Hartman, George W.: "The Central Business District: A Study in Urban Geography," *Economic Geography,* vol. 26, pp. 237–244, 1950.

Horwood, Edgar M., and Ronald R. Boyce: *Studies of the Central Business District and Urban Freeway Development,* University of Washington Press, Seattle, Wash., 1959.

Jonassen, C. T.: *Downtown versus Suburban Shopping,* Special Bulletin no. x-58 Bureau of Business Research, Ohio State University, Columbus, Ohio, 1953.

Murphy, Raymond E., and J. E. Vance, Jr.: "A Comparative Study of Nine Central Business Districts," *Economic Geography,* vol. 30, pp. 301–336, 1954.

———— and ————: "Delimiting the CBD," *Economic Geography,* vol. 30, pp. 189–222, 1954.

————, ————, and Bart J. Epstein: "Internal Structure of the CBD," *Economic Geography,* vol. 31, pp. 21–46, 1955.

Parkins, A. E.: "Profiles of the Retail Business Section of Nashville, Tenn., and Their Interpretation," *Annals of the Association of*

American Geographers, vol. 20, pp. 164–175, 1930.

Philadelphia City Planning Commission, *Philadelphia Central District Study,* Philadelphia, 1951.

Rannels, John: *The Core of the City,* Columbia University Press, New York, 1956.

Ratcliff, Richard U.: *The Madison Central Business Area: A Case Study of Functional Change,* Wisconsin Commerce Papers, vol. 1, no. 5, Bureau of Business Research and Service, University of Wisconsin, Madison, Wis., 1953.

Russwurm, Lorne H.: "The Central Business District Retail Sales Mix," *Annals of the Association of American Geographers,* vol. 54, pp. 524–536, 1964.

U. S. Bureau of the Census, *Intra-City Business Census Statistics for Philadelphia, Pa.* (prepared under supervision of Malcolm J. Proudfoot, Research Geographer) May, 1937.

———, Central business district statistics reports, 1958; major retail centers reports, 1963.

Weiss, Shirley F.: *The Central Business District in Transition,* Research Paper no. 1, City and Regional Planning Studies, Department of City and Regional Planning, University of North Carolina, Chapel Hill, N.C., 1957.

William-Olsson, W.: "Stockholm: Its Structure and Development," *Geographical Review,* vol. 30, pp. 420–438, 1940.

CHAPTER **16**

Manufacturing and the city

IN every city, at least some land is used for manufacturing. The proportion of the city's area so occupied is small—seldom more than 5 per cent—but the activity is much more important than its limited space needs suggest. Sometimes it serves only the community; in other words, the manufacturing may be entirely nonbasic as the term was used in an earlier chapter. But often it is of such character and proportions that it dominates the city's economic base. Harris, in his functional classification of United States cities, found manufacturing cities to be by far the most common type (see p. 131).

Of course, not all manufacturing is confined to urban areas. Nevertheless, so much of the manufacturing activity of the country is in or at the edges of cities that it becomes an important topic for consideration by the urban geographer.

As with other types of urban land use, there is a dichotomy in the urban geographer's interest in manufacturing. He wishes to gain an understanding of the patterns of distribution of cities based on the extent and characteristics of manufacturing, but he is at least equally interested in intracity patterns based on manufacturing. In both cases, his ultimate objective is to arrive at generalizations regarding the city.

Manufacturing Defined

Though the general meaning of *manufacturing*—changing the *form* of materials for the purpose of making them more useful or more valuable—is a matter of common knowledge, the ramifications and limitations of the term are not so well known. For this reason, the description of the manufacturing division given in the *Standard Industrial Classification Manual* [1] is quoted here:

[1] *Standard Industrial Classification Manual*, U.S. Bureau of the Budget, 1957.

The manufacturing division includes those establishments engaged in the mechanical or chemical transformation of inorganic or organic substances into new products, and usually described as plants, factories, or mills, which characteristically use power driven machines and materials handling equipment. Establishments engaged in assembling component parts of manufactured products are also considered manufacturing if the new product is neither a structure nor other fixed improvement.

The materials processed by manufacturing establishments include products of agriculture, forestry, fishing, mining, and quarrying. The final product of a manufacturing establishment may be "finished" in the sense that it is ready for utilization or consumption, or it may be "semifinished" to become a raw material for an establishment engaged in further manufacturing. For example, the product of the copper smelter is the raw material used in electrolytic refineries; refined copper is the raw material used by copper wire mills; and copper wire is the raw material used by certain electrical equipment manufacturers.

The materials used by manufacturing establishments may be purchased directly from producers, obtained through customary trade channels, or secured without recourse to the market by transferring the product from one establishment to another which is under the same ownership. Manufacturing production is usually carried on for the wholesale market, for interplant transfer, or to order for industrial users, rather than for direct sale to the domestic consumer.

Printing, publishing, and industries servicing the printing trades are classified as manufacturing industries.

There are various borderline cases between manufacturing and other activities. These, too, are summed up in the manual, to which the reader is referred for further details.

Industry, a term occasionally used in this chapter as well as elsewhere in the book, is a broader term than manufacturing. Using the term industry in its broadest sense, we speak of the agricultural industry and the resort industry, and, as in the above quotation, manufacturing industries. Frequently, industry is used as a synonym for manufacturing, as in the expression "industrial diversity"; and sometimes, as in "organized industrial districts," it is used to include manufacturing along with wholesaling, storage, and even transportation. Since manufacturing is the more exact term it should be given preference wherever practicable.

Census Sources for the Study of Manufacturing in the City

In the investigation of manufacturing geography of the urban complex, just as in other phases of urban geography, statistical data play an important role. As usual we turn to the possibilities of the United States Census, since such data have greater comparability than statistics from any other source. Volume III of the Census of Manufactures, Area Statistics,[2] is logically the first source to be considered, but the Census of Population, too, must be looked into.

The Census of Manufactures and summary totals

For each standard metropolitan statistical area, each county, and each city of 10,000 or more population, a summary total is given in the Census of Manufactures for each item of information indicated in Table 16.1, except where this would expose the operations of an individual company (see page 322). Where a standard metropolitan statistical area extends across a state line summary totals are given for the portions on each side of the line as well as for the stand-

[2] At the time of this writing, the most recent Census of Manufactures that had been published was the one for 1958. Two others had been issued since World War II, one in 1947 and the other in 1954. Final area statistics for the 1963 *Census of Manufactures* will become available during 1966 in the state report series, MC63(3)–1 to 51; subsequently, these reports will be assembled in vol. iii, *Area Statistics*, which is scheduled for publication early in 1967.

Table 16.1   Form showing information given for standard metropolitan statistical areas, counties, and cities of over 10,000 inhabitants

Standard metropolitan statistical area, county, and city	1958									1954	
	Establishments, number		All employees		Production workers			Value added by manufacture, adjusted ($1,000)	Capital expenditures, new ($1,000)	All employees, number	Value added by manufacture, unadjusted ($1,000)
	Total	With 20 or more employees	Number	Payroll ($1,000)	Number	Man hours	Wages ($1,000)				

SOURCE: U.S. Bureau of the Census, Census of Manufactures: 1958, vol. III, Area Statistics.

ard metropolitan statistical area as a whole.

Measures of manufacturing activity
At this point it might be well to look more closely at the types of information given in the table that are of most value in studying manufacturing. Number of employees, value added by manufacture, and number of establishments with twenty or more employees are the three most important items for this purpose.

PRODUCTION WORKERS AND TOTAL EMPLOYEES   Employment data, obtained by asking companies how many persons they employ in each establishment,[3] are reported in two forms, "all employees" and "production workers." The latter is limited more closely to people actually engaged in the manufacturing process.[4] Therefore, data

on production workers have generally been considered of more value in studying the location and volume of manufacturing than data on all employees. But the proportion of non-production workers is said to have grown significantly in recent years because of such factors as automation and computerization. Such developments argue in favor of total employees as the better measure.

VALUE ADDED BY MANUFACTURE   "Value added by manufacture,"[5] according to the Census Bureau, ". . . is considered to be the best value measure available for comparing the relative economic importance of manufacturing among industries and geographic areas."[6] Thus, if the value added by manufacture for one city is twice that

[3] An establishment is the operation of a company (or an individual) at one location engaged in one distinct line of activity. "In 1958, as in earlier years, a minimum size limit was set for including establishments in the census. Reports were required from all establishments employing one or more persons at any time during the census year. . . ."
[4] The Bureau of the Census, in the 1958 *Census of Manufactures*, defines "production and related workers" as follows: "Workers (up through the working foreman level) engaged in fabricating, processing, assembling, inspection, receiving, storage, handling, packing, warehousing, shipping (but not delivering), maintenance, repair, janitorial, watchman services, product development, auxiliary production for plants' own use (e.g., power plant), record keeping, and other services closely associated with these production operations at the establishment covered by the report are included. Super-

visory employees above the working foreman level are excluded from this category."
[5] According to the 1958 *Census of Manufactures*, value added by manufacture in the 1954 census and those of earlier years was obtained "by subtracting the cost of materials, supplies and containers, fuel, purchased electric energy, and contract work from the value of shipments for products manufactured plus receipts for services rendered. . . . For 1958, this measure of value added was adjusted by taking into account the following items (a) value added by merchandising operations (that is, the difference between the sales value and cost of merchandise sold without further manufacture, processing, or assembly) plus (b) the net change in finished goods and work-in-process inventories between the beginning and end of the year. The resulting figure is the adjusted value added by manufacture."
[6] U.S. Bureau of the Census, *Census of Manufactures: 1958, General Summary*, p. 13.

for another we can say that the first city has twice the volume of manufacturing activity that the second has.

NUMBER OF ESTABLISHMENTS "Number of establishments," as a measure of manufacturing activity, is chiefly useful in determining the average size of producing units (production workers per establishment) and the average volume of manufacturing activity (value added by manufacture per establishment). Number of establishments is used alone, too, to indicate the number of producing units in various manufacturing activities. But since establishments vary greatly in size, the number of establishments in a locality is not a very good measure of the importance of the activity represented. That is why, in most tables in the Census of Manufactures, the Census Bureau shows, in addition to number of establishments, the number with twenty or more employees.

The Census of Manufactures and industry groups and industries

The categories of Table 16.1 show only manufacturing as a whole and give no basis for discriminating between different types of manufacturing. For standard metropolitan statistical areas with considerable manufacturing and for counties with a certain amount of manufacturing development, however, the 1958 Census of Manufactures gives data by industry groups and industries.

Major industry groups The Standard Industrial Classification system is followed in establishing industry groups. To begin with, there are twenty major industry groups, each with a two-digit number. They appear in the 1958 Census of Manufactures as follows: 20, food and kindred products; 21, tobacco products; 22, textile mill products; 23, apparel and related products; 24, lumber and wood products; 25, furniture and fixtures; 26, paper and allied products; 27, printing and publishing; 28, chemicals and allied products; 29, petroleum and coal products; 30, rubber and plastic products, not elsewhere classified; 31, leather and leather products; 32, stone, clay, and glass products; 33, primary metal industries; 34, fabricated metal products; 35, machinery, except electrical; 36, electrical machinery; 37, transportation equipment; 38, instruments and related products; and 39, miscellaneous manufacturing. Each of the two-digit industry groups can be divided into three-digit industry groups and these in turn broken down into individual industries at the four-digit level.

Standard metropolitan statistical areas with 190,000 or more manufacturing employees For each standard metropolitan statistical area reporting 190,000 or more manufacturing employees for 1958, data under the headings shown in Table 16.1 normally are given for each major (two-digit) industry group and for industry groups (three-digit) and for individual industries (four-digit) as well. For example, for the Detroit Standard Metropolitan Statistical Area, which had 405,035 manufacturing employees in 1958, data are given for the major industry group 20, food and kindred products, as well as for all other major industry groups, since all happen to be represented. But in addition there are three-digit and four-digit data. Thus, 20, food and kindred products, is subdivided as follows: 201, meat products (2011, meat-packing plants; 2013, prepared meats; 2015, poultry dressing plants); 202, dairy products (2024, ice cream and frozen desserts; 2026, fluid milk); 203, canned and frozen foods (2033, canned fruits and vegetables; 2035, pickles and sauces); 205, bakery products (2051, bread and related products); 208, beverages (2082, malt liquors; 2086, bottled and canned soft drinks); 209, other food preparations (2094, grease and tallow; 2098, macaroni and spaghetti; 2099, food preparations, not elsewhere classified). Similar details are given for all other major industry groups insofar as they are represented in a particular standard metropolitan statistical area, except in those few cases where the operations of individual companies would be revealed or where changes in the classification system have resulted in non-comparable data.

Standard metropolitan statistical areas with 40,000 to 190,000 manufacturing employees Data are given in somewhat less detail for standard metropolitan statistical areas with between 40,000 and 190,000 manufacturing wage earners. The breakdown is only at the two- and three-digit levels. Thus for the Minneapolis–St. Paul Standard Metropolitan Statistical Area, with 135,136 manufacturing employees in 1958, all of the major industry groups except 21, tobacco products, are represented. Each, in turn, is broken down still further. Food and kindred products, for example, is subdivided into 201, meat products; 202, dairy products; 203, canned and frozen foods; 204, grain mill products; 205, bakery products; 207, candy and related products; 208, beverages; and 209, other food preparations. But this is as far as the breakdown goes. Again, of course, as with the standard metropolitan statistical area of 190,000 or more manufacturing employees, some data are withheld.

Industrial counties In addition to industry statistics for standard metropolitan statistical areas with 40,000 or more manufacturing wage earners, the Census of Manufactures gives two- and three-digit data for each county for each industry group that has at least five hundred manufacturing employees, where this can be done without disclosing the figures of individual companies.

Industrial county data supplement the standard metropolitan statistical area data in two ways. First, they provide industrial information for the principal counties of some of the smaller standard metropolitan statistical areas, many of which are, in fact,

one-county areas. Consider the Rockford, Illinois, Standard Metropolitan Statistical Area, which consists of only one county, Winnebago. Since the Rockford Standard Metropolitan Statistical Area had only 39,297 manufacturing employees in 1958, for example, it did not qualify as a standard metropolitan statistical area with 40,000 or more manufacturing employees, so only the summary totals were given that are available for every standard metropolitan statistical area, every county, and every city of 10,000 or more population. But Winnebago County did have several industry groups (two-digit and some three-digit) that have five hundred employees or more each, and, for these, additional data were given. They furnish the best census manufacturing details that are available for Rockford. Otherwise there would be published for the city and for the standard metropolitan statistical area only the summary totals referred to earlier.

But having two- and three-digit industry-group data by counties for certain industrial groups also is of value in another way. These data provide information on the county-to-county variations in industrial structure within the large multicounty standard metropolitan statistical areas. Thus, in addition to two-, three-, and four-digit data on industry groups for the Chicago Standard Metropolitan Statistical Area, some data by industry groups (two-digit and some three-digit) are published for each of the six counties that make up the area. This makes possible some differentiation of the interior of the Chicago Standard Metropolitan Statistical Area on the basis of manufacturing.[7]

[7] It just happens, in this case, that all six counties are "industrial counties." Often some of the counties making up a standard metropolitan statistical area are not. For example, in the Minneapolis–St. Paul, Minn., Standard Metropolitan Statistical Area, Hennepin and Ramsey are industrial counties. The other three—Anoka, Dakota, and Washington Counties—are not, so only summary manufacturing totals are available for them.

Independent cities Some cities, such as Baltimore, St. Louis, and the larger Virginia cities, are independent and not parts of counties. The Census Bureau treats these cities as if they were counties. For each of them, two- and three-digit data are given on the same basis as for industrial counties, and for each state in which these independent cities occur and qualify they are listed in the same table as the industrial counties. Where the city is large enough to have a standard metropolitan statistical area, statistics are given on this basis too.

The Census of Manufactures and disclosure

It was pointed out earlier that the Census Bureau cannot publish any statistics that disclose information reported by individual companies. Summary data for small cities or even counties are also sometimes withheld for this reason. The same rule makes it impossible to show details regarding some individual industries, industry groups, or even major industry groups. Items at the major industry-group level, however, rarely have to be withheld or consolidated with others; it is more often necessary to withhold industry-group (three digit) data; but four-digit (individual industry) data suffer first and most from the disclosure regulation. It is worth noting that if an industry or industry group is listed at all, the number of establishments is never withheld.

The Census of Population

Although the Census of Manufactures is considered the most important source for data regarding manufacturing in the city, the Census of Population, too, has statistics that bear on the subject. For the most part these, like the Census of Manufactures data, do not differentiate the interior of the city.

Data for urban units Data for urban places, cities, standard metropolitan statistical areas, and urbanized areas are available at three levels in the Census of Population. Employment totals for durable goods manufacturing and non-durable goods manufacturing are given for urban places of 2,500 to 10,000 population. Totals are available of all persons employed in manufacturing, and for each of fourteen manufacturing industry groups as well (Table 16.2), for standard metropolitan statistical areas, for urbanized areas, and for cities of 10,000 or more population. For standard metropolitan statistical areas with 100,000 or more population, the fourteen industry groups are broken down in considerable detail.

It should be kept in mind that data in the Census of Population are obtained from individuals by asking the kind of business or industry in which they are employed. Therefore, such information has the disadvantage of being reported by place of residence rather than place of work. On the other hand, the problem of disclosure does not enter in as it does in the Census of Manufactures, and there is the added advantage that, in the Census of Population, a breakdown of manufacturing into four-

Table 16.2   Manufacturing industries listed in the 1960 *Census of Population*

Furniture, and lumber and wood products
Primary metal industries
Fabricated metal industries (including not specified metals)
Machinery, except electrical
Electrical machinery, equipment, and supplies
Motor vehicles and motor vehicle equipment
Transportation equipment, except motor vehicles
Other durable goods
Food and kindred products
Textile mill products
Apparel and other fabricated textile products
Printing, publishing, and allied products
Chemical and allied products
Other non-durable goods (including not specified manufacturing.)

SOURCE: U.S. Bureau of the Census, *Census of Population: 1960*, vol I, *Characteristics of Population*, state volumes, table 75.

teen major groups is given for places as small as 10,000 in population.[8] Data are given, too, by urbanized areas, whereas this census area does not appear at all in the Census of Manufactures.

Data for census tracts One final item remains to be mentioned: the number of people engaged in manufacturing as a whole and in each of nine manufacturing industry groups is given by census tracts. But since, like all Census of Population statistics, the data are given by place of residence, they are of limited value to the geographer interested in patterns of manufacturing in the city.

Use of Census Data at the Intercity Level

Census of Manufactures and Census of Population data dealing with manufacturing in urban centers are frequently used in geographic research. In many such studies, concern has been with whole urban units—corporate cities, standard metropolitan statistical areas, or urbanized areas—without regard for variations within the urban agglomeration. The work has been focused on such tasks as comparing, characterizing, and classifying urban centers from the standpoint of manufacturing and on regionalizing on the basis of manufacturing in cities.

Delimiting the manufacturing belt

City data from both the Census of Manufactures and the Census of Population have been used in studies aimed at delimiting the American manufacturing belt. Sten de Geer's pioneer effort along this line was based on wage earners in manufacturing in towns of 10,000 population or more.[9] Hartshorne, too, used cities of 10,000 population or more, but felt that a correction should be made to eliminate ubiquitous (nonbasic) manufacturing activity.[10] Using the United States Census of 1929 as his source, he subtracted from the total number of manufacturing wage earners in each city a number equal to 10 per cent of the total population of the city, defining as an "industrial city" one in which at least five hundred manufacturing workers remained. These remaining workers, Hartshorne reasoned, were employed in manufacturing for markets beyond the city itself. Alfred Wright based his delimitation of the manufacturing belt on value added by manufacture in "all cities over 10,000 population and all manufacturing districts listed in the census of manufacturing. . . ."[11] Though no generally agreed method of delimiting the American manufacturing belt was arrived at through these and several other related studies, they serve to illustrate one type of use by geographers of census data dealing with manufacturing in cities.

Functional classifications of cities

Data from the Census of Manufactures and the Census of Population have been used in distinguishing manufacturing cities in functional classifications (see Chapter 8). Harris depended primarily upon the Census

[8] For example, for Huntington, Ind., a city of 16,185 population in 1960, the Census of Manufactures showed, for 1958, the total number of manufacturing establishments, the total number of persons they employ, the total number of production workers they employ, the total value added by manufacture in the establishments, etc., but no information whatever is given regarding the nature of the manufacturing. The Census of Population, on the other hand, shows the number of people residing in Huntington in 1960 who gave their employment as falling in each of the fourteen manufacturing industries listed in Table 16.2. Apparently, metal industries and machinery are outstanding in the manufacturing picture, especially electrical machinery.

[9] Sten de Geer, "The American Manufacturing Belt," *Geografiska Annaler,* vol. 9, pp. 233–359, 1927.

[10] Richard Hartshorne, "A New Map of the Manufacturing Belt of North America," *Economic Geography,* vol. 12, pp. 45–53, 1936.

[11] Alfred J. Wright, "Manufacturing Districts of the United States," *Economic Geography,* vol. 14, p. 198, 1938.

of Manufactures and the Census of Business in arriving at his classification, though he made secondary use of industry-group data from the Census of Population; Ohlson and, later, Jones, depended almost entirely upon the Census of Manufactures and the Census of Business in differentiating manufacturing and industrial cities; Nelson, on the other hand, based his manufacturing specialization upon industry-group data from the Census of Population. So, too, did Alexandersson.

Of particular interest with respect to Alexandersson's work is the fact that, using industry-group data from the Census of Population, he analyzed thirty-six of the industry groups listed under manufacturing and presented maps of many of these specialties. Thus he made distribution maps of furniture and lumber towns, textile towns, apparel towns, chemical manufacturing towns, food manufacturing towns, and several others. His technique of distinguishing between the city-serving and city-forming components for each activity type, including each of the various lines of manufacturing, and for grading the urban centers was described in Chapter 8 (see pages 125 to 126).

The manufacturing ratio

In addition to their classification of cities, Ohlson and, later, Victor Jones used Census of Manufactures data for deriving an interesting ratio.[12] It is called the *manufacturing ratio* and is the percentage that employment in manufacturing in a city

[12] Grace M. Kneedler Ohlson, "Economic Classification of Cities," *The Municipal Year Book*, International City Managers Association, Chicago, 1945, pp. 30–38 and table IV, repeated in some later issues; Victor Jones, "Economic Classification of Cities and Metropolitan Areas," *The Municipal Year Book*, International City Managers Association, Chicago, 1954, p. 81, repeated in some later issues; and Victor Jones, Richard Forstall, and Andrew Collver, "Economic and Social Characteristics of Urban Places," *The Municipal Year Book*, International City Managers Association, Chicago, 1963, pp. 94–95.

makes up of the aggregate employment in the city in manufacturing, retail and wholesale trade, and selected services. The data on manufacturing are obtained from the Census of Manufactures; those on trade and services from the Census of Business. The manufacturing ratio purports to show by a single number the relative importance of manufacturing in a city. As might be expected, the highest ratios are for small, specialized manufacturing cities, often, in reality, industrial satellites to which workers commute from the central city and suburbs, whereas the lowest ratios are those of urban centers that for one reason or another are notably non-manufacturing in their specialization (Table 16.3).

Such ratios can be calculated for incorporated urban centers of 10,000 population or more and for standard metropolitan statistical areas. They cannot be used for urbanized areas, however, since manufacturing and business statistics are not given for these units. Moreover, though useful, the manufacturing ratio may give the wrong impression of an urban center, since it takes account only of employment in manufacturing, retail trade, wholesale trade, and selected services. For an urban center where there is substantial employment in mining, transportation, public administration, or other activities not covered by the Census of Manufactures or Census of Business, the manufacturing ratio will be too high. It should be kept in mind that what the ratio shows is the relative importance of manufacturing employment among several types of employment. It does not purport to compare places as to the absolute importance of the manufacturing process.

The location quotient

Census data are used, too, to measure the extent to which a type of manufacturing is concentrated in an area.[13] The *location*

[13] United States National Resources Planning Board, *Industrial Location and National Resources*, 1943, p. 107.

Table 16.3 Manufacturing ratios for forty urban centers for 1958

Urban center	Ratio	Urban center	Ratio
Ames, Iowa	20	Lynn, Mass.	72
Asheville, N.C.	18	Memphis, Tenn.	36
Atlanta, Ga.	33	Milwaukee, Wis.	55
Atlantic City, N.J.	12	Moscow, Idaho	6
Austin, Tex.	17	New York, N.Y.	43
Baltimore, Md.	44	Philadelphia, Pa.	52
Boston, Mass.	37	Phoenix, Ariz.	25
Chicago, Ill.	49	Pittsburgh, Pa.	37
Clairton, Pa.	79	Princeton, N.J.	7
Cleveland Heights, Ohio	15	Rochester, Minn.	35
Columbus, Ohio	47	Sacramento, Calif.	17
Dearborn, Mich.	73	San Francisco, Calif.	27
Denver, Colo.	30	Sarasota, Fla.	17
Detroit, Mich.	48	Seattle, Wash.	47
East Chicago, Ind.	90	Steelton, Pa.	89
East Lansing, Mich.	3	Swissvale, Pa.	84
Flint, Mich.	64	Tonawanda, N.Y.	82
Fresno, Calif.	20	Tulsa, Okla.	30
Gary, Ind.	68	Wallingford, Conn.	74
Kansas City, Mo.	36	Washington, D.C.	14†

NOTE: These ratios are only for political units, although Jones and Forstall give ratios for standard metropolitan statistical areas as well; the forty urban centers listed represent a considerable range in type, however. Most of the large cities have only moderately high ratios. The very highest are associated with satellites such as Steelton, Pa., and East Chicago, Ind. Resort centers, university towns, and high-quality suburbs have low ratios.

† City includes significant employment in government operated manufacturing not covered in the Census of Manufactures.

SOURCE: After Victor Jones, Richard L. Forstall, and Andrew Collver, *Municipal Year Book*, Chicago, 1963.

quotient expresses the degree of this concentration. Though we are interested here chiefly in manufacturing, the idea is one that is by no means restricted to manufacturing but can be used to measure concentration in any kind of distribution. The location quotient is a measure of relative importance rather than of absolute importance.

Census of Manufactures and the location quotient For any type of manufacturing in a standard metropolitan statistical area the quotient can be found by the following formula based on Census of Manufactures data: [14] (Production workers in a

manufacturing group in an SMSA/Production workers in same manufacturing group in USA) ÷ (All manufacturing production workers in the same SMSA/All manufacturing production workers in the USA)

Suppose, for example, the location-quotient idea is applied to the motor vehicles and equipment group for the Detroit Standard Metropolitan Statistical Area for 1958. Data are obtained from the Census of Manufactures and the formula for the location quotient reads:

$$\frac{\dfrac{101,848}{458,220}}{\dfrac{295,788}{11,644,213}} = \frac{.2223}{.0254} = 8.75$$

The fraction .2223/.0254 can be interpreted as follows: 22.2 per cent of the production

[14] The calculation could be based, instead, on value added by manufacture, or, for that matter, on total employees in manufacturing.

workers in motor vehicles and equipment manufacturing in the United States are concentrated in the Detroit Standard Metropolitan Statistical Area, but only 2.5 per cent of all production workers in manufacturing in the United States are concentrated there.[15] If the numerator and denominator were identical, the final value would be the whole number 1, indicating that the standard metropolitan statistical area had the same proportion of the national total of production workers in the particular industry as it had of the national total of all manufacturing. If the number were less than 1 it would indicate a deficiency, that is, that the standard metropolitan statistical area is doing less than its share of this type of manufacturing, with the departure from 1 indicating how great this deficiency is. For certain industries the location quotient is 0 for many standard metropolitan statistical areas, since none of that particular type of manufacturing is carried on; on the other hand, some types of industry are carried on to some degree in every city and for such industries the location quotient is never 0. Values over 1 indicate concentration proportionately; and a value of 8.75, such as that for motor vehicles and equipment in the Detroit Standard Metropolitan Statistical Area, indicates

[15] The formula may also be written:

$$\frac{\dfrac{\text{Production workers in a manufacturing group in an SMSA}}{\text{All manufacturing production workers in the same SMSA}}}{\dfrac{\text{Production workers in the same manufacturing group in the USA}}{\text{All manufacturing production workers in the USA}}}$$

Mathematically, this is equivalent to the formula given in the text. The resulting fraction is .34433/.03985 = 8.75. The difference between the two formulas lies in what can be read from the fractions. This one tells us that 34.4 per cent of the manufacturing employees in the Detroit Standard Metropolitan Statistical Area are engaged in the manufacture of automotive vehicles and equipment, and 4 per cent of all industrial employees in the United States are engaged in similar activities.

a very considerable concentration of the industry, almost nine times the area's proportionate share. Generally speaking, the basic (as opposed to nonbasic) types of manufacturing will tend to have location quotients that depart furthest from unity.

An obvious limitation of the location quotient as it has been calculated here is the withholding of data in the Census of Manufactures. We cannot, for example, calculate the location quotient for motor vehicles and equipment for the Flint Standard Metropolitan Statistical Area since data are given only for major industry groups (two-digit) for that area. This is an unusual situation, since the Flint Standard Metropolitan Statistical Area had 57,536 manufacturing employees in 1958, considerably more than the 40,000 needed to qualify it for three-digit data (see pages 320 to 321). The situation reflects the high degree of manufacturing specialization in Flint with the consequent problem of avoiding disclosure of operations.

The best that can be done, in this case, is to calculate the location quotient for transportation equipment, the two-digit major industry group of which motor vehicles and equipment is a subdivision. The location quotient for transportation equipment is found to be 8.7, showing a high degree of concentration, which obviously reflects the importance of automobile manufacturing.

Number of establishments can be used in calculating the location quotient, but since establishments vary greatly in size this procedure is not recommended.

Census of Population and the location quotient In the foregoing paragraphs the implication has been that the location quotient for manufacturing concentrations must be based on Census of Manufactures data. Actually, however, it can be based, instead, upon industry-group data from the Census of Population, with, often, results not very different from those based on Census of

Manufactures data. Thus if 1960 *Census of Population* industry-group data are used in calculating the location quotient for motor vehicles and equipment for the Detroit Standard Metropolitan Statistical Area, the result is found to be 9.45—not too different from the quotient of 8.75 based on the 1958 *Census of Manufactures.*

It must be kept in mind that Census of Population data are based on where people live, in contrast to Census of Manufactures data which are given according to the location of factories in which people work. The latter, obviously, is a much more realistic basis for a location quotient as regards manufacturing activity.

Adaptations of the location quotient Various adaptations of the location-quotient idea may occur to the reader. For example, a ratio could be applied to all manufacturing in a standard metropolitan statistical area in order to get an idea of the importance of the area in manufacturing. In this case the ratio might be:

$$\frac{\dfrac{\text{Manufacturing production workers in the SMSA}}{\text{Manufacturing production workers in the USA}}}{\dfrac{\text{Population of the SMSA}}{\text{Population of the USA}}}$$

Ratios of over 1 would indicate a concentration of manufacturing; ratios of less than 1, a deficiency. The location quotient can be used, too, in studies of localization of manufacturing in districts within a city where separate data are available for such districts.[16]

Location quotient versus absolute importance Finally, another limitation of the

location quotient should be mentioned. Suppose the total number of production workers in a certain community is small but the proportion of these workers in a certain industry is large. The result would be a high location quotient even though in absolute terms the industry finds small representation. In short, it must be kept in mind that the location quotient shows relative concentration only.

Manufacturing magnitude and intensity

For the geographer the various types of census data are not ends in themselves. The matter of interest is how they can be most effectively put to use in gaining, for example, an understanding of the distribution of manufacturing in the United States. This was the general objective of a study by John H. Thompson which, though it is manufacturing geography, is also urban geography since it involves a classification of standard metropolitan areas.[17]

Not satisfied with any single criterion for measuring manufacturing activity, Thompson used what he called a multiple-criteria method in a study of fifty selected standard metropolitan areas.[18] By this method he arrived at *magnitude* and *intensity* ratings for the standard metropolitan areas.

Magnitude ratings The magnitude rating of a standard metropolitan area, according to Thompson, was based on three factors: all employees in manufacturing, salaries and wages, and value added by

[16] Use of the location quotient is by no means restricted to studies of the distribution of manufacturing. The technique can be applied equally well, for example, to wholesaling or to retailing. Thus one could determine whether a city stood out among cities for its wholesaling, or, if data were available, whether a certain district or certain districts stood out among others in the city in this respect.

[17] John H. Thompson, "A New Method for Measuring Manufacturing," *Annals of Association of American Geographers,* vol. 45, pp. 416–436, 1955. Standard metropolitan areas are used throughout this discussion and that of the following article since they represent work done before standard metropolitan statistical areas came into existence.
[18] Thompson used fifty of the fifty-three standard metropolitan areas which had over 40,000 people employed in manufacturing in 1947. The three which he omitted were New York–Northeastern New Jersey, Chicago, and Philadelphia.

manufacture. For each factor he used a fixed base which was an average of that factor for 1939 for the fifty standard metropolitan areas with which he worked.[19] The fixed base resulting from all employees in manufacturing was 70,000; for salaries and wages, 100 million dollars; and for value added by manufacture, 200 million dollars. The magnitude rating based on all employees in manufacturing was expressed by the following equation: $M_1 = En/70,000 \times 100$, in which M_1 is the magnitude and En is the number of manufacturing employees in the area to be rated. Similar equations were used for M_2, the magnitude based on salaries and wages, and M_3, the magnitude based on value added by manufacture. But since the value of salaries and wages in each of these two cases was based on 1947 data (the date of the latest Census of Manufactures at the time of the study) it was necessary to use a conversion factor K in each case to convert to 1939 dollars. Finally, the three magnitudes were averaged to obtain a single, multiple-criteria magnitude rating for the standard metropolitan area being considered.[20]

Intensity ratings

Intensity, which Thompson used to represent the importance of manufacturing in the economy, was also an average of three criteria. These were (1) ratio of all employees in manufacturing to total employed in all industry groups, (2) ratio of all employees in manufacturing to total population, and (3) ratio of value added by manufacture to total population (value added per person). Fixed bases were used which were the averages of each of these criteria for the fifty standard metropolitan areas in 1939. They amounted to 0.300, 0.110, and $310, respectively. The intensity rating for the ratio of all employees in manufacturing to total employed in all industry groups was expressed as $\dfrac{\left(\dfrac{En}{Tn}\right)}{.300} \times 100$, where En is all employees in manufacturing and Tn is the total employed in all industry groups. The ratings of the other two criteria were similarly calculated except that in the third equation value added by manufacture had to be multiplied by a conversion factor to convert to 1939 dollars.

Comparing the standard metropolitan areas

Thompson arranged his magnitude ratings into Class A, Class B, etc., through Class J. Similarly, he arranged the intensities into Classes I through X (see Table 16.4). Further work in his study involved showing in tables, groups, and maps the comparative standings of the fifty standard metropolitan areas for 1939 and 1947 and changes from 1939 to 1947.

Industrial diversity and industrial specialization

Another example of the use of Census of Population industry-group data is a study by Allan Rodgers of industrial (manufacturing) diversification in the United States.[21] Many cities claim manufacturing diversity and many others seek to achieve it, no doubt because of the widespread belief that a diversified community is less likely to suffer

[19] Standard metropolitan areas were not established until the 1940s, but the Bureau of the Census compiled 1939 data for them, publishing the results in the 1947 *Census of Manufactures*. Thompson chose 1939 rather than 1947 as his base year because a more accurate total of people employed in all industry groups could be obtained for 1939.

[20] A question that might well be raised here is, Are the three magnitude factors really of equal significance? This is implied by averaging them as Thompson has done. An alternative procedure would be to weight the three differently, but what should their relative weights be? The same problem arises regarding the averaging of the three intensity ratings discussed in the following subsection.

[21] Allan Rodgers, "Some Aspects of Industrial Diversification in the United States," *Economic Geography*, vol. 33, pp. 16–30, 1957.

Table 16.4   **Manufacturing magnitude and intensity of the Pittsburgh Standard Metropolitan Area for 1947**

Magnitude

$$M_1 = \frac{337,974}{70,000} \times 100 = 482.8$$

$$M_2 = \frac{1,023,913,000 \ (K_1)}{100,000,000} \times 100 = \frac{540,893,000}{100,000,000} \times 100 = 540.9$$

$$M_3 = \frac{1,707,918,000 \ (K_2)}{200,000,000} \times 100 = \frac{1,014,232,000}{200,000,000} \times 100 = 507.1$$

$$M_m = \frac{482.8 + 540.9 + 507.1}{3} = 510.3\text{—Class C}$$

Intensity

$$I_1 = \frac{337,974}{764,900 \ (.300)} \times 100 = 147.3$$

$$I_2 = \frac{337,974}{2,174,000 \ (.110)} \times 100 = 141.3$$

$$I_3 = \frac{1,707,918,000 \ (K_2)}{2,174,000 \ (310.)} \times 100 = \frac{1,014,232,000}{2,174,000 \ (310.)} \times 100 = 150.6$$

$$I_m = \frac{147.3 + 141.3 + 150.6}{3} = 146.6\text{—Class IV}$$

SOURCE: After John H. Thompson, "A New Method for Measuring Manufacturing," *Annals of the Association of American Geographers*, vol. 45, pp. 422 and 423, 1955.

in times of depression. Rodgers set out to investigate the degree of diversification within the major industrial areas of the United States and also to study some effects of diversification on local economic development.

What is industrial diversity? He found that there was, in the first place, no general agreement regarding the meaning of the term diversification. In its broadest sense it has been defined as the presence in an area of a great number of different types of manufacturing. Thus *absolute diversification* might involve equal employment in all manufacturing groups, but this would obviously vary tremendously with the kinds and numbers of manufacturing groups considered. There can even be manufacturing

diversification of a sort within a single group. To take one example, a town might be specialized in shoe manufacture, but its various factories might specialize in different styles of shoes for different markets.

Rodgers says that the composition of manufacturing in an area is important too. Thus some types of manufacturing are more sensitive to seasonal and cyclical fluctuations of employment than others. Finally, it may be important in the economic health of a community whether there is a single establishment in a field or many establishments. With many small firms, the overall effect on the community of a failure due to poor management may be minimized. On the other hand, the concentration of employment and production in a few larger firms may provide an advantage of local economies of scale which may be important in the competitive position of an area.

Use of standard metropolitan areas with substantial employment Rodgers felt that in view of the wide variety of factors to be considered, any measure of diversification must represent a compromise. It should use a large number of varied manufacturing groups as a base, and should be computed through measuring deviations from some norm which is considered a diversified pattern. He decided to work with standard metropolitan areas since in many ways they were true functional entities and since he was concerned only with the major lineaments of the United States manufacturing pattern. Of the 168 standard metropolitan areas used by the Census Bureau in 1950, only 93 were included in Rodgers's study. These were the only standard metropolitan areas in which manufacturing employment exceeded 20,000 according to the 1950 *Census of Population*. Together they accounted for over 92 per cent of the total manufacturing employment in all standard metropolitan areas and for almost two-thirds of all manufacturing employment in the United States in 1950. For the 93 metropolitan areas included in the study, Rodgers used industry-group data for twenty-two groups listed under manufacturing in table 79 of the 1950 *Census of Population* (see Table 16.5). This breakdown of manufacturing is in greater detail than that in table 35 of the Census of Population which was used by Nelson and by Alexandersson (see Chapter 8), but was available only for standard metropolitan areas and for cities of 100,000 or more population.

Rodgers's technique Rodgers's method of computation of what he calls the *crude diversification index* for the Indianapolis area is shown in Table 16.5. From the Census of Population he obtained the employment for each of the twenty-two groups and then calculated the percentage that

each of the twenty-two made up of their total. These percentages were ranked in descending order (part B of Table 16.5). Then progressive totals were arrived at: largest percentage; largest plus second largest; this total plus third largest; etc. Addition of the progressive totals gave the crude index of diversification for the Indianapolis Standard Metropolitan Area. For twenty-two manufacturing groups the crude index for maximum specialization in an area (a single group employing the entire manufacturing labor force) would be 2,200. The minimum specialization—that is, with equal

Table 16.5   Calculation of crude index of diversification for Indianapolis Standard Metropolitan Area

PART A

Manufacturing group	Employment by manufacturing group	% of total manufacturing employment
Lumber and wood	831	1.08
Furniture	1,085	1.41
Stone, clay, and glass	1,200	1.56
Primary metals	4,092	5.32
Fabricated metals	6,256	8.13
Machinery except electrical	9,596	12.47
Electrical machinery	10,256	13.33
Transportation equipment (except motor vehicles and equipment)	4,444	5.78
Motor vehicles	7,488	9.73
Professional equipment	636	0.83
Miscellaneous durable	1,571	2.04
Food and kindred	8,712	11.32
Tobacco	43	0.06
Textiles	1,996	2.59
Apparel	1,524	1.98
Paper and allied	2,262	2.94
Printing and publishing	5,101	6.63
Chemical and allied	6,300	8.19
Petroleum and coal	424	0.55
Rubber	2,210	2.87
Leather	173	0.22
Not specified	744	0.97
Total	76,944	100.00

PART B

Ranked percentages	Progressive totals
13.33	13.33
12.47	25.80
11.32	37.12
9.73	46.85
8.19	55.04
8.13	63.17
6.63	69.80
5.78	75.58
5.32	80.90
2.94	83.84
2.87	86.71
2.59	89.30
2.04	91.34
1.98	93.22
1.56	94.88
1.41	96.29
1.08	97.37
0.97	98.34
0.83	99.17
0.55	99.72
0.22	99.94
0.06	100.00

Crude diversification index	1,697.71

SOURCE: After Allan Rodgers, "Some Aspects of Industrial Diversification in the United States," *Economic Geography*, vol. 33, 1957.

employment in all manufacturing groups—would be about 1,150. The crude index for the Indianapolis Standard Metropolitan Area proved to be 1,697.71 or, as a rounded figure, 1,698.

Rodgers points out that the crude indices by themselves give no relative indication of the degree of diversity of an area since they lack a reference level. Therefore, he computed what he called *refined indices*. The base selected was the distribution of employment by manufacturing groups for all ninety-three areas combined and treated as a unit. The crude diversification index for this unit (computed just as in Table 16.5) was 1,553. The refined index for each standard metropolitan area was found by the following formula:

$$\frac{\text{Actual crude index} - \text{crude index for the 93 areas combined}}{\text{Crude index for least diversity} - \text{crude index for the 93 areas combined}}$$

For the Indianapolis Standard Metropolitan Area the refined index equals:

$$\frac{1,698 - 1,553}{2,200 - 1,553} = 0.224$$

For convenience, Rodgers considered the refined index as a whole number, in this case 224.

The rank order resulting The refined indices, as Rodgers points out, can vary from 0 (maximum diversity) to 1,000 (minimum diversity). Zero for any standard metropolitan area would mean that the area conformed exactly to the pattern for the ninety-three standard metropolitan areas treated as a unit. A score of 1,000 would mean that the area had only one manufacturing group of the twenty-two groups here considered. The Indianapolis Standard Metropolitan Area had a refined index of 224, thus showing a high degree of diversity. Actually, the ninety-three areas ranged in refined indices from Philadelphia, with an index of 39, almost complete diversity as measured in terms of the combined average, to 934 for Flint, presumably with a high degree of concentration on motor vehicles (Table 16.6). Statistical tests confirmed the idea that diversity tends to increase with population.

Evaluation of the method Rodgers points out certain limitations and certain balancing virtues of his index of diversification. Thus, although a high index implies a limited number of manufacturing groups, it gives no indication whether each manufacturing group represents one or several specific types of manufacturing. And the index fails to bring out certain critical facts about the composition of industry in an area, such as employment in durable versus that in non-durable goods. But the tech-

Table 16.6   Refined diversification indices for ninety-three standard metropolitan areas for 1950. The lower the number, the greater the diversity

Philadelphia, Pa.	039	Duluth–Superior, Minn.	428
St. Louis, Mo.	090	Allentown–Bethlehem–Easton, Pa.	430
Los Angeles, Calif.	114	Richmond, Va.	431
Boston, Mass.	118	Reading, Pa.	440
Trenton, N.J.	148	Wilmington, Del.	445
New Orleans, La.	152	Lincoln, Neb.	447
Cincinnati, Ohio	167	Portland, Maine	453
New York, N.Y.	173	Chattanooga, Tenn.	456
San Francisco, Calif.	173	Springfield, Ohio	456
Memphis, Tenn.	215	Seattle, Wash.	458
Dallas, Tex.	218	Erie, Pa.	462
Chicago, Ill.	224	Hartford, Conn.	462
Indianapolis, Ind.	224	Phoenix, Ariz.	467
Atlanta, Ga.	229	El Paso, Tex.	474
Baltimore, Md.	235	Harrisburg, Pa.	481
Denver, Colo.	238	Brockton, Mass.	492
Buffalo, N.Y.	243	Rochester, N.Y.	498
Springfield–Holyoke, Mass.	250	Roanoke, Va.	505
Kansas City, Mo.	257	Austin, Tex.	505
York, Pa.	261	Orlando, Fla.	564
Louisville, Ky.	261	Raleigh, N.C.	564
New Haven, Conn.	274	San Jose, Calif.	567
Minneapolis–St. Paul, Minn.	280	Hamilton–Middletown, Ohio	569
Altoona, Pa.	295	Kalamazoo, Mich.	575
Columbus, Ohio	298	Tacoma, Wash.	578
Huntington, W. Va.	298	Fort Worth, Tex.	580
Cleveland, Ohio	301	New Bedford, Mass.	589
Little Rock, Ark.	301	Pittsburgh, Pa.	600
Jacksonville, Fla.	303	Springfield, Ill.	603
Lancaster, Pa.	312	Fort Wayne, Ind.	606
Stamford–Norwalk, Conn.	320	Asheville, N.C.	612
Worcester, Mass.	335	Birmingham, Ala.	615
Portland, Ore.	337	Stockton, Calif.	617
Nashville, Tenn.	351	Rockford, Ill.	621
San Antonio, Tex.	351	Lowell, Mass.	624
Waco, Tex.	354	Wichita, Kans.	629
Des Moines, Iowa	355	Evansville, Ind.	632
Milwaukee, Wis.	363	South Bend, Ind.	641
Bridgeport, Conn.	369	Sacramento, Calif.	649
Grand Rapids, Mich.	369	Binghamton, N.Y.	651
Toledo, Ohio	372	Galveston, Tex.	652
Utica–Rome, N.Y.	374	Canton, Ohio	655
Shreveport, La.	380	New Britain, Conn.	655
Miami, Fla.	383	Saginaw, Mich.	658
Salt Lake City, Utah	388	Savannah, Ga.	669
Houston, Tex.	393	Lorain, Ohio	677
Racine, Wis.	397	Washington, D.C.	683
Providence, R.I.	402	Cedar Rapids, Mich.	683
Albany–Schenectady, N.Y.	403	Topeka, Kans.	683
Oklahoma City, Okla.	406	San Diego, Calif.	689
Jackson, Miss.	414	Sioux City, Iowa	692
Syracuse, N.Y.	416	Detroit, Mich.	700
Tulsa, Okla.	417	Greensboro–High Point, N.C.	700
Lexington, Ky.	420	Davenport, Iowa	702

SOURCE: After Allan Rodgers, "Some Aspects of Industrial Diversification in the United States," *Economic Geography*, vol. 33, 1957.

nique described does seem to give a good basis for comparison of areas according to manufacturing diversity and should make it possible to study the effects of diversification and specialization on the economic development of cities.

Distribution pattern of manufacturing diversity Rodgers found that no really broad regions of the country—such as the Northeast or the Middle West—stand out

as regions of either diversity or specialization (Figure 16.1). Nevertheless, there are significant elements in the pattern. The large urban agglomeration extending from Baltimore to New York is diversified. On the other hand, notable areas of specialization are apparent in the basic steel region of western Pennsylvania and eastern Ohio and in the motor-vehicle-producing area of southeastern Michigan. It is pointed out, too, that in the less highly industrialized

Fig. 16.1 No really broad regions of the country stand out as areas either of manufacturing diversity or of manufacturing specialization. Cf. Table 16.6. (After Allan Rodgers, "Some Aspects of Industrial Diversification in the United States," *Economic Geography*, vol. 33, 1957, fig. 2.)

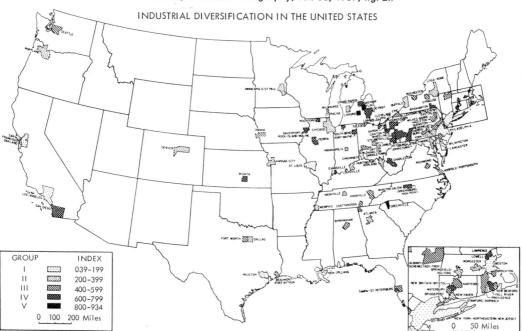

INDUSTRIAL DIVERSIFICATION IN THE UNITED STATES

GROUP	INDEX
I	039–199
II	200–399
III	400–599
IV	600–799
V	800–934

0   100   200 Miles

0   50 Miles

sections of the nation the regional metropolises are highly diversified. Atlanta, Dallas, Kansas City, Minneapolis–St. Paul, and Denver are examples of this tendency.

Other phases of Rodgers's study Rodgers also discussed historical changes in diversification patterns, the role of diversification in local economic development, and seasonal and cyclical variations. Finally, he discussed problems for further research. Some of these were in the form of questions:[22]

> . . . Are there more sensitive measures of diversification that can be used which would reveal more of the industrial composition of individual areas, particularly with regard to their emphasis on cyclically sensitive manufacturing types? Would diversification indices for "basic" types of manufacturing be of greater value than a measure based on the total manufacturing complex? Is there any direct measurable relationship between diversification and employment in urban service activities? What are the effects of diversification on intra-regional income differences?

Rodgers goes on to suggest that in particular we need to know more about the relative effects of diversification and specialization on specific manufacturing areas.

Other aspects of manufacturing cities at the intercity level

There are several other important matters with which the urban geographer is likely to concern himself when comparing, characterizing, and contrasting manufacturing centers.

Product types of manufacturing cities For instance, he is interested in the distribution of different types of cities based on what is manufactured. We can dismiss, of course, the nonbasic manufactures, which tend to occur in all cities roughly in proportion to population. But let us consider

the vast array of lines of manufacture based on markets beyond the city's boundaries.

Some of these lines of basic manufacture stand out, giving cities and their regions recognized reputations. One thinks immediately of Pittsburgh, Youngstown, and other cities of Ohio and western Pennsylvania where the manufacture of iron and steel and their products is dominant; of the textile mills and related manufactures of New England cities; of the predominance of flour milling and meat packing in the cities of western portions of the Middle West; of the automobile manufacturing in the Lower Lake cities; and of various other examples of cities' partaking of regional dominance in some line of manufacture. There are other less conspicuous cases of individual cities known for specialties that do not extend to other cities of the region in which they occur. Alexandersson made all this more concrete when he showed on maps the distribution of the furniture and lumber towns, the primary metal towns, and other urban centers classified by manufacturing specialties.[23]

In reality, most manufacturing cities represent a combination of several types of manufacturing. It would seem that such combinations, if they could be recorded for each standard metropolitan statistical area, might exhibit some interesting distribution patterns. Even so, there would be difficulties; for instance, for some places most of the employment falls in the indefinite categories: other durable goods or other nondurable goods.

Factory location at the intercity level The inquiry regarding manufacturing at the intercity level involves another question: Why are certain manufacturing industries located in City X, or, at least, why are they operating successfully there? Why aren't they in some other city? The answer may

---

[22] *Ibid.*, p. 30.

[23] Gunnar Alexandersson, *The Industrial Structure of American Cities,* University of Nebraska Press, Lincoln, Nebr., 1956.

be so different for different types of manufacturing and for different types of cities
that we can do little more here than hint
at the possibilities.

Many factors may be involved—the
availability of materials (sometimes true
raw materials, but, nowadays, more often
the products of previous manufacture);
power and fuel sources and costs; natural
features, such as the presence of an ocean
harbor or a navigable river; nature, location, and extent of markets; transportation
facilities, service, and costs; and labor (not
only general availability, but cost and quality as well). And such a list is just a start.
As the National Resources Planning Board
put it:

> . . . Although certain manufacturing in-
> dustries do owe their location to the domi-
> nant influence of a particular requirement,
> the majority cannot be properly treated
> without careful consideration of a multi-
> tude of production and organizational fac-
> tors . . .[24]

Not infrequently the location of a certain
manufacturing industry in a city has been
more the result of historical accident than
of any logical weighing of pros and cons,
and the continued success of the industry in the location may best be explained
by inertia and a high degree of locational
tolerance. Many factories would have been
equally successful in any of a number of
other cities, at least in the same region.
Once established, a factory has linkages to
markets, raw materials, and labor supply
which in themselves are locational advantages. Nevertheless, increasing attention is
being paid to scientific procedures for plant
location. This will be referred to further
in the next chapter.

The city's labor force

The labor force
of a city is a human resource. Thus it might
well have been discussed in the chapter on

people in the city. But the chief interest
in a city's labor force is likely to be in connection with manufacturing. Size and quality of the labor force may do much to hold
factories that are already present and to
attract new ones. Hence, the subject is
treated here even though, of course, the
availability and quality of labor are important in business and other activities as
well as in manufacturing.

DEFINITIONS The labor force, as defined
in Census of Population volumes, consists of
all persons fourteen or more years old who
hold jobs or are available for employment,
plus members of the Armed Forces on
active duty. It is the civilian labor force
with which we are concerned here. The experienced civilian labor force is made up
of employed workers and experienced unemployed workers.[25]

LABOR-FORCE DATA IN CENSUS OF POPU-
LATION A good deal of information regarding the civilian labor force is available in
the Census of Population. The data include
number, age distribution, sex, marital status,
race, occupation, industry, class of worker,
employment status, place of work, earnings
by industry and sex, and several other items.

HOW DATA VARY WITH CITY SIZE Availability of these various items of information varies greatly with city size. Some of
the simplest labor-force data are given for
urban places of 2,500 or more population;
slightly less condensed statistics are available for standard metropolitan statistical
areas, for urbanized areas, and for urban
centers of 10,000 population or more; and
still more elaborate data are published for
standard metropolitan statistical areas of
100,000 or more population. But much
labor-force information is available only for
standard metropolitan statistical areas of
250,000 or more population. What has been
said will serve to give a general idea of the

[24] United States National Resources Planning
Board, Industrial Location and National Resources,
1943, p. 2.

[25] For further details regarding definition of the
labor force and its components, see introductory
text of Census of Population: 1960, vol. I, Characteristics of the Population: Detailed Characteristics.

information available regarding the labor force in the Census of Population volumes, but it is only through assembling the labor-force information for two or three cities of substantially different sizes that one comes really to understand the possibilities and limitations of these data.

OTHER LABOR-FORCE DATA AND OTHER SOURCES There are other aspects of the urban labor force that we might be interested in. Educational level is one of these. Here labor-force information must be supplemented by data available for the population as a whole, since details regarding educational level are given only on this basis. The proportion of skilled labor, another item of interest, cannot be determined with exactitude but can be inferred, to some degree, from the detailed occupational breakdown and from median earnings by manufacturing groups.

The census volumes are not the only sources of labor-force information. Indeed, there are important facets of the picture—for example, unionization of labor—in which the Census Bureau is of little help. Here non-government sources sometimes prove of value. And state and city sources may add to the picture.

Intracity Patterns

Unfortunately, from the standpoint of the student of urban geography, statistics relative to manufacturing from either the Census of Manufactures or the Census of Population give little basis for differentiating the interior of the city. An exception to this is found where the urban agglomeration is made up of several political units. In that case some manufacturing data may be available for each political unit within the urban agglomeration, though, if the several units are small, only from the Census of Population or as summary totals from the Census of Manufactures. In fact, the smaller urban centers involved may be too small for much data to be given.

The only census basis for studying variations within the corporate city is the information for industry groups by census tracts. However, as was pointed out earlier, all Census of Population data are by places of residence. There may be some factories, especially in the older industrial cities of the country, where most of the employees live nearby and where industry-group data by tracts would reflect at least vaguely the general patterns of manufacturing in the city. But certainly this would be the exception. With the mobility that now characterizes the labor force in the average city it is unlikely that many people live in or very near the census tract in which they work.

Data sources and field work

Differentiation of manufacturing in the interior of the corporate city, therefore, has to be based almost entirely on city or state data or on field work. Such statistics have little or no countrywide comparability, which is a marked disadvantage, but they serve a purpose that no nationally secured data do.

City and state sources Most cities have a record of the principal manufacturing concerns, the major products of each, and the number of employees. Ordinarily, the last of these is not given in exact figures but in size groups something like this: A, 1,000 or more employees; B, 500 to 1,000 employees; C, 250 to 500 employees; D, 50 to 250 employees; E, less than 50 employees. The details of these divisions may vary greatly from city to city, and generally the data are given only for the incorporated city.

Some states collect and publish data for manufacturing. Massachusetts issues a directory of manufactures which shows manufacturing concerns by name, products, and size class for each minor civil division; and the state of Pennsylvania issues intermittently an industrial directory that shows for each county by classes of manufactures the names and addresses of concerns and their exact employment totals. Whether or not such city and state directories give factory addresses, it is a simple matter to get these addresses locally and to construct maps showing by proportional symbols employment in manufacturing or in some particular kind of manufacturing. Sometimes, where there are several branches of a company in a city, only one gross employment total is given, but generally it is possible through city directories or otherwise to obtain locally the information necessary to divide the employment between individual plants.

Field work in intracity studies Though some statistical data are basic to the study of manufacturing, more direct methods of obtaining these data and other information are often necessary when attention is focused on the interior of a particular city. Field work, supplemented by such standard sources as the *Sanborn Atlas* and the latest air photographic coverage, though not involved in city classifications and work on intercity patterns, is indispensable for intracity studies of manufacturing. It was pointed out in Chapter 11 that the field mapping of manufacturing, or of any other specific type of land use for that matter, may be incidental to the making of a general land-use map or may be carried on separately.

In any event, field mapping serves several useful purposes. First of all, the actual locations of areas of manufacturing land use in the city are plotted, thereby giving a basis for studying the intracity manufacturing pattern and for calculating proportions of various manufacturing land uses. When this is done for several cities on the same basis, generalizations become possible. What, for instance, is the average proportion of the urban area devoted to manufacturing in various types and sizes of manufacturing cities? How is the manufacturing land distributed?

The same field-mapping operation can yield other types of information about manufacturing in the city. The nature of the products and the names of the concerns can be recorded, thus simplifying the plotting of employment data, which, incidentally, may be checked and supplemented in the field. The actual floor area used for each establishment may be obtained at the same time, thus giving the basis for the floor area ratio, a useful measure of the intensity of manufacturing use of land, obtained by dividing the total floor area of buildings by the total lot area.[26] It is possible, too, to observe and record the shapes or appearances of the factories. Interviews, carried on at the same time as the field work, can give a good deal of additional information needed for an understanding of the location of the plants and the nature of their operations. And, of course, field mapping is invaluable as a basis for observing the grouping of different types of factories and the association of factories with other forms of land use.

Distribution patterns of manufacturing within the city

Patterns of the distribution of manufacturing inside the city are a prime concern of the urban geographer.

Patterns in two cities Manufacturing within the city is not evenly distributed. In York, Pennsylvania, which the writer of this book studied several decades ago,[27] a casual visitor might think he had found an essentially even distribution, but closer inspection revealed a more logical pattern (Figure 16.2). The principal factories were strung out along railroad lines which crossed in such a way as to reach out in

[26] Use of the FAR in business zoning was discussed on p. 278.
[27] Raymond E. Murphy, "Johnstown and York: A Comparative Study of Two Industrial Cities," *Annals of the Association of American Geographers*, vol. 25, pp. 175–196, 1935.

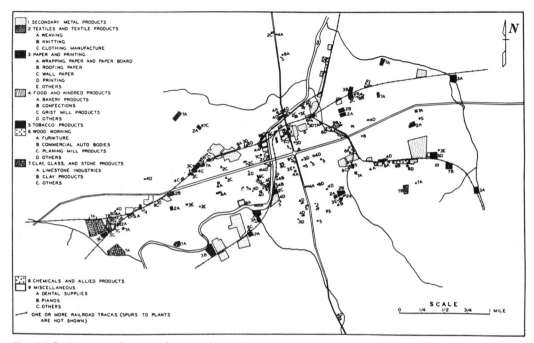

Fig. 16.2 Location of principal types of manufacturing in York, Pa., 1934. (After fig. 12 in Raymond E. Murphy, "Johnstown and York: A Comparative Study of Two Industrial Cities," *Annals of the Association of American Geographers*, vol. 25, 1935.)

four directions from near the center of the city. Lighter manufacturing was widely scattered over most of the remainder of the city, though not represented in the highest-quality residential district which lay to the south. Moreover, York is an old city, and there had been no zoning and little else to restrict the location of factories.

Albert Ballert, writing a decade later about manufacturing in Toledo, Ohio, a city five times as large as York, described the manufacturing establishments as localized in four major and several minor areas (Figure 16.3).[28] Three of the major areas are within the city and form northeast–southwest belts "roughly paralleling the two sides of the Maumee River and the New York Central right-of-way, which leads to Detroit." The fourth major area of localiza-

tion is along the northern border of the city, chiefly just outside the boundary.

Ballert goes on to describe the major areas of concentration. The chief one is the western belt along the New York Central right-of-way. Here, as can be seen from the map, are many of the largest concerns. Among them are the plants of more than a dozen of the city's best-known companies. Many of the products are associated with the automotive industry, which is not surprising since the plants are along a rail line that leads directly to Detroit. Portions of the central and eastern belts of manufacturing are discontinuous; Ballert goes into detail only about the commercial zone of the former and the lower river east shore section of the latter. The lower river east shore has older and heavier industries than most of the remainder of Toledo. These industries include the manufacture of pig iron, coke, and petroleum products as well

---

[28] Albert G. Ballert, "The Primary Functions of Toledo, Ohio," doctoral dissertation, University of Chicago, 1947, pp. 168–178.

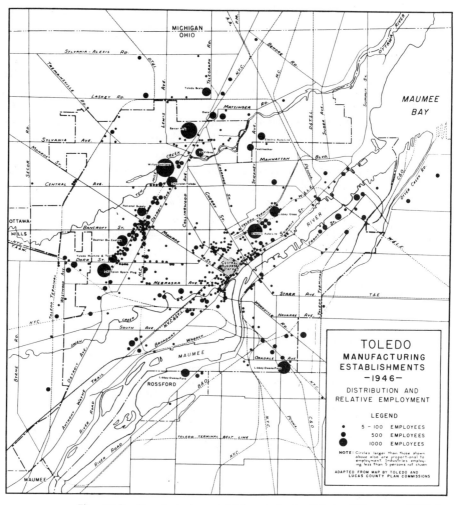

Fig. 16.3 Manufacturing establishments in the Toledo, Ohio, area, 1946, by number of employees. (After fig. 23 in Albert G. Ballert, "The Primary Functions of Toledo, Ohio," doctoral dissertation, University of Chicago, Chicago, 1947.)

as ship building. The commercial zone in the central belt (a zone of blight between the central business district and the residential portions of the city) shows a predominance of light manufactures intermingled with commercial activities.

The northern industrial fringe of the city was the area of most recent industrial growth at the time Ballert wrote. The availability of large blocks of land at a reasonable price appears to have been the chief attractive element operative in the area.

Several other industrial developments were beginning in other peripheral positions around the city.

The pattern generalized The patterns for York and Toledo obviously have little in common, and it is unlikely that the manufacturing patterns of other cities would show much similarity to either of the two. This raises the question, Can the pattern of manufacturing in the city be reduced to definite terms to the degree that business land use has been? Is there a city manufacturing structure such as Proudfoot described for retailing? This is hardly to be expected. Retailing is predominantly local in its appeal, so it benefits from nearness to customers; it follows that demand should result in similar responses to like situations throughout the city. Manufacturing would probably result in repetitive developments of this sort if it were entirely for local consumption, its products sold directly to consumers, but, of course, such is not the case.

Further consideration suggests, however, that we are dealing with two levels of generalization. The patterns described for the two cities are simple surface patterns, the products of casual observation. But there is another type of pattern, that involving underlying similarities based on locational influences. This is at the site level. To what extent is there a pattern of manufacturing establishments at the site level that is reasonably repetitive from city to city? Certain probable elements of such a pattern can be pointed out (Figure 16.4). It is believed that most of them could be identified in York and Toledo as well as in other cities.

OLDER MANUFACTURING DISTRICTS IN THE CENTRAL CITY For instance, most manufacturing cities have a few (possibly one or two or three) rather well-defined, long-established factory concentrations or districts within the central city, the sizes of the districts and the degree of concentration of plants varying from city to city. Usually,

Fig. 16.4 Schematic diagram of a middle-sized American manufacturing city, showing examples of the various situations in which plants typically occur. Numbers and letters refer as follows: *Older developments:* 1, manufacturing district (*a,* on waterfront, *b,* at waterfall, *c,* on railroad); 2, central business district (*a,* light manufacturing serving the central business district, *b,* loft-type factories in outer portion); 3, scattered factories in residential areas; *More recent developments:* 4, industrial district resulting from clearance and redevelopment, may or may not be organized or planned; 5, outlying industrial area, may or may not be organized or planned. Approximate edge of central business district is marked by broken-line circle; dotted line sets off zone of loft factories.

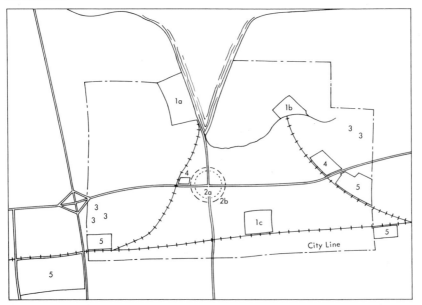

these districts contain some of the city's largest factories, often the factories that have given the city much of its reputation in manufacturing.

Such factory districts have originated in various ways. Some were localized originally by the presence of navigable water, and the industries often reflect the waterfront site. Petroleum products manufacture, the manufacture of iron and steel, and other heavy manufacturing and processing operations related to imports are common along waterfronts.[29]

In other cases, for example, in some of the New England cities, waterfalls were important in the original manufacturing development. Though this source of power is no longer used, the falls explain the present location of the manufacturing districts.

But ready availability of rail facilities has probably been the most important of all bases for localizing the major manufacturing districts in cities. Railroad sidings have been extended and spurs constructed, but such developments ordinarily have not gone far from the main lines. Usually, the major districts follow the principal railroad lines which often, of course, have followed val-

[29] How many lines of manufacturing represented on a waterfront really need to use the waterfront? This and a number of other questions dealing with waterfront manufacturing are raised by Arthur F. Loeben in "Philadelphia Waterfront Industry," which appeared in the *Geographical Review*, vol. 47, pp. 272–273, 1957, and was based on a report by W. A. Douglas Jackson (see reference list at end of chapter). The Philadelphia waterfront manufactures are classified by Jackson into tidewater-based industries, river water-using industries, and tidewater-related industries. Tidewater-related industries utilize the cheap water transportation but do not depend on it so wholly as tidewater-based industries. Many port cities have waterfront industrial belts. Although they are likely to extend well beyond the city's corporate limits, they are part of the urban area's industrial complex and hence within the province of the urban geographer. It would be worthwhile to study the waterfront manufacturing of some other cities and to see the degree to which they conformed to Jackson's findings for Philadelphia.

leys. Such districts frequently have linear or strung-out shapes relating to the railroads even in flat areas where relief is no factor.

Though typically of early origin, some of the older manufacturing areas of the central city have continued to grow. For example, in an active industrial city, the waterfront factory district may still be expanding.

CENTRAL BUSINESS DISTRICT MANUFACTURING A second though minor element in the picture of older manufacturing areas is factory development in the central business district. Light manufacturing is characteristic. The types are chiefly those that depend on the centrality the central business district has to offer and can afford to pay for it, such as newspapers, and other activities, such as job printing, that benefit by proximity to the industries that require centrality.

Loft-type factories at the edge of the district represent a sub-type of central business district manufacturing. Garment manufacture, for example, is in this position in some large cities, profiting by nearness to showrooms.

SCATTERED FACTORIES IN RESIDENTIAL AREAS In most cities, factories, singly or in small clusters, are scattered throughout the poorer residential areas of the city, inherited from a time when no one thought much about a logical arrangement of land uses. Generally, the industries represented in these locations are light, not requiring railroad service, and frequently they are community or service industries, e.g., a local bakery or a local ice-cream plant.

INDUSTRIAL DISTRICTS RESULTING FROM CLEARANCE AND REDEVELOPMENT Though no exact line can be drawn, the types of manufacturing described include most of the older factories of the city. The several types still to be discussed are in general of more recent origin. For example, a few industrial districts have resulted from recent clearance and redevelopment in the older, more run-down sections of cities. Such developments may be in old industrial areas, but, more likely, they are in areas that had been characterized by mixed functions. Such redeveloped factory districts may border the central business district or may be some distance from it.

OUTLYING INDUSTRIAL AREAS   Another element in the manufacturing picture of the city is the outlying industrial area. Such developments are usually of moderately recent origin and are located in the outer portions of the city or even just beyond the city line. The latter location is favored because land is likely to be available and cheaper, taxes lower, and regulations less stringent than inside the central city. Plants of outlying industrial areas are often large. Airplane factories, chemical plants, and other space-using types are characteristic. Heavy industries may be found in a waterfront belt far beyond the limits of the central city. Sometimes the city boundary has been extended to include outlying industrial areas originally located just beyond the city line.

ORGANIZED INDUSTRIAL DISTRICTS   Lastly, we come to the most recent development, the organized or planned industrial district. A single great manufacturing establishment is itself a planned industrial district, and such one-company towns as Hershey, Pennsylvania, and Kohler, Wisconsin, are carefully planned. But the modern organized industrial district as here described is designed to attract an assemblage of small and medium-sized plants.

> An "organized" or "planned" industrial district is a tract of land which is subdivided and developed according to a comprehensive plan for the use of a community of industries, with streets, rail lead tracks, and utilities installed before sites are sold to prospective occupants.
>
> The comprehensive plan must provide for adequate control of the area and buildings through restrictions and zoning with a view to protecting the investments of both developers of the district and industries occupying the improved sites.[30]

[30] Theodore K. Pasma, Organized Industrial Dis-

The term industrial park is probably best restricted to a large and elaborately organized industrial district. In practice, however, it has come to be used as synonymous with organized industrial district, or, popularly, even in preference. An industrial park is the dream of many a small, tax-burdened community.

The location of an organized industrial district is generally carefully chosen. Railroads have developed a number of organized districts in order to increase the freight on their lines; but others have been developed as private districts, local community group districts, and districts organized by various combinations of railroads, private interests, and community groups. Railroads are no longer considered essential for such a district. Now location on freeways, especially near interchanges, often is desired. Industries of almost any type may occupy the areas, wholesale establishments and storage yards as well as manufacturing, but zoning restrictions commonly assure that noise, smoke, and offensive odors be avoided. Landscaped grounds, parking areas, and new, one-story factory buildings are typical. The sites may be sold or disposed of on long-term leases. Often there are close relationships between the concerns represented in an organized industrial district, the finished product of one factory being the raw material of another.

Organized industrial districts are analogous to controlled shopping centers (pages 263 to 264) and to housing subdivisions (pages 393 to 394) as units of residential development. They are often at the edge of the city or just outside, since there is rarely enough space for them inside the central city. But where space permits, organized industrial districts may be developed inside the central city, and redevelopment of areas of deterioration may open space inside the city for such districts. Obviously, then, or-

tricts: A Tool for Community Development, Area Development Division, Office of Technical Services, U.S. Department of Commerce, 1955, p. 1.

ganized industrial districts are not locationally distinct from some of the other manufacturing areas; the distinction is based instead upon the planning of the development.[31]

A PRELIMINARY ATTEMPT What has been presented in the preceding paragraphs is a highly tentative attempt to generalize about manufacturing in the city. It is admittedly crude and preliminary. But by classifying the areas of industrial development in a number of cities in some such manner, we should be able to improve upon the generalizations.

The pattern in great cities The pattern is much more complex in large cities. Moreover, not all development is taking place at the edge of the city, with only occasional replacement in the city interior, as has been implied. In Chicago, for example, large areas hitherto inefficiently or incompletely used are being developed for manufacturing. This probably reflects in part the influence upon Chicago of the newly improved St. Lawrence Seaway.

On the other hand, recent industrial growth in the Boston agglomeration has been greatest at the western edge. Route 128, following a circumferential course near the western border of the Boston Urbanized Area, has proved especially attractive to industrial concerns, particularly near the intersections with highways radiating from downtown Boston. These are *outlying industrial areas* in terms of the schematic diagram, Figure 16.4.

In summary, large cities are more complex than smaller ones and hence cannot be expected to reflect as exactly a standard pattern. Nevertheless, even in large cities the manufacturing pattern probably can be resolved into identifiable site types.

[31] For further details regarding organized industrial districts, see *ibid.* Also see Robert L. Wrigley, Jr., "Organized Industrial Districts," *Journal of Land and Public Utility Economics*, vol. 23, pp. 180–198, 1947.

Product types within the city

If a map were made showing the extent of each manufacturing plant in the city and, by color or patterns, showing the product groups by plants, the picture presented usually would be a highly complex one. Site types could be identified, and the major elements of distribution pointed out and explained as was done for York and for the Toledo area. Even specific explanations might not be too difficult in some cases—one factory was obviously located long ago to take advantage of a waterfall; the cement plant at the edge of town marks the location of an outcrop of special-quality limestone; a candy factory was the creation of one man whose family had owned the particular site for several generations. But it would be a complex task, indeed, to determine exactly why every plant was located precisely where it is and would hardly add enough to our general picture to be worth the effort.

In an attempt to bring some order out of the complexity, however, we might be interested in applying measures of concentration. Are some types of manufacturing concentrated in certain districts of the city? Where data can be assembled, this can be tested by means of the location quotient:

$$\frac{\dfrac{\text{Employees in X manufacturing group in district}}{\text{Employees in X manufacturing group in city}}}{\dfrac{\text{Employees in all manufacturing within district}}{\text{Employees in all manufacturing in city}}}$$

Values over 1, you will recall, indicate some concentration; the higher the number, the greater the concentration.

It should be noted, too, that manufacturing does not stand alone. How is its distribution related to the distribution of other activities in the city—to commercial areas, to transportation, and to residential areas? These relationships are certainly within the scope of the urban geographer's inquiry.

Other items for investigation

There are many other topics that might

be investigated in connection with manufacturing in the interior of the city.

Linkages Linkages, or relationships
between plants, is one of these. Examples
are a factory and a machine shop that serves
it, and the relationships between a large
manufacturing concern and smaller ones
that do subcontracting for it. The pattern
of linkages may be extremely difficult to
work out, at least in any detail, but some
appreciation of it is essential to an understanding of the manufacturing complex of
a city or district. The whole matter seems
to present some interesting research challenges.

Morphology, function, and age Morphology, function, and age may be reflected
in the manufacturing picture of a city. Thus
certain primary types of manufactures—e.g.,
blast furnace operations and cement manufacture—have such distinctive form elements that they can ordinarily be recognized at a glance. To what extent is this
true of other types of manufacturing?

In the study of York, Pennsylvania, referred to earlier in this chapter, it was found
that most of the weaving mills were old
brick buildings several stories in height.
The city's hosiery manufacture, on the other
hand, was carried on in newer, lower,
brighter buildings. Also, the textile and textile products factories as a group occupied
only one-seventh as much land as metal
products manufactures while employing
about two-thirds as many workers.

With current emphasis upon single-
story factory buildings surrounded by ample
parking space and parklike grounds, many
of these differences are disappearing. Nevertheless, it might be worthwhile in any one
city to see what distinctive features remain
as indicators of manufacturing types. Are
the remaining morphological differences between establishments more the result of the
plant's age or of the nature of the manufacturing specialty?

The labor force at the intracity level

In earlier pages of this chapter it was
pointed out that details regarding the labor
force are important in the study of manufacturing. There the concern was with
labor-force characteristics that might differentiate one city from another. The larger
the city, the greater the detail the Census
of Population contains regarding the labor
force. But, it might have been added, the
larger the city, the less realistic it is to think
of a single labor force, since people do not
care to travel across a large city in going
to work. Thus, though a primary concern
for a city of 200,000 might be the labor force
for the municipality as a whole, for a city
the size of Chicago the problem would be
more nearly one of the nature of the labor
force of that section of the city in which,
let us·say, a factory is to be located.

Labor force by manufacturing groups
Some data of this sort have already been
referred to (see page 336). The Census of
Population records by census tracts the
number of persons who give their employment as falling in each of nine manufacturing groups. This, to a certain degree, gives
the existing distribution in the urban area
of people with some experience in each of
various general fields of manufacturing.

Where people work There is another
item of interest in connection with the manufacturing labor force. In the 1960 *Census of
Population* volumes there are some data on
where people work. For the first time, one
can determine how many of the employed
persons of an urban center work inside the
county of residence and how many work
outside. Also, by census tracts, data are
given on those who work inside the central
city (or cities) of a standard metropolitan
statistical area, what proportion lives in the
remainder of the standard metropolitan
statistical area (in each of the several counties where more than one county is in-

volved), and what proportion lives outside the standard metropolitan statistical area. These data refer to all sorts of employment, but for places that are predominantly manufacturing centers movements of the manufacturing labor force can be inferred.

Changing Manufacturing Patterns

Many of the statistics useful for studying current manufacturing are also available for several past censuses, so the manufacturing picture can be studied for a specific period in the past as well as for a succession of periods.

The change through time considered by Thompson and Rodgers

Two of the studies discussed earlier involved the past to some degree. Thompson, though primarily concerned with presenting a technique, applied this technique to both 1939 and 1947 data;[32] and Rodgers, though concentrating chiefly on 1950 conditions, did some work with historical changes in diversification.[33]

Changes in census reporting

One problem that arises in studying changing patterns is that from one census to the next there are likely to be some changes in terminology and in ways of presenting information. This means that anyone working with data for more than one period must study the volumes of the census carefully to make sure he is attaining the maximum that is possible in continuity and comparability. Rodgers, for instance, when he attempted to study changes in diversification patterns over several decades, found difficulties of this sort.

Intercity shifts in manufacturing

Not all factories are in urban locations, but a large percentage of them are. It is not illogical, therefore, to concentrate on urban

[32] Thompson, *op. cit.*, pp. 424–436.
[33] Rodgers, *op. cit.*, pp. 22–24.

areas in studying gains and losses in manufacturing.

Such gains or losses may be thought of as absolute, e.g., the loss when textile mills close down in a small New England city. Or they may be thought of as relative, e.g., when a city gains in number of manufacturing employees but at a lower rate of increase than the United States as a whole. Then we say the city has lost relatively.

Percentage gain or loss versus relative change If we were to use Census of Manufactures data and calculate the percentage increase or decrease from, say, 1958 to 1963 in all employees or in value added by manufacture for different cities or standard metropolitan statistical areas, the results might not be very significant. If the period were one of general growth nearly all the standard metropolitan statistical areas or cities would show percentage gains, with the percentages likely to be highest for small cities or small standard metropolitan statistical areas which had small totals to begin with. It is easier to achieve a large percentage gain from a small base. This is a disadvantage of using percentage change; it tends to make the gains or losses of small producers appear large and hence gives a misleading picture. Note, for example, that for a city with only 500 manufacturing employees, the addition of 500 more would amount to a 100 per cent gain; for a city with 50,000 manufacturing employees, the 500 would mean only a 1 per cent gain.

A more useful technique for analyzing such gains and losses involves the relative-change idea, which has been used in several places in this book. We might calculate the percentage of the United States total production workers that a standard metropolitan statistical area had in 1958 and the percentage of the United States total that it had in 1963. The difference between these two percentages, though not a percentage itself, is an index of relative change.

Plus figures indicate relative gain and minus figures, relative loss.

A map on this basis for manufacturing in the United States for 1958–1963 period would show relative gain or relative loss for various urban areas. It would show which cities increased in importance in the country's manufacturing picture and which lost, thus presenting a pattern that would merit investigation. Or such a map could be based on the cities of only one section of the country, such as New England, or even on a city and its suburbs. Note, however, that suburbs can be included only when they have populations of 10,000 or more, since in the Census of Manufactures even summary manufacturing data are not given for smaller places.

Reasons for manufacturing concerns entering or leaving a city

Another approach to the matter of manufacturing gains or losses is based on a study of the movements of specific concerns into and out of any one city. Obviously, this involves local data and local field work. What new factories have come into the urban area in the last decade and what reasons did the firms have for selecting the city? What firms have left in the last decade and what reasons do they give for having left? Where did they go and why? Some combination of questionnaires and interviews is generally called for in this type of investigation.

Changes within the urban agglomeration

Within each individual urban area, too, the manufacturing picture is changing. The most common shift is a movement outward from the central city to the suburbs and satellites, where land is often cheaper and more abundant, taxes lower, and regulations less onerous. In addition to the factories that they may acquire in this way, the suburban areas are likely to be more attractive than the central city for manufacturers moving into the area from elsewhere or for new factories just getting started.

Fortunately, data furnished by the Census Bureau give a fairly good basis for studying this movement. Our question becomes: Have the central cities of standard metropolitan statistical areas been losing out in manufacturing compared with the remainder of the standard metropolitan statistical areas? The necessary data can be obtained from the Census of Manufactures, which gives number of establishments, number of production workers, and value added by manufacture for the standard metropolitan statistical area as a whole and for the central city or cities of each standard metropolitan statistical area.

Suburbanization of manufacturing in standard metropolitan areas

The problem of suburbanization of manufacturing in standard metropolitan areas was the subject of a special study by Evelyn Kitagawa, a demographer, and Donald Bogue, a sociologist. Their results were published in 1955.[34]

Kitagawa and Bogue's basic concern was with contrasting the amount of manufacturing in the central city or cities of each standard metropolitan area with that in the remainder of the area. This remainder, that is, the standard metropolitan area minus the central city or cities, they referred to as the "ring." For the purposes of their study, "suburbanization" referred to the process which results in an increasing proportion of a standard metropolitan area's manufacturing (or other activity) being located in its ring. Using Census of Manufactures data they worked out the change in degree of suburbanization of manufacturing for the "principal standard metropolitan areas of 1940" for 1929 to 1939 and for 1939 to 1947.[35] Separate calculations were made

[34] Evelyn M. Kitagawa and Donald J. Bogue, *Suburbanization of Manufacturing Activity within Standard Metropolitan Areas,* Studies in Population Distribution no. 9, Scripps Foundation, Miami, Ohio, 1955.

[35] Actually, the term standard metropolitan area was not in use until 1949, but the Census Bureau

for each of the three standard measures of manufacturing variation—production workers, value added by manufacture, and number of establishments—since each, Kitagawa and Bogue said, reflects a somewhat different aspect of manufacturing activity. Though the results differed somewhat for the three measures, Kitagawa and Bogue found that there had been a definite increase in the proportion of manufacturing in the ring in the 1929–1939 interval, but that the proportion had remained essentially unchanged for the 1939–1947 period. Population, they found, suburbanized noticeably during both intervals.

But the study went far beyond these simple determinations. For instance, Kitagawa and Bogue used various statistical techniques (multiple regression, analysis of variance, analysis of covariance, etc.) in attempts to correlate shifts in manufacturing within the standard metropolitan area with other factors, such as population and population characteristics as given in the Census of Population. This was done in order to see how manufacturing shifts are associated with changes in the general structure of the community.

The authors contended, too, that in grouping all standard metropolitan areas in order to reach a general conclusion about what is happening in the ring versus the central city or cities, much information was lost, since the standard metropolitan areas varied so much.[36] The results were, therefore, of little value when applied to the problems or plans of a specific city. However, generalizations arrived at in the Kitagawa and Bogue study are formulated, as far as is possible, in terms that permit their application directly to the problems or

plans of specific cities. In line with this purpose, data for the central cities and rings of all standard metropolitan areas in the country are included in appendix tables of their study.

Suburbanization of manufacturing since 1947 The study just described carried the story through the 1947 *Census of Manufactures,* but was concluded too early to take the 1954 or 1958 censuses into account. Did suburbanization of manufacturing continue? Table 16.7, based on production workers in manufacturing in twenty standard metropolitan statistical areas, suggests that it did, at least in some degree. In seventeen of the areas, the land outside the central city or cities gained in its proportion of the production workers between 1947 and 1954. In thirteen of the areas, there was a similar gain between 1954 and 1958.

Reasons for variations in suburbanization of manufacturing The fact that in most standard metropolitan statistical areas suburbanization of manufacturing has been going on is hardly surprising. It seems to represent a continuation of a trend that has been under way for several decades with a slight interruption between 1939 and 1947—the period of World War II.

But why is manufacturing so much more suburbanized in some standard metropolitan statistical areas than in others? Some possible reasons are listed in Table 16.8. One might be able to match some of the reasons with individual cities. For example, one might safely assume that topography is of considerable importance in accounting for the high degree of suburbanization of industry in the Pittsburgh Standard Metropolitan Statistical Area. There simply has not been enough flat land for expansion inside the legal city. In Boston, the virtual impossibility of annexing adjacent land goes far toward explaining the high degree of suburbanization of manufacturing. But an-

has outlined standard metropolitan areas as they would have been for these earlier years and assembled manufacturing data for them.

[36] Information was lost, too, through not considering suburbanization except to the ring, since, in many urban areas, suburbanization goes on outside the ring.

Table 16.7   Percentage of manufacturing production workers employed
              outside the central city or cities in twenty standard metro-
              politan statistical areas and their earlier equivalents in
              1947, 1954, and 1958

SMSA or earlier equivalent	1947	1954	1958
Albuquerque, N. Mex.	31.0	54.0	39.8
Atlanta, Ga.	27.5	39.0	40.9
Boston, Mass.	48.0	66.0	69.1
Chicago, Ill.	30.0	35.0	33.7
Cleveland, Ohio	17.0	30.0	31.5
Davenport–Rock Island–Moline, Ia.–Ill.	31.0	40.0	41.1
Denver, Colo.	10.0	9.0	33.4
Flint, Mich.	2.5	20.0	32.1
Hartford, Conn.	35.0	60.0	67.6
Indianapolis, Ind.	14.0	24.0	22.8
Minneapolis–St. Paul, Minn.	14.0	22.5	26.6
New York–Northeastern New Jersey	33.5	37.0	34.5
Omaha, Neb.	7.8	9.8	16.1
Philadelphia, Pa.	39.0	44.0	45.3
Phoenix, Ariz.	64.0	53.0	43.0
Pittsburgh, Pa.	76.0	78.0	77.6
Richmond, Va.	19.0	16.0	18.0
San Francisco–Oakland, Calif.	44.0	50.0	49.9
Seattle, Wash.	9.0	20.0	29.9
Wichita, Kans.	44.0	66.0	70.9

SOURCE: Data from U.S. Bureau of the Census, Census of Manufactures. No attempt
has been made to take into account possible central city expansion through annexation,
or official changes in extent of standard metropolitan areas or standard metropolitan
statistical areas during the period involved.

Table 16.8   Possible reasons for an unusually high degree of suburbanization of manufacturing
              in some standard metropolitan statistical areas

1. Topography   A central city located in hilly country with narrow valleys may have little land suitable for factory sites. Under such circumstances factories may have extended along the valleys or onto other outlying land beyond the city limits.

2. Late manufacturing development   Cities that have had little manufacturing and are now belatedly attracting factory development may have little room for such activities except beyond the city border. This tendency is accentuated by the great space needs imposed by modern factory design. In older cities, new industries seem to prefer to erect new buildings in the suburbs rather than to remodel vacant ones in the central city.

3. Manufacturing type   Certain types of manufacturing, such as oil refineries, steel mills, meat packing plants, and aircraft factories with test-flying fields, may create nuisances to such a degree that location beyond the city's boundaries is imperative.

4. Nonfocused transportation   Along a harbor front, navigable river, canal, or belt railroad the advantages for manufacturing are spread out for a long distance. This can lead to extensive decentralization. Truck transportation also has the potentiality of being nonfocused. (See Point 6.)

5. Annexation difficulties   Some central cities are in sections of the country where annexation of surrounding land is essentially impossible. This is especially true in New England. Under such conditions a high degree of suburbanization of manufacturing is normal.

6. Extensive highway transportation facilities

Table 16.8 *(continued)*

With well-designed freeways and other modern highway facilities, factory development is less restricted to the central city.

7. **Government policy** Some metropolitan areas experienced much of their manufacturing growth with the development of defense plants during World War II and were thus subject to government policy of avoiding concentration. After the war, some of these suburbanized plants converted to civilian goods.

8. **Tax laws** In some metropolitan areas, manufacturing plants have been located outside the central city in order to avoid paying the high taxes of the city or taxes to both the city and the county.

9. **Failure of former factories** As old manufacturing operations located in the central city die from obsolescence or other causes their facilities and space are often converted to parking or other nonmanufacturing uses. This has the indirect effect of suburbanizing manufacturing.

10. **Zoning** Where the zoning ordinance of the central city fails to set aside enough land or large enough parcels of land for manufacturing, development in suburban areas is encouraged.

11. **High land values in central city** The high costs of factory sites inside a city may result in industries locating just outside the city.

12. **Satellite manufacturing cities** In some cases manufacturing may be highly concentrated in the central city and in one or two adjacent satellite cities which are not quite large enough to be classed as central cities but may have had their factories as long as the central city itself. These satellite cities may have a suffi-

cient share of all manufacturing so that industry is highly suburbanized.

13. **Location of central business district** In a few standard metropolitan statistical areas the central business district of the central city may be very near one of the corporate boundaries. Where manufacturing plants are arrayed around the central business district a considerable proportion may thus lie outside the central city.

14. **Definition of standard metropolitan statistical area boundaries** There is considerable variation in size and nature of counties included in standard metropolitan statistical areas. If a very large and densely populated county is included, a large amount of industry outside the central city may also be included. This means a high degree of suburbanization of manufacturing.

15. **Promotion by railroads** In some standard metropolitan statistical areas railroad companies have promoted manufacturing growth on sites strung out along their rights-of-way and therefore extending out of the city. This may have resulted in a fairly high degree of suburbanization of manufacturing.

16. **Rural labor force** In some instances a substantial rural and suburban labor force may tempt industrialists to move their factories to suburban locations.

17. **Factory design and space requirements** The relatively large space needs of new factories for plant construction, parking facilities, etc., often favor a suburban location.

18. **A single-industry city** When a city is essentially a single-industry city, new manufacturing may actually be discouraged by the dominant firm and may be forced to occupy suburban positions.

SOURCE: Modified from list in Evelyn M. Kitagawa and Donald J. Bogue, *Suburbanization of Manufacturing Activity within Standard Metropolitan Areas*, Studies in Population Distribution no. 9, Scripps Foundation, Miami, Ohio, 1955, pp. 121–123.

other factor helps to explain the increase in suburbanization in the Boston area since 1947: Route 128, which follows an arcuate course in the outer portions of the Boston Standard Metropolitan Statistical Area, has become famous for the many factories it has attracted. A high degree of suburbanization of manufacturing in a standard metropolitan statistical area is likely to be associated with a combination of several of

the factors listed and possibly with others not included in the list.

The Los Angeles Standard Metropolitan Statistical Area presents an interesting problem in the matter of suburbanization of industry. Fifty-three per cent of the area's production workers were employed outside the central city in 1954. This is surprising in view of the huge area of Los Angeles, itself. The city's area is more than twice that of Chicago and nearly ten times that of Boston. We might expect, therefore, that the Los Angeles Standard Metropolitan Statistical Area would show considerable centralization of manufacturing. Why is this not so?

Several contributing explanations have been suggested.[37] For one thing, there are several large aircraft manufacturing concerns which are dispersed for safety reasons and because of their need for extremely large sites. The Los Angeles system of freeways has made it possible for factories to operate efficiently outside the central cities, and the railroads have been active in developing sites outside the city. Since 1950, the government has requested that plants be dispersed for reasons of national defense, and this has been a factor in the situation. Another reason is the rapid growth of population in some of the areas adjacent to Los Angeles. Firms have located in the suburban areas in order to capitalize on the available labor supply.

Of course, the opposite situation prevails in some standard metropolitan statistical areas, with manufacturing showing a high degree of centralization. Some of the possible reasons for this situation have been summed up in Table 16.9. As an example, we can take the Omaha Standard Metropolitan Statistical Area, in which only 9.8 per cent of the production workers were employed outside the central city in 1954.

It is reported that, prior to World War II, 50 per cent of the land within Omaha's city limits was zoned for industry although a great deal of the area so zoned was not actually in industrial use.[38] Much of the wartime expansion took the form of extra working shifts in the meat-packing and cold-storage plants which dominate Omaha's manufacturing. A few factories developed outside the city limits, but they were very much the exception. In 1945 the city zoned

[37] Kitagawa and Bogue, op. cit., p. 97.
[38] Ibid., pp. 103–104.

the territory within a 3-mile belt outside the city limits, but this zoning provided only an insignificant amount of industrial land. Residential development preceded industry in the suburbs and this, it is said, brought about a resistance to industrial expansion there as well as resulting in an actual barrier to such development in some cases. New industry found it more convenient to locate inside the city limits since industrially zoned land with good railroad access remained there.

Supposedly, though, industry may tend to suburbanize to a greater degree in the Omaha area in the future, owing to the lower tax rate outside the city limits and the large space needs of some industries. From Table 16.7 one might infer that by 1958 some of this suburban industrial expansion had already taken place.

Other challenges in the problem of suburbanization of manufacturing Although the bases for city variations in suburbanization of manufacturing are of interest, the urban geographer would like to go further. For instance, if we were to plot the proportions of suburbanization for all standard metropolitan statistical areas on a United States map, would we find any marked regional tendencies? If so, with what factors might the pattern be correlated?

Particularly challenging, too, are great changes in the proportion of suburbanization (Table 16.7). Why did Hartford, Albuquerque, and Wichita increase so markedly in suburbanization of manufacturing in the 1947 to 1954 interval? And why did Phoenix decrease during this period and also between 1954 and 1958? [39]

[39] Phoenix had an area of 17.1 square miles in 1950; by 1960 it had expanded its limits to 110 square miles. Although we do not know how much of the annexation took place prior to the 1958 *Census of Manufactures,* annexation might easily account for the increased centralization of manufacturing.

Table 16.9   Possible reasons for an unusually low degree of suburbanization of manufacturing in some standard metropolitan statistical areas

1. **Topography** In a hilly area the central city may contain the only land suitable for most types of manufacturing. Swamps and lowlands subject to flooding also may keep industry inside a city. Or, all of the waterfront area suitable for port activities and water-oriented industries may be inside the city's boundaries.

2. **Utilities** Factories require water, sewage disposal, gas, electric power, and fire protection. These may be available only from the central city which may be reluctant to provide facilities for suburban areas. Under semi-desert conditions, particularly, the central city may be the only part of the standard metropolitan statistical area where water and other utilities are available.

3. **Early industrialization** Some cities founded as industrial centers grew up around factories, thus producing a centralized pattern of manufacturing. This centralized pattern may have been maintained despite recent trends toward suburbanization.

4. **Use of old buildings** Industry sometimes expands by taking over old warehouses or old factory buildings left by earlier industries. Some cities that have become industrialized only recently have done so by conversion to factory use of old, centrally-located buildings. Such developments would result in centralization of manufacturing.

5. **Growth through expansion of existing plants** In some standard metropolitan statistical areas most of the expansion of manufacturing volume has come about through expansion of old, well-established firms located in the central city.

6. **Single-industry or single-firm towns** Where a single industry or single firm dominates manufacturing employment, it is often located within the city limits and is closely identified with the central city. This may be done to such a degree that the city administration and financial interests have actually discouraged the coming of other industries that might conceivably have located in less centralized portions of the urban area.

7. **Zoning** The early adoption of a zoning program that made liberal provision for manufacturing has favored centralization in some cities.

8. **Original area of city** Other things being equal, we should expect that a city whose boundary was liberally drawn to begin with would have a relatively low degree of suburbanization of manufacturing.

9. **Annexation** Some states have liberal provisions by which central cities can annex adjacent territory. Such additions bring industries inside the city's boundaries, thus reducing the percentage of workers employed outside the central city or cities.

10. **Revival of industrial development** Some cities had large manufacturing developments before the depression of the early 1930s. They were centralized since that was the pattern of the time. World War II brought a resurgence of manufacturing which tended to use renovated facilities in the central city, and this pattern of centralization has been maintained.

11. **Type of manufacturing** Some types of manufacturing, such as jewelry and garment manufacture, seek a central location to be near other industries, near suppliers, or near a market. This favors localization of these kinds of manufacturing not only within the city but within the city's central area.

12. **Focused transportation** Where transportation facilities are highly focused upon the city but only limited outside the city's boundaries, industries are likely to be centralized. This is the antithesis of point 4 in table 16.8.

13. **Small number of plants** If a metropolitan area contains only one or a few important manufacturing plants and these lie inside the central city, manufacturing may appear to be highly centralized although the total number of persons employed may not be great.

14. **Cheap labor from slum areas** In some larger cities factories develop to use the cheap labor from slum areas at the edge of the central business district. This favors location of manufacturing within the city's central area.

SOURCE: Modified from list in Evelyn M. Kitagawa and Donald J. Bogue, *Suburbanization of Manufacturing Activity within Standard Metropolitan Areas*, Studies in Population Distribution no. 9, Scripps Foundation, Miami, Ohio, 1955, pp. 123–124.

Smaller study units desirable Although the contrast of central city or cities with the remainder of the standard metropolitan statistical area (Table 16.7) forms a practicable basis for studying the changing manufacturing pattern of the metropolis, it has the disadvantage of neglecting differences in small areal units in the area. It would be desirable to base the calculations on minor civil divisions and even on subdivisions of the central city. But manufacturing data even in summary totals are given only for cities of 10,000 or more population, and where many political units surround the central cities and make up much of the total agglomeration only a few may be that large.

Anyone wishing to study the suburbanization of manufacturing in the Chicago Standard Metropolitan Statistical Area, for example, faces exactly this problem. Outside the central city there are some cities of 10,000 inhabitants or more, but much of the area is made up of villages and cities too small for manufacturing data to be given.

Sometimes it is possible to supplement United States Census data with information from special local sources. In a study of suburbanization of manufacturing in the Chicago area, for example, Martin Reinemann supplemented Census of Manufacture data with information obtained from the records of the Territorial Information Department of the Commonwealth Edison Company of Chicago.[40] This made it possible to use some smaller unit areas and to study the movement of industries into these areas (Figure 16.5).

Summary

In this chapter manufacturing was considered as a basis for comparisons of cities and for studying patterns of distribution of cities; and manufacturing patterns within

[40] Martin W. Reinemann, "The Pattern and Distribution of Manufacturing in the Chicago Area," *Economic Geography*, vol. 36, pp. 139–144, 1960.

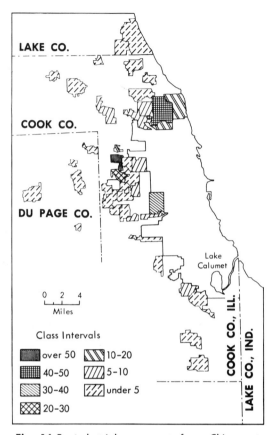

Fig. 16.5 Industrial movement from Chicago to suburban-fringe zone, from 1946 to June, 1954, by suburban units and number of plants that arrived. (After Martin W. Reinemann, "The Pattern and Distribution of Manufacturing in the Chicago Area," *Economic Geography*, vol. 36, 1960, fig. 3.)

the city were discussed at even greater length. Moreover, changes in the intercity manufacturing pattern were considered as well as changes in the patterns within urban areas.

The next chapter will go beyond analysis of the present scene in presenting something of the work of communities and private interests in bringing about changes in the industrial character of urban areas.

Selected References

Alexandersson, Gunnar: *The Industrial Structure of American Cities*, University of Nebraska Press, Lincoln, Neb., 1956.

Ballert, Albert G.: *The Primary Functions of Toledo, Ohio,* doctoral dissertation, University of Chicago, Chicago, 1947.

Cramer, Robert E.: *Manufacturing Structure of the Cicero District, Metropolitan Chicago,* Research Paper 27, Department of Geography, University of Chicago, Chicago, 1952.

De Geer, Sten: "The American Manufacturing Belt," *Geografiska Annaler,* vol. 9, pp. 233–359, 1927.

De Meirleir, Marcel J.: *Manufactural Occupance in the West Central` Area of Chicago,* Research Paper 11, Department of Geography, University of Chicago, Chicago, 1950.

Florence, P. Sargant: *Investment, Location and Size of Plant,* Cambridge University Press, Cambridge, England, 1948.

Gold, Robert N.: *Manufacturing Structure and Pattern of the South Bend–Mishawaka Area,* Research Paper 36, Department of Geography, University of Chicago, Chicago, 1954.

Hartshorne, Richard: "A New Map of the Manufacturing Belt of North America," *Economic Geography,* vol. 12, pp. 45–53, 1936.

Hoover, Edgar M.: *The Location of Economic Activity,* McGraw-Hill Book Company, Inc., New York, 1948.

Jackson, W. A. Douglas: *Philadelphia Waterfront Industry,* report submitted to Department of Commerce, City of Philadelphia, August, 1955.

Jones, Victor: "Economic Classification of Cities and Metropolitan Areas," *The Municipal Year Book,* International City Managers Association, Chicago, 1954, pp. 27–36, 62–72, 81–108; and repeated in several later issues.

——— and Richard L. Forstall: "Economic and Social Classification of Metropolitan Areas," in *The Municipal Year Book,* International City Managers Association, Chicago, 1963, pp. 31–44.

———, ———, and Andrew Collver: "Economic and Social Characteristics of Urban Places," in *The Municipal Year Book,* International City Managers Association, Chicago, 1963, pp. 85–157.

Kitagawa, Evelyn M., and Donald J. Bogue: *Suburbanization of Manufacturing Activity within Standard Metropolitan Areas,* Studies in Population Distribution no. 9, Scripps Foundation, Miami, Ohio, 1955.

Loeben, Arthur F.: "Philadelphia Waterfront Industry," *Geographical Review,* vol. 47, pp. 272–273, 1957.

Murphy, Raymond E.: "Johnstown and York: A Comparative Study of Two Industrial Cities," *Annals of the Association of American Geographers,* vol. 25, pp. 175–196, 1935.

Pasma, Theodore K.: *Organized Industrial Districts: A Tool for Community Development,* Area Development Division, Office of Technical Services, U.S. Department of Commerce, 1954.

Prior, Roger A., and Murray D. Dessel: *Diversification of Manufacturing Employment for States and Metropolitan Areas,* Business and Defense Services Administration, Office of Area Development, U.S. Department of Commerce, 1960.

Reinemann, Martin W.: "The Pattern and Distribution of Manufacturing in the Chicago Area," *Economic Geography,* vol. 36, pp. 139–144, 1960.

Rodgers, Allan: "Some Aspects of Industrial Diversification in the United States," *Economic Geography,* vol. 33, pp. 16–30, 1957.

Standard Industrial Classification Manual, U.S. Bureau of the Budget, 1957.

Thompson, John H.: "A New Method for Measuring Manufacturing," *Annals of the Association of American Geographers,* vol. 45, pp. 416–436, 1955.

U.S. Bureau of the Census, *Census of Manufactures, Area Statistics.*

U.S. National Resources Planning Board, *Industrial Location and National Resources,* 1943.

Wright, Alfred J.: "Manufacturing Districts of the United States," *Economic Geography,* vol. 14, pp. 195–200, 1938.

Wrigley, Robert L., Jr.: "Organized Industrial Districts," *Journal of Land and Public Utility Economics,* vol. 23, pp. 180–198, 1947.

CHAPTER **17**

Manufacturing expansion

THE last chapter closed with a section on changing manufacturing patterns. But there is an aspect of the study of manufacturing in urban centers which requires looking at change from a different angle. What is being done and what can be done by manufacturing concerns, individual communities, and other interested groups such as railroads to change the manufacturing pattern to their advantage? The answer involves several possibilities: new industrial development on new sites, expansion of existing industries, replacement of existing plants, use of old floor space.

Manufacturers, either through their own efforts or through real estate agents, are constantly looking for locations for expansion, or places where new or relocated plants can be operated profitably; community promotional groups are eager for industrial expansion; and railroads are trying to attract industrial developments to sites along their lines so that their freight business will be increased. It is worth noting that these three are not completely independent and rival efforts. Thus, manufacturers looking for sites must deal with communities where industry is wanted. The railroads, on the other hand, join forces with certain communities to attract manufacturers. At any rate, it is with these various attempts to change the manufacturing pattern that this chapter deals.

Manufacturers Looking for New Locations

The initial impetus for industrial growth in a community is likely to come from manufacturing concerns that wish to establish new branch factories or even to move their entire operations to new locations. Of course, it is the American tradition that in any community a small factory may spring up due to local initiative, and it may be a prodigious success. But nowadays such spontaneous developments are likely to be a minor part of the overall picture. The major urge comes instead from larger concerns, often great corporations.

Not many years ago the finding of a new location might have been assigned to almost anyone. Often such haphazard methods worked, at least for a number of years. In fact, some surprisingly "good" locations were found, but others were satisfactory only while locational methods in general were poorly developed. Then a competitor moved his plant to a really superior location and trouble began.

Now, at least with very large concerns, the best modern methods of plant location are used. Mistakes are still made, but efforts are directed toward minimizing the margin of error in locating new plant sites. Plant locating has become big business. Large corporations have their own staffs working on new locations, or they may hire location consultants.

A detailed study of requirements for the new plant is followed by a thorough search for the right site. The search is likely to be focused at first on a two- or three-state area and then on the proper state. Companies often do a good deal of checking at the state level—on such matters as voting records of senators and congressmen, the state's tax policies, workmen's compensation costs, and the ratio of strikes to nonfarm population. In addition many states have organizations such as industrial development bureaus that collect information and attempt to get companies to locate within their boundaries.

This is not urban geography, but it is close to industrial geography. The next step, however, is near to urban geography: focusing on the community. Here, of course, comparative costs are important. But there are many other things to consider. A long

checklist is likely to be followed, covering such subjects as community progressiveness; government; labor costs; labor relations, including annual labor turnover; community services and facilities; social, cultural, and educational conditions; tax rates; zoning; and many other topics. Questionnaires used may cover literally hundreds of relevant points. Nevertheless, it is in comparing communities that most mistakes are made, partly because it is hard to get specific objective local data and partly because the company executives often do not know just what questions to ask.

Within the community the choice frequently narrows down to sites that local real estate men and others have on record. It is less common for the national concern or the firm of location consultants to conduct a site survey of its own in the community. To a large degree this is up to the local people who are anxious to get factories. In any event the local sites available are subjected to a variety of tests based on the specific requirements of the company, the aim being to select the exact site best suited to its needs.

The Community and Manufacturing Expansion

In spite of the activities of big companies searching for places to establish new plants, the community must eventually be brought into the picture. Whether it is a place of 10,000 population or a large city, the community ordinarily must agree to the establishment of a plant. It is the attitude and actions of communities that concern us here. What role do they play in manufacturing expansion?

Why industrial growth is desired

Though the citizens of high-quality residential suburbs usually do not want industrial growth, the people of almost all other communities want new factories or expansion of old ones. Why? Partly because it means a broadening of the tax base. This, in turn, means more money available to pay for necessary community services which are constantly expanding. A second reason for desiring industrial expansion, and a paramount one in some communities, is that industrial growth will mean sustained or possibly expanded employment opportunities. New basic industries in themselves mean more jobs, and, through the employment multiplier effect (see page 99), growth in basic industries brings an expansion in nonbasic activities, with increased job opportunities in these lines.[1] Finally, too, sheer growth is impressive. Rightly or wrongly, most people feel that it is good for the urban center in which they live to grow.

The small community The prospect often is so attractive for a small community that the matter is not adequately thought through. There will be tax money from the new factories, it is true, and more employment opportunities, but there will be expanded costs due to the presence of the new industries. Moreover, the town leaders often do not realize that the workers who move in may occupy cheap houses and, therefore, may not pay property taxes in proportion to the added service costs to the community that will result from their presence, particularly costs for schooling. Nor are they likely to think of the other growing pains that will result. Balanced against all this is the increased tempo of the community: more jobs, more people, more business for the stores.

The situation in the city In cities, the problem is less direct though the motives often are much the same. More tax money

[1] It is contended by some that the reverse is equally true, that well-developed services (nonbasic activities) serve to attract basic industries (see pp. 110–111).

and additional jobs are involved. Ordinarily, less space for manufacturing is available in the city, so it may be more a matter of keeping up than of any considerable industrial expansion. Generally, however, there is manufacturing land that can be put to more efficient use through replacing obsolete buildings with new ones, and possibly factory space can be made available through clearance and redevelopment. In any event the motivation is likely to be chiefly a financial one.

The central city's plight Added tax revenue is often sorely needed by the central city, with its increasing municipal costs. Indeed, the complaint is a general one that the central city typically has rapidly increasing costs for which the suburbs are partly responsible. But, ringed in by suburbs and with little unused land remaining, the city has scant opportunity to broaden its tax base. In fact, more often than not, more and more land is being used for public and quasi-public purposes and is, therefore, being removed from the tax rolls. Thus the tax base is shrinking.

How the central city gains by suburban industrial growth Even when the industrial growth comes to suburban communities rather than to the central city, the latter may still benefit. The stores and banks in the central city gain by the increased business of the region. More and more the economic relationships between central city and suburbs are being reflected in steps toward regional cooperation.

Choice of industries

In spite of their desire for industries, most communities tend to be selective in the matter. Though it is not feasible to specify exact lines of manufacturing, they want factories of desirable types. Industries are favored which pay a substantial amount of taxes and, at the same time, involve little by way of <u>smoke, dirt, or other obnoxious qualities</u>. Moreover, they should pay high enough wages so the workers will live in homes of sufficiently high value to provide through taxes at least enough revenue to pay for the community services required. There is a tendency, too, nowadays, to prefer industrial parks to single-plant developments.

Tax-exempt industries, for example research laboratories operated by the government, have the disadvantage of paying no direct taxes, but usually the local government is reimbursed for direct services received—such as police and fire protection. Moreover, such establishments often pay high wages. As a result the workers live in better than average houses, thus contributing more than their share of community taxes.

Responsible individuals

In the community, various groups or individuals may be responsible for the effort to obtain industries. The planning department of a city or town may make a study of the situation, or the industrial committee of the chamber of commerce, or some private promotional group. Such groups normally consult the local real estate people about possible industrial sites available in the community and do valuable work in promoting industrial development. But it has been relatively unusual for them to take the basic step of carrying out an inventory of potential industrial sites. Such a survey requires technical skills often beyond those of the urban groups interested in acquiring new industries.[2]

[2] A study of this sort for the Cincinnati area was carried out under the direction of Victor Roterus for the City Planning Commission of Cincinnati in 1946. The Cincinnati study, though not discussed here, was valuable in setting up the methodology for the potential industrial sites inventory of the Springfield, Mass., area described in the following pages. The Cincinnati study also involved an estimate of future industrial land requirements.

An Inventory of Potential Industrial Sites [3]

The study that is described here was instigated by a promotional organization consisting of bankers and other businessmen of Springfield, Massachusetts.[4] These people realized that the amount of business conducted in the city depended not only upon the prosperity of the city itself, but upon that of surrounding municipalities as well. The owners of a new factory in any one of the nearby communities pay taxes on the factory only to the community in which it is situated, but the increased business activity resulting from the presence of the new industry benefits the banks and stores of the central city as well as those of the individual community. Therefore, the promotional group decided to sponsor an inventory of potential industrial sites not only in Springfield, itself, but also in a number of adjacent towns.

Political structure as background

Nine communities were covered by the survey: the cities of Springfield and Chicopee, and seven towns (Figure 17.1 and Table 17.1). As in most of New England, each community consists of a sizable area, several square miles in extent (see Appendix A). It may be mostly built up or it may be largely rural, with one or two or more villages or urban areas within its borders. The area that is not built up consists of farmed land, woodland, and waste. Each of the separate communities has school, highway, fire protection, and other

[3] Pages 357–364 are based on the author's "The Industrial Sites Inventory: An Example of Applied Geography," *Festskrift till Olof Jonasson*, Gothenburg School of Economics Publications, no. 1, pp. 125–133, 1959.
[4] The office and field work of the study was carried on by three geographers experienced in urban land-use study—G. W. Schultz, Grady O. Tucker, Jr., and James E. Vance, Jr.—under the direction of the author of this book.

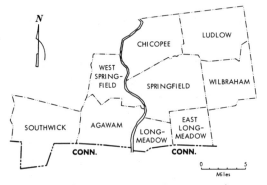

Fig. 17.1 The inventory area. Two cities and seven towns in western Massachusetts were included.

services to maintain, and the administrative officials of each are worried about the tax rate of their town or city. New factories mean more tax money. Hence nearly every city and town is striving to obtain new industries, at least new industries of desirable types.

Other elements of background

Other elements of background important in the survey included relief features, the availability of transportation facilities, and the extent of such town services as water supply and sewage disposal. It was also necessary to know something of the current land use and zoning.

Relief Relief features were particularly important in the survey. The area in the vicinity of Springfield is rolling, glaciated country, cut approximately in half by the Connecticut River. Tributary streams have multiplied the variety of features—hills separated by swampy lowlands; occasional sections of flat, sandy terrace; and, along the Connecticut River, a floodplain of varying width, which, because of periodic flooding, is of little value for industrial sites except where protected by dikes.

Transportation facilities The area is well served with transportation facilities. Railroads reach into all the communities except one, and paved highways crisscross the area. The highway system was considered as significant as the railroads, since many modern factories do not require rail connections, finding it sufficient to be well served by trucks. Especially noteworthy is the presence of the Massachusetts Turnpike, a limited-access superhighway which takes an east-west course across the northern part of the area, north of the center of Springfield. It has four interchanges within the area studied.

Municipal services All of the communities have municipal water, and sanitary sewers serve all but one. However, in several of the communities, such services are restricted to certain areas.

Current land use and zoning Finally, current land use and current zoning had to be considered as part of the background. Some of the communities surveyed had only limited built-up areas, with much of their land in farms and woods. The city of Springfield was at the opposite extreme; there, only limited areas remained to be developed. All of the communities had zoning bylaws, with the amount of land zoned for industry ranging from 16 or 17 per cent for one of the towns to none at all for two of them. In most cases, however, the land zoned for industry was poor, generally swampy and inaccessible.

Table 17.1   Characteristics of the nine Massachusetts communities studied

Name	Political status	Area, sq mi	Population (1950)
Agawam	town	24.35	10,166
Chicopee	city	24.04	49,211
East Longmeadow	town	13.04	4,881
Longmeadow	town	9.62	6,508
Ludlow	town	28.48	8,660
Southwick	town	31.79	2,855
Springfield	city	33.08	162,399
West Springfield	town	17.54	20,438
Wilbraham	town	22.51	4,003

Definitions

Agreement upon some definitions was a necessary early step in the work. For instance, just what is an *industrial site?* The purpose of the survey was to focus on those pieces of land that presented the greatest potential assets for industrial development. Each such separate area was considered a "site." Thus little attention was paid to property lines or land values, and each separate area was regarded as a site even though it might consist of several lots owned by as many individuals. This is a special use of the term site, and it needs to be clearly understood to appreciate the methods and findings of the inventory.

The term industrial as here used means essentially "manufactural." No attempt was made to specify the kind of manufacturing. Certainly, not all kinds of manufacturing, even among the lighter types that characterize New England, have exactly the same needs, but an attempt to distinguish between sites on this basis would have gone far beyond the time and money allotted for the survey. Instead, the sites were delimited on the basis of their advantages for industry in general rather than for specific types of industry.

In addition, the promoters of the inventory were not thinking in terms of a giant corporation wishing to establish a very large plant. Such a corporation might well be interested in some of the better sites outlined in the survey, yet such a concern could level hills, fill swamps, build roads—in short, *make* itself a suitable site almost anywhere. But for the average manufacturer just getting a start or developing a branch plant, it is essential to find the most favorable site possible. Likewise, for an industrial park of modest dimensions a suitable site is extremely important.

Materials used

The inventory was based on the use of air photos at a scale of 1 inch to 1,000 feet and United States Geological Survey topographic maps enlarged to the same scale. To supplement these maps and air photos, local maps and data were used, as well as soil surveys, geological bulletins, and other scientific reports. Conferences were held with town officials, representatives of the railroads, and other individuals who knew the locality. But office work with the photographs and maps and work in the field formed the real heart of the survey.

Site delimitation

Slope The first step in the actual task of site delimitation consisted of outlining on the topographic sheets all areas that had slopes of less than 6 per cent, that is, less than 6 feet difference in elevation for each 100 feet of horizontal distance.[5] This is an arbitrary limit. For some types of industrial plants, sites with slopes of 7 or 8 per cent might be usable, but in the Springfield area sites with moderate slope combined with other favorable qualities are numerous, so there was little incentive to use sites with more than 6 per cent slope. The areas thus outlined varied in size from a few acres to several hundred acres. They were the raw material for further analysis. These tentative sites were then tested on the basis of other limiting factors, and retained unchanged in size, reduced in area, or eliminated. The application of these factors is described in the following paragraphs.

Poor drainage and flood hazards Possible sites were ruled out if they were deficient in drainage or subject to flood. The extent of poorly drained areas was determined from study of topographic sheets and aerial photographs plus checking in the

[5] Through the use of the scale and contour interval of a topographic map, it is an easy matter to construct a slope indicator that shows the spacing of contours which represents a 6 per cent slope. By moving this scale over the map, one can see where the contours are more widely or more closely spaced than this, and hence can outline the areas of 6 per cent or greater slope.

field. Land subject to periodic floods was also eliminated, but this was a difficult determination to make since periodic floods are hard to define. In the Springfield area survey, land was considered unsuitable for industrial sites if it had been flooded in 1936 or 1938 (record recent years of high water in western Massachusetts at the time of the inventory) and had not since been protected by the construction of dikes.

Accessibility Sites had to be reasonably accessible. Highways rather than railroads were considered the basis for accessibility, since, even if a railroad reached a piece of land, it would have to be accessible by highway, too. The rule followed in the inventory being described was that a site had to have a frontage of at least 150 feet on a public road of moderate grade, that is, not more than 5 per cent. Related to accessibility was the factor of shape. A narrow strip of land would obviously make a less favorable site than one that was more nearly equidimensional, yet the requirement of shape is hard to express. In the inventory, this limit amounted largely to a subjective judgment.

Freedom from intensive use Moreover, the land could not be intensively used. Intensive use can be variously defined. In the survey here described, it included land built up in residences, commercial buildings, and factories, as well as cemeteries, parks, school grounds, golf courses, public playgrounds, military installations, watershed reservations, and other similar public and quasi-public holdings. In addition, land was considered intensively used if it was within 100 feet of an isolated residence or a cluster of buildings, though this did not apply to isolated barns or similar structures reached only by field roads. Highways and railroads were regarded as extreme cases of intensive use. They were obviously unavailable for industrial use and also served as boundaries between potential sites. Thus no

site could cross a highway or railroad right-of-way, and the same was true of the right-of-way of a power line or a trunk gas line or a major aqueduct.

Agricultural land Farmland was considered potentially available for conversion to industrial use. Certain types of agricultural use in the Springfield area—e.g., tobacco raising—yield large returns per unit of area, but have proven to be displaceable by urban-type uses.

Site boundaries The various limiting factors described served to fix site boundaries. A site, as finally delimited, might be bounded by a steep slope, the edge of a swamp, the beginning of intensively used land, a road or railroad right-of-way, or one of the other features mentioned. Similarly, a site could not cross a major stream. It was decided, too, that although a site might cross a town or county line it should not cross a state line, since states are likely to differ considerably in tax practices and in laws regulating manufacturing.

Minimum size of site Finally, a size limit was applied. After the sites were outlined on the basis of the factors described, many were too small to be of much value. A 3-acre minimum was decided upon.[6]

The place of field work

Much of the delimitation process was carried out in the office through the use of topographic maps, air views, and the like. In the office, too, maps of town water and town sewerage systems were studied to determine their availability for the various sites. But a field reconnaissance of the tentative sites was considered essential. Not only did field work check the slope, drainage, and other natural conditions, but it was invaluable in determining whether or not the sites

[6] For an industrial sites inventory confined to a city, where space is a precious commodity, a minimum of 1 acre or even ½ acre might be more desirable.

were still available. The topographic maps were out of date and the air views had been taken three years prior to the survey. Housing developments had preempted sites which the maps and air views showed to be unoccupied. Thus, as a result of the field check, many of the tentative sites were eliminated. The remaining sites were numbered independently for each city and town.

During the field check, too, additional details were obtained regarding the sites that remained. A sheet was filled out for each potential site (Table 17.2). On it essential details regarding the site were summarized as a basis for judging its quality, and additional information was re-

corded that might be valuable to prospective users of the sites as well as to community groups and others interested in promoting manufacturing development.

Quality rating of sites

It was apparent that among the sites remaining some barely justified inclusion as potential industrial sites, whereas others were well endowed with desirable attributes. In view of this fact, it seemed that some system of quality rating would add to the value of the inventory. Four quality classes were decided upon: A, B, C, and D. The distinctions between these four classes are brought out in Table 17.3. Addition of

Table 17.2   Site sheet used in the Springfield area survey

_____ (city or town)

SITE NO.:_____QUALITY RATING:_____DATE OF SURVEY:_____REVISED:_____

LOCATION:_____

SIZE:_____acres. Frontage: Total_____ft;   _____ft continuous on _____ (road or street)

SHAPE:_____

SURFACE CONDITIONS:
   Prevailing slope:_____%; Surface configuration:_____
   Surface material:_____; Drainage:_____

UTILITIES (X, on site; Y, off site but not more than 2,500 ft distant):
   Water: (___). _____in. main; approx._____ft from site
      Location of nearest main:_____
   Sewerage: (___). _____in. main; approx._____ft from site
      Location of nearest main:_____
   Gas: (___). _____in. main; approx. _____ft from site
      Location of nearest main:_____

TRANSPORTATION:
   Road: Direct access to_____road; _____ft wide
                        (surfaced; unsurfaced)
   R.R.: Probable connection on_____R.R.

LAND USE:_____ PRESENT ZONING:_____

LAND USE OF ADJACENT AREAS:_____

REMARKS (including any special features):_____

OWNER(S) OR AGENT(S) IF DETERMINED:_____

Table 17.3   Criteria for determining quality rating of sites

	A	AR	B†	C†	D†
Acreage	10 or more	10 or more	5 or more	*	*
Shape	Favorable	Favorable	*	*	*
Railroad	Rail connection not considered feasible	Rail connection appears feasible	Rail connection not considered feasible	Rail connection not considered feasible	Rail connection not considered feasible
Highway	400 ft continuous frontage on surfaced road at least 18 ft wide	On surfaced road at least 18 ft wide	300 ft continuous frontage on surfaced road at least 18 ft wide	200 ft continuous frontage on surfaced or unsurfaced road at least 14 ft wide. If unsurfaced, the road must be within 1,000 ft of a 14-ft or wider surfaced road	*
Drainage	Moderate or dry	Moderate or dry	Moderate or dry	*	*
Surface configuration	Uniformly level 0–3% slope	Uniformly level 0–3% slope	Uniformly level 0–3% slope	*	*
Municipal water	Available on frontage	Available on frontage	Within 2,500 ft	Within 2,500 ft	*
Sanitary sewer	Available on frontage	Available on frontage	*	*	*
Special features	Not behind dike	Not behind dike	Not behind dike	*	*

* No requirements other than those for all sites.

† BR, CR, and DR were used to indicate sites where railroad connection appeared feasible.

an R to any one of the four ratings meant that railroad connections appeared to be feasible.

Of course, this or any other rating system is arbitrary and does not necessarily reflect the usefulness of sites for specific, prospective manufacturers. For example, no site could have an AR or an A rating if it did not have a sanitary sewer on its frontage, yet a manufacturing concern might prefer to put in its own sewage disposal plant. Similarly, a slight difference in the degree of slope of the land might result in a site being given a quality rating of C rather than B, although for a particular factory the slightly greater slope might make little difference.

The quality rating should be considered a useful indicator of the relative values of the sites. D sites might be regarded chiefly as a reserve; but a site from any one of the higher ratings could be just what was needed by some specific concern.

Results of the survey

The primary product of the survey for each of the nine communities was a map of potential industrial sites with the rating of each. The map of Chicopee, for example, showed fifty-two potential industrial sites ranging in size from 3 to 82 acres (Figure 17.2).[7] Of these, only three were A sites;

[7] The base map for each town and city was made from United States Geological Survey topographic sheets, because the location and relief features of each site could best be seen on such a map.

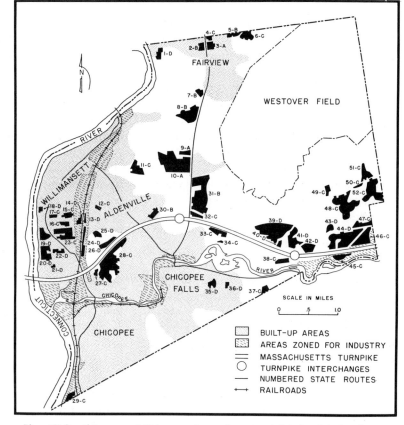

Fig. 17.2 This map of Chicopee shows the potential industrial sites for one of the nine communities. Quality rating is shown for each site. (See Table 17.3.)

six were B sites. No one of the nine was adjacent to a railroad.

But the information furnished did not stop with the maps. For each of the nine communities, there were, in addition, a detailed site sheet for each site, a summary table listing all sites with their locations and characteristics, and other tables listing the sites in order of size and by quality ranks. Similar information was summed up on maps and in tabular form for the Springfield area as a whole. Two other general tables were presented. In one of these the sites for which rail connections are possible were listed, and in the other the sites lying near interchanges on the Massachusetts Turnpike.

The number of sites

The number of potential industrial sites found in each town and city may seem excessive, e.g., the fifty-two in Chicopee. However, this number would have been greatly reduced if certain other factors could have been taken into consideration in the survey. For instance, an occasional site was held in several parcels, which might make its acquisition impracticable. Or a site might be part of a large property held as a unit and not available for sale piecemeal, or the title to a property might be unclear. But considerations related to ownership and availability were beyond the scope of the survey.

However, since only black and white illustrations are used in this book, contours are not shown on Fig. 17.2.

Zoning and existing land uses limited the number of potential sites still more. Some sites lay so close to high-quality residential areas or to schools or to other areas of incompatible uses that factories would be inadvisable and would be forbidden by any properly written zoning law. Moreover, wise zoning is supposed to restrict land for industry to certain portions of a town or city, and certainly not to spot it here and there. Hence, zoning, if properly applied, would considerably reduce the number of potential sites.

Values of the inventory

The industrial sites inventory could be justified on several grounds. The original problem—differentiation of the best potential industrial sites in a prescribed area— was definite and challenging. The general method, area analysis, was unquestionably geographic. To accomplish the objectives of the project, an elaborate system had to be set up for focusing on the most suitable pieces of land. The system was developed, the sites determined, and the results classified so as to answer effectively the original problem.

It must not be forgotten, however, that the project was applied research sponsored by a group of businessmen. Hence, its practical values are of interest. First of all, the inventory served as a guide to planning. The potential industrial sites outlined were far too numerous and extensive to justify holding any large number of them in reserve for industry. Nevertheless, armed with the knowledge of where their best industrial resources lay and with the advice of their local planning boards, the various individual communities were in a position to change their zoning so as to include some of their best potential sites in their industrial zones. In Chicopee, for example, at the time of the survey only six of the city's fifty-two potential sites were included in areas zoned for industry, and these did not

include any of the A or B sites. Immediate attention to such matters was considered important because communities were competing for industry, and manufacturers were demanding better and better sites. The same qualities that make a site desirable for industry often make it a prime location for housing and, sometimes, for commercial development. The inventory showed the leaders in each municipality where their best space resources for industry lay. From there on it was up to them whether or not they should take steps to safeguard the industrial future of their community.

The results of the inventory were of direct value, too, to the businessmen who promoted the study. They were interested in the economic growth of the whole Springfield area since it meant increased business for the city. It was to the advantage of this group that each town should know where its best industrial land was located and that some of the best of it be zoned or otherwise reserved for industry. Moreover, when a manufacturer asked about the location of a suitable site the promoters could point out quickly just where within the area he could find the exact conditions he wanted.[8]

General applicability of the technique

It must be obvious to the reader that a screening technique such as the one described here has to be adjusted to meet various situations. In the Springfield area, relief was a particularly important factor for outlining sites and distinguishing among them, but the same factor would be of little value in a flat area. There, possibly, drainage would be a more important control, or location on navigable water or the nature of current land use.

---

[8] If the survey area had been larger it might have been advantageous to file the information on punch cards so that a site with the desired combination of characteristics could be quickly pinpointed. Such a punch-card system would make it easier, too, to keep the records up to date.

How Railroads Attack the Problem

Thus far we have spoken of the industrialist seeking a site and the local community groups trying to attract him. But these are not the only interests that may be involved. Some railroads have active industrial development departments; it is the task of these departments to survey the areas along their lines and work up details regarding land available for industrial development in and near the various communities. The purpose of this sort of work is to increase the activity along the railroad and thereby increase the traffic to be handled. The railroad may own some of the land recommended or it may not. Typically, the industrial development department of the railroad works in close cooperation with the local city administration and with any promotional organization, governmental or private, that may be in existence.

For each community surveyed, a brochure is likely to be prepared by the railroad. It covers information that the average manufacturer might want if he were thinking of locating a plant there. One such report, for instance, is centered on a Middle Western city of 14,000 or 15,000 population. The brochure begins with a chapter on the general situation. In this chapter a very general statement about the city and its neighbors and its railroad and highway facilities is followed by some facts regarding topography, local economy, population, and labor. The second chapter deals with factors affecting industrial location. Here the topics discussed are transportation, raw materials, coal (availability via the railroad), oil (from nearby refineries), gas, electric power, water supply, waste disposal, city services, and taxation. A third chapter, "Manpower and Living Conditions," covers established industries of the area, labor situation (in more detail than in the first chapter), wage rates, community facilities (schools, churches, etc.), and cli-

mate. A fourth chapter or section deals with the industrial sites.

Three sites are recommended. These have acreages of 32.5, 58, and 156, respectively. The arrangement and details of the sites are depicted on a composite topographic map that is bound into the brochure. The properties are shown, also, on a reproduced air photo or photomap. Ownership of the sites is discussed. One site is owned by the railroad, but the others are privately held, one in several ownerships. The advantages and possible handicaps of the several properties are discussed.

Another report, this one dealing with a city of some 55,000 population, covers much the same background information. In this report, however, the attractions of an industrial park, under the sponsorship of a local industrial development corporation, are discussed, as well as those of several individual sites that are not part of the industrial park. All are so located that they can be served by the railroad. Here, the city planning commission has apparently cooperated closely with the railroad, and the local industrial development corporation is prepared to assist any company interested in locating a plant in the area.

Zoning and Manufacturing Expansion

But manufacturing expansion in a community is not just a matter of the manufacturer finding the right community and an attractive site. There is another factor that affects patterns of manufacturing expansion: local zoning. Dorothy Muncy has pointed out an interesting paradox in this regard.[9] On the one hand, cities, large and small, court the manufacturer, even going so far as to offer him free sites, tax-free buildings, or free rent. On the other hand,

[9] Dorothy A. Muncy, "Land for Industry: A Neglected Problem," *Harvard Business Review*, vol. 32, no. 2, pp. 51–63, 1954.

local zoning and land policy frequently seem designed to thwart him.[10]

Industry versus housing in the courts

Muncy tells of the case of a Connecticut community, Newington, that wished to attract industry. Newington, like other New England towns, has a substantial area, 14 square miles in fact, and in the early 1950s had a population of about 10,000. The town proceeded to zone an area of over 600 acres along the railroad for industrial use and amended its zoning code to prohibit the erection of housing in that area. But a developer had a 30-acre parcel of which 18 acres lay in the tract zoned for industry, and he wanted to build houses on his land. He brought suit, and the court ruled in his favor, chiefly on the ground that residences represent a higher use of the land than does industry.

Modern industry should take the lead

This situation, according to Muncy, can best be corrected by industrial leadership. The industrialist is in a strong bargaining position. He should make his wishes known. Modern factories require larger sites, desirable locations, good transportation, protection from encroachment by other uses, pollution controls, and a place in the community plan. Modern industry is in a position to play a dynamic role in the future of industrial zoning by insisting on these advantages.

Increasing land needs of industry

Muncy goes on to speak of the increased land needs of industry today. Modern factory buildings are likely to be single-story, requiring much more space than the factory of yesterday. Moreover, they are likely to be landscaped, so that the properties are rightly called parks. Expanded employee

facilities including cafeterias, dispensaries, hospitals, and the like are characteristic, as well as extensive parking lots. This trend toward more space is being speeded up by developments in modern technology. The trend is so great that adequate area for expansion ranks high on the modern industrialist's list of site characteristics. On the other side of the coin is the growing land shortage not only in the older urban-suburban sections, but in the peripheral portions of most urban areas as well.

Faults in zoning codes and land policy

Zoning codes and land-use policy are too often hostile to the growth of manufacturing. The problem is not just that industrial land is given no protection from residential encroachment, as in the Newington case, but also that unrelated commercial structures and even junkyards are allowed to invade the dwindling supply of good industrial land in the urban area. The residences that do develop in such a region usually lack many of the community services of good residential neighborhoods, and thus slums are bred. All too often, too, the land that is zoned for industry in a town is poor, swampy, subject to flooding, inaccessible, or otherwise undesirable. Thus present zoning is likely to set only poor land aside for industry while permitting the willful or misguided exploitation of good industrial sites for non-industrial purposes.

Obsolete classification

An obsolete classification of industry adds to the trouble. Most zoning codes recognize two types of industrial land use: heavy and light. Heavy manufacturing is either excluded entirely or restricted to the poorer districts. But the modern trend is away from this restriction. Plants should be judged, it is now claimed, on the basis of performance standards. Thus, some factories classed as heavy industry may be far preferable to light manufacturing plants less carefully planned.

---

[10] A similar, though much more local, paradox is seen in the fact that most people in the average town speak up for industrial expansion, but don't want it in their part of the community.

Bedroom towns Muncy cites further the plight of many "bedroom towns." All too often these have grown with little regulation. When eventually it is decided that the town needs factories to broaden its tax base and give workers a wider choice of jobs, inadequate space remains available for such use.

Unprotected sites Industries are often worst off when located in unzoned areas. They may have had plenty of space at first, but suddenly find themselves in the path of rapidly expanding metropolitan development. Eventually, such plants may be surrounded and choked by low-grade commercial development and inferior housing. Because of experiences such as this, industrialists often prefer to locate just inside the city limits.

A suggested program Muncy also discusses some of the elements of what she regards as a positive program for remedying the faults of zoning and land policy as they affect industrial growth. One of the first steps is the prohibition of residential building in industrial districts, whether the industry is heavy or light. To zone and thus hold land exclusively for industry, however, requires proof that it is needed for industry. This involves a careful analysis of past and present trends in manufacturing in the community, keeping in mind the growing space needs of modern industry and the physical suitability of potential sites for industrial development.[11] But the individual owner ordinarily cannot afford to hold potential industrial land as a long-range investment. A development corporation, an industrial foundation, or some other organization of businessmen should be formed to purchase and hold such land until it is needed.

Also pointed out as of prime impor-

tance in planning for the industrial future of a community are good transportation facilities. There is the need, too, of providing through zoning space for off-street loading and parking. And because planning for industrial growth cannot stop at the boundary of a central city, some sort of regional planning organization is an added help in a progressive program.

The Struggle for Industry Will Continue

The struggle that has been discussed is by no means over. Manufacturers will continue to look for the best possible sites for expansion, and states, and communities within states, will continue to do their utmost to attract the plants that will benefit them most. Railroad companies will continue their efforts to attract factories to the vicinities of their own lines, though probably with diminishing success as industry becomes less and less railroad-oriented and more and more dependent upon the truck.

Since manufacturing often furnishes more direct support to the city than any other activity, it was considered worthwhile in this chapter to depart from the general tone of the book. Instead of considering somewhat passively the nature of urban manufacturing patterns and how they are changing, the emphasis has been upon efforts to alter the patterns.[12]

Selected References

Breese, Gerald: *Industrial Site Selection: Burlington County, N.J.: A Case Study of Existing and Potential Industrial Location,* Bureau of Urban Research, Princeton University, Princeton, N.J., 1954.

Calef, Wesley C., and Charles Daoust: *What Will New Industry Mean to My Town?*

[11] A possibility to be kept in mind is that of "linked industries." If large enough tracts are preserved, interdependent factories may be attracted and an industrial district planned accordingly.

[12] The author has had personal experience with the types of problems discussed in this chapter, since he directed the Springfield area sites study and also worked on zoning ordinances for several central Massachusetts communities.

Area Development Division, Office of Technical Services, U.S. Department of Commerce, 1955.

City Planning Commission of Cincinnati, *Industrial Land Use: Present and Future,* Cincinnati, Ohio, 1946.

Fulton, Maurice: "Plant Location: 1965," *Harvard Business Review,* vol. 33, no. 2, pp. 40–50, 1955.

"Location Analysis," *Dunn's Review and Modern Industry,* April, 1956, pp. 61–63, 67–70.

Muncy, Dorothy A.: "Land for Industry: A Neglected Problem," *Harvard Business Review,* vol. 32, no. 2, pp. 51–63, 1954.

Murphy, Raymond E.: "The Industrial Sites Inventory: An Example of Applied Geography," *Festskrift till Olof Jonasson,* Gothenburg School of Economics Publications, no. 1, Göteborg, Sweden, pp. 125–133, 1959.

Roterus, Victor, Scott Keyes, and Raymond Van Schaack: "Future Industrial Land Requirements in the Cincinnati Area," *Annals of the Association of American Geographers,* vol. 36, pp. 111–121, 1946.

CHAPTER **18**

Urban
residential patterns

UNDOUBTEDLY, more of the city's land is used for residences and associated grounds than for any other single purpose, but it is difficult to get any consensus as to exactly what proportion of the average city's area is so occupied. Fisher and Fisher suggest that it amounts to 30 per cent of the total city area;[1] Bartholomew, in the fifty-three central cities he studied, found that residential use accounted for an average of 39.61 per cent of the total developed area of the city.[2] At least as important as space occupied, however, is the fact that urban areas contain the homes of over two-thirds of the country's people.

Residences and Residential Land Use Defined

At first glance, it seems hardly necessary to define *residences* and *residential* land use.[3] Certainly, the houses that line the streets are residences, and the land on which the houses are built is in residential use. Nobody would dispute the fact that the same designations could be applied to apartment houses and their grounds. But what of hotels and motels? Such seemingly transient residences are commonly regarded as commercial, but they are not exclusively so. Hotel or motel quarters used as a person's regular place of abode are considered residences. But there are all gradations between commercial establishments, as represented by the ordinary transient hotel or motel, and unquestionable residences; just

[1] Ernest M. Fisher and Robert M. Fisher, *Urban Real Estate*, Holt, Rinehart and Winston, Inc., New York, 1954, p. 307.

[2] Harland Bartholomew, *Land Uses in American Cities*, Harvard University Press, Cambridge, Mass., 1955, p. 26. "Developed area" is defined by Bartholomew as total city area minus vacant and water areas.

[3] Residences are referred to collectively as "housing," as in the U.S. Census of Housing.

as there are residences with an office or two, or some other line of business (see page 193). In field mapping, the exact distinction is often difficult to make.

Housing Units and Residential Land Use at Two Levels

The discussion of residences and residential land use deals with patterns at two levels. At one level, patterns of city distribution based on residential characteristics concern the urban geographer. Even more, however, he investigates residential patterns at a different level, those of the interior of the city.

United States Census Data on Housing

Whether the focus is on city similarities and differences based on residential characteristics or on internal residential patterns of the city, standardized statistics are of prime concern. For residential patterns there is one outstanding source. This is the Census of Housing which has been conducted by the Bureau of the Census at the time of each of the last several decennial censuses. Less directly, the Census of Population, since it deals with where people live, contributes to the story of residential patterns.

The housing unit

The *housing unit* is basic to data in the Census of Housing and hence to any discussion of residential land use. Quoting from the 1960 *Census of Housing:*

> A house, an apartment or other group of rooms, or a single room is regarded as a *housing unit* when it is occupied or intended for occupancy as separate living quarters, that is, when the occupants do not live and eat with any other persons in the structure and there is either (1) direct access from the outside or through a common hall, or (2) a kitchen or cooking equipment for the exclusive use of the occupants of the unit.

The inventory of housing units includes vacant as well as occupied units. Newly constructed vacant units were included if all exterior windows and doors were installed and the final usable floors were in place. Dilapidated vacant units were included provided they were still usable as living quarters but were excluded if they were being demolished or if there was definite evidence that such action was contemplated. Trailers, tents, boats, and railroad cars were included in the housing inventory if they were occupied as housing units but were excluded entirely if they were not so occupied. The housing unit of 1960 replaced the dwelling unit of 1950.[4]

Group quarters

According to the Census Bureau:

> Occupied quarters which do not qualify as housing units are classified as group quarters. They are located most frequently in institutions, hospitals, nurses' homes, rooming and boarding houses, military and other types of barracks, college dormitories, fraternity and sorority houses, convents, and monasteries. Group quarters are also located in a house or apartment in which the living quarters are shared by the person in charge and five or more persons unrelated to him.

In field mapping, areas occupied by group quarters may fall under "institutional land use" or some other non-residential category in spite of the fact that they perform a residential function.

Intercity data

The chief intercity housing data are in the state and small areas reports of the 1960 *Census of Housing;* the reports are published for all states. For each state,

[4] The housing unit is believed to encompass more completely all private living quarters than its predecessor, the dwelling unit. For details of this difference see the introductory text in any city blocks report, state and small areas report, metropolitan housing report, or census tract report.

housing-unit data are shown for standard metropolitan statistical areas, urbanized areas, and urban places of 1,000 inhabitants or more.[5] Each state volume covers occupancy characteristics, such as tenure, vacancy status, color of occupants, number of persons per occupied dwelling unit; structural characteristics, such as number of rooms and the year the structure was built; condition of unit; plumbing facilities, such as water supply and toilet and bathing facilities; equipment and fuels, including heating equipment, air conditioning, television sets, washing machines; heating fuel, cooking fuel, and water heating fuel; and financial characteristics, including value and rent. The detail is greatest for standard metropolitan statistical areas and least for places of 1,000 to 2,500 inhabitants.

Intracity data

Fortunately for anyone wishing to study housing variations within the city, some of the same data are available by city blocks (Table 18.1), which are the smallest units of the Census of Housing (see Appendix B). Only a limited number of characteristics are given, it is true, compared with those available for standard metropolitan statistical areas, urbanized areas, and places of 2,500 population or more, but these block data do make possible the study of some of the variations in residential patterns within the city to a degree that is not permitted by census data for commercial and manufacturing land uses. Maps of the various cities are

Table 18.1   Data given for each block in each city blocks report of 1960 Census of Housing

Total population

All housing units by condition and plumbing
    Total
    Sound
        Total
            With all plumbing facilities
            Lacking some or all facilities
    Deteriorating
        Total
            With all plumbing facilities
            Lacking some or all facilities
                With flush toilet
                No flush toilet
    Dilapidated

Occupied housing units
    Owner occupied
        Total
        Average value (dollars)
        Average number of rooms
    Renter occupied
        Total
        Average contract rent (dollars)
        Average number of rooms
    Occupied by non-white
    1.01 or more persons per room

available with the block data reports (Figure 18.1). These maps show the individual blocks of the city with identifying numbers.

Census tract reports, which are joint publications of the Censuses of Population and Housing, contain, for each tract, considerably more elaborate intracity housing data than are given for each city block.

Other Sources

Non-census sources yield little data for studying urban residential patterns, probably chiefly because of the sheer magnitude of the task of collecting such data. However, in the individual city, information may be available on welfare, juvenile delinquency, and other similar matters, and it is of interest to see the degree of asso-

[5] This policy is not followed consistently for New England. For example, in the case of Leicester, Mass., a town in Worcester County with a population of only 8,117 in 1960, two "urban places" are outlined, Leicester and Rochdale, and some "selected characteristics of housing units" are given for each in the Massachusetts States and Small Areas report. In contrast, no housing data are given for all or any portions of the town of Shrewsbury (population 16,622) in Worcester County or for West Springfield (population 24,924) in Hampden County.

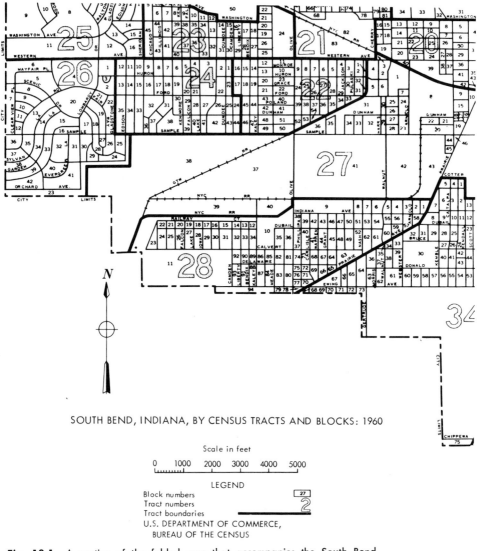

SOUTH BEND, INDIANA, BY CENSUS TRACTS AND BLOCKS: 1960

Scale in feet

0   1000   2000   3000   4000   5000

LEGEND

Block numbers
Tract numbers
Tract boundaries

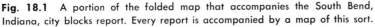

U.S. DEPARTMENT OF COMMERCE,
BUREAU OF THE CENSUS

Fig. 18.1 A portion of the folded map that accompanies the South Bend, Indiana, city blocks report. Every report is accompanied by a map of this sort.

ciation between such social factors and certain residential characteristics.

Field mapping

Field mapping is by no means to be ruled out in studying patterns of residential characteristics, especially those of residential land use itself. The geographer may carry on such mapping in any one city or in several cities which he is studying, thus arriving at data on proportions of residential land use,[6] as well as extent of areas devoted to single-family, two-family, and multifamily structures. The findings can be compared with similar data from other cities since residential land use is often mapped by planners, and hence such information is likely to be available on maps or in summary form. Certain other residential char-

[6] For mapping gross residential land use, air photographs and Sanborn maps may save considerable field time (see p. 189).

acteristics can be taken account of in the mapping, for example, space between structures. But in spite of the undoubted value of field mapping, the results lack the comparability of census findings. Unfortunately, however, the Census Bureau does not assemble data on residential land use, just as it does not collect data on the use of land for manufacturing or for business.

The American Public Health Association appraisal technique

In any discussion of residential field mapping, attention should be called to a field survey method for evaluating residential areas which was first described in the literature in the 1940s and has been widely used in selecting areas for urban renewal programs.[7] This method, the American Public Health Association (APHA) appraisal technique, involves two separate appraisals, one dealing with dwelling conditions and the other with quality of the environment. A penalty scoring system is used to rate a structure and its surroundings in terms of various features that are indicative of urban blight.

The method may be further described as follows: The dwelling-unit [8] appraisal is based on the individual dwelling and includes, among others, items on deterioration, maintenance and state of repair, safety and sanitation, adequacy of heating and lighting, and degree of room crowding. The

[7] American Public Health Association, Committee on the Hygiene of Housing, *An Appraisal Method for Measuring the Quality of Housing: A Yardstick for Health Officers, Housing Officials and Planners:* part I, "Nature and Uses of the Method," 1945; part II, "Appraisal of Dwelling Conditions," 1946; part III, "Appraisal of Neighborhood Environment," 1950. See, also, Philip Darling, "A Short-cut Method for Evaluating Housing Quality," *Land Economics,* vol. 25, pp. 184–192, 1949.

[8] At the time the APHA technique was developed, the dwelling unit was still the standard residential unit of the Census Bureau, so it is used here. In 1960, however, it was replaced by the housing unit, which would be used now if the technique were being applied.

environmental-quality appraisal covers such items as land crowding; front feet of inimical uses in the block; adequacy of water and sewerage facilities in the block; adequacy of schools, recreation areas, and other communal facilities in the area; and the extent of hazards and nuisances from traffic, railroads, and factories. The scores from the two appraisals can be combined to give a *housing score*. The technique can be used either for a complete house-to-house coverage of an urban area or a sampling of the area. A block may be found to correspond to any one of the following quality grades: A, excellent to good; B, acceptable; C, questionable; D, substandard; E, unfit for habitation.

Patterns of City Distribution Based on Residential Characteristics

Cities differ from one another in residential characteristics. Some contain unduly large proportions of houses built long ago; some have higher proportions of home ownership than others; some are distinguished by higher average values of owner-occupied units; some are characterized by higher proportions of deteriorating and dilapidated housing units; some have larger percentages of single-unit structures; and some exhibit more vacancy than others. As was pointed out earlier, such data by urban centers are available in the state and small areas reports of the Census of Housing.

The urban geographer is interested in distribution patterns of cities based on such residential characteristics. Are there regional contrasts? Do cities of the South, for example, differ from those of the Middle West or Northeast in proportions of home ownership? In proportions of substandard housing units? And, of course, the urban geographer wants to know with what other variations these patterns are associated.

There has not been much research by urban geographers at this intercity level; indeed, there has been little dealing with any residential patterns. Nevertheless, several intercity studies by geographers are referred to at appropriate points in the following pages, and intercity residential variations seem to offer good opportunities for additional research.

General Pattern of Residential Land Use in the City

But intercity patterns are only part of the story. What is the general picture presented by residential land use in the interior of the city? In the first place, in nearly every city, residential land use, as it has been defined here, is the largest single element on the land-use map. "Nearly every" is used advisedly, since there are a few small "cities" almost entirely industrial, which have managed to remain politically distinct from the areas in which most of their employees reside.[9] These small cities may have little land used for anything except factories and, perhaps, wholesaling. Though governed as units, such places are in reality only parts of cities.

Let us consider, instead, the pattern of residential land use in the average American city. A few housing units may be found just inside the central business district, especially on upper floors, but the district is largely devoid of residences (see Figures 10.1 and 10.2). It appears as a blank area on a population dot map of the city.

Just beyond the edges of the central business district the map commonly shows a belt of considerable density. There are often old residences in portions of this belt, grand houses of long ago, sometimes partly given over to beauty parlors or other lesser commercial uses and not infrequently operated as rooming houses. But these houses are in the minority. More typically, the belt has tenements and other low-quality residences which constitute the city's slums. Parts of the area, in some of the larger

cities, are undergoing redevelopment and have acquired a number of modern apartment houses. Typically, throughout the belt, yards are extremely limited or nonexistent.

Beyond the belt bordering the central business district and stretching in all directions through the corporate city and on into the suburbs are vast areas of predominantly residential land use. Density of housing tends to decrease with distance outward, and there is correspondingly more yard space around dwellings. But residential use, though predominant, is by no means continuous. Secondary commercial areas and ribbons of commercial development along important streets interrupt the expanse of residences, and so, too, do factory areas and areas of other land uses. There are various degrees of intermingling of these other types of land use with the residential use, and there are the ubiquitous streets which, in the average city, occupy almost as much land as the residential function.

Finally, scattered over the adjacent countryside, are individual homes of people who gain their entire livelihood from work in the city. These houses, too, in a sense, are part of the intracity residence supply, but they are not considered further here.

Theoretical Explanations of Residential Patterns

The pattern of residential land use of the city as just described may seem to exhibit little evidence of any rationality or guiding theme. But it will be recalled that several students of the city would argue differently. Theories have been advanced regarding the arrangement of city functions, theories in which residential land use plays a prominent role. Does residential land along with other land uses tend to occur in successive zones centered on the central business district? Or is the residential pattern better understood in terms of sectors, some of which have residences of high

[9] The city of Vernon in the Los Angeles Urbanized Area is a striking example. See pp. 422–424.

quality and tend to maintain this character as the city expands outward? Or do the residential areas develop chiefly around certain nuclei and take their characters from these nuclei?

These theories were discussed in Chapter 12 and will not be repeated here. However, it may be interesting to keep them in mind as the intracity residential patterns are considered in the present chapter.

Intensity Patterns

One of the most critical characteristics to be studied in connection with patterns of cities is intensity or density of residential spacing. This is partly a matter of the type of structure (Figure 10.1). Single-family residences obviously represent a lower density of residential land use than two-family or multifamily structures. But there is an additional point. Even among areas having a single type of structure, such as single-family houses, there may be considerable variation in spacing.

Types of structures

The difference between single-family structures and structures built for two or more families is fundamental to any study of urban residential land use. In his study of fifty-three central cities, discussed earlier in this book (see pages 194 to 196), Bar-

tholomew found that single-family dwellings accounted for much more of the land than two-family and multifamily houses together (Table 18.2).

Bartholomew pointed out, moreover, certain ratios that are relevant here. Thus single-family dwellings seem to occupy a fairly constant proportion of the developed area of the city up to a city size of about 250,000; in larger cities than this, the proportion of the area used for single-family dwellings declines. The ratio of land occupied by single-family dwellings to total population tends to decrease with city size. This is to be expected, since the single dwelling unit on a large lot is not practical in large cities. On the other hand, Bartholomew found a distinct tendency for the percentage of the city's total developed area used for multifamily dwellings to increase with increase in total city population; and he found that the larger the city the greater the ratio of multifamily land use to population.

Intracity distribution of common structural types

Even more than in possible relationships between the three types of dwellings and city size, the urban geographer is interested in patterns of distribution. How are the different structural types of dwellings with their associated density characteristics

Table 18.2   Importance of three types of dwellings in relation to total developed area and total residential area in 53 central cities

Type of use	Percentage of total developed area	Percentage of total residential area
Single-family dwellings	31.81	80.29
Two-family dwellings	4.79	12.11
Multifamily dwellings	3.01	7.60
Total residential	39.61	100.00

SOURCE: After Harland Bartholomew, Land Uses in American Cities, Harvard University Press, Cambridge, Mass., 1955, p. 46.

distributed throughout the city? According to Fisher and Fisher:

> . . . Apartment or tenement houses usually cluster near the center of the community [around the edges of the central business district] and also along lines of rapid transport, such as subways or highways. Generally, the oldest multifamily structures stand close to strategic points at which transportation facilities have been available for the longest period of time.
>
> Single-family residences predominate in suburban regions as well as in other areas adjacent to multifamily structures. . . .[10]

No information by city blocks regarding distribution of structural types of dwellings is available from the Census Bureau. But data are given by census tracts on numbers of units in structures, so the proportion of one-unit structures in each tract may be determined (Figure 18.2), or the proportion of one-unit plus two-unit structures.[11] The proportion generally is greatest in outer portions of the city; in short, intensity tends to vary inversely with distance from the city center.

Special types of housing

There are also special types of housing with their own density characteristics. For example, there are row houses in which one wall of a house is shared with the neighbor to the right, and the other wall is held in common with the neighbor to the left. These are especially numerous in older sections of Philadelphia and Baltimore. In New England there is the "three-deck-

er"—a three-story, three-family house. And there are other local types that carry concomitant densities. The origin, spread, and present extent of such special housing types would make worthwhile subjects of study for the urban geographer.

Spacing of structures

The actual spacing of structures cannot be determined from United States Census sources since the Census Bureau does not record areas. It is possible in the field to concentrate on mapping this single element of intensity—space between structures—though this has more meaning if the sizes of structures are in some way mapped at the same time, possibly as a ratio of area occupied by structure to total lot area. Such ratios, averaged for each block, might form the basis for a useful map of spacing of structures.

Patterns Based on Census of Housing Data

The intensity patterns described in the preceding section are based only in part on Census of Housing data. A number of other residential patterns which will now be discussed are based almost entirely on these housing statistics. But it should be noted that the data are for housing units. Since they take no account of yards, they do not fully describe residential land use.

Ownership patterns

Ownership is a characteristic of urban housing for which data are rather easily available. Thus, the numbers of owner-occupied and renter-occupied housing units are given by census tracts and by blocks, and a map on this basis can be made for any city or for part of a city and compared with other intracity patterns. One might, for example, make a map showing the proportion of rented units by census tracts (Figure 18.3) or even by census blocks. Does the percentage tend to be high or low in high-quality sections of the city (com-

---

[10] Fisher and Fisher, op. cit., p. 321.

[11] As the various characteristics of housing units are considered, the limitations of census tracts must be kept in mind. Although they are, according to the Bureau of the Census, "generally designed to be relatively uniform with respect to population characteristics, economic status, and living conditions," nevertheless, the average tract typically exhibits considerable diversity. Therefore, characteristics plotted by tracts may fail to show local areal variations that are really substantial. On the other hand, data available by city blocks are extremely limited.

pare with Figure 18.5)? Or is there any consistent relationship? Is the percentage of home ownership higher on the periphery of the city than nearer the center (Figure 18.3)? Is it higher in single-unit or in multi-unit sections of the city (Figure 18.2)? Even though some of the answers may seem obvious, investigations of the consistency of such general relationships are worthwhile.

Similar percentages can be worked out for individual cities on the basis of state and small areas data.[12] Should one expect the percentage of rentals to vary by functional type of city? Should suburbs, satellites, and central cities have typical but contrasting percentages? Do such proportions vary with city size?

Also included in the housing inventory is public housing. It is renter-occupied housing operated by a housing authority or corporation which is government financed. After World War II, public housing was built chiefly for veterans, but this phase of the public housing demand has almost disappeared. Recent projects have been intended chiefly for those with low incomes and with middle incomes and for old people. What should be expected to control the distribution pattern of such housing within the city? Would such housing be more characteristic of some types of cities than of others?

Age patterns of structures

Age of structures, like other residential characteristics, can be studied on an intracity basis or for cities as units.

Are the oldest and the newest residential buildings in a city likely to be found close together? Or are the oldest structures segregated in certain parts of the city and the newest in others? Data on when the

urban residential structures were built are available by census tracts on the basis of three periods: 1950 to March, 1960; 1940 to 1949; and 1939 or earlier. This information can be plotted in any of several ways, and the resulting patterns can be compared with other distribution patterns for the city. (See, for example, Figure 18.4, which should be compared with Figures 18.2, 18.3, 18.5, 18.7, and 18.8.) [13]

Through the use of data from the state and small areas reports, cities can be compared as to the proportions of residential structures built at different times. Here the breakdown is a little more detailed: 1955 to March, 1960; 1950 to 1954; 1940 to 1949; and 1939 or earlier. The detail is greater still for standard metropolitan statistical areas, urbanized areas, and cities of 50,000 population or more.[14]

Value and rent

Average value of owner-occupied housing units and average rent for renter-occupied units have interesting patterns of variation in the city. The blocks of highest median values mark the high-quality sections of the city; and the highest median rentals indicate the location of the best of the city's rental areas. Similar though somewhat more detailed data are available for census tracts (Figure 18.5). The median-values map for Worcester by census tracts shows a pattern which characterizes many cities—with low values in the older central portion of the city and higher values in the newer and more recently built-up areas.

Valuation data and rental data are given for individual cities in the state and small areas reports. These data make possible the answers to some interesting ques-

[12] A map in colors issued by the U.S. Bureau of the Census shows for 1960 by standard metropolitan statistical areas the relative proportions of occupied housing owned and rented. Central cities are contrasted with the remainder of the standard metropolitan statistical area in each case.

[13] Consider also, in this connection, Burgess' concentric zones described in Chap. 12.

[14] A map in colors issued by the U.S. Bureau of the Census shows for 1960 by standard metropolitan statistical areas the proportion of housing built before 1950. Central cities are contrasted with the remainder of the standard metropolitan statistical area in each case.

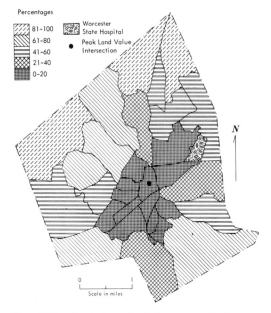

Fig. 18.2 Proportion of all housing units in one-unit structures, by census tracts, Worcester, Massachusetts, 1960. Obviously, the proportion is small in the central, older areas of the city, but increases with distance outward from the center. (Data from 1960 *Census of Population* and 1960 *Census of Housing*.)

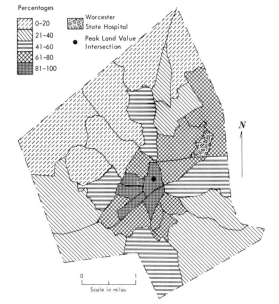

Fig. 18.3 Rented housing units as percentages of all occupied housing units, by census tracts, Worcester, Massachusetts, 1960. (Data from 1960 *Census of Population* and 1960 *Census of Housing*.)

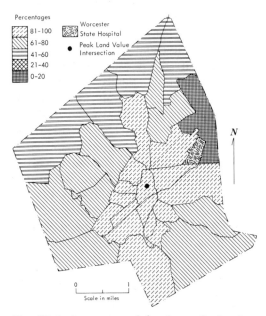

Fig. 18.4 Percentage of housing units in structures built before 1940, by census tracts, Worcester, Massachusetts, 1960. The newer housing is in northern areas of the city. (Data from 1960 *Census of Population* and 1960 *Census of Housing*.)

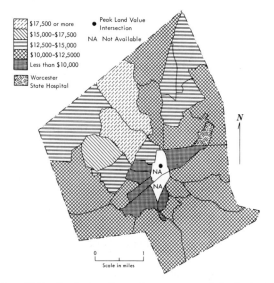

Fig. 18.5 Median values of owner-occupied single-unit structures, by census tracts, Worcester, Massachusetts, 1960. (Data from 1960 *Census of Population* and 1960 *Census of Housing*.)

tions. Do cities of high median housing values characterize certain sections of the country? Are such high values particularly characteristic of some functional types of cities? And is the intracity range of housing values greater for some sections of the country than for others? This last question was answered in the affirmative by Roland Fuchs.

Patterns of intraurban variation of residential quality In a study of variations in the intracity range of housing values, based on 1950 housing data,[15] Fuchs faced a difficulty inherent in these data: How can value of owner-occupied units and rent of renter-occupied units be reduced to equivalent terms so that city maps can be made or housing-cost figures arrived at for a city on a single basis?

The answer is somehow to convert housing values to rents or vice versa. Fuchs, who chose to base his maps upon rents, points out that estimated sale price can be converted to an estimated rental figure by employing a real estate rule based upon the close relationship between rents and property prices. "It is often stated as a general rule of thumb that a property is worth one hundred times the monthly rent or that it should rent for one percent of the cost of the property."[16] Fuchs applied this conversion method to the 209 cities for which block statistics were published for 1950, making certain adjustments, which are described in his article, for "open-end" categories.[17]

Using statistical techniques, Fuchs first calculated degrees of relative internal variation in residential quality (as reflected in

rental figures) for each of the 209 cities.[18] At this point he decided to base further work on central cities (of standard metropolitan areas) since they appeared to reveal more significant differences in amount of variation than non-central cities. He discovered that for central cities there were indeed substantial regional differences in the intraurban variation of residential quality (Figure 18.6). The range was greatest in the Southeast and in southern New England, and least in the Middle West and West. Further work demonstrated that intracity variation was significantly associated with several urban characteristics. Most significant was a direct association with the percentage of low-income families and a negative association with the percentage of dwelling units that were owner-occupied.

Differentiating high-quality residential areas and slums Most residential areas in the city are neither of very low nor of extremely high quality. Nevertheless, extremes attract more interest than averages and give rise to more intriguing questions. How, for instance, can we distinguish the areas of high-quality housing, and how can we differentiate slums?

HIGH-QUALITY HOUSING The definition of high-quality housing in the city presents difficulties, since Census of Housing data are focused chiefly on substandard housing characteristics. The only census data showing intracity variations in residential quality in local detail are those in city blocks reports (Table 18.1). Average value of owner-occupied housing can be reduced to rent equivalent, but one must be content with approximate results.

Other problems, too, are involved in differentiating high-quality housing. For example, just where should the lower limit of high quality be drawn, and how? One might take the whole range of housing values for all cities and consider some fraction, perhaps the upper one-fourth, as high-qual-

[15] Roland J. Fuchs, "Intraurban Variation of Residential Quality," *Economic Geography*, vol. 36, pp. 313–325, 1960.

[16] Leevern Johnson, "The Appraisal of Homes," *Appraisal Journal*, vol. 24, p. 516, 1956.

[17] Open-end categories can best be defined by two examples. In the 1960 census tract housing data, the highest value class given is "25,000 or more" and the highest rental class, "150 or more."

[18] Coefficients of variation were computed.

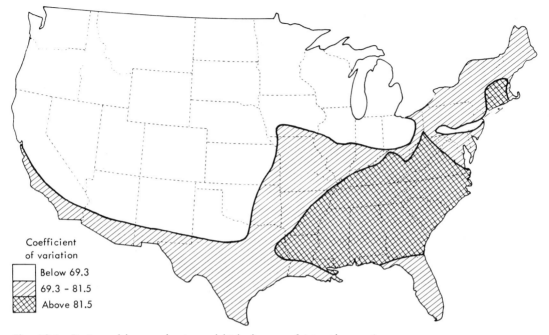

Coefficient
of variation

Below 69.3
69.3 – 81.5
Above 81.5

Fig. 18.6 Regions of low, moderate, and high degrees of intraurban variation of residential quality in central cities, 1950. Southern New England and
much of southeastern United States exhibit a high degree of variation. (After
Roland J. Fuchs, "Intraurban Variation of Residential Quality," *Economic
Geography*, vol. 36, 1960, fig. 5.)

ity housing. But should such a determination be based on values for all cities in the
nation? In that case, any one city might be
found to have very little high-quality housing, or half or more of its housing might
rate as high quality. One might decide, instead, for the particular city being studied,
to base the inquiry upon relative quality
within the city; then only the housing values of that single city would be considered.

Can the delimitation of high-quality
housing in a city be accomplished through
a field approach? What are the telltales of
high quality? A basic one, of course, is the
number of housing units in each structure.
High quality normally is associated only
with single-unit structures, though most
single-unit structures are not of high quality. Garage capacity per single-unit structure is generally considered a further index
of quality. What other field criteria might
be used?

SLUMS   Since most of the Census of
Housing data are aimed at outlining the
low-quality areas of the city it is no great
task to focus in a general way on the bad
and the very bad housing areas. Whether
these areas are *slums* or not is a matter of
definition. A slum seems to be generally
defined as an area where dwellings predominate which are so inferior as to be
detrimental to safety, health, or morals. But
there is no accepted statistical definition of
a slum, whereas the term *substandard
housing*, referring to dilapidated and deteriorating housing units, is rather generally
accepted. To what degree can areas of such
substandard housing be called slums? [19]

[19] It has been suggested that a slum might be defined by a high degree of substandardness, rather
like defining the hard core of the central business
district through the use of higher index values than
those required for defining the central business
district in general.

The pattern of condition of structures

As is clear from the foregoing discussion, one of the most important characteristics of urban housing is the condition of housing units. Census of Housing data available by blocks make it possible to show on a map the percentage of housing units that are substandard (deteriorating or dilapidated) in each block as contrasted with those that are sound. Or, if desired, the percentage that is dilapidated only may be shown; this is the lowest category of condition differentiated in the Census of Housing data.

Are housing units that are rated as deteriorating or dilapidated scattered at random over the city or are they concentrated in certain areas? In a study of Richmond, Virginia, carried out several decades ago, Homer Hoyt showed that, as might be expected, blocks with poor housing conditions were located predominantly in the valleys and on low ground elsewhere and were correlated rather closely with the low-rent areas of the city.[20]

As with data on other housing characteristics, data on substandardness of housing are available by larger units as well as by blocks. They are, of course, available by census tracts, and tracts rather than blocks are used here and throughout this chapter simply because use of the tract scale is more practicable. The map that may be constructed from these tract data shows that substandard housing has a tendency to occur in the older, central portions of the city where the proportion of single-unit structures is low and where rentals make up a high percentage of the housing units (Figure 18.7; compare with Figures 18.2 to 18.5). Data for urban places of 1,000 population or more, obtainable from state and small areas bulletins, make it possible to study relationships between substandardness and other housing characteristics at the intercity level.

A study of substandard housing Much of the interest in housing in recent years has focused on inadequate living quarters. It is a concern that is likely to grow, since provision of proper housing is one of the goals of the current war on poverty. The geographer, naturally, is interested in the patterns of distribution of these poor housing conditions both at the intercity and the intracity levels. Substandard urban housing in the United States, as recorded in 1950 *Census of Housing* publications, was studied some years ago by two geographers, Hartman and Hook, on an intercity basis.[21] The authors began with three questions: (1) What are the proportions of substandard housing in United States cities with populations of 10,000 or more? (2) How are the proportions of substandard housing in these cities areally distributed over the country? (3) How closely are patterns of certain other phenomena, such as low family income, associated with the distribution of substandard urban housing? Substandard housing was defined as housing that was either dilapidated or lacked basic sanitary amenities. The percentage of such housing was obtained by subtracting from 100 the percentage of dwelling units with hot running water, with private toilet and bath, and not dilapidated, as given in the 1950 *Census of Housing.*

Cities differ considerably in their proportions of substandard housing. Hartman and Hook found the proportions to vary from 0.2 per cent for University Heights, Ohio, a high-quality suburb of Cleveland, to 73.6 per cent for Helena, Arkansas; with

[20] *Structure and Growth of Residential Neighborhoods in American Cities,* U.S. Federal Housing Administration, 1939, pp. 34–48. The block data used were the results of "real property inventories" carried on by the Federal government in the 1930s. The present Census of Housing is an outgrowth of these early real property inventories.

[21] George W. Hartman and John C. Hook, "Substandard Urban Housing in United States: A Quantitative Analysis," *Economic Geography,* vol. 32, pp. 95–114, 1956.

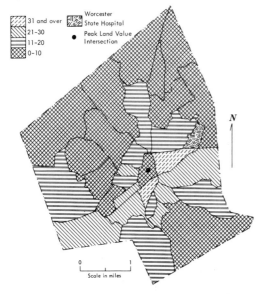

Fig. 18.7 Percentages of all housing units that are substandard (deteriorating or dilapidated), by census tracts, Worcester, Massachusetts, 1960. (Data from 1960 *Census of Population* and 1960 *Census of Housing*.) Note, however, that tracts form a particularly poor basis for focusing on substandardness since they represent averages. Within an individual tract that, as a whole, shows little substandardness there may be a number of blocks or of neighborhoods with notably poor housing.

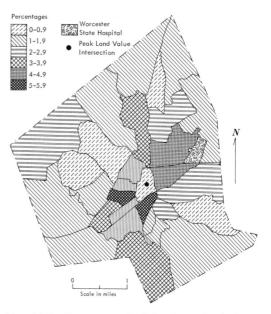

Fig. 18.8 Percentage of all housing units that are vacant and available, by census tracts, Worcester, Massachusetts, 1960. (Data from 1960 *Census of Population* and 1960 *Census of Housing*.)

a median of 22.2 per cent (Waynesboro, Pennsylvania).

The percentages of substandardness of all the cities under study were plotted on a map of the United States. In spite of discrepancies, it was apparent that substandardness of housing showed definite regional variation (Figure 18.9). For instance, cities with the highest percentages of substandardness were concentrated primarily in Southeastern United States, in the same general area in which Fuchs found the highest degree of intraurban variation of residential quality (see Figure 18.6), and along the lower Rio Grande Valley. Cities in most of Northeastern United States, in the Western two-fifths of the country, and in peninsular Florida showed the lowest percentages of substandardness.

But establishing the facts that there is

a considerable variation in the proportion of substandard housing in American cities and that there is regional differentiation in substandardness was only the beginning of the study. In addition, the associations between substandardness and a number of phenomena regarded as possibly related to it to a significant degree were checked statistically. Factors that were found to be relatively closely associated with substandardness were the proportion of families with low income and the proportion of certain family types restricted in choice of residence. The authors pointed out that age of residential structures and percentages of labor force unemployed appeared to be relevant factors, although this could not be demonstrated statistically, possibly because of certain difficulties inherent in the use of the types of data available.

The filtering-down process Closely related to substandardness of housing is the *filtering-down process*. It may be de-

REGIONS OF SUBSTANDARDNESS URBAN HOUSING

0 – 28% West, Northeast Florida
28 – 44% Midwest marg. Northeast marg.
44 +% Rio Grande, Southeast

Fig. 18.9 Regions of substandardness of urban housing, based on proportion of dwelling units that were substandard according to data in the 1950 *Census of Housing*. There are a number of cities that did not conform to the regional patterns. Nevertheless, the regions shown represent the predominant situation. (After George Hartman and John C. Hook, "Substandard Urban Housing in the United States: A Quantitative Analysis," *Economic Geography*, vol. 32, 1956, fig. 3.)

scribed most simply as the passing down of housing to successively lower-income groups as adequate supplies of housing for upper-income groups are produced.[22] Theoretically, filtering down continues until the bottom of the housing market—that is, the lowest price-quality level—is reached. In the long run, a surplus of housing (reflected in vacancies) will accumulate at this market level until uneconomic units are demolished or removed from the housing market.

The filtration idea is also closely related to the Burgess and Hoyt models of city growth described in Chapter 12. Both Burgess and Hoyt postulated that growth of

the city takes place outward from a central focal point, and, as new houses are constructed and occupied on the outer edges of the city, housing in the central areas tends to decline in value and quality. Theoretically, then, the bottom of the market should be located in the residential area that fringes the central business district.[23]

[22] Richard U. Ratcliff, *Urban Land Economics*, McGraw-Hill Book Company, Inc., New York, 1949, pp. 321–334.

[23] For some time students of American cities have been aware of an interesting paradox. Land values tend to drop with distance from the city center while family income tends to rise. The paradox is that the well-to-do live on cheap land while the poor live on expensive land. Thus the urban area grows like a tree in cross-section. What will happen as, through urban renewal, more and more new, high-income central housing becomes available? Will the well-to-do suburban dwellers move to the center and then start shifting outward again, thus

But just as the Burgess and Hoyt models do not apply uniformly to all cities, neither does the filtration concept apply to all. In fact, it is often argued that there are so many deviations from the generally expected process that filtration is an almost totally inadequate remedy for the problem of housing for lower-income groups as well as for the removal of substandard housing.

Housing vacancy patterns

Vacancy is another characteristic that is important in studying housing. From data in the city blocks report for any city the percentage of vacancy by blocks can be calculated, and the resulting map can be compared with those of tenure, value, rent, number of rooms, condition of structures, and other relevant characteristics of housing. What is the nature of the distribution of residential vacancies within the city? To what extent do concentrations of vacancies occur in areas of substandard housing and to what extent in areas of new and as yet unoccupied housing? And what are the relationships with the other patterns of characteristics of housing units? With social, economic, and demographic patterns?

Housing vacancy data are available in greater detail by census tracts. Here the primary division is between "available vacant" and "other vacant" (Figure 18.8; compare with Figures 18.2–18.5 and 18.7). The former are those units that are on the market for year-round occupancy; other vacant units include "dilapidated units, seasonal units, units rented or sold and awaiting occupancy, units held for occasional use, and units held off the market for other

reasons." The available vacant units are further subdivided into available for sale only and available for rent. Though vacancy maps based on census tract data are much less fine-textured than maps based on block data, the former are more convenient to work with. Moreover, as pointed out earlier, there are available, by tracts, various other data to which tract housing data are often meaningfully related.[24]

A study of intra-city vacancy patterns

In a study of vacancy patterns in five cities, an attempt was made to determine the relationships between unoccupied housing, the concentric zone and sector models, and the filtration concept of housing.[25]

Census tract data and data collected from other sources were used to examine the relationships between variations in vacancy rates and a number of other factors thought to be significant in explaining the patterns of unused housing. The five cities studied were Baton Rouge, Louisiana; Fort Wayne, Indiana; Rockford, Illinois; Savannah, Georgia; and Worcester, Massachusetts. Among the findings of the study, it was noted that the precise nature of the interrelationships between the distribution of vacancy rates and the hypothesized factors differed from city to city and also regionally. Thus, in the three Northern cities, there were a number of similarities. In general, high rates of vacancy in these cities occurred in the older, low-quality, low-income, residentially mobile, central residential areas of the city. These areas, in general,

---

generating, in the long run, a convectional flow? See William Alonso, "The Historic and the Structural Theories of Urban Form: Their Implications for Urban Renewal," *Land Economics*, vol. 49, pp. 227–231, 1964. A question might be added here. In many of the larger urban areas the central cities have much higher proportions of Negroes than the suburbs, a trend that is continuing. How will this affect the possible return of the well-to-do to central areas of the city?

[24] It should be noted that the only vacant units figure available on a block basis is obtained by subtracting the sum of owner-occupied and renter-occupied units from total housing units. The result is not a count of vacant units on the market. Instead, it includes all types of vacant units—those available for sale or rent as well as dilapidated units, seasonal units, and units held off the market for various reasons.

[25] Carolyn J. Ryan, "Intra-city Patterns of Residential Vacancy Rates," unpublished doctoral dissertation, Clark University, Worcester, Mass., 1964.

had also experienced population losses. Low vacancy rates occurred in the newer, owner-occupied, higher-income, residentially stable, peripheral sections of the city, which had gained population in the last decade.

The two Southern cities, Savannah and Baton Rouge, were quite different from the three Northern ones. The Southern cities had to be treated separately because of vacancy rate and other residential differentials between white and non-white residential areas of the city. Analysis of vacancy rates in these cities had to take cognizance of the differences between the white and non-white groups of tracts.

In the three Northern cities, the spatial outlines and the relationships between varying degrees of vacancy accorded well with the theories of Hoyt and Burgess. One tentative conclusion reached was that concentrations of vacancy in the older, central residential areas of the three Northern cities were the result of normal city growth processes. As new houses, conforming to changes in residential tastes and demands, were constructed and occupied in the peripheral sections of the city, the central residential areas declined in value, lost population, and were left with surpluses of unused housing.

Intercity patterns of housing vacancy
The study described was undertaken at an intracity level of generalization, although studies of vacancy or of any other housing characteristics may be undertaken at intercity levels as well.[26] And other questions relating to this level of generalization might be posed. How do patterns of city distribution on the basis of proportions of vacancy

[26] Housing vacancy data are available in state and small areas bulletins for most places of 1,000 population or more, in more detail for every place of 2,500 or more population, and in even greater detail for standard metropolitan statistical areas, urbanized areas, and cities of 50,000 population or more.

compare with patterns based on other housing characteristics? How does residential vacancy within cities vary regionally throughout the United States? Do the overall city vacancy rates vary by functional type of city? Is there any relationship between rates of vacancy and rates of unemployment?

The pattern of overcrowded housing units

The last of the housing characteristics to be discussed separately is a measure of overcrowding: the number of persons per room in dwelling units. In state and small areas reports and in census tract reports this information is given in some detail. In city blocks bulletins it is represented by a single limiting measure: housing units with 1.01 or more persons per room. This is a figure which has been much used in planning; as an exact dividing point it probably has been overrated. Regardless of the exact limiting value used, however, or whether the tract or the block is under consideration, it is found that the more crowded housing units are concentrated in the poorer sections of the city.

Other residential characteristics and patterns

A number of other housing characteristics, too, are summarized in the Census of Housing. Thus, there are data on white versus non-white occupants of housing units. This information is available by blocks, and it is summed up by census tracts and for all places of 1,000 population or more. In general the proportion of housing units with non-white occupants varies inversely with housing quality. Average number of rooms per housing unit per block, another measure of quality, may be expected to run highest in high-quality residential areas.

Another characteristic brought out by the Census of Housing is the year when the present residents moved into the housing unit. These data are given by census tracts for the following intervals: 1958 to March, 1960; 1954 to 1957; 1940 to 1953; and 1939 or earlier. It would appear that high proportions of recent arrivals might be found in either of two rather different types of areas: localities of very recent housing construction or areas of low housing quality. Similar data are available in state and small areas reports for places of 2,500 or more population.

And there are still other housing details available by tracts and summed up for urban places that reflect in one way or another on housing conditions: the presence or absence of a basement, the nature of heating equipment, and automobiles available.

Housing Characteristics and Quality

All of the housing characteristics described are to some degree measures of quality. They have been extensively used to focus on those parts of the city where some program of housing improvement is indicated.

But the patterns which have been discussed are of a good deal of interest for more scientific reasons also. Which ones are most closely related? And do they relate to patterns based on population characteristics, land-use data, or other phenomena?

Geographic City versus Corporate City in the Study of Housing Characteristics

The foregoing discussions of housing characteristics dealt, in each case, with the corporate city. This was largely a matter of convenience. Moreover, it was felt that patterns for the corporate city brought out the chief principles involved. But it would have been entirely possible and in many respects preferable to work with a larger area that would have more nearly approximated the geographic city. This might be done in either of two ways.

One would be to work with census tracts. The area around most tracted cities has itself been tracted, and summary housing data are available for each of these tracts just as they are for the tracts of the corporate city. But there are several difficulties. For one thing, the maps in census tract reports commonly show the city and tracts surrounding the city at different scales. Even if the two maps can be properly blended, for many cities it may be difficult to use a scale large enough to show the small tracts that are likely to occur near the city center and yet include the large tracts of the countryside. Moreover, some of the outlying tracts may include considerable open country and thus not be at all comparable to the tracts of the corporate city. For small tracted cities, it may be added, it is unlikely that the surrounding countryside will be tracted.

A second procedure is to use summary data from the state and small areas reports. When this is done for Buffalo and adjacent places, some interesting contrasts become apparent (Figure 18.10). Buffalo, the core city, and Lackawanna just to the south, have much higher proportions of rented units than most of the surrounding smaller places. But smaller incorporated urban places sometimes occur only sporadically around a core city, especially if the city is small, and the unincorporated areas, though bordering the city, cannot be taken account of at all.

Residential Regions

Though it is of obvious value to study urban patterns based on each of the various housing characteristics, such an analysis has its limitations. The geographer will strive for some sort of unit areas by which the city's residential sections can be considered, areas that will be more comprehensive than single-factor regions and yet more meaningful than such divisions as blocks, tracts, or wards.

Geographers have made some attempts

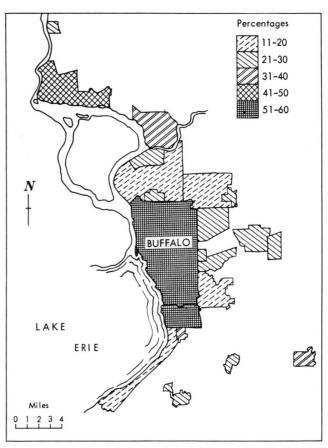

Fig. 18.10 Rented housing units as percentages of all occupied housing units in the Buffalo area, by urban places. The city of Buffalo and the small city of Lackawanna have larger proportions of rentals than any of the other political units represented. There are some areas of suburban development in adjacent townships, but for these no separate housing data are available. (Data from 1960 *Census of Housing*.)

at developing regions based on urban residential land use. Pierre Camu, for example, reported on a field study by geographers that involved a classification of house-type areas in the suburban region of Montreal.[27] His six categories were areas with row houses of 2 or 3 stories, apartment houses, single houses of 2 or 3 stories, single houses of 1 to 1½ stories, duplex houses, and, lastly, a mixture of house types (Figure 18.11).

The areas were also grouped, and for each group certain statistics were assembled rather like those furnished by the Census of Housing of the U.S. Census Bureau. Another geographer, in a study of Belfast, Northern Ireland, divided the city into regions based on type and age of housing combined with the presence or absence of shops.[28] But in spite of such efforts, geographers have done little by way of devel-

[27] Pierre Camu, "Types de Maisons dans la Région Suburbaine de Montréal," *The Canadian Geographer*, no. 9, pp. 21–29, 1957.

[28] Emrys Jones, "The Delimitation of Some Urban Landscape Features in Belfast," *The Scottish Geographical Magazine*, vol. 74, pp. 150–162, 1958.

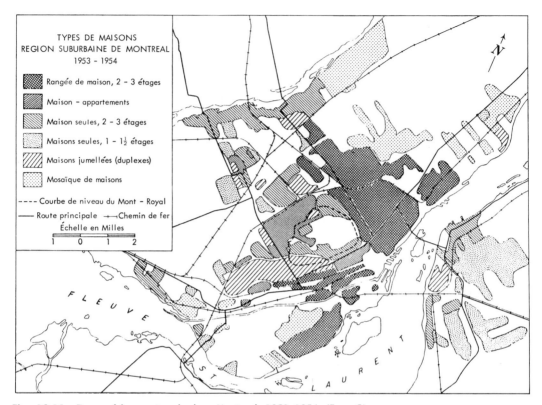

Fig. 18.11 Types of houses in suburban Montreal, 1953–1954. (From Pierre Camu, "Types de Maisons dans la Région Suburbaine de Montréal," *The Canadian Geographer*, no. 9, 1957, fig. 1.)

oping new methods of regionalizing the residential areas of cities. Possibly this is because the idea of the neighborhood long ago gained such popularity as the areal unit for studying urban residential land use.

Neighborhoods of the City

The *neighborhood* is a concept that is particularly difficult to pin down. Nearly half a century ago McKenzie, a sociologist, wrote, "Probably no other term is used so loosely or with such changing content as the term neighborhood, and very few concepts are more difficult to define." [29] A sur-

vey of the literature of recent years suggests that his statement still holds true.

A sociological concept?

The geographer may be tempted to dismiss the neighborhood from his field of study on the ground that it is a matter for the sociologist, and indeed it does seem chiefly to connote social relationships between people. "The emphasis of his [the sociologist's] interest, to be sure, is on the social rather than the spatial dimension; he is intent upon the investigation of 'neighboring' . . . [his] interest in the neighborhood has always been related to his interest in means of social control." [30] McKenzie

[29] R. D. McKenzie, "The Neighborhood: A Study of Local Life in the City of Columbus, Ohio," *American Journal of Sociology*, vol. 27, pp. 344–345, 1921–1922.

[30] Svend Riemer, in a symposium, "Frontiers of Housing Research" appearing as a supplement in *Land Economics*, vol. 25, p. 69, 1949.

referred to the neighborhood as "a patch of common life within the larger community, which is sufficiently differentiated from the city as a whole to be thought of as a unit." [31]

But the neighborhood, today, is by no means exclusively a sociological concept. There has always been popular usage, of course; in addition, planners have found the neighborhood a convenient unit for their studies of housing, though the neighborhood as they think of it may depart considerably from the sociologist's concept. In any event it is an areal unit of the city, so it is a direct concern of the urban geographer.

Neighborhoods in a New England city

Probably every city has some areas that are called neighborhoods, at least in the general sense of the term. They are areas that, for one reason or another, have come to be known by separate names whether or not they evidence any considerable degree of social integration.

In Worcester, Massachusetts, for example, there are Columbus Park, College Hill, Greendale, Vernon Hill, Tatnuck, Union Hill, Great Brook Valley, Westwood Hills, and some thirty or forty other neighborhoods (Figure 18.12). It would be hard to determine when the names originated, but the extent of the acceptance of most of them is evidenced by real estate advertisements in the Worcester evening paper. When an apartment is advertised for rent or a house for sale in almost any one of these neighborhoods, people not only know the location but also can infer something of the place's desirability from what is generally known of the neighborhood.

Types and classifications of neighborhoods

A person who knows Worcester will know the bases for a number of the city's neighborhoods. All are residential areas, of course, but they differ in other respects.

[31] McKenzie, op. cit., p. 352.

Several are known as concentrations of ethnic groups (see Creveling's study described on pages 179 to 182); at least two of the neighborhoods mentioned are centered around one or two prominent factories; still another is a low-cost public housing development; another is the highest-quality housing area in the city; and one has a college as its nucleus.[32]

But these are popular neighborhoods that in a sense just grew. There are several other types. For instance, there are "planners' neighborhoods" and planned neighborhoods, and still others conceived for one or another special purpose.[33]

Differentiating popular neighborhoods

Though neighborhoods such as those in Worcester are known in a general way, it is not easy to mark them off on a map. The central area of the neighborhood may be agreed upon, but what about the edges, and what is the nature of the area between it and the next adjacent well-known neighborhood? One can work out from the central area of the neighborhood and, through questions at individual houses, perhaps on a sampling basis, find the approximate line beyond which people no longer think of themselves as belonging in the neighborhood. But this may leave areas of indiffer-

[32] It may be of interest in this connection to review the multiple nuclei concept of city structure discussed on pp. 214–217.

[33] Robert Klove, in a study of a Chicago suburban area, used what he called "homogeneous neighborhoods." He defined a homogeneous neighborhood as "a group of contiguous subdivided blocks occupied by residential dwellings of similar type, size, use density, age, and quality of occupancy." Klove pointed out that the neighborhoods he outlined were not independent community areas, nor were they intended as neighborhoods in that sense. Most of them did not have their own stores, churches, schools, or parks. His neighborhoods averaged eighteen blocks in size and a population of 369. See Robert C. Klove, *The Park Ridge-Barrington Area: A Study of Residential Land Patterns and Problems in Suburban Chicago,* doctoral dissertation, private ed., University of Chicago Libraries, Chicago, 1942, p. 30.

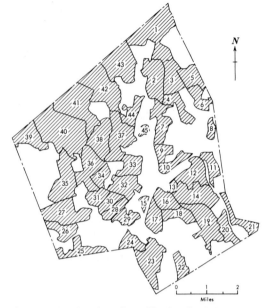

Fig. 18.12 Residential neighborhoods of Worcester as delimited by the Worcester Planning Department. The numbers refer to neighborhoods as follows: 1, Summit; 2, Burncoat; 3, Greendale; 4, Beverly Road; 5, Great Brook Valley; 6, Brookside; 7, Brittan Square; 8, Wigwam Hill; 9, Chandler Hill; 10, Shrewsbury Street; 11, Lakeview; 12, Bloomingdale; 13, Oak Hill; 14, Hamilton; 15, Island; 16, Union Hill; 17, Vernon Hill; 18, Rice Square; 19, Sunderland; 20, South Grafton Street; 21, Pinecrest; 22, Oakland Heights; 23, Quinsigamond Village; 24, College Hill; 25, Heard Street; 26, Ludlow; 27, South Worcester; 28, University Park; 29, Cambridge; 30, Woodland; 31, Columbus Park; 32, Piedmont; 33, Elm Park; 34, Beaverbrook; 35, Mill Street; 36, June Street; 37, Salisbury Park; 38, Westwood Hills; 39, West Tatnuck; 40, Tatnuck; 41, Salisbury Heights; 42, Westchester; 43, North Worcester; 44, Chadwick Square; 45, North Street.

Fig. 18.13 Planning districts as delimited by Worcester Planning Department. Compare with Figure 18.12. Note that all of the city is covered by the planning districts whether residential or nonresidential.

ence that do not really belong in any neighborhood.

The planning approach

A number of decades ago people interested in planning and housing research conceived the idea of using the neighborhood as the basis for their work. In recent years, it has been used considerably as an areal unit in deciding which areas in the city are suffi-

ciently substandard to justify applications for Federal funds for redevelopment, as well as for other purposes. The neighborhood, as adapted for planning purposes, can probably be most readily defined by the following quotation:

The neighborhood unit plan, in brief, is the effort to create a residential neighborhood to meet the needs of family life in a unit related to the larger whole but possessing a distinct entity characterized by the four strictly local factors:

1. A centrally located elementary school which will be within easy walking distance—no more than one-half mile—from the farthest dwelling.

2. Scattered neighborhood parks and playgrounds to comprise about 10 per cent of the whole area.

3. Local shops to meet daily needs, grouped together at accessible points on the periphery of the neighborhood.

4. A residential environment—that community-created resultant, the product

in part of a harmonious architecture, careful planting, centrally located community buildings, and special internal street system with deflection of all through traffic, preferably on thoroughfares which bound and clearly set off the neighborhood.[34]

It represents a compromise between the neighborhood concept of the sociologist and the popular neighborhood usage such as that described for Worcester, with due recognition of the present city realities of schools, streets, and the like.

The neighborhoods that have been outlined in so many cities have not been areas that necessarily measure up to the sociologist's ideas of a neighborhood, but they have been, at least, units of convenience for planning. The methods of delimiting these unit areas have by no means been standardized, though certain broad elements seem to be agreed upon.

Communities and neighborhoods of Cincinnati

An example of such a delimitation for Cincinnati was published in the 1940s.[35] The Cincinnati metropolitan area was considered to consist of twenty-four distinguishable "communities" (Figure 18.14). An average community was visualized as a fairly large area, 1,000 to 2,000 acres in extent, set off from surrounding areas by recognizable topographical or functional boundaries, and containing a present or potential population (perhaps 20,000 to 40,000 persons) large enough to support one junior high school with an accompanying playfield available for community use, and one dominant shopping district

with a rather complete assortment of goods and services.

Each community consisted of several more or less distinguishable neighborhoods. A neighborhood was described as perhaps 400 to 500 acres in extent; with an existing or anticipated population of 4,000 to 8,000 persons; an elementary school with children's playground; possibly additional playgrounds; one or more small local parks; and one or more shopping centers offering limited goods and services which are frequently used by the average family. The twenty-four communities covered by the master plan of Cincinnati contained a total of ninety-four neighborhoods.[36]

The approach in general

The delimitation described for Cincinnati is by no means unique, nor is it presented as a model of what should be done. Inquiry from planners, however, and examination of studies that have been made, suggest that somewhat similar methods have been used for neighborhood determination in many cities. An elementary school usually is taken as the core of the neighborhood. The traditional popular neighborhood pattern, too, such as that described for Worcester on pages 389 to 390, is followed in a general way.

Several other guides seem to be used. Thus, size of the neighborhood is likely to be expressed in number of families: 1,000 to 2,500 has been suggested as an average. Topographic breaks are sometimes relied upon to fix the outer boundaries, or the presence of rivers or other streams. Major arterials, even more, are used. But beyond the use of a few such elements one can find

[34] James Dahir, *The Neighborhood Unit Plan: Its Spread and Acceptance,* A Selected Bibliography with Interpretative Comments, Russell Sage Foundation, New York, 1947, p. 16.

[35] City Planning Commission, Cincinnati, Ohio, *Residential Areas: An Analysis of Land Requirements for Residential Development 1945 to 1970,* Cincinnati, December, 1946, and *Metropolitan Master Plan, Cincinnati, 1948.*

[36] Other neighborhoods were recognized which, because of isolation or restricted opportunity for expansion and population growth, could never be expected to achieve the standards of a full community or to become a component neighborhood of a community. They were referred to as "isolated neighborhoods," even though some were found in combinations of two or more.

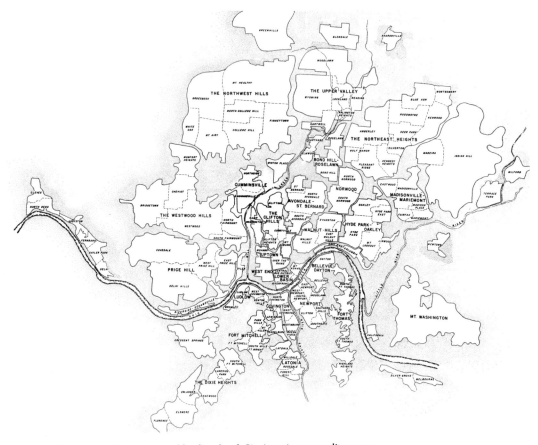

Fig. 18.14 Communities and neighborhoods of Cincinnati metropolitan area.
(From City Planning Commission, *Residential Areas*, Cincinnati, Ohio, 1946,
fig. 2.)

little by way of a standard method for delimiting neighborhoods. Delimitation in any
one city remains a highly subjective procedure.

Neighborhoods and planning Planners commonly delimit neighborhoods for
practical rather than scientific reasons. Having delimited the neighborhoods they then
attempt to characterize each through data
published in city blocks reports (Table
18.1). The method is simple. Take the case
of vacancy. For each neighborhood, the
number of housing units is totaled, and
since block data reports also give the number of occupied housing units, these, too,

can be totaled for the neighborhood as a
whole. Subtracting occupied housing units
from total housing units gives the number
vacant. Then, of course, it is easy to calculate the percentage of vacancy for the
neighborhood.

Condition and overcrowding may be
similarly analyzed. For the former, the percentage of all housing units in the neighborhood that are deteriorating or dilapidated
is calculated; for the latter, the percentage
of houses that have more than 1.01 persons
per room. And calculations can be made for
percentage of housing units in each neighborhood that are occupied by nonwhites,
and the percentage that are rented rather

than owned. In this way, figures are arrived at that characterize the neighborhood in a number of respects.[37]

But the facts regarding one neighborhood alone are not sufficient. What is wanted is a comparison of neighborhoods in order to focus on those most needing attention. To this end similar calculations are made for each of the neighborhoods of the city. From such work various measures result for each neighborhood. They are summed up in tables and often in maps and graphs. From these the planner makes his case for those neighborhoods needing clearance and redevelopment, rehabilitation, or conservation. But this is put too simply. Further study is needed in the field as well as in the office in order to focus on the exact areas of the selected neighborhoods that need one or another of these levels of treatment.

Planning districts versus neighborhoods
There has been a tendency in recent years to use *planning districts* rather than neighborhoods (Figure 18.13). This is because the neighborhood system is based only on residential areas, and thus leaves out areas of high concentration of factories or other non-residential use. In contrast, planning districts cover the entire city area. But even if the city is divided into planning districts, it is the neighborhood that is of chief interest in urban residential studies.

Changing Residential Patterns

Urban residential patterns are constantly changing. What is the nature of these changes?

Interior change

Changes in the residential pattern in

[37] For a field method of identifying residential blight by blocks see the discussion of the APHA technique, page 373. Of course, such block data can be aggregated for neighborhoods.

the interiors of cities involve little new building in new areas since so little open space remains. But, more and more, in the older areas of the city, urban renewal is going on. This may involve conservation, or rehabilitation, or clearance and redevelopment (see pages 205 to 206), depending on how run-down a residential area may be.

Sometimes another form of legal action is involved. Thus in 1964 it was reported that the mayor of Boston favored the repeal of an old statute that limited the heights of buildings in the Back Bay area of that city. This change was being sought to allow the construction of high-rise apartment buildings which was not feasible under existing law. This would increase the tax base of the city and, at the same time, help to hold some of the city's more well-to-do people who had been moving to the suburbs. It might even in small degree help to revitalize the retailing function in Boston's central business district which lay adajcent to the area under consideration.

Suburban growth

Probably the most impressive phenomenon associated with urban residential land use in recent decades has been the growth of suburbs. While most cities have been standing still in population or actually losing, the suburban areas have been gaining rapidly. The phrase "explosion to the suburbs" is a particularly apt description of what has been occurring.

The growth of residences in the suburbs has been characterized by two contrasting approaches. Homes are being built by individuals who buy a lot and hire a builder to erect the house that they want. This is likely to be true of the highest-priced suburban homes, but some low-priced houses are built on this same plan. In other suburban areas whole groups of houses are being built by developers. Such developments are generally known as subdivisions, and have been referred to as the residential equivalent of controlled shopping centers and organized or planned industrial districts. They are characterized by houses of a good deal of uniformity and hence economies of construction.

In most suburbs as well as inside the city, residential growth is subject to certain regulations—subdivision control, which requires adequate widths of streets, surfacing, and the like; zoning; and building codes. Such regulations are important. Where growth is uncontrolled, haphazard development may result, and subdivisions may consist of houses whose values do not reach the break-even point. That is, their values may be so low that the taxes from them are not equivalent to the cost of the services they require.

Other urban residential problems

Among the problems resulting from urban residential growth is a tangled skein of residential and transportation difficulties. There is, of course, the enormous problem of moving the growing masses of suburban dwellers to and from the city. But one of the answers to this—the building of new expressways and freeways which require broad pathways—has brought a further residential problem: where can the people go who are displaced by these new routes? This problem goes hand in hand with another: when the slums near the city's center are displaced through clearance and redevelopment, fewer housing units are likely to remain. Where can the displaced people be relocated?

Selected References

American Public Health Association, Committee on the Hygiene of Housing, *An Appraisal Method for Measuring the Quality of Housing: A Yardstick for Health Officers, Housing Officials and Planners:* part I, "Nature and Uses of the Method," 1945; part II, "Appraisal of Dwelling Conditions," 1946; part III, "Appraisal of Neighborhood Environment," 1950.

Beyer, Glenn H.: *Housing: A Factual Analysis,* The Macmillan Company, New York, 1958.

Blumenfeld, Hans: "Correlation between Value of Dwelling Units and Altitude," *Land Economics,* vol. 24, pp. 396–402, 1948.

Calef, Wesley: "Student Mapping of an Area of Multi-Story Buildings," *Journal of Geography,* vol. 50, pp. 233–239, 1951.

Camu, Pierre: "Types de Maisons dans la Région Suburbaine de Montréal," *The Canadian Geographer,* no. 9, pp. 21–29, 1957.

City Planning Commission, Cincinnati, Ohio, *Residential Areas: An Analysis of Land Requirements for Residential Development 1945 to 1970,* December, 1946.

Dahir, James: *The Neighborhood Unit Plan: Its Spread and Acceptance* (A Selected Bibliography with Interpretative Comments), Russell Sage Foundation, New York, 1947.

Darling, Philip: "A Short-cut Method for Evaluating Housing Quality," *Land Economics,* vol. 25, pp. 184–192, 1949.

Fuchs, Roland J.: "Intraurban Variations of Residential Quality," *Economic Geography,* vol. 36, pp. 313–325, 1960.

Garrison, William L., et al.: *Studies of Highway Development and Geographic Change,* University of Washington Press, Seattle, Wash., 1959, esp. sec. III.

Hartman, George W., and John C. Hook: "Substandard Urban Housing in the United States: A Quantitative Analysis," *Economic Geography,* vol. 32, pp. 95–114, 1956.

Hodge, Gerald: "Use and Mis-use of Measurement Scales in City Planning," *Journal of American Institute of Planners,* vol. 29, pp. 112–121, May, 1963.

Jones, Emrys: "Delimitation of Some Urban Landscape Features in Belfast," *Scottish Geographical Magazine,* vol. 74, pp. 150–162, 1958.

Klove, Robert C.: *The Park Ridge-Barrington Area: A Study of Residential Land Patterns and Problems in Suburban Chicago,* doctoral dissertation, private ed., University of Chicago Libraries, Chicago, 1942.

McKenzie, R. D.: "The Neighborhood: A Study of Local Life in the City of Columbus, Ohio," *American Journal of Sociology,* vol. 27, pp. 145–168, 344–363, 486–509, 588–610, 780–799, 1921–1922.

Ratcliff, Richard U.: *Urban Land Economics,* McGraw-Hill Book Company, Inc., New York, 1949, esp. chap. 11.

Stokes, Charles J.: "A Theory of Slums," *Land Economics,* vol. 38, pp. 187–197, 1962.

Structure and Growth of Residential Neighborhoods in American Cities, U.S. Federal Housing Administration, Washington, D.C., 1939.

U.S. Bureau of the Census, *Census of Housing: 1960,* city blocks reports.

—— *Census of Housing: 1960,* state and small areas reports.

—— *Census of Population: 1960,* and *Census of Housing: 1960,* census tracts reports.

Federal Housing Administration, *Structure and Growth of Residential Neighborhoods in American Cities,* 1939.

CHAPTER 19

Other urban patterns and associated land-use problems

IN THE last six chapters, transportation patterns in relation to the city, urban business patterns, urban manufacturing patterns, and urban residential patterns have been considered. There remain a number of urban activities that should be discussed at least briefly: education, religious activity, recreation, city government, and possibly one or two others. Vacant areas, too, though vacancy is not an urban activity and can hardly be considered a land *use*, are important since they represent the city's dwindling growing space.

While no breakdown is available in regard to typical land-use proportions in cities for the several activities mentioned, Bartholomew gives some relevant information based on data for fifty-three central cities.[1] According to his averages, urban recreation (as represented by parks and playgrounds) accounted for 3.77 per cent of the total city area, and public and semipublic property, 6.11 per cent. He classified as public and semipublic property everything associated with direct city administration (such as the city hall, police and fire stations, and other city buildings); government property at the county, state, and Federal levels; public and private schools; churches and church property; and a miscellany including libraries, cemeteries, charitable institutions, clubs, fraternal organizations, and the like. He does not, unfortunately, give information as to the relative amounts of land used for the various types of public and semipublic property. Much more important than any of these categories in terms of space occupied are vacant areas, which, according to Bartholomew's data, average 30.10 per cent of the city area. In addition, water areas occupy an average of 14.05 per cent of the total city

[1] Harland Bartholomew, *Land Uses in American Cities,* Harvard University Press, Cambridge, Mass., 1955, table 3.

area, but are so sporadic in occurrence that they are given no further attention in this chapter.

It is apparent from the foregoing that little separate data are available on urban land used by the various activities which are treated in this chapter. In some cases such information can be supplied by field mapping. But, after all, land use is only part of the story. There are other aspects of the several activities which can be studied and which present some interesting problems. As in the discussion of the several major urban activities, the concern here is with intercity as well as intracity patterns.

Urban Educational Patterns

What urban patterns related to education can be mapped and studied? We are concerned here with formal education carried on in schools.

Census data and characterization of the city as a whole

One level of approach is for the city as a whole. Publications of the U.S. Bureau of the Census are of some value. The Census Bureau gives information by cities on specific years of school completed, on median school years completed, and on the number of students at different levels in school. Do areal patterns of cities based on these factors vary regionally? And how do these patterns of distribution correlate with patterns of cities differentiated on the bases of other factors?

Census data and educational patterns of individual cities

Data similar to those just described are available by census tracts for individual cities. Through use of tracts, the patterns of median educational level (Figure 19.1), of specific years of school completed, and of levels of those attending schools can be plotted and studied for each city. To what other distribution patterns might they be found to be related?

Patterns of pre-college education

Location and classification of schools A logical first step in studying the educational patterns of a city is to locate the schools on a map and classify them as to type. Are they public or private? If the latter, are they church schools and if so of what denominations? What levels are represented? What is the total enrollment at each school? And so on.

Land actively used for school sites Land used for school sites is a topic that can be investigated. The gross total of land so used might be calculated as a ratio to city population, and such ratios compared with similar figures for other cities.

The individual sites, too, can be considered. Are there many small sites, or just a few large ones? Often there are striking contrasts here. In a study of education in two areas in the Chicago Metropolitan District, Philbrick found that within the village of Winnetka (2,454 acres) there were nine educational land plots aggregating 80.55 acres.[2] Bridgeport, a "community" in the city of Chicago with an area of 1,631 acres, had nineteen individual parcels of educational land, but these totaled only 20.56 acres. School sites varied in size from 2.07 to 30.4 acres in Winnetka and from 0.19 to 2.02 acres in Bridgeport. How can these differences be explained?

Such information gains greatly in geographic value when the school sites are considered in relation to the functional areas that surround them. Usually, schools occur in predominantly residential areas, though sometimes they are situated in localities of mixed uses. In the discussion of neighborhoods in the preceding chapter, it

[2] Allen K. Philbrick, *The Geography of Education in the Winnetka and Bridgeport Communities of Metropolitan Chicago*, Research Paper 8, Department of Geography, University of Chicago, Chicago, 1949, pp. 13–14.

was pointed out that in planners' delimitations of neighborhoods the elementary school frequently is taken as a core feature.

School administration patterns Patterns of school administration are another subject for possible investigation in connection with urban educational patterns. This sort of inquiry is, in a sense, a phase of political geography. What is the pattern of school districts through which the public schools of the city are administered, and what are the areas from which pupils must logically be served? Though urban school districts commonly have boundaries that conform to city boundaries, they may include some areas outside the corporate limits of the city, since school districts operate with a large degree of independence under state laws.

All this, of course, has to do with public schools. Roman Catholic schools, usually the largest element among the private schools, have their own administrative systems. They have their own service areas, set and administered by the diocese. Non-denominational private schools are less likely to have fixed service areas. Private schools, denominational or otherwise, are subject to some degree of control by the state, but fix their own locations and service areas.

The transportation factor A study of the transportation factor in relation to the location of schools and the residences of pupils carries our thinking still further. The home residences of pupils attending each school may be plotted. This amounts, of course, to delimiting service areas (see Chapter 4). Normally, the higher the level of the school the larger its service area. Elementary schools are more numerous and commonly more dispersed in order to be nearer the homes of pupils. Sheer distance is not so important as the time-distance relationship, which takes account of the means of travel to school. Even the planning of the most effective routes for school buses is a

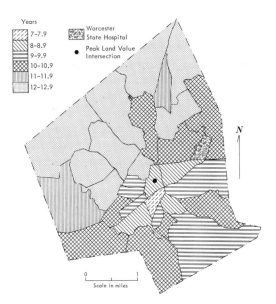

Fig. 19.1 Median school years completed by adult population resident in Worcester, Massachusetts, in 1960, by census tracts. (Data from 1960 *Census of Population* and 1960 *Census of Housing,* Census Tracts, Worcester, Mass., Standard Metropolitan Statistical Area.) This map should be compared with those in Chapter 18 showing the characteristics of housing units.

subject in which the geographer's approach may be helpful, though the overall problem is more a task for the planner.

School location problems But studies of administrative patterns and transportation patterns are less basic than actual location of schools. Usually the first step in school location analysis involves plotting the distribution of children of school age on a map showing existing school buildings together with maximum effective capacities of the buildings. In the simplest case it is assumed that all students attend public schools. Using each school building as a center, a circle is drawn with its radius equal to the maximum distance students are expected to travel. The elementary schools will have smaller radii than junior high or senior high schools.

It now becomes possible to see whether

or not the existing schools are well situated to serve the city's needs. The relatively unserved areas normally will show the direction in which the city is expanding and hence where new schools may be needed, but they may reflect, in some cases, poor locations of existing schools. On the other hand, such a map might show that some areas are overserved, with schools nearer one another than seems necessary. Map study would have to be supplemented by field inquiry to get a clear picture of the situation.

An obvious next step is to attempt to correct any flaws in the current situation. It may be found that some of the schools are old and inadequate and that it may be desirable to build new schools in the same places. Or perhaps the location of an old school might not be good enough to justify reusing the site. These are the sorts of findings that may result from a survey of urban educational patterns. At this point, of course, the present and probable future location of school population must be taken into account. In addition, the availability of sites near the points that seem most logical for school locations and matters of zoning are likely to be important in the location decisions. Also, transportation and possible school bus routes must be considered, especially in view of the trend toward larger schools drawing from larger areas. Finally, it should be noted that the provision of adequate and well-located schools is not a problem for which there is any final answer. Never-ending study and attention are required.

Consolidation and its effects The modern trend toward consolidated schools has greatly altered location patterns and must be taken into consideration in any site selection. In the lower grades, children are likely still to attend a nearby school; the greatest effects of consolidation can usually be seen at higher levels. In the city, it partly involves special types of schools, though consolidation of regular public schools is common too. But it is in suburban areas that consolidation is likely to have had its greatest effects. There the attempt may be made, for example, to find a site where a senior high school can serve a wide area, possibly including several distinct municipalities. This change of pattern has been enforced, ordinarily, by a state department of education, through which state and Federal assistance to education is dispensed.

Private schools In most cities, private schools, particularly denominational schools, siphon off some of the pupil load so that not so great a public school capacity is required as would normally be the case. But where the denominational school pupils are drawn chiefly from certain restricted sections of the city this is a variable that must be taken into consideration in public school location work. And administrations of denominational schools, trying to have their schools keep pace with the changing population picture, have to use some such analytical methods as those described.

Ethnic groups and segregation Ethnic groups and the problems of segregation also must be considered in studying patterns associated with education. Though some information on ethnic and racial groups can be worked out from census tract data and though a more elaborate map of this sort can be constructed from interview data (see Figure 10.6), such information is not always readily available regarding school children. For example, the proportion of Negroes among the pupils is a matter of record in some states and cities, but not in others. Areal variations in this proportion are, of course, the chief basis for the current difficulties regarding segregation in public schools. The problem can be stated something like this: Are Negro pupils in the city concentrated in just one or two of the public schools? If so, to what extent are they so concentrated? And are these schools inferior in quality to the other city schools? Of course, the residences of the pupils must be considered in relation to the distribution of schools to obtain a complete picture of segregation or lack of it.

Research problems The discussion of patterns of pre-college education can lead to various problems for research. For example, in a certain city, public schools share the burden of pre-college education with a system of Roman Catholic schools. How is the city's public school pattern affected? We may assume that less gross public school space will be needed than if there were only public schools. But are the public school buildings spaced similarly over the city regardless of the fact that in some areas a large proportion of the children go to Roman Catholic schools? And are the public school service areas similar in size all over the city? This is just one of many specific inquiries involving pre-college education patterns that might be worth following up.

Universities and colleges and related problems and patterns

Most cities of substantial size have one or more universities or colleges, and these present geographic problems rather different from those associated with pre-college education. Each institution has, for example, a service area that may be interesting to study, based on sources of students.[3] Another problem has to do with the space needs of these institutions. Some are fortunate enough to have lands that far exceed their present or probable future needs. But where this is not so, and the university is a growing one, its presence may result in an area of blight in portions of the city bordering the university property, particularly at

the points of greatest expansion of the university grounds (see page 144).[4]

Universities, like elementary schools and secondary schools, the government, and other public and quasi-public users of land, present to a city the problem that the property is not subject to taxation, and hence they do not directly contribute to the support of the community (see pages 203 to 204). However, there is often an arrangement whereby the university, to cover fire protection and policing, makes some payment to the city in lieu of taxes.

Research on university and college educational patterns of the city Consideration of the university and college educational patterns of cities can easily lead to some interesting research problems. For instance, service areas based on origins of students can be studied. One would expect a contrast between community colleges, on the one hand, presumably drawing pupils almost entirely from the city and its immediate vicinity, and the state university, which has the whole state as its service area and often reaches far beyond. Moreover, private colleges and universities have certain inherent characteristics that cause their service areas to differ from those of either level of government-supported school. The average large private university probably has a service area larger than that of most state universities of comparable size. On the other hand, why do some state universities draw pupils from far beyond the boundaries of the states in which they are located? University reputation, natural and other attractions of the locality in which the university is situated, level of out-of-state tuition, and no doubt various other factors enter in. And how do the source

---

[3] Preparatory schools, which might have been discussed under pre-college education, are more like colleges in some of these respects than they are like public schools.

[4] To a certain degree public schools, hospitals, and even churches may have a depressing effect on residential quality in adjacent areas though such influences are certainly not so great as those resulting from adjacency to an expanding university.

areas of graduate students differ from those of undergraduates? An intriguing idea involves a historical approach: plotting the source areas of a university for different time periods. Have there been substantial changes from time to time and what do they reflect?

These ideas regarding service areas are just a few of the various possible research problems on the geography of college and university education that might be undertaken.

Educational expansion

It is generally agreed that the United States is entering a period of great school expansion both at the pre-college and college levels. This means that more and more attention will have to be paid to the patterns and problems associated with urban educational geography.

Urban Patterns Related to Religion and to Religious Land Use

Religion and religious land use present other urban patterns, the investigation of which involves some real challenges. There are a number of possible lines of attack which present varying degrees of difficulty.

Nature and limitations of data

Unfortunately for anyone interested in studying the geographic expressions of religion, data are limited and not very reliable. No information on religious beliefs is collected by the U.S. Bureau of the Census. Officials of the Bureau have never felt free in the regular census to direct to individuals a query concerning religious preference or affiliation, although it is a possibility that has often been discussed. A mandatory question on this point might be considered to violate constitutional rights, and if an answer were optional the response to other census questions would be undermined.

The best data thus far made available were published in New York (1956–1958) by the National Council of Churches of Christ in the United States. The data were assembled from participating religious bodies and were based chiefly on the year 1952. Responses could not be obtained from a number of religious groups, but these were mostly small denominations, probably not amounting in total to more than 20 per cent of the church membership in the United States. Another limitation is inherent in the different criteria for church membership used by various church groups. And it must always be kept in mind that the statistics are based on membership as reported by churches and not on information on religious preference obtained directly from individuals. Of the eighty bulletins published, series D, Denominational Statistics by Standard Metropolitan Areas, is of most direct value to the urban geographer.[5] No information is given for areas smaller than the county and standard metropolitan area.

Intercity studies

The data for standard metropolitan areas make possible intercity comparisons on the basis of church membership. Maps can be drawn up comparing standard metropolitan areas on the basis of the major religious groups (Figure 19.2) or on the basis of any one of the individual church groups for which data were assembled. To make very precise comparisons between church membership and other standard metropolitan area characteristics, however, would suggest an exactness out of keeping

[5] For details regarding the possibilities and limitations of these statistics on the religious geography of the United States, see Wilbur Zelinsky, "The Religious Composition of the American Population," *Geographical Review*, vol. 50, pp. 272–273, 1960, and his "An Approach to the Religious Geography of the United States: Patterns of Church Membership in 1952," *Annals of the Association of American Geographers*, vol. 51, pp. 139–193, 1961.

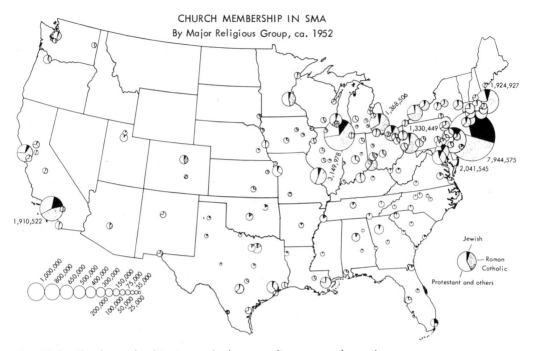

CHURCH MEMBERSHIP IN SMA
By Major Religious Group, ca. 1952

Fig. 19.2 Church membership in standard metropolitan areas, by major religious group, ca. 1952. (After fig. 2 in Wilbur Zelinsky, "An Approach to the Religious Geography of the United States: Patterns of Church Membership in 1952," *Annals of the Association of American Geographers*, vol. 51, pp. 139–193, 1961.)

with the quality of the membership statistics.

Distribution of denominations within the city

The study of intracity religious geography presents even greater difficulties. The first idea that is likely to occur to the student interested in patterns related to religion and the city interior is the making of a map showing peoples of various religious denominations.

Map of single denomination More practically, since it would be difficult to deal with members of many denominations on one city map, one group at a time might be considered. The map might, for example, take the form of a dot map of the distribution of Presbyterians within the

city, or Presbyterians could be presented as a proportion of the total population of each areal unit of the city or as a proportion of total recorded church membership. Here statistics on religion by enumeration districts or census tracts would be very useful. But, as was pointed out, the Census Bureau is of no help in this matter, and the work of the Council of Churches did not extend beneath the county and the standard metropolitan area levels.

Predominant groups as determined through sample interviews Another possibility is a generalized map of predominance of denominations that might conceivably result from a sampling procedure such as that described earlier in this book for making a cultural-regions map (see pages 179 to 182). Since the question would be regarding the group predominating in an area rather than the faith of the individual, it might encounter less resentment than a direct question to the individual on a United States Census schedule.

Distribution patterns of members of denominations A more exact map of the members of single denominations is possible if the church administration of that denomination in the city is willing to make available lists of congregation members and their addresses. A simplification might consist, in each case, of showing the congregation by tracts on a map through the use of a census tract street index (see Appendix B).

Such maps for different denominations should bring out some meaningful differences. The highly organized system of one denomination might be reflected in the discrete service areas of the churches. Another denomination in contrast might show much more overlapping of service areas. A denomination with a small membership in a city might be able to support only one church. Ideally, this would be centrally located, but such a central location might be too expensive. Also, it might be considered unnecessary, since for its particular denomination the one church has a monopoly.

Related patterns The individual distributions discussed, whether intercity or intracity, are not merely ends in themselves. To what other patterns are they related? Such a study might be of particular interest, for example, where plotting from rolls of the several churches of a denomination in a city gave a complete picture of the distribution of members of that denomination. If the plotting had been done by census tracts, it should then be possible through plotting other available tract data to see just what socioeconomic characteristics were associated with the distribution of the denomination, and how the several congregations of the denomination differed in their relationships to these characteristics. More broadly, if the memberships of several denominations were plotted by tracts, then the denominations could be compared and contrasted according to distribution patterns as well as according to relationships to socioeconomic characteristics. Data regarding the latter are available from the census, but it should be kept in mind that considerable local information, too, is assembled by census tracts (see discussion of census tracts in Appendix B).

Distribution of churches and church-used property

Perhaps the simplest approach to a study of the distribution of organized religions in the city is through the construction of a map showing the various church structures by denominations. A step further would be to show the space used by each denomination. In each case, the basis is direct field mapping, so a minimum of cooperation is required. A difficulty arises if areas used are to be mapped: some denominations, for example Roman Catholics, typically have their schools on the same property as their churches, so it is hard to keep religious land use and educational land use distinct. In mapping, one may have to meet this problem by a subjective division of properties of this sort. But despite such difficulties, a map showing church land is fairly easy to achieve.

The several denominations can be compared and contrasted as to extent and distribution patterns of their properties, and possible relationships between these patterns and other patterns of land use, cultural-group patterns, and other socioeconomic patterns can be investigated. It is particularly interesting to look at the church-used properties through time. For example, the population distribution, street patterns, and transportation systems of earlier periods may go far in explaining the present location of church properties.

The pattern of religious institutions in Cincinnati

A study of patterns of religious institutions in Cincinnati was conducted in the late 1940s by Wesley A. Hotchkiss.[6] It serves to illustrate some of the ideas that have been discussed.

Location in accordance with proportional representation in population The different religious groups, according to Hotchkiss, tend to have patterns of location within Cincinnati in accordance with their proportional representation in the populations of different areas of the city. Roman Catholics are represented in each community of the city and in some parts of each neighborhood.[7] Their school-church combinations serve definite parishes. The institutions of Judaism in contrast are strikingly concentrated. They are located in certain predominantly Jewish communities, lying northeast of the central business district of the city. The churches of the six major Protestant denominations, when taken as a group, are neighborhood institutions with at least one church of the group in each neighborhood and with tendencies toward interchanging of membership and toward a common strategy for church development programs.

Smaller Protestant denominations The largest of the smaller denominations of Protestantism are predominantly Negro and therefore are located in the Negro areas. There are small "white" denominations also, however, with their churches located so as to serve city areas larger than

communities, thus getting as complete coverage as possible with a few churches. Finally, there are some denominations with just one or two churches; these tend to be located downtown, at the focus of the transportation system, where they can draw from the entire city.

Factors in church location patterns In summarizing church location patterns, Hotchkiss points out that once a religious group has decided to build in a particular section of the city many factors are involved in selecting the site, including availability of vacant land, price of real estate, transportation pattern, the presence or absence of compatible forms of land use, and various others. Hence, he concludes, it can hardly be said that each religious group has its own specific pattern of church location. Locational patterns, Hotchkiss says, exist only as general tendencies associated with certain religious groups.

Protestant denominations and the community shopping center Among the Protestant denominations there is a tendency to locate within or near the community shopping center, but there is a notable exception to this rule. The churches of the Episcopal group generally have been located in residential sections away from the actual business center of the community. The appeal of this church has been to a small, selected segment of the total population, so the church has not felt the need of advertising its presence to the general community. However, the Episcopal Church is now changing its policy in this regard, and presumably the sites it selects in the future will be more like those utilized by other denominations.

The Church of the Nazarene is another exception to the general rule mentioned, but for different reasons. Like the Episcopal Church it tends to be in residential areas, but instead of being located in established residential areas near the center

---

[6] Wesley A. Hotchkiss, *Areal Pattern of Religious Institutions in Cincinnati*, doctoral dissertation, Research Paper 13, Department of Geography, University of Chicago, Chicago, 1950.

[7] For the meaning of "community" and "neighborhood" as used here see pp. 391–392. A map of the communities and neighborhoods of Cincinnati is presented as Fig. 18.14.

of the community, Nazarene churches are likely to be in peripheral residential areas where homes are more recent and of lower quality. The group is forced to these less expensive locations because of the lower economic level of its typical constituency.

Catholic and Jewish churches and locational factors Hotchkiss also speaks of the locational tendencies regarding Roman Catholic churches and Jewish synagogues. The synagogues are not generally located in close proximity to community shopping centers, but are scattered throughout the residential areas of the predominantly Jewish communities. The chief concern is accessibility to the Jewish population which is distributed over the entire area of each community. Roman Catholic churches are more commonly associated with transportation nuclei which usually coincide with shopping centers. These institutions are conspicuous in the communities both because of their central positions and their large sizes.

Changing values of church locations Hotchkiss also points out that the city is constantly changing and that the superior church location of today may be a poor location in the future if the congregation decreases or if it expands in an unexpected direction. Some of the greatest changes have occurred in the downtown areas. Though a downtown location still is valued by many denominations, churches there have in general been displaced from the more valuable sites by more intensive uses of the land.

Changing patterns

The urban patterns related to religion, like most other patterns of human geography, change rapidly. This adds to the complexity, but also to the interest of studies of these patterns.

Changing membership totals To the extent that data on membership by denominations are available we can see how the gross total of church members is changing in different cities and how the various groups contrast in growth or decline. But data that are available regarding membership in different denominations are not strictly comparable, as was pointed out earlier in this chapter. Moreover, one is inclined to doubt whether such data for past periods and for the present are sufficiently on the same basis for the measures of change to be very reliable.

Changes in different sections of the city Of particular interest, though often very difficult to obtain, are data on how the proportions of various denominations are changing in different sections of the city. But even mapping of the current distribution of one denomination in the city is sufficient to show generally how the pattern has changed since the church buildings were located. It may, for instance, show that the church buildings are poorly located to serve the present membership of the denomination. It may be that so many of the congregation of a church have moved to the suburbs that a similar relocation of the church may be indicated. The problem of locating a new church site may be solved by mapping techniques much like the problem of locating a new school.

Changes in extent and location of church-used land The extent of church-used land is not a true measure of sizes of congregations, nor does the pattern of church-used property necessarily reflect the pattern of membership. Nevertheless, changes in such property represent information that, in most places, is a matter of record and therefore can be obtained. How are the pattern and extent of church-used land changing in the city? And how does this differ by denomination? These questions might be followed by a third: Why are such changes important? For one thing, the geographer, from the nature of his discipline, is interested in areal patterns and in changes in such patterns. But there are more directly practical reasons for his interest in this case. Church administrations need this sort of information in planning for the future, and such changes are of practical interest, too, to the city. It was pointed out in an earlier chapter that religious land, like land for schools and other public and semipublic purposes, is not subject to taxation (see page 203). Increases or decreases of land used by churches affect the city's tax base accordingly.

Urban Recreation and Urban Recreational Land Use

The discussion of urban educational patterns dealt only with formal education carried on in schools, and the discussion of urban patterns related to religion considered only organized religion. In like manner, the discussion of urban recreational land use will be confined to the organized phases of recreation. For the most part, too, it will deal with what is commonly called "outdoor recreation."

Geographers' work on recreation

Though geographers have worked on recreational land use, their published research has not dealt directly with such use in the city. Instead, it has been concentrated on lake- and seashores and wilderness areas and the like to which people go to escape the city.[8] It is often said that the greatest recreation centers are the great cities, but little work has been done on this aspect of the topic.

Urban areas classified as recreational

Urban areas classified as recreational

"embrace a wide variety of uses [or use types] including parks, playgrounds, community centers, outdoor theaters, camp sites, beaches, golf courses, tennis courts, gymnasiums, arboretums, zoological gardens, scenic and historical sites, pleasure resorts, and open spaces of various kinds."[9] They include publicly owned lands but also privately owned areas open to public or semipublic use. However, only publicly owned recreational areas will be considered here. Public recreation lands overlap with educational land in that school playgrounds may be available for public use especially during vacations, and to some extent school administrations may depend on the availability of nearby public playgrounds.

Standards

According to the National Park Service, each city should have at least 1 acre of park or recreational space, either within the city or immediately adjoining its boundaries, for each hundred persons. Also, it has been suggested that of the total area of the city no less than 10 per cent should be devoted to public recreation.[10] It is probable that few cities meet these recommended minimum standards, but really objective comparisons of cities in this matter are difficult. In the first place, studies for which such information is reported may be based on different city concepts, and in the second place, terms such as "accessible park or recreational space" and "public recreation" may be variously defined in different studies.

Another suggested urban recreation standard is a population per acre factor for each type of park, varying from 1,000 persons per acre for outlying parks to 500 persons per acre for parks in tenement-

---

[8] In this connection see Preston E. James and Clarence F. Jones (eds.), American Geography: Inventory and Prospect, Syracuse University Press, Syracuse, N.Y., 1954, pp. 251–255.

[9] Donald H. Webster, Urban Planning and Municipal Public Policy, Harper and Row, Publishers, New York, 1958, pp. 166–167.

[10] Local Planning Administration, The International City Managers Association, Chicago, 1948, p. 165.

house districts, the service radius of each park not to exceed one mile. Also recommended is one acre of play area for each 1,500 to 2,500 of population beyond school age (the higher figure for low density areas and the lower for congested districts); and the following minimum play space for each child enrolled in schools: (1) elementary schools, 75 square feet; (2) junior high schools, 100 square feet; (3) senior high schools, 200 square feet.[11]

Bartholomew's findings

The most readily available general data on urban recreational land use are those of Bartholomew. In fifty-three central cities studied, he found, on the average, about 7 per cent of the developed area or 3.77 per cent of the total city area (or 0.46 of an acre per hundred persons) devoted to "parks and playgrounds." [12]

According to Bartholomew, there is a tendency for the percentage of city land in parks and playgrounds to increase with city population.[13] As he points out, the countryside is close at hand in small communities, so the demand for public parks and playgrounds is less than in large crowded cities. On the other hand, often in the large city much of the park and playground space is in one or two large holdings instead of being distributed over the city in accordance with population and may, therefore, be less available to the people than the area figure alone would suggest.

Intercity studies

Several lines of geographic research dealing with recreation in urban areas appear promising. Some of these are intercity in character. For instance, the amount of recreational space could be related to city size and the anomalies studied. Or cities could be studied in terms of the generally

[11] *Ibid.*, p. 167.
[12] Bartholomew, *op. cit.*, tables 3 and 4. In other tables similar data are presented for thirty-three satellite cities and nine "urban areas."
[13] *Ibid.*, pp. 66–67.

accepted standards of recreational space mentioned above. It is important that exact definitions be established so that the comparisons are significant.

As a follow-up of the foregoing, it would be interesting to see how the amount and proportion of urban land used for recreation is changing in different cities and the reasons for these changes.

Intracity recreational studies

There are various possible types of investigation of urban recreation within a city. Sample areas from throughout the city might be studied in detail in order to determine the types of recreational land available, the degree of utilization of the recreational resources, and similar information.

A second type of study might involve the hierarchy of facilities for recreation: those for very young children, the equivalent, almost, of backyard play facilities; playgrounds for somewhat older children who can travel farther; and so on up the scale to adult facilities. Such a study probably would require mapping and evaluating quantitatively each of the types of recreational areas available in various parts of the city. It might be found, for example, that some sections of the city are inadequately supplied with recreational areas for very young children but adequately supplied with golf courses, riding parks, or other facilities for adults. It would be interesting, if possible, to spot on the map, or on an overlay, cases of juvenile delinquency for the last several years, to see whether high delinquency rates correspond to areas of deficient playground facilities.

Land for recreation

Fortunately, recreation does not always compete seriously for space with other types of land use. Flat, well-drained sites can be used for parks and playgrounds, of course, but so can land that is not much in demand for other purposes. Parks, for example, may include deep ravines, steep hillsides, and rocky promontories, and areas which border lakes and streams and are difficult to drain or subject to flood may be of value for recreation at least during some seasons. But all recreation areas should be reasonably accessible in order to be of maximum value to the people of the city.

Land Use for Government

A certain amount of land in every city is used in connection with various levels of government. The establishments from which city affairs are conducted include the city hall; police and fire stations; highway department buildings; utility service buildings, such as pumping plants, power stations, sewage disposal plants; and various other areas and structures. Some of these establishments are gathered near the center of the city, possibly with branches farther toward the edge, especially if the city is a large one. Other establishments, such as those in the utility-service category, are more typical of the city's edge.

In any one city (or in a group of cities) it would be of interest to map and classify the areas devoted to such direct city government uses and to study how the types and total amounts of such land have been changing. Is the proportion of city land thus used increasing in the average city? Where this happens, the tax base to this extent is declining, since land used by the city does not yield tax revenue. Of course, this is equally true of the land and structures associated with organized education and organized religion, and they too are on the increase. How does the extent of land used for city government vary with city size? Only studies in a number of cities, using comparable city concepts and comparable definitions of use classes, could give reliable information on such points.

It would be entirely possible, too, to analyze the city's patterns of government lands at other levels; for example, of the central post office and its branches, of the county courthouse that is found in nearly every American city, and of the state government buildings in state capitals.

Minor Urban Patterns

There are various other lesser urban activities and land uses with which the urban geographer may be concerned. For instance, he may be asked about the location of a new library. Libraries do not occupy much land, but techniques may be used rather like those suitable for selecting school locations. Cemeteries, on the other hand, occupy enough land so they are often considered a somewhat incongruous use of land in a crowded city.

The cemeteries of Chicago

Cemetery land utilization in Chicago was described by William D. Pattison in 1955.[14] His major findings are considered here since they suggest lines of inquiry regarding cemetery geography that might be followed in other cities.

Preliminary view In the early 1950s seventy cemeteries were receiving Chicago's dead. They were situated in the Chicago Urbanized Area (as of 1950), but fewer than one-third of the seventy were inside the legal limits of the city. In all, the cemeteries occupied 12 square miles of land. Thirty-nine, according to Pattison, were owned by corporations organized for profit, twenty-six by churches, three by fraternal societies, and two by non-profit cemetery associations.

History of development The history of Chicago's cemeteries began early in the nineteenth century. Burials had been largely

[14] William D. Pattison, "The Cemeteries of Chicago: A Phase of Land Utilization," *Annals of the Association of American Geographers*, vol. 45, pp. 245–257, 1955.

haphazard—along both banks of the Chicago River, in the windblown sands at the mouth of the river, and some near individual houses—before Chicago, with a population of somewhat more than 3,000, obtained its first charter in 1835. Two burial tracts were ordered laid out, one north and the other south of the town. By 1850 the city had reached a population of 30,000 and was expanding rapidly. The city government had established a new cemetery 2 miles north of the center of the city to which the contents of the older municipal cemeteries had been moved. A Jewish burial society had purchased part of this new cemetery's acreage, and the Roman Catholic Church had founded a separate cemetery nearby.

There is nothing today to mark the cemeteries of 1850. Between 1850 and 1900 all three of the cemeteries of the earlier years had disappeared, but others had taken their places or been added to make a total of twenty-seven. The city cemetery was first abolished, giving way to three privately owned non-sectarian cemeteries invested in by well-known civic leaders. By 1900, ten more privately owned cemeteries were founded; three new cemeteries had been opened by the Catholic Archdiocese of Chicago; and several Jewish cemeteries had been organized. The picture was further complicated by German, Bohemian, and Polish Catholic parishes banding together to found cemeteries; and by the establishment of a Bohemian fraternal cemetery and four Lutheran cemeteries. During the 1850–1900 period, too, several cemeteries were evacuated and relocated at more distant sites.

Between 1900 and 1950 the number of cemeteries grew from twenty-seven to seventy. Of the forty-three added, thirty-three were business enterprises. Of the remainder, some were founded by the Catholic Archdiocese or by groups of Catholic parishes organized on the basis of national origin; and Lutheran and Jewish cemeteries and a Lithuanian fraternal cemetery were added.

Reasons for establishing new cemeteries Pattison points out that there has been no conscious overall coordination of cemetery growth, but that certain reasons for the growth can be discerned. Since 1835, he says, the total amount of available burial space has been more than sufficient for the needs of Chicago as a whole, but burial space attractive to particular population groups has had to be added from time to time. Thus additional Catholic cemeteries were developed after 1900 to supplement an archdiocese cemetery already in existence. New cemeteries have been added, too, to afford burial space nearer to the homes of interested families. Others have been added because of a desire for segregation of the dead according to religion and still others to maintain a national distinction. Exclusionist policies by most established cemeteries have resulted in the establishment of Negro cemeteries. Changing decorative taste has resulted in the creation of some new cemeteries operated for profit.

Profit-making cemeteries Pattison says that a notable feature of cemetery expansion, particularly since 1900, has been the increase in profit-making cemeteries. All of the reasons cited, he says, have been operative in their multiplication. The general market has been expanding except for Roman Catholic families and most Lutheran families, who have been consistently diverted by the availability of cemeteries specifically for these religious denominations. In the 1930s some business-operated Jewish cemeteries were opened, suggesting a weakening of Jewish allegiance to the religious and fraternal organizations of their group.

Some locational factors Pattison examines the problem of cemetery location against the backgrounds of municipal control, transportation, and land. The government of Chicago since its establishment has been generally inclined to exclude cemeteries. One argument used in the early decades of the city's history was that the presence of cemeteries was prejudicial to health. Another motive for government opposition has arisen from the fact that land dedicated to burial is not subject to property tax, which in many cases would be considerable. At any rate, the addition of cemeteries to city territory in the last half century has come about only through annexation of areas that have cemeteries and through the granting of special permits. The prohibition has been more definitely spelled out in recent years. An ordinance passed in 1931 makes it unlawful for anyone to establish, enlarge, or alter the boundaries of any cemetery in the city or within a mile thereof. There remains the possibility of cemetery acreage being increased through an extension of the city limits, but the prohibition has not stopped at the city line. Neighboring towns and villages also are empowered to forbid the establishment of cemeteries, and Cook County has been increasingly reluctant to grant permits. It seems probable that no further permits will be granted except where extreme need can be shown to exist.

Transportation also has been an important factor in cemetery location. Generally, cemetery founders have sought remoteness from the center of the city, but have shown a decided preference for locations on or near main lines of transportation. At first, cemeteries were established along main highways; from the coming of the railroads, about 1855, until about 1920, the preference was for locations alongside railroad lines. The alignment of these railroads left open large wedges of countryside, and it is in these wedges, near well-traveled highways and now intensively used, that

almost all cemeteries founded since 1920 have been located.

Landform settings of cemeteries Founders of cemeteries in the Chicago area tried where possible to select land that was well drained, easy to excavate, and capable of supporting plant life. In many instances they were able to locate on sandy beach ridges marking the shores of Lake Chicago, which existed in glacial times. However, nearly every cemetery has some portion that is low and poorly drained, and difficult digging characterizes parts of others.

Extent and rate of use of cemetery land Some facts regarding the extent and rate of use of cemetery land are worth pointing out. Of the 7,700 acres allotted to cemeteries in the Chicago Urbanized Area, 2,000 acres are occupied by graves. This discrepancy is accounted for by the fact that the founding and expansion of cemeteries have usually not been in direct response to the need for more burial space. Instead, land well in excess of current needs has been bought in order to anticipate other real estate buyers and to guarantee long life for a cemetery. Then the land has been developed as needed, with the drainage, landscaping, and building of roads, service buildings, and the like that are required. About 25 per cent of developed cemetery land is given over to such non-burial uses.[15] Also, some cemetery land is idle and will never be used. For instance, there are some lots that were purchased, but for some reason never used or sold.

Methods of economizing on space Relief from future pressure on burial space is offered by three devices. One of these is the reuse of graves after a specified time. This is not practiced anywhere in the United States. A second method of saving space, the placement of coffins one above another,

[15] *Ibid.,* p. 256.

is practiced at only one cemetery in the Chicago area. The third device, cremation, though increasing, is opposed by the Catholic Church in the United States and by Orthodox Judaism, and is rare among Negroes. About 8 per cent of all the Chicago dead are cremated at the present time. But all together these ways of economizing on space for burial have been of small effect. The consumption of land for burial in the Chicago area is proceeding at the rate of about 25 acres per year.

Broader aspects of cemetery problems

Although Pattison confined his investigation to the Chicago area, his discussion suggests questions about cemeteries elsewhere as well. For instance, does the proportion of space used by cemeteries vary with city age? It might be assumed that the older cities would have a number of completely filled cemeteries as well as cemeteries currently in use. In spite of the apparent disadvantages of the presence of cemeteries in crowded urban areas where space is at a premium, there is one offsetting factor. The cemetery remains a type of open area relieving the monotony of the congested, built-up city.

Vacant Land

Another type of open area in the city is vacant land. Such land is a critical subject for study since it is, in a sense, an important raw material for city expansion and change. Mapping and classification of vacant land, therefore, become a very practical exercise.

The first step is a matter of definition. Vacant urban land usually is taken to include all land that is not in definite urban use. Built-up areas obviously are not vacant and neither are city parks or golf courses. On the other hand, land in non-urban use, for example, a truck farm, is classed as vacant according to the definition suggested

here. Farms are rare inside city boundaries unless the city is considerably overbounded. Even then, those farms that remain are likely to be just inside the city's border and to be short-lived. There is other vacant land which, though available for urban use, for some reason is unused. Such land is particularly important because it includes the band of speculative and transitional holdings around the expanding edge of the city. Part of this belt may lie inside the city boundaries, but part lies outside, along the edge of the geographic city.

The study of vacant land is particularly susceptible to field work and to air-photo analysis. In such an analysis, a decision first has to be made about the sizes of areas to be mapped. It is often impracticable to map every vacant lot; in fact, a minimum of an acre may have to be set. But, of course, such decisions depend on size of the city and scale of the inquiry.

Normally, some sort of land classification is used in such a study. Slope, nature of subsoil, the presence or absence of bedrock at or near the surface, drainage, and other, similar factors are assessed so that the possible utility of the vacant parcels can be determined.[16] A knowledge of other qualities, too, such as accessibility, zoning, ownership, and view, is valuable in a vacant-land evaluation. And it should be kept in mind that conditions change. Even swampy or steeply sloping land or an area of bedrock outcrop may be in demand for house sites as population increases.

Because of limited time, the vacant-land survey may have to be restricted to the corporate city. The same is true, of course, if the city is underwriting the study. Otherwise, suburban areas, too, can be included. Here there may be pressures to leave some of the land in green belts or otherwise not

[16] See "An Inventory of Potential Industrial Sites" on pp. 357–364. A somewhat different set of considerations may enter in when use for other than industrial purposes is contemplated.

actively used for urban purposes, and in some suburban areas zoning to encourage the continuation of farming has been set up. But such barriers to urban expansion are usually futile.

Selected References

Bartholomew, Harland: *Land Uses in American Cities,* Harvard University Press, Cambridge, Mass., 1955.

Hotchkiss, Wesley A.: *Areal Pattern of Religious Institutions in Cincinnati,* doctoral dissertation, Research Paper 13, Department of Geography, University of Chicago, Chicago, 1950.

Myers, Richard A., "How a Council of Churches Uses Census Tract Data," Bureau of the Census Working Paper No. 13, Papers Presented at the Census Tract Conference, September 8, 1962, pp. 20–66, Washington, D.C., 1962.

Pattison, William D.: "The Cemeteries of Chicago: A Phase of Land Utilization," *Annals of the Association of American Geographers,* vol. 45, pp. 245–257, 1955.

Philbrick, Allen K.: *The Geography of Education in the Winnetka and Bridgeport Communities of Metropolitan Chicago,* doctoral dissertation, Research Paper 8, Department of Geography, University of Chicago, Chicago, 1949.

Zelinsky, Wilbur: "An Approach to the Religious Geography of the United States: Patterns of Church Membership in 1952," *Annals of the Association of American Geographers,* vol. 51, pp. 139–193, 1961.

———: "The Religious Composition of the American Population," *Geographical Review,* vol. 50, pp. 272–273, 1960.

CHAPTER 20

The political factor and growth of the city

THROUGHOUT the United States as in most other countries there is an increasing number of large urban agglomerations. Nearly all are growing in area and in population, but it is a growth that is extremely difficult to measure since such agglomerations have no exactly defined boundaries.[1] Nevertheless, some of the most interesting problems of urban America are associated with this growth. It is fitting, therefore, that this final chapter should focus on the political units that make up the urban agglomerations.

Though often seeming to be a continuous city, rarely is one of these urban agglomerations, at least if it is of substantial size, governed as a single unit. Instead, the administration or jurisdiction is likely to be divided among one or two central cities and a number of other civil units. For a very large agglomeration the gross number of administrative units may be phenomenal. Each unit is a uniform region since it has a prevailing government distinct, to some degree, from that of any of its neighbors. Unlike the urban agglomerations, these political units have defined boundaries, and there are definite area measurements and definite population data for them. Estimates of population totals of urban agglomerations are based on these political units.

The political units that share administration of the urban agglomeration are of several types, even though each is under a state government and generally is a subdivision of a county. At one extreme is the central city. Many an urban agglomeration has only one central city; a few have two or even three. There are also small cities, villages, towns, and the like. And there are townships, or their equivalents, only portions of which lie within the agglomeration. In this chapter we are considering the char-

[1] Each urban agglomeration is a geographic city as discussed in Chap. 2.

acteristics and problems of the individual units of this administrative hotchpotch as they coexist.

It was brought out in an earlier chapter that city size is usually measured by city population total rather than by city area. In the following pages, therefore, unless otherwise specified, growth and decline refer to changes in population totals of corporate units. The urban geographer is concerned with the growth and decline of the urban political units that make up the agglomeration since the size of such a unit helps to characterize it as an element of the urban complex and affects its role in interaction between the units. And population changes for each urban agglomeration as a whole are important, since the expanding edge of the geographic city is the "shatter zone" of urban America.

The concern here is not with the economic reasons for growth or decline of the individual urban units, important though these reasons may be. Such underlying bases for change have been implied in earlier chapters and discussed at length in many books about cities. Here we are concerned, instead, with what might be called the mechanics of change.

The City within Static Boundaries

We can begin with the simplest case of change, the change in size of a city (or other urban unit) within static political boundaries. This is a relatively simple situation and by no means just a hypothetical one. Though many cities expand by annexing land, thus adding whatever population the annexed areas may have, some cities are unable to add land and population by annexation. For them, all population changes must take place within unchanging boundaries.

Components of change

In cities with static boundaries, the components of change are simple. One is natural increase or decrease, gotten by comparing births with deaths for the period. These statistics are assembled annually for each political unit. A second element is gain or loss resulting from ordinary in-migration versus ordinary out-migration; a third is gain or loss of military personnel. Still another possibility is an increase in local college and university enrollment.

Gain within static boundaries

When the resultant of the foregoing factors is a net gain, just where do the additional people live? How do they fit into the city? How is the increase accomplished in terms of space? Obviously, additional housing units are necessary on some basis. For one thing, where there are unused areas in the city, additional dwellings may be constructed. Or if there are no such areas available, the intensity of housing may be increased through the replacement of single-family houses with multifamily dwellings.[2] Of course the accommodation of a greater total population may be accomplished by a combination of these processes: new housing may be built in formerly unused areas, and, in other portions of the city, multifamily dwellings may replace single-family homes.

Examples in New England Examples of city population increases in the 1950–1960 interval, without any annexations having taken place, are difficult to find, since nearly all cities have been adding at least some area by annexation. But this is not true in New England, where annexation is essentially impossible, and most of the larger cities are running out of desirable

---

[2] Zoning can play an important role in city growth. For example, if additional areas are zoned for multifamily housing there may be a larger increase in population in the available urban space than would be possible if only single-family houses were built.

living space. In fact, because of such limitations as well as growing obsolescence, these old cities, in a number of instances, are unable to hold the populations they now have.

A few of the smaller New England cities started out with areas well in excess of their needs and they still have ample space. An example is Concord, New Hampshire. With an area of 65.5 square miles and static boundaries, it has been gaining moderately in population, the total amounting to 27,171 in 1940, 27,988 in 1950, and 28,991 in 1960. It might be assumed that the people represented by this gain were accommodated chiefly through new houses on new sites, since there is ample room for such expansion in Concord. But apartment house development has been moderately active too.

One large New England city, Springfield, Massachusetts, gained in population in the 1950–1960 interval. From 162,399 in 1950 the total had climbed to 174,463 by 1960. Springfield has a moderately large area and the site of the city is fairly level. Nevertheless, it would be interesting to find out just how the city was able to grow in population at a time when most New England central cities were suffering population losses. Why didn't the newcomers settle in the suburban towns as they are doing in so many New England urban areas?

Examples outside of New England
Population increase without annexation is rare outside of New England, too, at least among large and moderate-sized cities.[3] In the first place, outside of New England, most cities annex at least small bits of land from one decennial census to the next. But some large cities have fixed boundaries, for reasons that will be pointed out later. With few exceptions they suffered

[3] A cursory check shows only New Orleans and St. Paul among cities of substantial size to have gained in population without annexation.

the fate of so many central cities: they lost in population.

Loss within static boundaries

Population loss within static boundaries is more common than population gain, and a number of the cities involved are large and important ones. Most of the larger New England cities fall in this category, and it is significant that losses without boundary changes were registered, too, by some of the major cities elsewhere in the country in the 1950–1960 interval. Among them were Baltimore, Buffalo, Cleveland, Detroit, New York, Philadelphia, Minneapolis, San Francisco, St. Louis, and Washington, D.C. Some of these large cities outside New England coincide with counties (Philadelphia, San Francisco), and expansion of the border of such a county is difficult. Others, for example, Baltimore, St. Louis, and Washington, D.C., have independent status and thus encounter great difficulty expanding at the expense of neighboring areas; and still others are completely walled in by smaller places that have become incorporated.

The components of change mentioned earlier account for loss just as they do gain. There are deep-seated economic reasons for loss, such as a decline in employment possibilities. But there are also more immediate, local bases for cities losing in population. For one thing, urban redevelopment may result in the destruction of dense, low-quality housing, thus displacing some of the city dwellers without providing residences elsewhere. These people may be driven to the suburbs or somewhere else outside the central city. To an increasing degree, too, new freeways or expressways are using space, thus leaving less room for people in the city. Expansion of the areas used for city government, for schools, and for churches also lessens space available for residential purposes. And growing obsolescence in older cities, rendering the housing less desirable, may reduce the residential potential still more. Unless these influences are balanced by the building of new housing units and the displacement of single-family houses by multifamily structures, there is literally less room for people in the city. Thus an actual disappearance of housing space and a decline in the quality of remaining housing may cause population decline.

The City within Changing Boundaries

But the boundaries of cities do not ordinarily remain static from one census period to another. Instead, most cities add some land through annexation, and the inhabitants of that land become part of the city's population. This is a possibility that must be kept in mind whenever an urban center is found to have gained rapidly in population. So, to the components of change for the average city (see page 414), another must be added: How many people are living in the territory or territories annexed by the city during the period between censuses?[4] We are still, of course, dealing with the political or corporate city.

The process of annexation

Normally, annexation is a very ordinary procedure. Most cities are underbounded. The geographic city is steadily outgrowing the corporate city so the corporate city must periodically add pieces of land around its borders if it is not to fall too far behind. Such annexations are carried on in conformance with the laws of the state in which the city is situated. Such increments of area

with their included populations may, in many cases, be sufficient to offset the population decline that seems to have been normal to most central cities in recent years.

More exactly, one of several situations is possible. The central city may have gained in population and the added population of the annexed area merely serves to swell the amount of increase. Or the addition of some population through annexation may not be enough to balance decreases in the central city, so the latter may sustain a net loss. Often, however, the addition results in a net population gain for a city that would otherwise have suffered a decrease.

It is an interesting fact that the acquisition by a city of only 1 or 2 square miles often involves a number of separate annexation actions. For example, the 6½ square miles that San Jose, California, acquired in 1959 was the result of 124 successful annexation actions; Fresno, California, used 92 such actions to acquire a little more than 3 square miles; and Rockford, Illinois, 53 to absorb less than 1½ square miles.[5] On the other hand, in the same year, four of the seven cities annexing the largest amounts of territory did so through from one to three successful actions.

It is beyond the scope of this book to go into detail regarding annexation procedures. In New England, of course, boundaries have been essentially unchangeable for many years, but elsewhere procedures vary greatly from state to state. In general, they involve a favorable vote by the people of the area to be annexed as well as by the people of the annexing city. The more populous an area is and the more highly organized its government, the more difficult it is likely to be to get agreement from the people to have their area annexed.

Sometimes the request for annexation comes from fringe-area residents and sometimes from officials of the city that is to

---

[4] Actually, an urban center may have to give up some territory and this may contribute somewhat to loss. In practice, however, whenever there are boundary adjustments the larger urban unit usually ends with a net gain in area and population. Small towns are constantly incorporating so that they can resist annexation or even annex territory themselves. Even so they may be absorbed by a larger neighbor. But it is chiefly unorganized territory or small civil units of the lowest status that are annexed.

[5] See *The Municipal Year Book*, International City Managers Association, Chicago, 1960, p. 52.

annex; not infrequently, subdividers initiate the action. Objections on the part of the people of the areas to be annexed may be based on the prospect of having to pay higher taxes or on doubts regarding the quality of services they can expect. Occasionally, the owners of a factory and adjacent lands lying just beyond the city line may fight annexation in order to avoid the higher taxes and more onerous regulations that are likely to result. But the objections do not always come entirely from the area to be annexed. The city voters or the city administrators may have their doubts, too, owing to the low quality of the area under consideration or to the expense of extending water, sewerage, and other services into the area.

Abnormalities in annexation

There are, unfortunately, various obstacles in the path of normal, orderly expansion of the corporate city. These are of several types.

The situation in New England New England, for example, is more generally hostile to annexation than any other section of the country, a fact which is rooted in the area's town structure. Typically, all of the land in a New England state is divided into towns and cities (see Appendix A), which are strong governing units. Their citizens are likely to resent bitterly the idea of giving up any land to larger neighbors. It would require nothing short of an act of a state legislature to bring about anything of the sort, and there is little likelihood of any one of these governing bodies of New England attempting to force such a shift of land from one administrative unit to another.

So, as a result of the town structure, annexation can play little part in the growth of a New England city. In a list of annexations of one-fourth square mile or more by cities of 5,000 or more population in 1962, not a single New England urban

center appears among the 216 annexing cities.[6]

State and county lines in relation to annexation There are various situations outside of New England, too, where annexation is impeded. A state line, for example, is an impregnable barrier: nowhere has a city been able to annex areas lying in another state. County lines are less serious barriers. Ordinarily, corporate cities do stop at such lines, but there are several exceptions. Atlanta, Georgia, for example, extends from Fulton County into Dekalb County; and Oklahoma City now extends into four counties.

Smaller corporate units as barriers The most common barrier to corporate city expansion, however, consists of smaller incorporated units at the edge of the city. In most of the country's crowded areas outside of New England, the incorporation of one after another of these smaller urban units is gradually choking off the possibility of further expansion of the major city. Cleveland is completely closed in in this way, and there are only one or two points remaining along Chicago's corporate boundary where further expansion is not blocked by incorporated units. In fact, the difficulty seems to be endemic to large cities, no doubt because the same attractive forces that resulted in development of the city have encouraged smaller places to spring up around it and to incorporate.

This does not mean that further expansion of the central city is impossible. The city and a smaller community may agree on annexation of the latter, but the process is less likely and more difficult than when open township or county areas are in direct contact with the city. Also, of course, the state can act to bring about an annexation, but this is generally a legal rather than a practical possibility.

[6] See table II in *The Municipal Year Book*, International City Managers Association, Chicago, 1963.

Enclaves and exclaves Some small municipalities, though able to resist absorption, have been surrounded by the central city in its annexation program. Thus Highland Park and Hamtramck form *enclaves* in Detroit, University Park and Highland Park in Dallas, and San Fernando in Los Angeles; and there are many others.

Less commonly, the central city may own a piece of land entirely separate from the main body of the city. Such an *exclave* might result, for example, if the city acquired an outlying airport. More often, though, the central city manages to acquire a strip of land connecting it with the outlying area.

Reaching out to an objective Expansion of the corporate city does not always take the form of an orderly spread outward. An early example of this was Los Angeles' march to the sea. There were several possible ports for the growing city, but none had adequate protected water and, besides, downtown Los Angeles lay about 20 miles inland.[7] Finally, in 1899, the Federal government began construction of a breakwater at San Pedro. But when the breakwater was finished and certain other harbor improvements completed, commerce did not boom, chiefly because of still inadequate port facilities; and neither San Pedro nor Wilmington, its neighbor to the northeast, had the necessary millions to build and maintain a modern seaport.

It became clear that Los Angeles would have to pay for the port if there were to be an adequate one. Annexation of San Pedro and Wilmington appeared to be the only answer. Though the people of the two small cities were reluctant to be absorbed, the prospective economic advantages eventually overcame this reluctance. There remained the 15 miles between Wilmington and Los Angeles. But Los Angeles annexed a strip of land nearly 15 miles long and only ½ mile wide reaching to the northern boundary of Wilmington, and this made possible the annexation in 1909 of the two small cities. Los Angeles had become a seaport. Additional water frontage in the San Pedro area was acquired later through further litigation, but the point of particular interest here is the famous "shoestring" annexation by which Los Angeles became a real seaport. A study of the urbanized area maps in the 1960 *Census of Population,* particularly for cities in states where there has been most activity in annexation, reveals other instances of shoestring annexations (see, for example, the maps of several urbanized areas in Texas).

Rapid annexation in the Southwest For rapidity and size of urban annexations, Oklahoma, Texas, and California have been particularly outstanding (Table 20.1). Houston annexed 187.6 square miles of territory in 1956, thus establishing a record that still holds for area annexed in a single year. Oklahoma City, though not totaling this amount for a single year, has been even more phenomenal for the extent to which it has increased in area through annexation. From 50.8 square miles in 1950, Oklahoma City had grown to 321.5 square miles in 1960. In 1962, it reached an area of 620.16 square miles.[8] Thus Oklahoma City had become by far the largest city in area in the United States. It extended into four counties and exceeded by more than 160 square miles its nearest rival, Los Angeles, which had held the record in city area for many years. Though Oklahoma City gained also in population, reaching a total of 355,000 in 1962, this population gain was insignificant compared with the city's enormous areal gain.

[7] For a discussion of the Los Angeles struggle for a port see Willis H. Miller, "Competition for the Ocean Trade of Los Angeles," *Economic Geography,* vol. 13, pp. 325–333, 1937.

[8] John C. Bollens, "Metropolitan and Fringe Area Developments in 1962," *The Municipal Year Book,* International City Managers Association, Chicago, 1963, p. 54.

Table 20.1   Cities annexing 5 square miles or more of land, 1958–1962, inclusive

City	sq mi annexed	City	sq mi annexed
Alabama		**Georgia**	
Mobile	68.55	Macon	36.00
Auburn	9.75	Savannah	32.53
Jasper	7.72	Columbus	13.80
Anniston	6.75		
Huntsville	6.00	**Idaho**	
Cullman	6.00	Pocatello	6.25
Arizona		**Indiana**	
Phoenix	184.98	Michigan City	15.00
Flagstaff	56.27	Indianapolis	8.39
Tucson	47.03		
Tempe	9.36	**Iowa**	
Glendale	9.04	Cedar Rapids	14.27
Mesa	8.12		
Scottsdale	7.00	**Kansas**	
Winslow	6.12	Wichita	28.25
Arkansas		**Kentucky**	
Little Rock	18.00	Lexington	6.51
California		**Louisiana**	
San Diego	136.37	Shreveport	9.37
Sacramento	47.19		
San Jose	25.86	**Michigan**	
Redwood City	24.97	Grand Rapids	16.07
Hayward	21.97	Lansing	13.13
Oceanside	16.88		
Riverside	12.37	**Mississippi**	
Palo Alto	11.66	Jackson	19.30
Santa Ana	8.19	Meridian	16.00
Fresno	7.56	Tupelo	7.00
San Bernardino	6.66	Picayune	6.25
Union City	6.09		
Orange	6.03	**Missouri**	
Whittier	5.50	Kansas City	200.80
Palm Springs	5.48	Independence	36.25
Seal Beach	5.40	St. Joseph	14.00
		St. Charles	6.25
Colorado		Malden	5.00
Denver	8.35		
Aurora	5.80	**Nebraska**	
		Lincoln	7.13
Florida			
Gainesville	36.24	**Nevada**	
Daytona Beach	29.03	North Las Vegas	12.50
West Palm Beach	22.00	Las Vegas	11.45
Tampa	13.85		
Fort Lauderdale	7.67	**New Mexico**	
Ormond Beach	7.03	Albuquerque	12.23
Cocoa	6.04	Alamogordo	11.44

Table 20.1   Cities annexing 5 square miles or more of land, 1958–1962 inclusive (*continued*)

City	sq mi annexed	City	sq mi annexed
North Carolina		Lubbock	45.21
High Point	39.60	Port Arthur	25.88
Charlotte	33.53	Amarillo	23.99
Raleigh	16.85	Wichita Falls	22.03
Asheville	7.00	Grand Prairie	20.46
Burlington	5.22	Waco	15.97
		Abilene	15.00
Ohio		Fort Worth	13.63
Toledo	22.17	Athens	13.00
		Killeen	12.50
Oklahoma		Monahans	12.00
Oklahoma City	357.72	El Paso	10.40
Norman	176.11	Houston	10.39
El Reno	160.50	Midland	10.18
Edmond	51.37	Garland	9.91
Midwest City	18.50	Baytown	8.94
Shawnee	11.28	Texarkana	6.44
Tulsa	6.40	Laredo	6.25
Oregon		**Virginia**	
Springfield	5.50	Norfolk	13.50
		Portsmouth	10.00
South Carolina			
Charleston	9.79	**Washington**	
Greenville	6.95	Everett	12.34
		Richland	5.00
Tennessee			
Nashville	49.37	**West Virginia**	
Memphis	12.64	Charleston	19.00
Columbia	6.21		
		Wisconsin	
Texas		Madison	21.53
Dallas	52.14		
Corpus Christi	49.00		

SOURCE: Based on data reported by city officials and published in annual issues of *The Municipal Year Book*. Many cities annexed smaller areas.

The annexation activity of several smaller cities in central Oklahoma was in some respects even more spectacular. In 1961, Norman, which had a population of 34,000 people, annexed 174 square miles, the second largest amount ever annexed by any American city in one year. This gave Norman the largest land area of any city with less than 250,000 population in the United States. In 1962, El Reno, a city of 11,000 population, lying a short distance west of Oklahoma City, annexed the most land added by any municipality in the nation during that year, 160.5 square miles.[9] This amounted to an increase of 3,210 per cent in the city's area, the largest percentage increase in area ever attained by any American city through annexation in a twelve-month period. A local official reported that the reason for this large annexation was "large city encroachment." It is significant that both Norman and El Reno

[9] Its population increase was far less spectacular: from 11,000 to about 12,000.

are in the Oklahoma City Standard Metropolitan Statistical Area. The people of these smaller cities evidently were affected by the example of their large neighbor, or, more likely, they wished to avoid eventually being annexed by it.

Conditions favoring rapid annexation

In summary, annexation is a way of dealing with problems of the fringe around the central city, but its extensive use requires that two conditions be fulfilled. "They are the availability of a liberal annexation law and the existence of sizable and adjacent unincorporated territory." [10]

Preoccupation with problems of annexation is relatively recent. Until about 1900, American cities added land by annexation with no particular difficulty. Beginning at approximately that time, however, people's attitudes toward annexation began to change, and many states adopted provisions that made annexation more difficult. Annexations became less frequent and were mostly limited to small, unincorporated areas just outside the city's borders. But a resurgence followed World War II, chiefly because of the tremendous spurt in suburban development. As a result, each of the states now has constitutional and statutory provisions for annexation, but these vary greatly.

An example of a liberal annexation law is that of Texas where any city of more than 5,000 population may, by majority vote, adopt a home-rule charter. This includes provisions for annexing fringe territory. Most of the Texas home-rule charters allow the city to annex contiguous unincorporated territory by simple council action with no action whatsoever necessary in the territory to be annexed.[11] This ease of areal growth

[10] John C. Bollens, "Metropolitan and Fringe Area Developments in 1960," *The Municipal Year Book*, International City Managers Association, Chicago, 1961, p. 58.

[11] Chester W. Bain, "The Annexation of Fringe Territory," in *A Place to Live*, The Yearbook of Agriculture, Washington, D.C., 1963, p. 458.

is particularly striking when contrasted with the situation in New England, where boundaries are essentially rigid. Since most annexed areas have some population, it is apparent that annexation is an important factor to take into account, particularly when comparing the growth rates of cities in New England with those of cities of the Southwest. Even if the annexed areas are sparsely populated, they provide a potential for city growth, and suburban growth is checked by absorption of the areas where it might occur.

Areal growth studies of cities

For many urban areas, studies of areal growth of the political city should be particularly rewarding. This could be done through a succession of maps showing the extent of the city at various periods. What were the steps involved in each addition? Did the proposal come from people in the annexed area or from the city administration or from developers? What were the arguments pro and con? Any resulting generalizations, however, would be somewhat limited in application by variations in state annexations laws.

A study of growth of the political city would not be feasible for the average New England city or for a city that, from the beginning, was coincident with a county or was an independent city and still holds to its original limits. But many cities have grown through annexation, piece by piece, and for them such a study would be an interesting record of the forces that have molded the present political unit.

Growth of Smaller Political Units of the Agglomeration

The foregoing discussion has focused particularly on the central city of an urban agglomeration. But there may be more than one central city, and the agglomeration might contain, also, smaller cities and villages.

Problems of growth

The smaller cities, it may be assumed, grow in much the same ways as the dominant city, but there are some significant differences. Generally speaking, they can annex additional land less easily than the large city. Moreover, most such places are younger than the central city and are likely to show the effects of zoning. Lot size regulations may do much to determine growth possibilities and so, also, can the extent to which zoning may limit multifamily housing.

These smaller non-central cities are often poorly balanced economically. In some, so little land is used for industry or business that the community is restricted almost entirely to a dormitory function. In others, nearly all of the land may be devoted to industry or business. As a result, some of the smaller communities are almost weirdly specialized.

The Vernon Area

A study of a community in the vast, complex Los Angeles urban area illustrates this point. The city of Vernon, located about 2 miles southwest of the central business district of Los Angeles, was the subject of a paper published in 1952 by Howard Nelson.[12] In the study he attempted particularly to determine how much the local municipal boundaries were reflected in the urban land-use pattern.

Variability of political units characterizes the area (Figure 20.1). Los Angeles borders Vernon on the north and west, and unincorporated county territory adjoins it on the southwest and northeast. The cities of Huntington Park and Maywood are adjacent on the south and southeast, with Bell a short distance away; and inside the boundaries of the city of Vernon are two

[12] Howard J. Nelson, "The Vernon Area, California: A Study of the Political Factor in Urban Geography," *Annals of the Association of American Geographers*, vol. 42, pp. 177–191, 1952.

blocks of unincorporated county territory. Nelson refers to this metropolitan mosaic of Vernon and its neighbors as the Vernon Area.

On a map of residential land use, the city of Vernon has the appearance of an almost empty island. According to Nelson's calculations, scattered houses occupy less than 1 per cent of the developed area, as compared with nearly 40 per cent devoted to residences in the average city (see Table 11.1, page 195). The few houses are mostly old, unpainted structures; and the population of Vernon, never large, dropped from a high of 1,269 in 1930 to 229 in 1960. This is particularly significant, since Vernon is in the midst of one of the fastest growing urban areas in the United States. The residential development that characterizes surrounding urban centers seems to stop at the Vernon city line.

Commercial concentrations, too, though well developed in the Vernon Area, are almost entirely absent from Vernon itself. There is no real commercial core or shopping district, just a few widely scattered commercial establishments—chiefly isolated restaurants, banks, and filling stations serving the daytime needs of people employed in the city. The total commercial land, according to Nelson, is only about one-fourth the usual percentage. In contrast, portions of the Vernon Area surrounding the city of Vernon show normal commercial development.

Industrial land use in Vernon presents quite a different picture. Nelson refers to the city as a peninsula of industrial land almost surrounded by a sea of land used for non-industrial purposes. Nearly 75 per cent of the developed land in the city is devoted to packing houses, oil processing plants, steel fabricating mills, breweries, fruit and vegetable packing houses, and other manufacturing and wholesaling. This is in contrast to about 6 per cent in manufacturing and wholesaling in the average city. Nelson

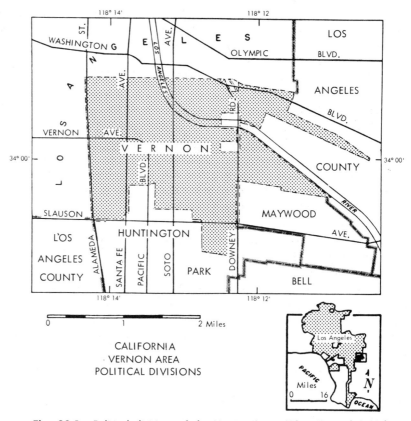

Fig. 20.1 Political divisions of the Vernon Area. (After Howard J. Nelson, "The Vernon Area, California: A Study of the Political Factor in Urban Geography," *Annals of the Association of American Geographers*, vol. 42, 1952, fig. 2.)

estimates the total industrial employment in the city of Vernon as about 60,000, equal to the employment in all occupations characteristic of a city of 150,000. Obviously, many, many more industrial workers must come into Vernon each day than sleep in the city.[13] But, in any event, it is clear that Vernon is highly specialized in industry, and the city boundary to a noticeable degree marks the edge of this area of specialization.

There are several other ways in which the city of Vernon stands out. It has a dense network of railroad tracks, and tracks and rail yards occupy over twice the space that

they do in the average city. The railroad network coincides in general with the city of Vernon, with much less concentration in neighboring areas. Though truck terminals are outstanding, Vernon has only about one-third the usual area found in streets.

There is little public land and there are few public buildings in Vernon, whereas in the neighboring areas public land and buildings are found in normal proportions.

There was nothing about the site of the city of Vernon that would make it any different from its surroundings; rather its specialization might be attributed to <u>historical accident</u>. Several ranchers living in the area are said to have sensed its qualities for

---

[13] Thus it might be referred to as an extreme case of a satellite.

industrial development, and were responsible for railroad spurs being extended from the Southern Pacific and for lumber yards and the first manufacturing plants being built. These men resisted annexation of the area, and eventually, in 1905, it was incorporated as the city of Vernon.

Almost immediately, Vernon assumed a unique character. Saloons, prizefighting, and Sunday baseball developed. Thus almost from the beginning Vernon stood out from its neighbors, which tended from the start to be balanced communities. The sporting function of Vernon declined with the coming of prohibition, but factories had been developing almost from the beginning, and Vernon became more and more specialized as an industrial center. This function has grown by migration of industries into the city, and selective annexations have brought more industries and have tended to leave residences out. Moreover, the rapid increase in the price of land has made residential land use uneconomical. Industrial development has been encouraged by low taxes; Vernon has the lowest rate of any city in California. This is possible partly because of the high valuation of industries and partly because lack of significant population makes most public services unnecessary.

In other respects, too, Vernon shows its industrial specialization. The police and fire departments are specialized in protecting industrial property, and water and power costs have been kept low. In 1951, the city council was responsible to only 139 persons, most of whom were said to be employees of the city. But they had the power to regulate industries with a total value of several hundred million dollars.

Such extreme functional specialization is unusual even among the smaller cities of urban agglomerations. But there are many other cases of almost as great specialization in one direction or another. They are possible because such small cities do not stand alone but, instead, are elements of agglom-erations which, it may be assumed, are reasonably balanced economically.

Fragmented Political Structure

The earlier pages of this chapter have dealt largely with the growth of individual cities. But the large urban agglomeration is vastly more complicated than any one city. Typically, it consists of a central city or cities surrounded and hemmed in by a complex of smaller units, the whole assemblage roughly approximating the geographic city.

Each agglomeration as a complex of administrative units

The urbanized area is the nearest Census Bureau equivalent to the urban agglomeration or geographic city, so it is to the urbanized area we must turn for the best enumeration of the political units that make up the agglomeration. A few examples may make the picture clearer. Judged on the basis of urbanized areas, in the great urban agglomeration that centers on Chicago 2 states are represented, as well as 6 counties, 49 townships, 10 towns, 30 cities, and 110 villages.[14] In the Boston urban cluster only 1 state is involved, but 3 counties are represented as well as 18 cities and 59 towns. For the Los Angeles agglomeration, there is only 1 state but there are 2 counties and 85 cities. Another of the urban agglomerations, that centering at Pittsburgh, is situated entirely in Pennsylvania, but the administrative units making up the area include 3 counties, 10 cities, 45 townships, and 105 boroughs.

The terminology, of course, differs with the nomenclature of the particular locality. Perhaps most unusual is that of the New Orleans agglomeration, where, in addition to the state of Louisiana, 4 cities, 3 parishes,

[14] This does not take account of more than 400 school districts and 235 special tax districts. See Malcolm J. Proudfoot, "Chicago's Fragmented Political Structure," *Geographical Review,* vol. 47, p. 111, 1957.

11 wards, 1 town, and 1 unincorporated place are represented. But regardless of the varying terminology, the picture of the average large agglomeration tends to be a complex of varied political units sharing the administration of what is in reality one great city.

Mobility of the fragmented city

The picture is complicated in many cases by being anything but static. The pattern of administrative units of the Boston area, it is true, is essentially immobile, since in New England, town and city boundaries have been essentially unchanged for many years.[15] But there are changes in population going on in the Boston area, with the outlying towns gaining relatively.

In agglomerations outside of New England, also, the mobility takes the form of relative growth of outlying minor civil divisions, but in addition new corporate units are likely to appear. Thus for the Los Angeles agglomeration the Census of Population shows a substantial list of new suburban cities that were incorporated between 1950 and 1960, and even in the Chicago area numerous boundary adjustments were recorded.

But whether new suburban units develop or whether there is just a relative population increase of existing political units, the outward shift of population is tremendously significant and has given rise to various descriptive designations. The process is most commonly referred to as suburbanization, but one hears, also, of flight to the suburbs, explosion to the suburbs, and urban sprawl.

Inefficiencies of fragmentation

The really remarkable thing, however, is that here is a great area of urban density that might be expected to function as a single city but in which, instead, the many political units go their several ways. Policing, fire protection, utilities—these are but a few of the many types of activities where difficulties arise. It is obviously inefficient to have distinct developments of each of these services for the many small political units that commonly make up a great urban agglomeration.

The chief sufferer, though, is likely to be the large core city. As one writer put it, "Cities no longer are defined by walls, but often the legal boundaries are almost as restrictive, for they are established by law, and the city's jurisdiction does not extend beyond them."[16]

The question may be asked: What difference does it make whether or not a city's legal boundaries coincide with its sociological and economic boundaries? After all, the entire area is under some type of government. Why should a city and the surrounding urban developments be placed under one government?

To begin with, the disadvantages to the central city as fringe areas incorporate around it are fairly obvious. Characteristically, the older residential and business sections of the city fall into disrepair as residents and business firms move to sites outside the central city, where taxes are lower, transportation not as congested, and parking areas feasible. As the city's tax base declines, the per capita share of government cost increases and falls more heavily on those who remain. At the same time, through the growth of smaller corporate units all around it, the city may be entirely shut off from expansion through annexation which might make possible the further growth of factories and commercial establishments and thus an augmented tax base.[17]

[15] See Raymond E. Murphy, "Town Structure and Urban Concepts in New England," *The Professional Geographer*, vol. 16, no. 2, pp. 1–6, March, 1964.

[16] Bain, *op. cit.*, p. 454. Ideas from Bain's article are used freely in this discussion of the inefficiencies of fragmentation.

[17] Annexation, however, is not always a solution to economic ills. Some central cities have declined to annex territories that were haphazardly developed

Equally important, according to some, is the fact that the growth of fringe areas deprives the city of strong civic and political leaders. The suburbanite, at the same time, has no direct voice in the management of the affairs of the city of which he is in reality a part and in which ordinarily he earns his living. Most large cities have a few high-quality suburbs in which the leaders of the central city's businesses, industries, and professions reside.

Willy-nilly the core city is serving more and more as the metropolis for the whole agglomeration. It provides services and functions for the suburbanite when he is in the city; streets and traffic control to get him in and out of the city, police and fire protection, water supply, and sewage disposal. These and other needs of the central city tend to increase with the size of the population agglomeration, yet the suburbanite ordinarily does not help to pay for them directly. It is partly to serve the suburbanite that, in the central city, more and more land is being absorbed for public and quasi-public buildings, and of course such uses mean that the land is nontaxable. The suburbanite earns his living in the city, and some cities have used a payroll tax as a means of making the fringe dweller help pay for the cost of central city government. Even the expanded retail activity which might logically be expected to afford some degree of compensation for the central city's difficulties is undermined by the relative growth of shopping centers in the suburbs. In view of the foregoing facts, it is not surprising that the central city often takes the position that the fringe areas and the city itself represent a community of interest and therefore should be merged into a single political unit.

In many agglomerations the central city is losing population both relatively and absolutely. Loss of population may in some

and hence, presumably, would increase the financial burden of the city beyond what the new areas might contribute in taxes.

respects be a desirable readjustment to changed conditions. On the other hand, it reflects in part the depressing effects of a declining tax base and of an increased burden of services furnished by the city for the people of both city and suburbs but paid for by the central city alone.

But sympathy should not be restricted to the central city. The suburbanite is paying indirectly. The reverse side of the coin is seen in the fantastic per capita rise of municipal debts of the suburbs, which have had to shoulder the burden of expanding schools, streets, and utilities, with a relatively small share of the commercial-industrial tax base. In other words, fragmentation produces a variety of inequities for all. In the aggregate, it does not benefit anyone in particular, and it may greatly decrease the economic efficiency of metropolitan services.

Chicago as an example

The difficulties of one central city, Chicago, were discussed graphically by Malcolm J. Proudfoot a few years ago.[18] The real Chicago, that is, the urban agglomeration, according to Proudfoot, is a true metropolis—healthy, expanding, and prosperous—but the central city has ceased to grow. The city of Chicago, which once provided the government for the geographic city, is now only one of a number of local political units. It is burdened by gerrymandered representation and overlapping executive, legislative, and legal machinery.

> . . . It is kept weak by the overrepresented rural and downstate interests that dominate the Illinois General Assembly, the Illinois Senate, and the Illinois Supreme Court. It contributes far more in taxes than it receives in revenues, and it is hamstrung by inequitable budgetary control exercised by the state.
>
> These downstate interests commonly view with alarm any attempt to strengthen Chicago. They have kept the city in hand by discriminatory legislation, easily passed because the democratic, if not the legal, requirements of proportional representa-

[18] Proudfoot, *op. cit.*, pp. 106–117.

tion have been evaded. . . . The real Chicago has been further weakened by the shortsighted antagonism and obstruction of many of its suburban residents, whose satellitic, not to say parasitic, municipalities form a continuous retaining wall of separate political and legal autonomy around the central city.[19]

According to Proudfoot, Chicago's plight, though serious, is by no means unique. He points out that numerous local government units are the fate of most of our largest urban agglomerations. But in Chicago the problem is further aggravated by internal fragmentation of the corporate city of Chicago. Thirteen autonomous government units are involved, he says, and their jurisdictions are further subdivided into fifty "well-nigh autonomous" wards. One-third of the population of the real Chicago resides outside the arbitrary limits of the central city; this one-third and the two-thirds living in Chicago have common problems that cry out for metropolitan solutions.

Possible Solutions

The problems arising out of political fragmentation of urban agglomerations are numerous and obvious. The question arises, What can be done about this archaic way of governing the urban area? Answering this question is the business of the political scientist rather than the geographer. But just as the urban geographer is interested in the fragmented political structure of the urban agglomeration, so, too, is he interested in ways in which the pattern of administrative units is changing or may change as attempts are made to reach a more efficient governing system for the urban area.

Amalgamation into a single city

One thinks immediately of a rather obvious solution: amalgamation into a single city. Surely this would lead to greater overall efficiency. Indeed, where a moderate-

sized city has one or two small neighbors, union may be brought about through agreement and possibly a vote. But all too often, in the very large agglomeration, the people of the small units cherish their independence. Their desire to remain separate may be reasonable, since the smaller unit may have better government, better schools, and lower taxes than the central city. There may also be less laudable motives, such as the desire to keep certain official jobs which would disappear with consolidation. Much of the opposition to amalgamation, therefore, must be attributed to our democratic system.

State action is another way in which consolidation can be brought about. But in some states this would require changing the state constitution and the small incorporated units are likely to have too much political strength for any such drastic action to be practicable. Proudfoot pointed out all too vividly the sort of opposition that is likely to line up against the "big city."

Special districts

Though complete amalgamation into a single city may be impracticable in most cases, it is unlikely that any very large agglomeration of political units exists without some degree of cooperation. At least some of the smaller units are likely to have working arrangements with each other or with the central city for policing or fire protection or sewage disposal.

Frequently, broader cooperation is undertaken for certain specific services. Thus the Sanitary District of Chicago handles sewerage for Cook County's population both in the central city and in the many smaller municipalities, and the Metropolitan Water District of Southern California brings water from the Colorado River to serve many communities in the Los Angeles area.[20] Other examples of such cooperation

[19] *Ibid.*, pp. 111–113.

[20] Charles R. Adrian, *Governing Urban America*, 2d ed., McGraw-Hill Book Company, Inc., New York, 1961, p. 283.

are the Massachusetts Metropolitan District Commission, which furnishes sewage, water, and park services to Boston and its neighbors in the Boston agglomeration; and the Massachusetts Bay Transit Authority, established to operate rapid transit, trolley, and bus lines serving the seventy-eight independent municipalities of the Boston metropolitan area and also to help the railroads continue commuter service in the area. Such metropolitan special districts are increasing in number and importance. Each represents a large nodal region based on a single service or on several services and overlying a complex of smaller regions, each of which is an administrative unit. However, such special districts may exist for a long time without leading to any broader cooperation.

City-county consolidations

One plan for solving the city's difficulties is city-county consolidation within county limits. Under this scheme, city and county police, attorneys, clerks, treasurers, and health, welfare, and other departments can be combined, thus saving the taxpayer money. New York City has had essentially this form of city-county consolidation for many years, though it has not been carried far enough to result in the maximum economies possible under the system.[21] Other examples of longstanding city-county consolidations of this sort are the city of New Orleans, the city of Philadelphia, the city and county of San Francisco, the city and county of Denver, and the city and county of Honolulu. The last of these consolidations to be enacted, that of the city and county of Honolulu, dates from 1907. But the city-county consolidation, though it has involved no very large cities since 1907, is by no means dead. Thus, in 1962, the city of Virginia Beach and Princess Anne County, Virginia, consolidated into the city

of Virginia Beach, and South Norfolk and Norfolk County merged into the city of Chesapeake.[22]

There is another type of city-county consolidation in which the city attains separate status from the county in which it is located. The county then has no more control over the city than it does over another county. Each city, in addition to its normal city functions, performs for the city the other types of services that are usually performed by a county. This, then, is a case of consolidation of city-county functions within city limits.

Virginia can be said to have started the movement toward cities being separate from their counties. Though cities independent of counties have existed there since 1708, it was not until 1906 that the plan was formalized as it is in operation today.[23] Now any Virginia city that reaches a population of 10,000 is a first-class city and hence automatically independent of the county in which it is located. A city that reaches a population of between 5,000 and 10,000 is a second-class city, but it may apply to the courts to become a first-class city and hence to have independent status. In 1960, Virginia had thirty-two independent cities, ranging in size from Norfolk, with a population of 304,869, to Norton, with 5,013.

The only two large cities that have become independent from the counties in which they are situated are Baltimore, which was able to separate from Baltimore County about the middle of the nineteenth century, and St. Louis, which was separated from St. Louis County in 1876. In each, the city's government represents city-county consolidation within city borders. An entirely separate government prevails in

[21] John A. Rush, The City-County Consolidated, published by the author, Los Angeles, 1940, pp. 207–228.

[22] Sollens, "Metropolitan and Fringe Area Developments in 1962," in The Municipal Year Book, International City Managers Association, Chicago, 1963, p. 49. It is interesting to note that the two consolidations eliminated all unincorporated areas adjacent to the city of Norfolk, thus blocking further annexations by that city.

[23] Rush, op. cit., p. 204.

the county that surrounds the city. The idea behind the separation is that the county is largely rural and thus unsympathetic to the problems of the city dwellers.

City-county consolidations either within the county or within city borders have the disadvantage that neither system is well equipped to cope with the growth and incorporation of suburban cities and villages. The independent Virginia cities, thanks to Virginia's liberal annexation laws, are not so seriously handicapped in this respect as some other cities. In Virginia, a suit at law for annexing an area adjacent to one of the cities may be initiated by a municipality, by 51 per cent of the voters of the area under consideration for annexation, by the governing body of the county, or by the governing body of a town desiring to be annexed by a city.[24] Even under Virginia's annexation laws, however, a city may be walled in through the rise of new incorporated units.[25]

Metropolitan federations

A type of urban area government which has developed since World War II is rather like the city-county consolidation but gives more voice to constituent communities.[26] This is sometimes called a *metro system* because it is based on a metropolitan area.

Metropolitan Toronto The municipality of metropolitan Toronto, popularly called Metro, was incorporated in 1953. The city of Toronto in its earlier years met the problem of urban expansion by absorbing the suburbs that developed. From 1883 until 1914 there was an annexation every two or three years, either of independent municipalities, such as Yorkville and West Toronto, or of the urbanized strips of the large rural townships that surrounded Toronto. But beginning about 1920 the Toronto City Council halted this process of gradual amalgamation. Thereafter, as areas around Toronto became urban they did not look forward to annexation by Toronto but, instead, developed their own municipal structures. By 1930, Toronto and vicinity consisted of the present thirteen divisions (Figure 20.2).

[24] For a further discussion of the Virginia annexation system see Bain, *op. cit.*, pp. 457–458.
[25] See footnote 22 above.

[26] The following discussion is based largely on *Metropolitan Toronto: Ten Years of Progress, 1953–1963*, prepared for the Metropolitan Toronto Council by the staff of the Toronto Planning Board and published in June, 1963.

Fig. 20.2 The municipality of metropolitan Toronto consists of the central city, five townships, four towns, and three villages.

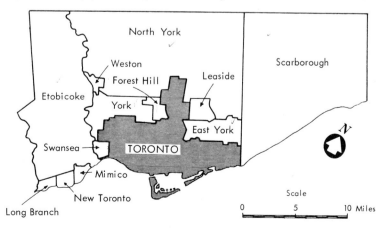

THE MUNICIPALITY OF METROPOLITAN TORONTO

In the late forties and early fifties, difficulties came about in the matter of services. For instance, in suburbs such as North York, denied physical access to Lake Ontario, water had to be supplied from wells, and sewage disposal was based on septic tanks. As the suburban developments grew, these methods not only were incapable of meeting the demand but also were considered dangerous to health. The system of intermunicipal agreements for the provision of services broke down under the strain. Moreover, there was nothing to commit the city to any capital expenditure for expansion of services.

Various possible solutions to the growing problem were discussed before the Ontario Municipal Board. The city of Toronto requested the province to amalgamate the city with the suburbs and the urbanized sections of the three large suburban townships, but this was opposed by all but one of the twelve suburban areas. In 1953, the Municipality of Metropolitan Toronto Act was passed, bringing together Toronto, five townships, four towns, and three villages (Figure 20.2). It established a Metropolitan Council of twenty-four members, twelve from the city of Toronto and twelve from the suburbs.

The legislation gave the new level of government many responsibilities while maintaining for the thirteen area municipalities (Toronto and the twelve others) their separate identities. The central authority took under its jurisdiction responsibility for major regional services. These included:

> The wholesale supply and purification of water, provision of major storm and sanitary sewers and the control of water pollution, responsibility for basic education costs, public transportation and the major road network, regional planning, administration of the county jail and the lower courts, public housing, regional parks, homes for the aged, and the care of indigent hospital patients and neglected children.

The metropolitan budget is raised by a levy upon the thirteen individual municipalities in the ratio that the total assessment of each municipality bears to the aggregate assessment of the entire metropolitan area. To make sure that the levy would be equitable, the new metropolitan corporation was given the responsibility of reassessing every individual property in the thirteen municipalities on precisely the same basis.

Has the Toronto experiment worked? An appraisal at the end of the first full decade of operations listed three principal achievements.[27] First, and in many respects the foremost, accomplishment of the Metropolitan Council, the report pointed out, has been the realization of a solid expression of support for the general concept of metropolitan government in the Toronto area. A second major Metro achievement has been the resolution of a series of specific service crises. These crises were particularly in the water supply, water pollution control, and education services. Third, among the principal achievements of the Council has been "the provision of a capital financial capability that has helped the Toronto metropolitan area meet the demands of its burgeoning growth."

But Metro Toronto has its difficulties as well as its achievements. In the appraisal it was stated that Metro's three major problems are:

> a growing imbalance in the economic resources, and burdens, between Metro's member municipalities; the failure to achieve a cohesive spirit of metropolitan unity among these members; and the reluctance on the part of Metro and its members to deal decisively with a number of important commitments and responsibilities.

A variety of possible changes in the existing organization have been considered. One is the amalgamation of all thirteen

[27] Frank Smallwood, *Metro Toronto: A Decade Later*, Bureau of Municipal Research, Toronto, 1963.

local municipalities into one large metropolitan city. A second alternative would attempt to preserve the essence of Toronto's original metropolitan federation concept through consolidation of the thirteen municipalities into four or five enlarged and more equalized boroughs. A possible third alternative, return to conditions as they existed prior to 1953, is not favored by any significant group. Toronto's metropolitan government has compiled an impressive record. Nevertheless, studies are under way toward making Metro more effective during its second ten years.

Dade County–Miami (Metro) The first serious attempt in the United States at a metro type of government involved Miami and Dade County, Florida, the Miami Standard Metropolitan Statistical Area. There were efforts in 1945, in 1947, and again in 1953 to effect a city-county consolidation on the theory that elimination of the city of Miami as a separate unit of government would reduce the tax load and provide better services. The 1953 proposition would have abolished the city and assigned all of its functions to the county. The plan was defeated at the polls, but a later proposal, presented as a constitutional amendment, was accepted in 1957. It transformed the county government into a metropolitan government.

The charter provided for two distinct levels of government for Dade County—municipalities, which would administer local services not requiring metropolitanwide authority, and the county, which would administer metropolitanwide services which transcended municipal boundaries. There were twenty-six municipalities in 1957, with the city of Miami having a much greater population than any other.

According to Metro's charter:

> The metropolitan government has authority to provide arterial and other roads, bridges, tunnels, and parking facilities and to enforce master plans for traffic and parking control. It can furnish air, water, rail, and bus terminals, port facilities, and public transportation systems. It can prepare and enforce comprehensive plans for the development of the county; provide uniform police and fire protection; supply parks, cultural facilities, hospitals, and uniform health and welfare programs; establish and administer housing in depressed areas; and construct integrated sewerage and water supply programs.
>
> The metropolitan government also is empowered to establish, coordinate, and enforce zoning regulations that are necessary. for public protection and can set minimum standards for all governmental units in the county for the performance of any service or function . . .[28]

Under the terms of the charter, municipalities in Dade County remain in existence until their voters decide otherwise. The municipalities exercise all powers relating to their local affairs which do not require metropolitanwide authority as outlined in the charter.

Metro seems to be at least reasonably successful thus far. In spite of repeated attempts to amend the charter so as to strengthen the municipalities at the expense of the county, the metropolitan government is still in existence; in fact, if anything, metropolitan control has been strengthened. The basic problem is how to enable Metro to provide new and better countywide services and at the same time furnish municipal-type services to unincorporated areas of the county with the cost of these services to be borne by the recipients. In the future a complete merging or amalgamation of Miami and Dade County seems likely. Then the unincorporated areas will get more municipal-type services but will have to carry a greater share of the tax burden of the county (or of the city if by then amalgamation into a single city has taken place).

[28] John C. Bollens, "Metropolitan and Fringe Area Developments in 1957," *The Municipal Year Book*, International City Managers Association, Chicago, 1958, p. 45.

Other federations and consolidations
Partly, no doubt, owing to the examples set by Toronto and Miami–Dade County, other consolidations and federations are being considered in urban agglomerations throughout the United States and Canada.[29] They are of interest as efforts at various levels to cope with the problem of fragmented jurisdictional structure.

Changing Patterns in Relation to the Political Factor

This chapter has dealt with the mechanics of growth of the political units that make up urban agglomerations, and it has emphasized the inefficiencies and other difficulties inherent in the fragmented structure of large agglomerations. Particularly, the predicament of the central city walled in by small independent corporate units has been stressed, though it was pointed out that the individual suburb, too, suffers under the fragmented system. And the transcending problem has been posed: How can the fragmented political structure of the urban agglomeration best be brought into line with the realities of the geographic city?

The trend toward fragmentation has been augmented by centrifugal development. The geographic city is spreading outward in a wave that generally leaves obsolescence and decline in its wake. Not only central cities but also the incorporated suburbs of the inner ring are losing population. The urban agglomerations are continuing to grow, however, because of increases in the van of the wave. Two-thirds of the increase in population of the United States between 1950 and 1960 occurred in the outlying portions of standard metropolitan statistical areas. It is in these outlying parts, too, that additional political units are incorporating, thus increasing the problems of political fragmentation.[30]

One solution of the fragmented political pattern problem is for the central city to incorporate far beyond its immediate needs, but this is possible only where annexation laws are liberal and where there is much adjacent unincorporated territory. It is not feasible for our largest agglomerations.

Steps taken for Toronto, for Dade County and Miami, and for a number of other cities toward some sort of workable consolidation of the geographic city are encouraging. At least the problem is recognized and solutions are being attempted.

One of the principal difficulties results from the mobility of the agglomeration. Where city and county are partially or completely merged, the answer, it must be realized, is only a temporary one. What will happen as additional built-up areas develop beyond the county line? Even in Oklahoma City, which has extended its boundaries so widely, small corporate units beyond the new boundaries are annexing territory and may eventually block the central city's expansion. A federation of the central city and the smaller municipalities appears the best solution, particularly if provision can be made to add other built-up areas automatically as the geographic city expands.

The whole matter of the relations between political units within the geographic city differs so greatly regionally and by states and even from one urban complex to the next that any overall answer is probably impossible. But this adds to the challenge. For the urban geographer interested in the

---

[29] Still another variety of federation or consolidation was achieved in Tennessee in 1963. Davidson County, in which the city of Nashville is situated, became Nashville and Davidson County. Under this arrangement Nashville became the urban services district of the new county; there was no longer a legally defined area with the name "Nashville," although it was expected that the name would continue in popular usage. (For details regarding this and similar current developments see issues of *The Municipal Year Book*.)

[30] This situation holds good for most of the country; it does not apply in New England, of course, since there all the land is already divided into towns and cities.

political phases of his subject there are great opportunities in the study of the jurisdictional patterns of urban agglomerations.

Selected References

Adrian, Charles R.: *Governing Urban America*, 2d ed., McGraw-Hill Book Company, Inc., New York, 1961.

Bain, Chester W.: "The Annexation of Fringe Territory," in *A Place to Live*, The Yearbook of Agriculture, Washington, D.C., 1963, pp. 454–459.

Miller, Willis H.: "Competition for the Ocean Trade of Los Angeles," *Economic Geography*, vol. 13, pp. 325–333, 1937.

The Municipal Year Book, International City Managers Association, Chicago. Issued annually.

Murphy, Raymond E.: "Town Structure and Urban Concepts in New England," *The Professional Geographer*, vol. 16, no. 2, pp. 1–6, March, 1964.

Nelson, Howard J.: "The Vernon Area, California: A Study of the Political Factor in Urban Geography," *Annals of the Association of American Geographers*, vol. 42, pp. 177–191, 1952.

Northam, Ray M.: "Declining Urban Centers in the United States: 1940–1960," *Annals of the Association of American Geographers*, vol. 53, pp. 50–59, 1963.

Proudfoot, Malcolm J.: "Chicago's Fragmented Political Structure," *Geographical Review*, vol. 47, pp. 106–117, 1957.

Rees, Henry: "A Growth Map for the Manchester Region," *Economic Geography*, vol. 23, pp. 136–142, 1947.

Rush, John A.: *The City-County Consolidated*, published by the author, Los Angeles, 1940.

Schnore, Leo F.: "Municipal Annexations and the Growth of Metropolitan Suburbs, 1950–60," *The American Journal of Sociology*, vol. 67, pp. 406–417, 1962.

Smallwood, Frank: *Metro Toronto: A Decade Later*, Bureau of Municipal Research, Toronto, 1963.

A

Governmental structure in New England

AT A number of points throughout this book, New England is singled out for special treatment because of certain unique characteristics. The standard metropolitan statistical area of New England, for example, is defined differently from that of the remainder of the country; and consideration of the urbanized area, of suburbs, of the rural-urban fringe, and of several other topics must take New England's uniqueness into account. At the heart of this necessity for special treatment is New England's government structure.

New England town or city versus Middle Western township We may take Massachusetts as a typical New England state. All of the land in the Commonwealth of Massachusetts is divided into towns and cities. These towns and cities are rather like the civil townships of the Middle Western states in that each has a sizable area—15, 20, 30, or more square miles (Figure A.1). Each is a part of a county, just as the Middle Western township is, and, just like the Middle Western township, the Massachusetts town may be largely rural, but have one or more villages or built-up areas.

Here the likeness ends. In the Middle Western township, the built-up areas exist as separate legal units variously called towns or villages, depending upon the locality—or, in some cases, cities. Though the township performs certain functions for the built-up areas, each of them is, to a considerable degree, a self-governing, legal unit, different from the remainder of the township, which usually is almost entirely rural. For many purposes both the built-up unit (town, village, or city) and the rural township depend upon the county. In fact the civil township has been losing more and more of its governmental function. In Iowa and Oklahoma, for example, townships now exist in name only.

In contrast, the Massachusetts town or city —which in area is often comparable to the township of the Middle West—is a strong governing unit, considerably stronger than the county. But the built-up sections or villages, of which there may be one or several within the town, though they may have separate names, have no separate legal identities. The town (or city) as a whole is the governing unit, a fact that is reflected in a single town (or city) hall, a single highway department, and a unified school system.

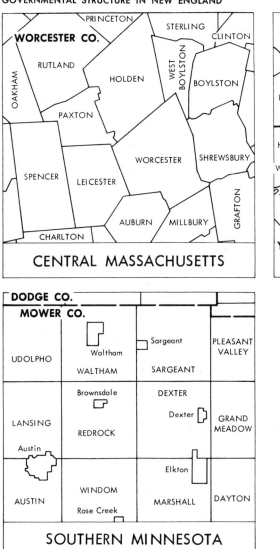

Fig. A.1 Minor civil divisions in central Massachusetts, southeastern Pennsylvania, and southern Minnesota. In Massachusetts, all the land is divided into towns and cities and these form the minor civil divisions. In Pennsylvania, cities, boroughs, and townships are the minor civil divisions; in Minnesota, cities, villages, and townships. The predominant north-south and east-west trends of most of the township and county lines in Minnesota reflect the township and range land survey system.

The town of Leicester, Massachusetts Leicester, a town in Worcester County in central Massachusetts, may be taken as an example (Figure A.2). With an area of nearly 25 square miles, its 8,000 people are concentrated chiefly in three villages—Leicester Center, Cherry Valley, and Rochdale. The land between the villages is largely rural; scattered clusters of houses occur, though usually these clusters are too small to have acquired distinct names. The most interesting thing about the three villages, though, is the fact that they have no separate legal existences, as villages do in most other parts of the country. On topographic maps of the United States Geological Survey and on other large-scale maps of Leicester, the names of the villages are shown, but the villages have no fixed bound-

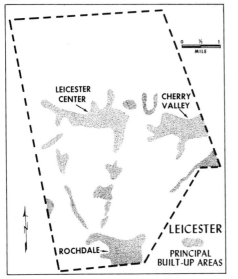

Fig. A.2 One of the Massachusetts towns appearing in Fig. A.1, Leicester, is here shown on a larger scale. Note the three built-up clusters—Leicester Center, Cherry Valley, and Rochdale. They have names, but no legal existences or definite boundaries; the town as a whole is the legal unit.

aries. The town, unlike the township in the Middle West, is a strong governmental unit, and the affairs of the entire town, including those of the three villages, are settled from the Town Hall at Leicester Center, commonly referred to as "The Center."

Massachusetts cities The foregoing remarks apply to most Massachusetts cities, too, since in all but one or two cases they are former towns that have acquired city charters. The smaller cities usually have several built-up areas within their borders, just as Leicester does, built-up areas that have names but no separate legal status. Chicopee, for example, a city of approximately 60,000 population in 1960, borders Springfield in the Connecticut Valley. Portions of Chicopee's 25 square miles are essentially rural; other areas are built up and these have separate names—Chicopee, Chicopee Falls, Aldenville, Willimansett, Fair-

view (see Figure 17.2). But these villages have no boundaries and no separate legal status. Instead, the whole area, once a town, forms the city of Chicopee, and is governmentally a single unit.

The larger cities have filled more of their land. This is particularly true of Boston. A town until 1822, it grew by annexation of several adjacent areas in the nineteenth century, and the names of some of the annexed towns still are used for the corresponding sections of the city. But Springfield and Worcester grew in population within their original boundaries and became cities. They did not acquire additional territory through annexation; indeed, for some years past, annexation by New England cities has been virtually impossible. The neighboring towns and cities have no inclination to give up their independent status or any of their territory. There are cities outside of New England which, for one reason or another, cannot expand through annexation, but in New England the boundaries are particularly inelastic.

Governmental structure elsewhere in New England The structure that has been described holds good in general for other sections of New England, but there are minor exceptions. A considerable portion of the interior of Maine, for example, is not organized into towns and cities, and small portions of New Hampshire and Vermont depart from the normal New England pattern. But these variations occur in the more remote portions of the three states. In Connecticut, a few boroughs appear as subdivisions of towns, but for the most part the regular town and city pattern prevails. Moreover, each city in Connecticut coincides with a town of the same name, the two governments performing slightly different functions. This is true, for example, with the city and town of New Haven. But these are minor variations that do not detract seriously from the overall pattern of New England town structure. Rhode Island, it may be added, is much like Massachusetts in its conformance to the standard New England pattern.

B

Administrative
and census
divisions of the city

FORTUNATELY for anyone interested in differentiating the interior of the city, data of one sort or another are available for a number of divisions of the urban area. Such divisions include wards, precincts, school districts, and other areas involved in city administration. And they include, also, areas that are of interest chiefly because they are units for which data are collected by the U.S. Bureau of the Census. The latter group consists of census enumeration districts, census tracts, and city blocks. The boundaries of no one of the types of divisions mentioned are reflected, ordinarily, in land-use differences or in other directly observable features. Nevertheless, a knowledge of the several types of divisions is necessary if one is to be prepared to make effective use of all available city statistics.

Local versus Census Bureau divisions and data   The data available for the first group of divisions, those involved in city administration, are from local sources, except in the case of wards. Population totals by wards are assembled by the Census Bureau for those cities that have wards, and, for 1960, were published in a special supplementary report of the Census of Population, covering all cities of 10,000 population or more. For the three types of Census Bureau units—census enumeration districts, census tracts, and city blocks—data are collected for various cities on similar bases. Such data are likely to be of much more value in studying the American city than statistics assembled by local agencies, since the former lend themselves better to city comparisons which can lead to valid generalizations. Nevertheless, for some problems it may be necessary to use locally collected data. The important thing is to realize the possibilities and limitations of each type of urban divison.

Maximum areal coverage desirable   To be of the utmost value in urban geography, administrative and statistical divisions should afford coverage of the entire urban area. Thus, subdivisions of the urbanized area or of the standard metropolitan statistical area are preferable to divisions available for the corporate city only. It is not surprising, however, that the ideal rarely prevails. In a city of substantial size, most or all of the types of divisions discussed in this appendix are likely to be repre-

sented in the incorporated city, but some of
them stop at the city line.

Administrative Divisions of the Incorporated City

The city's administrative divisions, important though they may be in the life of the
city, are ordinarily not of much concern to the
geographer. But for studies of the voting pattern in the city and occasionally for other research purposes they may be very important.
Many American cities are divided into wards
(or their equivalents), voting precincts, police
precincts, and school districts. Sometimes the
police precincts and school districts are not
correlated with the city ward structure, but the
voting precincts are usually segments of wards.

Wards and voting precincts

Wards and other divisions which take the
place of wards in some cities and the voting
precincts into which these areas are divided
are the administrative divisions of most concern here. They are of value chiefly for the
study of voting patterns.

Wards in Worcester, Massachusetts The
nature of wards may be made clearer by the
example of Worcester, Massachusetts (Figure
B.1), a city which had a population of 186,587
in 1960. The city is divided into ten wards by
well-defined lines such as streets. No attempt
is made to attain homogeneity within wards,
except possibly political homogeneity. Although, originally, each ward sent a member
to the City Council, under proportional representation, which prevailed in Worcester when
this appendix was being written, the nine members of the council are elected at large. But
although this function of the ward is no longer
important, the ward remains a unit from which
a member is sent to the State Legislature.

According to law, Worcester's wards are
supposed to contain approximately equal numbers of voters. Every tenth year Worcester, by
vote of the City Council, may make a new
division of its territory into wards in order to
keep the number of voters per ward equal.
However, such action is often delayed. In September, 1963, it was pointed out in an editorial
in a Worcester paper that, though Ward 8
had 5,042 registered voters and Ward 7 had
12,532, each had one representative in the
Massachusetts House, an obviously inequitable
representation.

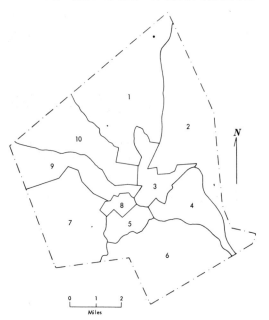

Fig. B.1 Wards for Worcester, Massachusetts,
1960. They ranged in population from 12,408 for
Ward 8, to 28,131 for Ward 2. Each ward is divided
into voting precincts which are of value in studying
the voting patterns of a city.

Voting precincts in Worcester, Massachu-
setts Each of Worcester's ten wards is, in
turn, divided into voting precincts. Precinct
boundaries have been changed four times in
the last twenty-five years. For instance, a revision in September, 1951, resulted in the addition of 28 new voting precincts for a total of
105 for the city as a whole.

How ward populations vary Since wards
were set up originally to serve the municipal
government, which was based upon the election of councilmen or aldermen from various
parts of the city, an attempt was made to have
each ward contain the same number of voters.
For this reason, wards within a single city usually have comparable population totals. They
may differ greatly in area to accomplish this.
However, ward populations vary considerably
from city to city, particularly in cities of different sizes. Large cities usually have more persons per ward. For instance, ward populations
in Chicago ranged from 48,030 to 132,824 in
1960, whereas wards in Wood River, Illinois, a
village with a population of 11,694, contained
only 2,000 to 3,000 persons each.

Limitations of wards and voting pre-

cincts One serious drawback to the use of ward and voting precinct data is that these subdivisions of a city can readily be changed in shape and size. In fact, frequent changes of this sort are necessary if the areas are to continue to represent uniform voting strength, but a result is that the patterns of administrative divisions may change substantially even from one voting period to the next and may be unrecognizable after twenty or thirty years. Also, these political subdivisions are subject to the vagaries of political pressure and the use of gerrymandering. This means that wards sometimes have peculiar and irrational shapes which may limit their value as statistical areas. Nevertheless, ward and precinct data should not be overlooked as possible bases for useful research.

Not all cities have wards Not all American cities are divided into wards. In most states some cities are so divided and others not. Where the ward does not exist, some other type of administrative area normally takes its place. For instance, New York City, Los Angeles, and San Francisco have assembly districts for which population data are given; Bridgeport, Connecticut, has voting districts; Washington, D.C., has police precincts; and Bellingham, Washington, uses "census county subdivisions." [1]

Police precincts and school districts

Some data are likely to be available locally by police precincts and by school districts. An annual list of all residents by police precincts is prepared in some cities. Annual school censuses are often taken by school districts, and the data are carried into the preschool age brackets in order better to estimate classroom and teacher needs for the coming years. These school census figures may tell a significant story about the sizes of families in different school districts and the characteristic age structures of families.

In some localities the school district pattern may even exercise an observable influence on land use. Thus, school districts sometimes are laid out independently of other types of divisions. Different parts of a single urban area may lie in different school districts, and a single district may lie partly inside and partly outside the corporate city. The school districts levy

[1] The whole system of local administrative divisions is so varied that anyone using these divisions must look into the special situation that prevails in the particular city and state under consideration. See footnote 11, p. 14.

taxes and the rate is sometimes substantially higher in a district than in the one adjacent to it. Where this occurs the school district pattern may be reflected in the location pattern of factories and other forms of land use.

Census Divisions of the City

Because of the limitations of administrative divisions, the Bureau of the Census long ago set up its own divisions by which comparable data are assembled for cities as part of the decennial censuses of population and housing. There are three of these systems of census divisions. Two of the three, census enumeration districts and census tracts, are purely creations of the Census Bureau. The third, the city block, is a normal unit of city structure which the Bureau of the Census has adopted with some minor variations as a statistical area for the presentation of selected housing data. These three divisions are discussed in detail in the following paragraphs.

Census enumeration districts

The enumeration district as a building block A census enumeration district (ED) is the smallest area for which census data are tabulated, with the exception of the city block which is used only in the Census of Housing. Enumeration districts are thus the basic units of which all other census areas (except the city block) are made up.

Rules regarding boundaries To avoid any possibility of confusion, the Census Bureau follows certain rules regarding enumeration district boundaries. The first requirement is that each enumeration district be bounded by streets or other definite, easily identifiable features. Political boundaries such as city lines form somewhat of an exception to this rule since they are often unmarked except where they cross major streets. Enumeration districts are so laid out that their boundaries never cross political lines such as a county boundary or that of a city or other minor civil division. In addition to not crossing political boundaries, the boundaries of enumeration districts never cross the boundaries of such special-purpose census areas as census tracts, urbanized areas, or census county divisions.

Size expressed in population As a result of the fact that the enumeration district boundaries cannot cross the boundary lines of any of the statistical areas for which data are to be published, some enumeration districts are abnormally small or sparsely populated. But the desired population for each enumeration district in urban areas is about 1,000. Most enumeration districts contain approximately 250 housing units.

Availability of data   Unfortunately, the Bureau of the Census does not publish data by enumeration districts. However, enumeration district data on population and on population and housing characteristics may be purchased from the Bureau. This is complete count data; sample data by enumeration districts were not tabulated. The information can be provided in several forms—reproduced tables, magnetic tape, or microfilm. Enumeration district maps, too, can be purchased.

Boundaries lack permanence   Another limitation of enumeration districts as statistical areas is that they do not have permanent boundaries. If an enumeration district from the previous decennial census satisfies all other requirements and has had little change in population it may be used in the new census, but many of the districts are changed from one census period to the next to conform with changes in population distribution.

Census tracts

It is highly desirable for many purposes to have the city or the city and vicinity divided into fairly small statistical areas which, unlike census enumeration districts, have some degree of permanence (Figure B.2). To meet this need the census tract was originated early in this century.[2] Though a census tract may occasionally consist of only one enumeration district, the average is more nearly four, and census tracts are relatively permanent.

The scope of census tracting   All cities of 50,000 or more population are eligible for census tracts. Where the principal central city has a population of 100,000 or more the Bureau has encouraged tracting of the entire standard metropolitan statistical area, and in some instances this has been approved even where the chief central city has less than 100,000 inhabitants. There are 180 or more urban areas in the United States and Puerto Rico that have been tracted and further extensions of the system are planned. In most instances the whole standard metropolitan statistical area has been included.

[2] See latest *Census Tract Manual* of the Bureau of the Census.

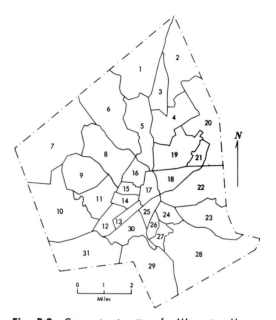

Fig. B.2   Census tract pattern for Worcester, Massachusetts, 1960. The thirty-one tracts ranged in population from 9,531 for Tract 22 to 2,846 for Tract 21, which is coincident with the Worcester State Hospital. Note that the tracts tend to average greater in area with distance from the city center. This reflects the greater population density that prevails near the center of the city combined with the desire to outline tracts that will have approximately equal numbers of people. Normally, one census tract is made up of about four enumeration districts and each of these in turn of some fifteen blocks, though this latter number can vary considerably. The census tract system has been extended to surrounding towns, but only Worcester's tracts are shown here.

The local committee   The development of census tracts in any area requires an active local committee. The Census Bureau has promoted this approach to the census tract plan since it is felt that local people know an area best and that local groups are the chief users of census tract data. Therefore, it is important that they approve of the tract layout. This local approach has been carried even further: for the 1960 census, local census tract committees were invited to divide their census tracts into enumeration districts—following Census Bureau criteria, of course, and subject to Census Bureau approval.

Population   When census tracts for American cities are laid out, several general rules with respect to population totals are kept in mind. Tracts should be approximately equal in population. They should contain between 2,500 and 8,000 persons each, but may have somewhat more where a high degree of homogeneity makes it undesirable to subdivide a tract. The average census tract has a population of about 4,000, which is four times the average enumeration district total for urban areas.

permanent institution, such as a prison, sanitarium, or military installation, may be recognized as a separate tract if it has more than 1,000 residents. Non-institutional tracts with less than 2,500 inhabitants must have special justification. For instance, local census tract committees are asked to outline a central business district tract (which can have far less than 2,500 inhabitants) for each of the large cities or, in the very large city, a group of tracts to approximate the central business district.

Tract boundaries Other factors too are taken into account in establishing the pattern of tracts. Some of these have to do with tract boundaries. Since they are also the boundaries of enumeration districts which must be followed in the field by enumerators, census tract boundaries should follow permanent and easily recognized lines. They may be streets, highways, railroads, rivers, canals, and the like, or reasonably permanent political lines. Features that form major barriers making ordinary access from one side to the other difficult—for example, a cliff, a broad river, or a major arterial—make good tract boundaries. Moreover, it is regarded as undesirable to have one part of a tract located on a high hill and the remainder in a valley, since the area thus outlined would not make a very good district for any local agency and it is hoped that, increasingly, all sorts of local groups will use the tracts.

Homogeneity An attempt is made, also, to enclose in each tract an area that is fairly homogeneous in population characteristics such as race, national origins, economic status, and living conditions.

Boundaries based on compromise Obviously, it is impossible to have homogeneity of racial and nationality characteristics and of economic status within the tract, to have good tract boundaries, and yet to maintain the ideal in number of inhabitants. Sometimes certain expedients are adopted with regard to census tract population. For example, if the population is growing rapidly in a part of the city, then it may be desirable in that area to lay out tracts with considerably less than the average population. Or, if a certain section of the city seems to stand out as an area of considerable homogeneity in population characteristics, and, in addition, is somewhat isolated physically and fairly static in population, it may be decided to create a single tract even though the population total is as great as 8,000 or 9,000. Significant homogeneity of population within tracts, it must be admitted, is often more of an ideal than a reality.

Permanency of tracts Once tracts are established for a city and its neighboring areas they should remain fixed if they are to be of maximum value for studying changing social and economic patterns. But sometimes the boundaries of tracts have to be changed. For instance, if land is annexed to the city, it may be necessary to change the boundaries of tracts so as to include the new territory, though often it is possible to solve this problem by the creation of new tracts. Sometimes, too, rapid growth of population in a tract may make its subdivision into two or more smaller tracts desirable.

In rare instances, it may be decided to revise the tract pattern in order to divide a city into more homogeneous units. This happened in New Haven, Connecticut, which had first been laid out in tracts at the time of the 1940 census, but was re-tracted later so that its pattern of census tracts for 1950 was substantially different from that of the earlier year. Such drastic changes are avoided, if possible, since tracts are of the most value where they have remained essentially unchanged for several successive census periods.

Census data by tracts For most of the tracted areas, separate reports are published giving data by tracts on basic population and housing characteristics. According to the Census Bureau:

The population items are: race and color, nativity and parentage, foreign stock and country of origin, age, relationship to head of household, marital status, married couples and families, school enrollment, years of school completed, residence in 1955, income in 1959, employment status, occupation, industry, class of worker, place of work, and means of transportation to work. The housing items are: tenure of housing unit, color of occupants, vacancy status, number of persons in the unit, persons per room, year moved into the unit, number of units in structure, year structure built, basement in structure, number of rooms, condition and plumbing, number of bathrooms, heating equipment, automobiles available, value of property, contract rent, and gross rent. Some of these items were enumerated on a complete-count basis and others were collected for a sample of persons and housing units.

There is additional, tabulated, unpublished data by tracts, photocopies of which can be purchased at cost from the Bureau of the Census. The census tract report for each area contains a map, in several sections if the city is a very large one, showing the pattern and numbering of the tracts.

Local data by census tracts In addition to the data published by the Bureau of the Census, many cities collect statistics of various sorts through their community agencies, and it has proved useful to fit these data into the census tract structure so they may be readily compared with census data. It is advisable as a preliminary to plotting such data to prepare a census tract street index. This usually is done by the local planning board. The census tract street index shows for every house number the number of the census tract in which it is located, which in turn makes it possible to plot rapidly data that have been assembled on a street address basis. Health data, juvenile delinquency statistics, church affiliation, welfare data, school censuses, social service data, and a variety of other public and semipublic records are now often kept by census tracts.

Data for individual establishments, too, when available by street addresses, may readily be plotted by tracts when a census tract street index is available. A manufacturing concern may wish to show on a map the home locations of its employees so it can compare the pattern with patterns of economic and social characteristics plotted by tracts; the administration of a city library may want to know where its users live; and this same kind of data may be plotted for a magazine's subscribers, for a store's customers, for the users of a utility, and the like. Such distributions are valuable for their own sake as well as for comparison with other community data and with tract data from the United States Census.

Census tract data and the study of change. Some of the most unique aspects of census-tract use involve the comparison of data for successive decennial censuses, or, in the case of locally collected data, statistics for successive collection periods whatever they may be. The value of such an approach is that we can see what shifts are in progress.

Variety of users Many different agencies and many different kinds of people use census tract data. Social scientists are probably the chief users on a purely scientific and research basis, but there are many fields of endeavor in which census tract statistics have proved of value. Among these are various official city departments and agencies, business interests, social service agencies, health groups, and a variety of others. The reader is referred to the latest *Census Tract Manual*, available from the Census Bureau, for more detailed lists of users of census tracts.[3]

Community areas The number of census tracts is so great in some very large cities or standard metropolitan areas that special groupings are desirable. In New York City and Chicago, according to the Census Bureau, it has been the practice to combine census data by tracts into larger areas for which the data are published locally. The Census Bureau recommends that where such special groupings are necessary the census tract committee of the urban area be asked to secure local agreement on a general-purpose grouping of the tracts into larger units which might well be known as "community areas."

City blocks

The smallest unit for which any census data are published is the city block, and the material available on this basis is restricted largely to selected housing data from the Census of Housing. Such statistics by blocks were published in 1960 for each city or urban place which had a population of 50,000. In addition, a number of smaller places were included in the program through agreements whereby the cost of collecting and publishing information was paid for by the city govern-

[3] A Census Tract Library is maintained in the Geography Division of the Bureau of the Census. All persons and organizations using census tract data in their research are asked to send a copy of any resulting publication to the library, where it can be consulted by anyone interested.

ment. A city map showing block numbers accompanies each block housing report. Census tracts, too, are shown, and the block data in the several tables in each report are arranged by blocks within tracts.

Information available The 1960 *Census of Housing* provides in the city reports the following information for each block:

> Total population, number of housing units classified by condition and plumbing, tenure of occupied units, average value and average number of rooms for owner occupied units, average contract rent and average number of rooms for renter occupied units, number of units occupied by nonwhites, and number of units with 1.01 or more persons per room.

All of the items were enumerated and tabulated on a 100 per cent basis for the statistics in the report.[4]

Research value Block housing data are of real value in urban research even though

[4] For further details see the city blocks report for any city, 1960 *Census of Housing*.

they are restricted topically. For any given city, block housing data give a basis for the most fine-grained distribution patterns that can be derived from any United States Census data. Moreover, block housing data are available for 1940 and 1950. Although some of the items for which data are given have changed, there is sufficient comparability so that some interesting shifts can be studied. However, one of the most valuable items, total population by blocks, was first available for the 1960 census, so comparisons on this basis will not be possible until the 1970 census data are issued.

Reliability Unfortunately, block housing statistics are not so reliable as most census data. The Census Bureau points out that each block count is the work of a single enumerator, and that he may have misunderstood his instructions or may have used the wrong block number. Occasionally, for example, a number of dwelling units are shown for a block that is a park or otherwise unused for housing. Where block data are combined in tract totals, however, the percentage of error is likely to be small.

Index

Index